BRITISH FAMILY NAMES

Their Origin and Meaning

WITH

LISTS OF SCANDINAVIAN, FRISIAN, ANGLO-SAXON
AND NORMAN NAMES

BY

Rev. HENRY BARBER, M.D., F.S.A.

AUTHOR OF

'FURNESS AND CARTMEL NOTES,' 'THE CISTERCIAN ABBEY OF MAULBRONN,' 'SOME
QUEER NAMES,' 'THE SHRINE OF ST BONIFACE AT FULDA,' ETC.

'What's in a name?'—*Romeo and Juliet.*
'I believe now, there is some secret power and virtue in a name.'
BURTON'S *Anatomy of Melancholy.*

SECOND EDITION, ENLARGED

PUBLIC LIBRARIES LINCOLN

LONDON
ELLIOT STOCK, 62 PATERNOSTER ROW, E.C.
1903

D0240233

M 6011
(929.4)

(2)

CONTENTS

PREFACE TO THE FIRST EDITION

THE following pages are offered to the public in the belief that they will be found useful to those interested in the study of names or engaged in compiling family histories.

Although the vast catalogue of British surnames may not have been exhausted, yet by many years' labour more than eight thousand representative modern names, extracted from directories, newspapers, voting lists, etc., have been traced to their source, and when it is remembered that this includes the numerous variations and ramifications of these patronymics, the extensive scope of this work will then be appreciated.

The utility of the lists of ancient names to the student of local etymology must at once be apparent, whilst to the genealogist (whether British, Colonial, or American) the revelations as to the transformation of family names will be of the utmost service.

H. B.

RAVENSTONE,
    ASHBY-DE-LA-ZOUCH.

vii

PREFACE TO THE SECOND EDITION

ANOTHER edition being demanded, an effort has been made to present it in a cheap and popular form.

The book has been revised, enlarged, and improved; and, besides additional information in the introductory part, the number of family names has been brought up to over ten thousand.

Many errors have been rectified, but the writer is conscious of defects still existing, which time, experience, and further research may help to overcome.

He takes this opportunity of thanking his numerous correspondents, in all parts of the world, for their kind and encouraging communications.

BOOKS CONSULTED

Abel, H. F. Otto. Die deutschen Personen-Namen. Berlin, 1889.

Bailey, N. German and English Dictionary. 2 vols. 8vo. Jena, 1810.

Bartholomew, J. Gazetteer of Great Britain. Edin. 1887.

Bosworth, Rev. J. Anglo-Saxon Dictionary. Lond. 1868.

Buchanan, W. Scottish Surnames. 8vo. Glasgow, 1820.

Burke's Peerage and Baronetage.

Camden Society. Lists of Foreign Protestants and Aliens. 1862.

Chambers's Etymological Dictionary. Lond. 1868.

Charnock, R. S. Patronymica Cornu-Britannica. 8vo. 1870.

Cleasby and Vigfusson's Icelandic-English Dictionary. Oxf. 1874.

Directories of Belgium, Denmark, Germany, Holland, Normandy, Norway, Sweden.

Domesday Book.

Edmunds, F. Names of Places. Lond. 1869.

Ellis, Sir H. Introduction to the Study of Domesday Book. 2 vols. 8vo. Lond. 1833.

Ferguson, R. Surnames as a Science. 8vo. Lond. 1884.

Finlayson, J. Surnames and Sirenames. 8vo. Lond.

Fishwick, H., F.S.A. Rochdale Surnames.

Frey, A. B. Names, Nicknames, and Sobriquets. 8vo. 1888.

Guppy, H. B. Homes of Family Names. 8vo. Lond. 1890.

Halliwell, J. O. Dictionary of Archaic Terms. 2 vols. Lond. 1868.

Hardy, T. D. Rotuli de Oblatis et Finibus, *temp*. Regis Johannis. 8vo. Lond. 1835.

Hardy, T. D. Rotuli Normanniæ. 8vo. Lond. 1835.

Innes, C. Some Scotch Surnames. 4to. Edin. 1860.

Islands Landnáma-bók.

Joyce, P. W. Irish Names of Places. 2 vols. 1883.

Kelly's County Directories of England.

Kemble, J. M. The Names, Surnames, and Nicknames of the Anglo-Saxons. 8vo. Lond. 1846.

Koolmann, T. D. Wörterbuch der Ostfrieschen Sprache. 3 vols. Norden, 1882.

Long, H. A. Personal and Family Names. 8vo. Lond. 1883.

Lower, M. A. Patronymica Britannica. Lond. 1860.

Matheson, R. E. Surnames in Ireland. Dublin, 1894.

Matheson, R. E. Synomyms of Irish Surnames. Dublin, 1890.

Moisy, H. Glossaire comparatif Anglo-Normand. Caen, 1889.

Moisy, H. Noms de famille Normands. Paris, 1875.

Moore, A. W. Surnames and Place-names of the Isle of Man. 8vo. Lond. 1890.

Morris, T. E., LL.M. Welsh Surnames, " Bygones." Oswestry, 1899-1900.

Murray's Handbook of Normandy, with Maps. 8vo. Lond. 1854.

O'Hart, J. Irish Pedigrees. 8vo. Dublin, 1876.

Palgrave, Sir F. Normandy and England. 4 vols. 8vo. Lond. 1851-64.

Planché, J. R. The Conqueror and his Companions. 2 vols. Lond. 1874.

Registrar-General's Reports, England and Scotland, 1890-94.

Rotuli Hundredorum. 2 vols. fol. A.D. 1273.

Round, J. H. Calendar of Documents in France, A.D. 918-1206, vol. i. 8vo. Lond. 1899.

Searle, W. G. Onomasticon Anglo-Saxonicum. Camb. 1897.

Sharpe, R. R. Calendar of Wills, Court of Husting, 1258 to 1688. 2 vols. 8vo. Lond. 1889.

Sims, C. S. Scottish Surnames. 1862.

Taylor, Rev. I. Words and Places. Lond. 1865.

The Norman People. 8vo. Lond. 1874.

Vigfusson, Dr G. Sturlinga Saga. Index of Names in vol. ii. 8vo. 1878.

Worsaae, J. J. A. Danes in England. 8vo. Lond. 1852.

Yonge, C. M. History of Christian Names. 8vo. Lond. 1884.

INTRODUCTION

'A painful work it is and more than difficult, wherein what toyle hath been taken, as no man thinketh, so no man believeth, but he that hath made the trial.'—ANTHONY A WOOD.

DURING a lengthened research in studying the place-names of the Danelagh, the writer accumulated a great number of names from ancient sources necessary for unravelling the tangled skein of local etymology.

It occurred to him that these might be utilised in the treatment of British surnames, and his first idea was to publish the lists with an introductory chapter on the origin of surnames, for the use of students of this branch of archæology, who were in need of such things, for easy reference.

With this view the author wrote an article in the *Antiquary* (September 1891), in order to draw attention to the subject, as Lower's 'English Surnames' is both out of date and altogether unreliable.

After this he met with, for the first time, the last-mentioned author's 'Patronymica Britannica,' a more ambitious work, and a great improvement upon the previous attempt, but still deficient in precise information and investigation.

The dictionary form, however, seemed to be the best for ready reference, and he thought a few examples, to show the way in which he had wrought out the names, would be of service to those who are interested in this important study. Hence it came about that this work has gradually grown until it assumes its present proportions.

The chief object has been, as far as possible, to avoid anything like guess-work or fancy interpretation, and to seek for a definition among such sources as seemed likely to supply it; so that, when a word could not be referred to any reasonable origin, it was put on the shelf until time, experience, and discovery should verify it.

Besides the works of reference which he consulted, he found it necessary to prepare, for his own use, the lists of names already mentioned, and these have been of so much service that he trusts they will be found equally available for all those who wish to enter upon this arduous but fascinating task.

In addition to these he has examined directories and maps of Great Britain, Norway, Sweden, Denmark, Holland, Flanders, Germany, Normandy, etc.

Many a name that seemed to defy all explanation was found to be that of some obscure village, so disguised as to be almost past

A

recognition. Who, for instance, would expect to see Sevenoaks in
Snooks, St Olave's Street in Tooley Street, St Etheldreda in Tawdry,
D'Eagles in Diggles, Wilburgham in Wilbraham, Tuberville in Trouble-
field, Longueville in Longfellow, Longchamps in Longshanks, Blondeville
in Blomfield, Adburgham in Abraham and Abram, Renshaw in
Wrencher and Wrinch, Wymondham in Wyndham?

Indeed, as Mr Lower truly says:

'Corruptions which many family names have undergone tend to baffle alike the
genealogical and etymological inquirer.'

The following will serve as illustrations of the corruption to which
names are liable. The family name of Weewall occurs frequently in
the parish register of Peckleton, Leicestershire, and between 1735 and
1750 there are many variations of the spelling, scarcely two entries
being alike. It appears as Whewaugh, Whewvaugh, Wheevaw, Weway,
Weewaa, Wheewhal, Whewwhaw, Whealwhal, Weewal, Wheelwall. In
the North of England it took the form of Whewell.

The name of the great English dramatist is generally spelt Shakes-
peare, but there are many ways of spelling the name according to
English orthography. Here are a few of them as appearing in old
documents : Shakspere, Shaxpere, Shakspire, Shaxspere, Schaksper,
Shakespere, Shakspeare, Schakespeyr, Shaxespeare, Shagspere, Shax-
pur, Shaxsper, Shaksper, Shackspeare, Saxpere, Shakespire, Shakespeire,
Shackespeare, Shakaspear, Shaxper, Shakspear, Shaxpeare, Shakspeere,
Shaxbure, Shackspeyr, Shakespear, Schakesper, etc.

Goodwin is found in ancient documents as Godewyn, Godin, Godwin,
Godwyn, Goodwen, Goodwin, Goodwyn, Goodwyne.

Bugge as Buci, de Bougy, de Bucy, Bugi, Boci, Bogge, Busse, Boge,
Bouche, Boughe, Buggey, Bussey, Bogg, Boag, Boake, Bogue, Beucy,
Beucey, Boogie, Bugey, Buggy, Buggie, Bukie, Bouky, Boog, etc.*

Yule appears as Yovele, Youhill, Youille, Youle, Yowell, Yewell, Youell,
Yuell, Yewle, Yeule, Jouel, Jowel, Jewell, Jule, Yull, Juler, etc.

Applethwaite as Ablewhite, Ablett, Ebblethwaite, Hebblethwaite,
Hepplewhite, etc.

Job as Jopp, Jupp, Jubb, Juby, Jubey, Chubb, Chope, Jupp, Jupe.

Mr W. P. Phillimore, M.A., B.C.L., in 'Notes on Finnimore,
Phillimore, and their Allied Surnames,' gives fifty-nine different ways
of spelling the former, and thirty-four of the latter surname.

* The arms of Bugge, Bouge, Bugey, or de Bougy, are :—Or on a fesse sable three
water bougets ar. This is a play upon the name, but it gives the early pronunciation.

BRITISH SURNAMES

'This is a subject which involves many curious questions of antiquarian interest, bearing upon the language, habits and pursuits of our countrymen in bygone days. It is one, also, that immediately concerns every man who feels an honest pride in being called by his father's name.'—*Notes and Queries*, vi. 201.

'To find out the true originall of surnames is full of difficulty.'—CAMDEN.

MUCH speculation has arisen as to the date when surnames were first used in this country. It is now pretty well admitted that they began to be adopted about A.D. 1000.

According to Lower, the practice commenced in Normandy, and gradually extended itself to this country; but the use of surnames was occasionally hereditary among the Anglo-Saxons before the Conquest, and the general adoption of family designations.

In the time of King Edward the Confessor there was among the Saxon tenants in Suffolk one Leuric Hobbesune. Suert Magno or Manni, Godric Poinc, Tedricus Pointel, Siuuard Rufus, Stigand Soror also occur.

At the time of the Domesday Survey they were becoming more numerous, for both the tenants in chief and the under-tenants possessed them. Thus we find Alwin Dodesune, Godric Cratel, William Goizenboded, William Hosed, Hugo Lasne, Walter Achet, Osmund Angevin, Roger Arundel, Bernard Barb, Walter Bec, Hugo Bolebec, William Bonvaslet, Aluin Coc (bedellus), William Denomore, Roger Deramis, etc.

Various writers have treated the subject of British surnames in different ways, from Camden and Lower downwards. Some have produced very amusing articles by grouping the most extraordinary names they could find together, as the names of birds, beasts, flowers, objects in common use, trades, etc.

A few have made some attempts to give the derivations of well-known names according to their own classification, ignoring altogether the possibility of many being traced to extremely ancient sources.

Names which betoken association with territorial possession and occupations, and Christian names also, are not difficult to distinguish; but the oldest names of all are those which belong to the Norse or Frisian settlers, except such as are probably of Celtic or British origin.

It is a well-known fact that many family names are peculiar to certain localities, where they have remained for many generations, as can be proved from the old church registers. The spread of railways and the increased facilities for locomotion in every way are fast altering the old state of things, however, especially where there is a sudden development of one or more local industries, causing a great influx of strangers.

In remote country places, and particularly in agricultural districts,

3

many of the old family names still remain—some, indeed, are seldom found in any other part of England.

In one district in England a marked peculiarity in the names of the people exists. This is known as the Danish Settlement (Danelagh), already referred to.

Here, as might be expected, is a strong Norse element, and this distinction is more clearly marked the farther east one goes, as the names have not undergone the modification so often found in the west, since in many cases the original Scandinavian form prevails.

The family nomenclature of this part of the country undoubtedly requires particular treatment. It is not surprising, therefore, to discover many personal names, either of pure Norse families or of places or qualities.

In East Anglia a large proportion of the family names are mono-syllabic. This singularity is so striking that it forces itself upon the most casual observer. Perhaps it is owing to the large infusion of names of Dutch and Flemish origin.

Moreover, strangely enough, the local pronunciation of names of persons and places has long outlived the many orthographical changes which took place in our written language while men spelt words phonetic-ally, or as fancy dictated. Accordingly, we find in old records, from Anglo-Saxon charters and Domesday Book to later times, strange varia-tions, in some cases making the derivation from the original source by no means easy,

All this is very interesting to the student of British surnames, who looks at the subject, not on the humorous side only, but in its historical, etymological, ethnological, and topographical aspect.

The language—dialect if preferred—of the North of England is to this day full of words and expressions which can only be explained by the help of the Icelandic, as the representative of the old Northern languages spoken by the Scandinavian settlers in England. The colonization of Iceland was included in that stream of emigration which began to leave Norway A.D. 852, and spread along the coasts of Normandy, England, Ireland, and Scotland up to the end of the eleventh century. For about four hundred years afterwards the old Norse tongue was locked up in that remarkable Northern island, and preserved almost incorrupt, while the mother-country became affected, and its original language considerably modified, by contact with other European nations.

In a sort of Domesday Book, compiled by the authorities in Iceland (Islands Landnámá-bók), there was, among other matters recorded and deposited in the cathedral of Reykyavik, a roll of the names of the original settlers (of which perhaps a third are women) and the lands they occupied, making about five thousand proper names.

This remarkable document, which has been preserved, throws great light upon the derivation of many personal and local names in Scotland and Northern England hitherto considered to be obscure, and it is as necessary to the antiquary as the so-called ' Roll of Battell Abbey' or the Domesday Book of the Conqueror. It is, in fact, the chief storehouse for genealogical knowledge.

The study of the Icelandic, in its relation to old and provincial English and its comparison with Swedish, Norwegian, Danish, Frisian, Flemish, and German, has opened out a wonderful field of never-ending interest, and made us acquainted with things we never before dreamed of in connection with this subject.

In the course of his researches the writer has picked up a few odds and ends of information which may perhaps be useful to others. It is possible to derive some instruction and to extract no little amusement from the carrying out of a train of speculation on the origin of names, so, if these details appear somewhat dry, it is to be hoped they will be set down as a humble effort to deal as carefully with a special and difficult subject as the nature of the materials within reach and limited qualifications for the task will permit of. It may appear to some, possibly, that the importance of the old Norse has been over-estimated, and not enough credit given to the Anglo-Saxon.

Perhaps it is so; but, besides the names of places, it must be admitted that very many modern English words show early Northern influence, and even in Anglo-Saxon times the language was so blended with Scandinavian words that there were often double expressions for the same thing.

It seems clear that the Frisian dialect of the Low German gives the best idea of the original so-called Anglo-Saxon, for it is the modern representative of the language of old Dutch Friesland, whence so many of those who settled in England (after the departure of the Romans) came.

This appears to be borne out by the fact that the early English missionaries (notably St. Boniface) made their way to that country because it was the home of their fathers, and there was no more difficulty with the language than in the case of a citizen of the United States visiting Britain.

It will be seen that even at this early period names were derived from localities, occupations, personal and mental qualities and peculiarities as nicknames, social relations, etc. Further, in common with the Teutonic races, the Norse used diminutives, or pet names, which afterwards stuck to the individuals so designated and became family names.

The terminations ing, kin, and son, so common in English names, are derived from the Norse, *ingr*, *kyn*, and *sonr*, the *r* being dropped in compounds. The Danish make the last *sen*. Also *kyn* must not be confounded with the diminutive-endings: Germ., *chen;* Fris., *ken* and *ke;* Flem., *kin;* which have quite a different meaning and are used in pet names chiefly.

The diminutives, Frisian, ken, ke, ock, and cock;* Norman French,

---

* There has been much controversy over the termination 'cock.' It appears to be derived from the Frisian *gök* or *kök*, a foolish, silly, awkward person, hence the Scotch *gowk*. The Fris. *Jankök* (Johncock) is equivalent to the German *Hans Wurst*. At first applied to children as a check to thoughtlessness, it would become gradually used as a diminutive. *Cock* and *ock* are akin to *ke*. In some cases cock is a corruption of *cot* found in local names.

et, ette, let, ot, otte, ell; Old Norse, i, a, ki, ka, gi, ga, ungr, ingr, lingr, should be noted.

It will be useful to apply the test of the old world sources to the family names of this country, comparing them in the first instance with those of the Northern nations, the Scandinavians (Danes so called), the Frisians (*i.e.* Saxons), the Old English (Anglo-Saxon) in Domesday Book, and, in the second place, with existing names in Northern Germany, Sweden, Denmark, Normandy, Holland, and Flanders.

In addition to these quarries, which the writer will endeavour to work, it may be mentioned that there are many names which clearly bear the stamp of foreign origin, and have not yet been so entirely metamorphosed but that their Continental source may be discovered. An Act of the Irish Parliament (5 Edw. IV., c. 3, A.D. 1465) ordained that every Irishman dwelling betwixt or amongst Englishmen in the counties of Dublin, Myeth, Vriel, and Kildare, should dress like Englishmen and take an English surname, of a town (as Sutton, Chester, etc.), or colour (as white, black), or art (as smith, carpenter, etc.), or office (as cook or butler), and he and his issue should use the same under a specified penalty. Thus, O'Gowan became Smith and MacIntyre Carpenter, etc. Most surnames will be found to come under one or other of the following heads:

1. Nicknames.	5. Trade names.
2. Clan or tribal names.	6. Christian names.
3. Place-names.	7. Foreign names.
4. Official names.	8. Foundling names.

I.—NICKNAMES

'You had not your name for nothing.'—*Old Proverb.*

Unquestionably the oldest names of all are those derived from by-names, given on account of a strong peculiarity of figure, feature, or character, deed of prowess, eccentricity of dress, speech, or carriage.

Among primitive nations the slightest deviation from the ordinary course of life or difference among his fellows was enough to mark a man, especially where a striking cognomen was readily applied. Fleetness of foot, a mighty hunter, skill in the use of a particular weapon, or the very opposite, gave rise to a name implying praise or contempt. Indeed, the most trifling cause served to invent a title by which a man was distinguished from his contemporaries. When King Magnus assumed the Highland dress he become known as Berbeinn (Bareleg) among his followers, and this is preserved to us in the modern though Puritan-sounding Barebones.

A man became notorious on account of a fearful scar upon his leg, hence he was called Orra-beinn (Scar-leg), which we see in Horrabin to this day.

In the Orkneys the Norse Earl Einar gained the *soubriquet* of

'Turf-Einar' (Torf-Einarr) from having taught the Norsemen to dig peat, he having probably learnt it himself from the Gaelic tribes in Scotland.

Blund and Blunt (Blunðr, dozing, slumber), Brock (Bróki), Hannay (Hani, a cock), Hacker and Harker (Hákr), Harfoot (Héra-fotr, a Danish king), Read, Reader (Hreðr), Rell (Hrella), Rooke (Hrúkr), Root (Hrútr), Hook (Húkr), Catt (Köttr, a cat), Kemp, Camp (Kampi, a champion), Capps, Capper (Kappi), Kimber (Kimbi), Cropper (Kroppr), Maxey (Maxi), Masey, Macey (Mási), Monk (Munki), Orry (Orri, a moor fowl), Peak, Pick (Pík), Payne (Peini), Ramm (Ramr, strong), Spurr (Spörr, a sparrow), Stott (Stoti, foolish), Sandys (Sandi), Sellers, Sell (Selr, a seal), Silver (Silfri), Strong (Strangi), Scarth (Scarði, hare-lip), Skinner (Skinni), Scory (Skorri), Skeat, Skett (Skyti, a marksman, a shooter), Stubbs (Stubbi), Syers, Siers (Syr), Young (Ungi), Horrocks (Örrek) are familiar names derived from old Norse nicknames.

Among these also may be classed pet names. In girls Sigga from Sig-riðr, Gunna from Guð-run, Inga from Ing-unn, Imba from Ingi-björg, Gudda from Guð-riðr, etc.

In boys Siggi from Sig-urðr, Gvendr from Guð-mundr, Simbi from Sigmundr, Brynki from Bryn-jólfr, Steinki from Stein-grimr, Mangi from Magnus, etc.

A list of these will be found in the appendix to the Norse names.

The Anglo-Saxons also had their nicknames. In Codex Dipl. are Godwine Rust (rustiness), Toui hwita (white), Towi reâda (red), Brihtric geonga (younger), Þurcyl hwita, Þurcyl blâca, Godwine reâda, Eâdgyfu swanhals (Edith the swan-necked), Æðelflœd hwite, Harald Hâranfôt (harefoot), Þurcyl myranheâfod (mareshead) Eâdrîc streôna (the acquirer), from streôn (treasure), Eâdberht Pren (priest), Oda se gôda (the good), Ælfgâr se gyldena (the golden) Ælfrîc Prœt (ingenious), Anfrid ccocesfôt (cocksfoot). Also Mol or Mûl (mule), Leofing (dear-ling, darling), hwœde (gentle), Tâte (tender), Enede (duck), Crâwe (crow), Coifi, Coefe, Coefig, Cêfig (the bold or active one), Dun (dark), Mucel (big), Brorda (swordsman), Cnebba (with a beak), Stefna (with a stem or prow—a ship-owner), Pâda (with a tunic), Buc (stag), and even Bucge and Bycge were used as by-names.

Of pet-names or diminutives there are Totta for Torthelm, Sicgga for Sigiberd, Æti for Eâdsige, Ælle for Ælfwine, Odda for Ordgâr, Podda, Dudda, Bubba, Tudda, Obe, Offa, Ibe, Beda, Becca, Beonna, Acca, Heca, Lulla, may have had a similar origin.

Of later date may be mentioned that of Fortescue, said to have been bestowed on Sir Richard le Fort, one of the leaders of the Conqueror's army at the Battle of Hastings, who had the good fortune to protect his chief by bearing before him the *escue*, or shield.

The name of Plantagenet, borne by eight successive kings of England, originated with Fulke or Foulques, Count of Anjou, about the twelfth century, who went on a pilgrimage to Jerusalem, and wore in his helmet, as a mark of his humility, a piece of *planta genista*, or broom. Arm-strong and Strongitharm arose from some feat of strength; Santerer was one who had been to the Holy Land (Saint Terre); Romer, one who had been to Rome; Palmer, a pilgrim, etc.

Again, Applejohn, Brownjohn, Littlejohn, Micklejohn, Prettyjohn, Properjohn, Upjohn, etc., are probably of this class. The French have Beaujean, Bonjean, Grandjean, Grosjean, Henryjean, Klinjean, Mallejean, Neujean, Petitjean.

II.—CLAN OR TRIBAL NAMES

'My foot is on my native heath and my name is MacGregor.'—SCOTT.

According to the Rev. Dr. Todd:

'Clan signifies children or descendants. The tribe being descended from a common ancestor, the chieftain, as the representative of that ancestor, was regarded as the common father of the clan, and they as his children.'

The Gaelic *Mac*, the Irish *O*, the British *Ap*, the Norse *ungar*, the Frisian *ingar* and *en*, the Anglo-Saxon *ing*, the Norman *Fitz*,* are all indications of a family name.

'By Mac and O you'll always know
True Irishmen, they say;
But if they lack both "O" and "Mac,"
No Irishmen are they.'

The ancient tribe of Waring or Wearing, the Vœringi or Veringen, originally from what is still called the Vœringifjord in Norway, formed the celebrated Varangian Guard of the Byzantine Emperors, which was afterwards recruited largely from the North, and especially from Britain.

The following list, compiled from 'Words and Places,' by the Rev. Isaac Taylor, and from 'Surnames as a Science,' by Mr R. Ferguson, will be found to contain ancient Scandinavian and Frisian family names, with the Old English or Anglo-Saxon suffix.

A reference to and comparison with the Icelandic names of the Landnámábók and the Saxon tenants of Domesday Book will prove of great assistance to the reader.

Mr Taylor points out settlements of these families in England, Normandy, and Germany. Some of these are corruptions of the genitive *an*, as Pœccing for Pœccan.

A

Ading	Arring	Æcling	Ælping
Alding	Arting	Æfing	Æscing
Aldring	Æbing	Ælcing	Æscling
Anning	Æbling	Æling	Æsling
Anting	Æcering	Ælfing	Æting
Arling			

* Verstegan is of opinion that the prefix Fitz originated in Flanders. It is remarkable that it is now unknown in France, and that it does not occur in the ancient chronicles of that country (Noble).

The generally accepted idea is that it is derived from the Latin *filius*, Fr. *fils*, old Norman Fr. *filz, fiz, fitz*. It has been used to distinguish the illegitimate children of kings and princes of royal blood. Many Irish families substituted Fitz for Mac in Norman times.

B

Bæbing	Beorning	Bocing	Brisling
Bæding	Beorhting	Bofing	Briting
Bædling	Berling	Boling	Bruning
Bæling	Bermaring	Bonding	Bryding
Bafing	Berring	Bonning	Bucing
Basing	Bessing	Bosing	Buding
Beccing	Billing	Brahcing	Bulling
Belling	Bing	Branting	Burring
Belting	Binning	Bressing	Busling
Benning	Birling	Bridling	Bydeling
Beofing	Bitering	Brihtling	Byrting
Beoring	Blœcing	Brimming	Bytting
Beorling	Bobbing	Brining	

C

Cæding	Cearling	Cnudling	Coling
Cæging	Cenesing	Cocing	Cressing
Cæssing	Cenning	Coding	Cridling
Calling	Centing	Cofing	Cubing
Camering	Cerring	Colling	Culling
Ceading	Cifing	Coping	Cylling
Ceadling	Cnotting	Coring	Cyrtling
Ceaning			

D

Dæfing	Denning	Dinning	Doring
Dælling	Deorling	Dinting	Dunning
Darting	Diceling	Dissing	During
Dedding	Didding	Docing	Dycing
Deming	Dilling	Doding	

E

Eadling	Ecging	Elming	Epping
Eagling	Ecling	Elring	Ercensing
Eardling	Eding	Elsing	Essing
Earming	Efing	Emming	Etting
Eastring	Elcing	Eoring	Evering
Eberding	Elling	Eorping	

F

Fearing	Feorming	Freling	Fring
Fearning	Fincing	Frescing	Froding
Ferring. *See*	Finning	Fresting	Fyling
Wæring	Folcing	Frilling	

G

Gæging	Geofening	Gilling	Gisling
Garing	Gerling	Ging	Golding
Gealding	Gestinge	Gipping	Gystling
Gedding			

H

Hæcing	Halling	Hensing	Horing
Hæding	Hanesing	Heoring	Horning
Hæfering	Haning	Hereling	Hucing
Hægling	Hearding	Hiceling	Huding
Hæsling	Hearing	Hilling	Hunding
Hæssing	Helling	Hocing	Huning
Hæsting	Helveling	Honing	Hunting
Hafocing	Heming	Hopping	

I

Iceling	Illing	Ipping	Ising
Ifing	Imming	Iring	Isling

L

Læcing	Leasing	Lidling	Loding
Læfering	Leding	Ling	Lofing
Leafing	Ledring	Locing	Lulling

M

Mading	Mæting	Merling	Motting
Mæding	Malling	Milling	Mundling
Mægling	Manning	Mincing	Mutling
Mæring	Mecing	Minting	Mycging
Mæssing	Melling	Molling	Myrcing

N

Næcing	Nolling	Notting	Nyding
Nedding			

O

Ofing	Ossing

P

Pæccing	Pætring	Petling	Poling
Pæfing	Paling	Pipering	Porning
Pælling	Peging	Piting	Puning
Pæting	Penning	Pocling	

R

Ræding	Ricling	Ripling	Rossing
Ræfning	Riding	Rising	Rowing
Ratling	Rifing	Rocing	Rucing
Renning	Rilling	Roding	Ruscing
Ricing	Rimming	Rolling	Rusting

S

Sæling	Scearding	Sepping	Stufing
Sandling	Scearing	Serring	Sulling
Sandring	Sceding	Sinning	Surling
Sceacling	Scyrling	Snoring	Swanning
Sceading	Scyting	Snoting	Swefeling
Sceafing	Seafing	Specing	Sycling
Sceafling	Sealfing	Stæning	Sydling
Scealing	Seaxling	Stelling	Syfing
Sceaning	Secging		

T

Tæding	Terring	Toding	Trumping
Tæling	Thorning	Torting	Tucing
Tæting	Tilling	Tring	Tutling
Teorling	Ting		

U

Uffing	Uling	Upping

V

Veorling (Feorling)

W

Wacering	Wealcing	Wendling	Wiscing
Wading	Wealcring	Weording	Witling
Wælsing	Wealding	Wiccing	Witting
Wæpling	Wealdring	Wickling	Wræning
Wæring	Wealing	Wiging	Wrihting
Wasing	Wearning	Willing	Wylfing
Wating	Wedering	Wining	Wylring
Watring	Welling	Wipping	

III.—PLACE-NAMES

' A local habitation and a name.'—Midsummer-Night's Dream.

It was the custom of the Norsemen and the Saxons to give their names to the lands upon which they settled.

Hence it is that so many towns and villages in England as well as in Normandy show the name of the original occupier who appropriated the soil by right of conquest, and the prefix is generally found in the possessive case common to all Teutonic nations.

After the Norman Conquest the followers of William, among whom the land was divided, adopted the title of the manor or estate granted to them by the king.

These afterwards became their family names.

Ivo de Taillebois was made Baron of Kendal, but his descendant, William, assumed the style of de Lancaster. Robert de Tours became Robert de Lowick from his English estate, as, in like manner, William le Fleming was William de Aldingham from his lordship of that manor, and Nigel, younger son of Robert de Statford, inheriting the manor of Gresley, in the county of Derby, took the name and was known as Nigel de Gresley. This last family is one of the very few remaining of those who have retained their lands since the Conquest.

In the reign of Henry VIII., Welsh gentlemen, who had not done so in Norman times, adopted the name of their estates. It is very likely that in after-years change of residence was usually the cause of the bestowal of the original abode as a surname.

About the thirteenth century another way of adopting place-names sprung up, as is seen from the registers of wills in the Court of Husting, London, A.D. 1258 to 1358, at Lincoln and other cities.

The word 'atte,' as implying residence, if not possession, crept in, and thereby arose such names as Atte Boure, Atte Brig, Atte Hash, Atte Hay, Atte Kirkstile, Atte Lane, Atte Maydens, Atte Stile, Atte Well. Indeed, this custom may be traced back to Anglo-Saxon times, for in a charter, No. 775 of the Codex Dip., there occurs Eâdmar æt Burhâm, and in No. 492, dated about 960, we have Godwine æt Fechâm, Eâdric æt Hô, Ælfgâr æt Meâpahâm.

William Atwater was Bishop of Lincoln in 1574.

In course of time the *de* and the *atte* were dropped, as the persons using them lost their estates or changed their place of abode; but retaining the surname, they wandered into various parts of the country as fancy or necessity led them.

Hence it happens that many extraordinary surnames, which have been a puzzle to investigators hitherto, and almost defy derivation, are found to be traceable to some obscure spot in Great Britain or France.

Richard Verstegan wrote in 1673

> 'In Foord, in Ham, in Ley, in Tun
> The most of English surnames run.'

But it is only a partial statement, as we know. Also, as Camden says,

> 'By Tre, Ros, Lan, Car, Pol, and Pen,
> Ye shall know the most Cornishmen,'

is true as far as it goes, for many other local names in that county have given names to families.

Names derived from localities are more common in England and Scotland than in Wales and Ireland.

IV.—OFFICIAL NAMES

'I am become a name.'—TENNYSON.

When the country became settled under Edward the Confessor, and the Norsemen, Saxon, and Welsh lived together with something like a suspension of their international feuds, the land was brought into a semblance of law and order, and, consequently, offices of influence and responsibility arose.

Bright, Steward, and Despencer are names of this period. They all mean the same thing. *Bryti* is the Norse and Dispensator the Latin equivalent of Steward.

Lagman (lawgiver), Fawcett (Forseti, judge), Alderman, Reeve, Sheriff, Tabberer (Tabarðr, a Tabard), Chamberlain (Camerarius), Chancellor (Canceler), Chaplain (Capellanus), Clerk (Clericus), Deacon (Diaconus), Beadle (Bedellus), Latimer (Latinarius, or interpreter), Miles (Miles, a soldier), Marshall (Marescal), Redman (Radman), Sumner or Somner (Chaucer's Sompnoure, a summoner or apparitor), Poynder (a bailiff), Parker (Park-keeper), Palliser (Park-pailings keeper), Franklin (a free-holder), Vavasour or Valvasour* (an office or dignity below a baron and above a knight), Arblaster (Balistarius), Botiler (Butler), etc.

Some, such as Abbot, Bishop, and Scripture-names, may have originally been given to play-actors who took the parts in mediæval times, as people now speak of the Ober-Ammergau actors by their stage names.

V.—TRADE NAMES

'A rose by any other name would smell as sweet.'—*Romeo and Juliet.*

As might be expected, a man's occupation gave him notoriety, especially if he were skilled in his handicraft.

Even among primitive nations there seems to have been a tendency to adopt this mode of distinguishing an artificer by his calling.

The Norse *Skapti*, originally a shaft-maker, became a nickname, and afterwards a personal name as Scapti and Scafti, the Scotch form of which is Shafto. *Sneypir* (a snipper), gives us Snapper ; *Dengir* (one who whets), Denger ; *Kembir* (a comber), Kimber; *Smið* (a smith), etc.

The Anglo-Saxon *Bæc-ere* (baker), *Cu-hyrde* (cowherd), *Feormere* (farmer), *Fiscere* (fisher), *Fugelere* (fowler), *Fullere* (bleacher), *Sceáphyrde* (shepherd), *Sàpere* (sailor), *Webere* (weaver), etc.

In Domesday Book occur Arbalistarius (a crossbowman), Aurifaber (goldsmith), Arcuarius (bowyer), Artifex (workman), Accipitrarius (fal-coner), Cocus (cook), Carpentarius, Censorius, Cubicularius (groom of the chamber), Dapifer (a server), Faber (smith), Forestarius, Harparius, Ingeniator, Joculator, Larderius, Lorimarius (bridle-maker), Monialis, Machinator, Medicus, Ostiarius (usher), Porcarius (swineherd), Piscator

---

* The Norman kings had an officer who kept ward at the entrances and borders of the realm, *ad valvas Regni.*

(fisher), Pincerna (butler), Portarius (porter), Stalrus, Staller (groom), Stirman, Scutularius (page), Scriba, Tonsor, Venator (huntsman).

In middle English times we find, according to Lower, Massinger (Fr., Massager, a messenger), Pottinger (apothecary), Brownsmith (a maker of 'brown bills'?), Nasmith (nail-smith?), Ferrier and Farrier (horse-shoer), Jenner (joiner), Furner (Fr., Fournier, a baker), Lavender (Fr., Lavandier, a washerman), Pullinger (Fr., Boulanger, a baker), Pointer (a maker of 'points,' an obsolete article of dress), Pilcher (a maker of pilches, the great coat of the fourteenth century), Shearman and Sharman (one who shears worsteds, fustians, etc.). They sheared the roughest off the nap of cloth before it was done by machinery. Caird (a travelling tinker), Maunder (a beggar), Kidder and Kidman (a pedlar ; N., *kyta*, to hawk, deal), Crowther (one who plays upon the crowd ; Welsh, *crwth*, a rude sort of violin), Polter and Pulter (poulterer), etc.

It is open to question, however, whether some of the names popularly ascribed to occupations, such as Arkwright, Baker, Barber, Beadle, Botwright, Butcher, Carter, Cartwright, Cooper, Carver, Collier, Driver, Dyer, Fidler, Fuller, Glaisher, Iremonger, Leadbeater, Packer, Painter, Pinder, Pointer, Plummer, Potter, Poulter, Plowright, Nailer, Osler, Sawyer, Seaman, Shearer, Sharman, Shearman, Sheppard, Skinner, Tanner, Tinker, Tucker, Turner, Tyler, Walker, Wheeler, Warrener, etc., will not bear a different interpretation. The reader is invited to study these names in their proper places.

In England there is one Smith in every seventy-three persons, in Scotland one in sixty-eight.

VI.—CHRISTIAN NAMES

'What is your name?'—*Tempest*, Act iii. Sc. 1.

When Christianity spread among the northern nations in the eleventh century, a baptismal name followed as a matter of course, and for a long time was the only one possessed by the individual upon whom it was conferred. Thus John, Peter, and Paul were great favourites, and those who were named in this way transmitted the Christian name to their descendants, who became known as Janson, Johnson, Peterson, Patterson, Polson, etc. (N. *sonr*, pl. *synir*). In Wales and Cornwall, as well as in Denmark, Friesland, and the Netherlands, the final *s* alone served to mark the fact that it had become a patronymic. Indeed, it is remarkable that a large proportion of the family names of Wales should be those of Teutonic, Christian, and other names, and is difficult to account for, as there is no evidence of a special legislative enactment (as was the case in Ireland) requiring the inhabitants of the Principality to adopt such designations as would be understood by the English. Mr T. E. Morris thinks 'there are sufficient grounds for believing that the Teutonic names of the (Norman) invaders were gradually adopted, first by the large landowners of Wales, a class which included noblemen and gentry, then by their retainers and tenants, and finally by the ordinary common people.'

Whether the final *s* indicates the family name or not, it makes the plural, even if it does not represent *synir*, *son*, or *sen*, and it seems quite natural for us, in these days, to speak of the Whites, the Browns, the Smiths, the Robinsons, and even the Joneses, the Edwardses and Thomases.

In some instances the Christian name is undoubtedly a contraction of the Latin form in use in early English times, for it is very common to find in old documents John's for Johannes, Will's for Willelmus, Ricard's for Ricardus, Edward's for Edwardus, Phillip's for Philippus, Jacob's for Jacobus, etc.

Of these names there are also many diminutives and modifications, as Jon, Ion, Jan, Jane, Jennis, Jenner, Jenkin, Jinks. In like manner we find Pete, Peet, Pate, Pett, Pitt, Pittar. Also Paul, Spaull, Powell, Pull, Pulley, Powley, Pollyn, Poll, Pole, Pullein, Pulleyne, Poole, etc.

Jones is the second most common name in England.

VII.—FOREIGN NAMES

' I cannot tell what the dickens his name is.'—*Merry Wives of Windsor*, Act iii. Sc. 2.

Some of these are undoubtedly Norman, others are more recent, and may presumably be set down to Huguenot and other refugee emigrants, or to the influx of followers of the Orange or Hanoverian Dynasties.

Edward III. was the first to promote woollen manufacture in England. He brought seventy families of Walloons for the purpose in 1331. A colony of Flemings was established in Pembrokeshire in the reign of Henry I. There is a list of the names of ' Foreigners' in the town and county of Cambridge in the year 1440, including French, Dutch, Flemish, Irish and Scotch. French and Flemish names came into N.-W. Lincolnshire and S.-E. Yorkshire with Vermuyden and the draining of 'The Levels' in the seventeenth century. The Irish Parliament in 1674 passed an Act granting letters of naturalisation to French and Flemish Huguenot refugees. Colonies were founded at Dublin, Kilkenny, Portarlington, Waterford, Cork, and Lisburn. In 1709 a fleet was sent to Rotterdam by Queen Anne, which brought over about 7000 German emigrants from the Palatinate of the Rhine. About 3000 were sent to North America, the remainder, except a few families which remained in England, settled principally in the County of Limerick.

It is well known, moreover, that many French prisoners of war during the reign of George III. married or formed other ties during their captivity, and when peace was restored, remained in this country. To these may be added those who have been attracted to Great Britain by greater facilities of trade, or more political or individual liberty than they found at home.

Many names bear a close resemblance to such as are at present existing in the North of Germany and in the Low Countries—a large number, indeed, being very little changed.

The question arises, Are they direct importations, or are they derived through Frisian sources?

There is no doubt about many Frisian names having spread along the southern shore of the Baltic, for the prevalence of the diminutive 'ke,' in contradistinction to the German 'chen,' is transparently obvious. Nevertheless, many of them are difficult to trace, either through the Frisian, or those of ancient Scandinavia as found in Iceland.

Further research may possibly throw more light upon this interesting but complicated subject.

Of these foreign names many have become naturalised in this country. The earliest instances occur among the Norman tenants in chief in Domesday Book.

Those of more recent times will be readily distinguished as Aufrere, Beauchamp, Caux, Drew, Durrant, Frere, Grand, Jacques, Le Neve, Motte, Pettit, Roche, Sant, Vipond, etc.

Sir W. Russell brought over settlers from Holland to drain the Cambridgeshire Fens. At Thorney there is a French Register of Baptisms, 1653 to 1727.

The intimate relationship between Scotland, France, and the Netherlands, which existed before and after the time of the ill-fated Queen Mary, will account for the presence of names in Scotland which are clearly derived from the latter countries.

VIII.—Foundling Names

'Phœbus, what a name!'—Byron.

There is every reason to believe that we are indebted to the parish beadle and the workhouse officials for many extraordinary and even ridiculous names which cannot be derived from any known sources. They have been evolved from the imagination of the Bumbles of a past generation, as Charles Dickens shows us in 'Oliver Twist,' and they remain a puzzle to all who would attempt to clear them up, unless they are classed in this section.

Indeed, it is a convenience to have a receptacle of this sort in which to stow away, until further research comes to our aid, such names as philologists cannot yet account for, except upon the supposition that the ingenuity of the public servants has suggested them. Some of those which have been a source of wonder to many for a long time, and were supposed to be foundling names, can now be shown to possess a real historical signification.

Possibly, by-and-by, more may be rescued, but in the meantime they must be classified somehow, and it is better to put them on the unknown list rather than invent a fanciful origin which may be, after all, mere guess-work.

According to Burns' 'History of Parish Registers,' p. 80, an Act was passed in the second year of George III., 1761-2, specially directing that children received in a workhouse were, in cases where their names were unknown, to have surnames given them by the overseers and churchwardens.

That there was a custom of naming foundling children after the parishes where they have been picked up is proved by the entries in the registers of several of the London City churches. The Registers of the

Temple, London, show that in that district alone, between 1728 and 1755, no less than 104 foundlings were christened, all of whom were surnamed Temple or Templer. Nicholas Acons, after the parish of that name, and Benetfink, Orgar, Sherehog, with many others, exist as surnames which may be all traced to this source. Other stray children have been named from the circumstances under which they were found.

Over the signature of 'Peter Lombard,' a writer in the *Church Times* has recently drawn attention to the registers of St Mary Woolnoth where are these entries: 'A male child was found in our parish with a penny in his hand, and was named accordingly Henry Penny.' 'A child found in the alley between the church and the stocks on the morning of St John's Day was named John Before Day.'

A girl who was so picked up was christened Anne Monday, after the day of the week, and a boy who was laid 'atte Mr Garrett's dore' was christened 'John Bynight.' Such names as Christmas, Easter, Lammas, Paske, etc., may have been suggested by the season when a child was found.

Lower gives, among other instances, Jack Parish, Tom Among-us, and Napkin Brooker as the names bestowed by the parish authorities on foundlings. The last-mentioned, it is stated, was found by the side of a brook, tied up in a napkin.

Allbone (from Holburn?) and such names as Lilywhite and Sweetapple may belong perhaps to this category.

At the baptism of the children first taken into the Foundling Hospital, which was on the 29th March 1741, it is recorded that 'there was at the ceremony a fine appearance of persons of quality and distinction. His Grace the Duke of Bedford, our President, their Graces the Duke and Duchess of Richmond, the Countess of Pembroke, and several others, honouring the children with their names and being their sponsors.' For long after this it was the fashion to come down to the Foundling on a Sunday morning to be sponsor to a child, and to give it a name quite incongruous with its station and fortune. A child was left with a £50 note pinned to its clothes, and it was called Japhet Newland from the name of the governor of the Bank of England, Abraham Newland, on the note. The last child taken in when the parliamentary control ceased was named Kitty Finis!

A lady sends that of a family named Haycock. She was told that the father was found as an infant deserted under a haycock. The name is not uncommon, and may be otherwise accounted for. There is a hill in Cumberland called Haycock, and Hayo and Heie are Frisian personal names, to which may be added the diminutive 'cock.' Indeed, Heij-Koch is a Dutch proper name.

ABBREVIATIONS

N. Old Norse (Icelandic), S. Swedish, D. Danish, F. Frisian, Dch. Dutch, Fl. Flemish, Fr. French, G. German, A.S. Anglo-Saxon, N.-Fr. Norman-French, D.B. Domesday Book, p.n. personal name, n.n. nickname, loc. n. local name.

OLD NORSE PERSONAL NAMES

FROM ISLANDS LANDNÁMA-BÓK (THE ICELANDIC BOOK OF SETTLEMENT)
AND OTHER SOURCES

(*Revised by Professor Hjalmer Petersen of Christiania*)

A

Abraham (Bp.)
Adam
Aðisl
Aðrianus
Afvaldr
Agnar
Agni
Aistein
Albert
Aldis (f.)
Alexius
Álfarekkar or Halfrekkar
Álfarinn
Álfdis (f.)
Álfeiðr (f.)
Álfgeirr
Álfgerðr (f.)
Álfjótr or Ulfjótr
Álfr
Áli
Álrekr
Álöf (f.)
Ámundi
Án
Áni
Anti-cristr

Are (Ari)
Arinbjörn
Armoðr
Arnaldr
Arnbjörg
Arnbjörn
Arndis (f.)
Arneiðr (f.)
Arnfinnr
Arnfriðr (f.)
Arngeirr
Arngerðr (f.)
Arngrimr
Arngunnr
Arnhaldr. See Arnaldr
Árni
Arnis
Arnkatla (f.)
Arnkel
Arnlaug (f.)
Arnlaugr
Arnleif
Arnljótr
Arnmoðr
Arnoddr
Arnóra (f.)

Arnórr
Arnriðr
Arnsteinn
Arnþjófr
Arnþóra. See Arnóra
Arnþórr. See Arnórr
Arnðruðr (f.)
Arun
Ása. See Æsa
Ásbera (f.)
Ásbjarnarsynir
Ásbjörg (f.)
Ásbjörn
Ásborg (Asbjörg)
Ásbrandr
Ásdis (f.)
Ásgautr
Ásgeirr
Ásgerðr (f.)
Ásgrimr
Áshildr (f.)
Ási
Áskell, n.n.
Askr
Áslákr, n.n.

Áslaug (f.)
Ásleif (f.)
Ásleikr
Ásmóðr
Ásmundr
Ásný (f.)
Ásolfr
Ásrauðr
Ásta (f.)
Ástriðr (f.)
Ásvaldr
Ásvarðr
Ásvör (f.)
Atli
Audolfr
Audr (f.)
Auðunn
Aun
Aungull
Aunundr. See Önundr
Aurlyger. See Örlygr
Auzor. See Özurr
Ásvaldi
Ávaldr
Ávangr

From other sources

Aðils. *A.S.* Eadgils (a king) Angan-tyr, p.n. *A.S.* Ongentheow
Akra-carl, cogn. Aska-spillir, cogn.
Akra-spillir, cogn. Auðr (f.), p.n.
Ali-karl, n.n. Auðunn, p.n. *A.S.* Eâðvin
Amb-höfði, n.n. *See* Hjart-höfði Aust-rænn, n.n.
Amloði (Hamlet)

B

Baldvini	Bjargey (f.)	Blót-mar	Briann or Brann
Bálki	Bjarnaðr	Blund-Ketill	(Gaelic)
Barbara	Bjarneyja	Blundr, n.n.	Bryngerðr
Bardi	Bjarnharðr	Blæingr	Brynhildr (f.)
Bardr	Bjarnheðin	Bogi	Brynjólfr
Bárekr	Bjarni	Bolli	Brodd-Helgi
Barna, n.n.	Bjarnvarðr. *See*	Borgillðr (f.)	Broddi
Baugr, n.n.	Bjarnharðr	Bót	Broddr
Beda	Bjartmarr	Bótey (f.)	Brunda-Bjalfi
Beinir	Bifra, n.n.	Bótolf	Bruni
Beiskaldi	Bjolan (Gaelic)	Bragi	Brunólfr
Bekan (Gaelic)	Bjólfr	Brandax	Brúsi
Bera (f.)	Bjollok (f.),	Brandi	Bröndólfr
Berðlu, n.n.	(Gaelic)	Brandr	Budli
Bergðis (f.)	Birna (f.)	Brandönundr	Burislafr
Bergljót (f.)	Birningr	Brattr	Bægifótr
Bergr	Birtingr	Braut-Önundr	Böðmóðr
Bergþora (f.)	Bitru, n.n.	(Svia-Konungr)	Bódólfr
Bergþor	Björg	Breidar-Skeggi	Bödvarr
Bersi	Björn	Breidr	Böggvir
Bjaðmakr	Björnolfr	Brennu-Kári	Bölverkr
(Gaelic)	Bla-kinn	Bresasynir	Börkr
Bjálfi	Blígr	Bresi	

From other sources

Bak-skiki, cogn. Blá-ber, cogn. Brimstein, n.n.
Barka-bazi, cogn. Blá-hattr, cogn. Bróki, n.n.
Berbeinn, cogn. Blá-siða, cogn. Bryti
Beiskaldi, n.n. Blá-tönn, cogn. Bullu-fótr
Beit-stokkr, cogn. Blígr, cogn. Buttr
Deli, cogn. Blunðr, cogn. Buttraldi
Berserkr, n.n. Bog-sveigr, cogn. Bui. *D.* Boye
Bersi, p.n. Bófi, n.n. Bægi-fótr, cogn.
Bifr, cogn. Bragi Boðvildr
Birtingr, n.n. Brák, n.n. Böggull, n.n.
Bitra, cogn. Brikar-nef, n.n. Böl-viss, n.n.

D

Dadi	Dalkr	Dómarr	Duf-þakr (Gaelic)
Dagr	Dalla (f.)	Drafdritr (Gaelic)	= Dofnakr
Dagrun	Darri	Drafli	Dugfus (Gaelic
Dagstyggr	Digr-Ormr	Drumb-Oddr	Dygvi [Dufgus)
Dala-alfr	Dís. *See* Dýs	Dufan (Gaelic)	Dýrfinnr (f.)
Dala-kollr = Hof-	Dofnakr	Dufnall (Gaelic)	Dýri
kolli (?)	Dómaldr	Dufniall (Gaelic)	Dýs (f.)

From other sources

Dampr
Dapi, n.n.
Dengir, cogn.

Drettingr, cogn.
Dyðrill or Dyrðill, n.n.

Dyntill, cogn.
Dytta, cogn.

E

Eadmund. *See*	Eldjárn	Erný (Eirný)	Eyja (f.)
Jatmundr	Elfraðr	Erplingar	Eyjarr
Edna (f.)	Elina (f.)	Erpr	Eyjolfr
Egill	Elliðagrimr	Errubeinn	Eylaugr
Eiðr	Endridi	Evarr. *See* Ævarr	Eymundr
Eilifir	Enoc	Exna-Þorir. *See*	Eyrný (f.)
Einarr	Erlendr	Yxna-Þorir	Eysteinn
Eindriði	Erlingr (dim. of	Eydis (f.)	Eyvindr (a jarl)
Eiríkr	Jarl)	Eyfreyðr	Eyvör (f.)
Eirný	Erlygr	Eygerðr (f.)	Eyþjófr
Eldgrímr			

From other sources
Eysill, n.n.

F

Falgerðr (f.)	Finnbjörn	Flosi	Freysteinn
Falki	Finnbogi	Flugu-Grimr	Freyviðr
Fastný (f.)	Finngeirr	Foka	Frið-Froði (Dana-
Faxa-Brandr	Finni	Fostolfr	Konungr)
Faxi	Finnr	Frayr (Freyr)	Friðgerðr
Feilan (Gaelic)	Finnvarðr	Freygerðr (f.)	Friðleifr = Odd-
Fenkell	Fiska-Finnr	Freyja. *See* Fraija	leifr
Fjarska = Fiska(?)	Fjölnir	Freyleif. *See*	Friðmundr
Fiðr	Fjörleif (f.)	Fjörleif	Friðrekr (Frith-
Filippus	Fleinn	Freyer	recr)
Finna (f.)	Flóki	Freysgyðlingr	Fróði

From other sources

Fasi, n.n.
Fisk-reki, n.n.

Fola-fótr, n.n.
Freys-goði, n.n.

Fuð-hundr, n.n.
Fugl

G

Galmi
Galti
Gamli
Garðar, or
   Garðarr
Garða-Snorri
Gaukr
Gautr
Gautrekr
Geirbjörg (f.)
Geirhildr = Geir-
   riðr (f.)
Geiri
Geirlaug (f.)
Geirleifr
Geirmundr
Geirný (f.)
Geirolfr
Geirr
Geirriðr (f.)
Geirröðr
Geirsteinn
Geirþjofr
Geitir
Gellir (Gaelic)
Gerdr (f.)

Gerpir
Gestr (f.)
Gjaflaug
Gjafvaldr
Gils
Gisl
Gisli
Gisroðr
Gizur
Glædir
Glámr, or Glam-
   maðr, n.n.
Gleðill, n.n.
Gljómall (Gaelic)
Glíru-Halli
Glúmr
Gnupa
Góa (f.)
Goðormr-Goddi
Goðrun (f.)
Godun. *See* Jódis
Gollnir
Gormr
Corr
Goti
Goðiscolkr (Bp.)

Goðmundr =
   Guðmundr
Goðröphr
Grafar-leifr
Granni
Graut
Greipr. *See* Gripr
Grelöd (f., Gaelic)
Grenjaðr
Grettir. *See* Ófeigr
Grima (f.)
Grímkell
Grímólfr
Grímr
Grimssynr
Grjótgarðr
Gripr
Gris
Gróa (f.)
Guðbjörg (f.)
Guðbrandr
Guðhormr. *See*
   Guttormr
Guðiskolkr. *See*
   Goðiscolkr
Guðlaug (f.)

Guðleif (f.)
Guðmund
Guðný (f.)
Guðriðr (f.)
Guðrikr
Guðrun (f.)
Guðröðr
Guðormr
Gufa (Gaelic)
Gufi
Gull-Þorir
Gunnarr
Gunnbjörn
Gunnhildr (f.)
Gunnlaugr
Gunnólfr
Gunnsteinn
Gunnvaldr
Gunnvör
Gunn-Þjólfr
Guttormr = Guð-
   hormr
Gyða (kona)
Gyðja
Gyrða
Göngu-Hrólfr

From other sources

Galli and Gallaðr, n.n.
Galpin, n.n.
Gapa-muðr, n.n.
Geit-heðinn
Geit-skór, n.n.
Gellini, n.n.
Gestr
Gisl, Gisli, p.n. by metathesis ; Gils
   —as Þor-gils, Auð-gils, Spá-gils,
   Her-gils
Gleðill, n.n.
Glenna, n.n.
Gloppa, n.n.
Glúmr, n.n.
Gnúpa = Gnufa

Goddi, n.n.
Gormr, contr. of Goð-ormr.
   A.S. Guthrum
Grá-barði, cogn.
Graut-nefr, n.n.
Greifi, n.n.
Gríss, n.n.
Gull-hjálmr, n.n.
Gull-höttr, n.n.
Gull-knapper, n.n.
Gull-kroppr, n.n.
Gull-skeggr, n.n.
Gull-tanni, n.n.
Gurpr, n.n.

H

Hafgrimr	Haukr (berserkr)	Hildi-björn	Hreinn
Hafliði	Hávarðr	Hildi-brandr	Hrifla
Hafljótr	Hávarr	Hildi-grimmr	Hringr
Hafnar-Ormr	Heðin	Hildigunnr (f.)	Hríseyjar
Hafr, n.n.	Heggr	Hildir	Hrisi, n.n.
Hafrsteinn	Heiðr	Hildiriðr (f.)	Hróaldr-hryggr
Hafsteinn	Heimir (jarl)	Hildi-tannr, n.n.	Hróarr
Hafþora (f.)	Heimlaug (f.)	Hild-ólfr	Hróðgeirr
Hafþorr	Heimrekr (Bp.)	Hildr	Hróðmarr
Hagbarðr	Helga (f.)	Hjörleifr	Hróðný (f.)
Haki	Helgi	Hjörr	Hróðólfr (Bp.)
Hákon	Helgu-Steinnarr	Hjörtr	Hroi
Háleygar	Helias	Hlenni	Hrojn, n.n.
Hálfdan (King)	Hella-Björn	Hlif	Hrólfr
Hálfr (K.)	Hellu-Narfi	Hlödverr	Hrollaugr
Hallaðr (jarl)	Herborg (f.)	Hnaki	Hrolleifr
Hallbera (f.)	Herdis (f.)	Hnokan (Gaelic)	Hrómundr
Hallbjörg (f.)	Herbrandr	Hofgarða	Hrónarr
Hallbjörn (f.)	Herfinnr	Hof-Kolli	Hrossbjörn
Halldis (f.)	Hergils	Holbarki, n.n.	Hrosskell
Halldora (f.)	Hergrimr	Hólmfastr	Hrútr
Halldórr	Hergunnr (f.)	Hólmfriðr (f.)	Hrærekr
Hallfreðr	Herjólfr	Holmgöngu-	Hudar-Steinarr
Hallfriðr (f.)	Herlaugr	Hrafn	Húnbogi
Hallgerðr (f.)	Herleifr	Holmgöngu-	Hundi
Hallgils	Hermoðr	Máni	Hundólfr (jarl)
Hallgrima (f.)	Hermundr	Holmgöngu-	Hungerð (f.)
Hallgrimr	Herrauðr	Starri	Hunrauðr
Halli	Herriðr	Hólmkell	Hvati
Hallkatla	Hersteinn	Holm-Starri	Hvítserkr
Hallkell	Hervarðr	Holmsteinn	Hyrna, n.n.
Hallormr	Hertili	Holta-ɏorir	Hyrningr
Hallr	Hervör (f.)	Holti, n.n.	Hý-nefr, n.n.
Hallsteinn	Her-ɏjólfr	Hraði	Hækingr
Hallvarðr	Her-ɏruðr (f.)	Hrafn	Hængr, n.n.
Hallveig	Hesta-Gellir	Hrafna-Floki	Hæringr
Hallvör	Heyjángrs-Björn	Hrafnhilðr (f.)	Hofða-ɏórðr
Háls	Heyjángs-Björn	Hrafnkell	Höggvandi, n.n.
Hamall	Hjaldr (K.)	Hrafsi	Höggvin - Kinni,
Hamundr	Hjallkárr	Hramn	n.n.
Haraldr (K.)	Hjalmgerðr (f.)	Hrani	Högni
Hardrefr	Hjalmólfr	Hrappr	Hörða-Kari
Hárekr	Hjálmun-Gautr	Hrefna (f.)	Hörðr
Harri	Hjálp (kona)	Hreiðarr	Höskuldr
Hásteinn	Hjalti		

From other sources

Haddinja-skati, n.n.
Hak-langr, n.n.
Hali, n.n.
Hamðir
Hani, n.n.
Harð-beinn, n.n.
Harð-jaxl, n.n.
Harð-magi, n.n.
Hausa-Kljúfr, n.n.
Hákr, n.n.
Hálfr, n.n.
Hálfs-rekkr, n.n.
Há-fæta, n.n.
Há-nefr, n.n.
Heikil-nefr, n.n.
Heið-rekr (King)
Hein, n.n. *D.* King
Hemingr
Hera-fólr, n.n. *D.* King
Herjan

Herj-ólfr. *A.S.* Here-
  woll
Hiði
Hildingr
Himaldi, n.n.
Hjálmr
Hjálmgeirr
Hjálgrimr
Hjálmgunnr
Hjálm-týr
Hjalm-gerðr
Hjörr
Hjörtr
Hlöðr
Hnúfa, n.n.
Hol-muðr, n.n.
Horti, n.n.
Hrani
Hreða, n.n.
Hregg-viðr

Hreimr, n.n.
Hrella, n.n.
Hrókr
Hrúga, n.n.
Hrúkr, n.n.
Hugi, p.n.
Hundingi
Hundsfótr, n.n.
Húkr, n.n.
Hvitr. *D.* Hvid.
Hvit-beinn, n.n.
Hvita-skald, n.n.
Hvita-ský, n.n.
Hvita-kollr, n.n.
Hvita-leðr, n.n.
Hækill, n.n.
Hænsa-Þorir, n.n.
Hæru-kollr, n.n.
Höd-broddr, n.n.
Höttr

I

Idunn (f.)
Illugi
Indriði
Íngjaldr
Íngibjörg (f.)
Íngigerðr (f.)
Íngileif (f.)

Íngi-marr
Íngi-mundr
Íngimundarsynr
Íngiriðr (f.)
Íngolfr
Ínguðr (f.), or
  Ingvoldr

Íngunn (f.)
Íngunnr (f.)
Íngvarr. *See*
  Yngvarr
Íngvildr. *See*
  Yngvildr

Íngyoldr. *See*
  Inguðr
Ísgerðr (f.)
Ísleifr (Bp.)
Ísólfr
Ísrauðr
Ivarr

From other sources

Imi

Isja, n.n.

Ístru-magi, n.n.

Ísungr, n.n.

J

Jakob
Jarngerðr (f.)
Jatmundr. *See*
  Eadmund
Játvarðr (Edward).
  K. of Eng.

Jóan. *See* Jón
Jódis (f.)
Jófreiðr
Jófriðr (f.)
Jóhann (Bp.)

Jólgeirr
Jón
Jóra (f.)
Jóreiðr (f.)
Jórunn (f.)

Josteinn
Jökull
Jörundr
Jösurr
Jötun-Björn

From other sources

Jarn-hauss, n.n.
Jarn-hryggr, n.n.

Jarn-saxa, n.n.
Jarn-skjöldr, n.n.

Jólfr (a name of Odin)

K

Kaðall (Gaelic)	Kjarran (Gaelic)	Knöttr	Korni
Kaðlin (f., Gaelic)	Kjarfalr (Gaelic)	Koðrán	Krafla
Kálfr	Kjartan (Gaelic)	Kolbeinn	Krákneflingar
Kald-munnr, n.n.	Kjarvalr	Kolbjörn	Kraku-Hreiðarr
Kali (Gaelic)	Kimbi, n.n.	Kolbrún	Kristofórus
Kalman (Gaelic)	(Gaelic)	Kolfinna (f.)	Krókr, n.n.
Kamban, n.n.	Kjöl-fari, n.n.	Kolgrima (f.)	Kroppa, n.n.
(Gaelic)	Kjölvör (f.)	Kolgrimr	Krumr
Kampa-Grímr	Kjötvi	Kolka, n.n.	Kymlingar
Kári	Klaufi	Kolli (Gaelic)	Kræklingar
Karl	Kleppjarn	Kollr	Krömu-Oddr
Karli	Kleykir, n.n.	Kollsveinn	Kúgaldi
Karlsefui	Klyppr	Kolr (Bp.)	Kuggi
Kárr	Klæingr	Kolskeggr	Kveld
Katla	Klöku	Kolssynir	Kvistr
Kaun	Knappi, n.n.	Koltherna	Kýlan (Gaelic)
Ketilbjörn	Kneif, n.n.	Kolumba	Kögurr, n.n.
Ketill	Knútr	Konáll (Gaelic)	Körmlöð (Gaelic)
Ketilriðr (f.)	Knýtr, n.n.	Kori (Gaelic)	Körtr, n.n. (Karta)
Kjallakr (Gaelic)	Knörr	Kórmakr (Gaelic)	Köttr, n.n. (a cat)
Kjallæklingar			

From other sources

Kaggi, n.n.	Kerling	Kolbeinn, n.n.
Kakali, n.n.	Kesja, n.n.	Konr
Kambari, n.n.	Kiðlingr, n.n.	Kráka, n.n.
Kamb-höttr, n.n.	Kiðlings-munnr, n.n.	Kráka-nef, n.n.
Kampi, n.n.	Kikini, n.n.	Kregð, n.n.
Kappi, n.n.	Kikr, n.n.	Krepp-hendr, n.n.
Karls-ungi, n.n.	Kirjalax	Krista, n.n.
Kastan-razi, n.n.	Kisi, n.n.	Kristin (f.), Christina
Katrin (f.)	Kjötvi, n.n.	Krist-röðr
Kauða (f.) n.n.	Klaka	Krist-rún
Kaupungr, n.n.	Klápr = Kláfr, n.n.	Kroppr, n.n.
Kausi, n.n.	Klemus	Kumbi, n.n.
Ká-beinn, n.n.	(Clements)	Kussa, n.n.
Kárhöfðaðr, n.n.	Kliningr, n.n.	Kutiza, n.n.
Kegill, n.n.	Kló, n.n.	Kúgaðr, n.n.
Keikan, n.n.	Knerra, n.n.	Kúgi, n.n.
Keis, n.n.	Knúi, n.n.	Kúla-nefr
Kekkja = Kökkr, n.n.	Knarra-bringa, n.n.	Kveld-úlfr, n.n.
Kembir, n.n.	Kobbi, pet n. Jacob	Kylli-nef, n.n.
Keppr, n.n.		

L

Lambi	Leik-goði, n.n.	Ljúfina (f.)	Lunan (Gaelic)
Laugarbrekku,	Leó (Keisari)	Ljoðhattr	Lunda-Steinarr
n.n.	Lina (f.)	Ljoðinn	(jarl)
Lecný (Lækný),	Ljódarkeptr	Ljoðmundr	Lýtingr
or Leikny	Ljót (f.)	Loka-senna, n.n.	Lækný. *See*
Leðrháls	Ljótólfr	Loki, n.n.	Lecný
Leggjaldi, n.n.	Ljótr	Lón-Einarr	Lög-Skapti
Leiðolfr	Ljótunn	Lopþæna (f.)	Löngu-bak, n.n.
Leifr	Ljúfa (Kona)	Loptr (Bp.)	

From other sources

Lafranz (Laurence)	Leggr	Lygra, n.n.
Laf-skeggr, n.n.	Leira, n.n.	Lyngvi
Lang-beinn, n.n.	Lindi-áss, n.n.	Lyrgr, n.n.
Langa-spjöt, n.n.	Lín-seyma, n.n.	Lyrtr, n.n. (lurtr)
Lang-brók, n.n.	Líri, n.n.	Lyst-Knappr, n.n.
Lang-höfði, n.n.	Ljóð-horn, n.n.	Lysu-Knappr, n.n.
Lang-nefr, n.n.	Ljómi, n.n.	Lög-maðr
Láfi, pet n. (Oláfr)	Lúndi, n.n.	Lömbungr, n.n.
Láki, pet n. (Þrolákr)	Lúfa, n.n.	

M

Mábil (f.)	Maria (f.)	Melpatrekr	Mos-hals, n.n.
Maddaðr (K.,	Markús	(Gaelic)	Munnr, n.n.
Gaelic)	Martein (Bp.)	Miðfjarðr, n.n.	Myra-Knjukr
Magnús	Má-scári, n.n.	Mjöll (f.)	Myrgjol (f.,
Magr-Helgi	Mein-frettr	Módólfr	Gaelic)
Mág-Snorri	Mela-Snorri	Moð-skegg	Myrkjartan (K.,
Mána-Ljotr	Melkorka (f.,	Moeiðr (f.)	Gaelic)
Máni. *See* Menni	Gaelic)	Molda-Gnúpr	Mýrun
Már	Meldun (jarl	Moldi, n.n.	
Margret (f.)	Scot., Gaelic)		

From other sources

Magni	Málga, n.n.	Mundi, pet n.
Magr, n.n.	Mál-spakr, n.n.	Murta, n.n.
Manar-menn (Manx-	Mási, n.n.	Munki, n.n.
men)	Mein-akr, n.n.	Myntari, n.n.
Mangi (Magnus)	Mein-fretr, n.n.	Mögr, p.n. *See*
Manni, n.n.	Menni, n.n.	Mágr
Mar-drap, n.n.	Mikill	Mör-landi, n.n.
Mat-Krákr, n.n.	Mikla, n.n.	Mör-nefr, n.n.
Maull, n.n.	Mildi, n.n.	Mör-strútr, n.n.
Maxi, n.n.	Mjo-beinn, n.n.	Möttull, p.n.
Mág (Mac, Mc)	Mjóvi, n.n.	(Finnish King)

N

Naððoðr	Náttfari	Nesja-Knjukr	Njáll (Gaelic)
Nafar-Helgi	Nefsteinn	Niðbjörg (f.)	Njörðr
Nagli	Nereiðr (jarl)	Nikolás	Norr (K.)
Narfi			

From other sources

Nef, n.n.	Nes-konungr, p.n.	Næfra-maðr, n.n.
Nefja (f.), n.n.	Njosnar-helgi, n.n.	Nörtr, n.n.

O

Oblauðr	Oddleifr	Orð-lokarr, n.n.	Órækja
Oddbjörg (f.)	Oddmarr	Ormarr	Ósk
Oddbjörn	Oddný	Ormhildr (f.)	Ósku (f.)
Oddfriðr (f.)	Oddr	Orms-tunga, n.n.	Óspakr
Oddgeirr	Ófeigr	Ormr	Ósvaldr (K.)
Oddi	Óláfr	Orny (f.)	Ósvífr (Osyfr)
Oddkatla	Óleifr	Orrabeinn	Otryggr
Oddlaug	Óli	Orra-skáld, n.n.	Óttarr
Oddleif (f.)	Ólöf		

From other sources

Opin-sjoðr, n.n.	Orri, n.n.	Oxi, p.n.

P

Páll	Parak, n.n.	Patrekr (Gaelic)	Pétr
Papar (Gaelic)	Paschalis	Petrus	Philippus

From other sources

Paktin, n.n.	Pitlor, n.n.	Prest-mágr, n.n.
Pálnir, p.n.	Pík, n.n.	Prúði, n.n.
Peini, n.n.	Plógr, p.n. (*D.*)	Pung-elta, n.n.
Petarr	Plytr, n.n.	

R

Ráðormr	Rannveig (f.)	Refr (a fox)	Rodolfr. *See*
Rafn	Ráðormr	Ref-skeggr, n.n.	Hródólfr
Rafnkell	Rauða-Björn	Reginleif	Roðrekr
Rafsi	Rauð-bekri, n.n.	Reidarr. *See*	Rólf. *See* Hrólfr
Raförta (f.,	Rauð-feldr, n.n.	Hreidarr	Rotinn, n.n.
Gaelic)	Rauðr	Reistr	Rudolphus
Raga-broðir, n.n.	Rauð-skeggr,n.n.	Reyðr-siða, n.n.	Ruðu-Ulfr (Bp.)
Ragi	Rauðúlfr	Reyni-björn	Ruggi, n.n.
Ragnarr (K.)	Rauðum-skjaldi,	Reyr-Ketill	Runolfr
Ragnheiðr (f.)	n.n. (red shield)	Rifla	Rútr. *See* Hrútr
Ragnhildr (f.)	Raumr	Rjúpa (f.)	Rögnvoldr (jarl)
Rang-látr, n.n.	Raunguðr		

From other sources

Rafa-Kollr, n.n.
Ramr, n.n.
Rand-eiðr (f.)
Rang-muðr, n.n.
Ranka (Ragnheiðr)

Rand-verr
Regg-búss, n.n. (Wen-
   dish)
Reikall, p.n.

Remba, n.n.
Ruza, n.n.
Rykill, n.n.
Rympill, n.n.

S

Salbjörg (f.)
Salgerðr (f.)
Samr
Saurr, n.n.
Saxi
Sela-Kálfr
Sel-Þórir
Semingr
Sigarr (K.)
Sigfastr
Sigfús
Sighvatr
Sigmundr
Signý
Sigriðr (f.)
Sigtryggr
Sigurðr (Bp.)
Sigvaldi
Sigvatr
Sigvör
Símon
Sjóni, n.n.
Skagi
Skáld-Helgi
Skáldhrafn
Skáld-Refr
Skalla-Grimr
Skálp-hæna, n.n.
Skamkell
Skapti
Skarpheðinn
Skati
Skefill = Skemill
Skegg-ávaldi
Skegg-broddi
Skeggi, n.n.
Skjalda-Björn

Skjaldbjörn
Skálgr
Skiði
Skinna-Björn
Skjöldólfr
Skolmr
Skopti
Skorargeirr
Skorri
Skota-Kollr, n.n.
Skrof-Skrofi
Skrof-uðr, n.n.
Skuli
Skúmr
Skútaðar-Skeggi
Skæringr
Sleitu-Helgi
Slettu-Björn
Smiðkell
Smiðr
Smiðskeggi
Snar-fari, n.n.
Snepill
Snertlingar
Snjallr. *D.*
   Snolde
Snjallsteinn
Snorri
Snæbjörn
Snækollr
Snælaug (f.)
Snörtr
Sokki, n.n.
Solveig (f.)
Sólvör
Sóti
Spá-Kona, n.n.

Spak-Böðvarr
Spana (f.)
Spörr, n.n.
Stafngrimr
Starkaðr
Starri
Steigar-Þorir
Steinbjörn
Steinfirðr
Steingrimr
Steini
Steinmóðr
Steinn
Steinnar (jarl)
Steinólfr
Steinrauðr
Steinuðr. *See*
   Steinunn
Steinvör
Steinþórr
Stephanus (Bp.)
Stigandi, n.n.
Stórólfr
Stoti, n.n.
Strangi, n.n.
Stúfr
Sturla
Styrbjörn
Styrkárr
Styrmir
Styrr
Sulki (K.)
Sumarliði
Sunnólfr
Súrr
Surtr

Svana (f.)
Svanlaug (f.)
Svanr
Svart-höfði
Svarðkell
Svarta-þurs, n.n.
Svartr
Svasi
Svavarr
Svegðir
Sveinbjörn
Sveinn
Sveinúngar
Sverlingr. *A.S.*
   Swerthing
Svið-balki
Sviðu-Kári
Svigna-Kappi, n.n.
Svína-Böðvarr
Svinhaga-Björn
Svörfuðr
Sæbjörn
Sæhildr (f.)
Sælingr, n.n.
Sæmundr
Sæuðr (Sæunn)
   (f.)
Sæ-úlfr (Sjólfr)
Sökkólfr
Sölgi (K.)
Sölmundr
Solverr (Sölvarr)
   (K.)
Sölvi
Sörkvir-Svarkr
Söxólfr

From other sources

Salt-eyða, n.n.
Samr, n.n.

Sandi, n.n.
Saup-ruðr, n.n.

Sel-byggr, n.n.
Selr, n.n.

Sepill, n.n.
Sið-nefr, n.n.
Siggi (Sigurðr)
Signjótr
Silfri, n.n.
Sjaundi
Skakki, n.n.
Skam-fótr, n.n.
Skam-háls, n.n.
Skammi, n.n.
Skarði, n.n.
Skati, n.n.
Skat-Kaupendi, n.n.
Skála-glam, n.n.
Skáldi, n.n.
Skálf
Skálgr, n.n.
Skári, n.n.
Skemill = Skefill
Skeið-Kollr, n.n.
Skeifr, n.n.
Skekill, n.n.
Sker-auki, n.n.
Skerðingr, n.n.
Skerja-blesi, n.n.
Skin-hringr, n.n.
Skinni, n.n.
Skinn-vefja, n.n.
Skirvill, n.n.
Skíðungar (the descendants of Skíði)
Skífa, n.n.
Skjómi, n.n.
Skjöldr
Skol-beinn, n.n.
Skoppr, n.n.
Skorpa, n.n.
Skorri, n.n.
Skota, n.n.
Skota-Kollr, n.n.

Skotti, n.n.
Skógungar, n.n.
Skólmr, n.n.
Skrafari, n.n.
Skratt-hanki, n.n.
Skrauti, n.n.
Skrápi, n.n.
Skreyja, n.n.   *D.*
Skryde
Skrill, n.n.
Skrukka, n.n.   *D.*
Skrog
Skrúð-hyrna, n.n.
Skúma (f.), n.n.
Skúmr, n.n.
Skvaðra, n.n.
Skvaldri, n.n.   *S.*
squallia
Skúli
Skyti, n.n.   *D.* Skytte
Skæla, n.n.
Slafsi, n.n.
Slaga-Kollr, n.n.
Slakki, n.n.
Slandri, n.n.
Slappi, n.n.
Slefa, n.n.
Sleggja, n.n.
Sleppi, n.n.
Slinkr, n.n.
Slókr, n.n.
Slyngr, n.n.
Smetta, n.n.   *D.*
Smutte
Snákr, n.n.
Snati, n.n.
Sneypir, n.n.
Snjólfr (Snæ-úlfr)
Snoppa-langr, n.n.
Snókr, n.n. *See* Snákr

Snuin-bruni, n.n.
Snæ-þryma, n.n.
Soddi, n.n.
Sopi, n.n.
Spá-Kona, n.n.
Spraka-leggr, n.n.   *D.*
Sprade
Spýtu-leggr, n.n.
Stag-brellr, n.n.
Stag-nál (f.), n.n.
Standali, n.n.
Stand-eykr, n.n.
Steðja-Kollr, n.n.
Steypir, n.n.
Stigandi, n.n.
Stigr, n.n.
Stiku-bligr, n.n.
Storgr, n.n.
Storka, n.n.
Stoti, n.n.
Strangr, n.n.
Stri-nefr, n.n.
Strylltr, n.n.
Stubbi, n.n.
Stangar-högg, n.n.
Stöpuðr
Súrr, n.n.
Svaði, p.n.
Svagi, n.n.
Sveiði, n. of a sea king
Sveimr, n.n.
Sveinki (Sveinungr)
Sveltir, n.n.
Sverrir
Sviðr-balki, n.n.
Sviðandi = Sviðingr, n.n.
Svín-höfði, n.n.
Syrja (f.) n.n. (sori)
Sýr, n.n.

T

Talkni
Tanni
Tasaldi, n.n.
Teitr
Tindr
Tinforni
Tjörfi

Tófa (f.)
Tófi
Torf-Einarr (jarl)
Torfi
Torráðr
Tor-tryggr
Trandill, n.n.

Trefill, n.n.
Trolli, n.n.
Trumbu-beinn, n.n.
Tryggvi (K.)
Tumi
Túngu-Kári

Túngu-Oddr
Túngu-Steinn
Tunhani
Tvennum-brúni, n.n.
Tyrfingr

From other sources

Tabarðr, n.n.
Tölu-sveinn, n.n.
Tandri, n.n.
Tann-gnjóstr, n.n.
Tann-grisnir, n.n.
Tann-refill, n.n.
Tann-skári, n.n.
Tálgi, n.n.
Táta
Tin-forni, n.n.
Tin-teinn, n.n.
Titlingr, n.n.
Tiðinda-Skopti, n.n.
Tjörn-skinn, n.n.
Tjúgu-skegg, n.n.
Todda (f.), n.n.

Tosti
Toti
Tottr, n.n. *D.* Tommel-tot
Tóki. *D.* Tyge, *Lat.* Tycho
Tónn, n.n.
Trausti
Tré-bót, n.n.
Tre-telja, n.n.
Trúðr, n.n.
Trú-fast, n.n. of K. Athelstan
Tronu-beinn, n.n.
Tulkari, n.n.
Tungu-goði, n.n.
Tunni, n.n.
Tysti = Tosti, n.n.
Tyza, n.n.

U

Uggi
Úlfarr
Úlfeiðr
Úlf-hamr
Úlf-heðinn

Úlf-heiðr (f.)
Úlf-hildr (f.)
Úlf-Kell
Úlfljótr
Úlfr

Úlfrun (f.)
Una (f.)
Uni
Unnr

Úrækja
Úspakr
Útryggr

From other sources

Ubbi. *A.S.* Ubba, Uffa
Uðr
Ull-höttr, n.n.
Ulli, dim. of Erlendr
Ull-serkr, n.n.
Ull-strengr, n.n.

Ungi, n.n.
Urðar-Köttr, n.n. = Hreysi-Köttr
Urðar-steinn, n.n.
Urka, n.n.
Úrr, n.n.

V

Vaði
Valbrandr
Valdis (f.)
Valgarðr
Valgautr
Valgerðr (f.)
Vali
Valla-Brandr
Valla-Ljótr
Valþjoflingar
Valþófr
Valþýflingar
  (Valþýfingr)

Vand-raðr
Vanlandi (K.)
Vápni
Vatnarr (K.)
Vebjörn
Vébrandr
Védis (f.)
Véðormr. *See*
  Veþormr
Veðra-grimr
Veðr, n.n.
Véfreyðr
Végeirr

Végestr
Vékell
Vélaug (f.)
Vélcifr
Vémundr
Vény (f.)
Vermundr
Vestarr
Vestcinn
Vestliði
Vestmaðr
Vetrliði
Véþormr

Véþörn
Viðarr
Vifill
Víga-Barði
Víga-Bjarni
Víga-Glumr
Víga-Hrappr
Víga-Skuta
Viga-Sturla
Víga-Styrr
Vígbjoðr
Vigdis (f.)
Vígfús

Viglundr	Vilbaldr	Vilmundr	Vorsar
Vigsterkr	Vilburg (f.)	Vilraðr	Vorsa-Úlfr
Vikarr	Vilgeirr	Visburr (K.)	Væpnlingar
Vikinga-Kari	Vilgerðr (f.)	Vívill	Völu-steinn
Víkingr	Vilhjálmr		

From other sources

Vaggaldi, n.n.	Veljungr = Vælungr,	Við-leggr, n.n.
Vagn	n.n.	Viggjar-skalli, n.n.
Val-frekr, n.n.	Vendill	Vippa (f.), n.n.
Vandill	Vendill-Kráka, n.n.	Víg-ólfr
Vágr	Vesall, n.n.	Væringi (the Warings)
Vei	Vettir, n.n.	Vörsa-Krákr, n.n.
Veðr, n.n.	Við-finnr	Vöttr, p.n.
Veili, n.n.		

Y

Ýnglingar	Ýngvi	Ýr (Yri), (f.)	Ysja (f.), n.n.
Ýngvarr	Ýngvildr (f.)	Yxna-Þorir	

Þ

Þángbrandr	Þorbjörn	Þórhildr (f.)	Þórormr
Þengill	Þorbrandr	Þórhrolfr	Þorsteinn
Þiðrandi	Þórdis (f.)	Þóriðr. *See*	Þorsteinnsbjörn
Þjóðarr	Þórðr	Þuriðr	Þórunn
Þjóðgerðr (f.)	Þórelfr (f.)	Þórir	Þorvaldr
Þjóðhildr (f.)	Þórey (f.)	Þorkatla (f.)	Þorvarðr
Þjóð-mar. *G.*	Þorfiðr (Máni)	Þorkell	Þór-vé (Þor-veig)
Ditmar	Þorfinna (f.)	Þorketill	Þorviðr
Þjóðrekr. *G.*	Þorfinnr	Þorlakr	Þórvör (f.)
Deitrich	Þorgautr	Þorlaug (f.)	Þráin
Þjökka (f.), n.n.	Þorgeirr	Þorleif (f.)	Þrándr
Þjóstarr	Þorgerðr (f.)	Þorleifr	Þrasi
Þjóstólfr	Þorgestr	Þorleikr	Þraslaug (f.)
Þóra (f.)	Þorgils	Þorljót (f.)	Þróndr. *See*
Þórálfr	Þorgnýr	Þorljótr	Þrándr
Þóralldr. *See*	Þorgrima (f.)	Þormoðr	Þröstr
Þórhallr	Þorgrímr	Þornjótr	Þuriðr (f.)
Þórarinn	Þorhaddr	Þórný (f.)	Þussasprengir, n.n.
Þórarna (f.)	Þórhalla (f.)	Þórodda (f.)	Þyna (f.), n.n.
Þorbergr	Þórhalli	Þoroddr	Þöngull, n.n.
Þorbjörg (f.)	Þórhallr	Þórólfr	

From other sources

Þak-raðr = Þakk-raðr, p.n. *G.* Tan-   Þausnir, n.n.
  cred   Þegjandi, n.n.
Þas-ramr, n.n.   Þenja, n.n.

Þing-bitr, n.n. Þrúða, Sig-Þruðr (f.)
Þing-höttr, n.n. Þumli, n.n.
Þjálfi Þura, Þuriðr (f.)
Þjóri, n.n. *D.* tyr Þurs, n.n (a giant). *D.* Tosse
Þjóti, n.n. Þvari, n.n.
Þórðr Þveit, p.n. (Thwaite). *D.* Tvæde
Þrjúgr. *D.* Tryge Þyrni-fótr, n.n.
Þruma, n.n. Þömb, n.n.

Æ

Æði-Kollr, n.n. Æsa (f.)
Ægileif (f.) Ævarr

O

Ögmundr Ön. *See* Aun Önundr Ösyfr. *See*
Ögurr Ondott (f.) Örlygr Ósvifr
Ögvaldr. *See* Öndottr-Kraka Örn Öxna-megn, n.n.
 Afvaldr Öngr Örnólfr Öxna-Þorir. *See*
Ölfuss, n.n. Öngull. *See* Örrek, n.n. Yxna-Þorir
Ölmóðr   Aungull Örv-öndr, or Özurr
Ölmæðlingar Önn Örvhendr, n.n. Öþr. *See* Auðr
Ölver

From other sources

Ölbogi, n.n. Örðig-skeggi Örkn-höfði, n.n. Örra-beinn, n.n.
Örðigr, n.n. Ör-eiðr, n.n. Ör-nefni

PET NAMES—GIRLS

Ása, from Ás-laug Jóra, from Jóreiðr
Ásta, from Ás-triðr Kata, from Katrin
Disa, from Val-dís, Vig-dís, Her-dís Lauga, from Guð-laug
Dóra, from Hall-dóra Manga, from Margrét
Friða, from Holm-friðr Ranka, from Ragn-eiðr, Ragn-hildr
Geira, from Geir-laug Sigga, from Sig-riðr
Gudda, from Guð-riðr Sissa, from Sig-þruðr
Gunna, from Guð-rún Tobba, from Þor-björg
Imba, from Ingi-björg Valka, from Val-gerðr
Inga, from Ing-unn, Ingveldr Þrúða, from Jar-þruðr, Sig-þruðr
Jóka, from Jó-hanna Þura, from Þur-iðr

PET NAMES—BOYS

Arni (Arnc), from Örn Bersi, from Björn
Ási, from Ás-mundr Bjarni, from Björn
Atli, from Attila Björsi, from Björn
Bensi, from Benedikt Brynki, from Bryn-jólfr

Daði, from David
Erli, from Erl-indr (Erlingr)
Eyvi, from Eyj-ólfr
Fusi, from Víg-fús
Gamli, from Gamel
Goddi, from compounds in Guð
Grimsi, from Grímr
Gutti, from Guðormr
Gvendr, from Guð-mundr
Helgi, from Há-leygr
Ingi, from compounds in Ing
Jónsi, from Jon
Karli, from Karl
Keli, from Ɖor-kel
Kobbi, from Jacob

Láfi, from Óláfr
Láki, from Ɖor-lákr
Laugi, from Gunn-laugr
Mangi, from Magnus
Mundi, from Ás-mundr
Ragni, from compounds in Ragn
Runki, from Rún-ólfr
Sebbi, from Sig-björn
Siggi, from Sig-urðr
Simbi, from Sig-mund
Snorri, from Snerrir
Steinki, from Stein-grímr
Sveinki, from Sveinn
Tumi, from Thomas
Valdi, from Ɖor-valdr

FRISIAN PERSONAL AND FAMILY NAMES

A

Abbo, m.; fam. n., Abben, Abena
Adde, m.; Adda, f.; fam. n., Adden
Ade, m.; fam. n., Aden, Adena
Afke, f. dimin. *See* Efke, Eveke, from Eva
Agatha, f.
Agge, m.; fam. n., Aggen
Agt, Agte, f. dimin. of Agatha
Aisso, Aisse, Eisse, m.; fam. n., Aissen, Eissen
Albert, Albarts, Albardus, Albertus (Albrecht), m.; fam. n., Alberts, Albers; f. Albertje
Alerk (Alarich, contraction of Athalarich), m.; fam. n., Alerks, Alers, Ahlers
Alle, m.; fam. n., Allen, Allena

Almôd, Almôth, Almt, f. (Allmuth)
Alt, m.; fam. n., Alts
Amel, m.; fam. n., Amels. Comp. Amala, Amalia, Amalung, etc.
Amke, m. and fam. n. *See* Hamke
Anke, f. (Antje), from Anna, as also Anken, Aennchen, Annechin
Anna, f.
Arend, Arnd, Arndt, m. (Arnold); fam. n., Arends
Arjen or Arien, m.; fam. n., Arjens, Ariens, Arjes
Arkonâ, Arkenâ, fam. n., from Arko
Arrel, Arl. *See* Harrel
Athe, m.; fam. n., Athen. *See* Ade, Atte
Atte, Atto, m.; fam. n., Attena

B

Baino, Beino, m.; fam. n., Bainen, Beinen
Bantje, m.; fam. n., Bantjes, dimin. of Banno
Bärend, Bêrend, Bernd, m.; fam. n., Bärends, Berend, a contraction of Bernhard

Bauke, Bâwke, Bâfke or Bâvke, f. dimin. of Old *F.* Bavo; fam. n., Bavink
Beelke, Belke, dimin. of Bele
Beino. *See* Baino
Bela, f.
Bele, Behl, Beil, Bill, m.

Belemar, Biletrud
Bêner, m. ; fam. n., Bêners
Benge, m. ; fam. n., Bengen
Bêninga, Bênenga, fam. n.
Benno, m. ; Benna, f.
Berend. *See* Bärend
Bôdewîn, m. Comp. Bouduin, Balduin, Boldewin
Boko, m. *N.* Baugr
Boldewîn

Bôle, Boele, m. ; fam. n., Bôlen, Bolema
Bôleke, Bôlke, Bolkes, dimin.
Bonno, m. ; fam. n., Bonnen
Boys, Boye, Boy, m. ; dimin. Boyke ; fam. n., Boyen, Boyinga, Boyink, Boyunga
Brûno, m. ; Brûnke and Brûntje, f. ; and fam. n., Brûninga, Brûns, Bronsema, and Brûnken

D

Datter, m.
Dedde, m. ; fam. n., Dedden
Dêtlêf, m.
Detmer, m.
Dever. *Dch.* Dieven
Deverke, dimin. f.
Dîderik, Dîdrîk, Dîdrîch, Dîderk, Dierk, Dirk, m. (Dietrich)
Dîko or Dyko, m. ; fam. n., Dîken, Dyken, Dikena, Dykena

Dîle, Diele, m. ; fam. n., Dielen (Dil.)
Dirk, Dierk, m. ; f. Dirktje, Dirtje ; fam. n., Dirks, Dirksen, Dirken, Dierken
Djure, m. ; fam. n., Djuren ; f. Djurke, Jurke
Djurelt and Durelt, m.
Dodo, m. ; f. Doda ; fam. n., Doden, Dodens, Dodena

E

Ebbe, m.
Ebbo, m.
Ebo, Ebbo, Ebe, Eppo, Eve, m. ; f. Ebbe, Eveke ; fam. n., Eben, Even, Eppen, Ebeling
Edde, m. ; fam. n., Edden
Edo, m. ; dimin. Edje ; fam. n., Eden, Edinga
Edsard (Esdert ?), m. ; fam. n., Edsards, Edzards, Esderts
Egbert, Ebbert, m. ; fam. n., Egberts, Egbers
Egge, m. ; fam. n., Eggen
Eibo, Eibe, m. ; fam. n., Eiben
Eiko, Eike, m.
Eilert, Eilt, m. ; fam. n., Eilerts, Eilers, Eilts, Eils (contraction of Egilhardt, Ailhardt)

Eimo, Eime, m. ; fam. n., Eimers
Eint, Eent, m. ; fam. n., Eints (Aginhardt ?)
Eka, Eke, Ekea, Eckea, f.
Ele, Ehle, m. ; fam. n., Ehlen
Elle, m. ; Ella, f. ; Ellen, fam. n.
Eme, Emo, Ehme, and Eimo, m. ; fam. n., Emen, Ehmen, Emminga ; dimin. Emke ; fam. n., Emken
Emminga, Emmius, fam. n.
Emmo, Emme, m. ; Emma, f.
Eppo, m. ; Eppen, fam. n.
Ernst, m.
Esdert. *See* Edsard
Eta, Etta, f. dimin. Ettje
Eve, Ewe, Aeve, m.

F

Faukc, m.
Fekko, Fêko, Feyko, Fekke, m. ; fam. n., Fekken, Feyken, Feikena

Feyen, fam. n.
Feyke, m. ; Feyken, fam. n.
Fia, dimin. of Sophia, dimin. Fiake, Fîke

C

Fimmo, Fimme, m.; fam. n., Fimmen

Flamê, Flâm, a Fleming

Fôke, Fauke, m.; Fôken, fam. n.

Fokke, Fokko, m.; Fokka, f.; Fokken, Fokkena, fam. n.

Folerk. *See* Folrick

Foletta, f.

Fôlke, f.

Folkerd, m. (Folk-ward); Folkerds, Folkers, fam. n.

Folkmar, m.

Folpmer, m.

Folpt, Fulpt, m.; Folpts, fam. n.

Folrâd, Fulrâd, m. (Vollrath, Folkrâd)

Fôlrîk, Fôlrîch, Fôlerk, m.; Folrichs, Fôlerks, Fôlers, fam. n.

Frërk, Frêrk, m.; Frërksen, fam. n., from Frêrik, Frederik

Frese or Frêse, a *F*.

Fulbrand, m.

Fulf, m.

Fulke, f., or Fulka, Fulleke, from Fulla, Folla

Fulko, m., from Fullo

G

Gaiko. *See* Geiko

Galt, m.

Gâlt, m., contraction of Garrelt, Garlt, Gerlt

Garbrand, Garbert, m.

Garrelt, Gerrelt, m.; Garrelts, Garrels, Gerrelts, Gerrels, fam. n. (Garhold, Gerhold)

Geiko, Gaiko, Gayko, Geike, m.; Geiken, fam. n., from Geio, Gayo

Gerd, m.; dimin. f. Gerdtje; fam. n., Gerdes, contraction of Gerhard. Also Gerjet, Gêjert, Gert, and Gerriet

Gerdrût, Gädrût, f. (Gertrude)

Gerke, m.; Gerken, fam. n.

Gërman, old fam. n.

Gêske, f. dimin. of Gêso, Gêsa, Giso (Gîsbert)

Grendel, Grennel; f. dimin. Grendelke, Grennelke

Greta (Margaretha), dimin. Gretje

Grôn, fam. n.

Grönefeld, Grönfeld, fam. n.

Gronewold, Gronwold, fam. n.

H

Habbo, m.; Habben and Habbinga, fam. n.

Haddo (Hatto), m.; Haddinga, fam. n. *See* Heddo

Hagen, m.; Hagena, fam. n.

Hamke, dimin. of Hamo; fam. n. Haming

Harm, m. (contraction of Hermann); f. dimin. Harmke; fam. n., Harms, Harmens

Hâro, Hâre, m.; Hâren, Haringa, Harringa, fam. n.

Harrell, Harle, m.

Hayo, m.; Hayung, Heyungs, Hayunga, fam. n.

Hebe, f. dimin. Hebeke, Hêbke, Hëpke

Heddo, Hedde, m.; Hedden, Heddinga, fam. n.; Heddo, *A.S.* Bishop, A.D. 676

Heie, Hei, m. *See* Hayo

Heiko or Haiko, m.; Heikens, Heiken, Heikena, Haiken, Hayken

Hein, m.; Heine, Heinen, fam. n. (from Heinrich)

Heini

Heink, m. *See* Hein

Heite, Heit, m.; Heits, fam. n.

Helmer, m.; Helmers, fam. n.

Herman, m.

Hêro, Hêre, Herre, m.; Hêren, Herren, fam. n.

Hester (Esther)

Hibbo, Hibbe, m.; Hibben, fam. n.
Hidde. *See* Hiddo
Hiddo, m.; Hidden, fam. n.
Hilke, f. dimin. of Hille, Hilla, Hilda
Hillerd, Hillerk. *See* Hillrich
Hillmer, Hilmer, m.; Hillmers, fam. n.
Hillrich, Hillrik, Hillerk, Hillerd, m.; Hillrichs, Hillerks, Hillers, Hillern, fam. n.

Hima, f.
Himke, dimin. of Hima
Hinderk. *See* Hinrich
Hinrich, m.; Hinrichs, Hinnerks, Hinners, Hinnerssen, Hünerssen, fam. n.
Hiske, f.
Hoot, m.; Hoots, Hôting, Hooting (from Hotbert)

I

Ibo, Ibe, Ihbe, m.; Iben, Ibben, Ibeling, fam. n.
Ide
Idje, Itje, f. dimin. of Ida
Idse, Itse, Idze, m.; Idsen, Itzen, Idsinga, fam. n.
Igge, m.; Iggen, Iggena, fam. n.
Ikke, Ikka, Ika, f.
Iko, Ike, m.; Iken, Ikena, fam. n.
Imel, m.; Imels, fam. n.

Imke, f., also Immeke, dimin. of Imme
Imme, Immo, m.; Immen, fam. n.
Ine. *See* Ino
Ing, Ingo, Inguio, m.
Inka, f.
Ino, Ine, Ihno, m.; dimin. Inke, Ihnke; fam. n., Inen, Ihnen; Ino, *A.S.* King, A.D. 727
Ippo, Ippe, m.; Ippen, fam. n.

J

Jabbo, Jabbe, Jabe, m.; Jabben, fam. n.
Jak, m., also fam. n.; dim. Jäkchen
Jakub, Jakup, m.
Jan, m.; Janna, Jantje, f.; Jansen, Janssen, Jenssen, fam. n.
Jasper, m.; Jaspers, fam. n.
Jelle, m.; Jellen, Jellena, fam. n. (from Jellrich?)
Jellrich, Jellrik, Jellerk, m.

Jetta, f. dimin. Jettchen
Jibbo, m.; Jibben, fam. n.
Jimme, m.; Jimmen, fam. n.
Jochem, Jofen, m. (Joachim)
Juist. *See* Jûst
Jürgen, Jürjen, contraction of Jürn, m. (Görgen), also Jörg; fam. n. Jürgens, Jürjens, Jürns
Jurke, f.
Just, loc. and fam. n.

K

Karsten, Kersten, Karsen, Kassen, Kasjen, from Kristjan (Christian); fam. n., Karstens, Karsens, Kassens, Kasjens
Kasper, m.

Kâtje, f. dimin. of Kate, Catherina
Kês, m., contraction of Cornelius
Klâs (Klaus), Niklâs, m.
Klûn, Kluin, fam. n.

L

Lambert, Lampert, Lambrecht, m.
Lanbert, Lanpert, Lantpert, m.

Lübbert, m.; Lubberts, Lübbers, fam. n.

Lübbo, m.; Lübben, Lübbena, fam. n.; dimin. Lübke; fam. n., Lübkes
Lûdowig, Lûdewig, Lûdwig, m.; Lûdowigs, Lûdewigs, Lûdwigs, fam. n.
Lûdo, m.
Lüitje, m.; Luitjens, fam. n.

Lüke, m.; Lüken, fam. n., contraction of Lüdeke, Ludeke, Liudeke, dimin. of Ludo, Lindo, etc.
Lükke, f. *See* Lüke
Lûks, m. (Lucas)
Lüppo, Lübbo, m.; dim. Lüpke; fam. n., Lüpkes
Lûth, m. (Lütet); Lûitje, f.

M

Machelt, f. (Machtild)
Machtild, Mechtild, f.
Magrêta, f. (Margrêta)
Maike. *See* Marê
Mammo, Mamme, m.; Mammen, Memmen, Mamminga, Memminga, fam. n.
Manno, Manne, m.; Manninga, fam. n.
Marê (Maria), dimin. Marêken, Marêke, Maike
Margrêta, Margrêt, Magrêta, Magrêt, Megrêt, Mergrêt, contraction Grêta; dimin. Grêtje
Meinert, Mênert, contraction Meint, Meent, m. (Meinhard); Meinerts, Meiners, Meints, Meents, fam. n.
Meino, m. (Magino, Megino)
Memke, Mêmke. *See* Memmo.
Memkes, Mêmkes, Mimkes, fam. n.

Memmo, Mémo, Méme, m.; Memmen, Memminga, fam. n.
Mêne, m.; Mênen, fam. n.
Menje, f. dimin. of Menna
Menko, Menke, m.; Menken, fam. n.
Menno, Menne, m.; f. Menna; Mennen, Menninga, fam. n.
Mense, Mens, m.; Mensen, Mensinga, fam. n.
Mês or Mêwes, contraction of Bartolomaeus
Meta, Metta, f. dimin. Metje
Mêwes. *See* Mês
Mia, f. (Maria); dimin. Mîke, Mîtje
Michel, m.
Mimke, Mimmke, m. (Mimeken, Mimmeken)
Mimste, m.

N

Nanno, Nanne, m.; Nannen, Nan ninga, fam. n.

Nâtje, f., contraction of Annatje, dimin. of Anna
Nôme, Nôm, m.

O

Ode, Odo, m.; Odens, Odenga, Odinga
Okko, Ocko, Okke, m.; Okka, f.; Okken, Okkinga
Ommo, m.; Ommen, Omkes, fam. n.
Onke, Onneke, dimin. of Onno; fam. n., Onkes, Onnekes

Onno, m.; Onna, f.; Onnen, fam. n.
Ontje, m.; Ontjes, fam. n., from Onno
Ordgîs, Ortgîs, Oortgies, Oorthgies, Oordgiese, m.
Ortwin, Oorthwin, Ooordwin, m.
Otte, Otto, m.; Otten, fam. n.

P

Paul, m. ; Pauls, Paulsen, fam. n.
Peta, f.
Peter, m.; dimin. Peterke, f.; Peters, Petersen, fam. n.

Poppe, m. ; Poppen, Poppinga, fam. n. ; dimin. Popke, Popken
Poppe, Duke of Friesland, was slain in battle by Charles Martel in 734

R

Reent, m. ; Reents, fam. n.
Reimer, m. (Regimar) ; Reimers, fam. n.
Reiner, m. (Reinhard) ; Reiners, fam. n.
Reinhard, m.
Reint, m. ; Reints, fam. n.
Rembold, m.
Remmer, m. ; Remmers, Remmerssen, fam. n.

Rewert, m. ; Rewerts, fam. n.
Rikkerd, Rikkert, m. (Richard) ; Rikkerts, Rikkers, fam. n.
Rôlf (Rodolf), m.; Rôlfs, fam. n.
Rötger, m. (Hrodgar) ; Rötgers, fam. n.
Rumke, m., contraction of Rumo or Hrom ; Rumkes, fam. n.
Rummert, m.; Rummerts, Rummers, fam. n.

S

Sebo, m. ; Seba, Sebens, fam. n.
Sibet, m.
Sibo, m.; Siebens, fam. n.
Sikko, Sikke, m.; Sikkens, Sikkinga, fam. n.

Swêerd, Swêert, m.; Swêerds, Swêerts, Swêers, fam. n.
Swîthert, Swittert, Switer, m.; Switers, Switters, fam. n.

T

Tado, Tade. *See* Thado and Tjado
Tako, m. ; Takes, fam. n., contraction Tâks, Takens
Tale, Talea, f. dimin. Tâlke
Taletta, f.
Tammo, Tammo, m. ; Tammen, Tamminga, fam. n.
Tanno, m. ; Tannen, fam. n.
Tâtje, f.
Tebbo, Tebbe, m.; Tebben, fam. n.
Tetta, f. dimin. Tetje

Têwes, m., contraction of Matheus. Comp. Mes
Thado, Tado, Thade, Tade, m. ; Thaden, Taden, fam. n.
Tjado, Tjade, m.; Tjaden, fam. n.
Tjârd, Tjard, Tjârt, m. ; Tjârds, Tjards, Tjârts, fam. n.
Tjarko, m.; Tjarks, fam. n.
Tjetmer, m. ; Tjetmers, fam. n. (Dietmar)
Tönjes, m. (Antonius)

U

Ubbo, Ubbe, m. ; Ubben, Ubbinga, fam. n.
Udo, Ude, m.; Uden, fam. n.

Ufo, Ufe, Uvo, Uffo, Uffe, m.; Ufen, Uven, Uffen, fam. n.; dimin. Ufke ; Ufkes, fam. n.

Uko, Üko, Uke, m.; Uken, Ukena, fam. n.

Ulerk (Ulrich), m. ; Ulerks, Ulers, fam. n.

Ulferd, Ulfert, m.; Ulferds, Ulferts, Ulfers. The Dutch form is Olferd, Ulferd, Ulverd, Ulverdus Ulrîk. *See* Ulerk

W

Warner, m. (Werner) ; dimin. Warntje ; Warners and Warntjes, fam. n.

Wêert, m. ; Wêerts, Wêers, Weiers, fam. n.

Wêrda, Wiarda, fam. n.

Wêt, m. ; Wêts, fam. n.

Wilbert, m. ; Wilberts, Wilbers, fam. n.

Wildert, contraction Wilt, m.

Wilhelm, contraction Wilm, m. ; Wilms, fam. n.

Wilko, Wilke, m. ; Wilken, fam. n.

Wît, Wiet, dimin. Witje, Wietje, m.; Wîts, Wiets, Wîtjes, Wietjes, fam. n.

Wîterd, Wîtherd, Wîthert, m.

Wobbo, Wobbe, Wobbi, m.; dimin. f. Wobbeke, Wobke ; fam. n., Wobbena, Wobben.

Wolbrecht, m. ; Wolbrechts, Wolbergs, fam. n.

Wübbo, m. ; Wübbens, Wubbena, fam. n. ; Wübke, dimin. f.

NAMES OF PERSONS ENTERED IN DOMESDAY BOOK AS HOLDING LANDS *TEMP*. KING ED. CONFR.

A

Aben	Adeluuald	Ægduuardus	Ælfleda
Abet	Adelwoldus	Æileua	Ælfric
Abo	Ademar	Æilmar	Ælgar
Achebranni	Adestan	Æilmer	Ælger
Achestanus	Adjuuar	Æilmund	Ælget
Achi	Adret	Æilric	Æli
Achil	Adstan	Ællard	Ælmar
Achins	Adstanus	Ældeua	Ælmer
Acolf	Adulf	Ældid	Ælmund
Acum	Æchebrand	Ældiet	Ælnod
Acun	Ædelflete	Ældit	Ælric
Adam	Ædeldreda	Ældred	Ælsi
Adeldreda	Ædgeua	Ældreda	Ælstanus
Adelmus	Ædi	Ældret	Æluert
Adelid	Ædmundus	Ælfag	Ælueua
Adelinge	Ædricus	Ælfec	Æluin
Adeliz	Æduinus	Ælfelm	Æluric
Adelo	Ædwardus	Ælfer	Æluuacre
Adeold	Æduui	Ælfeth	Æluuard
Adelric	Ædwoldus	Ælfled	Æluui

Æluuin	Ainar	Alfa (Notts)	Alsicus
Ælwius	Aiolf	Alfac	Alsius
Æluuold	Airaf	Alfag	Alstan
Ærefast	Airet	Alfah	Altei
Ærgrim	Aischil	Alfeg	Altet
Æstanus	Aisil	Alfeih	Alti
Ætheldreda	Aiulf	Alfer	Altor
Æthericus	Aki	Alferd	Alwardus
Æthesi	Ala	Alfgerus	Alued
Ætmarus	Alanus	Alfhilla	Aluena
Ætnod	Albani	Alfidis	Aluene
Agelmarus	Alberic	Alfit	Aluer
Agebred	Albernus	Alfled	Aluerd
Agelricus	Albertus	Alfleda	Aluerle
Ageluuard	Albricht	Alflet	Alueron
Agemund	Albus	Alfnod	Aluert
Agenulfi	Alcerl	Alfric	Aluet
Aghemundus	Alchel	Alfriz	Aluied
Aglete (Linc.)	Alchemont	Alfsi	Aluiet
Aieluert	Alchen	Alfuuinus	Aluin
Aifride	Alcher	Algar	Alun
Ailad	Alcheris	Algerus	Alunold
Ailarduo	Alcherl	Algod	Aluol
Ailbernus	Alchetel	Algrim	Aluold
Ailbric	Alchil	Alham	Aluort
Ailbriht	Alcolm	Alid	Alur
Aildeig	Alcot	Aliet	Alured
Ailet	Alcude	Alli	Aluret
Aileua	Aldebert	Allic	Aluric
Ailhalle	Alded	Allric	Aluuacre
Ailid	Alden	Almær	Aluuald
Ailida	Aldene	Almar	Aluuard
Ailiet	Aldeuuif	Almer	Aluuart
Ailith	Aldgid (f.)	Almund	Aluuen
Ailm	Aldi	Almunt	Aluui
Ailmar	Aldid	Alnod	Aluuid
Ailmer	Aldiet	Alnoht	Aluuin
Ailmundus	Adolfus	Alnold	Aluuol
Ailof	Aldred	Alnot	Aluuold
Ailred	Aldreman	Alnoth	Aluuric
Ailric	(Linc.)	Alous	Amod
Ailsi	Aldret	Alrebot	Amund
Ailuerd	Aldvi	Alredi	Anand
Ailuert	Alduin	Alreforda de	Anant
Ailucua	Aldulf	Alret	Anaut
Ailuuard	Alebric	Alric	Ancholfus
Ailward	Alebrix	Alris	Andrac
Ailwi	Alestan	Alselmus	Andreæ
Aimar	Aluesdef	Alsi	Andreas

Angarus
Angerus
Angot
Anschil
Anscot
Ansculf
Ansfrid
Ansfrig
Ansgar
Ansger
Ansgot
Ansketill
Anund
Anunt
Ape (Som.)
Appe (Wilts)
Arcebald
Arcenbald
Archel
Archetel
Archii
Archilbar

Archisti
Ardegrip
Arduin
Ardul
Ardulf
Aregri
Aregrim
Aret
Arfastus
Aric
Arich
Arling
Arnebrand
Arnegrim
Arnenger
Arnui
Arnul
Artor
Arulf
Asa
Ascer
Ascha

Aschi
Aschil
Aschilbar
Asci
Ascored
Aseloc
Asford
Asfort
Asgar
Asgot
Asi
Aslac
Asli
Assemann
Assorin
Asul
Asulf
Athelwold
Atilie
Atserus
Atsur
Attile

Atules
Audoen
Auduid
Audulf
Auegrin
Auelin
Aueue
Augustinus
Auic
Auitius
Aured
Ausgar
Austin
Autbert
Auti
Avigi
Awart
Azelinus
Azer
Azor
Azur

B

Baco (Linc.)
Bada (Derb.)
Bade
Bain
Balchi
Baldeuin
Baldric
Balduin
Bar
Barch
Bardi
Bared
Baret
Barn
Barne
Basin (Yorks)
Basine (Yorks)
Batoc
Batsuen
Bedel
Bedling
Belam
Belehorne

Belrap
Benedict
Benne
Benz
Beorus
Ber
Berchinges de
Bercsi
Bere
Berguluer
Bern
Bernac
Bernard
Berne
Bernolt
Bernalf
Berrnar
Bers
Bertor
Bertunt
Besi
Beso
Besy

Beteslau
Bettice
Biche (Devon)
Biga
Bil
Bisi
Blac
Blach
Blache
Blacheman
Blachemer
Blacre
Blacsune
Blacuin
Blacun
Blacus
Blakeman
Blancar
Blund
Boche
Boda
Boddus
Bode

Bodin
Boding
Boi
Boia
Bole
Bolest
Bolla
Bolle
Bollo
Boln
Bolne
Bonde
Bondi
Bondo
Bondus
Borda
Boret
Borgered
Borgeret
Borred
Borret
Boso
Bosteinn

Bot
Boti
Botild
Botius
Botiz
Bou
Boui
Brand
Brandulf
Branduna
Branting
Branuuine
Breme
Bresibalt
Bretel
Bricfrid
Brichtmar
Bricmar
Bricmær
Bricnod
Bricsi
Bricsic
Bricsmar
Bricstan
Bricstec
Bricsteg
Bricstouuard (Som.)
Bricstual
Bricstuard
Bricstuin
Bricstul
Brictere
Bricteua
Brictic
Brictmar

Brictmer
Brictolf
Brictred
Brictric
Brictsuin
Brictuald
Brictuard
Brictui
Brictuid
Brictuin
Brictuold
Brictuolt
Brictuuard
Bricxtric
Brideuuold
Briford
Brihferd
Brihmar
Briht
Brihtman
Brihtmar
Brihtnoth
Brihtnot
Brihtric
Brihtuold
Brihtwald
Brinot
Brisid
Brismar
Brisnod
Bristec
Bristei
Bristeuuard
Bristoaldus
   (Devon)

Bristui
Bristuin
Bristuoldus
Bristuuard
Briteua
Britfleda (f.)
Britheue
Brithmar
Brithwold
Britmar
Britnod
Britric
Brixe
Brixi
Brixtuin
Brocles
Brode
Broder
Brodo
Brodor
Brodre
Bruhioc
Brumage
   (Northants)
Bruman
Brumanbeard
Brumann
Brumar
Brun
Brune
Brunesune
Brungar
Brungart
Brunier
Bruniht

Bruning
Bruno
Brunus
Brunwin
Bu (Yorks)
Bubba
Buge (Notts)
Bugered
Bughered
Bugo (Notts,
   Yorks)
Bului
Bunda
Bunde
Bundi
Bundo
Burc
Burcard
Burch de
Burchard
Burchart
Burchric
Burkart
Burgel
Burgered
   (Devon)
Burli
Burnes
Burnod
Burred
Burrer
Burret
Burric
Burro
Busch (Herts)

C

Cabe
Cadiand
Caduualent
Cædd
Caflo
Calpus
Camerarius
Camp
Campa
Campo

Cana
Canceler
Candovre
Cane
Canistre
Cano
Cantuin
Canud
Canus
Canut

Capellanus
Capin
Capus
Carentoch
Cari
Carle
Carlesone
Carleunda
Carlo
Carman

Caron
Caschin
Cassa
Caua
Cauua
Cecus
Cedd
Cedde
Celcott
Celeinus

Celestan	Chenui	Clarebold	Colne
Cellinc	Chenuicelle	Cliber	Colo
Celmar	Chenvichelle	Clibert	Colocar
Celred	Chenvin	Cloch	Coloen
Celric	Chenut	Cnud	Cols
Cerret	Chepin	Cnut	Colsegc
Certesyg	Cheping	Cobbe	Colsuan
Ceruel	Cheric	Coc	Colsuein
Cestre	Cheteber	Code	Coluin
Ceterith	Chetel	Codolf	Colvin
Chelbertus	Chetelbar	Codricus	Commend
Chenegar	Chetelbern	Coduius	*Constabularius*
Chenestan	Chetelbert	Cofsi	Coolf
Cheneue	Chilbert	Cola	Coolle
Cheneuuard	Chiluert	Colben	Copsi
Chenias	Chinesi	Colbert	Corbun
Chenicte	Chinestan	Colbrand	Costellin
Chening	Chinias	Cole	Couta
Chenisi	Chiping	Colebran	Crac
Chenistre	Chit	Coleg	Crin
Chenna	Chitel	Colegrim	Croc
Chenp	Cild	Coleman	Crucan
Chenric	Cille	Colgrim	Cubold
Chentis	Cilleham de	Colgrin	Cudulf
Chentiscus	Cilt	Colibertus	Cunlf
Chentuinus	Clac	Colle	Cutbert
Chenuard	Claman	Collnic	

D

Dachelin	Derinc	Don	Dunestan
Dacus	Dering	Done	Dunne
Dagobertus	Derolfus	Donne	Dunniht
Dainz	Derstanus	Donning	Dunninc
Dane	Deule	Donno	Dunning
Danemund	Doda	Dons	Dunno
Dedol	Dode	Dore	Duns
Dedou	Doding	Dot	Dunstan
Deincora	Dodo	Doth	Durand
Delfin	Dolesuuif	Dotus	Durilda
Dena	Dolfin	Dringlel	Dustan
Dene	Domne	Drogo	Duna (f.)
Depekin	Domniz	Drondus	Dunen
Derch	Domno	Duglei	

E

Eadmund	Earne	Ecchebrand	Edded
Eaduin	Ebrard	Ecchefrid	Eddeua
Ealgar	Eburg	Eculf	Eddeva

Eddid	Eilaf	Elsi	Ernuin
Eddied	Eilsberie	Elstan	Ernuit
Eddiet	Eileua	Elsuid	Ernulf
Edduin	Eilmer	Eltor	Ertein
Eddulf	Eilric	Eluena	Eruastus
Edeldreda	Eingar	Eluin	Esber
Edelmund	Einulf	Eluine	Esbern
Edelric	Eiric	Eluolt	Escelf
Edeluuold	Eiulf	Eluret	Eschet
Edena	Elaf	Eluric	Escul
Ederic	Elded	Elurilde	Escule
Edestan	Eldeua	Eluuacre	Esgar
Edeulf	Eldid	Eluuar	Esket
Edgar	Eldildæ	Eluuard	Eskmeld
Edged	Eldit	Eluui	Esmoda
Edgida	Eldred	Eluuin	Esnar
Edic	Eldret	Eluuold	Esneburn
Edid	Elduif	Engelri	Essocher
Ediet	Elduin	Engelric	Essul
Edilt	Eleua	Enisan	Estan
Edina	Elfac	Epy	Estarcher
Edlouedief	Elfag	Erchebrand	Estmunt
Edmær	Elfeg	Erding	Estori
Edmar	Elfelm	Erfast	Estorp de
Edmer	Elfelt	Ergrim	Estred
Edmund	Elfer	Eric	Etgar
Ednod	Elfgiva	Erich	Etmar
Ednoth	Elfin	Erlebald	Etnod
Edred	Elflet	Erlechin	Etone
Edric	Elfric	Erlenc	Etsius
Eduin	Elgar	Erne	Euchill
Eduuard (Cild,	Elget	Erneber	Eudo
Cilt.)	Eli	Ernebold	Euing
Eduui	Eliard	Ernebrand	Eur
Edwin	Eliert	Erneburne	Eureuu-
Eduunus	Eliet	Ernegrin	acre
Eduuold	Elintone	Erneis	(Devon)
Eduuolt	Elmær	Ernesi	Euroac
Edzi	Elmar	Erneuin	Eustachius
Egbert	Elmer	Erneuui	Eustan
Egbrand	Elmund	Erni	Euuacre
Egilfride	Elnoc	Erniet	Ewen
Egfride	Elnod	Ernold	Ewicman
Eghebrand	Elous	Ernu	Ezi
Eglesham, Abbatia	Elric	Ernui	Ezui
de (Glouc.)			

F

Faber	Finegal	Frauuin	Frodo
Fader	Fisc	Frebertus	Frogerus
Fanchel	Fitel	Fredebern	Fuglo
Fardan	Fitheus	Frederic	Fulbert
Fardein	Floteman	Fredghis	Fulcard
Fargrim	Forn	Fredgis	Fulcher
Fastolf	Forne	Fredgist	Fulcheric
Fech	Forst	Fredregis	Fulchi
Feche	Fot	Fredri	Fulchri
Feg	Fradre	Fregis	Fulcoi
Fegarus	Frambolt	Fregist	Fulcui
Felaga	Fran	Freowin	Fulghel
Fenchel	Frane	Freuuin	Furcard
Fenisc	Frano	Fridebert	Fursa
Fin	Franpalt	Friebern	Fyach
Fin (danus)	Franpold	Friebert	

G

Galterus	Ghida	Godefrid	Godton
Gam	Ghil (Yorks)	Godel	Godtovi
Game	Ghilander	Godelent	Goduin
Gamebar	Ghile	Godeman	Goerth
Gamel	Ghilebrid	Godere	Gogan
Gamelbar	Ghilemicel	Goderic	Gola
Gamelcarle	Ghilepatric	Goderus	Golde
Gangemere	Ghille	Godessa	Golderon
Gardulf	Gida	Godestan	Goldinus
Garle	Gilemichel	Godet	Goldstan
Gellinge	Giraldus	Godeua	Goldus
Genret	Girardus	Godeurt	Golegrim
Genuis	Giroldus	Godeva	Golleue
Genust	Gislebertus	Godgeua	Golnil
Genut	Giso	Godhit	Golstan
Gerinus	Gitda	Godid	Goltoui
Gerling	Gladewin	Godil	Goluin
Germund	Gladuin	Godinc	Gonchel
Gernan	Gladuine	Goding	Gonchetel
Gerneber	Gleuuin	Godiva (Countess	Gondrede
Gernebern	Glouuec	Warwick)	Gonhard
Gerold	Glunier	Godman	Gonnar
Gert	God	Godmar	Gonneu-
Gest	Goda	Godmund	uate
Getda	Godbold	Godo	Gonni
Gethe (f.)	Goddua	Godred	Gonnil
Gethne	Gode	Godric	Gonuerd
Gheri	Goded	Godrid	Gort

Gos
Gosfrid
Gosp
Gospatric
Gotil
Gotild
Gotius
Gotlac
Gotone
Gotra
Gouti
Gozelin
Grene
Greslet
Greue
Gribol
Grichetel
Grifin

Griketel
Grim
Grimbald
Grimber
Grimbert
Grimbold
Grimchel
Grimchil
Grimmus
Grimolfus
Grimulf
Grimus
Grinchel
Grino
Grossus
Grud
Grunulf
Grut

Grutt
Guda (f.)
Gudda
Gudeta
Gudmund
Gudmunt
Gudret
Gueda
Guerd
Guert
Gueth
Guiolf
Gulbert
Guluert
Gunchil
Gundulf
Guneuuare
Gunnar

Gunner
Gunneuuate
Gunni
Gunnild
Gunning
Gunnor
Gunnulf
Gunre
Gunuer
Gunuert
Gunuuar
Gunward
Gurert
Guret
Gurt
Guthac
Gutmund

H

Hache
Haco
Hacon
Hacun
Hademar
Hadeuui
Hadimar
Haduic
Hadulf
Haduuin
Haemar
Hagana
Hagane
Hagris
Haimer
Haiminc
Hairand
Hakena
Haldan
Haldein
Halden
Haltor
Hambe
Haminc
Haming
Handone
Hannart
Hapra
Har
Hard

Hardechin
Hardecnut
Hardewin
Harding
Hardul
Hardulf
Haregrim
Haregrin
Harold
Harparius(Camb.
  Aluui)
Hasten
Hauuard
Hauuart
Heche
Hedned
Hedul
Helewis
Helga
Helge
Helghi
Helghin
Helins
Helmelea
Heltor
Henricus
Her
Herald
Herbert
Herch

Herc
Heremannus
Hereuuard
  (Linc.)
Hereuuoldus
Herfast
Herfrid
Herfrind
Herleng
Hermann
Hernetoc
Herold
Herolf
Herueus
Herulfus
Hildeuert
Hobbesune Leu-
  ricus (Suff.).
  See Obbesune
Hoch
Hofward
Hoga
Holangar
Holchetel
Holefest
Holmo
Holt
Holund
Homdai
Honeuain

Horim
Horling
Horne
Horolf
Hosmund
Houden
Hugo
Hunman
Huna
Hunchil
Hundic
Hundin
Hunding
Hundulp
Hune
Hunef
Hunepot
Huni
Huning
Hunneue
Hunni
Hunnic
Hunnit
Hunnith
Hunta
Hunus
Husteman
Huthtrad
Huthtret
Hveche

I AND J

Jadulfus	Ingefrid	Inguare	Judichel
Jalt	Ingelric	Ingulf	Juin
Jaul	Ingemund	Johannes (danus)	Juing
Ilbert	Ingeuuar	Joseph	Juo
Ineuuar	Ingolf	Jouin	Justan
Ingar	Ingrede	Iric	Justin

K

Kee (Norf.)	Kerinc	Ketelbern	Keueua
Keneuuard	Ketel	Ketelbert	Kochaga
Kenoldus	Ketelber	Keteluua	Kochagana
Kenric			

L

Ladulf	Lefquena	Leuard	Leustan
Lag	Lefric	Leue	Leuuard
Laghemann	Lefriz	Leuecild	Leuuare
Lagman	Lefsi	Leueclai	Leuui
Lambe	Lefsida	Leuecol	Leuuin
Lambecarl	Lefsinus	Leuedai	Leuuold
Lambertur	Lefsius	Leuefa	Leuuord
Lanbecarl	Lefstan	Leuegar	Leuuric
Lanc	Lefsune	Leuget	Ligul
Lancfer	Leftan	Leueno	Ligulf
Lanch	Lefwin	Leuenod	Lihtwin
Lanchei	Leimar	Leueric	Linbald
Lang	Leising	Leueron	Linxi
Langabein	Leisini	Leuestan	Liseman
Lange	Leit	Leuesuna	Lisius
Langfer	Leman	Leuesunas	Liuing
Langfere	Lemar	Leuet	Liuric
Lant	Lemer	Leuetuna	Liuuard
Lasciuus	Leodmer	Leueua	Lochi
Ledi	Leofleda	Leuid	Locre
Ledman	Leofric	Leuiet	Lodric
Ledmar	Leofsi	Leuiget	Lofe
Ledmer	Leofstan	Leuild	Longus
Ledric	Leofsun	Leuinc	Lord
Leduui	Leomer	Leuin	Loten
Leduuin	Leonestan	Leuing	Ludi
Lefchil	Lepsi	Leuolt	Ludri
Lefcill	Lesinc	Leured	Lufchel
Lefelm	Lesing	Leuret	Lurc
Leffcilt	Lesius	Leuric	Lustuin
Lefflet	Lestan	(Leofric, the last	Luttin
Lefled	Leswin	Bp. of Crediton,	Luuare
Leflet	Let	transferred his seat	Luuede
Lefmer	Letfled	to Exeter by per-	Luuet
Lefolt	Leua (f.)	mission of K. Ed.	Luuetote
		Confr., 1050.)	

M

Maban	Mannicus	Menleua	Moding
Machel (Yorks,	Mannig	Merde	Moduin
332)	Mannius (Swert)	Merdo	Moithar
Machern	Manno	Merefin	Molleve
Machus	Manstan	Meresuuet	Monulf
Macus	Mansuna	Mereuin	Morcar
Madoch	Mapesone	Merken	Moregrim
Magbanec	Marculf	Merlesuain	Morewin
Magne	Martinus	Merlesuen	Morfar
Magno (Suert)	Maruaen	Meruen	Morganau
Mainard	Maruuen	Meruin	Moruant
Maino	Matheld	Meurdoch	Morulf
Mal	(Devon)	Micelenie	Mule (Yorks)
Malet	Mathila	Michaelis	Mulo
Malf	(Devon)	Michahel	Munding (Suff.)
Malgrim	Mauna	Milda	Mundret
Malgrin	Melc	Milegrim	Munulf
Man (Yorks)	Meldona	Milnegrim	Murdac
Mancus	Melduna	Modephefe (f.)	Murdoc
Manegot	*Mellessam de*	Modeva	Muscham
Manesuna	(Suff., 409)	Modgeva	Musla
Manna	Melmidoc	Modinc	

N

Nicholaus	Niuelig	Noriolt	Novi
Nigell	Niuelin	Norman	

O

Obbesune. *See*	Offers	Ordgar	Ormer
Hobbesune	Offo	Ordin	Ornod
Ocsen	Offram	Ording	Orthi
Oda	Ofl	Ordinc	Oruenot
Ode	Oghe	Ordmær	Orulf
Odeman	Oin	Ordmar	Osber
Oderus	Oiranti	Ordmer	Osbern
Odeua	Olbolt	Ordoff	Osbert
Odfrid	Olf	Ordric	Oschetel
Odil	Olgrim	Ordui	Oschil
Odincar	Olketel	Ordulf	Osfert
Odincarl	Olvva (f.)	Orduuold	Osford
Odo	Oluius	Orgar	Osgar
Odulfus	Oluuard	Orgrim	Osgod
Ofchetel	Oluuin	Orm	Osgot
Offa	Olviet	Ormar	Osiar
Offels	Orde	Ormchetel	Osier
Offerd	Ordec	Orme	Osiet

Osketel · Oswar · Otho · Oudon
Oslac · Osuuard · Othon · Oudulf
Osmar · Osui · Otre · Ouen
Osmer · Osuid · Otro · Ouiet
Osmund · Osuuol · Otti · Oune
Ostebrand · Oswald · Oualet · Outbert
Ostula · Otbert · Oudencar · Outi
Osul · Otburuilla · Oudfride · Ouu
Osulf · Ote · Oudgrim · Ouuine
Osuuald · Othen

P

Padda · Paulin · Peurel · Pinchengi
Pagan · Pauli · Phin · Pinslan
Pagen · Pbochestan · Pic · Poinc Godricus
Pallinus · Perci · Pileuuin · Pointel Tedricus
Pat (Ches.) · Perlo · Pin · Pur

R

Rachenild · Ratho · Rausnar · Ringulf
Rada · Rauan · Rauuen · Robert
Radboda · Rauecate · Rayner · Roc
Radolf · Rauechel · Reder · Roches
Radulf · Rauechet · Redulf · Roger
Rænold · Rauechetel · Rees (Ches.) · Rold
Rafrid · Rauechil · Regifer · Rolf
Rafuuin · Ravelin · Reider · Rolft
Ragenal · Raven · Reimbald · Roschel
Ragenald · Rauen · Reinbald · Roschet
Ragenalt · Rauenchil · Rembald · Roschil
Ragenild · Rauene · Renold · Rot
Ragenot · Rauengar · Restef · Rotbert
Rainald · Rauensuar · Restelf · Rotlesc
Rainbald · Rauensuard · Reuensuard · Roulf
Rainer · Raues · Reuer · Rozo
Ram · Rauesard · Ricard · Rufus Siuuard
Ramechil · Rauesue · Rinbold · Ruillic
Rannulf · Raulfus · Ringul · Ruschil
Rasrid

S

Sac · Saiet · Salvage · Sauin
Sæmar · Sailt · Samar · Saul
Sagar · Saisi · Saolf · Saulf
Sagera · Saisil · Sared · Sauord
Sagrim · Salecoe · Saric · Sauuard
Saiard · Salomon · Sarpo · Sauuata
Saied · Salpus · Sauard · Sauuin

Saũuold	Seuuard	Sorches	Stergar
Saxa	Seuuart	Sorchoued	Sterr
Saxi	Seuuen	Soror Stigandi	Sterre
Saxo	Seuui	Sort	Stichehare
Saxulf	Seuuin	Sorte	Stigand
Saxwin	Seward	Sortebrand	Stikestac
Sbern	Sexi	Sortocol	Stilla
Scaldefort	Sibe	Sota	Stille
Scalpi	Sichet	Soteman	Stingand
Scanchel	Sidgar	Sotinz	Stori
Scapius	Sigar	Sparhauoc	Stou
Scelfride	Sighet	Sperhauoc	Strami
Scemund	Sigred	Sperri	Stramun
Scet	Simon	Sperun	Strang
Sceua	Simond	Spieta	Strangulf
Scheit (Norf.)	Simund	Spille	Stric
Scipti	Sinod	Spirites	Strui
Scireuold	Sired	Spirtes	Struostun
Scirold	Siret	Sport	Stubart
Sclula	Sireuuald	Spretman	Stur
Scotcol	Sireuuold	Sprot	Suain
Scotecol	Siric	Sprotulf	Suan
Scotel	Sirof	Spuda	Suardcol
Scoua	Sistain	Spur	Suart
Scroti	Sistric	Staigrim	Suartcol
Scrotin	Siuard	Stainulf	Suartin
Scula	Siuargent	Stam	Suartric
Scule	Siuerd	Stanard	Suaue
Sech	Siuert	Stanart	Sudan
Seduin	Siulf	Stanchil	Suein
Segar	Siuuard	Stanfled	Suert
Segrida	Siuuart	Stangrim	Suerting
Seiar	Siuuin	Stanhard	Suet
Selecolf	Siuuold	Stanhart	Sueteman
Seleuuin	Siuurad	Stankar	Sueting
Selua	Smail	Stanmar	Suetman
Semær	Smalo	Stannechetel	Suetth
Seman	Smer	Stanuin	Suga
Semar	Smert	Stapleuin	Suglo
Semer	Smeuuin	Stari	Sumersul
Sendi	Snellinc	Starling	Summerde
Sercar	Snerri	Stauhart	Summerled
Seric	Snoch	Stein	Suneman
Serlo	Snode	Steinchetel	Suuain
Sessi	Snot	Steinulf	Suuarger
Seubar	Soartin	Stepi	Suuen
Seuen	Sol	Stepiot	Suwart
Seulf	Sonneua	Ster	Swert
Seuuar	Sonulf	Stercher	Syric

T

Taini, Teini,	Tochi	Tormord	Tunne
Teigni	Tochil	Torn	Turber
Taldus	Tocho	Toroi	Turbern
Tallgebosc	Tof	Torol	Turbert
Tarmoht	Toiswald	Torolf	Turbran
Tedgar	Toka	Torp	Turbrant
Tedric	Toke	Torsus	Turch
Tedricus	Tokesone	Tort	Turchel
Teit	Tol	Toruerd	Turchetel
Tela (f.)	Tolf	Toruert	Turchil
Tenus	Toli	Torulf	Tureuert
Teodric	Tona	Tosti	Turgar
Teolf	Tone	Tostil	Turgis
Teos	Tonna	Toti	Turgisle
Tepechin	Tonne	Tou	Turgod
Tepekin	Tono	Toue	Turgot
Terus	Tope	Touet	Turgrim
Thol	Topi	Toui	Turi
Thole	Topic	Touilda	Turketel
Tholi	Tor	Toul	Turkil
Thor	Toradre	Toulf	Turlog
Thoret	Torber	Touni	Turmod
Thori	Torbern	Toxus	Turmund
Thouus	Torbert	Trasemund	Turold
Thuinam	Torbrand	Trasmund	Turolf
Thurbern	Torbrant	Trauuin	Turorne
Thure	Torchel	Trec	Turot
Thuri	Torchetel	Trumin	Turstan
Thurmer	Torchil	Tube	Turstin
Thurmot	Tord	Tuffa	Turtin
Tidulf	Tored	Tuini	Turued
Tihell	Toret	Tumi	Turuer
Tisellin	Toreth	Tumme	Turuerd
Toc	Torfin	Tunbi	Turuert
Tocha	Tori	Tuneman	Turuet
Tochæ	Torif	Tunna	Turulf
Toche			

V

Vbe	Vital	Vlchil	Vlfeg
Vctebrand	Vitel	Vlestan	Vlfeih
Vctred	Viulf	Vlf	Vlfelm
Vdebrun	Vlbert	Vlfac	Vlfenisc
Vdeman	Vlbold	Vlfah	Vlfer
Vgelbert	Vlchel	Vlfar	Vlfert
Vgheta	Vlchet	Vlfchetel	Vlfenisc
Vibald	Vlchetel	Vlfech	Vlfiet

Vlfketel
Vlflet
Vlfmer
Vlfon (Sussex)
Vlfra
Vlfret
Vlfric
Ulfriz
Vlfstan
Vlfus
Vlfwin
Vlgar
Vlgrim
Vlketel
Vlmar
Vlmær

Vlmer
Vlnod
Vlnoth
Vlric
Ulsi
Vlsiet
Vlstan
Vlsuin
Vlsy
Vltain
Vltan
Vluara
Vluard
Vluer
Vlueron

Vluert
Vluerun
Vluena
Vluied
Vluiet
Vluin
Vluoi
Vluret
Vluric
Ulwar
Vluuard
Vluuen
Vluui
Vluuic
Vluuiet

Vluuin
Vluuinchil
Vluuold
Vluured
Vlvi
Vnban
Vnfac
Unlot
Vnspac
Vntani
Vntan
Vnton
Vrleuuine
Vstred
Uthtret

W

Wacra
Wada
Wade
Wadel
Wadelo
Wadels
Wado
Waga
Waih
Wailoff
Walduin
Walle
Wallef
Walleus
Wallo (Ches.)
Walraue
Walræuen
Walt
Waltef
Walteif
Walter
Walteu
Wana
Wand
Wants
Wardham
Warrena, Will de
Waso
Wateman
Wdebrun
Wege

Weghe
Weinhou
Weleret
Welgrim
Welland
Welle
Uuelp
Welp
Welrauen
Wenesi
Wenestan
Wenhou
Weniet
Wenning
Vuenoit
Wenric
Werden
Wester
Westre
Wetman
Wgulafra
Whita
Wiber
Wibert
Wichigus
Wichin
Wicling
Wicnod
Wicolf
Wicstric
Wictric

Widard
Widegrip
Widenesci
Wider
Widuis
Wiet
Wifare
Wifle
Wiflet
Wig
Wiga
Wigar
Wige
Wigha
Wighe
Wiglac
Wigod
Wigot
Wihenoc
Wihtgar
Wightmar
Wihtred
Wihtric
Wiking (Suff.)
Wilac
Wilaf
Wilde
Wilcgrip
Willa
Wimarc
Wimer

Wine
Winegod
Winemar
Wincstan
Winge
Winterled
Wintrelet
Wintremelc
    (Alricus)
Wirclmus
Wiscar
Wisg
Wisgar
Wislac
Wistan
Wistric
Wit
Uuit
Uuitc
Witg
Witgar
Wither
Withgar
Withmer
Withri
Witlac
Witric
Wiuar
Wiuara
Wiuelac
Wiulf

Wlbald
Wlf
Wlfah
Wlfric
Wlgar
Wlmær
Wlmar

Wlmer
Wlnod
Wlsi
Wlsin
Wlstan
Wluard
Wluar

Wleua
Wlui
Wluin
Wlured
Wluric
Wluuar
Wluuard

Wluuen
Wluui
Wlwi
Wluuin
Wnulf
Wordron

NAMES OF TENANTS IN CHIEF IN DOMESDAY BOOK

A

Abetot de
Achebranni
Adam
Adeldreda
Adeling
Adeliz
Adobod
Adrecide
Ældeva
Ældred
Agebric
Agemund
Ailmar
Ailrun
Ailunard
Aincurt de
Aiulf
Alan

Albamarla de
Albani
Alberic
Albert
Albingi de
Albus
Alden
Aldit
Aldred
Aldvi
Alestan
Alfhilla
Alfildis
Alfred
Algar
Alis
Almar
Almer

Almund
Alnod
Alric
Alselin
Alsi
Alverd
Aluers
Aluena
Alvied
Aluiet
Alured
Aluric
Alward
Alwi
Alwin
Alwold
Andeli
Anschetil

Ansger
Ansgot
Arches de
Archil
Arcis de
Aregrin
Areti
Artor
Arundel
Aschil
Ascuit
Asinus
Asne
Audoen
Autbert
Azelina
Azor

B

Bade de
Badpalmas de
Baignard
Balduin
Balgiole
Bangiard
Bano de
Barbatus Hugo
Bastard
Batailge de la
Bech de
Bedford de
Belcamp de

Belet
Bella Fago de
　(Beaufoy)
Belmont de
Belot
Belvaco de
Benz
Benzelin
Berchelai de
Berchingis de
Bereville de
Bernai de (Nor-
　mandy)

Bernard
Berneres de
Bernerus
Bersers de
Bertone de
Bertram de
Bevrere de
Bigot
Bituricensis
Blunders
Boci de
Bohun de
Bolebec de

Bolle
Bollo
Bomene de
Bonvalest
Bosch de
Boscnorman de
Breteville de
Bricteua
Brictoward
Brictric
Brictuin
Brimor de
Brismar

Brito	Bruning	Buenvaslet de	Burun de
Bruis Robertus	Bucfestre de	Buge (Notts)	Buruolt
de (Yorks)	Buci de	Buiville de	Busli de
Brun	Budi de	Burci de	

C

Cadomo de	Ceterith de	Clibert	Crass, Norman
(Caen)	Chana, Lewin	Coci de	Cratel, Godric
Cahainges de	Chelbert	Cola	Credun, Wido de
Cailgi	Chenvin	Colebern	Creneburne de
Cambrai de	Cheping	Colegrim	Crispin, Milo
Canut	Chetel	Collinc	Christina (f.)
Carbonel	Chetelbern	Colsvain	Croc
Carentoch de	Chetelbert	Colsuen	Croiland de
Carle	Chievre, Wm.	Colsuin	Cudulf
Carnot	Chilbert	Columbels de	Cvenild
Cedda, S.	Cicestre de	Colvin	Curbespine de
Cernel de	Croches de	Corcelles de	Curci de
Certesyg de	Claville de	Cormelies de	Cutbert
Cestre de	Clec, Godwin	Corniole, Wm.	

D

Dalari de	Doai de	Donne	Dreimes de
David	Dodesone, Alwin	Donno	Drogo
Derman	Dodid	Dons	Dunning
Dispensator	Dodo	Dovre de	Durand
Dive de	Dolfin	Dowai de	Dwai de

E

Eadmund	Edred	Eldred	Ernald
Ebrard	Edric	Elfain	Ernebern
Ebrulf	Eduin	Elmer	Erneis
Eddeva	Eduard	Elnod	Ernui
Eddid	Edwi	Elric	Ernuin
Eddiet	Edwin	Elsi	Ertald
Eddulf	Eglesham de	Elward	Esnebern
Edeua	(Eynsham, in	Equarius	Eudo
Edgar	Oxfordshire)	Erchenger	Eustachius
Ediet	Eldild	Eric	Excsse de
Edmund	Eldit	Erleching	

F

Fafiton	Ferendon de	Forne	Fresle, Richard
Falcisc de	Flamme	Fossard	Frodo
Fcircrcs dc, or	Flanbard	Fossart, Nigel	Fulcher
Ferieres	Flandren	Fouuer, Ansger	Fulcred
Fenisc, Ulf	Flavus	Framen, Rudulf	

G

Galterus	Girold	Goizenboded,	Greno or Grenon.
Game	Giselbert	Wm.	*See* Gernon
Gamel	Goda (f.)	Goismer	Grentebrige de
Gand de	Gode	Golde	Grestain de
Gant de	Godebold	Gonduin	Gretuilla de
Gerin	Godefrid	Gosbert, Hugo	Griffin
Gernio	Godescal	Goscelmus	Grimbald
Gernon	Godeua	Gospatric	Grim
Ghilo	Godmund	Gozelin	Gudmund
Gifard	Godric	Granetarius	Gunduin
Gilo	Goduin	Greistein de	Gunfrid
Girard	Goisfrid	(France)	Gurnai
Girbert			

H

Hagheburn	Hardulf	Herald	Hispaniensis,
Hago	Haregrin	Herbert	Alured
Haimeric	Harold	Herbrand	Holmo de
Haldein	Hascoit	Hereford de	Hortone de
Haluille de	Hascoith	Herion de	Hosed, Wm.
Hamelin	Hascolf	Hermer	Hugo
Hamo	Helion, Her-	Herveus	Hugolin
Handone de	veus de	Hesding	Humfrid
Hardinc	Henricus	Hghbern	Hunfrid
Harding	Heppo		Hunger

I and J

Ida (Countess	Illinge	Insula de	Iveri de
of Bologne	Ingald	Johannes	Ivichel
Jeanio	Ingania de	Isac	Ivikel
Ilbert	(Engaine)	Iseldis	Justen
Ilbodo	Ingulf	Judhel de Tote-	
		nais (Totness)	

K

Ketel

L

Laci de	Lawirce. *See*	Leuric	Loges de
Lanchei de	Wirce	Leutfrid	Lorz de
Landri	Leduin	Leuuin	Losward
Landric	Lefstan	Ligult	Lovet
Lanfranc	Legat	Limesi de	Loveth
Lanheie de	Leuena	Liof	Luith
Lasne, Hugo	Leviet	Lira de	Luri de
Latimarus	Levild	Liseman	Lusorüs de
Launire de	Leving		

M

Madoc	Maldrith	Medehal de	Molebec de
Magnavilla	Malet	Melchisan de	Monneuile de
(Mannwille)	Malf	Mellend de	Montagud de
Maigno	Maminot	Merde de	Monteburg de
Maino. *See*	Mantel	Mereuuin	Montfort de
Manno	Mappesone	Merleberge de	Montgomery de
Mal. *See* Malf	Martin	Mert	Morin
Malaopa	Matheus	Micelenie de	Mortemer de
Malcolun	Mathild	Moduin	Mucelgros de
Maldoith	Mauric	Moion de	Musard
Maldred	Mauritaniensis		

N

Nicolaus	Nigel	Niger	Norman

O

Oaura	Oilgi de	Osbern	Oswold
Obarvilla de	Oirant de	Osgot	Otha
Odard	Olaf	Osiet	Otho
Odburville de	Ordgar	Oslac	Otto
Ode	Ordric	Osmer	Ou· de
Odin	Ordui	Osmund	Outi
Odo	Orlatelle	Ostreham de	Ouus
Odolin	Orm	Osward	Ow de
Oger			

P

Pagen	Peret	Pilardintone de	Pointel de
Pagenel	Persore de	*Pincerna*	Pomerei de
Pancevolt	Peverel	Pinel	Porth de
Parcher, An-	Picot	Piperellus. *See*	Pugnant
schitil	Pictavensis	Peverel	Puingiant
Percehaie	Pierani de	Poillgi de	Puintel
Perci			

Q

Quintin, S. de

R

Rabellus	Rames de	Rayner	Roelent
Radulf	Ramesy de	Reinbald	Roger
Ragenald	Ramis de	Restold	Rolf
Rainald	Rannalf	Ricard	Romenel de
Rainbald	Ravelin	Riucirc	Rotbert
Rainburgis	Raven	Robert	Rothais (f.)
Reinbuedcurt de	Ravenchil	Rodmund	Ruald
Ramechil			

S

Saiet	Saward	Sibold	Stigand
Saieva	Sawin	Sigar de Cioches	Stirman
Saisselin	Sawold	Siric	Stratfort de
Salceid de	Sbern	Siuard	Sturmid
Salceit de	Scalers de (or	Soartin	Suain
Salebi de	d'Echallers)	Sortebrand	Suarding
Salmur de	Schelin	Spech (or	Suarting
S. Quintin de	Scohies de	Espec?)	Suen
Sanson	Scrope	Sperri	Sueno
Saric	Scudet	Stanard	Surdeual de
Sariz	Sedret	Starcolf	Suuen
Sasford	Seric	Stefan	Svain
Sasselin	Seuard	Steinulf	Swan
Saulf			

T

Tailgebosch	Thomas	Tor	Totenais de
Tedfort de	Tison	Torber	Tovi
Tehell	Tisun	Torbern	Turbern
Teodric	Tochi	Torchil	Turbert
Tetbald	Todeni de	Tored	Turchil
Tezelin	Toenio de	Tornyg de	Turstui
Theodric	Tona	(Thomey)	Turstun

U and V

Valbadon de	Ver de	Vlbert	Vlmar
Valonges de	Verdun de	Vlchel	Vlnod
Valonis de	Verli de	Vlf	Ulsi
Vctred	Vernon de	Vlfric	Vluiet
Vdi	Vis de Lew	Vlgar	Vluui
Veci de			

W

Wadard	Wanz	Widuile de	Wirce de
Wado	Warene de	Wielard	Wislac
Walchelin	Warwell de	Wigar	Wit
Waldin	Wateman	Willelm	Wlmar
Waleram	Wateuille de	Wiltune	Wluin
Waleran	Waula	Winemar	Wlwi
Waleric	Wibert	Wintremelc	Wrehantune de
Walter			

NAMES OF UNDER-TENANTS OF LANDS AT THE TIME OF THE DOMESDAY SURVEY

A

Aba (Northts.)	Ailuuacre	Alnulf	Anger
Abba (Norf.)	Aincurt de	Alred	Ansger
Abel (Kent)	Airard	Alric	Ansgered
Abernon de	Aistan	Alselin	Ansgot
Abetot de	Aitard	Alsi	Anslepe de
Abraham	Aiulf	Altet	(Northampt.)
Acard	Alam	Aluerad	Ansleuile
Achet, Walterus	Alan	Aluered	Appeuile
Acun	Albengi de	Aluena	Archil
Adam	Alberi	Aluiet	Archis
Adelard	Alberic	Alulf	Arcis de
Adeledmus	Albert	Alured	Arda de
Adelelmus	Albin'	Aluric	Ardulf
Adelina	Albold	Aluuard	Arling
Adelold	Albus	Alward	Armenteres
Adelolf	Alcher	Alwart	Arnald
Adelulf	Alde	Alwewe	Arnegrim
Adelwin	Alded	Aluui	Arni
Adeluuold	Aldelin	Aluuin	Arnuf
Adestan	Alden	Aluuold	Artur
Adolf	Aldi	Amalric	Arundel, Roger
Adret	Aldred	Ambrose	Asc' (Ascelin)
Ældcua	Aldrie	Amelfrid	Aschil
Ældred	Alelm	Amelger	Ascolf
Ælfelm	Alencun	Amerland	Aselin
Ælgot	Alestan	Aman	Asford
Ælmer	Alflet	Amund	Asfort
Aelons	Alfred	Anchitill	Aslac
Ælric	Alfric	Andeli de	Aslen
Ælucue	Alfrid	Andreas (Cornw.)	Asne
Æluuard	Algar	Anger	Asso
Ærnold	Alger	Angevin, Osmund	Asuert
Agemund	Alich	Anschetill	Avenel
Aguet	Allic	Anschill	Auesgot
Agenulf	Almær	Anschitil	Ausgustin
Aghemund	Almar	Ansegis	Avigi
Agnes	Almer	Ansel	Auigi
Ailbold	Almfrid	Anseredus	Auti
Ailmar	Almod	Ansfred	Azelin
Ailric	Alno	Ansfrid	Azo
Ailuard	Alnod	Ansgar	Azor

B

Baderon
Bagod
Baignar
Baignard
Bainard
Baingiard
Bainiard
Baldeuin
Baldric
Balduin
Balt
Barb, Bernard (Heref.)
Barbes de
Baret
Baro
Basset
Basuin
Beatrix
Bec, Walter
Bech de
Belcamp de
Belencun' de
Belet
Belfago
Belfou
Bellafago
Beluard
Benedict
Benthelm
Benzelin
Berard
Berchelai de
Berdic

Berengarius
Bereuuold
Berger
Bernai de
Bernar
Bernard
Berner
Bernulf
Berold
Berruarius
Bertran
Beruold
Beuerde
Beulf
Big
Bigot
Blach
Blacheman
Blancard
Blancus
Blechu
Bleio
Blize
Blohin
Bloiet
Blon
Blond
Blosseuille de
Blund
Bodin
Bolebec, Hugo
Bollo
Bondi

Bono
Bonuaslet, Willm.
Borci
Bordin
Borel
Boret
Borghill
Bosc de
Boscroard de
Boselin
Boso
Boteric
Boter
Boti
Botild
Braiboue de
Braiose de
Brant
Bretel
Breteuile de
Bricmær
Brictmar
Brictmer
Brictolf
Brictred
Brictric
Brichelf
Brictuin
Brictuuard
Brien
Briend
Brienz
Brion

Brisard
Brismer
Bristeua
Bristist
Bristoald
Bristoard
Brito
Brixi
Brodo
Bruman
Brun
Brunard
Brunel
Brungar
Bruning
Brunnuin
Bruno
Bucard
Buci de
Buerd
Bueret
Buissel
Bundo
Burci de
Burdet
Burghard
Burnard
Burnart
Burneuill de
Bursigni de
Busch
Busli de
Buter

C

Cada' de (de Cadamo)
Cadio
Cadomi
Cadomo de
Caflo
Cahainges de
Caisned de
Calpus
Caluus
Calvus

Candos de
Cardon
Cardun
Carnot'
Caron de
Carun de
Cedde
Celric
Celsi de
Cepe
Chacepol

Chemarhnec
Chenesis
Chenret
Cheping
Chernet de
Chetel
Chetelbar
Chetelbern
Chetelburn
Cheure
Cioches de

Clarebald
Clarenbald
Claron
Clauile de
Clavilla de
Clodoan
Coc, Aluuin (bedellus)
Coci de
Cola
Colbert

Colegrim
Colevil de
Colgrim
Collo
Colo
Colsuain
Colsuan

Coluin
Colvin
Conded
Constantin
Corbelin
Corbet
Corbin

Corbun
Corcel de
Co'rp
Credun, Wido
  de
Crispin, Milo
Croc

Cruel
Cudhen
Culling
Curcan de
Curci de
Cus

D

Daniel, Roger
  (Suss.)
Dauid
David
Denomore, Wm.
Denuers, Wm.
Depeiz, Guerno
Deramis, Roger
Dereman
Dereuuen

Derinc
Derisbou, W.
Derman
Deuais, Robt.
Deuernu' (De
  Vernon)
Doda
Doddus
Dodeman
Dodemund

Dodesone, Alu-
  uin (Herts.)
Dodin
Dodo
Dolfin
Domnic
Donecan
Doneuuald
Donno
Douenold

Douuai de
Dreuues, Amal-
  ric de (Wilts)
Drogo
Dudeman
Dunning
Dunstan
Dur'
Durand
Dynechaie

E

Eadvuun
Ebrard
Ecchebrand
Eddeua
Eddid
Eddiet
Eddille
Eddulf
Edelo
Ederic
Edgar
Edied
Edmar
Edmund
Ednod
Edred
Edric
Eduin
Eduuard
Eduui
Egbert

Egbriht
Ehelo
Eideua
Eileua
Eiluuard
Einbold
Elbert
Eldeid
Eldred
Elduin
Elfin
Elfric
Elfrid
Eli
Elinant
Elmar
Elmer
Elmui
Elmund
Elnod
Elric

Elsi
Eluard
Elward
Eluui
Eluunin
Engelbric
Engeler
Engenold
Engelulf
Enisan
Enisant
Er (Ermen-
  hald)
Erchebrand
Erchenbald
Erenburgis
Erfast
Erluin
Ermenhald
Ermenfrid
Erm'iot

Ernald
Ernegis
Erneis
Ernold
Ernolf
Ernucion
Ernui
Ernuin
Ernulf
Ernuzen
Ertein
Escalers de
Ettard
Eudo
Euen
Euerwin
Eurard
Eurold
Euruin
Eustachius

F

Fabri
Faderlin
Fadrelin

Faeicon
Faeto
Falcus

Farman
Fastrad
Fatat

Fech
Feggo
Felcher

Felger
Ferme
Ferron
Firmat
Fla'bard
Fla'mart
Fla'mens
Flanbard
Flandr'
Flavus
Flint

Floc de
Folcheran
Folcran
Folet
Forist
Fragrin
Frane
Franco
Frano
Fredgis
Fredo

Frodo
Froger
Froissart, Wm.
Frumond
Fulbert
Fulbric
Fulcard
Fulche
Fulcher
Fulchered
Fulcho

Fulco
Fulcoin
Fulcold
Fulcran
Fulcred
Fulcui
Fulcuin
Fulkered
Fulo
Furic

G

Gadinc
Gadio
Gadomo de
Galicer
Galt'
Galterus
Gamas
Game
Gamel
Gamelin
Gand de
Gaosfrid
Garenger
Garin
Garmund
Garner
Gatelea
Gaufrid
Gaurinc
Gausfrid
Gerald
Gerard
Gerbodo
Gerelm
German
Germund
Gerneber
Gernon
Gerold
Geron
Gherui
Gifard

Gifart
Gildre
Gingom
Girald
Girande
Girard
Girold
Giron
Gisbert
Gislebert
Gislold
Giso
Glauill
Gleduin (Leic.)
Gleu (Bedf.)
Glodoen
Godard
Godebold
Godefrid
Goderet
Goderun
Godescal
Godeue
Godid
Godinc
Goding
Godman
Godmund
Godric
Goduin
Godzelin
Goisbert

Goisfrid
Goislan
Goislen
Goismer
Goldwin
Goleman
Gollam
Golstan
Gondran
Gonfrid
Gonther
Gosbert
Goscelin
Goscelm
Goselin
Gosfrid
Goslin
Gospatric
Gotwin
Goze
Gozel
Gozet
Grai de
Grando
Grantcurt
Grapinel
Greno
Grentmaisnil
de
Grento
Greslet
Grichel

Grichetel
Grifin
Griketel
Grim
Grimbald
Grinon
Gros
Gualter
Guarin
Gudhen. *See*
Cudhen
Gudmund
Gueri
Gveric
Guerlin
Guert
Guibert
Gvihu'mar
Gulaffra
Gulbert
Gulfer
Gulfered
Gummar
Gunduin
Gundulf
Gunequata
Gunfrid
Gvnhar
Gunner
Guntard
Gunter
Gutbert

H

Hacun	Heldered	Herion, Tihell	Hosed
Hadeuuin	Heldred	de	Hotot de
Hadulf	Heldret	Herlebald	Houard
Hagebert	Heldric	Herlebold	Huard
Haimard	Helduin	Herleuin	Hubald
Haimer	Helgod	Herman	Hubb'
Haiming	Helgot	Hermenfrid	Hubert
Haimo	Helio	Hermer	Hubold
Halanant	Helmer	Hernold	Hveche
Halsard	Helto	Herold	Hugo
Hame	Hengebald	Herolf	Hugol'
Hamelin	Henric	Herpul	Hugolin
Haminc	Herold	Heruen	Hunald
Hamo	Herbert	Hesdinc	Hunfrid
Hamon	Herbrand	Hesding	Hunger
Hardeuuin	Herding	Hezelm	Hunnit
Harding	Hereberd	Hildebrand	Hunulf
Harold	Hereuuard	Hosdena de	Hurant
Hato	Herfrid	Hosdenc de	Huscarle

I AND J

Jacob	Inganie	Johannes	Junain
Jagelin	Ingelbald	Jouin	Junan
James	Ingelbert	Iric	Junen
Jarnacot	Ingelram	Isac	Iuo
Idhel	Ingelran	Iseldis	Ivo
Ilbert	Ingelric	Isenbard	Iuran
Ilbod	Ingenulf	Iseuuard	Iurei
Ildebert	Ingrann	Ispania de	Iuri
Ilduin	Ingulf	Judhell	Ivri
Ingald	Johais	Judichel	Iward
Ingelra'n	Joh's	Juhell	Iuuein
Ilgerus			

K

Keresburg de

L

Lacei de	Langetot de	Laurentius	Leftan
Lachelin	Langhetot de	Ledman	Lemar
Laci de	Lanzelin	Ledmar	Lemci
Lambert	*Lardarius*	Leflet	Lepsi
Lanbert	Latin	Lefric	Lestan
Landri	*Latinarius*	Lefsi	Letard
Landric	Latinus	Lefsun	Lethelin

Letmar	Leuuard	Lira de	Losoard
Leucilt	Lewes	Liseman	Losuard
Leuegar	Leuui	Lisoisus	Louel
Leuenot	Leuuine	Locels de	Louet
Leueua	Leuuric	Loder	Ludichel
Leuiet	Liboret	Lodouuin	Ludo
Leuinc	Ligulf	Loeruic	Lundonie de
Leuing	Limesi de	Lof	Lunen
Leuric	Lincole de	Loges de	Lungus
Leusin	Liof	Loher	Lusorio de

M

Machar	Manasses	Mellend de	Moriland
Machinator	Manbodo	Melling de	Morin
Machus	Manneuille de	Merc de	Moriton de
Maci	Mara de	Merde de	Mortemer de
Madoc	Marcher	Mereuin	Mortuing
Maigno	Marci de	Merlebey	Morua
Mainard	Marcud	*Miles*	Moruant
Mainfrid	*Marescal*	Modbert	Moruuin
Maino	Martel	Moion de	Mosters de
Maiulf	Mascerel	Molebec	Motbert
Malauill	Mascherell	Monetar	Moyses
Malbedeng	Mater	Monfort de	Mucedent de
Maldoit	Mathild	Monulf	Mucelgros de
Malet	Matheus	Moran	Muceull
Malf	Mechenta	Morcar	Mundret
Malger	*Medicus*	More de	Murdac
Malus Vicinus	Meinard	Morel	Musard
Maminot	Meinfrid		

N

Nardred	Nicolaus	Nogiold	Norun
Nauuen	Nigel	Norgiot	Noui
Nemore	Noiers de	Norgot	Nouuers de
Nepos	Noies de	Norman	Nubold
Nicol			

O

Oburuilla de	Odo	Oilgi de	Oluu'
Odard	Odon	Oismelin	Orbec de
Odarus	Offa	Olaf	Ordmær
Odbert	Offels	Olbald	Ordmar
Odburcuilla de	Offran	Ole de	Ordric
Oddo	Oger	Olf	Ordulf
Odelin	Ogis	Olgi de	Orduui
Odin	Oidelard	Oliuer	Orenet
Odmus	Oilard	Olnei de	Orenge de

Orgar	Osgot	Osuuold	Otho
Orger	Oslach	Otbert	Otto
Orm	Osmund	Otbold	Oudchel
Ormar	Osulf	Otburville de	Ouethel
Orme	Oswald	Othelin	Outi
Ornod	Oswar	Othem	Ow de
Osbern	Osuuard	Othingar	Ou
Osbert	Osuuic		

P

Pagan	Peccatu'	Picot	*Pistor*
Pagen	Perapund de	Pictavensis	Pleines
Paisfor	Perci de	*Pincerna*	Poingiant
Paisforere	Periton de	Pinchengi de	Pointel
Pancefold	Pertenai de	Pinc'u'n'	Polchehard
Pantul	Pcsserara	Pinel	Pomerei de
Pantulf	Peteuin	Pipe (Som.)	Ponther
Papald	Petrus	Piperell	Ponz
Parisiac	Peverel	Pipin	Port de
Parisiacenis	Peurel	Pirot	Pugnant
Parler	Phanexon	*Piscator*	Pungiant
Passaq'			

Q
Quintin

R

Rabboda	Ramis de	Reinfrid	Rictan
Rabel	Randulf	Reinold	Ricuard
Rademar	Rannulf	Remir	Riculf
Rademer	Rardulf	Renald	Rippe
Radfred	Rasrid	Renbald	Risboil de
Radman	Ratho	Renelm	Riset de
Radulf	Rauemer	Reneuuald	Riuold
Radus	Rauen	Renold	Riuualo
Rafri	Rauengar	Renuuar	Roald
Raimar	Rauenot	Restald	Robert
Raimund	Raynald	Restold	Rodbert
Rainald	Rayner	Restolt	Rodeland de
Rainalm	Raynold	Ret	Roder
Rainbald	Raynouuard	Ribald	Rodulf
Rainbert	Reduers de	Ricaiard	Rog'e
Rainbold	Reger	Ricar	Roger
Rainelm	Reimund	Ricard	Rogo
Rainer	Reinbald	Richer	Rogus
Rainfrid	Reinbert	Ricoard	Rohard
Rainold	Reiner	Ricolf	Roic

Rold
Rolf
Rolland
Romenel de
Roric

Ros de
Rotbert
Rotroc
Rozel'

Rozelin
Ruallon
Rualon
Rufus

Rumald
Rumbold
Rumold
Runeuille

S

Sacheuilla de
Sæfrid
Safrid
Sagar
Sagrim
Saiet
Saieua
Sais de
Salmur de
Salo
Salomon
Sanson
Sasfrid
Sasgar
Sasuualo
Sasuuard
S. Leger
S. Quintin
S. Sansone de
Saucnie de
Sauigneio de
Sauigni de
Saulf
Sauuard
Sauuold
Saxlef

Schelin
Schelm
Scohies de
Scolland
Scoua
Scriba
Scudet
Scutet
Sedred
Segrim
Seibert
Seifrid
Semar
Semer
Sencler de
Sent Cler de
Sentebor de
Seolf
Septniuels de
Seric
Serlo
Sessibert
Seward
Seuuen
Seuui
Sigar

Silua de
Silvester
Simon
Simond
Simund
Sinod
Sired
Sireuuold
Siric
Siuert
Siuuard
Siuuate
Smalavill de
Soies de
Sotus
Spec
Spech
Sprottulf
Stable
Stanard
Stanart
Stannechetel
Stantone de
Stauhart
Stefan

Stenulf
Stirman
Stoches
Sturm'
Sturmid
Sturstan
Suain
Suan
Suarting
Suartric
Suausey de
Suauis
Suen
Suertin
Suerting
Suetin
Sueting
Suetman
Sufreint
Suin
Sumeri de
Surd've
Suttuna
Suuan
Suuen

T

Taccham de
Tædald
Tailgebosc
Taissel de
Talebot
Talliebosc
Tame de
Tascelin
T'chetel
Tebald
Tedald
Tedbert

Tedbold
Tedric
Tehel
Teher
Teodbald
Teoderic
Teodric
Teodulf
Terbert
Tetbald
Tetbaud
Tezelin

Tham de
Thochi
Tidbald
Tiger
Tinel
Tirel de
Tirus
Toche
Tochi
Tochil
Todeni de
Toeni de

Toka
Toli
Tonne
Tor
Torchill
Tored
Toret
Torgis
Tornai
Torold
Torstin
Tosard

Tosti	Troarz de	Turbern	Turlauillade
Toui	Tual	Turchetil	Turmit
Touilt	Tuder	Turchil	Turold
Traillgi de	Tumbi	Turgar	Turstan
Tralgi de	Tur	Turgis	Tursten
Trauers	Turald	Turi	Turstin
Troard de	Turbat		

U and V

Vagan	Verley de	Vlf	Vlueua
Valbadon de	Verli de	Vlfac	Vluiet
Vallibus de	Vernon de	Vlfchetel	Vluric
Valonges	Vill'o de	Vlketel	Vluuard
Valongies de	Vinitor	Vlmar	Vlwart
Valonis de	Uis de Leun	Vlmer	Vluui
Vals de	Uisdelups	Vlnod	Vluuin
Uctebrand	Visolupi	Vloi	Vnifrid
Vctred	Vitalis	Vlric	Vrfer
Veci	Vitard	Vlsi	Vrso
Venables de	Vlchel	Vlstan	Vruoi
Venator	Vlchetel	Vltbert	Uttal
Ver de	Vlestan	Vluard	Uual' de

W

Wachelin	Walo de	Wateuile de	Widelard
Wadard	Walscin	Wazelin	Wido
Wal' de	Walter	Wazo	Widr
Wala	Waluille de	Wenelinc	Wielard
Walbert	Wanceio de	Weneuc	Wigar
Walchel	Wanz	Wenric	Wigemore
Walchelin	War' de	Werelc	Wiger
Walcher	Waras de	Werenc	Wighen
Walcin	Wareger	Werestan	Wigot
Waldin	Warene de	Wert	Wihanoc
Walen	Wareng'	Wesman	Wihomarc
Walenn	Warenger	Westone	Wihtmar
Walenses	Warenna de	Wgulafra	Wihuene c
Waler'	Wares de	(W. Gulafra)	Wihumar
Waleram	Waribold	Wiard	Wihvmarc
Waleran	Warin	Wibald	Wilard
Walicher	Warinbold	Wiberg	Willac
Walifrid	Warinc	Wibert	Willelm
Wallef	Warmund	Wicard	Wimarcæ
Walo	Warner	Wichin	Wimerus
Walon' de	Wast	Widald	Wimund
Waloniencis de	Wasunic	Widard	Wineman

E

Winemar	Witbert	Wizo	Wluuard
Wintrehard	Witburg	Wlb'tus	Wluui
Wiscand de	Witsand de	Wlric	Wluuold
Wisgar	Wituile de	Wlsi	Wodeman
Wissand de	Hugo	Wlueua	

Y

Ymfrid (Humfrid)

NORMAN NAMES

A GREAT deal has been written about the Roll of Battell Abbey and the companions of the Conqueror, which is doubtless of great interest to those who claim to be descendants of the persons therein recorded.

There was such a roll suspended in the great hall of the building, and it bore the names of 645 knights, but it has disappeared long ago, as well as the other relics of the battle, which were removed to Cowdray, and perished in the great fire there in 1793.

There are several copies more or less imperfect. The lists which appear to be the most authentic are: Duchesne's list, taken from the abbey charter, containing 405 names; Leland's collection, with 498 names; Magny's catalogue, with 425 names; Delisle's, with 485 names. These are all of a much later date than the Conquest, probably *temp.* Ed. I.

Of the great array of time-honoured names very few are now borne by direct representatives. They exist rather among the old gentry than in the peerage. In the majority of cases the later descendants of illustrious families have sunk into poverty and obscurity unconscious of their origin, and this was more likely to be the case with the younger branches, since the name or title of the family went with the elder line that inherited the estates.

The following names have been collected from the lists above mentioned. Many of them will be found in Domesday Book, and where such is the case they may be considered to be genuine followers of the Conqueror. It is obvious that those which compare favourably with Domesday Book are the most reliable, and others which do not stand that test may be looked upon as of later date. The names of some of the Flemings who accompanied William are also included in this list.

Much doubt has long existed as to the authenticity of the several versions which have appeared at different times, claiming to be a roll of the names of the Norman invaders who survived the battle of Hastings, but it is manifest that many of those recorded, even if they were ever upon the original document deposited with the monks of Battell Abbey, are not found to correspond with either the tenants-in-chief or the under-tenants of Domesday Book at the time of the Survey (A.D. 1086). On the other hand, the last mentioned—of whom there is a great number —have hardly a place upon the roll.

It is well known that the heralds of the fourteenth and fifteenth centuries were not scrupulous in adding names to the list.

Queen Isabella of France, the consort of Edward II., introduced in her train many personages bearing surnames previously unknown in England.

The Rotuli Normanniæ, R. Hundredorum, and R. de Oblatis et Finibus, *temp.* Regis Johannis, Testa de Neville, Pipe Rolls, etc., are valuable evidence as to Norman names. The place-names of Normandy have been added.

The asterisk denotes a tenant-in-chief.

A

Abbeville. Appeville; a loc. n. *D.B.* Appeuile, de Oburvilla

Abell. *D.B.* Abeel, loc. n., Belg.

Aimeris. *D.B.* Haimeric *

Aincourt. *D.B.* de Aincurt.* Agincourt; a loc. n.

Akeny. *D.B.* Acun (?). Acquigny, Aucun, loc. n.

Albeny. *D.B.* Albani *

Amay (Johannes Ame). Amécourt (?), loc. n.

Amerenges

Amouerduile, Aumarill, Amundeville, loc. n.

Angenoun. Angennes; a loc. n.

Angers, Aunwers. *D.B.* Anger. Angers; a loc. n.

Angewyne. *D.B.* Angevin Osmund

Angilliam, Aungcloun. Angoulême; a loc. n.

Anuay. Aunay, loc. n.

Archere. *D.B.* de Arcis,* de Arques, loc. n. France

Arcy, D'Arcie, Darcy,* from de Ardreci. *D.B.*, T.C. (Lincs.)

Argentoune. David de Argentomo in *D.B.* Reginald de A., Sheriff of Camb. 5 Rich. I., Argentan; a loc. n.

Arundel. *D.B.**

Arwerne

Aspermound

Aspervile

Audeley. *D.B.* Andeli * (?). Andelys; a loc. n.

Audeville or Adryelle (?). Adervielle; a loc. n.

Auenant, Avenele. *D.B.* Avenel

Aumarle. *D.B.* de Albamarle *

Avereris. *D.B.* de Iveri *

Aybeuare (John Aubry). Aubevoye, loc. n.

B

Bagott. *D.B.* Bagod

Bailif. Le Bailli

Baillol. *D.B.* Balgiole.* Bailleul; a loc. n.

Bainard, Byngard. *D.B.* Bangiard *

Baious, or Baus. Bayeux; a loc. n.

Baloun. Bâlines, loc. n.

Banastre, Banestre; a loc. n.

Banet or Benny. *D.B.* de Bano * (?)

Barchampe. Beauchamp, loc. n.

Bardolfe

Barduedor

Barnivale, Berenvile, Burneville, Burinell. *D.B.* de Burneuill. Barneville; a loc. n.

Barrett, Baret. *D.B.* Baret
Bary, Barre, Barry. Berry; a loc. n.
Bascoun. *D.B.* Basuin (?)
Baskerville, Bacqueville; a loc. n.
Basset or Bassey. *D.B.* Basset
Bastard. *D.B.**
Baudewin, Baudin, Baldwin. *D.B.* Balduin,* Count of Flanders
Baupere. Beauport; a loc. n.
Beauchamp. *D.B.* de Belcamp
Beaumont. *D.B.* de Belmont (?), de Bomene*; a loc. n.
Beauvise or Bevers. Beauvais; a loc. n.
Beelhelme, Bealum. Bellême; a loc. n.
Beisin. Bessin; a loc. n. *D.B.* Basuin (?)
Beke. *D.B.* de Bech.* Bec-Hellouin; a loc. n. or Beeck, Belg.
Belefroun. Beauvron; a loc. n.
Belesur. Bellecourt; a loc. n.
Beleuers, Belliéres; a loc. n.
Bellet. *D.B.* Will. Belet (Hants). Harvey Belet lived *temp.* K. Steph.
Bellew. *D.B.* Belot.* Bellou, loc. n.
Bellire. Balleroy; a loc. n.
Berners. *D.B.* de Berners.* Bernières; a loc. n.
Bernon. *D.B.* Bernar (?)
Berteuilay. Berthouville (?), loc. n.
Bertin. *D.B.* de Bertone.* St Bertin; a loc. n.
Bertram. *D.B.* de Bertram,* Robert Vicomte, 1047
Beteruile or Breteville. *D.B.* de Breteville. Bretteville; a loc. n.
Beurey or Bevery. *D.B.* de Bevrere* (a Fleming)
Bevill, Belevile. Belleville; a loc. n.
Bigot. *D.B.**
Bikard, Bekard. *D.B.* Brictoward.* Briquesart; a loc. n.

Biroune. *D.B.* de Burun.* Biron; a loc. n.
Blondell or Blundel. *D.B.* Blunders* or Blond (?)
Bluet. *D.B.* Bloiet. Briqueville la Blouette; a loc. n.
Blunt, Blundet, or Blounte. *D.B.* Blunders.* Blandain; a loc. n.
Bodin, Bidin. *D.B.* Bodin. Beaudéan; a loc. n.
Boels. Bouelles, loc. n.
Bohun. Bohon; a loc. n. *D.B.* de Bohun*
Bois. *D.B.* de Bosch* (*Fl.*), Busch, or Bois, loc. n., Belg.
Bondeville. Bonneville; a loc. n. *D.B.*
Bonett. Bonnat; a loc. n., *Fr.*
Bonrett. Bonnart; a loc. n., Belg.
Bonueier. Bonnières; a loc. n.
Boranvile. Bérengeville (?), loc. n.
Botelere, a loc. n., Belg.
Botevile or Boyville. *D.B.* Botild(?). Bouille; a loc. n. (?)
Boundes. *D.B.* Bondi (?) or Bundo (?)
Bounilaine
Bourcher. *D.B.* Borci (?) Boursières; a loc. n., Burgund.
Brabason or Brabaion. *D.B.* de Braibone. Brabençon (Brabant)
Bracy. Brecy; a loc. n.
Braibuf. *D.B.* de Braiboue
Braine. *D.B.* Brien. Brionne; a loc. n., or Braine, Belg.
Brand. *D.B.* Brant
Braunch. St Denisde Branche; a loc. n.
Bray, loc. n., also Belg.
Brazard. Brassehaet; a loc. n., Belg. *D.B.* Suss., Hants, Berks, Wilts, Dors.
Brebus
Brent. *D.B.* Brant
Breton. *D.B.* Brito*
Brette. Bretteville (?); a loc. n.
Broilem. Breuilpont (?), loc. n.
Broleuy. Broglie; a loc. n.

Brouce, Brus, Brutz, Bruys. *D.B.* Robertus de Bruis* (Yorks). Breux, loc. n., now Brix.

Browe, Broy. Breux, loc. n.

Bryan. *D.B.* Brion. Brionne; a loc. n.

Buffard. Bouffey; a loc. n. Or Beaufour

Burdett. *D.B.* Burdet

Burdon. *D.B.* Buerd (?). Beaudoin, loc. n.

Bures. *D.B.* Buret (?). Bures; a loc. n.

Burgh, Bourg; a loc. n.

Busard. *D.B.* Bucard. Buzet; a loc. n., Fland.

Bushell. *D.B.* Buissel. Buscel; a loc. n.

Bushy or Bussey. *D.B.* de Buci.* Bougy, Buchy, loc. n.

Busseuille, Boseville. *D.B.* de Buiville.* Boscherville, Beuzeville, loc. n.

Buttecourt. *D.B.* Buter. Butot, loc. n.

Bysey. *D.B.* de Buci.* Buzy; a loc. n.

C

Cammile. *D.B.* de Cormelies.* Cormeilles; a loc. n.

Camois, Camoys. Camous; a loc. n.

Camvile, Cameville; a loc. n.

Caperoun. Rad. Capron, 1180

Carbonelle. Chabannes; a loc. n. *D.B.* Carbonel

Carevile, Coruyele. Courville; a loc. n.

Cateray, Cartrait. *D.B.* de Ceterith.* Cauterêts; a loc. n.

Cauncy, Chauncy. Canchy; a loc. n.

Chaiters, Chartres. Chartres; a loc. n.

Challouns. Challones; a loc. n.

Chamberay. Chambrais; a loc. n.

Chamberlain (Camerarius)

Chambernoun or Chaumberoun. Cambernon; a loc. n.

Champney, Champnais, Chawnes. Champigny, loc. n.

Chanduit, Chaudut. Chanday; a loc. n.

Chantelow (Cantelupe?), Cauntelow. Canteloupe; a loc. n.

Charles, Chaleys. Chalais; a loc. n.

Chaumont, a loc. n.

Chaundos. Chanday; a loc. n. *D.B.* de Candos

Chaward, Chaworth. Chauvincourt (?), loc. n.

Chawent, Chauunt. Chaumont (?); a loc. n.

Cheine, Cheines, Cheyni. *D.B.* Chenesis. Chênée and Chiny, Flanders. Chaignes, Le Chesne, loc. n., *Fr.*

Chereberge. Cherbourg; a loc. n. Cherecourt

Cholmeloy. Chamblac, loc. n.

Chopis, Chapes; a loc. n.

Clarell. *D.B.* de Claville (?). Clavelle, Cléville, loc. n.

Cleremaus, Clerevals; a loc. n. Clerenay

Clifford. *D.B.* Clibert (?)

Clinels

Coinvile. Cornouailles (?); a loc. n.

Columber. *D.B.* de Columbels.* Colomby; a loc. n.

Colvile. *D.B.* de Colevil. Colleville; a loc. n.

Comin, Comeyn. Comines; a loc. n.

Conderay. Connerré; a loc. n. (?)

Conestable (De Gand)

Corbett, Corbet. *D.B.* Corbet

Corbine, Corby. *D.B.* Corbin. Corbie; a loc. n., Corbais, Belg.

Coville. Couville ; a loc. n.
Cressy, Crescy. Crécy ; a loc. n.
Creuquere, Crevecuer. Crevecœur ;
  a loc. n.
Cribett

Cuily ; a loc. n.
Curly, de Curleio ; a loc. n.
Curson, Courson. *D.B.* de
  Curcan
Curtenay, Courteny, loc. n.

D

Dabernoune. *D.B.* de Abernon
Dabitott. *D.B.* de Abetot *
Dakeny. Acquigny ; a loc. n.
Dalseny
Dambleton
Damnot, Damot. Motteville (?),
  loc. n.
Damry, Damary. Amory, near Caen,
  loc. n.
Daniel. *D.B.* Roger Daniel (Suss.)
Danway. Hanouard (?), loc. n.
Darell. Airel, near St Lo, loc. n.
Daubeney. *D.B.* de Albingi.*
  Aubigné ; a loc. n.
Daueros, Deveroys
Dauntre, Dautry
Dauonge, Daverenge. Avranches ;
  a loc. n.
Davers. *D.B.* Denvers (?) ; Anvers,
  la Manche, loc. n.
Deheuse, De la Huse. Héas and
  La Hisse, loc. n.
De la Bere. Labouheyre (?) ; a
  loc. n.
De la Hill
De la Hoid, De la Hay. La Haye ;
  a loc. n.
De la Linde, Lindebeuf, loc. n.
De la Planche. Planquery ; a
  loc. n.
De la Pole. St Pol de Léon ; a
  loc. n.
De la Vache, De Wake. La
  Vacherie, loc. n.

De la Vere. *D.B.* de Ver.* Ver ;
  a loc. n.
De la Ware. Wierre ; a loc. n.
Delaund. La Londe, loc. n.
Delaward. *D.B.* de War'
Delee, Del Isle. Ille ; a loc. n.
Denaville. Dénestanville, loc. n.
Derey. *D.B.* Derinc (Fleming)
Desny, Diseny. Isigny ; a loc. n.
Devaus. Vaux ; a loc. n.
Deverelle. Vireville ; a loc. n.
Devereux. Évreux ; a loc. n.
Devile, Deyville. Déville ; a
  loc. n.
Devise. *D.B.* Devais. Vaacey,
  loc. n.
Disard, Disart. Deserte ; a loc. n.
Dispencere, Dispenser. *D.B.* Dis-
  pensator *
Dive. Dives ; a loc. n. *D.B.* de
  Dive *
Dodingsels, Dodingle. *D.B.* Do-
  did * (?)
Doiville. Ouville, loc. n.
Druel. Ruelle ; a loc. n.
Drury. Rouray ; a loc. n.
Duilly, Duylly. *D.B.* de Oilgi (?).
  Ailly ; a loc. n.
Dulce. Dolcé ; a loc. n.
Dunchamp. Encamp ; a loc. n.
Dunstervile. Dénestanville, loc. n.
Durand, Durant. *D.B.* Durand.*
  Douvrend (?), loc. n.
Durange

E

Engaine. Enghien ; a loc. n. *D.B.* *
Estrange, Destranges (Breton)
Estriels

Esturney
Estuteville, Estoteville. Etréville (?),
  loc. n.

F

Facunburge. Fauquembergues, loc. n.

Fauecourt. Fallencourt, loc. n.

Fenes. *D.B.* Fenisc Ulf.* Fains, Fiennes, loc. n.

Fermbaud. *D.B.* Ferme (?)

Ferrerers. *D.B.* de Ferieres.* Ferrère; a loc. n.

Fichet, Fichent

Filberd, Filebert. St Philbert; a loc. n.

Finere

Fingez

Fitz Aleyn. *D.B.* Alan *

Fitz Auger. De Agou (?) *D.B.* Aguet

Fitz Browne. *D.B.* Brun *

Fitz Eustach. *D.B.* Eustachius *

Fitz Fitz

Fitz Fouk. *D.B.* Fulche

Fitz Geffrey. *D.B.* Gaufrid

Fitz Henrie. *D.B.* Henricus *

Fitz Herbert. *D.B.* Herbert *

Fitz Hugh. *D.B.* Hugo *

Fitz John. *D.B.* Johannes *

Fitz Laurence. *D.B.* Laurentius

Fitz Marmaduke

Fitz Morice. *D.B.* Mauric *

Fitz Otes. *D.B.* Otho (?) *

Fitz Pain. *D.B.* Pagen *

Fitz Peres. *D.B.* Peret *

Fitz Philip

Fitz Rainold. *D.B.* Rainald *

Fitz Rauf, Rafe. *D.B.* Rolf *

Fitz Rewes. *D.B.* Rufus (?)

Fitz Roand. *D.B.* Rohard (?)

Fitz Robert. *D.B.* *

Fitz Roger. *D.B.* *

Fitz Simon. *D.B.*

Fitz Thomas. *D.B.* *

Fitz Walter. *D.B.* Walter *

Fitz Waren. *D.B.* Warin

Fitz William. *D.B.* Willelm *

Flamville. *D.B.* Flamme.* Flamanville; a loc. n.

Fleschampc

Fleuez or Flevez. *D.B.* Flavus *

Folioll, Filiol. Folleville (?), loc. n.

Foliot, Filiot. *D.B.* Folet

Folville. Folleville; a loc. n.

Formay. Formerie; a loc. n.

Formibaud. *See* Fermbaud

Forz, Forges (?), Belgium

Fouke. *D.B.* Fulche

Fourbeville

Freville, Fryville. Fréville, loc. n.

Frisell, Fresell. *D.B.* Fresle, Richard.* Fresville; a loc. n.

Frisound, Frisoun

Front de Bœf. Daubeuf (?), loc. n.

Furnieueus, Forneux. Furnaux, Belgium

Furnival, Furnivaus; a loc. n.

G

Gamages. *D.B.* Gamas (?). Gamaches; a loc. n.

Garre, Karre. Gare; a loc. n.

Gaugy, Gorgeise, Georges, Gourges Gaunson

Gaunt, Kaunt. *D.B.* de Gand,* *Fl.* Gand; a loc. n.

Gernoun. *D.B.* Gernon.* Gernon de Montfichet

Giffard, Gifard. *D.B.* Gifard *

Glateuile. *D.B.* Glauill

Goband, Gobaude. *D.B.* Godebold * (?)

Gobion, Gubioun; a loc. n., Britt.

Golofre, Galofer. *D.B.* Gulaffra, Gulfer. Goulafrière, loc. n.

Gower, Goher; a loc. n.

Grammori, Grymward (?)

Graunson. Grandchain (?), loc. n.

Graunt. *D.B.* Grando. Le Grand

Gray. *D.B.* de Grai; a loc. n.

Greile, Greilly. Gresillé, Anjou

Grendon, Graundyn

Grenet. *D.B.* Granetarius. Grenade ; a loc. n.

Greneuile, Geneville. Granville ; a loc. n.

Grensy

Gressy, Gracy. Graçay ; a loc. n.

Griuel. Greuville, loc. n.

Guines, a loc. n.

Gurdon, Gerdoun ; a loc. n.

Gurley. *See* Curly

Gurnay, Gurney. *D.B.* Gurnai, Gournay. Gurney, loc. n.

Gurry. Gueures, loc. n.

H

Haket. *D.B.* Walter Achet. Achiet ; a loc. n.

Hamelin. *D.B.**

Hamound. *D.B.* Amund, Hamont(?), loc. n., Belgium

Hanlay, Haulley. Aulnay (?), loc. n.

Hanville. Anneville, loc. n.

Hardell

Harecourt, Harcord. Harcourt ; a loc. n.

Harewell, Hareville. Ardouval (?), loc. n.

Hastings. Hastingues ; a loc. n., island in the river near Bayonne

Haunsard. Hanouard, loc. n.

Haurell, Hurel. Eurville (?), loc. n.

Hauteny, Hautein. Autigny, loc. n.

Hayward. Hauwaert, loc. n., Belgium

Henoure

Hercy, Herey. Herseaux (?), Belgium, or Hericy, Norm.

Herioun, Heroun. *D.B.* de Herion.* Héron le, loc. n.

Herne. Hern, loc. n., Belgium

Heryce. Heriz ; a loc. n.

Houell. Houville, loc. n., *Fr.*

Husee. Useé, or Houssaye ; a loc. n.

J

Januile

Jarden, Jardyn (De Gardino), 1189

Jasperuile

Jay (De Gaio or Gai)

Jeniels

Jerconuise

K

Kancey

Karrowe

Keine, Kanæs. Kain, loc. n., Belgium. Cahaignes, Norm.

Kenelre

Keveters

Kimaronne, Kymarays

Kiriell (De Criol)

L

Lacy, Lascy. *D.B.* de Laci.* Laissey or Lessay ; a loc. n.

Lane, Lenias. Lens ; a loc. n.

Lascales, Lascels. Lacella ; a loc. n.

Latomer, Latymer (Latinarius)

Laumale, La Muile. Lamballe (?) ; a p. n.

Leded

Lemare, Lymers (?). *D.B.* Lemar. Limours ; a loc. n.

Liffard

Limers, Limesey, Limousin ; a loc. n. *D.B.* de Limesi.* Limours ; a loc. n.

Linnebey. Lindebeuf, loc. n.

Lisours. Lisieux (?) ; a loc. n., *Fr.*

Loious. De Loe (?)
Longechampe. Longchamps ; a loc. n., Belgium
Longespes
Longueuale, Longville, Logevile. Longueville ; a loc. n.
Lorancourt. Loraine (?) ; a loc. n.
Loriage
Loterell. Loudervielle ; a loc. n., *Fr.* (?)
Loueney, Loveyne, Lovein, Lovan.

D.B. Leuuin.* Lieuvin ; a loc. n., *Fr.* Louvain, loc. n., Belgium
Louerace, Loverak. Louvres ; a loc. n. Leuric *
Loveday, Leuetot, Lovetot. *D.B.* Leviet * (?), Loudet and Louvetot, loc. n., France
Lovell. *D.B.* Laval ; a loc. n.
Lownay. Luynes ; a loc. n. (?)
Loy, Loif. Louye, loc. n.
Lucy, Luse. Lucy ; a loc. n.

M

Maiell. *D.B.* de Medehal*
Maine, Maoun. *D.B.* Maino.* Mayne ; a loc. n.
Mainell. Ménilles, loc. n.
Maingun (?). *D.B.* Maigno
Mainwaring, Mesnil-Warin, loc. n.
Malebranch, Malebys (?). Malbise
Maleheire. Mellier ; a loc. n., Belg.
Maleherbe, Maleberge. Malesherbes ; a loc. n.
Maleluse. Malause ; a loc. n.
Malemaine, Maumasin. Malmaison ; a loc. n.
Malemis. Malines (?), Fland.
Malet. *D.B.* Malet.* Melet ; a loc. n., Fland.
Maleuile. Malcville ; a loc. n. *D.B.* Malauill
Malevere. Maulévrier ; a loc. n.
Mallony. Malaunay ; a loc. n.
Mallop. *D.B.* Mala opa
Mandut, Maudiet (?). Mauduit, loc. n.
Mangisere
Maniard, Mainard. *D.B.*
Manlay
Manse, Monceus (?). *D.B* Manasses (?). Manage ; a loc. n., Belg.
Manteuenant. Mainenon ; a loc. n.
Mantolet, Montelent. *D.B.* Mantel.* Manthelon, loc. n.
Manuile, Meneville. *D.B.* de Manneuille. Manneville, loc. n.

Marceaus. *D.B.* de Marci.* Marsous ; a loc. n.
Mare, Marre. *D.B.* de Mara. St Maure ; a loc. n. (?)
Marmilon, Marmion ; a loc. n.
Marny. Mauny, loc. n.
Martcinc. *D.B.* Martin.* St Martin ; a loc. n.
Martinaste. Martinvaast ; a loc. n.
Massey. *D.B.* Maci. Massay ; a loc. n.
Matelay. Madeleine - de - Nonacourt (?), loc. n.
Mauches. Monchaux (?), loc. n.
Mauclerke
Maularde
Maulay, Maule, Morley. Marley ; a loc. n.
Maulicerer. Mauleverer (?), loc. n.
Maunchenell, Mauncel. Mansel, loc. n.
Maundervile, Maundeville. *D.B.* de Manneville.* Mondeville ; a loc. n.
Maurewarde
Mauveysin. Mauvezin ; a loc. n.
Meintenore
Meletak. Melite ; a loc. n.
Meller. Le Meillur
Melun. *D.B.* de Mellend.* Melen, loc. n., Belgium
Menere, Maners (?). Le Manoir, loc. n.
Menpincoy, Mounpinson

PUBLIC LIBRARIES LINCOLN

Merke, Merkenfell. *D.B.* de Merc. Marques (?), loc. n.
Miriel. Mirville; a loc. n.
Mohant. Moen (?); a loc. n., Belg. Moion, Norm.
Monchenesey, Mountheusey
Monhout. Manéhouville (?), loc. n.
Montfichet. *See* Muschet, Mussett
Monthermon, Maihermer
Montrauers, Mountravers. Montaure (?), loc. n.
Morell. *D.B.*; a loc. n.
Moren. *D.B.* Morin.* Morainville, loc. n.
Moribray, Mowbray. Moutbray; a loc. n. Maubray, loc. n., Belgium. Moubrai, Norm.
Morleian. *D. B.* Moriland (?). Morillon; a loc. n.
Morreis, Mourreis, Murres. *D.B.* Mauric.* St Maurice, loc. n.
Mortimere. *D.B.* de Mortemer; a loc. n.
Mortiuale, Mortivaus. Motteville(?); a loc. n.
Morville; a loc. n.

Mouett, Movet. Mouettes, loc. n.
Mouncey. Monchy (?), loc. n.
Mountagu. *D.B.* de Montagud.*
Montaigu; a loc. n., Belg.
Mountbother. *D.B.* Manbodo
Mountford. Montfort; a loc. n. *D.B.* de Montfort*
Mountgomerie. *D.B.* de Montgomery. Monte Goumeril, loc. n.
Mountlovel, Maulovel. Malleville(?), loc. n.
Mountmarten, Mortimaine. Montmain, loc. n.
Mountsoler, Mounsorel (?). Moncello
Mourteney, Morteyn. *D.B.* Mortuing. Mortain; a loc. n.
Mowne, Mooun, Moine, or Mohun. Moyon; a loc. n. *D.B.* de Moion
Musarde. *D.B.* Musard.* Bretagne
Muse. *D.B.* Musard.* Moux (?); a loc. n., *Fr.*
Musegros. *D.B.* de Mucelgros
Musett, Muschet. Mozet (?), loc. n., Fland.

N

Navimere. *D.B.* Nemore (?)
Nefmarch, Newmarch. Neufmarché, loc. n.
Neile, Fitz-Nele. *D.B.* Nigel. Nagel, loc. n.
Neiremet
Nembrutz
Nermitz. Neumarché (?); a loc. n.
Neville, Nereville. Neuille and Néville, loc. n.

Newborough, Newburgh. Neubourg; a loc. n.
Noers, Neuers. Noyers; a loc. n. (?). *D.B.* de Noiers
Norbet, Newbet. *D.B.* Nubold (?)
Norice. Norrey; a loc. n.
Normaville. Normanville, loc. n.
Nusetys

O

Oisell. Oissel; a loc. n.
Olenel, Otinel (?). *D.B.* de Olney (?). Aulnay (?), loc. n.
Olibef. Elbœuf; a loc. n.

Olifard, Olifant. *D.B.* Oliver
Orioll. Orival (?), loc. n.
Otevell. Octeville, loc. n.
Ounall. Ouainville, loc. n.

P

Paifrere. *D.B.* Paisforere
Paignel or Panel. *D.B.* Pagenel*
Paiteny
Pampilium. Papillon, Pavillon, loc. n.
Pantolf. *D.B.* Pantulf
Patefine, Parthenay ; a loc. n.
Paucy. Poey le Houn ; a loc. n.
Pavley, Paveley. Pavilly ; a loc. n.
Peccell
Peche. *D.B.* Pecchaie. Le Pecq ; a loc. n. and Belg.
Peito. Poitou ; a loc. n.
Pekeny. Picquigny ; a loc. n.
Penecord. Piencourt, loc. n.
Percelay, Perechay. *D.B.* Percehaie.* Perche, loc. n.
Percivale. Puisenval (?), loc. n.
Percy. *D.B.* Perci.* Percy ; a loc. n.
Perepound, Pierrepoint. *D.B.* de Perapund
Perere, Perrers. Perrières, loc. n.
Pershale
Perot, *D.B.* Peret,* Pirot
Pery, Perier, Bretagne

Petiuoll. Petiville, loc. n.
Pevrell. *D.B.* Peverel.* Pierreval (?), loc. n.
Phuars, Fours, loc. n.
Picard. Picardy ; a loc. n.
Pigot, Pygot. *D.B.* Picot.* Picot Avenel
Pinchard, Punchardoun, Pinkadoun. Punchardon or Pincherdoun, loc. n.
Pinel. *D.B.** Pinterville (?), loc. n.
Pinkenie. *D.B.* de Pinchengi
Placy, Place. Plessis ; a loc. n.
Plukenet. Plangcnoit, loc. n., Belgium
Pomeray. *D.B.* De Pomerie.* Pommeraie ; a loc. n.
Poterell. La Poterie (?), loc. n.
Pounce, Poynce. *D.B.* Ponz. Pontoise (?) ; a loc. n.
Power, Poer. *D.B.* de Porth * (?). Portes, loc. n., or Puers, Belg.
Preaus. Preaux, loc. n.
Preulirlegast
Pugoy, Pugoys. *D.B.* Pugnant (?). Puchay (?), loc. n.
Putrill. Futerel (?)

Q

Quinci, Quyncy, Quincé, Maine, loc. n.
Quintini. *D.B.* de St Quintin.* St Quintin ; a loc. n.

R

Raband. *D.B.* Rabbada
Raimond. *D.B.* Raimund
Rait. *D.B.* Ret. Reeth ; a loc. n., Belg.
Randvile. Ranville ; a loc. n.
Rastoke. Rusticus (?)
Richmound. Richemont, loc. n.
Ridell
Rie, Ry. Rhuys, loc. n.
Rigny
Rinuill, Reynevile. Regneville, loc. n.
Ripere, Ripers. *D.B.* Rippe

Risers, Rysers. *D.B.* de Riset
Rivell. *D.B.* Rivvuls. Riville, loc. n.
Rivers. Reviers, loc. n. *D.B.* Riveire.* Rivière, Belg.
Rochford. Roquefort, loc. n.
Rokell. Rocheville ; a loc. n.
Romilly ; a loc. n.
Ronde. De Rotundo, Norm.
Ros. *D.B.* de Ros. Rosay (?), loc. n.
Roselin. *D.B.* Roselent,* Rozelin. Rouisillon ; a loc. n.

Rougere. *D.B.* Roger. Rochers; a loc. n.

Rous, Rothais (?) or Roic (Roys). Roux, loc. n., Belg.

Rushell, Rozel, Russell. Risle; a loc. n. *D.B.* Rozel

Ryan. Royan, loc. n. Ruyen, Belg.

S

Saluin. *D.B.* Sawin* (?). Silvanus

Sanctes, Sainct Tesc. St Eustache (?), loc. n.

Sandvile. Sandouville, loc. n.

Sanford. Sancourt (?), loc. n.

Sauay. *D.B.* de Sais (?), or de Soies (?)

Saulay, Souley. Soule; a loc. n.

Saunay. *D.B.* de Sauigni. Savigny; a loc. n.

Sauncey. *D.B.* de St Sansone

Saunsouerre. *D.B.* de Saucnei. St Saire (?), loc. n.

Say. Sées or Saie; a loc. n.

Seffe. *D.B.* Seifrid (?)

Seguin, Sengryn. Serquigny, loc. n.

Senclere. *D.B.* de Sencler. St Clair; a loc. n.

Sent Albin. St Aubin; a loc. n.

Sent Amond. St Amand, loc. n.

Sent Barbe. *D.B.* de Barbes. St Barbe-sur-Gaillon: a loc. n.

Sent Cheveroll, Soucheville. *D.B.* de Sacheuilla. Sacquenville, loc. n.

Sent George. St Georges-sur-Fontaine, loc. n.

Sent John, St Jean. St Jouin, loc. n.; Sent Jean, Flanders

Sent Legere, St Ligiere. St Léger, loc. n.

Sent Les. Lez; a loc. n.

Sent Martin; a loc. n.

Sent More. *D.B.* de More. St Maur, loc. n.

Sent Omere. St Omer, loc. n.

Sent Quintin. *D.B.* de St Quintin*

Sent Scudemore. Escudemore, loc. n.

Sent Vile. Sainneville, loc. n.

Sheuile. Seuilly (?); a loc. n.

Sieward. *D.B.* Siuuard

Sirewast

Snylly. St Helier (?), loc. n.

Somerey, Someray. *D.B.* de Sumeri. Somery; a loc. n.

Somerville; a loc. n., Caen

Soreglise

Sorell. Surville (?), loc. n.

Souch. Sauchay (?), loc. n.

Sourdemale, Surdevale. *D.B.* Sourdeval; a loc. n.

Sucheus

Sules, Soules, Solers. Selles (?), loc. n.

Suremounte. Saumont, loc. n.

T

Talbot. *D.B.* Talebot

Taket or Takel. Tocqueville (?), loc. n.

Tankervile. Tancarville; a loc. n.

Tanny, Tany

Tardevile

Tarteray

Tavernez. Le Tavernier

Tenwis

Tercy. Tessé (?); a loc. n.

Thorney. *D.B.* Tornai. Tournay; a loc. n.

Thornille. R. Tornelvie

Tibtote, Thibtot; a loc. n.

Tinel. *D.B.* Tinel

Tinevile

Tirell. *D.B.* Tirelde

Tisoun. *D.B.* Tisun.* Dison, Belg.

Toget, Tuchet. Touchet; a loc. n.

Tolet. De Toleta, Norm.

Tollemach, Tolimer.   Tolemer ; a loc. n.

Tolous.   Toulouse ; a loc. n.

Tomy.   De Thelomeio (?)

Torell.   *D.B.* Torchill (?).   Tocqueville (?), loc. n.

Tortechappell

Totelles

Touke,   Tuk.   *D.B.*   Tochi.* Touques ; a loc. n.

Touny, Tony.   *D.B.* Tona.*   Tonnay ; a loc. n.

Tracy ; a loc. n.

Traies, Thays

Trainell

Travers.   *D.B.* Trevieres, loc. n.

Travile.   Trouville, loc. n.

Tregos.   Tregoz ; a loc. n.

Trenchevile

Trenchilion

Treverell, Treville (?)

Trison

Trivet

Trousbut

Trussell

Trylly.   *D.B.* de Traillgi

Turbevile.   *D.B.* Turberv, loc. n.

Turley

Turvile.   Tourville ; a loc. n.

Tyriet.   Turretot (?), loc. n.

V

Vaberon

Valence ; a loc. n.

Valenger, Valenges.   *See* Wallangy, Valognes ; a loc. n.

Valers ; a loc. n.

Valingford

Valiue.   Valliquerville (?), loc. n.

Vanay.   Vannes ; a loc. n.

Vancorde, Venecorde

Vasderol

Vauuruile.   Varaville ; a loc. n.

Vaux, loc. n.

Vavasour.   Vavassor, Norm., 1180

Veirny.   Vernet ; a loc. n.

Venables, loc. n.

Vendore, Venour.   Vendres ; a loc. n., or Venator

Veniels.   Vénesville (?), loc. n.

Verdeire, Verders, Verdour

Verdoune.   Verdon ; a loc. n.

Vere.   Ver ; a loc. n.

Verland.   Verlaine, loc. n., Flanders

Verlay, Werlay.   Verlée, loc. n., Flanders

Vernoun.   Vernon ; a loc. n.

Vernoys.   Vernai ; a loc. n.

Veroun.   Verune ; a loc. n.

Verrere.   *See* Ferrer

Vesey, Vessay.   *D.B.* de Vesci *

Vian.   Vienne ; river

Viez.   *D.B.* de Uis (?).   Wieze, Belg.

Vilan.   Vilaine ; a river.   Villainville, loc. n.

Vinoun.   Veinions ; a loc. n.

Vipont.   Veteriponte ; a loc. n.

Viville, Wyville, Wivell.   Virville (?), loc. n.

Umfravile.   Amfreville, loc. n.

Vnket

Vrnaful

Vrnall.   Verneuil ; a loc. n.

Vschere.   Le Huissier, Ostarius

W

Wacely, Wely.   Vesly (?), loc. n.

Wafre.   Wavre, loc. n., Belgium

Walangy, Valenger.   *D.B.* de Valonges.*   Valognes ; a loc. n.

Waloys, Valers (?).   *D.B.* de Wals. Valailles (?), loc. n.

Wake, Wace (?).   Wace ; a loc. n.

Wamerville

Ward. *D. B.* Wiard. Weerd, Belg.
Wardebois, Warroys (?)
Wareine, Warrene. *D.B.* de Warene,* Warenger. Varengeville, loc. n.
Wate. Le Waite, 1180

Watelin
Watevil, Waterville. *D.B.* de Wateuile.* Vatteville ; a loc. n.
Werdonell
Wermelay
Wespaile. Wespelaer, loc. n., Flanders

ALPHABETICAL LIST OF BRITISH SURNAMES

A

ABBISS. *N.-Fr.* De Abbacia; a p.n.
1198, R. de A.; 1272, Rot. Hund.

ABBOTT. Dimin. of Abb.; or *see* official names.

ABBS. *F.* Abbo; *D.B.* Api, Appe, Aba, Abba, Abo; *G.* Aber, Ahber, Haber; *Dch.* Abas, Abbing, Appij; *Fl.* Abas, Abs, Abts; p.n. (mighty). From a Gothic stem *aban* (to have power). *See* Abbiss

ABDALE. From Abbeydale; a loc. n., Yorks

A'BECKETT. From Beckett; a loc. n., Berks; Atte-Beckett

ABELL. F.om Abeele; a loc. n., Belg., or *D.S.G.* Abel; *Fl.* Abbeele, Abeels; *Dch.* Abels, Eble; *G.* Abel, Ebel; *D.B.* Abel; p.n.
Abell is on the Roll of Battell Abbey. Abel, tenant in *D.B.* (Kent); *A.S. abal* (?) (strength)

ABERCORN. A loc. n., Linlithgow

ABERCROMBIE. A loc. n., Fife

ABERNETHY. A loc. n., Elgin, Fife, Moray, Perths.

ABIGAIL. *A.S.* Abagisl (?) (mighty hostage)

ABLE. *See* Abell

ABLETT. *N. Fr.* De Abelot; a p.n.; Camb. Rot. Hund., 1274; or *see* Ablewhite

ABLEWHITE. From Applethwaite; a loc. n., Cumb., Westmd.

ABLEY. From Abberley; a loc. n., Worcest.

ABNEY. A loc. n., Derbysh.; *D.B.* Habenai

ABRAHALL. From Aberhalc; a loc. n., Mongomeryshire

ABRAM. A loc. n., Lancs., formerly Adburgham

ABSELL. *Fl.* Absil; a p.n. *See* Abbs

ABY. A loc. n., Lincs.

ACHESON. *See* Atkinson

ACHMUTY. From Auchtermuchty; a loc. n., Fife

ACKERS. *A.S.* Acca, Æcca; p.n. (edge, point); *Fl.* Hakkars; fam. n.

ACKMAN, AIKMAN. *N.* Ögmundr (sharp, terrible director); *A.S.* Agemund; *G.* Egmond; *D.* Hageman; *Dch.* Haagman; *Fl.* Haakman; p.n.

ACLAM. A loc. n., Yorks; *D.B.* Aclun, Achelum
Roger de Aclum in Rot. Obl. et Fin. K. John

ACLAND. A loc. n., Devon
De Acland was settled there *temp.* Hen. II. Also de Accalen

ACORNS. *Dch.* Akens; a p.n.

ACRES. *See* Ackers

ACTON. A loc. n., Chesh., Middlx., etc.; *N.-Fr.* Burnell, 1086

ADAIR. From Adare (?); a loc. n., Limerick

ADAMS. *A.S. Fr.* Adam; *Fl.* Adams; p.n.

ADCOCK. *A.S.* Adda, Hadda; *F.* Adde; *G.* Hädicke; p.n. Dim. of Adda; or *see* Addicott Atte-Cocke, Court of Husting, 1258

ADCROFT. From Addiscroft; a loc. n., Cornw.

ADDERLEY. A loc. n., Salop. De Dunstanville held it Hen. I.

ADDERTON. From Atherton; a loc. n., Lancs. Or Edderton, Ross

ADDICOTT. From Adcott; a loc. n., Salop

ADDINGTON. A loc. n., Kent, Northants., Surrey. De Abernon, 1086

ADDISON. *See* Addy

ADDLEY. *See* Adderley

ADDY, ADE, ADEY. *F.* Ade; *A.S.* Ada, Æddi, Eada; *S.* Adde; *Dch.* Ade, Adee; p.n. (father's ancestor). Welsh form of Adam

ADEANE. From Atte-Dean. Dean; a loc. n., Glost., Hants, etc.; or *F.* Adde, Adden; p.n. *See* Dean

ADENEY. *See* Adney

ADLAM. *See* Headlam; or *A.S.* Adhelm, Eadhelm, Ealdhelm, Æthelhelm; p.n. (noble helm)

ADLINGTON. A loc. n., Lancs.

ADNEY. A loc. n., Salop

ADSHEAD. From Adsett; a loc. n., Glost.

AFFECTION. *Fr.* Afchain; *A.S.* Æfic (Ælfic), p.n. Dim. of Elf

AFFLECK. A loc. corruption of Auchinleck, Ayrshire

AGACE. *See* Aggs

AGATE. *G.* Agath; a p.n. *Old G.* Achgoz (Goth); or *see* Hackett

AGGAS, AGGS, AGGIS, AGGUS. *A.S.* Aga, Agis; *F.* Agge; *D.* Ager, Acker; *G.* Hakus; p.n. Perhaps from *Old G.* Hadgis (war hostage); or *ac, ag, ecg* (edge, point, as of a weapon)

AGG. *N.-Fr.* Auge; a p.n. De Augo, Norm., 1200; Eng., 1199; Oxfd., 1249

AGGER, AGAR. *See* Egarr

AGNEW. From Aigneaux, near Bayeux. *N.-Fr.* Agneau; *Fl.* Agnier; p.n., Winchester, 1148; Wigtown, Scotl.

AGUTTER. *A.S.* Agatho, Ægteard, Agtard; p.n. *ag* (point, edge); *hard* (strong)

AHEARNE. *See* Heron

AIKEN. *See* Eykin

AILSBY. From Aylesby; a loc. n., Lincs.

AINGER. *See* Angier

AINSLIE. *Dch.* Enslie; a p.n. or *see* Ansley

AINSWORTH. A loc. n., Lancs.

AIREY. From the Castle of Airey, Norm.

AISHFORD. *See* Ashford

AISTROP. From Aisthorpe; a loc. n., Lincs.

AITCHISON. *See* Atkinson

AKEHURST. *See* Akhurst

AKENHEAD. From Aikenhead; a loc. n., Lanark

AKERS. *See* Ackers and Aggs

AKHURST. From Hawkhurst; a loc. n., Kent

AKISTER. From Acaster; a loc. n., Yorks

ALABASTER. Albastre, Court of Husting, 1258. *See* Arblaster

ALAN. Scot. p.n. (cheerful)

ALBAN. *D.* Allbahn; *D.B.* Alban; p.n. *See* St. Aubyn

ALBIN. *A.S.* Albuin; *Fl.* Albouin; p.n. (elf-friend); or *see* Alban

ALBISTON. From Albaston; a loc. n., Devon

ALBRIGHT. *A.S.* Æthelbeorht, Alberct, Albert; *Dch.* Albregt; *G.* Albrecht; p.n. *æl-beorht* (noble, illustrious)

ALBRIGHTON. A loc. n., Salop

ALDERDISE. *See* Allardyce

ALDERTON. A loc. n., Northants, Wilts

ALDHAM. A loc. n., Ess., Suff., Yorks

ALDINGTON. A loc. n., Kent

ALDIS. *N.* Aldis (Alfdis), elf-goddess. Or *see* Allardyce

ALDOM. *See* Aldham

ALDRED. From Aldreth ; a loc. n., Camb. Or *A.S.* Ealdred ; a p.n., *eald-ræd* (aged counsellor)

ALDRICH. *A.S.* Alderich, Ealdric ; p.n. (old ruler). Or *see* Aldridge

ALDRIDGE. A loc. n., Staff., Suff.

ALDWINCKLE. A loc. n., Northants

ALDWORTH. A loc. n., Berks

ALECOCK. *A.S.* Ail, Æthel (noble) ; *F.* Alle ; *G.* Alker ; *D.* Halck ; *Dch.* Alchen ; *D.B.* Alchen, Alcher, Alcot ; p.n., dimin.

ALESBURY. *See* Aylesbury

ALEXANDER. *Dch.*, *G.* p.n. ; *Fr.* Alexandre ; a p.n.

ALFORD. A loc. n., Lincs, Somers.

ALFRED. *N.* Elfraðr ; *A.S.* Ælfrede (fairy counsellor) ; *D.B.* Alured, or Alvred ; *D.* Allert ; p.n.

ALFREE. *N.-Fr.* Alveré, Caen, 1195 ; *A.S.* Ælffrith ; a p.n. (peaceful elf)

ALGAR, ALGER. *N.* Álf-geirr ; *Dch.* Algie, Allgäuer ; *A.S.* Algar, Ælfgar, Elfgar, Elgar ; *G.* Allger ; p.n. (Elfspear)

ALINGTON. A loc. n., N. Wales, Wilts

ALKER. From Altcar ; a loc. n., Lancs

ALLAN. *See* Allen

ALLANBY. *See* Allonby

ALLARD. *A.S.* Alhard, Ealheard (all strong) ; p.n. ; *N.-Fr.* Aelart. *See* Allott

ALLARDYCE. A loc. n., Kincardineshire

ALLBERRY. From Alderbury ; a loc. n., Wilts

ALLBON. *See* Alban

ALLBROOK. A loc. n., Hants

ALLBUTT. *A.S.* Ælbeorht ; *Fl.* Albert, Albot ; p.n., Alburtt, a Fl. Prot. ref., Lond. 1618. *See* Albright

ALLCARD. *See* Allgood

ALLCHIN. From Haulchin ; a loc. n., Fland. Or *Fl.* Halkin ; *Dch.* Halk ; *D.B.* Alchen ; p.n. Dimin. of *N.* Halli ; a p.n.

ALLCHURCH. From Alvechurch ; a loc. n., Worcest.

ALLCOCK. *See* Alecock

ALLCORN. From Alchorne ; a loc. n., Suss. (?)

ALLDAY. *A.S.* Alda, Ealda (old) ; p.n. Or *see* Halliday

ALLDIN. From Halden ; a loc. n., Kent ; *N.-Fr.* Alden, 1195. Or Irish McAldin

ALLDRITT. *See* Aldred

ALLEN. *A.S.* Al, Æthel (noble) ; *F.* Alle, Allen ; *Dch.* Alink ; *D.B.* Alan ; *Fr.* Allain ; a fam. n.

ALLENGAME. *See* Allingham

ALLERTON. A loc. n., Yorks

ALLERY. *See* Elleray

ALLETT. *See* Allott

ALLEYNE. Welsh Aluyen ; Irish Allwin, Alain ; Gaelic Aluinn ; Manx Aalin ; *S.* Alin ; p.n. (fair, beautiful). Or *see* Elvin

ALLFLAT, ALLFAT. *A.S.* Ælffet, Ælfrith, Alvert ; *Fl.* Aelvoet ; *Dch.* Alphert ; p.n. (peaceful elf)

ALLGOOD. *A.S.* Ælfgod, Algod ; p.n. (elf Goth) ; a Fl. Prot. ref. n., Lond. 1618

ALLINGHAM. A loc. n., Kent

ALLINGTON. A loc. n., Devon, Dorset, Lincs, Salop, Hants, Wilts

ALLISON. *See* Allen

ALLKIN. From Alken ; a loc. n., Belg. ; Halkyn, N. Wales. Or *see* Allchin

ALLMAN. From Allemagne, near Caen. *Norm.* or *A.S.* Ælfman, Ællman (elfman) ; *D.S.* Ahlman ; *Fl.* Aleman ; *G.* Hallman ; p.n. ; Prot. ref., Lond. 1618

ALLMARK. *See* Almack

F

ALLNATT, ALLNUTT. *A.S.* Ælnoth, Ælfnoth (elfbold) ; *D.B.* Alnod ; p.n.

ALLONBY. A loc. n., Cumb.

ALLOTT. *N.* Hallaðr ; *S.* Allart ; *D.* Allert ; *Dch.* Allot ; *Fl.* Allard, Allart, Hallart ; *N.-Fr.* Hallet ; p.n. ; a Hugt. n., Norwich, 1622, Lond. 1688. *See* Allard

ALLOWAY. A loc. n., Ayrshire

ALLPASS, ALLPRESS. Fam. n. of Alpe ; *D.* Alpers ; a p.n.

ALLSHORN. A loc. n.

ALLUM. From Hallam ; a loc. n., Derbysh.

ALLWARD. *N.* Hallvarðr ; a p.n. (hill-warder, watchman) ; or *A.S.* Ælfweard, Alward (elf warden)

ALLWAY. *See* Alloway or Holloway.

ALLWIN. *See* Alwyn

ALLWOOD. *See* Allward

ALLWORK. From Aldwark ; a loc. n., Yorks

ALLWORTH, ALLWORTHY. *See* Aldworth

ALLWRIGHT. *See* Alldritt

ALMACK. From Almeneches (?) ; a loc. n., Normandy

> There is a tradition that a Scotchman, coming to London, changed his name from MacAll to Allmack ! It may be so.

ALMENT, ALMOND. *A.S.* Almund, Ealhmund (Hall protector)

ALNWICK. A loc. n., Northbd.

ALPE. *N.* Hjálpr (a helper, saviour); *Fl.* Alpen ; *Dch.* Alphen ; *G.* Hallop, Hallup ; p.n.

ALPIN. Scot. (elf)

ALPORT. A loc. n., Derbysh.

ALSFORD. *See* Aylesford

ALSOP. A loc. n., Derbysh. ; *D.B.* Elleshope

ALSTON. A loc. n., Cumb. ; or *N.* Hallstein ; *Fl.* Alsteens ; *A.S.* Alstan, Alestan, Ealhstan (Hall the firm) ; p.n.

ALTHORP. A loc. n., Lincs, Northants

ALTMAN. *A.S.* Ealdman (old man) ; *G.* Altmann ; a p.n.

ALTON. A loc. n., Staffs.

ALTY. *A.S.* Alt, Alti, Eald ; *F.* Alt ; p.n. (old)

ALURED. *See* Alfred

ALVEN. *A.S.* Æthelwine, Ailwin (noble friend) ; or Ælfwine, Alwin (elf friend) ; *Fl.* Alvin ; p.n. *See* Elven

ALVEY. *N.* Halveig ; *A.S.* Ealhwig; *Dch.* Halfweeg; *G.* Hallwig ; p.n. (Hall-war)

ALVIS. From Alves; a loc. n., Elgin

ALWYN. From Halluin ; a loc. n., France. Prot. ref., Lond. 1618. Or *see* Alven

AMAS. *See* Ames

AMBLER. *A.S.* Amalhere ; a p.n. (old warrior)

AMEN. *Dch.* p.n. Or from Amagne ; a loc. n., France. *See* Ames

AMER. *See* Hamer

AMERY. *Fl.* Emery ; *G.* Emerich ; p.n. (work rule)

AMES, AMESS, AMIES, AMIS, AMISS. From Hamois ; a loc. n., Fland. Or Hiesmes, Normandy; *A.S.* Am, Em, Haim, Ham ; *F.* Emo, Eme ; *Dch.* Ameaz, Amsen, Emous, Amen ; *Fl.* Ameys ; *D.* Ham, Hemme ; *G.* Ameis, Emmes, Hems, Hemme ; p.n. (active) ; Hameus, a Flem. ref., Lond. 1618

> De Hames in Rot. Obl. et Fin. De Amias, Amyas, Amys, Court of Husting, 1288.

AMHERST. A loc. n., Kent

AMMAND, AMMON. From St Amand ; a loc. n., Norm. Or *see* Hammond

AMOORE, AMOR. From Atte-Moor

AMOOTY. *See* Achmuty

AMOS. *See* Ames

AMPHLETT. From Amflete ; a loc. n., Normandy

AMPS. *A.S.* Imper, Ingwar ; *Dch.* Ampers, Hampe ; p.n. (Frey's defence)

AMYS. *See* Ames

ANCIENT. *See* Innocent

ANDERTON. A loc. n., Cornw., Yorks

ANGEL. *D.*, *Dch.* p.n. *See* Inglis

ANGIER, ANGRE. A loc. n., Belg. ; *Fr.* Anger ; *D.* Anger ; *D.B.* Anger ; p.n.
> Angers in Roll of Battell Abbey ; Anger or Auinger (venator) in Rot. Obl. et Fin., K. John.

ANGLE. From Les Angles ; a loc. n., Norm. Or *see* Angel
> G. de Angle in Rot. Obl. et Fin. A.D. 1199, Ireland.

ANGLER. From Angleur ; a loc. n., Belg. Or *A.S.* Engelhere, Engeler ; p.n. (a warrior of the Angles)

ANGRAVE. From Hengrave ; a loc. n., Suff.

ANGUIN. *N.-Fr.* Angevin in *D.B.* From Anjou

ANGUS. Irish Aenghas ; a p.n. (excellent virtue)

ANKER. *D.* Anker ; *G.* Anke ; *Dch.* Hankart ; p.n. *See* Hanks

ANLEY. From Hanley ; a loc. n., Staffs. Or Andely, Norm.

ANLEZARK. From Anglezark ; a loc. n. (manor), Bolton, Lancs
> John Anglezargh, Duxbury, 1598 ; Robert Anzleark, 1680 ; John Anleyzargh, 1681.—*Chester Wills.* In Estham Register, Cheshire, are twenty-seven entries under Anglizer.

ANNABLE. *See* Hunnibell

ANNAN. A loc. n., Scotl.

ANNES, ANNESS, ANNIS, ANNISON. *A.S.* Anna, Enna (defender) ; *F.* Enno ; *D.B.* Enisan ; *Dch.* Annes ; *Fl.* Hanes, Hanneson, Anhes, Annez ; *D.* Hanisch, Annise ; p.n. Ennis, a Prot. ref., Lond. 1618

ANNESLEY. A loc. n., Notts
> Rd. le Breton held it, 1079. Ralph de A., with Reg. his son, founded Felley Abbey, 1152. From them descended Visct. Valentia, Jas. I., and Earls of Angelesey, Annesley, Mt. Norris.

ANSAR. *See* Ensor

ANSELL. *Old G.* Ansilor ; *Dch.* Ansel ; or *N.-Fr.* Ancelle ; p.n. (a servant)

ANSLEY. *See* Annesley

ANSON. *See* Hanson

ANSTEAD. From Henstead (?) ; a loc. n., Suff.

ANSTEY. A loc. n., Devon, Hants, Herts, Warw., Wilts

ANSTRUTHER. A loc. n., Fife
> Held by De Candel, formerly Malherbe.

ANTHONY. From St Antoine ; a loc. n., Norm.
> In Rot. Hund., 1272.

ANTILL. From Ampthill ; a loc. n., Beds. Or *Fr.* Antieul, Antil ; p.n.

ANTROBUS. A loc. n., Chesh.

ANYON. *See* Onions ; a Hugt. n., Lond. 1618

ANWYL. Welsh (beloved) ; or from Anneville ; a loc. n., Normandy

APLIN. *Dch.* Abeelen ; *Old G.* Abbilin ; p.n. Dim. of Abbo. *See* Abbs. Or *N.-Fr.* de Abelon, 1180

APPERLEY. A loc. n., Glost., Yorks

APPLEBEE. *See* Appleby

APPLEBY. A loc. n., Leicest., Lincs, Westmd.

APPLEGARTH. A loc. n., Dumfries

APPLEGATE. *See* Applegarth

APPLETON. A loc. n., Lancs, Norf., Yorks

APPLEYARD. *See* Applegarth

APPS. *See* Abbs

APRILE. *Fl.* April ; a p.n.

APTHORPE. A loc. n., Northants, Notts

AQUS. *See* Ackers

ARBER. From Arbre ; a loc. n., Belg. Or *see* Harbard

ARBLASTER. *D.B.* Arbalistarius (an officer of cross-bowmen)

ARBOURN. From Harborne ; a loc. n., Worcs.

ARBUCKLE. A loc. n., Lanark

ARBUTHNOT. A loc. n., Kincardineshire ; anciently de Arberbothenoth, a barony

ARCH. From Arches; a loc. n., France. *N.-Fr.* Arques; *D.B.* de Arches, de Arcis; p.n.
In Roll of Battell Abbey. Tenant in chief in *D.B.* Henry de Arches held land in Yorks *temp.* K. John. A Hugt. n., Lond. 1618.

ARCHARD. *N.-Fr.* Achard *A.S.* Archeard (Domfront, Norm. 1020); p.n. (strong hero)

ARCHBELL, ARCHBOLD. From Archibald; a p.n. *D.B.* Arcebald (a bold hero)

ARCHDALL. From Arkendale; a loc. n., Yorks

ARCHDEACON. From the office

ARCHER. *N.-Fr.* L'Archer; a p.n.
Richard le Archer and Nicholas Archer in Rot. Obl. et Fin., K. John.

ARCHIBALD. *A.S.* Eorcenbeald, Arcenbald; *G.* Erchanbald; p.n. (sacred prince)

ARDA. *A.S.* Ard, Eard, Heard; p.n. (hard, strong)

ARDEN. A loc. n., Lanark, Yorks

ARDILL. From Ardle; a river, Perth (?). Or Hartell, Worcs.

ARDLEY. A loc. n., Herts

ARGLES. *Dch.* Arkels; a fam. n. *See* Arkle. Arcklus; a loc. n., Holland

ARGYLE. A loc. n., Scotl.

ARKCOLL, ARKELL, ARKILL, ARKLE. *A.S.* Arcytel, Arkil; *Dch.* Arkel (noble Ketel); p.n.

ARKWRIGHT. *Old G.* Archarat (hero-counsellor); or *A.S.* Archeard, Arch-hart (strong hero); p.n.

ARLESEY. From Arlsey; a loc. n., Beds

ARLIDGE. From Arley; a loc. n., Warw. *D.B.* Arlege (?)

ARLINGTON. A loc. n., Suss.

ARLOSH. From Harlosh; a loc. n., Skye

ARMER. *G.* Armer, Hermer; *Fl.* Harmer; p.n. *See* Harmer

ARMES, ARMIS. *D.* Harms; *Dch.* Armes; p.n. *See* Armer

ARMFIELD. *S.* Armfelt; a p.n. Or Amfield; a loc. n., Hants

ARMITAGE. A loc. n., Staff.

ARMON. *N.* Hermundr; *A.S.* Arimund (warrior-protector); *Fr.* Armand; p.n.

ARMSBY. *See* Ormsby

ARMSTEAD. *See* Hampstead

ARMSTRONG. From Armston (?); a loc. n., Northants. Or from the Irish Lamb Laidir (strong arm); a n.n.

ARMSWORTH. A loc. n., Hants

ARNALL, ARNELL. *See* Arnold

ARNE. A loc. n., Dorset; or *A.S.*, *D.* p.n. (eagle)

ARNOLD. A loc. n., Notts, Wilts, Yorks; *D.B.* Ernehale. Or *N.* Arnhaldr (eagle-holder); *A.S.* Earnweald; p.n. A Prot. ref., Lond. 1618

ARNOTT. *Fr.* Arnaud; a Hugt. n., Lond. 1687

ARRAND. *A.S.* Arnold, Earnweald; *F.*, *Dch.*, *G.* Arend; p.n. (eagle ruler)

ARRINDELL. *See* Arundell

ARROWSMITH. *See* Athersmith

ARSCOTT. A loc. n., Salop

ARSTON. *See* Harston

ARTER, ARTHY, ARTHEY. *N.* Arnpórr; *A.S.* Arthur, Earnthor; *Fl.* Artur; p.n. (eagle Thor)

ARTIS. *N.* Hjörtr (a stag); *A.S.* Hart; *G.* Harter, Hart, Harte; *Fl.* Art, Arts, Artus; *D.* Hartig; *Dch.* Arts; p.n. Or *A.S. heard* (hard, strong)

ARUNDELL. A loc. n., Suss. R. Hirendale, Norm. 1198; also Fr. Hugt. n., Lond. 1618

ASBURY. From Ashbury; a loc. n., Berks, Devon. Or *see* Astbury

ASCOITH. *See* Askew

ASCOTT. A loc. n., Cornw.

ASH. *See* Dash

ASHBEE. *See* Ashby

ASHBRIDGE. From Agbridge; a loc. n., Yorks

ASHBURNER. *See* Ashburnham. Or
A.S. Æscbeorn; a p.n. (spear
bear)

ASHBURNHAM. A loc. n., Suss.;
D.B. Esseborne
Held by de Criol, 1086.

ASHBY. A freq. loc. n.

ASHCROFT. A loc. n., Yorks

ASHDOWN. From Ashdon; a loc. n.,
Ess.

ASHENDEN. A loc. n., Herts

ASHFIELD. A loc. n., Suff.

ASHFORD. A loc. n., Derbys.,
Devon, Hants, etc.

ASHLEY. A loc. n., Hants, Wilts

ASHMAN. *N.* Ásmundr; *D.* As-
mund; *G.* Assman; *Dch.* Asman; *A.S.* Asman, Osmund; p.n.
See Osmund

ASHMORE. A loc. n., Dorset, Wilts

ASHPITEL. From Ashbrittle (?); a
loc. n., Somers.

ASHPLANT. *See* Aspland

ASHPOLE. From Aspull; a loc. n.,
Lancs

ASHTON. A loc. n., Lancs, Hants,
Herts, Glos., Wilts

ASHURST. A loc. n., Kent, Lancs,
Suss.

ASHWELL. A loc. n., Herts, Rutl.,
Somers.

ASHWIN. *A.S.* Ascwine, Æscwine;
p.n. (spear friend)

ASHWORTH. A loc. n., Lancs

ASKER. *N.* Askviðr (ash-pole or
staff, spear); *D.* Askov; *S.* Asker;
Dch. Asscher; *D.B.* Ascuit; p.n.
Comp. Askew, Ascoith, etc.

ASKEW. A loc. n., Yorks; *D.B.* Asc-
with, Hascoith; p.n. (Ashwood)
Held by Fitz-Akaris after 1086.

ASKHAM. A loc. n., Notts, Lancs

ASKIN. *See* Erskine

ASKWITH. *See* Askew

ASPDEN. From Aspenden; a loc. n.,
Herts

ASPINALL. *Fr.* Espagnol; a p.n. (a
Spaniard); or a loc. n., Aspen-
hall (?)

ASPINWALL. *See* Aspinall

ASPLAND. *S.* Asplund, Espelund;
a loc. and p.n.

ASPRAY. From Esperraye; a loc. n.,
Norm.

ASSHETON. A loc. n., Ess.

ASTBURY. A loc. n., Ches.

ASTELL. From Astwell; a loc. n.,
Northants

ASTLEY. A loc. n., Lancs, Salop,
Warw., Worc.

ASTON. A loc. n., Glos., Hants,
Heref., Salop

ASTOR. *N.-Fr.* Fitz-Estur; a p.n.
Wm. Fitz-Estur, Norm. 1180, And.
Estor, 1198. Astor in Rot.
Hund.

ASTPREY. *See* Aspray or Astbury

ASTROP. From Asthorpe; a loc. n.,
Herts; Astorp; a loc. n., Sweden

ATCHLEY. From Atcherley; a loc. n.
Sir Roger Atcherley, Lord Mayor of
London, A.D. 1511.

ATCHIESON. *See* Atkinson

ATHAWES. From Atte-Hawes; a
loc. n. Athus; a loc. n., Belg.

ATHERLEY. From Hatherleigh; a
loc. n., Devon

ATHERSMITH. *F.* Athe; a p.n.,
and Schmid. Or *F.* Atteschmid,
the obsolete form of Ritterschmid,
an armourer, who belonged once
to the lower orders of nobility

ATHERSTONE. A loc. n., Warw.

ATHERTON. A loc. n., Lancs
Robert de Atherton, Sheriff of Lancs,
A.D. 1206.

ATHORNE. From Atte-Horn; a
loc. n. Or Haythorne
Horn was a corner or triangular piece
of land.

ATHORPE. From Authorpe; a loc.
n., Lincs

ATHOW. From Hathow; a loc. n.,
Lincs. Or *see* Atto

ATKINS, ATKINSON. *See* Atto

ATLAY. *See* Attlee

ATTENBOROUGH. A loc. n., Notts

ATTERBURY. A loc. n., Devon

ATTERSLEY. *See* Haddesley

ATTFIELD. *See* Hatfield

ATTHEL, ATTLE. *A.S.* Æthel; a p.n. (noble)

ATTHILL. From Atte Hill
A surname adopted as early as the fourteenth century from place of residence (at the hill). Or *see* above.

ATTLEE. From Atterley; a loc. n., Salop. Or Hatley, Camb.
Atte-Lee, Court of Husting, 1258.

ATTMORE. From Atte-moor (at the moor)

ATTO, ATTOE. *N.* Höttr (Hattr) (a hood); *F.* Athe, Haddo, Hatto; *A.S.* Atto; *G.* Hatto; *Fl.* Athée, Attout; *D.* Hatting; *Dch.* Ates, Atten, Atkins; p.n. Or *see* Addy

ATTREE. Atte-tree; loc. n.

ATTRIDGE. Atte-ridge; loc. n. Or *A.S.* Ætheric, Æthelric (noble ruler)

ATTS. *See* Atto

ATTWATER. Atte-water; loc. n.

ATTWOOD. From Atte-wood

ATTY. From Athiès, near Amiens. *See* Atto.
John de Atie or Athy, custodian of Limerick, 1311.

ATWELL. From Atte-welle; a loc. n.
Court of Husting, London, 1258-1358.

ATYEO. *A.S.* æt-ea (at water); a loc. n. *See* Yeo

AUBREY. *N.-Fr.* De Alebrai
Norm. 1198. Sir Reg. A. held lands in Brecknock, 1088. *N.-Fr.* Aubraye, a place planted with elders.

AUCHINLECK. A loc. n., Ayr

AUCHMUTIE. *See* Achmuty

AUCOTT. From Hawcoat; a loc. n., Lancs (?)

AUDLAND. From Audlem (?); a loc. n., Ches.

AUDLEY. A loc. n., Ess., Staffs., formerly Aldithley

AUDSLEY. *See* Audley

AUGER. From Orgières (?); a loc. n., France; or pays d'Auge. *G.* Augar; a p.n.; *Fr.* Augier; a Hugt. n.

AUKER. *N.* Haukr (a hawk); *G.* Hauk, Hauke; *Fl.* Haucq; *Dch.* Aukes; *A.S.* Heafeca; p.n.

AUKLAND. A loc. n., Dur.

AUSTEN, AUSTIN. *D.* Augustin; *D.B.* Augustin, Austin; p.n.

AUSTWICK. A loc. n., Yorks

AVANT. From Havant; a loc. n., Hants

AVELEY, AVELING. From Aveline; a loc. n., Belg. *Fl.* Evely; *Dch.* Evelein; *D.B.* Avelin; p.n.

AVENELL. *N.-Fr.*; p.n.; *D.B.* Avenel (under tenant)
W. Avenel, in Rot. Obl. et Fin., K. John. Auneuil (?); a loc. n., France.

AVERELL. From Haverhill; a loc. n. Suff. Or Avril, Norm.

AVERY. From Evreux (?); a loc. n., Normandy. *See* Every
Cecil de Evereus in Rot. Obl. et Fin., K. John. Havery; Hugt. n., Norwich, 1622.

AWDRY. From Audrieu, near Caen, Norm.

AXFORD. A loc. n., Wilts

AXHAM. From Hexham; a loc. n., Northd.

AXON. From Auxonne; a loc. n., France

AYBEL. *See* Abell

AYERS, AYRES. *N.* Eyar; *N.-Fr.* Le Heres; *Fl.* Eyer, Eyers; p.n. (island warrior)

AYLESBURY. A loc. n., Bucks

AYLETT, AYLOTT. *D.*, *F.* Eilert; *D.B.* Ailet; *Fl.* Heylaert; *G.* Heilert; p.n. *See* Aylward

AYLIFFE. *N.* Eilífr (ever living); *D.B.* Ailof, Eilaf; p.n.

AYLING. From Eeelen, Belg.; Hayling; a loc. n., Hants. Or *A.S.* Æling; a fam. n.; *Fl.* Elen, Eylen p.n.

AYLIVARD. *See* Aylward

AYLMER. *A.S.* Ælmer; a p.n. *See* Helm
Ailmar, a tenant in chief, *D.B.*

AYLWARD. *N.* Adelvardr; *A.S.* Æthelweard, Ailward (noble warden); *F.* Eilart; *D.* Eylard; *G.* Ehlert; p.n. *See* Aylett
Ailward in Rot. Obl. et Fin., K. John.

AYRTON. A loc. n. Yorks.

AYRE. From Ayr; a loc. n., Scotl.; Ere, Belg.; or Aire, France. *See* Ayers

AYSCOUGH. From Aysgarth; a loc. n., Yorks

AYSCUE. *See* Askew

AYTON. A loc. n., Berwick, Yorks

B

BAALAM, BAALHAM. From Baylham; a loc. n., Suff. Or Bellem; a loc. n., Fland; Bellème, France. *See* Bellamy
In Roll of Battell Abbey.

BAAS. *A.S.* Bass; *D.* Basse; *Dch.* Baas, Bas; *Fl.* Baes; p.n. (one in authority)
Le Bas in Rot. Obl. et Fin.

BABBAGE. *Fr.* Babiche; *G.* Babisch; p.n. (stranger)

BABBINGTON. A loc. n., Cornw., Northd., Notts, Somers.

BABBS. *A.S.* Babba (protector)
Babbe in Rot. Obl. et Fin.

BABER. A loc. n., Norf.

BACCHUS. *See* Backhouse

BACK. *A.S.* Bac; *Dch.* Bac, Bak; p.n. *See* Bagge. Or Welsh *bach* (little)

BACKHOUSE. *Dch.* Backhaus; a p.n.

BACON. *N.* Bekan (from the Gaelic); a p.n.
Bacun in Rot. Obl. et Fin., K. John.

BADCOCK. *A.S.* Bad, Bat, Beado; *D.* Badock; *G.* Badke, Batke; p.n. Dim. *beado* (war)

BADDELEY. From Baddiley; a loc. n., Ches.

BADGER. A loc. n., Salop. *D.B.* Beghesovre, Begesour, Bechesore

BADHAM. A loc. n., Cornw.

BADKIN. *Fl.* Batkin; a p.n. Dim. of Bad

BADLEY. A loc. n., Suff.

BADMAN. From Baudemont; a loc. n., Norm. Or *A.S.* Beadumund, Bademund; p.n. (war protector)

BAGGALLAY. *See* Baguley

BAGGE. *N.* Bögvir (a bag), or *bagga* (to hinder); *A.S.* Bag; *S.*, *Fl.*, *D.*, *Dch.* Bagge; *G.* Baake, Backe; p.n.
Bagge in Rot. Obl. et Fin., K. John.

BAGLEY. A loc. n., Berks, Salop, Somers.

BAGNALL. A loc. n., Staffs.

BAGOT. *Old G.* Badgad, Badgaut (battle Goth); *Fl.* Bygodt; *Fr.* Baguet; *D.B.* Baco, Bagod; p.n. *See* Bygod
Baggard, Bagod, Bagot, Bargard, Bigard, Bigod, Bigot, in Rot. Obl. et Fin., K. John.

BAGSHAW. From Bagshot; a loc. n., Surrey, Wilts

BAGULEY. A loc. n., Ches.

BAGWELL. *See* Bakewell

BAIGENT. *See* Bezant

BAILEY. From Belley, France. Or Beeleigh; a loc. n., Ess.; or *G.* Behlau; *Fl.* Beeli; p.n.; *Fr.* Baillé; a Hugt. n., Lond. 1688
Or it may be derived from the office of "bailiff," a title formerly applied to many feudal, municipal, and executive appointments. It also may have been "atte Bailey," the name given to the outworks of a castle.

BAIN. From Beyne; a loc. n., Belg. Prot. ref., Norwich, 1622. Or *see* Baines

BAINBRIDGE. A loc. n., Yorks

BAINES. From Baynes, near Bayeux, Norm. Or *N.* Beinir (legs, tall (?)); *F.* Baino, Beino; *D.* Behn; *S.* Been; *Fl.* Bayens, Beine, Beyns; *Dch.* Beens; *G.* Bens; *D.B.* Bain, Benz; p.n.

BAIRD. *N.-Fr.* Baiart ; a p.n.
 Godf. Baiard, Northbd. 1165. Bard,
 Visct. Bellamont, Chas. I., Scotl.,
 12th cent.

BAKE. *See* Beck

BAKER. *A.S.* Becca ; a p.n. (mat-
tock). Or *Fl.* Becker ; *G.* Becher ;
Dch. Becker, Beeke ; p.n. *See*
Beck, Becke, a Prot. ref. n.,
Norwich, 1622.
 It may be from *Dch.* Bakker ; a p.n. ;
 A.S. bæcere (a baker). Le Baker
 in Rot. Hund., vols. i. ii.

BAKEWELL. A loc. n., Derbysh.

BALCHIN. *D.* Balchen ; *Fl.* Bal-
caen ; *N.* Bálki (a beam) ; *D.B.*
Balchi ; *G.* Balcke ; p.n. ; or dim.
of Baldr

BALCOMBE. A loc. n., Suss.

BALDCOCK. *See* Balchin

BALDERS. *N.* Baldr ; *A.S.* Bald,
Bold (foremost, bold) ; *G.* Balder ;
D. Bald, Balle, Boldt ; *Dch.*
Balder, Bols, Bolt ; p.n.

BALDERSTON, BALDERSTON. From
Balderstone ; a loc. n., Lancs

BALDING. *D.*, *Dch.* Bolding ; fam.
n. of Bald. *See* Baldwin

BALDOCK. A loc. n., Beds

BALDRY. *A.S.* Baldric ; a p.n.
(bold ruler)

BALDWIN. *N.* Baldvinni (friend
of the god Baldr) ; *A.S.* Beald-
wine ; *G.* Baldin ; *Fl.* Bauduin,
Boldewin (bold friend)
 The name of the Counts of Flanders.
 Bawdwin is on the Roll of Battell
 Abbey, and Baldwin among the
 tenants in chief in *D.B.*

BALE. A loc. n., Norf.; also Besle,
France. *See* Bell

BALFOUR. A loc. n., Fife

BALLANTYNE. *See* Bannatyne

BALLARD. *A.S.* Bealdheard ; a
p.n. (strong)

BALLENGER, BALLINGER. *Fl.* Bel-
langer ; a p.n. Prot. ref. n.,
Lond. 1688

BALLOCH. Irish *ballagh* (the
freckled)

BALLS. *See* Balders

BALMER. From Balmire ; a loc. n.,
Cumb.

BAMBER. *See* Bambury

BAMBRIDGE. From Bembridge ; a
loc. n., Camb., Hants. Also
Bambrugge, Flanders

BAMBURY. From Bamburgh ; a
loc. n., Lincs, Northd.

BAMFORD. A loc. n., Lancs ;
Derbysh.

BAMFYLDE. A loc. n., Somers.

BAMPTON. A loc. n., Cumb., Devon,
Oxf., Westmd.

BANBURY. A loc. n., Oxon

BANCROFT. From Brancroft ; a
loc. n., Ches., Yorks. *See* Butler
 Held by Boteler.

BANE, BANEY. *See* Bain

BANFATHER. *N.* Bjarnvardr (bear-
ward). Or *see* Pennefeather

BANGER, BANGERT. *Dch.* Bangert ;
A.S. Bangeard (death-guard) ; p.n.

BANGHAM. *See* Banham

BANGS. From Banc, near Hon-
fleur. W. Bancs, Camb. 1203 ;
or *D.* Bang ; *G.* Banke ; *Dch.*
Bank ; p.n. *See* Banger

BANHAM. A loc. n., Norf.

BANISTER, BANNISTER. From Ban-
astre, now Beneter, near Etampes,
Norm.
 In Roll of Battell Abbey. Warin B.,
 baron of Newton, Lancs, *temp.*
 Wm. I. Adam B. in Rot. Obl. et
 Fin.

BANNING. *A.S.* Baningas ; a tribal
n. *Bana* (a slayer)

BANKS. A loc. n., Yorks. Or *see*
Bangs

BANNATYNE. From Ballindean ; a
loc. n., Perth. Or *see* Valentine

BANNER. *Dch.*, *A.S.* Bana (a
slayer) ; p.n.

BANNERMAN. *Dch.* Bonnerman ; a
p.n. *See* Banner

BANTHORPE. A loc. n.

BANTIN, BANTING. *Dch.* ; p.n. ;
G. Bantein ; a loc. n. *See* Pantin

BANYARD. *See* Banger

BARADALE. A loc. n., Ayrsh.

BARBEN. *See* Barbon.

BARBER, BARBOUR. From St Barbc sur Gaillon; a loc. n., Norm., where was the celebrated abbey of St Barbara; Barber or Barbour, a hamlet in Dumbartonshire. Or *Fr.* Barbe, Barbier, Barbare, Barberie, Barbry; *G.* Barber; p.n.
> Bernard Barb and de Barbes, tenants in *D.B.* St Barbe is on the Roll of Battell Abbey. William de St Barbara, Bishop of Durham, A.D. 1143. Le Barbier, Court of Husting, Lond. 1258.

BARBEY. *Fr.* Barbé, Barbet, Barbey; p.n. (bearded)
> Hugo Barbatus in *D.B.* (Hugh with the beard.)

BARBON. A loc. n., Westmd.

BARCLAY. *See* Berkeley

BARDELL, BARDILL. *See* Bardwell

BARDRICK. *D.B.* Baldric (foremost ruler); a p.n. Or *see* Brodrick

BARDSEY. A loc. n., Lancs
> Anciently de Berdesey, Byrdeseey.

BARDSLEY. A loc. n., Lancs

BARDWELL. A loc. n., Suff.

BARE. *See* Bear

BAREFOOT. *See* Barfoot

BARFF. A loc. n., Lincs

BARFITT, BARFOOT. *D.* Barfod; *N.-Fr.* Barfot; p.n.
> Norm. 1180, Rot. Hund.

BARGE. *Dch.*, *G.* Berg (a hill); p.n.

BARGMAN. *Dch.*, *G.* Bergmann (a miner); p.n.

BARHAM. A loc. n., Kent, Suff.

BARING. *A.S.* Beoring, Berring; fam. n. *See* Bear

BARKER. *N.* Börkr (bark); *S.* Barck; *Dch.* Barger; *Fl.* Barker; *G.* Barche; *N.-Fr.* Le Bercher; *D.B.* Barch; p.n.

BARKLEY. *See* Berkeley

BARKSHIRE. From Berkshire; the county

BARKUS. From Bargus; a loc. n., Cornw.

BARKWAY. A loc. n., Herts

BARKWORTH. From Barkwith; a loc. n., Lincs

BARLEE, BARLEY. A loc. n., Herts

BARLOW. A loc. n., Derbysh., Yorks

BARNABY. *See* Barnby. Or from Barnabas (?)

BARNACKLE. *N.* Bjornkell (bear-kettle)

BARNARD. *N.* Bjarnaðr (strong bear); *Fl.* Barnard; *D.B.* Bernard; p.n.

BARNBY. A loc. n., Suff., Yorks

BARNES. From Berners or Bernieres; a loc. n., Norm. Also a loc. n., Surr.

BARNETT. From Barnet; a loc. n., Herts; or *G.* Barnatt, Barnert; *Fl.* Bernert; p.n. *See* Barnard

BARNEWALL. *See* Barnwell

BARNEY. From Bernai, Norm.; loc. n., Norf.; or *N.* Bjárni, a p.n.

BARNICLE. *See* Barnackle

BARNSDALE. A loc. n., Yorks

BARNSLEY. A loc. n., Dorset, Yorks

BARNWELL. From Barneville; a loc. n., Normandy

BARON. A loc. n., Normandy

BARR. La Barre, Norm.; a loc. n., Ayrshire, Staffs; or *A.S.* Bar (a bear). *D.* Barr; *Fl.* Bar; *N.-Fr.* de la Barre; p.n.
> The Norman, de Dreux, assumed the name of de Barre from his manor of Great Barr. De la Barr, Hugt. n., Lond. 1618. Barre in Rot. Obl. et Fin.

BARRADALE. From Borrodale; a loc. n., Cumb.

BARRELL. *Fl.* Barel, Bareel; *D.* Baruël; *Fr.* Barill; p.n.; dim. of Bear. A Hugt. n., Cant. 1622

BARRET. *A.S.* Barath, Barcd, Baret; *Fr.* Barette; p.n.; *A.S.* beor-ræd (bear counsel); *N.-Fr.* barette, a measure of corn; seems unlikely

BARRIE. A loc. n., Forfar
BARRINGTON. A loc. n., Camb., Lincs, Somers. Or from Barenton; a loc. n., Normandy
BARROW. A freq. loc. n. Or *D.* Barroe; *Dch.* Barrau; *Fl.* Baro; p.n.
BARRY. A loc. n., Belg. Or *see* Barrie
In Roll of Battell Abbey.
BARSBY. A loc. n., Leics.
BARSTOW. From Barstone; a loc. n., Kent
BARTER. *See* Barth
BARTH. *D., Dch., Fl., G.*; p.n.; a contr. of Bartholomew
BARTHORP, BARTHROPP, BARTROP, From Barthorp; a loc. n., Lincs
BARTINGTON. *See* Partington
BARTLETT. *G.* Bartelt; *Fr.* Bartalot; p.n.; dimin. of Bartholomew
BARTLEY. A loc. n., Hants, Worcs.
BARTON. A freq. loc. n.
BARWELL. From Berville, Norm. Also a loc. n., Leics.
BARWIS, BARWISE. *A.S.* Beornwig (war-bear); *Fr.* Barvais; *G.* Barwisch; p.n.
BASAN. *See* Bezant
BASCOMB, BASCUM. From Boscombe; a loc. n., Hants, Wilts
BASE. *See* Bayes
BASEY. *See* Beazer
BASHALL. A loc. n., Yorks
BASHAM. From Barsham; a loc. n., Norf.
BASHFORD. From Bassford; a loc. n., Staffs.
BASIN, BASSIN. *See* Bass
BASKETT. From the *Fr.* Bassecourt; a loc. n. Or Bosquet; a p.n.
BASS. A loc. n., Invury, Haddington. Or *see* Baas
BASSANT. *See* Bezant
BASSETT. *N.-Fr.* (a dwarf); dimin. of Bass. Under tenant in *D.B.* Also Hugt. n., Sandwich, 1622
BASTABLE. From Barnstaple; a loc. n., Devon. Or *N.-Fr.* Wasteble; a p.n.

BASTARD. *Dch.* Bastert; *Fl.* Batard; p.n.
In Roll of Battell Abbey and in *D.B.* (baron), Devon. Wm. le Bastard held lands in Yorks *temp.* K. John.
BASTIN, BASTING. *Fr.* Bastien; *Fl.* Bastin; *Dch.* Basting; *D.* Bastian; p.n.; contr. of Sebastian
BASTOW. From Baston; a loc. n., Lincs
BATCHELDER, BATCHELOR. From Becelaere; a loc. n., Fland.; *Dch.* Baggelaar; *Fr.* Bachelier; *G.* Bachaly; p.n. Or *N.-Fr.* Bachlier, Bacheler (bachelor, esquire). Lewis Batchelier, Hugt. n., Lond. 1682.
BATE, BATES. *D.* Betz; *Dch.* Beets; *Fl.* Bette, Beths, Beetz, Bets; p.n.; Beez; a loc. n., Belg.
BATELEY. *See* Batley
BATEMAN. *S.* Betjeman; *Dch.* Betman; p.n. *See* Badman
BATGER. *See* Badger
BATH. A loc. n., Somers
BATHE. *A.S.* Bath, Beada; *Dch.* Bethe, Beth; p.n. (war)
BATHURST. A loc. n., Suss.
BATHY. From La Bathie, Norm. Or Welsh, Ab Adde (Adam)
BATLEY. A loc. n., Yorks
BATSFORD. A loc. n., Glost., Suff.
BATSON. *See* Bathy
BATT, BATTY, BATTYE. *See* Bathy
BATTAM. *See* Batterham or Badham
BATTCOCK. *See* Badcock
BATTELL, BATTLE. A loc. n., S. Wales, Suss. Or *N.-Fr.* Battaille; a p.n.
BATTEN. *N.-Fr.* Bethune or de Bethune; a p.n.
BATTERHAM. *See* Buttram
BATTERSBURY. From Battlesbury (?); a loc. n., Wilts
BATTERSBY. A loc. n., Yorks
BATTERSHALL. From Patishull (?); a loc. n., Staffs
BATTISCOMBE. From Bettiscombe; a loc. n., Dorset

BATTOCK.　*See* Badcock
BATTRUM.　*See* Buttrum
BAULY.　From Beoley (?) ; a loc. n., Worcest.　Or *see* Bowley
BAVE.　*Fr.* Bavay ; a loc. and p.n.
BAVEN, BAVIN.　From Bavent; a loc. n., Normandy ; *Fl.* Bawin ; a p.n.
BAWDEN.　A loc n., Cornw.　Or *see* Baldwin
BAWN.　*D.* Baun ; *Fl.* Bauwen ; p.n.　Or Irish *ban* (white)
BAWTREE.　From Bawtry ; a loc. n., Yorks
BAXENDALE.　A loc. n.
BAXENDEN.　A loc. n., Lancs
BAXTER.　The Scot. and N. Engl. form of Baker.　*A.S. bæc-estre*, a f. baker
BAYES, BAYS.　*Fl.* Baye ; *D.* Beyer ; *Dch.* Bes, Bey, Bies; p.n.　*See* Bee
BAYLISS.　*Fl.* Bellis ; a p.n.　Or Welsh ab Elis
BAYNES.　*See* Baines
BAYNHAM.　*See* Banham
BAYNTON.　A loc. n., Northants, Oxf., Yorks
BAZELEY.　*See* Beasley
BEACH.　*N.-Fr.* De la Beche ; a p.n. ; Goisfrid de Bech, t. in chief, Hertfd, 1086.　*See* Beck
BEACHAM.　From Beauchamp ; a loc. n. in the Cotentin, France
BEACOM.　*Dch.* Becküm, Beekum ; p.n.　Or *see* Beacham
BEADLE.　From Bedale ; a loc. n., Yorks ; or *N.-Fr.* Bedel, a p.n., Bucks, 1086
BEADMAN.　*See* Badman
BEADSMORE.　From Birdsmoor ; a loc. n., Dorset.　De Berdesmor, 1327
BEAMAND, BEMAND.　Welsh Ap Edmund ; a p.n.
BEAK.　*See* Bick
BEAL.　A loc. n., Yorks
BEALE.　A loc. n., Dur.
BEALES.　From Bealings ; a loc. n., Suff.
BEALEY.　From Beeley ; a loc. n., Derbysh.

BEAMENT.　*See* Beaumont
BEAMES.　*See* Beamish
BEAMISH.　A loc. n., Dur.
BEAN.　From Bienne ; a loc. n., Belg. ; *D., Dch.* Biene ; a p.n. (a bee).　Prot. ref., Norwich, 1622
BEANHAM.　*See* Baynham
BEANLANDS.　A loc. n., Cumb.
BEAR.　*N.* Bera (a bear); *A.S.* Beor ; *D.* Bjerre ; *D.B.* Bere ; *Dch., Fl.* Beer, Behr ; *G.* Behr ; p.n.　Or Baer ; a loc. n., Belg. ; Fl. ref., Lond. 1618
BEARCHELL.　From Bircholt (?) ; a loc. n., Kent
BEARCROFT.　A loc. n.
BEARD.　*See* Baird.　*Fl.* Baert ; a Hugt. n. ; Lond. 1618
BEARDMORE.　*See* Beadsmore
BEARDSHAW.　A loc. n.
BEARDSLEY.　From Buwardsley, Ches.　Or *see* Bardsley
BEARDSWORTH.　From Beardswood ; a loc. n., Lancs
BEARDWELL.　From Bardwell ; a loc. n., Suff.
BEASANT.　*See* Bezant
BEASEY.　*See* Bessey
BEASLEY.　From Beazley ; a loc. n., Warw.
BEASTON.　*See* Beeston
BEATON.　From Bethune in Artois ; *Fr.* Bethune; a p.n.　Or from Beighton; a loc. n., Derbys., Norf., Suff.
BEATTIE or BEATTY.　From the Irish Betagh (biadhtach), a public victualler ; p.n.　Or *A.S.* Betti ; a p.n.　*See* Bathy
BEAUMONT.　A loc. n., Belg. and Normandy.
　In Roll of Battell Abbey.　*D.B.* De Belmont, Bomene.　Rot. Obl. et Fin., K. John.
BEAVEN, BEAVIN, BEAVON.　*See* Bevan
BEAZER.　From Baisy ; a loc. n., France.　Or *Fr.* Bisez ; a p.n.
　Bisi or Bysey in the Roll of Battell Abbey.　*See* Bessey

BEBELL. *A.S.* Babel; a p.n. Dim. of Babba

BECCLES. A loc. n., Suff.

BECK. From Beeck; a loc. n., Belg.; *D.*, *S.*, *G.*, *Dch.* Beck; *Fl.* Baeck; p.n. Atte Becke, 1327
Beke on the Roll of Battell Abbey. De Bec, a tenant in chief, Walter Bec at the time of the Survey, in *D.B.* Bec and Bek in Rot. Obl. et Fin., K. John. Also Prot. ref., Lond., 1618; Norwich, 1622.

BECKETT. *A.S.* Beagheard; *Dch.* Beket; *Fl.* Beckaert, Becquart, Becquet; *N.-Fr.* Bechet, Béquet; p.n. (strong crown)

BECKFORD. A loc. n., Hants

BECKHAM. A loc. n., Norf.

BECKLEY. A loc. n., Hants, Suss.

BECKWITH. A loc. n., Yorks

BED. *N.*, *A.S.* Beda; *Fr.* Béde; *Fl.* Bette; *G.*, *Dch.* Beth; p.n. *See* Bathe

BEDALL. From Bedale; a loc. n., Yorks. Or *A.S. bidel*, a beadle

BEDDOE. *A.S.* Beada; *G.* Beddau; *Fr.* Bidaut; p.n. Or Welsh Ab Edward. *See* Bathe

BEDFORD. A loc. n., the county town

BEDINGFIELD. A loc. n., Suff.

BEDSON. From Bedstone; a loc. n., Salop

BEDWARD. Welsh, Ab Edward; a p.n.

BEDWELL. A loc. n., Beds

BEE. *D.*, *Dch.* Bie, Bye; *N.* Bui; p.n. *See* Bye (a neighbour)

BEEBEE. From Beeby; a loc. n., Leics.

BEECH. *See* Beach

BEECHEY. *See* Beeching

BEECHING. A loc. n., Suss., Wilts

BEECROFT. *See* Bearcroft

BEEDELL. *See* Bedall

BEEDEN. A loc. n., Berks or Bidon, Burgundy

BEEFORTH. From Beaford; a loc. n., Devon

BEEL. *A.S.* Bil; *Old G.* Bilo; *G.* Bill, Biel; *Fl.* Beel; p.n. (gentle)

BEER. A loc. n., Devon. Or *see* Bear

BEESLEY, BESLEY. *See* Beasley

BEESTON. A loc. n., Norf., Notts

BEETHAM. *See* Betham

BEETLES. *See* Bedall

BEETON. *See* Beaton

BEETS. *See* Bates

BEEVER. *A.S.* Beffa; *Fl.* Bevers; *Fr.* Biver; p.n. (a beaver)

BEGBIE. From Bigby; a loc. n.; Lincs

BEGG. *A.S.* Beg; a p.n. *See* Bigg. Or Irish p.n. (little)

BEHAG. *N.* Baugr; a n.n. (ring of a shield, also money); *A.S.* Beag; a p.n.; *Fl.* Behagel; p.n.; dim. Hugt. n., Sandwich, 1622

BEILBY. From Belby; a loc. n., Yorks

BEITH. A loc. n., Ayr, Renfrew. Or *G.* Bieth; a p.n.

BELCHAM. From Belchamp; a loc. n., Ess. *D.B.* De Belchamp; p.n. Or *Fr.* Beljambe; a p.n.

BELCHER. From Bellecourt; a loc. n., Normandy, near Perrone, and in Belg.
Bellesur in Roll of Battell Abbey.

BELDAN, BELDEN, BELDING. From Beltinge; a loc. n., Kent

BELFRAGE. From the Norman-French Beaufoy, Latinised into de Bella Fago. *D.B.* Belvaco, Belvou; p.n.

BELHAM, BELHOMME. *See* Baalam

BELL. *N.* Beli (obese); *F.* Bela, Bêl, Bele; *S.* Bell; *A.S.*, *Dch.* Bel; *Fl.*, *N.-Fr.* Baele, Beli; p.n. Le Bel in Rot. Obl. et Fin. (the handsome)

BELLAIRS. *See* Bellares

BELLAMY. A *Fr.* p.n. from Bellème; a loc. n. in Normandy. *D.B.* Belam; *D.* Beilum; *Fl.* Belemme; *Dch.* Bellm; p.n.; *Fl.* ref., Lond. 1618
Beelhelme in Roll of Battell Abbey.

BELLARS, BELLARES. From Bel-
laires; a loc. n., Belg.; *Fl.* Bel-
lers; a p.n.
Beleuers in Roll of Battell Abbey.
Hamon Bellars was a hostage to
K. John, A.D. 1216 (Whitwick,
Leics.). De Belhus and De Bello
in Rot. Obl. et Fin.

BELLASIS. A loc. n., Cornw.,
Northbd., Yorks; *Fr.* de Belas-
size; a loc. n., Norm.
Ballisise in Roll of Battell Abbey.

BELLCHAMBER. From Bellencombre
Castle, near Dieppe. Bernd. de B.
Suff. 1086, Ess. 1272. Rot. Hund.

BELLEW. *Fr.* Bellot; a p.n. From
Belleau; a loc. n., Norm.
Bellew in Roll of Battell Abbey;
Belot, a tenant in chief in *D.B.*
Gaufrid Belewe and Robt. de
Baleewe in Rot. Obl. et Fin., K.
John.

BELLIN. *A.S.* Bæling; *Fl.* Belin,
Bellen, Belyn; p.n. *See* Bell.
A Hugt. n., Lond. 1685

BELLINGHAM. A loc. n., Northbd.

BELLIS. Welsh Ab Ellis. *See*
Bayliss

BELLOE. *See* Bellew

BELLOWS. *See* Bellew

BELSCHES. *See* Bellasis

BELSHAM. *See* Belchamp

BELSHAW. *See* Belcher

BELUTEN. *See* Belston

BELSTON. A loc. n., Devon

BELTON. A loc. n., Leics.

BELWARD. *A.S.* Belweard, Bel-
uuard; p.n. (gentle guard)

BEMROSE. From Penhrôs(?); a loc.
n., Wales. Or Penrose, Cornwall

BENBOW. From Benningborough;
a loc. n., Yorks

BENCE. In Rot. Hund. 1272. *See*
Benson, Benns. A Hugt. n.,
Sandwich, 1662

BENDALL. *D.* Bendahl, Bendal;
Dch. Bendel; p.n. A loc. n. (?)

BENDELOW. *Dch.* Bentelaar; a p.n.
(one from Bendal)

BENDER. *D.*, *Dch.*, *Fl.*, *G.*; p.n.

BENDING. *D.* Benthin; *Dch.* Ben-
dien, Bentinck; p.n. *See* Benn

BENDON. From Benton; a loc. n.,
Northmbd. Or Benden; a Hugt.
n., Lond. 1618.

BENDY. *G.* Bendig; a p.n. (Benedict (?))

BENFIELD. From Benefield; a
loc n., Northants

BENFORD. From Bainsford; a
loc. n., Stirling

BENHAM. From Benholme; a
loc. n., Kincardine

BENINGFIELD. *See* Benfield

BENN, BENNETT, BENNY. Dimin.
of Benedict. Hugt. n., Lond.
1688

BENNION. Welsh, Apwenwyn (ap
Einion), *eynon* (just); a p.n. *See*
Beynon

BENNINGTON. A loc. n., Lincs

BENNISON. *See* Benson

BENSLEY. A loc. n., Ayr

BENSON. *N.* Benni and Bensi; *F.*
Benne (dimin. of Benedict); *S.*
Benzon; *D.* Bengtsen, Bendsen,
Benzen; *Dch.* Bense; *D.B.*
Benz; p.n.

BENSTED, BENSTEAD. From Binstead; a loc. n., Hants, Suss.

BENT. *D.* Bendt; a p.n. *See* Benn

BENTHALL. A loc. n., Salop

BENTHAM. A loc. n., Staffs.

BENTLEY. A loc. n., Yorks

BENWELL. A loc. n., Northbd.

BENYON. *See* Bennion

BERBIDGE. *See* Burbage

BERGAN, BERGEN. *See* Burgoyne

BERGIN. *See* Burgoyne

BERKELEY. A loc. n., Glos.

BERRALL. *See* Burrell

BERRETT. *See* Barret
Barrett in Roll of Battell Abbey.

BERRICK. *See* Berwick

BERRIDGE. From Berwick; a loc. n.,
Ess.

BERRY. A loc. n., Devon and
Normandy; or from the Irish
O'Beara; a p.n.

BERWICK. A loc. n., Ess., Northbd., Wilts

BESANT. *See* Bezant

BESFORD. A loc. n., Worc.

BESSELL. *A.S.* Besel. Dim. of Besa. *D.* Bestle; a p.n.

BESSEY. *A.S.* Besi; a p.n.

BEST. A loc. n., Holl. *D.*, *Dch.*, *Fl.*, *G.* p.n. De Best; *Fl.* ref., Lond. 1618

BESTOW. *See* Bastow

BESWICK. A loc. n., Yorks

BETHAM. A loc. n., Westmd.
Ralph de Betham was a benefactor to Furness Abbey, Hen. II.

BETHELL. *G.* Bethel; *Fl.* Beethel; p.n. Dim. *See* Bathe. Or Welsh Ab Ithell

BETSWORTH, BETTESWORTH. From Betchworth; a loc. n., Surrey

BETT. *Fl.* Bette; *Dch.*, *G.* Beth; p.n. *See* Bathe

BETTELEY. From Betley; a loc. n., Staffs.

BETTERIDGE. From Pettridge; a a loc. n., Kent. Or *A.S.* Beaduric; a p.n. (battle ruler)

BETTERTON. A loc. n., Berks

BETTS. *See* Bates

BETTY. *See* Beattie

BEVAN. From Bièvène; a loc. n., Belg. Or Welsh ab Evan
Bevan and Bevin occur in Rot. Obl. et Fin., K. John.

BEVERIDGE. *See* Berridge

BEVINGTON. A loc. n., Lancs

BEVINS. *A.S.* Bafing, Beofing; *Fl.* Beving; p.n.; fam. n. of Beever

BEVIS. From Beauvais; a loc. n., France
In Roll of Battell Abbey. W. Beaufiz de Rya in Rot. Obl. et Fin., K. John.

BEW. *See* Pugh or Boow

BEWICK. A loc. n., Yorks

BEWLEY. A loc. n., Westmd.

BEWSHER. *See* Butcher

BEX. *Fl.* Bex; *D.* Becks; p.n. *See* Beck

BEYNON. *See* Bennion

BEZANT. From Beausaint; a loc. n., Belg. Or *Fr.* Baisant; a Hugt. p.n. A Byzantine coin. In heraldry a disc without impress

BIBBINGTON. From Bebington; a loc. n., Ches.

BIBBY. *See* Beebee

BICHENS. *A.S.* Bic, Big; p.n. *See* Bigg

BICK. *A.S.* Bic, Big (a crown), chaplet; *Fr.* Bické, Bicqué; *G.* Bick; p.n.

BICKELL, BICKLE. *Fr.*, *Dch.* Bickel, Bichel; p.n. Dim. of Bic

BICKER. A loc. n., Lincs. *See* Bick

BICKERDYKE. A loc. n.

BICKERSTETH. From Bickerstaffe; a loc. n., Lancs; anciently Bykyrstath, Bekerstath

BICKERTON. A loc. n., Norf.

BICKFORD. A loc. n., Staffs.

BICKLEY. A loc. n., Kent, Worcest. Or Bickleigh, Devon

BICKMORE. From Bicknor; a loc. n., Glos., Heref., Kent

BICKNELL. From Bickenhall; a loc. n., Somers. Or Bickenhill, Warw.

BICKTON. From Bickton; a loc. n., Cornw., Devon, Hants

BIDDLE. *See* Biddulph or Bedall

BIDDLECOMBE. A loc. n.

BIDDULPH. A loc. n., Staffs.

BIDGOOD. From Bidacott (?); a loc. n., Devon

BIDMEAD. A loc. n.

BIDWELL. A loc. n., Beds

BIGG. *A.S.* *D.* Big; *G.* Bick; *Dch.* Bicker; a p.n. *See* Bick

BIGGADIKE. *See* Bickerdyke

BIGGAR. A loc. n., Lanarks

BIGGEN. A loc. n., Dur.

BIGGINS. A loc. n., Derbysh.

BIGGS. A loc. n. (?). Peter de Bixe in Rot. Obl. et Fin., K. John. *See* Bigg

BIGHAM. *See* Bingham

BIGNALL, BIGNELL. A loc. n., Staffs.

BIGSBY, BIXBY. From Bigby; a loc. n., Lincs

BILBOROUGH. A loc. n., Notts, Yorks

BILBY. A loc. n., Notts. Or Beilby, Yorks

BILL. *A.S.* Bil, Bill; *D.*, *G.*, *Fr.*, *Dch.* Bille; p.n. (a sword)

BILLETT. *N.-Fr.* Belet; p.n.

BILLING. A loc. n., Lancs, Northants, Yorks (contr. of Billingham); or *D.S.* Billing; *Fl.* Billen; p.n.
Billing, an ancient noble northern clan.

BILLINGTON. A loc. n., Staffs.

BILLYARD. *A.S.* Bilgeard; *Fr.* Billiard; p.n. A Hugt. n., Dover, 1622 (gentle protection)

BILTON. From Bilston; a loc. n., Staffs.

BINDLEY. A loc. n., Hants

BINDLOSS. *G.* Bindlos; a p.n. (bandless)

BINDON. A loc. n., Hants

BINGHAM. A loc. n., Notts. Held by De Buisli
Hugo and Robert de Bingeham in Rot. Obl. et Fin., K. John (Notts).

BINGLEY. A loc. n., Yorks

BINKS. *D.* Bing, Bink; *A.S.* Bing; *Fr.* Binne; *S.* Bing; *G.* Bieneck; *Dch.* Bing, Binger, Bink; p.n.
This patronymic gives the names to Bing (Suff.), Bingham (Notts), Bingley (Yorks), Bingen (Rhine), Binges (Burgundy).

BINLESS. *See* Bindloss

BINNEY. From Binnie; a loc. n., Linlithgow

BINNS. A loc. n., Roxburgh. Or from Binche; a loc. n., Belg.; *Dch.*, *Fl.* Bins; *G.* Binas; p.n.

BINSTEAD. A loc. n., Hants, Suss.

BINYON. *See* Bennion

BIRCH. A loc. n., Ess., Lancs, Salop, Yorks. Or *see* Burch

BIRCHALL. From Bircholt; a loc. n., Kent

BIRCHAM. A loc. n., Norf. Or Berchem, Belg.

BIRCHENOUGH. *A.S.* Burchenoth, Burgnoth; p.n. (courageous protector). Or *Dch.* Berkenhoff; a loc. and p.n. *A.S. birchenhof* (birch house)

BIRCHINGTON. A loc. n., Kent

BIRCHMORE. A loc. n., Warw.

BIRD, BIRT. *A.S.* Birht, Beorht; *D.* Bird; *Fl.* Burdo, Burth; *G.* Burde, Berto, Berdie; *Fr.* Bert; p.n. (bright)

BIRDSEYE. *See* Bardsey

BIRKENSHAW. A loc. n., Yorks

BIRKETT. *See* Borret

BIRKIN. A loc. n., Yorks
De Birchinges, a tenant in chief in *D.B.* John de Birkin held land in Yorks *temp.* K. John.

BIRKLE. From Birkhall; a loc. n., Aberdeen. Or Birkhill, Fife

BIRLEY. A loc. n., Heref.

BIRMINGHAM. A loc. n.
Held by Fulco Paynel *temp.* Hen. I. Peter de B. went to Ireland and was ancestor of the Earls of Louth.

BIRNIE. A loc. n., Elgin

BIRRELL. *See* Burrell

BIRTHWRIGHT. From Birthwaite; a loc. n., Westmd.

BISPHAM. A loc. n., Lancs

BISS. From La Bisse; a loc. n., Norm. Or *A.S.* Byssa, *bisi* (?) (busy); *S.* Bishe; p.n.

BISSELL. *N.-Fr.* Bichell; a p.n. (a hind). Or dim. of Biss. *See* Buscall

BISSETT. *Fr.* Bissot; *G.* Bissert; p.n. A Hugt. n., Lond. 1618
Biset in Rot. Obl. et Fin.

BISSICKS. Welsh Ab Isaac (?)

BISSMIRE. *G.* Bessemer; *Fl.* Pessemier; *A.S.* Bisimær; p.n. (Besi the famous)

BITTLESTON. From Biddlestone; a loc. n., Heref.

BIXBY. *See* Bigsby

BIZLEY. *See* Beasley

BIZZELL. *See* Bissell

BLABY. A loc. n., Leics.

BLACK. *A.S.* Blac, Blæc ; *D.* Black; *Fl.* Blake ; *Dch.* Blaak, Blak ; p.n. *See* Blake

BLACKABY. From Blackfordby ; a loc. n., Leics.

BLACKADDER. A loc. n., Scotl.

BLACKALL. A loc. n., Devon

BLACKBORN. *See* Blackburn

BLACKBURN. A loc. n., Lancs, Linlithgow

BLACKFORD. A loc. n., Devon

BLACKGROVE. From Blagrave ; a loc. n., Berks

BLACKLEDGE. *See* Bleackley

BLACKLOCK. From Black Loch ; a loc. n., Lanark, Renfrew, Stirling

BLACKMORE. From Blackmoor ; a loc. n., Somers.

BLACKSTONE. A loc. n., Devon

    Held by Alured le Breton, 1086.

BLACKTIN. From Blackden ; a loc. n., Ess.

BLACKWELL. A loc. n., Derbysh., Dur., Worc.

BLACRE. *Fr.* De Blacquiere ; a p.n.

BLADE. From Bleid ; a loc. n., Belg. Or *A.S.* Blæd ; *D.* Blad, Bladt ; *S.* Blad ; *Fl.* Bled ; *Dch.* Blad, Blatt ; *Scot.* Blate ; *G.* Blöde (blade of a sword) ; p.n.

BLADES. A loc. n., Yorks

BLADON. From Bladen ; a loc. n., Dorset

BLAGBURN. *See* Blackburn

BLAGDEN. *See* Blagdon

BLAGDON. A loc. n., Devon

BLAGG. *See* Black

BLAGROVE. From Blagrave ; a loc. n., Berks

BLAIR. A loc. n., Perth

BLAKE. *Dch.* Bleek ; *Fl.* Blieck ; *N.* *bleikr* ; p.n. (pale). *See* Black

    Walter Blacke. Rot. Hund. 1273.
    Le Blake in Rot. Obl. et Fin.

BLAKEMORE. From Blakemere ; a loc. n., Heref.

BLAKENEY. A loc. n., Glos., Norf.

BLAKESLEY. A loc. n., Northants

BLAKISTON. A loc. n., Dur.

BLAMIRE. *D.* Blumer ; *Dch.* Bloemer ; *Fl.* Bloemart ; a p.n. Or *N.* blá-mœr (blue moor), a poetical name for the sea

BLAND. *A.S.* Bland ; *Fr.* Blandre ; p.n. (blend, mixture, perhaps racial)

BLANDFORD. A loc. n., Dorset

BLANKLEY. From Blankney ; a loc. n., Lincs

BLATCH. *D.* Blache ; *G.* Blach, Blasche ; p.n. *See* Black

BLATCHLEY. From Bletchley ; a loc. n., Oxon, Salop

BLATHERWAYT, BLATHWAYT. From Bleathwaite ; a loc. n., Cumb.

BLATHERWICK. A loc. n., Northants

BLAXALL. A loc. n., Suff.

BLAXLAND. From Blackland ; a loc. n., Suff.

BLAY, BLEY. *See* Bly

BLAYDON. *See* Bladon

BLAYNEY. From Blaney ; a loc. n., Fermanagh

BLAZY. From St Blazey ; a loc. n., Cornw. and France. *Fr.* Blaise ; *Dch.* Blaze, Blazer, Bles ; *Fl.* Blaes, Blazy ; *D.B.* Blize ; p.n.

BLEACKLEY. From Blakeley ; a loc. n., Lancs

BLEANEY. *See* Blayney

BLEASBY. A loc. n., Lincs

BLEASDALE. A loc. n., Lancs

BLEASDELL. *See* Bleasdale

BLEASE. *See* Bliss

BLEBY. *See* Blaby

BLECHYNDEN. A loc. n., Hants

BLENCOE. From Blencow ; a loc. n., Cumb.

BLENKARNE. From Blencarn ; a loc. n., Cumb.

BLENKIN. *See* Blenkarne

BLENKINSOPP. A loc. n., Northbd.

BLENNERHASSET. A loc. n., Cumb. Held by De Tilliol *temp.* Hen. I.

BLESSLEY. *See* Blatchley

BLEW, BLOW. *G.* Blüh; a p.n.

BLEWITT. From Briqueville la Blouette; a loc. n., Norm. *Fr.* Bluet; *D.B.* Bloict; p.n. (cornflower)
> Bluat in Roll of Battell Abbey. Robert Bloet, Bishop of Lincoln. 1093. Robert Bloet held land in Wilts *temp.* K. John, 1201.

BLEZARD. *See* Blizard

BLICK. *N.* Blígr (shy); *S.* Blix; *D.* Blicker; *Fl.* Blieck; *G.* Blicke; *Dch.* Bliek; p.n.

BLIGH. *See* Blick or Bly. *N.* *bljúgr*; *S.* *blyg*; *D.* *bly* (bashful, shy)

BLIGHT. *A.S.* Blith; *D.* Blyt; p.n. (joyful)

BLISS. From Blois; a loc. n., Norm.
> W. de Bleys, Worcs., Rot. Hund. 1272.

BLIZARD. *A.S.* Blic, Plec, Plegheard; *D.* Blichert; p.n. (strong sword player)

BLOCK. *A.S.* Bloc; *D.* Blok; *Dch.*, *Fl.* Block; *Fr.* Bloc; p.n. (a block; one who lived in a log hut)

BLOCKIN. *See* Block; fam. n.

BLOCKLEY. A loc. n., Worcest.

BLOGG. *Dch.* Blog; a p.n. *See* Block

BLOMEFIELD. From Blomville, near Caen

BLOOD. *G.* Blöde; *Dch.* Blötc; p.n. *See* Blade

BLOOM. *S.* Blom; *D.* and *Fl.* Blom, Blum; *Dch.* Bloem, Blom, Blum; *G.* Bluhm, Blum, Blume; p.n. (a flower)

BLORE. A loc. n., Staffs.

BLOSS. *See* Blowers

BLOSSOM. *See* Bloxham

BLOTT. *A.S.* Blœdda; *S.* Blad; *Dch.* Blöte; p.n. *See* Blade

BLOUNT. *See* Blunt

BLOWERS. *D.* Bloes; a p.n. (naked)

BLOWEY. *See* Bloye

BLOXAM. From Bloxham; a loc. n., Lincs

BLOY, BLOYE. From Blois; a loc. n., Normandy

BLUDWORTH. From Blidworth; a loc. n., Notts

BLUETT. *See* Blewitt

BLUNDELL. *Fr.* Blondel; a p.n. Dim. of blonde (fair)
> Robert Blundel in Rot. Obl. et Fin., K. John.

BLUNT. *N.* Blundr (sleepy); a n.n.; *D.B.* Blund; a p.n.
> Blund in Rot. Obl. et Fin., K. John.

BLY. From Blaye; a loc. n., France. *G.* Blei, Bloy; *Dch.* Bleij; *D.B.* Bleio; p.n.

BLYTH. A loc. n., Northbd., Notts

BOAG, BOAK. *N.* Bogi (a bow, or bowshaped); *D.B.* Boche; *D.* Boeck, Booek; *Dch.* Bock, Boeg, Bok; *G.* Bock, Böge; p.n. Or *see* Bugg

BOARBANK. *See* Bowerbank

BOARD, BOORD. *A.S.* Bord, Brord (a sword); *Dch.* Bordes; p.n.

BOAREE. *Dch.* Boeree; *G.* Boerey; p.n. (rustic, countryman)

BOASE, BOAZ. *D.* Boas, Boese, Bohse; *Dch.* Boas, *Fl.* Boes; *Fr.* Bous; *G.* Boas, Boos; *A.S.* Boso; p.n.

BOAST. *Fr.* Bost, Boust; p.n.

BOATWRIGHT. *See* Botwright

BOBBIT. *Dch.* Bobbert; a p.n.

BOBBY. *A.S.* Bobba, Bubba; *G.* Bube, Bober, Bobisch; *D.* Bobe; *Dch.* Bobbe; *Fr.* Bobée; p.n. (a boy)

BOCOCK. *See* Boocock

BODDINGTON. A loc. n., Glos., Northants

BODENHAM. A loc. n., Wilts and Heref.

BODGER, BOGER. *N.-Fr.* Boschier; *G.* Böger; p.n.
> W. le Boghier, Rot. Hund. 1272.

G

BODGINER. *Fr.* Bodinier; a p.n. *boudinier* (a pudding maker)

BODILLY. A loc. n., Cornwall. *See* Baddeley

BODKIN. *D.* Bodecker; *Dch.* Boddeke; p.n. Dim. of Bode Bodkint in Rot. Obl. et Fin., K. John.

BODLE. *See* Boodle

BODLEY. *See* Badley

BODY. *N.* Boddi. Dimin. of Bödvarr (wary in battle). Or *A.S.* Boda, Boter, Boti, Bot; *Fr.* Bodé; *D.* Bodi, Bodin, Bott; *Fl.* Bodhy, Body; *G.* Bods, Bode, Böde; *S.* Bode, Bodin; *Dch.* Boddé, Bode, Bodt, Botter, Bott; p.n. (a messenger)

BOFFAY. From Beaufay; a loc. n., Norm.

BOFFIN. From Bovignes; a loc. n., Belg. Or *N.* Bófi; a p.n.; *A.S.* Bofing; a fam. n.; *Fr.* Boffin; a p.n.; Bovin, a Hugt. n., Lond. 1685

BOGERT. *Dch., Fl.* Bogaert; *Fr.* Boygard; *Dch.* Bogaardt; p.n. (bow guard). Hugt. n., Lond. 1681

BOGG. *See* Boag

BOGGERS, BOGGIS. A p.n.

BOGGS, BOGGERS, BOGGIS. *N.-Fr.* De Bogis or De Boges; p.n., 1180

BOGUE. *See* Boag

BOHANAN. *See* Buchanan

BOLDERS. *See* Balders

BOLES. *See* Bowles

BOLITHO. A loc. n., Cornw.

BOLIVER. Welsh Ab Oliver

BOLLAND. A loc. n., Yorks, Belg.; Boilantes, Norm.

BOLLARD. *A.S.* Baldred, Boldred; *Fr.* Boulard; a p.n. *See* Pollard

BOLLINGTON. A loc. n., Ess.

BOLSHAW. From Balsham; a loc. n., Camb.

BOLSOVER. A loc. n., Derbys.

BOLSTER. *See* Alabaster

BOLT. From Bolt or Bout, Norm. *N.-Fr.* De Boalt; *D.*, *Dch.*; p.n.

BOLTON. A freq. loc. n.

BOLUS. *See* Bowles

BOMPAS. From Bonpas, near Perpignan

BONALLACK. From Banhaglog; a loc. n., Montgomeryshire

BONAR. A loc. n., Sutherland

BONCHER, BONSHER. *N.-Fr.* Bonnechière (bon visage); a p.n.

BOND. *N.* Bondi (a yeoman); *D.* Bond; *S.* Bonde; *Fl.* Bondue; *A.S.* Bonde, Bondi, Bundi; p.n.

BONE. From Bohon; loc. n., Normandy. Or *Fr.* Bouhon; *Dch.* Boon; *G.* Bohn; *D.*, *Fl.* Bon; p.n. A Hugt. n., Lond. 1621 De Buun in Rot. Obl. et Fin.

BONEHILL. A loc. n., Staff.; or Bonhill, Dumbarton. Or *N.-Fr.* Bonnel; *Dch.* Bonel; p.n. A Hugt. n., Lond. 1618

BONFIELD. *See* Bonville

BONHAM. A loc. n., Somerset

BONIFACE. *Dch., G.* Bonifacius; *Fr.* Boniface; p.n. (well-doer)

BONIWELL. *See* Bonville

BONNER. From Bonnard; a loc. n., France. *Fr.* Bonnard, Bonneau, Bonheur; p.n. Hugt., Lond. 1618. Or *N.-Fr.* Bonnaire (courteous); a p.n. *See* Bunner

BONNETT. *Fr.* Bonnet; p.n. Bonnat and St Bonnet; loc. n., France Bonet in Rot. Obl. et Fin.

BONNEY, BONNY. *Fr.* Bonné; a p.n. (capped). Or *see* above

BONSALL. From Boncelles; a loc. n., Belg. Or Bonsall, Derbys.

BONVILLE. A loc. n., near Rouen, Normandy

BOOBY, BOOBYER. A loc. n. From *N.* Búibýr. *See* Boow

BOOCOCK. *Dch.* Boock; *D.*, *S.* Book; p.n. Dimin. of *N.* Búi; p.n. *See* Boow

BOODLE. From Bootle; a loc. n., Lancs, Cumb.; *D.B.* Bodele

BOOKER. *See* Boucher

BOOL. *Fr.* Boulle; a p.n. *See* Bull

BOOME. From Boom; a loc. n., Belg. *Dch.* Boom; a p.n.

BOON. *Dch.*; p.n. *See* Bone

BOORMAN. *See* Borman

BOORN. *See* Bourne

BOOSEY. From Bussey; a loc. n., Norm. *Fr.* Bussy, Buzi; *D.B.* Buci; p.n. A Hugt. n., Lond. 1684
> De Busey in Rot. Obl. et Fin., K. John.

BOOT. From Buat, a castle near Falaise, Norm. Or *see* Butter

BOOTH. A loc. n., Derbysh. Or *D.*, *Dch.*, *Fl.* Bude, Budde; p.n.

BOOTHBY. A loc. n., Lincs
> Held by de Tateshall, 13th century.

BOOTHROYD. From Bodewryd; a loc. n., Anglesey

BOOTON. *See* Button

BOOTY. From Bothey; a loc. n., Belg. Or *G.* Buthy; *Fr.* Boutez (straight-legged); p.n.

BOOW. From Bow; a loc. n., Devon. Or *N.* Búi (a neighbour); *D.* Boye; *F.* Boyo; *Fl.* Boey, Bohy; *G.* Boy; *D.B.* Boui, Boi, Bou, Bu; p.n.

BOOY. *See* Boow

BORHAM. From Boreham; a loc. n., Wilts, Ess., Suss.

BORKING. From Barking; a loc. n., Surr.

BORLAND. From Burland; a loc. n., Yorks

BORLAND. A loc. n., Perth

BORLASE. From Borlez; a loc. n., Belg.

BORMAN. *A.S.* Beorhtman; *Dch.* Boerman, Borman; p.n. (illustrious man)

BORN. A loc. n., Germ. Or *N.* Björn (a bear); *D.*, *Dch.*, *G.* Born; *N.-Fr.* Le Borne; p.n. Or *see* Bourne

BORNER. *Fr.* Borné; a p.n.

BORRADAILE. *See* Barradale

BORRET. *N.* Berg-harðr (?) (hard as a rock); *D.B.* Borgeret, Borgret, Borret, Burghard, Burred, Burret, Borred; *D.* Borregaard; *Fl.* Boret, Burkard; *G.* Burchardt, Burghardt; *Fr.* Bourret; *Dch.* Berkhout; p.n.

BORRINGTON. *See* Barrington

BORRIS. *See* Burrows

BORTHWICK. A loc. n., Edinburgh

BORWELL. *See* Barwell

BORWICK. A loc. n., Lancs

BOSCAWEN. A loc. n., Cornw.

BOSHIER. *A.S.* Boshere, Bossa; *G.* Boscher; p.n. (stall warrior)

BOSS. *A.S.* Bos, Bosa (stall keeper (?)); *Fr.* Bosse; *D.* Boss; *G.*, *Dch.* Bos; p.n.
> In Rot. Obl. et Fin.

BOSSEY. *Fr.* Bussis; a p.n. *See* above

BOSSOM. From Bosham; a loc. n., Suss.

BOSTEN. *See* Boston

BOSTOCK. A loc. n., Ches.

BOSTON. A loc. n., Lincs

BOSWELL. *Fr.* Bosseville; a p.n. Bosville; a loc. n., Normandy

BOSWORTH. A loc. n., Leics.

BOTFIELD. A loc. n., Salop

BOTHAM. From Bodham; a loc. n., Norf.

BOTHAMLEY. From Barthomley; a loc. n., Ches.

BOTHERWAY. *Dch.* Botterweg; a p.n.

BOTHWELL. A loc. n., Lanark. Or Botwell, Middlx.

BOTT. *N.-Fr.* Bot; a p.n., 1195. *See* Body
> Brien Bot in Rot. Obl. et Fin., K. John.

BOTTEN, BOTTING. A loc. n., Lancs. *N.-Fr.* Botin; a p.n., 1180

BOTTENHAM. From Bodenham; a loc. n., Wilts

BOTTERIL. From Bottereaux; a loc. n., Norm. *Fr.* Bottrel; a p.n.
De Boterell in Rot. Obl. et Fin.

BOTWRIGHT. *See* Bootheroyd. Or *A.S.* Botred; a p.n. (riding messenger)

BOUCHER. From Boursières; a loc. n., Burgund.

BOUGEN, BOUGHEN. From Bouchain; a loc. n., France. Or *see* Buggins

BOUGHAL. *See* Arbuckle

BOUGHEY. *See* Boag, Bugg

BOULT. *See* Balders

BOULTBEE. From Boulby; a loc. n., Yorks

BOULTER. *A.S.* Bealdhere (bold warrior); *Fr.* Bolté; a p.n. *See* Balders
W. Bulder, York, 1272. Rot. Hund.

BOULTON. From Bolton; a freq. loc. n., Lancs, etc.

BOUND, BOWN. *See* Bone

BOUNDY. From Bondy; a loc. n., France. Or *D.* Bonde; a p.n. *See* Bond

BOURKE, BURKE. *Fr.* de Burgo; a p.n.; Bourg; a loc. n., Normandy
Burgh in Roll of Battell Abbey; *D.B.* Burc, de Burck, tenants in chief

BOURNE. A loc. n., Devon, Lincs, Norf., Somers., Suff.

BOUSFIELD. From Bousville; a loc. n., near Pavilly, Norm.

BOUSTEAD. A loc. n., Cumb.

BOUTTELL. *Fr.* Boutel, Bouteille; a p.n.
Boteville in Roll of Battell Abbey.

BOVER. From Beauvais; a loc. n., France. *Fl.* Bouvier; *Dch.* Bouwer, Boeve; p.n. Or *Fr.* Beaufour (Beaufort); p.n.

BOVILL. From Bowell; a loc. n., Belg. Or *see* Boswell
De Bovill in Rot. Obl. et Fin., K. John.

BOWCH. From Buce; a loc. n., Norm. *Fr.* Bouche; a p.n.; *N.-Fr.* de Buce, 1180

BOWCHER. Hugt., Lond. 1685. *See* Boucher

BOWDEN. A loc. n., Ches., Leics., Northants, Roxburgh

BOWEN. Bovignes; a loc. n., Belg. *Fl.* Boen; *Dch.* Bowen; p.n. Or Welsh Ab Owen. *See* Boy

BOWERBANK. A freq. loc. n.

BOWERS. A loc. n., Staffs.

BOWES. From Boves; a loc. n., Norm.
J. de Bowes, 1180; Hugh de B., Notts, Willm. I.

BOWGEN, BOWGIN. *See* Bougen

BOWHILL. *See* Bovill

BOWKER. From Beaucaire; a loc. n., France. Or *G.* Bauke; a p.n. *See* Bowcher

BOWLER. *Fr.* Boulard; a p.n.

BOWLES. From Baulers; a loc. n., Belg. *F.*, *Dch.*, *Fl.* Boels; *D.B.* Bollers; p.n.

BOWLEY. A loc. n., Heref. Or *Fr.* Beaulieu

BOWMAR. *See* Beaumont

BOWRING. From Beauraing; a loc. n., Belg. *Fl.* Bauraing; a p.n.

BOWSER. *See* Boucher

BOWSKELL. From Bouskall; a loc. n., Cumb.

BOWSTEAD. *N.* Bú-stað (a dwelling); *S.* Bostad, Bystedt; *G.* Baustatte; loc. and p.n. *See* Boustead

BOWYEAR, BOWYER. *N.-Fr.* Bouvier, 1180; Le Boyer, Kent, 1250; *Dch.* Bowier; p.n.

BOX. A loc. n., Wilts. Or *D.*, *Fl.* Bock; *G.* Bochs; *Dch.* Box; p.n.
De Boxe in Rot. Obl. et Fin., K. John.

BOXALL. A loc. n., Herts

BOY. *N.* Búi (a dweller, neighbour); *A.S.* Boia; *S.* Boye; *D.* Boye; *F.* Boyo, Boye, Boy; *G.* Bühr, Böer, Böhr; *Fl.* Boes, Bour, Bues; *Dch.* Boh, Boeje, Buys, Buys; p.n.

BOYACK. *F.* Boyke (dimin. of Boy); *D.* Boëck; *Fl.* Boek; *D.B.* Boche (?); p.n.

BOYCE. *D.*, *Fl.* Boyes; a p.n. *See* Boy

BOYCOTT. A loc. n., Salop

BOYD. *Fr.* Boyard; a p.n. Or Gaelic *boidh* (fair-haired). Hugt. n., Lond. 1687

BOYDELL. *G.* Beudell; a p.n.

BOYER. *Fr.*; p.n. *See* Bowyer

BOYLE. From the Irish O'Baoighill; a p.n. Or Boelles (now La Buille, Norm.)

BOYLING. *Fl.* Boelin; a p.n.

BOYNES. *Fl.* Boyen; *Dch.* Bouwens; p.n.; fam. n. of Boy

BOYNTON. A loc. n., Yorks.
De Bruce held it 1129.

BOYS. *See* Boyce

BRABAZON. From Barbançon; a loc. n., Fland.

BRABBS. *Dch.* Braber; *Fl.* Brabandt; *G.* Brab, Brabender; p.n. (a native of Brabant)

BRABY. From Brawby; a loc. n., Yorks

BRACEBRIDGE. A loc. n., Lincs
De Arden held it 13th century.

BRACEY. *See* Brassey

BRACHER. *See* Brasier

BRACKENBURY. A loc. n., Lincs

BRACKETT. *Fl.* Brachert; *Fr.* Braquet; p.n. Dimin. of Bragg

BRACKLEY. A loc. n., Northants

BRADBEER. *See* Bradby

BRADBROOK. From Bradbridge; a loc. n., Suss.

BRADBURY. A loc. n., Durham

BRADBY. A loc. n., Derbysh., now Bretby

BRADDOCK, BRADOCK. From Broadoak; a loc. n., Cornw., Ess.

BRADDON. From Bradden; a loc. n., Northants, Somers.

BRADDYLL. From Bradwall; a loc. n., Ches. Or Bradwell (?); a loc. n., Derbysh.
Radulph de Bradel held land in Lincs *temp.* K. John.

BRADE. From Breda, a loc. n., Holland. *G.* Breede; *Fl.* Breda, Bret; *D.* Breede, Brede, Bret; *Dch.* Brade, Brat, Breda; p.n. Prot. ref., Lond. 1688

BRADING. A loc. n., Isle of Wight

BRADLAUGH. From Bradley; a loc. n., Lincs; *D.B.* Bredlow. Also Broadlaw, a mountain in Peebles

BRADLEY. A loc. n., Glost., Lincs, Wilts, Staffs., Yorks

BRADNAM. From Braddenham; a loc. n., Norf.

BRADRIDGE. *See* Brodrick

BRADSELL. From Breadsall; a loc. n., Derbysh.

BRADSHAW. A loc. n., Lancs

BRADSTOCK. A loc. n., Dorset

BRADWELL. A loc. n., Derbysh., Ess., Suff.

BRADY. From the Irish O'Braidaigh; a p.n.

BRAGG. *N.* Bragi (a hero); *S.* Brag; *D.* Bracker; *Dch.* Brakke; *Fl.* Brack; *Fr.* Bracq; *A.S.* Breg; p.n.

BRAHAM. A loc. n., Camb.

BRAIDLEY. A loc. n., Yorks

BRAIDWOOD. *See* Broadwood

BRAIKENRIDGE. From Brackenrigg; a loc. n., Cumb.

BRAILEY. From Breuillet; a loc. n., France

BRAILSFORD. A loc. n., Derbysh.

BRAIN. From Braisnes; a loc. n., France. Or Braine; a loc. n., Belg. *Fr.* Breyne; p.n.; Breon, a Hugt. n., Lond. 1688
In Roll of Battell Abbey. Matt. de Brain, Yorks, 1199.

BRAITHWAITE. A loc. n., Yorks

BRAKE. *N.-Fr.* De Brac, 1180. *Fl.* Braecke; p.n.

R. de la Brache, Bedf. 1199.

BRAKSPEAR. From Bran-spée or Branc-spée; a *N.-Fr.* term for a long sword used by the northern nations. Or Braceby (?); a loc. n., Lincs. *See* Shakespeare and Winspear

BRAMALL. A loc. n., Ches.

BRAMBLE. From Brambeley; a loc. n., Middlx. Or *see* Brimble

BRAME. *A.S.* Breme (renowned); *D.* Bram; *S.* Brehm; *Fl.* Brame, Brems; *Dch.* Brehm, Brem; *Fr.* Brame; p.n. Or *see* Braham

BRAMLEY. A loc. n., Yorks

BRAMMER. *G.* Bramer; *F.* Bremer; *D.* Brammer; p.n. *See* Brame

BRAMWELL. *See* Bramall

BRAN. *A.S.* Bren, Beorn (bear); *G.* Brann; p.n.

BRANCH. From St Denis de Branche; a loc. n., Norm. *Dch.* Branse; *Fl.* Branche; p.n. Branchon; a loc. n., Belg.

Braunch in Roll of Battell Abbey.

BRANCHFLOWER. *Fr.* Blanchfleur; a p.n. (white flower)

BRAND, BRANDER. *N.* Brandr; *D.* Brandt; *S.* Brander; *Dch.*, *G.* Brand; p.n. (a sword-blade); *N.-Fr.*; Norf. 1086

Brand in Roll of Battell Abbey and *D.B.* G. Prot. ref., Lond. 1618.

BRANDON. A loc. n., Norf., Suff.

BRANDRAM. From Brandrum; a loc. n., Monaghan. *N.-Fr.* 1198

BRANDRETH. A loc. n., Cumb.

BRANDUM. From Brantham; a loc. n., Suff.

BRANFORD. A loc. n., Worcest.

BRANSCOMBE. A loc. n., Devon

BRANSGROVE. From Bromsgrove(?); Worc.

BRANSTON. A loc. n., Hants, Leics, Lincs, Staffs.

BRANWHITE. From Brandthwaite; a loc. n., Cumb.

BRAS. A loc. n., Belg. *Dch.* Bras, Brass; *Fr.* Brasse; p.n.

BRASH. From Brages (?); a loc. n., Belg.

BRASIER, BRAZIER. From Bressuire; a loc. n., France. Or *G.* Breyesser; *Fr.* Brasseur; p.n. A Hugt. n., Norwich, 1622

BRASSEY. From Brachy or Brécy; loc. n., Normandy

Bracy in Roll of Battell Abbey. Robert de Brasey in Rot. Obl. et Fin., K. John.

BRATBY. *See* Bradby

BRATT. *See* Brade

BRATTLE. From Braithwell; a loc. n., Yorks. Or *see* Braddyll

BRATTON. A loc. n., Devon, Somers

BRAUNSTON. A loc. n., Leics, Northants

BRAY. A loc. n., Norm., Belg., Berks. *N.-Fr.* de Bray; *Dch.*, *G.* Bree; p.n.

Bray in Roll of Battell Abbey. Radulph de Bray in Rot. Obl. et Fin., K. John.

BRAYBROOK. A loc. n., Northants

BRAYSHAW. *See* Brasier

BRAZENDALE. From Braystonedale; a loc. n., Cumb.

BREACH. *A.S.* Brich (Beorht); *Fr.* Briche; p.n. (bright)

De Briche in Rot. Obl. et Fin., K. John.

BREAM, BREAME. A loc. n., Glost.

BREARLEY. A loc. n., Yorks

BREDDY. *See* Brady

BREE. *Dch.*; p.n.; Brye; a loc. n., Belg.; *Fr.* Briey. Or *A.S.* Bri (bright)

BREEDEN. *See* Breedon

BREEDON. A loc. n., Glost., Leics, Worc. Or Bridon. A Hugt. n., Lond. 1681

BREEKS. *See* Briggs

BREESE. *N.* Bresi; *S.* Braise; *D.* Bræs; *Fl.* Brees; *Dch.* Bres, Breys; *G.* Briese; p.n. Or *see* Brice (fire (?))

BREHENY. From the Irish Breathamh (a judge)

BRELY. From Brilley; a loc. n., Hunts

BRENCHLEY. A loc. n., Kent

BRERETON. A loc. n., Ches., Staffs.

BRETHERTON. A loc. n., Lancs

BRETT. *Fr.* Bret; a p.n.
> Le Bret in Rot. Obl. et Fin., K. John.
> Le Breton (?)

BRETTON. A loc. n., Yorks. Or *see* Britton

BREWER. From Brueria, now Breviere, near Caen, Norm. *Fr.* Bruyère; a p.n.
> William Briwere, a favourite of Hen. II., descended from Drogo de Bevreire, a Fleming, who held lands in Northants, Leics., Lincs, Norf., Suff., Yorks, *D.B.* Briwer in Rot. Obl. et Fin., K. John. Or *see* Bryer.

BREWIN. *A.S.* Bregwin, Archbp. Cant. 765; *Fl.* Bruin; p.n. (a ruler friend). Or *see* Brown

BREWSTER. The Scot. and N. Engl. form of Brewer

BRICE. From St Brice; a loc. n., Norm. Or *A.S.* Bris; *Fl.* Brys; a p.n. (bright). Or Welsh Ab Rhys; a p.n.

BRICKDALE. From Briquedale; a loc. n., Norm.

BRICKNELL. *See* Brignall

BRICKSTOCK. *See* Brigstocke

BRICKWOOD. From Bricket Wood(?); a loc. n., Herts.

BRIDE. *N.* Breidr; *D.* Bryde; *A.S.* Brada; *G.* Breit; p.n. (broad)

BRIDGES. An old way of spelling Bruges. *See* Briggs

BRIDGEWATER. A loc. n., Somers.

BRIDLE. From Bridell; a loc. n., Pembroke. Or *A.S.* Brithwall, Beorhfweald (bright ruler); *Fl.* Breydel; a p.n.

BRIERLEY. A loc. n., Glost., Yorks

BRIGGS. From Bruges; a loc. n., Belgium. *S.* Brügge; *Dch.* Brigg; *Fl.* Bruges; p.n. A Hugt. n., Lond. 1618. Atte Brigge, 1327
> Brig and de Brug occur in Rot. Obl. et Fin., K. John.

BRIGHT. *A.S.* Beorht, Brict; p.n. (bright, illustrious)

BRIGHTING. Fam. n. ; descendant of Bright

BRIGHTWELL. A loc. n., Suff.

BRIGNALL. A loc. n., Yorks

BRIGSTOCK. A loc. n., Northants

BRILEY. From Broilly; a loc. n. Norm.

BRILL. A loc. n., Bucks., Cornw. Or Brielle, Holl. ; *D.* Brill; *Fl.* Brille; *Dch.* Briel; *G.* Briehl; p.n. Prot. ref., Sandwich, 1622

BRIMBLE. From Bremble ; a loc n., Wilts

BRINE. From Brin; a loc. n., France. *See* Brain. Or *A.S.* Brine, Beorn; a p.n. (bear)

BRINKHURST. From Bringhurst; a loc. n., Leics.

BRINKLEY. From Brinklow; a loc. n., Warw.

BRINSLEY. A loc. n., Notts

BRISCOE. A loc. n., Yorks. Also de Birkskeugh, Cumb.

BRISCOMBE. From Brinscombe ; a loc. n., Somers.

BRISLEY. A loc. n., Norf.

BRISTOW. From Bristow, the ancient name of Bristol

BRITCHER. *Fl.* Brichard, Brichart ; *A.S.* Brictuard ; *G.* Brichta, Brieger ; *Fr.* Briche ; p.n. (illustrious guard)

BRITTON. *Fr.* Breton, Britton, le Breton ; *D.* Bretton ; *Fl.* Breting ; *D.B.* Brito ; p.n.
> Breton in Roll of Battell Abbey. Brito, Briton, le Briton in Rot. Obl. et Fin., K. John.

BROAD. *A.S.* Brod, Brorda; a p.n. (a sword)

BROADHEAD. From Broadheath; a loc. n., Lancs, Worcest.

BROADHURST. A loc. n., Lincs

BROADWAY. A loc. n., Dorset, Heref., Somers., Worcest.

BROADWOOD. A loc. n., Devon, Lanark

BROCK. From Broc; a loc. n., Norm. Or *N.* Broki; a n.n. (a badger); *S.* Brock; *D., Dch.* Broch, Brock; *Fl.* Brockx, Bruch; *D.B.* Broc; p.n.

> Robert le Broc and Ranulph de Broc in Rot. Obl. et Fin., K. John.

BROCKBANK, BROCKLEBANK. A loc. n., Cumb.

BROCKLEHURST. From Brocken-hurst; a loc. n., Hants

BROCKLESBY. A loc. n., Lincs

BROCKLEY. A loc. n., Suff.

BROCKSOPP. From Brockthrop (?); a loc. n., Glost.

BROCKWELL. A loc. n.

BRODICK. A loc. n., Bute

BRODIE. A loc. n., Nairn

BRODRIBB. From Bawdrip; a loc. n., Somers

BRODRICK. From the Welsh Ab Roderic. *See* Prhydderch

BRODY. From the Irish *brodach* (proud). Or *see* Brodie

BROGDEN. A loc. n., Yorks

BROMAGE, BROMEDGE. *See* Brom-wich

BROMLEY. A loc. n., Staffs.

BROMMELL. From Broomhill; a loc. n., Norf.

BROMWICH. A loc. n., Staffs.

BROOKE. A loc. n., Norf. Atte Broke

BROOKES, BROOKS. *A.S.* Bruc, Bruchyse; *Fl.* Broeckx; *G.* Brucks, Brucksch, Bruksch; *Dch.* Broeks; p.n. *See* Brock

BROOKHOUSE. A loc. n., Staffs., Yorks

BROOM. From Broome; a loc. n., Norf. Atte Brome, Court of Husting. Or *A.S.* Brum, contr. of Brunman; *D.* Brummer; *Dch.* Brom; *G.* Brumme; p.n. (brown man)

BROOMHALL. A loc. n., Worc.

BROOMHEAD. *See* Brummit

BROS. *N.-Fr.* Bros, 1180; Broche, 1198; p.n. *See* Brows

BROTHERHOOD. From Bough-rood (?); a loc. n., Radnor

BROTHERIDGE. From Brodrick (?); a loc. n.

BROTHERS. *N.* Broddr (a spike, sword); *A.S.* Broder, Brother; *Fl.* Broothaers; *Dch.* Broeders; p.n. Prot. ref., Sandwich, 1622

BROTHERSTON. *See* Brother-ton

BROTHERTON. A loc. n., Yorks

BROUGHAM. A loc. n., Westmd.

BROWN. *N.* Bruni (fire); *D.* Braun, Bruhn, Brun, Bruun; *A.S.* Brun; *F.* Brûno; *Dch., Fl.* Brun, Brune, Brown; *G.* Braun, Brun, Bruno; *Fr.* Brune, Bruné; p.n.; *N.-Fr.* Le Brun

> Brun, Bruni, Brunus in Rot. Obl. et Fin., K. John.

BROWNING. *F.* Brûninga; a fam. n.; *D.* Breuning, Bryning; *D.B.* Bruning; *Dch.* Bruning; *Fl.* Brunin; *G.* Brünig, Brüning; p.n.

BROWNJOHN. From Brongwyn (?); a loc. n., Cardigan

BROWNLOW. A loc. n., Ches., Lancs

BROWNRIGG. A loc. n., Cumb.

BROWNSWORD. From Brownswood; a loc. n., Wexford. Or *A.S.* Brunswith; a p.n.

BROWS. *Fl.* Browaeys; *G.* Brause; *D.B.* de Braiose; *Fr.* Brousse; p.n. *See* Bruce

BROXHOLM. A loc. n., Lincs

BRUCE. From Breux; a loc. n., Normandy (?); probably derived from the original Norse owner. Or *N.* Brúsi (a buck, he-goat); *D.* Bruse, Bruus; *S.* Bruse, Bruze; *Fr.* Brousse, de Brouas; *Fl.* Broos, Brouez; *Dch.* Brus, Brusse; *G.* Brusch, Brysch; p.n.

D.B. Robertus de Bruis, a tenant in chief (Yorks). The founder of the family of Brus of Skelton, from whom the Kings of Scotland and the family of Bruce, Earl of Ailesbury, are descended. His seal is engraved in the *Registrum Honoris de Richmond.* Bruys in Roll of Battell Abbey. Giles de Brewse, Bishop of Hereford, 1200. Adam, Peter, and William de Brus in Rot. Obl. et Fin., K. John.

BRUDENELL. From Bretignolles, near Alençon, Norm.

BRUFF. From Brough; a loc. n., Yorks

BRUMBRIDGE. From Broomridge; a loc., n., Northbd.

BRUMBY. *See* Bromby

BRUMMELL. *See* Brommell

B R U M M I T. *Dch.* Bromet; a p.n. Or Bramwith; a loc. n., Yorks

BRUNDRITH. *See* Brandreth

BRUNDSDEN. *See* Brundsdon

BRUNDSDON. From Brundon; a loc. n., Ess.

BRUNLEES. From Bronllys; a loc. n., Brecknock

BRUNT. From Brund; a loc. n., Staffs. Or *A.S.* Brunheard (Brown the strong); *Dch.* Brunt; *D.* Brund; *Fl.* Brunard; *Fr.* Brunet; p.n.

BRUNTON. A loc. n., Fife

BRUNYEE. *N.* Bruni (fire, burning); *Fr.* Bruné, Brunier; *Dch.* Brunje; *D.B.* Brunc; p.n. Fl. ref., Lond. 1618

BRUSH. *G.* Brusch; a p.n. *See* Bruce

BRUTON. *See* Brereton

BRYAN. From Brionne; a loc. n., Normandy. Or *see* O'Brien
Will. de Brion in Rot. Obl. et Fin., K. John, A.D. 1207.

BRYANT. From Breaunt; a loc. n., Norm. *Fr.* Briand, Briant; p.n.

BRYDGES. From de Bruges. *See* Bridges

BRYER. From Briar; a loc. n., France. *D.* Breyer; *Dch.* Bruijer; *Fl.* Breyer, Briers; *G.* Breier, Breyer; *Fr.* Brière, Bruyère; p.n. *See* Brewer

BUBB. *See* Bobby. Prot. ref., Sandwich, 1622

BUBBINGS. *See* Bobby
Descendants of Bobe. Comp. Bobbinger, a loc. n., Ess.

BUBEAR. *See* Boobyer

BUCHANAN. A loc. n., Fife

BUCK. *A.S.* Buc, Buga; *S., D.* Buck; *N.-Fr.* De Boc and Le Buc; p.n. *See* Bugge
Herlewin Buc in Rot. Obl. et Fin., K. John. Prot. ref., Lond. 1618.

BUCKBY. A loc. n., Northants

BUCKENHAM. A loc. n., Norf.

BUCKETT. *Fr.* Bouquet, Buchet; p.n. Dim. of Buck
Richard Bucket in Rot. Obl. et Fin., K. John. Also Hugt. n., Lond. 1685.

BUCKHURST. A loc. n., Ess., Lancs

BUCKINGHAM. The county town

BUCKLAND. A loc. n., Berks, Bucks, Devon, Hants, Herts, Kent, Surr., Wilts

BUCKLE. From Boucle; a loc. n., Fland. *G.* Buchal, Buckol; p.n. *See* Arbuckle

BUCKLEY. A loc. n., Bucks

BUCKNELL. A loc. n., Salop, Staffs.

BUCKTON. A loc. n., Yorks

BUCKWELL. A loc. n.

BUCKWORTH. A loc. n., Yorks

BUDD. *D., Dch.* Budde; *G.* Bude; p.n. *See* Body
Simon Bude in Rot. Obl. et Fin., K. John.

BUDDELL. From Budel; a loc. n., Belg.

BUDDEN. *Fr.* Boudain, Boudin; *G.* Budan; p.n.

BUDDERY. *Fr.* Butré; a p.n. *See* Butter

BUDDLE. A loc. n., Northbd.

BUDGEN. *See* Buggins

BUDGETT. *Fr.* Bugat; a p.n. Dim. of Bugg

BUDICOMB. *See* Puddicombe

BUGG. From Bouge; a loc. n., Belg. Or Bougy, Buchy, Normandy. *Fr.* Bougy, Bugué. Or *S.*, *D.* Bugge; *G.* Böger, Büge, Bugge, Buke; *Dch.* Boggia, Boeg, Büger, Bugers, Buggers (a bow); p.n.

Bushy on Roll of Battell Abbey. *D.B.* De Buci and Bugg, tenants in chief (Notts). Buge, Bugo, Saxon tenants. W. Bugge in Rot. Obl. et Fin., K. John.

The N.-Fr. forms are local; the rest may be possibly derived from the Danish as a n.n. *N. bygan*; *D. bugne*, to bend; *A.S. búgan*, to bow. In the dialect of the Midlands *bug* is used in the sense of set up, proud. *See* p. 2.

BUGGINS. *N.-Fr.* Bogin; *Fl.* Buchin, Bughin, Buyghens; p.n. *See* Bugg

BUIST. *N.-Fr.* Boiste or Buiste, 1198; *Fr.* Buisset; p.n.

BULBECK, BULBICK. From Bolbec; a loc. n., Normandy

D.B. de Bolebec, a tenant in chief. In Rot. Obl. et Fin., K. John.

BULCAMP. From Bulscamp; a loc. n., Flanders

BULCRAIG. A loc. n., Cumb.

BULFORD. A loc. n., Wilts

BULKLEY. From Bulkeley; a loc. n., Ches.

BULL. From Bulles; a loc. n., Belg. and Fr. Or *A.S.* Bul; *N.* Bolli; *F.* Bóle, Boele; *G.* Buhl, Bulla; *S.* Bolle; *Fl.* Bully, Buls, Boel; *Dch.* Boll, Boel, Bull; *D.* Bull, Bollé, Boelle; p.n. (a bull)

Richard Bole and Radulph Bule in Rot. Obl. et Fin., K. John. Prot. ref. n., Lond. 1618.

BULLEN. From Bologne. *Fr.*, *N.-Fr.* De Buliun, de Bolein, Boleyn; p.n. Or *F.* Bólen; *S.* Bollin; *Fl.* Bulens; *Dch.* Boelen; p.n.; Bolinnes; a loc. n., Belg.; *A.S.* Bolling, the fam. or tribal name of Bolli. Bollen, Prot. ref., Lond. 1618

BULLER. From Boulaere; a loc. n., Fland. *G.* Buller; a p.n.

Baldwin de Buller in Rot. Obl. et Fin., K. John.

BULLETT. *N.-Fr.* Bulete, Bolet; *Fr.* Boullet; p.n. Dim. of Bull

BULLIFANT. *See* Bullivant

BULLIMORE. From Bulmore; a loc. n., Wilts

BULLINGBROOK. From Bolingbroke; a loc. n., Lincs

BULLIVANT. From Polliphant; a loc. n., Cornw. Or *N.-Fr.* Belef-fant (good-looking); *Dch.* Belin-fante; p.n.

BULLOCK. *G.* Bullok; p.n. Dim. of Bull

BULLWINKLE. *Dch.* Belwinkel; a p.n. (bell-corner)

BULPIT. From Bullapit; a loc. n., Devon

BULPORT. A loc. n.

BULSTRODE. A loc. n., Bucks

BULTITUDE. *A.S.* Bealdthryth, Baldetrude; *Dch.* Boldoot; *Fr.* Bultot; p.n. (bold—true)

BULWER. From Bouloire; a loc. n., Normandy. *D.B.* Bulvi (?)

BUMPUS. *See* Bompas

BUNBURY. A loc. n., Ches.

BUNCE. *Dch.* Bunge; p.n. Dim. *See* Bunn

BUNGEY. From Bungay; a loc. n., Suff.

BUNKALL, BUNCKLE. A loc. n., Scotl. Or dim. of Bunn. *G.* Bunkale; a p.n.

BUNN. *A.S.* Bun, Buna (gushing, spirited)

BUNNER. From the Welsh Ab Ynyr; a p.n. Or *see* Bonner

BUNNETT. *Fr.* p.n. (hedge-sparrow)
BUNNEY. From Bougnies (?) ; a loc. n., Belg. Or *see* Bunn
BUNNING. *A.S.* Buna ; *Dch.* Buning ; p.n. ; *N.* *buna* (to gush as water, brisk) son of Bun
BUNTER. *D.* Bunde ; *Dch.* Bunte ; p.n. *See* Bond
BUNTING. *Fl.* Buntinx ; a p.n.
  Unfrid Bunting in Rot. Obl. et Fin., K. John. Fam. n. from Bunte.
BUNYAN, BUNYON. *Fl.* Bonichon, Bundgen ; *Fr.* Bonjean ; p.n. Dim. of Bunn (?)
BURBIDGE, BURBRIDGE. From Burbage ; a loc. n., Derbysh., Leics., Wilts
BURCH. *See* Burdge
BURDASS. From Burdiehouse ; a loc. n., Edinburgh
BURDEN. *Fr.* Bourdain, Bourdin, Bourdon ; p.n. From Burdinne ; a loc. n., Belg.
  Burdon in Roll of Battell Abbey ; *D.B.* Buerd (?). Bourdon in Rot. Obl. et Fin., K. John. *See* Bird.
BURDETT. *Fr.* Bourdet ; a p.n.
  Burdet in Roll of Battell Abbey and in *D.B.* William Burdet in Rot. Obl. et Fin., K. John. Hugt. n., Lond. 1685. *N.-Fr. bourdet* (a border).
BURDGE, BURGE. *D.*, *G.*, *Dch.* Berg ; p.n. Or *A.S.* Berch ; a p.n. (bright)
BURFIELD. From Burghfield ; a loc. n., Berks
BURFITT, BURFOOT. *See* Barfoot
BURFORD. A loc. n., Salop, Wilts
BURGESS, BURGIS. *Dch.* Burges, Burgess ; p.n. Burges is an old way of spelling Bruges
  In Rot. Obl. et Fin.
BURGOYNE. *N.-Fr.* Bourgain, Bourgogne ; p.n.
BURGRAVE. A loc. n., Lincs
BURKET, BURKITT. *See* Birkett
BURLEY. A loc. n., Hants, Rutl.
BURNABY. *See* Burnby
BURNBY. A loc. n., Yorks
BURNESS. *See* Burns

BURNETT. *A.S.* Beornheard ; *N.-Fr.* Burnard, Bernard ; p.n. (strong bear)
BURNHAM. A loc. n., Bucks, Ess., Lincs, Norf., Somers.
BURNINGHAM. From Briningham ; a loc. n., Norf. Or Birmingham
BURNS. A loc. n., Fife. Or *N.* Björn (a bear) ; *D.* Bjoern, Born ; *S.* Björn, Berns ; *Fl.* Burny ; *D.B.* Barn, Beorn, Burn, Bern ; p.n.
BURNSIDE. A loc. n., Westmd.
BURR. From Burgh ; a loc. n., Lincs, Norf. Or Bure, Belg.
  Prot. ref., Lond. 1687
BURRELL, BURRILL. From Burrell ; a loc. n., Yorks. Or *Fr.* Burel (a little house) ; *G.*, *Dch.*, *Fr.*, *D.B.* Borel ; p.n.
BURRIDGE. A loc. n., Devon
BURRIS. *See* Burrows
BURROWS. A freq. loc. n.
BURSTALL. A loc. n., Suff.
BURT. *N.-Fr.* Berte ; a p.n.
  Rot. Hund. 1272. *See* Bird.
BURTENSHAW. *See* Birkenshaw
BURTHNOT. *See* Arbuthnot
BURTON. A freq. loc. n.
BURWASH. A loc. n., Derbysh., Suss.
BURY. A loc. n., Belg., Lancs, Suff. Or Bourry, Norm.
BUSBY. A loc. n., Yorks
BUSCALL. From Buscel ; a loc. n., Normandy ; *D.B.* Buissell ; a p.n.
  Bushell in Roll of Battell Abbey.
BUSFIELD. *See* Bousfield
BUSH. Bosch, now Bois ; a loc. n., Fland. *S.* Busck ; *D.*, *G.* Busch, Busk ; *Fl.* Bosch ; p.n.
  Bushy in Roll of Battell Abbey. De Bosch, tenant in chief, and Busch (Hertf.), a Saxon tenant in *D.B.* Robert de Buscy in Rot. Obl. et Fin., K. John. Paul Bushe, Bp. of Bristol, 1542. Prot. ref., Lond. 1618.

BUSHBY. From Bushbury ; a loc. n., Staffs.

BUSHELL. *See* Buscall. A Hugt. n., Lond. 1618

BUSICK. From Buseck, a valley of Hesse Darmstadt. A noble German family of great antiquity
There is also a Fr. p.n., Busiquet. Boussac, a Hugt. n., occurs in London in 1685.

BUSKARD. *Fl.* Buysschært; *Dch.* Bosschaart ; *Fr.* Boisard ; *D.B.* de Boscroard (?) ; p.n.

BUSS. *D.*, *Dch.*, *Fl.* Bus ; a p.n.

BUSSEY. *See* Boosey

BUSZARD. From Buzet ; a loc. n. in Flanders. Or *Dch.* Boshart ; *Fl.* Bossaert; *Fr.* La Bussate ; p.n.
Buzard in Roll of Battell Abbey. Bossard, a Prot. ref., Sandwich, 1622. *See* Buskard.

BUTCHER. *D.*, *G.* Boettcher ; *Dch.* Boddekke ; *Fl.* Buker, Buscher ; *D.B.* Boscher; *Fr.* Boucher, Bucher ; p.n. *See* Boucher

BUTLER. From Bottelaere ; a loc. n., Flanders. Ireland, *temp.* Hen. II.
Botelere in Roll of Battell Abbey and Lib. Vit. Dur. Hugo Pincerna, 1066.

BUTLIN. *Fr.* Boutevillaine ; a p.n.

BUTT, BUTTER. *N.* Buttr (short) ; *D.* Butho ; *Dch.* Buter; *Fr.* Buteau ; *G.* Butte, Butter ; *D.B.* Buter, Butor ; p.n. Or *A.S.* Bothere ; a p.n. (warrior - messenger)
Roger But in Rot. Obl. et Fin., K. John.

BUTTANSHAW. *See* Birkenshaw

BUTTERFIELD. From Butterfell ; a loc. n., Cumb.

BUTTERICK. *See* Butterwick

BUTTERWICK. A loc. n., Lincs, Yorks

BUTTERWORTH. A loc. n., Lancs

BUTTERY. *N.-Fr.* Boteri ; a p.n., 1180
Buteri, Butery, Rot de Lib.

BUTTEVANT. A loc. n., co. Cork

BUTTIFANT. *See* Buttevant

BUTTLE. *See* Buddle. Butel, a Hugt. n., Lond. 1685

BUTTON. *Fr.* Boutin, Bouton, Butant ; p.n. *See* Budden

BUTTRUM. *D.B.* de Bertram ; a loc. n.
In Roll of Battell Abbey.

BUTTS. *Fl.* Budts, Buedts ; p.n. Fam. n. of Budd

BUXTON. A loc. n., Derbysh., Norf.

BUZZARD. *See* Buszard

BYARD. *See* Boyd

BYAS. From Biars ; a loc. n., Normandy. Or Biez, Belg. ; *Fr.* Bias ; a p.n.

BYE. A loc. n., Dorset. Or *see* Bee

BYERS. *See* Byas

BYFIELD. A loc. n., Northants

BYFORD. A loc. n., Heref.

BYGOTT. *Fr.* Bigot ; *Dch.* Biko ; p.n. *See* Bagot
D.B. Bigot, a tenant in chief. Bigot in Roll of Battell Abbey.

BYGRAVE. A loc. n., Herts

BYLES. From Bueil ; a loc. n., France. *G.* Beil ; *Fl.* Byl, Buyl ; *Dch.* Buijl ; p.n. A Hugt. n.

BYNOE. *See* Baines

BYRNE. From the Irish O'Broin ; a p.n. *See* Burns

BYRNEY. *See* Birnie

BYROM. From Byram ; a loc. n., Yorks

BYRON. From Biron ; a loc. n., Guienne, France. Or Buron, Norm.
D.B. de Burun, tenant in chief. Robert de Burun in Rot. Obl. et Fin., K. John. Biroune in Roll of Battell Abbey.

BYRTH. From Berth ; a loc. n., Heref. Or *Fl.* Berth ; a p.n. Or *see* Byworth

BYWATER
Radulph juxta aquam occurs A.D. 1170, Empingham, Rutl.

BYWORTH. A loc. n., Suss.

C

CABLE. *G.* Kabel; a p.n. *See* Keble

CABORN, CABOURNE. A loc. n., Lincs

CACKETT. *A.S.* Cœc; *Dch.* Cachet; a p.n. Dim. (a key)

CADBURY. A loc. n., Devon

CADDELL. From the Welsh Caddell (warlike). *Fr.* Cadel; a p.n.

CADDICK. From Catwick; a loc. n., Yorks

CADDIE, CADDY, CADE. *A.S.* Cadda, Ceada; *chad*, for *had* (war); *G.* Kade; *S.* Kadier; p.n.; *D.B.* Cœdd; a p.n.; Chad (?). Or *Fr.* Cadet. A Hugt. n., (younger)

CADEBY. A loc. n., Yorks

CADEY, CADY. *See* Caddy

CADGE. *See* Cage

CADOGAN. Welsh Cadwgan (war)

Kydwgan, Lord of Radnor, Hen. I.

CADWELL. *See* Caldwell

CAFFIN. *Fr.* Chaufin; a p.n. *N.-Fr.* Cauvin (a little calf). *See* Choffin

CAFFREY. From the Irish O'Craffrey, M'Caffrey; p.n.

CAGE. *N.* Kaggi, n.n. (a keg); *A.S.* Ceagga; *G.* Kage; *Dch.* Kagie, Keg, Keja; p.n. Or *see* Kay

CAHAN. *See* Caine

CAIGER. *See* Cage

CAIN, CAINE. From Cahaignes; a loc. n., Normandy. *Fr.* Cahen; *D.B.* de Cahainges. Or Irish O'Cathain; p.n.

W. de Kaynes in Rot. Obl. et Fin., K. John.

CAIRNS. From the Irish O'Cairn; a p.n.; *carn* (a heap, a little hill)

CAISEY. From the Irish Macasey; *eathaiseach* (valiant)

CAKE. *See* Keck

CAKEBREAD. Cæcbrid (bright key). Or *N. Fr.* Calcebued; a p.n.

CALCOTT. A loc. n., Wilts

CALCUTT. A loc. n., Warw.

CALDECOTE. A loc. n., Lincs, Monmouth, Northants, etc.

CALDECOURT. *See* Caldecot

CALDER. A loc. n., Lanark

CALDERBANK. A loc. n., Lanark

CALDERWOOD. A loc. n., East Kilbride, Scotl.

CALDWELL. A loc. n., Derbysh., Yorks, etc. *See* Coldwell

CALEY. *See* Cayley

CALL. From M'Call. *A.S.* Cal, Calla; *F.* Kalle; p.n. (a man)

CALLAGAN. Irish O'Callagan; *colgan* (?) (swordsman)

CALLANDER. A loc. n., Perth

CALLARD. *Fl.* Callaert, Callewaert; p.n.; *A.S.* cal - weard (man warden)

CALLIER. *See* Colyer

CALLIFORD. From Callford; a loc. n., Suff.

CALLIS. From Caleys; a loc. n., Picardy

CALLOW. A loc. n., Worcest.

CALLOWAY. *See* Galloway

CALLUM. *Gael.* (dove)

CALSTOCK. A loc. n., Cornw.

CALTHROP. From Colthrop; a loc. n., Glos. Or Calthorpe

CALTHORPE. A loc. n., Derbysh., Lincs, Norf.

CALVER. *N.* Kálfr (a calf); *G.* Kalfar; *D.B.* Calvus; p.n. Or from Calver (*D.B.* Caluore); a loc. n., Derbysh. Calfe, Flem. ref., Lond. 1618

CALVERLEY. A loc. n., Yorks

CALVERT. From Calbert; a loc. n., Norm. *A.S.* Ceolweard (keel, ship-guard); *Fl.* Callewaert; p.n.

CAMERON. A loc. n., Fife

CAMFIELD. From Camville; a loc. n., Norm.

CAMIDGE, CAMMIDGE. *See* Cammish and Gammage

CAMM. From Cam; a loc. n., Glos. Or Welsh *cam* (crooked)

CAMMELL. From Campell; a loc. n., Norm. Or *see* Gamble

CAMMISH. Manx, Cammaish. From MacHamish (James's son)

CAMP. From Campe; a loc. n., Norm. Or *N.* Kampi; n.n. (a bearded person); *S.* Camp, Kemp; *D.*, *Dch.* Kemp; *G.* Kampe. Or *A.S.* Camp, Cæmpa (champion); p.n. A Hugt. n., Lond. 1618

CAMPAIN. *D.*, *Dch.* Campagne, Campen; p.n. Or *see* Campion

CAMPBELL. *N.-Fr.* de Camville (de Campo Bello). Or *see* Gamble

CAMPION. *N.-Fr.* p.n.
> W. C. in Norm. 1184; Geof. C. in Eng. 1194. Rot. Cur. Reg. Flem. Prot. ref., Norwich, 1622. *See* Champion.

CANDY. From Candé; a loc. n. near Blois, Norm.

CANE, CANEY. *See* Caine

CANHAM. From Cainham; a loc. n., Salop

CANLER. From Cantley (?); a loc. n., Yorks

CANN. From Canne; a loc. n., Belg. Or Can, Norm.; *D.* Kann; *Fl.* Cahn; *G.* Kann; *Dch.* Canne, Kan; p.n.
> W. de Kanne and Ric. de Can in Rot. Obl. et Fin., K. John.

CANNELL. From Chenel; a loc. n., Norm. Also the Manx form of the Celtic MacConaill; Irish M'Connell. Canwell; a loc. n., Staffs

CANNER. *See* Cann

CANNON. *Fr.* Canonne; a p.n.; *N.-Fr. chanoine* (a canon)

CANNOT. *Fl.* Canoodt; *Fr.* Carnot; *N.* Knútr; *D.* Knud, Knuth; p.n. *See* Nutt

CANT. *See* Cannot and Gaunt

CANTER. *N.-Fr.* Cantor; a p.n. (a singer)
> Gaufrid C., Norm. 1180. Christn. le Chaunter, Rot. Hund. 1272.

CANTERFORD. From Kentford; a loc. n., Suff.

CANTLOW. From Canteleu; a loc. n., Normandy
> In Roll of Battell Abbey.

CANTRELL. *N.-Fr.* Cantrel, Chantrell; p.n. Also a Hugt. n., Lond. 1618
> William Chanterell, *temp.* K. John.

CANTWELL. *See* Canwell

CAPEL. From La Chapelle; a loc. n., Norm., Suff., N. Wales, S. Wales. Also a Hugt. n. Lond. 1618

CAPERN. *N.-Fr.* Capron; a p.n.
> Caperoun in Roll of Battell Abbey.

CAPES. *N.-Fr.* Cape, Capes; p.n.
> W. de Capes, 1199.

CAPON. *Fl.* Capon, Capen; *Dch.* Capoen; p.n.

CAPPER. *N.* Kappi; *Fl.* Cappe; *Dch.* Kappers; p.n. (a hero)

CAPPS. *See* Capes

CAPSTICK. From Copestake; a loc. n.

CARD. *A.S.* Carda; a p.n. (guard); *Fr.* Cardes. A Hugt. n., Lond. 1681

CARDELL. *See* Cardwell

CARDEN. From Carwarden; a loc. n., Ches. *D.B.* Cardun. Also *N.-Fr.* Cardon or Cardun; a p.n.

CARDEW. *See* Carthew or Cordeaux. Hugt. n., Lond. 1622

CARDIN. *See* Carden

CARDINAL. *Dch.* Cardinaal; *Fl.* Cardinael, Cardinal; p.n. *See* p. 12

CARDWELL. From Cardeville; a loc. n., Norm.

CARDY. *See* Cardin

CARELESS. From St Karles de Parcy; a loc. n., Norm. *Fr.* Carliez; *Fl.* Carles; *Span.* Carlos; p.n. From Carolus (Charles)

CAREW. A loc. n., Pembrokesh.
CAREY. *See* Carry
CARFRAE. A loc. n., Scotl.
CARGILL. A loc. n., Perth
CARLETON. A loc. n., Lancs, Yorks
CARLEY. *N.* Karli (carle, churl);
D. Carli ; *Dch.* Carlee ; *A.S.*
Carle ; p.n.
CARLILL. From Carlisle
CARLINE. *N.* Kerling (a woman);
S. Carling ; p.n. Or Carling ; a
loc. n., Germ.
CARLYLE. *See* Carlill
CARLYON. A loc. n., Cornw. Also
Carlehon, Bretagne, France
CARMAN. *A.S.* Carman ; *Fr.* Car-
manne ; *garman* (spearman) ; p.n.
CARMICHAEL. A loc. n., Lanark.
Or Cara Michil (a friend of St
Michael)
CARMODY. *See* Kermode
CARNABY. A loc. n., Yorks
CARNE. From Carn ; a loc. n.,
Cornw. Or *N. - Fr.* Caron,
Charun ; p.n.
CARNEGIE. A loc. n., Forfar
CARNELLEY. From Carnelles; a loc.
n., Norm. Or Irish M'Annally ;
a p.n.
CARNSEW, CARNZU. *Fl.* Carnseuw ;
a p.n.
CARON. *Fr.* Hugt. n., Lond. 1687
CARPENTER. *N.-Fr.* Carpentarius ;
a p.n.
Durand C., a t. in chief, *B.D.* Norf.
CARPUE. *Fr.* Carpiaux (young
carp) ; a p.n.
CARR. *N.* Kárr (curly hair); *S.*
Karr ; *G.* Karo ; *Dch.* Kar; p.n.;
A.S. Car. Or *see* Keir
CARRATT, CARRITT, CAROTTE ; *Fr.*
Carette ; a p.n. Dim. of Carr
CARRELL. From Caril; a loc. n.,
near Lisieux, Norm.
CARRICK. From the Irish *carraice*
(a rock). *See* Creak
CARRINGTON. A loc. n., Notts
CARROLL. From the Irish O'Cearb-
hoil, M'Carroll ; p.n.

CARRON. A loc. n., Stirling
CARRUTHERS. A loc. n., Dumfries
CARRY. *N.* Kári (the god of the
winds), *Fr.* Carré, Karré ; p.n.
Or Irish M'Carrie. Hugt. n.,
Lond. 1685. *See* Carr
CARSBOULT. *A.S.* Garbeald ; a
p.n. (spearbold)
CARSLAKE. A loc. n., Somers. Or
Carsac, Norm.
CARSLEY. From Kersley or Curs-
ley ; a loc. n., Warw.
CARSTAIRS. A loc. n., Lanark
CARSTON. *F., Dch.* Karsten; *D.*
Carsten; p.n. (from Christian).
See Casson
CARSWELL. A loc. n., Berks
CARTER. From the Irish M'Carter,
arta (great), M'Carthur, Mac-
Arthur. Or Castres ; a loc. n.,
France. Or *A.S.* Carda ; a p.n.
(guard) ; *G.* Kartte ; *N.-Fr.* Car-
tier ; p.n. Hugt., Lond. 1618
Ralph C. held a fief from the See of
Worcester, 13th cent. Caretarius
in Winch. *D.B.*
CARTERLEY. From Chartley. *D.B.*
Certelie ; a loc. n., Staffs.
CARTHEW. A loc. n., Cornw. Or
Catheux; a loc. n., Normandy
CARTHY. From the Irish Mac
Carthaigh ; a p.n. (*Carthac*, the
founder of a city). Or *see* Carter
CARTLEDGE. From Cartlett (?) ; a
loc. n., Glos.
CARTMELL. From Cartmel ; a loc.
n., Lancs
CARTWRIGHT. From Cauterêts ; a
loc. n., Norm. Or Catherick,
Yorks
Cartrait, Cateray in Roll of Battell
Abbey. De Ceterith, a tenant in
chief in *D.B.* De Cartray in Rot.
Obl. et Fin., K. John.
CARVELL. *N.-Fr.* De Carville ; a
p.n.
CARVER. *See* Calver
CARWARDINE. From Carwarden ;
a loc. n., Ches.
CARWITHEN. A loc. n., Cornw.

CASBOLT. *See* Carsboult
CASBURN. A loc. n. *See* Chase
CASE. *A.S.* Casa; *D.* Casse, Kasse; *Dch.* Kas, Käss, Caisse; *Fl.* Cas, Casse, Casy; p.n.; De la Case. Hugt. n.
CASEBOW. *Fr.* Cassabois; a p.n. (wood-breaker)
CASEMENT. *Fl.* Casman; a p.n.
CASEY. From the Irish *cathaiseach* (valiant). Or *see* Case
CASHMORE. From Cashmoor; a loc. n., Dorset
CASSELL. A loc. n., Flanders
     Hugo de C., Lond. 1130, Pip. Rolls.
CASSIDY. Irish p.n. (treasurer)
CASSON. *F.* Kassen, from Christian; *i.e.*, Kristjan, Kersten, Karsten, Karsen, Kasjen, Kassen; *D.* Kasten; *S.* Cassen; *Dch.* Carsten; *Fl.* Kastan, Casen, Cason; p.n.
CASTLE. *N.* - *Fr.* Castel; a p.n.
     Ino. de Castro, 1272, Rot. Hund.
CATCHPOLE, CATCHPOOL. From Cageypole; a loc. n., Dorset. Or Caterpole, Suff.
CATCHSIDE. From Catcherside; a loc. n., Northumbd.
CATER. *Fr.* Cattreux; a p.n.
     Walter Cater occurs in a deed A.D. 1076, Harl. MS. John de Catara, Beswick, Yorks, and Walter Catar his nephew in a deed 1 Steph. Chaitres in Roll of Battell Abbey (?).
CATESBY. A loc. n., Northants
CATFORD. A loc. n., Kent
CATHCART. A loc. n., Lanark
CATHEY. From Cathay; a loc. n., S. Wales. Or *see* Caddy
CATLING. *Fl.* Catelin; p.n. *See* Catt. A dim. Or Castelin; a loc. n., Norm.
CATLOW. *Fr.* Cathelineau (?); a p.n.
CATMORE. A loc. n., Berks
CATMUR. From Catmer; a loc. n., Ess. Or *see* Catmore
CATT. *N.* Köttr (a cat), n.n.; *A.S.* Catta; *N.-Fr.* Le Cat; *D.* Kett; *Dch.* Cate, Kat; *G.* Kathe, Katte; p.n.

CATTEE. *G.* Kathe, Kattey; *Fr.* Chaté; p.n. Or Irish M'Atee (high)
CATTEN. *Dch.* Kattan, Ketting; *S.* Kaeding; p.n.; fam. n. of Catt
CATTERALL. A loc. n., Yorks
CATTERMOLE. *N.* - *Fr.* Quatremeulles (?) *Dch.* Cattermolen; p.n.
CATTERSON. From Catherston; a loc. n., Dorset. Or *see* Cater
CATTLE. From Cattall; a loc. n., Yorks. Or *Fr.* Catel, Châtel; *N.-Fr.* Du Chastel; p.n.
CATTLEY. From Chatterley; a loc. n., Staffs
CATTY. *See* Cattee
CAUDLE. A loc. corr. of Caldwell, Derbysh. Also *N.-Fr.* Caldell or Caudel; p.n.
     W. C. Camb. 1272, Rot. Hund.
CAULFIELD. *N.-Fr.* de Calvel or Caville; p.n.
     Jas. Calfhill, Calvel, or Calfield, Bp. of Worcs. 1506
CAUNT. *See* Gaunt
CAUSTON. A loc. n., Warw.
CAUTLEY. From Caughley; a loc. n., Salop
CAUX. A loc. n., France
CAVE. A loc. n., Yorks.
     The family of De Cave was seated here for eleven generations from the Conquest.
CAVELL. *See* Caulfield
CAVENDISH. A loc. n. (a manor), Suff.
     It was assumed by the Norman knight, Gernon de Montfichet; *D.B.* Gernon. Gernun in Rot. Obl. et Fin.
CAVILL. From Cavill; a loc. n., Yorks. Or *see* Caulfield
CAWDWELL. *See* Caldwell
CAWKER. *N.* Kolka; a n.n. (coalblack); *D.* Kalckar; *G.* Kalke; *Fl.* Caukens; *Dch.* Kalker; p.n.
CAWLEY. *See* Macaulay
CAWS, CAWSE. *See* Caux
     Robert Cause, Gilbert de Cause, John de Cauz in Rot. Obl. et Fin., K. John.

CAWSTON, A loc. n., Norf., Warw.

CAWTHORNE. A loc. n., Yorks

CAXTON. A loc. n., Camb.

CAYLESS. *See* Careless

CAYLEY. From Cailli; a loc. n., Norm. *Fr.* Caillet; a p.n.

Hugh de Cuilly was Lord of Orby, Norf., *temp.* Edw. I. De Cailly in Rot. Obl. et. Fin. A Hugt. n., Sandwich, 1622.

CECIL. *Fr.* Cécile, Secelle; p.n.

Ancient spelling Sicelle, Cyssel. From St Cécille, or Sysseele, both loc. n. in Flanders.

CHACEMOOR. From Chackmore; a loc. n., Bucks

CHADD. *N.-Fr.* Cadd; *A.S.* Ceadda, Cedda; p.n.; *chad* for *had* (war); Celtic *cath, cad* (battle)

CHADWICK. A loc. n., Lancs

CHAFFE, CHAFFEY, CHAFY. *A.S.* Caefi, Coifi (active, bold). Or *N.-Fr.* Le Chauve; a p.n. (the bald); *Fr.* Chavée; p.n.; Chavet. Hugt. n., Lond. 1682

CHAFFER, CHAFFERS. From Chevrières; a loc. n., Norm.

R. de Cheveriis, Norm. 1195; W. de Caveres, Salop, 1272, Rot. Hund.

CHALCRAFT. *See* Calcraft

CHALK. A loc. n., Kent

CHALLACOMBE. A loc. n., Devon

CHALLICE, CHALLIS. *G.* Callas, Kallesse, Kalisch; *Dch.* Kalis; *Fl.* Calis; p.n. *See* Callis

CHALLINGWORTH. A loc. n., Glost.

CHAM. *See* Camp

CHAMBERLAIN. *N.-Fr.* Chambellan, Chamberlein; p.n. Hugt. n., Lond. 1618

CHAMBERS. From Chambray (?); a loc. n., Normandy. Or Camerarius (a chamberlain). A Hugt. n., Lond. A.D. 1618

De Cambray, De Camera, and Camerarius in Rot. Obl. et Fin., K. John.

CHAMLEY. From Chamilly or Chambly; a loc. n., Normandy

CHAMNEY. From Chamneis or Champneis, the ancient district of Champagne. *D.B.* Chemarnhee

In Roll of Battell Abbey. Champaney in Rot. Obl. et Fin.

CHAMPION. *Fr.* p.n.; a loc. n., Flanders

CHANCE. *Fr.* Chansay; a p.n.

W. de Chanes in Rot. Obl. et Fin., K. John.

CHANNON. A loc. n., Devon

CHANTER. *See* Canter

CHANTLE. *See* Gentle

CHAPLIN. *N.-Fr.* Capelen; a p.n.

W. Capellanus, Norm. 1180. *D.B.* 1086; York, 1202; Sleford, Lincs, 1443.

CHAPMAN. *See* Coopman

CHARD. A loc. n., Somers.

CHARITY. *Fr.* Charité; a p.n.

De Caritate in Rot. Obl. et Fin.

CHARLES. *Fr.* p.n.

CHARLEY. *Fr.* Charlet, Charlier; p.n.

CHARLTON. A loc. n., Berks, Glos., Kent. Oxf., Salop, Somers, Suss.

CHARNLEY. A loc. n., Leics

CHARRINGTON. From Charentonne; a loc. n., Normandy

CHASE. *D.* Jess; *Fl.* Jesse; *Dch.* Jes; *G.* Jesche; p.n. *See* Cheese

CHASTEN, CHASTENEY, CHASTY. *Fr.* Chastaigner. A Hugt. n., Lond. 1687

CHATBURN. A loc. n., Yorks

CHATER. *See* Chatto

CHATFIELD. A loc. n., Suss.

CHATT. *See* Chadd

CHATTAWAY. From Chitway; a loc. n., Wilts. Or *A.S.* Catwa; a p.n.; *catwig* (victorious in war)

CHATTERIS. A loc. n., Camb.

CHATTERLEY. A loc. n., Staffs

CHATTERTON. From Chadderton; a loc. n., Lancs

CHATTIN. *Fr.* Chattaine. A Hugt. n., Lond. 1618. *See* Chatwin

H

CHATTO. From Chatou; a loc. n., France. *Fr.* Chateau; *Dch.* Katto; *Fl.* Katto; p.n. *See* Chadd

CHATWIN. *See* Chetwynd

CHAYTOR. From Chatres; a loc. n., Norm.

CHEALES. From Cheal; a loc. n., Lincs

CHEAVIN. *See* Sheavyn

CHECKLAND. From Chachland; a loc. n., Scotl.

CHECKLEY. A loc. n., Staffs

CHEEK. *See* Chick

CHEESE. *A.S.* Cissa; *Fr.* Tsjisse; *Dch.* Chijs; p.n.; *gis* (a hostage) Chese in Hund. Rolls.

CHEESMAN. *A.S.* Gislmund; a p.n. (hostage protector)

CHEESWORTH. From Chisworth; a loc. n., Derbysh.

CHEESWRIGHT. *See* Cheesworth

CHEETHAM. From Chidham; a loc. n., Suss.

CHEFFINS. *A.S.* Ceofa; a p.n.; Ciwing; a fam. n. Or *N.-Fr.* *chevin* (a chub)

CHELL. A loc. n., Staffs. Or Chelles, France

CHENEREY. From St Ceneri; a loc. n., Norm.

CHENEY. Chênée, Chiny; loc. n., Flanders; Quesnay, Norm. *Fr.* Chesnais, Chesnée; *D.B.* Chenisis, Chenin; p.n.
Cheyne, Cheines, Cheyni in Roll of Battell Abbey. Robert de Chesney Bishop of Lincoln, 1147; Richard Cheyney, Bishop of Lincoln, 1562. William de Chesne in Rot. Obl. et Fin., K. John, 1208. *See* Cheyne.

CHERITON. A loc. n., Devon

CHERRY. *N.-Fr.* De Cerisy; a p.n.

CHESELDEN. From Chiseldon; a loc. n., Wilts

CHESLYN. *See* Cheselden

CHESNEY, CHESTNEY. *See* Chasteney

CHESSELL. *G.* Jessel; a p.n. Dim. *See* Cheese

CHESSON. *See* Jesson

CHESTERFIELD. A loc. n., Derbysh.

CHESTERTON. A loc. n., Camb.

CHETEL. *N.* Ketel (a kettle); *D.B.* Chetel; p.n.

CHETWODE. A loc. n. (a manor), Bucks

CHETWYND. A loc. n., Salop Held by De Verlai, 1086.

CHEVELEY. A loc. n., Camb.

CHEVERTON. From Chevington; a loc. n., Northbd., Worcest.

CHEW. A loc. n., Somers. Or *A.S.* Cheawa; a p.n. (chewed) (?)

CHEYNE. *See* Cheney

CHICK. From Chich; a loc n., Ess. Or *A.S.* Cich; a p.n.; *N. gygr* (a giant); *N.-Fr cec, chike*

CHICKALL. From Chicknall; a loc. n., Ess.

CHICKEN. *N.* Kikini (?); a n.n.; *A.S.* Cich; *Old G.* Ghikin; p.n.; *N. gygr* (?) (a giant)
W. Chikin in Rot. Obl. et Fin., K. John.

CHIDDICK. *See* Chadwick

CHIDLEY. From Chudleigh; a loc. n., Devon

CHIETHAM. *See* Cheetham

CHILD. From Schilde; a loc. n., Belg. Or *N.* Skjöldr; *D.* Skjold; *D.B.* Cild, Cilt; *Fl.* Child; *G.* Schild; *Dch.* Schilt; p.n (a shield). Or perhaps from *A.S. hild* (war), the aspirate often changing into *c*

CHILDERS. *A.S.* Cildas; fam. or tribal n.; *Dch.*, *Fl.* Schilders; a p.n. *See* Child

CHILDS. *See* Childers

CHILLCOTT. A loc. n., Somers.

CHILLEY. *N.* Gilli; *A.S.* Ghile, Gil, Gilo; *Fr.* Gillé, Gillet, Gilliet; a p.n. (servant)

CHILLINGWORTH. From Kilworth (Killingworth); a loc. n., Leics

CHILLINTON. From Chillington; a loc. n., Somers.

CHILLYSTONE. From Chellaston; a loc. n., Derbysh.

CHILMAID. *A.S.* Ceolmod ; a p.n. (ship courage)

CHILMAN. *A.S.* Ceolmund ; a p.n. (ship protector); *G.* Killmann ; *D.* Kielman ; p.n.

CHILTON. A loc. n., Berks, Suff., Somers.

CHILVERS. A loc. n., Warw.

CHIMLEY. *See* Cholmondeley

CHING. *A.S.* Cyne ; a p.n. (royal)

CHINNEREY. *See* Chenerey

CHIPCHACE. A loc. n., Northbd.

CHIPP. *A.S.* Ceapa, Cyppa ; *D.* Kib (?) ; p.n. (a merchant)

CHIPPENDALE. From Chipnall (?) a loc. n., Salop

CHIPPERFIELD. A loc. n., Herts

CHISHOLM. A loc. n., Inverness

CHISNALL. *Fr.* Chesnell (?) ; a p.n. (a caterpillar)

CHISSELL. *Fr.* Choiseuil (?) ; a p.n. (a form of *N. gisl* (a hostage (?))

CHISWELL. From Chishall (?) ; a loc. n., Ess.

CHITTAM. *See* Cheetham

CHITTENDEN. From Chittingstone ; a loc. n., Kent

CHITTOCK. From Chideock ; a loc. n., Dorset

CHITTY. *N.-Fr.* Cette ; *A.S.* Cyddi, Cyta ; a p.n. ; *Dch.* Chits ; *D.B.* Chit ; p.n. (a striver). *See* Kiddy Rot. Hund. 1272.

CHIVERS. From La Chievere ; a loc. n., Norm. Or *see* Chilvers

CHOAT. From Chute ; a loc. n. in Wilts. Or *Fl.* Jot (?) ; a p.n.

CHOFFIN. *Fr.* Chauvin ; a p.n. (bald). A Hugt. n., Lond. 1684. *See* Caffin

CHOLMELEY. *See* Cholmondeley

CHOLMONDELEY. A loc. n. (a manor), Ches. *D.B.* Calmundelai

CHOPE. *See* Jope

CHORLTON. A loc. n., Lancs

CHOULES. *A.S.* Ceola ; *Dch.* Jaulus (?) ; p.n. (ship man)

CHOWLER. *See* Choules

CHREES. From Chris, a dimin. of Christopher (?)

CHRIMES. *See* Grimes

CHRISTIAN. *A.S.* Cristthegn, Christthin ; *Fl.* Christaen ; *Dch.* Christan ; *S.* Christen ; *G.* Christian ; p.n. (a soldier of Christ

CHRISTIE. A p.n. for Christopher or Christian.

CHRISTOPHERSON. *S.* Kristofferson ; a p.n.

CHUBB. *See* Jubb

CHUBBOCK. Dimin. of Chubb

CHUCK. From Choques ; a loc. n., Fland. Or *G.* Schuch ; a p.n. (shy)

CHUDLEIGH. A loc. n., Devon

CHUGG. *A.S.* Cug ; a p.n. *See* Chuck. Or *G.* Schüge ; a p.n. (shy)

CHUMLEY. *See* Cholmondeley

CHURCH. Atte Cherche, Court of Husting, 1258

CHURCHER. From Churcham (?) ; a loc. n., Glost.

CHURCHILL. *N.-Fr.* de Curcelle ; a p.n. From Courcelles ; a loc. n., France and Belg.

De Corcelles, a t. in chief in *D.B.*

CHURTON. A loc. n., Ches.

CHUSEWORTH. *See* Cheesworth

CHUTTER. *A.S.* Cuda, Cuta, Cutha, Guda, Gutha, *gúd* (war) ; *G.* Chudy (?) ; p.n.

CINNAMON. *See* Symonds

CIRCUIT. *See* Sirkett

CIVILL. *Fr.* Civiel ; a p.n. (polite). Or *see* Saville

CLABOD. *Fl.* Clabots ; a p.n. (?)

CLABON. *Fr.* Cléban ; a p.n.

CLACK. *N.* Klökkr (bending, pliable); *Dch.* Kloek ; *A.S.* Clac ; p.n.

CLAMP. *See* Clampett

CLAMPETT. From Clampitt ; a loc. n., Cornw.

CLAPCOTT. A loc. n., Berks

CLAPP. *N.* Klápr (?) (a rough box); *D.* Klepsch; *S.* Klop; *Dch.* Klapp; *A.S.* Clapa; p.n.

CLARABUT. *N.-Fr.* Clarebald (brightly-bold); *Fl.* Clairbaut, Clerebaut; p.n. Prot. ref., Sandwich, 1622

CLARE. A loc. n., Cornw., Suff. Or Clères, France. *See* St Clair

CLARICOAT. From Clerewoodcott (?); a loc. n., Hants

CLARIDGE. From Clarach (?); a loc. n., Cardigan

CLARK. *D.*, *Fl.* p.n. (a cleric). Hugt. n., Norwich, 1622

CLATWORTHY. A loc. n., Somers

CLAUGHTON. A loc. n., Lancs

CLAVERING. A loc. n., Ess.

CLAWSON. *See* Closson

CLAXTON. A loc. n., Dur., Leics, Norf.

CLAYBROUGH. From Claybrooke (?); a loc. n., Leics

CLAYDON. A loc. n., Suff.

CLAYE, CLAY. A loc. n., Normandy. Or *D.* Klee; a p.n. De Clai in Rot. Obl. et Fin.

CLAYPOLE. A loc. n., Lincs

CLAYTON. A loc. n., Lancs., Yorks

CLEAK. *Fr.* Cliquet; a p.n. (millclapper)

CLEARE. *See* Clare

CLEARY. From the Irish *Cleireach* (a clerk)

CLEASBY. A loc. n., Yorks

CLEATHER. From Clitheroe; a loc. n., Lancs

CLEAVER. *Fr.* Clavier; *G.* Kliewer; p.n. (key bearer)

CLEEVE. A loc. n., Glos.

CLEGG. A loc. n., Lancs. Or Manx Clague, contracted from MacLiaigh (the leech's son)

CLEGHORN. A loc. n. near Carstairs, Scotl.

CLELAND. A loc. n., Lanark. *See* Cleveland

CLEMENTS. *Fl.* Clement; *G.* Clemens; p.n. Prot. ref. n., Lond. 1618

CLEMO, CLEMOW. *Fr.* Clement; a p.n.

CLENDINNING. *See* Glendinning

CLENT. A loc. n., Worcest.

CLERIHEW, CLEROWE. From Clairvaux; a loc. n. Aquitaine De Clervaus, 1272, Rot. Pip.

CLERY. *See* Cleary

CLERK. *N.-Fr.* Le Clerc; *Dch.* Clerk; p.n.

CLEVELAND CLIFFLAND. A loc. n., Yorks

CLEVELEY. A loc. n., Lancs

CLEVERDON. From Clevedon; a loc. n., Somers. Or Cleverton, Wilts

CLEVERLEY. *See* Cleveley

CLEWER. A loc. n., Berks

CLEWORTH. From Clayworth; a loc. n., Notts, Somers

CLIBRAN. *See* below

CLIBURN. A loc. n., Westmd.

CLICK. *G.* Klick; a p.n. *See* Cleak

CLIFF. A loc. n., Yorks, etc. De Clif, in Rot. Obl. et Fin.

CLIFFORD. A loc. n., Glos., Heref., Yorks

CLIFT. *D.* Klifoth; a p.n.

CLIFTON. A loc. n., Beds, Derbysh., Lancs, Notts, Somers, Staffs, Warw., Yorks

CLIMANCE. *See* Clements

CLIMO. *A.S.* Clima; a p.n. *See* Clemo

CLIMPSON. (Clementson (?)). *See* Clements

CLINCKETT. *Dch.* Klinkert; a p.n.

CLINGO. *G.* Klinger; *S.* Klinga; p.n. (a ringer, or a swordsman)

CLINTON. From Glinton; a loc. n., Northants

CLIPSTON. A loc. n., Northants, Notts

CLISBY. *See* Cleasby

CLIXBY. A loc. n., Lincs

CLOAKE, CLOAKIE. *Fr.* Cloquet; a p.n. (bell-flower). Clocke, a Hugt. n., Lond. 1618. Or *see* Clack

CLOD, CLODD. From St Claude, near Blois, Norm. Or *A.S.* Hlōd, Hlōth; p.n. (loud, famous)

CLOONEY, CLOWNEY. *See* Clunie.

CLOSE. Prot. ref. n., Lond. 1618. *See* Clowes

CLOSSON. *S.* Klason; *G., Dch.* Clauson; p.n. From Nikolaus. Prot. ref. n., Lond. 1618

CLOTHIER. *A.S.* Hlothhere; *Fr.* Chlother, Clotaire; p.n. Clothar, the name of a Frankish king. *Clod* for *loth* (fame); *hari* (warrior)

CLOUDESLEY. A loc. n., Warw.

CLOUDSDALE. From Clydesdale; a loc. n., Lanark

CLOUCH. A loc. n., Yorks. *N.* *Klofi*, a cleft or rift in a hill. Or from the Irish *cloch*, a stone

CLOUT. *D,* Kloth; *Dch.* Kloot, Kluit; p.n. *See* Clodd

CLOUTING. *G.* Klatting; *Dch.* Cloetingh; *Fl.* Cloeten; p.n. Descendants of Kloth

CLOVER. *N.* Klaufi (?) (awkward); *Dch.* Kloover; *D.* Klüver; p.n.

CLOW. *See* Cluff

CLOWES. Dimin. of Niklaus; *F.* Klás; *D.* Kloos, Klose; *Fl.* Claus, Cloes, Close; *Dch.* Kloos, Klous; *G.* Klaus, Klaas, Klaws, Klos, Klose; p.n.

CLUBB, CLUBBE. *A.S.* Cloppa; *G.* Kloebb, Klobe, Klober, Klupsch; *Dch.* Clob, Klop; *Fl.* Clop; p.n. (a loud speaker (?))

CLUCAS. From M'Lucas (a Manx name). Celtic MacLucais, the son of Luke

CLUCKIE. From Macluckie. *See* Luckey

CLUER. *See* Clewer

CLUES. *Dch.* Clüjs; a p.n. Or *see* Clowes

CLUFF. *See* Clough

CLULOW. Welsh Lleulu (?) (light)

CLUNE. From Clun; a loc. n., Salop. Or Irish M'Clune, *clones* (meadows)

CLUNIE. A loc. n., Perth

CLUSBY. *See* Gillespie

CLUSE. *See* Clowes

CLUTTEN. *See* Clutton

CLUTTERBUCK. A Flem. ref. n.; a loc. n. *A.S. hluttor beck*; *G.* *lauter-bach* (clearbrook)

Cloerterbooke was Sheriff of Glos. in 1586.

CLUTTON. A loc. n., Ches., Somers

CLYMA, CLYMO. *See* Clemo

CLYNE. A loc. n., Scotl. Or *D., G., Dch.* Klein; a p.n. (small)

CLYST. A loc. n., Devon

COACHAFER. *Fl.* Cauchefer; a p.n.; *Fr. cauchevis* (?) (a crested wren)

COATES. A loc. n., Edinbgh., Yorks

COBB. *N.* Kobbi, dimin. of Jakob. *A.S.* Cobba; *S.* Kobbs; *Dch.* Kop; *G.* Kobe, Kober, Kopp, Kopper; p.n.

Cobb in Rot. Obl. et Fin.

COBBETT, COBETT. Dimin. of Kobbi (Jakob); *Dch.* Cobet; *Fl.* Cobbaert; *G.* Kobitz; p.n. Or from Coubet; a loc. n., Norm. *See* Cobb

Hugo Coubite, Norm. 1180; Suff. 1340.

COBBLE, COBLE. *S.* Cobel; *Fl.* Copal; *G.* Kopple; p.n. *See* Cobbold

COBBLEDICK. From Coppledyke or Coupledyke; a loc. n., Lincs. Or Koppeldijk; a *Dch.* loc. n.

Hund. Rolls, Johann de Cupledick, Test. de Nev. Rob. de Cubbledick.

COBBOLD. *A.S.* Godbeald, Godbold, Godebold; p.n. (Goth prince or bold Goth)

COBLEY. A loc. n., Worcest.

COBON. From Coburn, a contraction of Cockburn

COCHRANE. A loc. n., Renfrew

COCK. *D.* Cock; *A.S.* Cocca;
Fr. Cocq; *Dch.* Kok; *G.* Koch;
S. Kock; *D.B.* Coc.; p.n.

Cocus in Rot. Obl. et Fin., K. John. As a surname it is frequent in Cornwall, so is probably derived from *B. coch* (red)

COCKAYNE. *See* Cocking. Or *Fr.*
Cocagne; *Dch.* Kocken; p.n.
Fam. n. of Cock

COCKBURN. A loc. n., Scotl.

COCKEN. *See* Cockayne

COCKER. *A.S.* Cocca; *Fr.* Cocard,
Coqueau; p.n. *See* Cock. A
Hugt. n., Norwich, 1622

COCKERELL. *Fr.* Cocquerel; a
p.n. From Cocherel; a loc. n.,
Norm. Or Cockerhill, Ches.

Richard Cokerell in Rot. Obl. et Fin.

COCKERHAM. A loc. n., Lancs

COCKERTON. A loc. n., Dur.

COCKETT. *Fl.* Kockaert; a p.n.
Dim. of Cock

COCKIE. *See* Cock

COCKING. A loc. n., Suss.

COCKLE. From Cockhill (?); a loc.
n., Somers. Or Kochel; a loc. n.,
Germ.   Cokele, a Prot. ref.,
Norwich, 1622.

COCKRAM. *See* Cockerham

COCKRILL. *See* Cockerell

COCKS. *See* Cox

COCKSEDGE. From Cockhedge; a
loc. n., Lancs

COCKSHAW. *See* Cockshott

COCKSHOTT. A loc. n., Salop

CODD. *Dch.* Kode; a p.n.

CODD, CODE. *A.S.* Cod, God; p.n.
See Goad. *Dch.* Kode; a p.n.
Hugt. n., 1618

CODEY, CODY. From Codhay; a
loc. n., Devon. Or *see* Codd

CODLING. A loc. n., Dur. Or
dim.

CODNER. From Codnor; a loc. n.,
Derbysh.

CODRINGTON. A loc. n., Glos.

Held by De Cantelupe, 1201.

COE. *Dch.* Coe, Koe; p.n.; *D.*
Koe (?) (a cow)

COFFEE, COFFEY. From the Irish
Cobhthaigh. Or *A.S.* Coifi, Cufa
(bold); *Fr.* Coffé; p.n.

COFFIELD. *See* Corfield

COFFIN. From Couvin; a loc. n.,
Belg. Or Couvain, Norm. *A.S.*
Cofin; a fam. n.; *Fr.* Coffin; a p.n.

COFIELD. *See* Coffield

COGGAN, COGGING. *Fl.* Coghen;
Irish Cogan; p.n.

COGGER. *N.* Kuggi (a cog); *G.*
Cogho; *Dch.* Kogghee; *A.S.*
Cogga; p.n. Coege, a *Fl.* ref.,
Lond. 1618

COGGINS. *See* Coggan

COGHILL. *See* Cargill

COGHLAN. From the Irish O'Coch-
lain; a p.n. (hooded man)

COGMAN. *See* Coggan

COGSWELL. From Coggeshall; a
loc. n., Ess.

COKE. *See* Cock

COKER. A loc. n., Somers.

Held by De Mandeville, 1203

COLBECK. A loc. n., Lincs. Or
Caldebec, Norm.

COLBORNE. *N.* Kolbjörn. *A.S.*
Colbeorn; p.n. (helm-bear)

Colebern, a tenant in chief in *D.B.*

COLBRANT. *A.S.* Colbrand; a p.n.
(helm-sword)

COLBY. From Coleby; a loc. n.,
Lincs, Norf.

COLCLOUGH. A loc. n., Staffs

COLCOMBE. From Challacombe;
a loc. n., Devon. Or Chalcombe,
Northants

COLDHAM. A loc. n., Camb.

COLDRON. *A.S.* Cold, Gold; *Old*
G. Goldrun; *Fr.* Caudron; p.n.
(gold-mystery)

COLDWELL. A loc. n., Northbd.
John Coldwell, M.D., Bp. of Salisbury, 1575.

COLE. *See* Colls
Richard Cole in Rot. Obl. et Fin.,
K. John. Also a Fl. ref., Lond.,
1618.

COLEMAN. *A.S.* Colman; p.n. (charcoal man). *See* Colman
In *D.B.* and Rot. Obl. et Fin. Or from *coll* (a helmet).

COLEMORE. A loc. n., Hants

COLERIDGE. A loc. n., Devon

COLES. *Fl.* Cools; a p.n. *See* Colls

COLGATE. A loc. n., Suss.

COLGAN. From the Irish *colg* (a sword), a swordsman

COLGROVE. A loc. n., Herts

COLK. *Dch.* Kolk *G.* Kalk; p.n. *See* Cawker

COLLACOTT. A loc. n., Devon

COLLAMBELL. From Colomby; a loc. n., Normandy. *D.B.* de Columbels; *Fr.* Colombel; p.n.
In Roll of Battell Abbey.

COLLEGE. From Colwich; a loc. n., Staffs. Or *Fr.* Collige; a p.n.

COLLETT. *Fr.* Collette; a p.n. (collar)

COLLIE, COLLEY. From Cuilly; a loc. n., Norm. *Fr.* Colleye. A Hugt. n., Lond. 1618

COLLIER. *See* Colyer

COLLING. A loc. n., Yorks. *A.S.* fam. n.

COLLINGBOURNE. A loc. n., Wilts

COLLINGRIDGE. From Collingham Bridge (?); a loc. n., Yorks

COLLINGTON. A loc. n., Heref.

COLLINGWOOD. From Callingwood; a loc. n., Staffs

COLLINS. *N.-Fr.* De Colince. From Coulonces; a loc. n., Norm. Or *see* Colling

COLLISHAW. *See* Cowlishaw

COLLS. *N.* Kollr and Kolr (the head); also a pet n. ("my boy"); *S.* Kull; *D.* Koelle; *G.* Kolla, Koller, Kolley, Kohl, Kohler; *Dch.* Koll; *D.B.* Col, Cola, Colo, Cols; *Fl.* Colas, Colles, Colle, Culus; p.n.

COLLYNS. *See* Collins

COLMAN. *N.* Kalman; *A.S.* Colman (helmet-man); *Dch.* Koelman; *G.* Kohlmann; p.n. *See* Colls
John Coleman in Rot. Obl. et Fin., K. John.

COLMER. *See* Colemore

COLOMB. From St Colomb; a loc. n., Cornw. Or Colombier, France

COLPUS. *N.* Kálfr (a calf); *Fl.* Calphas; *G.* Kalbas; *A.S.* Calpus; p.n.

COLQUHOUN. A loc. n., Dumbarton

COLSON. *Fl.* p.n. *See* Colls

COLTON. A loc. n., Lancs, Staffs Yorks

COLVER. *See* Calver

COLVILLE. From Colleville, near Bayeux
Gilb. de C., Suff. 1086.

COLWELL. A loc. n., Northumbd. *See* Colville

COLYER. From Collioure (?); a loc. n., France

COMAN. *Fl.* Coeman; a p.n.

COMBE. A loc. n., Glos.

COMBES, COOMBES. *N.-Fr.* Comes; a p.n.
Rot. Hund. 1272

COMERFORD. From Comberford; a loc. n., Staffs

COMFORT. A loc. n., Cornw. Or *see* Comerford

COMLEY. A loc. n., Salop

COMMERELL. From Comberwell (?); a loc. n., Wilts

COMPER. From Champier (?); a loc. n., Norm.

COMPTON. A loc. n., Dorset, Hants, Somers, Staffs, Wilts

COMYNS. From Comines; a loc. n., Flanders

CONDER, CONDY. *N.-Fr.* Condé; a loc. n., Normandy

CONDUIT. *See* Conder

CONE. From Cosne; a loc. n., France. Or *N.* Konr (noble); *Dch.* Con; *Fl.* Coen; p.n. Or Irish M'Cone

CONGDON. A loc. n., Cornw.

CONGRAVE. *See* Congreve

CONGREVE. A loc. n., Staffs

CONINGHAM. *See* Cunningham

CONINGSBY. A loc. n., Lincs

CONISBEE. *See* Coningsby

CONLEY. From Cononley; a loc. n., Yorks. Or *see* Conolly

CONNEL. Irish Connal; a p.n. (chief's courage)

CONNOR. From the Irish O'Conchobhair; a p.n. (endowed with strength)

CONNORTON. From Conderton (?); a loc. n., Glos.

CONOLLY. From the Irish O'Conghaile; a p.n. (chief courage)

CONQUEST. From Conquet; loc. n., Bretagne

CONWAY. A loc. n., N. Wales

CONYERS. From Coignieres, Isle of France

COOCH. *G.* Kütsch; *Fl.* Couche, *Fr.* Gouche; p.n. *See* Gooch

COOK. *A.S.* Cuc, Cucca; p.n. (quick, lively)

COOKSEY. A loc. n., Worcest.

COOMBE. A loc. n., Cornw., Devon, Hants, etc. Or Irish M'Combe

COOPER. From Cupar; a loc. n., Fife. Or *A.S.* Cuppa (a cup); *Fl.* Kupper; *Dch.* Cuyper; *N.-Fr.* De Cuper, Kooper; p.n. Coup'e in 1327.

COOPMAN. *A.S.* Copman; *Fl.* Coopman; a p.n. (a merchant, dealer)

COOTE. *A.S.* Cut, Cuth; *Fl.* Coet; *Dch.* Koot; *G.* Kutt; p.n. (noted, skilled)

COPE. *N.-Fr.* Coupe; *Dch.* Koop, Kop, Koope; p.n. Rot. Hund. 1272.

COPESTAKE. From Corpusty (?); a loc. n., Norf. *D.B.* Corpestig

COPESTICK. *See* Copestake

COPEMAN. *See* Coopman

COPLAND, COPELAND. *See* Coupland

COPLESTONE. A loc. n., Devon

COPPERTHWAITE. *See* Cowperthwaite

COPPING, COPPINGER, COPPON. *N.* Kaupungr; n.n.; *D.* Koeppen; *S.* Koppang; *Dch.* Koppen; a p.n. (a merchant). Flem. ref., Lond. 1618

COPSEY. *See* Cobb

CORAH. From Corrar; a loc. n., Salop

CORBET. *Fr.* p.n. (raven) Corbet, an under-tenant in *D.B.*, and in Rot. Obl. et Fin., K. John.

CORBY. A loc. n., Cumb., Lincs, Northants. Or Corbie, France; Corbais, Belg.

CORBYN. *N.-Fr.* Corbin; a p.n. (crow) Corbine, in Roll of Battell Abbey, and Corbin under-tenant in *D.B.*

CORCORAN. From the Irish *corcurach* (purple). *See* Cochrane

CORDINGLEY. From Cottingley; a loc. n., Yorks

CORDOCK. *Fr.* Cordeaux; a p.n.

CORDREY. *See* Cowderoy

CORDY. *Fr.* Cordeau; *Dch.* Cordes, Cordia; *G.* Korte; p.n.

CORE. *See* Cory

CORFIELD. A loc. n., Salop *See* Cornfield

CORKE. From Kork; a loc. n., Germ. *D.* Kork; *Dch.* Korch; *Fr.* Corque. Hugt. n., Lond. 1618

CORKHILL. From the Manx MacCorkyll derived from the Scandio-Celtic Macþor-Ketill or Þorkell. Or *see* Cargill

CORNELL. *N.-Fr.* Corniola; *Fl.* Cornehl; p.n.

CORNFIELD. *G.* Kornfeld; a p.n.

CORNFOOT, CORNFORD. *See* Cornforth

CORNFORTH. A loc. n., Dur.

CORNISH. From Cornesse; a loc. n., Belg. Or the county of Cornwall

CORNS. From the Irish Curran

CORNWALL. The county n. Or Cornville, Norm.

CORPE. From Corps; a loc. n., Norm.

CORRINGTON. From Corringdon; a loc. n., Dorset

CORSBY. *See* Cosbey

CORSER. *A.S.* Corsa; *N.Fr.* Corvesar; *G.* Korsawe; p.n. (tormentor (?))

CORY. *N.-Fr.* Coriei; *A.S.* Cari; p.n. Or Irish M'Corry

COSBEY. From Cosby; a loc. n., Leics

COSGRAVE. A loc. n., Northants

COSGROVE. *See* Cosgrave

COSHAM. A loc. n., Hants

COSSEY. From Cossy; a loc. n., Norf.; Coussey, France. Or *N.* Kausi; n.n. (a cat); *D.* Koese; *G.* Kosc, Kosig; *Dch.* Cossa; *Fl.* Cossé; p.n.

COSSHAM. A loc. n., Hants

COSSINGTON. A loc. n., Somers.

COSSINS. *See* Cozens

COSSTICK. *See* Copestick

COSTELLO. From Mac Ostello, descendants of Hostilio de Angulo, settled in Ireland *temp.* Hen. II. Or *G.* Gostelle; *Old G.* Costila; p.n.

COSTERTON. A loc. n., Scotl.

COTCHEIFER. *See* Coachafer

COTES. A freq. loc. n.

COTESWORTH. From Cottesford; a loc. n., Oxf.

COTHAM. A loc. n., Glos., Yorks

COTHER. *See* Cottew. Or Irish M'Cottar

COTON. A loc. n., Northants, Staffs

COTTAM. A loc. n., Lancs, Notts

COTTERELL, COTTERILL. *N.-Fr.* Coterel; a p.n.

COTTEW. *Fr.* Cotteau; *G.*, *Dch.* Kothe; *A.S.* Cotta; p.n. *See* Gotto

COTTINGHAM. A loc. n., Northants, Yorks

COTTLE. *N.-Fr.* Cotel; *Fr.* Coutelle; a p.n.

COTTON. A loc. n., Camb., Suff.

COTTY. *See* Cottew

COUCH. From Coucy; a loc. n., Norm.

COULLING. *See* Cowling

COULSON. A loc. n., Devon

COULSTON. A loc. n., Wilts

COULTHART. *D.* Coulthardt; *Fl.* Colleart; *Dch.* Collard; *A.S.* Colta, Couta; p.n.
Probably from the *N.* Kollotahart, a hart without horns.

COULTON. From Colton; a loc. n., Lancs

COUNSEL. *N.-Fr.* Consel; a p.n.

COUPLAND. A loc. n., Northumbd.

COURAGE. From Curridge; a loc. n., Berks. Or *Fr.* Correges. a Hugt. n.

COURCEY. *Fr.* De Courcy; a p.n.

COURTEEN. From Courtonne, near Caen. Surr. 1130; Ess. 1189

COURTNAY. From Courtenay; a loc. n., France
William de Curtenay, *temp.* K. John. Rot. Obl. et Fin.

COUSENS. *See* Cozens

COUTTS. *See* Cutts

COVEL. *Fr.* Chauvel; a p.n.

COVENTRY. A loc. n., Warw.

COVERDALE. A loc. n., N. Yorks

COVERLEY. *Fr.* Coveliers; a p.n.

COVINGTON. A loc. n., Hunts

COW. *Fr.* Cahu (?); a p.n. (owl). Or *see* Cowie

COWARD. *A.S.* Cuhard (strong, noble). Or from La Couarde, near Rochelle. *Fl.* Couard; *Fr.* Chouard; p.n. A Hugt. n., 1688
De Coarda occurs in Norm. 1198; Roger de Cowert, Rot. Hund. 1272.

COWDEROY, COWDRY. From Cordray; a loc. n., Norm. De Codria, 13th century

COWELL. From the Irish Mac Cathmhoil; a p.n. Or *N.-Fr.* Cauvel

COWES. *D.* Koese; *Dch.* Koes, Coes; *Fl.* Couez; *Fr.* Caux (?); p.n. A loc. n., Isle of Wight

COWIE. A loc. n., Kincardine

COWLAND. A loc. n., Edinbgh.

COWLEY. A loc. n., Bucks, Derbysh., Middlsx., Oxf., Staffs

COWLING. A loc. n., Suff., Yorks

COWLISHAW. From Cowlishall; a loc. n., Lancs

COWLS. *See* Colls

COWPERTHWAITE. A loc. n., Westmd.

COX. *Lat.* Cocus; *Fl.* Kockx; *Dch.* Koks, Kokx; p.n. *See* Cock

COXHEAD. From Coxyde; a loc. n., Belg.

COZENS. From Cusances; a loc. n., Norm.; Cosen, Belg. *Fr.* Cousin; *Dch.* Couzijn; p.n. Hugt. n., Lond. 1618

CRAB. *A.S.* Creba; *G.* Krappe; *Dch.* Krabb; *Fl.* Crab, Crabbe; p.n. (a crab)

CRABTREE. A loc. n., Devon

CRACK. *N.* Kráka *D.* Krage; (a crow); a n.n.; *A.S.* Crac; *D.* Krag; *Fl.* Crach; *Dch.* Kraak; p.n.

CRACKENTHORPE. A loc. n., Westmd.

CRACKNALL, CRACKNELL. From Craigneill; a loc. n., Edinbgh.

CRACROFT. A manor in Lancs

CRADDOCK. A loc. n., Devon. Or Cradoc, S. Wales.

It is probably a corruption of Caradoc, which was Latinised to Caractacus. Welsh *caradwg* (beloved).

CRAFER. *G.* Kreifer; *Fl.* Creve, Creyf; p.n.

CRAFT. *D.* Kraft; *Dch.*, *G.* Kraft, Kroft; p.n. (strength)

CRAGG. A loc. n., Yorks. Or *D.* Krag; a p.n. *See* Crack

CRAIG. A loc. n., Forfar

CRAIGIE. A loc. n., Ayrshire

CRAIK. A loc. n., Sutherland

CRAIKE. A loc. n., Dur., Yorks

CRAKE. A loc. n., Norf., Yorks

CRAMPTON. From Crompton; a loc. n., Lancs

CRANAGE. A loc. n., Ches. Or from Cranwich; a loc. n., Norf.

CRANBROOK. A loc. n., Kent

CRANE. From Crehen; a loc. n., Belg. Or Cranne, in Maine; *D.* Krener; *G.* Kren; *Fl.* Craen; p.n.

CRANEY. *See* Crane

CRANG. *See* Cranke

CRANK. A loc. n., Lancs. Or *D.* Kranker, Crenker; *Fl.* Craninck; *G.* Krancke; p.n. (ill)

CRANKSHAW. *See* Cronshaw

CRANMER. A loc. n., Devon; Cranmore, Camb.

CRANNIS. *G.* Krannisch, Krentsch; a p.n. Dim. *See* Crane

CRANSEN. *See* Cranston

CRANSTON. A loc. n., Edinbgh.

CRANWELL. A loc. n., Lincs. Or from Cramanville, Norm.

CRAPP. *See* Crab

CRASKE. *G.* Kraske; p.n. Dimin. of *D.*, *Fl.*, and *Dch.* Crass

CRATE. *A.S.* Creda, Creoda, Grid; *Dch.* Kret; *G.* Kreth; p.n. From *A.S. hræd* (ready, quick)

CRAUFORD. A loc. n., Lanark

CRAVEN. A loc. n., Yorks

CRAW. *A.S.* Crawe; a p.n. The Scottish form of Crow

CRAWFORD. A loc. n., Dorset, Lanark, Lancs

CRAWHALL. From Crakehall (*D.B.* Cracele); a loc. n., Yorks. Or Croxall, Derbysh., and Staffs

CRAWLEY. A loc. n., Bucks, Hants, Suss.

CRAWSHAW. A loc. n., Lancs

CRAZE. *Fr.* Crez; *Dch.* Kress; p.n.; Crest; a loc. n., France

De Cres in Rot. Obl. et Fin.

CREAK. From Creake; a loc. n., Norf.

CREAM. *See* Gream

CREAMER. *Fl.* Cremer, Crimmers; *G.* Kremer; *Dch.* Cramer, Cremer; p.n. *See* Grimmer. Prot. ref. n., Lond. 1618

CREASE. From the Irish M'Creech

CREASEY. *See* Cresey

CREAVEN. *See* Craven

CREECH. From Creich; a loc. n., Sutherld.; Criech, Fife; Crich, Derbysh. *See* Creak

CREED. A loc. n., Cornw. Or *see* Crate

CREEDY. Irish M'Creedy

CREEKE. *See* Creak

CREER. *See* Grier

CREIGHTON. A loc. n., Staffs

CRELLIN. From Crallan; a loc. n., Norm.

CRESEY. From Crécy; a loc. n., Norm.
Cressy is on the Roll of Battell Abbey, and a tenant in chief in *D.B.*

CRESSWELL. A loc. n., Northbd., Staffs. Or *N.-Fr.* De Croissiles; a p.n.

CREW, CREWE. A loc. n., Ches. Or *Fr.* Croux; a p.n.

CREWDSON. *A.S.* Creoda, Croda, Crud; *hrod* (glory); *Fl.* Crusen, Crutzen; p.n. *See* Croote

CREYKE. From Crayke; a loc. n., Yorks

CRIBBIN. From M'Robin

CRICHTON. A loc. n., Edinbgh.

CRICK. A loc. n., Northants. Or *see* Creak

CRICKET. *See* Critchett

CRIGLEY. *See* Critchley

CRINGLE. *N.* Kringla; a n.n. (a circle)

CRIPPS. From Crispin. *G.* Krips; a p.n.

CRISELL. *Dch.* Kressel or Kristel; a p.n. Dim. of Christopher

CRISP, CRISPIN. From St Crispin; a Norman-French loc. n.
Milo Crispin, a tenant in chief in *D.B.* Also in Rot. Obl. et Fin.

CRITCHETT. *N.-Fr.* Crichet, Cruchet, Criquet; p.n.

CRITCHFIELD. From Cruickfield (?); a loc. n., Berwick

CRITCHLEY. From Crickley; a loc. n., Glos.

CRITTENDEN. *See* Cruttenden

CROAGER, CROAKER. *See* Crocker

CROASDALE. From Croixdal; a loc. n., Normandy. Or Croxdale, Dur.

CROCKER. *N.-Fr.* Le Crochere; a p.n. (a cross bearer)
In Rot. Obl. et Fin. and Rot. Hund.

CROCKETT, CROCKITT. *N.-Fr.* Crochett; *Fl.* Crockaert; *Fr.* Croquet; p.n.

CROCKFORD. A loc. n., Kirkcudbright

CROCOMBE. From Crowcombe; a loc. n., Somers

CROFT. A loc. n., Cornw., Glos., Heref., Yorks. Or *Dch.* Kroft; a p.n. *See* Craft
Bernard de Croft in *D.B.*

CROKE. *See* Crocker

CROLY. *See* Crawley

CROMBIE. A loc. n., Fife

CROMIE, CRUMMIE. *See* Crombie

CROMWELL. A loc. n., Notts

CRONK. *G.* Krancke; p.n. *See* Cranke

CRONSHAW. From Cranshaws; a loc. n., Berwick

CROOK. A loc. n., Devon, Westmd., Dur. Or *N.-Fr.* Croc, Croch, Fitz-Croch; p.n.

CROOKENDEN. From Crookdean; a loc. n., Northd.

CROOKES. A loc. n., Yorks

CROOMBE. From Croome; a loc. n., Worcest., Yorks

CROOTE. From Crot; a loc. n., Norm. Or *A.S.* Creoda, Crud, Cryda; *Dch.* Kroode; p.n. *See* Crewdson
Grud, Grut, Grutt, Saxon tenants in *D.B.* R. Grut in Rot. Hund. 1272.

CROPPER. *N.* Kroppr; n.n. (a hump); *A.S.* Croppa; *S.* Cropps; *Dch.* Krop; *G.* Kropp, Kroppe; p.n.
Crop in Rot. Obl. et Fin. Also *N.-Fr.* S. de Croper, Northants, 1194.

CROSBY. A loc. n., Cumb., Lancs, Lincs, Westmd.

CROSHER. *See* Crocker

CROSLAND. A loc. n., Yorks

CROSS. From St Croix; a loc. n., Norm. *Dch.* Crosse; a p.n.
De St Cruce, Norm. 1180; de Cruce, Eng. 1199. Prot. ref., Croydon, 1618.

CROSSINGHAM. From Cressingham; a loc. n., Norf.

CROSSLEY. From Crosslee, Renfrew; or Crosslegh, Lancs

CROSSTHWAITE. A loc. n., Cumb.

CROSTON. A loc. n., Lancs

CROTHERS. *See* Carruthers

CROUCH. Atte Crouche, Court of Husting, 1258

CROUDACE. *See* Carruthers

CROUGH. *See* Crocker

CROUGHTON. A loc. n., Northants

CROWDER, CROWDY, CROWTHER. *A.S.* Creoda; *hrod* (glory); *Dch.* Kroode; p.n. Or *see* p. 13

CROWDSON. *See* Crewdson

CROWE. *See* Crocker

CROWHURST. A loc. n., Surr.

CROWLEY. From Crulai; a loc. n., France. Or *see* Crawley

CROWSHAW, CROWSHAY. *See* Crawshaw

CROWSON. *See* Crewdson

CROYDEN. *See* Croydon

CROYDON. A loc. n., Surr.

CROYSDALE. *See* Croasdale

CRUDGE. *G.* Crutge; *Dch.* Kruge; p.n. Dimin. of Crud. *See* Croote. Prot. ref., Lond. 1688

CRUDGINGTON. A loc. n., Salop

CRUM, CRUMMEY. *N.* Krumr; *Fr.* Crombez; p.n. (crooked, a cripple)

CRUMMACK. From Crummock; a loc. n., Cumb.

CRUMP. *See* Crum

CRUMPTON. *See* Crompton

CRUNDALL. From Crundale; a loc. n., Kent

CRUSE. From Creusanisy, Norm. *N.-Fr.* De Creus; a p.n.
De Crus in Rot. Obl. et Fin., Devon, 1199.

CRUSO. From Creusot; a loc. n., France. *Fr.* Creuseau; a p.n. Hugt. n., Norwich, 1622

CRUTCHER. *G.* Krutsche; a p.n. (a cross-bearer). Or *see* Crudge

CRUTHE. *See* Croote

CRUTTENDEN. A loc. n. Kent

CRUTWELL. From Crudwell; a loc. n., Wilts

CRYER. *G.* Kreyher; *Dch.* Kreije; p.n.

CUBITT. From Cowbitt; a loc. n., Lincs (*N. kúa-beit*, cow-pasture)
Pronounced locally Cubbitt, and written Cubyt as late as 1410. Or *see* Cobbett.

CUDBAR, CUDBY. *See* Cuthbert

CUDBY. A loc. n.

CUDDEFORD. From Cuttiford; a loc. n., Cornw.

CUDDEN, CUDDING, CUDDON. *D.* Gudden; a fam. n.; *Fl.* Guttin; a p.n.; *D.B.* Cudhen, Gudhen. *See* Goding. Or Irish M'Cudden

CUFF. *A.S.* Coifi, Cuffa; p.n.; *côf* (active, bold)

CUFFE. *See* Coffee

CUISHEN. *See* Cushion

CULHAM. A loc. n., Berks

CULL. *A.S.* Cula, Culf; *G.* Kulla; p.n. A form of hwulf

CULLEN. A loc. n., Banffs. Or from the Irish O'Coilean; a p.n.; *coilean* (a young warrior)

CULLEY, CULLY. From Couillet; a loc. n., Flanders
Cuilly in Roll of Battell Abbey. Hugo de Cuilly in Rot. Obl. et Fin., K. John. Or Irish M'Cully.

CULLING. *A.S.*; fam. n. of Cull

CULLINGFORD. *See* Cullingworth

CULLINGWORTH. A loc. n., Yorks

CULLYER. *Fr.* Coulier; a p.n. *See* Colyer

CULMER, CULMORE. From Cullamore; a loc. n., Staffs

CULPECK, CULPICK. From Kilpeck; a loc. n., Heref. Or *Fl.* Callepeck; a p.n. Dim. of Calp

CULPERWELL. From Culverwell (?); a loc. n., Devon

CULPIN. From *N.* Kolbeinn (?) (black legs) ; *A.S.* Colben ; p.n.

CULPIT. *Fl.* Calepet (?) ; a p.n.

CULY. *See* Culley

CUMBERBATCH, CUMBERPATCH. From Comberbach ; a loc. n., Ches.

CUMBERLEGE. From Cumberlow ; a loc. n., Herts

CUMBY. *N.* Kumbi ; n.n. (a chopper) ; *Fl.* Combe ; *Fr.* Combet ; p.n.

CUMMINGS. *See* Comyns

CUNDIL. From Cundall ; a loc. n., Yorks

CUNDY. *See* Condy

CUNLIFFE. From Concliffe or Cunliff ; a loc. n., Lancs. *N.* Gunleif ; *A.S.* Gunleof ; p.n. (war love)

CUNNEEN. From the Irish *coinin* (a rabbit)

CUNNINGHAM. A loc. n., Ayrshire

CUNNINGTON. A loc. n., Hunts

CUPISS, CUPPAGE. From Kippax (?) ; a loc. n., Yorks

CUPPER. From Kupp ; a loc. n., Germ. Or *see* Cooper

CURD. *A.S.* Curda (a staff) ; *G.* Kurde ; p.n.

CURE. *N.-Fr.* De la Cour ; a p.n.

John Cure, Rot. Hund. 1272.

CURL. *A.S.* Ceorl ; *D.* Curjel ; *S.* Correll ; *Dch.* Kurrell ; p.n. (a free man)

CURLING. *N.* Karl, Kerling ; *G.* Kerling ; p.n. *See* Curl

CURLY. A loc. n., Norm.

John de Curley in Warwickshire. Rot. Obl. et Fin., K. John.

CURNOCK. From Carnock ; a loc. n., Fife

CURNOW. *N.-Fr.* du Cournau ; a p.n.

CURRAN. Irish Cwaran ; a p.n. (sickleman, farmer)

CURREY, CURRIE. A loc. n., Edinbgh.

CURSHAM. From Corsham ; a loc. n., Wilts

CURSON, CURZON. From Courçon, near Caen.

Curson in Roll of Battell Abbey. De Curcan in *D.B.*

CURTAIN. *Fr.* Courtin ; a p.n. *See* Courteen

CURTIS. From Cortys ; a loc. n., Belg. Or *Fr.* Courtois ; a p.n. (courteous). Hugt., Norwich, 1622

CURTLER. From Curtley ; a loc. n., Northants. Or *G.* Gertler (a girdle-maker) ; a p.n. Curtelow, Fl. ref., Lond. 1618

CURWEN. *A.S.* Garwine ; *Old G.* Gerwin, Caroin ; *Fl.* Carroen ; p.n. (spear friend)

CUSACK. *Fr.* Queyssac ; a p.n. Or *see* Kissack

CUSSICK. *See* Cusack

CUSHING, CUSHION, CUSHON. *N.-Fr.* Le Cuchon ; a p.n.

CUSS. From Gouis or Gouvis ; a loc. n., Norm. *N.-Fr.* De Guz ; a p.n.

W. Cousche, Cust, or Cushe, Camb., 13th cent. Testa de N.

CUSTANCE. From Coutance ; a loc. n., Normandy

CUTBARTH. *See* Cuthbert

CUTCHER. *G.* Kutscher ; a p.n. (a coachman). Or *see* Goodyear

CUTFORTH. From Cuttiford ; a loc. n., Cornw.

CUTHBERT. *A.S.* Cuthbeorht, Cuthbryt (noted brightness). Or Guðbeorht (war bright) ; *D.B.* Cutbert ; p.n. *See* Gotobed

CUTLACK. *N.* Guðlaug (good play) ; *A.S.* Cuthlac, Guthlac ; *D.B.* Gotlac ; p.n.

CUTLER. *Fl.* Cotteleer ; a p.n.

Gaufrid de Cuteler in Rot. Obl. et Fin., K. John.

CUTMORE. *See* Catmur

CUTTER. *A.S.* Cuthere; *G.* Kutter; *Fr.* Coudeyre, Cuttier, le Couteur; p.n. (good warrior)

CUTTING. *See* Cudden

CUTTLE or CUTHILL. A loc. n., Haddington. Or *see* Cottle

CUTTS. *See* Coote

CYPHER. *See* Sypher

D

DABBS. *G.* Dabisch; p.n. *N.-Fr.* D'Abice; De Abbacia Rot. Hund.

DABLE. *Dch.* Debel; a p.n. *See* Daplin

DACK. *G.* Dach; *Fl.* Dache; *Dch.* Dake; p.n. *See* Day

DADE. *N.* Dadi; *A.S.* Dadda, Dado; *N.-Fr.* Dade; *Irish* M'Dade; *F.* Datter, Dede; p.n. (father)

DADFIELD. A loc. n.

DADY. *See* Dade

DAGG. *N.-Fr.* De Augo; p.n. *See* Day. Dague, Hugt. n., Cant. 1622

DAGGET. *A.S.* Dœgheard; *D.* Daugaard, Doggert; *Fl.* Degard; p.n. (glory-strong). Dackett, Flem. ref., Norwich, 1622

DAGLEY. *Fr.* Dachelet; a p.n. (?)

DAGNALL. From Dagnell; a loc. n., Worcest.

DAGWORTHY. From Dagworth; a loc. n., Norf.

DAINES. *N. Fr.* D'Aines; a p.n.

DAINTREE. From Daventry; a loc. n., Northants

DAINTY. *S.* Dente; *Fr.* Dantée; p.n. Or Anthée; a loc. n., Belg.

DAISLEY. From Disley; a loc. n., Ches.

DAKING. *N.-Fr.* De Akeny. From Acquigny, Norm. Or *Dch.* Dekking; p.n. *See* Deck

DALBY. A loc. n., Lincs, Yorks

DALE. A contraction of Dalzell. Or Atte-Dale

DALLAS. A loc. n., Elgin, Moray

DALLEY. *N.-Fr.* D'Ally; a p.n. From Ailly, Norm.

DALLINGER. *N.* Dellingr (dayspring); *G.* Döllinger; *Dch.* Dallings; p.n.

DALRYMPLE. A loc. n., Ayrshire. Gaelic *Dail-á-chruim-puill.* Anciently spelled Dalruimpuill, Dalrimpil.

DALTON. A loc. n., Dumfries, Devon, Dur., Lancs, Yorks

DALY. From the Irish *dal* (blind). Or from Dailly; a loc. n., Belg. and Scotl.

DALZELL. *See* Dalziel

DALZIEL. A loc. n., Lanark Anciently Dalyell, Dalvell.

DAMANT. *Dch.* and *G.* Diamant; p.n. *See* Dimond

DAMER. *A.S.* Dægmær; a p.n. (glory famed)

DAMPIER. From Dampierre; a loc. n., Normandy W. de Danpere in Rot. Obl. et Fin., K. John.

DAMS. *N.-Fr.* D'Ames; *G.* Dammas, Damis, Dams; *Dch.* Dammers; *Fl.* Dams; p.n. Prot. ref., Norwich, 1622. *See* Ames

DANBROOK. From Danbury (?); a loc. n., Ess.

DANBY. A loc. n., Yorks

DANCE. From Ans; a loc. n., Belg.; *G.* Dance; *Fl.* D'Ans, Danse; p.n.

DANCER. *A.S.* Denisheard (strong Dane). Or *N.-Fr.* D'Ancere; a p.n. From Anceres, Norm.; *Fl.* Dansaert; p.n.

DANDRIDGE. From Danebridge; a loc. n., Ches.

DANDY. *Fr.* Dandoy; a p.n.

DANE. *N.* Danir, *S.* Dann; *D.* Dehn, Dein; *G.* Denia, Deny; *A.S.* Dane, Dene, Dena; p.n. *See* Deyne

DANGAR. *A.S.* Denegær, Dengar (Dane-spear); *D.* Dankert; *G.* Danger; *Fr.* Danguet; p.n. Or *N.-Fr.* D'Angers. Prot. ref., Lond. 1618

DANGERFIELD. *N.-Fr.* Dangerville; a p.n.

DANIEL. *Fr.*; p.n. A Hugt. n., Lond. 1618; Norwich, 1622

DANKS. From Henges, near Amiens. De Henges in Rot. Hund.

DANN. *A.S.* Dan, Dene, Tan; *Fr.* Danne; p.n. *See* Dane

DANNAHY, DENNEHEY. *See* Deneher

DANNATT. *Fr.* Dannet; a p.n. Dim. of Dann

DANSIE. *See* Dance

DANSON. *D.* Dan : *S.* Dann; *Fl.* Danne; *G.* Dann; p.n. *See* Dane

DANVERS. From Anvers, La Manche, France
In Roll of Battell Abbey, *D.B.* and Rot. Obl. et Fin., K. John.

DAPLIN. *S.* Döbelin (Dahbelin); a p.n. Dapperling (a dwarf)

DARBEY, DARBY. From Derby; loc. n.
Dyrbye is a loc. and p.n. in Denmark.

DARCY. From de Ardreci, D'Arcie
A tenant in chief, *D.B.* (Lincs).

DARE. *A.S.* Deor, Diar, Dyre; *Fl.* Dare; *Dch.* Diere; p.n. *See* Dyer

DARK. *N.-Fr.* D'Arques; a p.n. *See* Arch

DARKIN. *See* Dorking

DARLING. *A.S.* Deorling, Derling; p.n. (beloved)

DARLINGTON. A loc. n., Dur.

DARLOW. From Darly; a loc. n., Derbysh.

DARNELL, DARNILL. *See* Dartnall

DARNTON. *See* Darrington

DARRAH. *See* Darroch

DARRELL. From Airel; a loc. n., Norm.

DARRINGTON. A loc. n., Yorks

DARROCH. From Darragh; a loc. n., Isle of Man. Irish, *dair* (oak)

DARTNALL. From Darnhall (?); a loc. n., Ches.

DARVALL, DARVELL. DARWALL, *N.-Fr.* D'Orival; a p.n.

DARWEN. A loc. n., Lancs. From the British Darwenydd, Derguint (Derwent). Or *A.S.* Deorwynn; a p.n. (dear friend)

DASENT. *Fr.* Dessaint; a p.n. *See* Sainty

DASH. From Assche; a loc. n., Belg. *Fr.* D'Assche; a p.n.
Roger de Asc in Rot. Obl. et Fin., K. John. De Ash, Court of Husting.

DASHPER. *Fl.* Deschepper; a p.n.

DASHWOOD. A loc. n.

DATE. *A.S.* Dœda; *Fr.* Dethy; p.n. *See* Dade

DAUBENY. From Daubigny; a loc. n., France. *N.-Fr.* D'Albini; a p.n.

DAUNT. *G.* Dohnt; a p.n.

DAUNTON. *N.-Fr.* Dantan, De Donton; p.n.

DAVAGE. *Fr.* Duverger; a p.n.

DAVENPORT. A loc. n., Ches.

DAVID. *Fr.*, *D.*, *Dch.*, *G.*; p.n.

DAVIE. *See* Davy

DAVIES, DAVIS. Welsh Ap Dafydd; Irish M'Daid; *Fr.* Devis; p.n.

DAVIN. Irish *Daimh* (a poet). Or *see* Devine

DAVITT. *Dch.* Dawit, Davijt; p.n.

DAVY. *Fr.* Dévé; a p.n.

DAW, DAWES. *D.* Dauc; *F.* Dauewes, Douwes; *G.* Thou, Dohse; p.n. Daw is also a dimin. of David

DAWBARN, DAWBIN, DAWBORN. *Fr.* Daubin; a p.n. *See* Daubeny

DAWBER. *A.S.* Dagobert, Dægbeorht; *Fr.* Daubert; p.n. (illustrious)

DAWBRY. A loc. n., Derbysh.

DAWDY. *See* Dade

DAWDRY. *See* Dordry

DAWLEY. *See* Daly

DAWKINS. *See* Daw. Dimin.

DAWSON. *See* Daw. Ger. Prot. ref. n., London, 1621

DAY. *N.* Dagr; *A.S.* Dag, Dæg; *S.* Daug; *G.* Dege; *Fl.* Day, Daye; p.n. (day, brightness, glory). Or from St John de Day, near St Lo

DAYNES. *See* Dane

DEACLE. From Achel (?); a loc. n., Belg. Or *see* Tickle

De Acle occurs in Rot. Obl. et Fin., K. John.

DEACON. le Dekene in 1327

DEADMAN. *N.* Þjoðmar (brave man); *D.* Dettmer; *Dch.* Dettman; *G.* Dittmann, Dittmer, Tiedemann; *A.S.* Dodeman, Dudeman

DEALY. *See* Daly

DEAN, DEANE, DENE. A loc. n., Hants, Northants, Roxburgh, Yorks

DEARDEN. A loc. n., Lancs

DEARING. *N.* Dyri (a deer); *A.S.* Deoring; fam. n.; *Dch.* Dieren; *S.* Dyring; p.n.

DEARSLEY. From Dursley (?); a loc. n., Glost.

DEARTON. From Dearden; a loc. n., Lancs

DEASE. *A.S.* Dis, Tis, Tisa; *Dch.* Dis; p.n. From the Goth. *thius* (a servant)

DEASON. *See* Dyson

DEATH. *Fr.* D'Ath; a p.n. Ath; a loc. n., Flanders

DEAVES, DIVES. A loc. n. in Normandy. *Fr.* Devis; a p.n.

Devise in Roll of Battell Abbey. *D.B.* de Dive.

DEAVIN. *See* Devine

DEBENHAM. A loc. n., Suff.

DE BURGH. *See* Bourke

DECENT. *See* Dasent

DECK. *G.* Deck, Decke, Decker; *Dch.* Dekker; p.n. *See* Day

DEDMAN. *See* Deadman

DEE. From St Die; a loc. n., France. *Dch.* Die; a p.n.

DEED. *A.S.* Did, Theod; p.n. (people)

DEEDES. *See* Dade

DEEKES. *See* Dicks

DEEKER. *Dch.* Dieker; p.n. *See* Dicks

DEEVES. *See* Deaves

DEEVEY. *See* Davy

DEIGHTON. A loc. n., Yorks

DELACHEROIS. *Fr.* Delacroix; a p.n.

DELAMERE. *Fr.* Delamare; a p.n.

DELANEY. *Fr.* Delanney; a p.n.

DELAROE. *Fr.* Delarue; a p.n.

DELAY. From the *Fr.* De la Haye; a p.n.

DELLAR. *A.S.* Dealla; *G.* Della (eminent); p.n.

DELMEGE. *Fl.* Delmez; a p.n. Or *see* Talmage

DELMER. *See* Delamere

DELOOHERY. Irish form of Delacroix

DELVE. From Delft; a loc. n., Holl. *Fl.* Delf. A Prot. ref. n., Lond. 1618

DEMER. *Fr.* De Meur; a p.n.

DEMPSER. *See* Dempsey

DEMPSEY. From the Irish *diomusach* (arrogant)

DENCH. *Fl.* Dengis; a p.n. *See* Ding, Danche. A Hugt. n., Lond. 1688

DENEHAN. *Fr.* Denain; a p.n.

DENEHER. *Fr.* Denier or Denoyers; p.n.

DENHAM. A loc. n., Beds, Roxburgh, Suff.

DENIFFE. *Fr.* Deneuve; a p.n.

DENLEY. A loc. n.

DENNENT. *Fr.* Denin; p.n. Denain (?)

DENNETT. *N.-Fr.* D'Anet; a p.n.

DENNEY. A loc. n., Stirling. Or Denée; a loc. n., Belg. *Fl.* Denis, Denie, Deny; p.n.

DENNINGTON. A loc. n., Norf., Suff., Yorks

DENNIS. St Denis; a loc. n., France. *Fr.* Denis; p.n. Hugt. n., Lond. 1682

DENNISON, DENNISTON. From Denerdiston; a loc. n., Suff. Or Denston, Staffs

DENNY. *See* Denney

DENSON. *See* Dennison

DENT. A loc. n., Yorks

DENTON. A loc. n., Lincs, Norf., Lancs, Northants, Northbd., etc. (16 places)

DERHAM. *See* Deerham or Durham

DERING. *See* Dearing

DERLYN. *See* Darling. Hugt. n., Norwich, 1622

DEROW. *Fr.* Derrieu; a p.n.

DERRICK. A contraction of Theoderic. Or *Fr.* Deryck, D'Eryc, or D'Heriche; p.n. Hugt. n., Norwich, 1622

DESBOROUGH. A loc. n., Northants

DEVANY. *See* Devine

DEVERELL. Deverill; a loc. n., Wilts. From Vireville (?); a loc. n., Norm.; Deverall, Cornw.
In Roll of Battell Abbey, Wm. de Deverell of Segelawe in Hund. Rolls, Hen. III.

DEVERY. *Fr.* Devereux; a p.n.

DEVILLE. From Daiville; a loc. n., Norm. *N.-Fr.* D'Eville; a p.n.
Devile and Doiville are on the Roll of Battell Abbey. Devle is in *D.B.*

DEVINE, DEVINNEY. *Fr.* Desvignes, Devine; p.n. Hugt. n., Norwich, 1622

DEW. *N.-Fr.* D'Eu; a p.n. *Lat.* De Augo, from Eu; a loc. n., Norm.

DEWDNEY. *See* Dudeney

DEWES. *Fl.* Dewys; a p.n. Hugt. n., Lond. 1618. *See* Dewey

DEWESBURY. From Dewsbury; a loc. n., Yorks

DEWEY. From Dhuy; a loc. n., Belg. Prot. ref., Lond. 1618
De Dwai. t. in chief, *D.B.*

DEWFALL. *Fr.* Duval. A Hugt. n., Lond. 1687

DEYNE. *D.* Dehn, Dein; *Dch.* Deen, Deene; *G.* Dane, Diehne; p.n. *See* Dane

DEYNES. *Fl.* Daens; a fam. n. *See* above

DIAPER. From Ipres; a loc. n., Fland. *N.-Fr.* De Ypre; a p.n.

DIBALL, DIBBLE. *See* Dipple

DIBBEN. *D.* Dibbern; a fam. n. of Dibb

DIBBS. *F.* Tibbe; *G.* Dibus; p.n. *See* Tipple

DIBDIN. From Dibden; a loc. n., Hants

DIBLEY. From Dipley; a loc. n., Hants

DIDOLL. *See* Dipple

DICEY. From Diss; a loc. n., Norf. It also appears as Disa, Disce, Disse

DICK. *See* Digges. Also a loc. n. From *A.S. dic*; *Dch. dijk* (a dyke, bank, mound) ·
W. de Dyck was Alderman of Edinburgh, 1296.

DICKENS, DICKMAN. *See* Dicks

DICKS. *F.* Diko, Dyko; fam. n., Diken, Dyken, Dikena; *G.* Dix, Dieck, Dicke; *Dch.* Diek, Dieker, Dikkers, Dikken; p.n. *See* Digges

DIDLICK. From Didling; a loc. n., Suss.

DIDSBURY. A loc. n., Lancs

DIDWELL. A loc. n.

DIFFEY. *See* Dive

DIGBY. A loc. n., Lincs

DIGGENS, DIGGES, DIGGON. *A.S.* Diga, Dycga (strong); *D.* Dige; p.n. *See* Dicks

DIGGLES. From Diggle; a loc. n., Yorks. Or Dikele, Fland.; D'Eagles, from L'Aigle, Norm., has been suggested

DILKE. *See* Tilke

DILL. *A.S.* Dilla (good); *Dch.*, *Fl.* Dille; *G.* Dill; p.n. *See* Teele

I

DILLON. From the Irish O'Dilm-hain; a p.n. (David)

DILWORTH. A loc. n., Lancs. Or *Fl.* Dielwart; a p.n.

DIMBLEBY. From Thimbleby; a loc. n., Lincs

DIMMER. *See* Dimon

DIMMOCK. From Dymock; a loc. n., Glost.

DIMON, DIMOND. *D.* Demandt; *Dch.* Dieman, Diamant; *G.* Demand, Demant, Diamant; *Fl.* Deman; *Fr.* Diman; *Old G.* Diomund; p.n. (servant-protector)

DIMPLE. A loc. n., Derbysh., Lancs

DIMSDALE. From Dinsdale; a loc. n., Dur.

DING. *N.* Dengir; cogn. *G.* Dinger; *Dch.* Denike, Dinger; *Fl.* Dengis; p.n. (one who whets)

DINGLEY. A loc. n., Northants

DINGWALL. A loc. n., Scotl.

DINHAM. A loc. n., Monmth.

DINNER. From Dinard; a loc. n., France. *Fr.* Diner, Dineur; *Fl.* Dinear; p.n.

DINSDALE. A loc. n., Dur.

DINSMORE. From Dinmore; a loc. n., Heref.

DINWOODIE, DUNWOODIE. A loc. n., Dumfries

DIPPLE. A loc. n., Devon. Or *see* Tipple

DIPROSE. *N.-Fr.* De Preaux; a p.n.

DISART, DISERT. From Izards; a loc. n., Norm. *N.-Fr.* D'Izard
In Roll of Battell Abbey.

DISBROWE. From Desborough; a loc. n., Northants

DISNEY. *N.-Fr.* D'Isigny; a p.n. From Isigny, Norm.

DITCHETT. From Ditcheat; a loc. n., Somers

DITCHFIELD. *G.* Dickfeld; a p.n.

DITCHLEY. A loc. n., Oxf.

DIVE. *Fr.* Dive; a p.n. *See* Deaves

DIVER. *N.-Fr.* Diveres; a p.n.
Rot. Hund. 1272.

DIX. *See* Dicks

DIXIE. *F.* Diko. Dimin. Dikje; p.n. Or *see* Dicey

DOAK, DOAG. *A.S.* Daga, Docca; *Dch.* Dooge; *Fl.* Docq; p.n. (day, *i.e.* bright, glorious)

DOBBIE. Dimin. of Robert. *Fl.* Doby. A Prot. ref. n., Lond. 1618

DOBBIN. *Dch.* Dobben; *G.* Dobin; p.n.; a fam. n.
Hugo Dobin in Rot. Obl. et Fin., K. John.

DOBBS. *See* Dobbie

DOBELL. *D.* Dobel; a p.n. Dim.

DOBNEY. *See* Daubeny

DOCKER. *Fr.* Docquet; a p.n. Or *see* Dockwra

DOCKERILL. A loc. n.

DOCKRAY, DOCKWRA. From Dockwray; a loc. n., Cumb.

DOD, DODD. *F.* Dodo; *A.S.* Dod; *D.* Dodt; *F.* Dodde; *D.B.* Dode; *Fl.* Dod, Dodd; p.n. *See* Dade
In Rot. Obl. et Fin.

DODDERIDGE. A loc. n., Sandford, Devon
Gilbert de Dodarig, A.D. 1218.

DODDING. *A.S.* Doding; a fam. n.; *F.* Doden. *See* Dodd
William Dodin (Worc.) *temp.* K. John.

DODINGTON. A loc. n., Kent, Lincs, Northants, Northbd.

DODSON. *D.B.* Dodesune; a p.n. *See* Dodd

DODSWORTH. *See* Dodworth

DODWELL. A loc. n., Hants, Warw.

DODWORTH. A loc. n., Yorks

DOE. *N.-Fr.* D'O. From the castle of O, Nerm.
J. and W. Doe in Rot. Hund. 1272.

DOGGETT. *N.-Fr.* Doget, Doket, Duket; p.n. Or *see* Dagget
Rot. Hund.

DOGOOD. *See* Toogood

DOIDGE, DOIG. *See* Doak

DOLAMORE. *See* Dolleymore

DOLBEN. From the *N.-Fr.* D'Albini; a p.n.

DOLEMAN. *A.S.* Doleman ; *N. dolgr* (foe) ; *D.* Dohlmann ; p.n.

DOLL. *Dch., A.S., G.* Doll ; a p.n. Dole, a Prot. ref., Norwich, 1622

DOLLAR. A loc. n., Clackmannan

DOLLAS. *See* Dallas

DOLLEYMORE. *N.-Fr.* De la Mare ; a p.n.

DOLLING. *G.* Dollen ; a p.n. ; fam. n. of Doll

DOLPHIN. *A.S.* Dolfin ; *N. dolgfinnr* (Finnish foe) ; *Fl.* Dolphin ; p.n. Dolfin, a tenant in chief in *D.B.*

DOMINY, DOMONEY. *G.* Domina ; a p.n. Dominic (Sunday child)

DONINGTON. From Donnington ; a loc. n., Leics

DONISTHORPE. A loc. n., Derbysh.

DONITHORNE. From Dinnethorn ; a loc. n., Devon

DONKIN. *See* Dunkin

DONNE. A loc. n., Perth

DONOGHUE. Irish (brown chief)

DONOUGH. *See* Donoghue

DORBEN. *See* Dawbin

DORDERY, DORDRY. From Audrey or Aldrey, Norm.

DORE. Dore ; a loc. n., Derbysh. Or *A.S.* Dor, Deor (dear) ; *Fr.* Doré ; *Dch.* Dórr, Dorre

DORKING. A loc. n., Surr.

DORMAN. From Dormans ; a loc. n., France. Or *N.* Vormundr (?) (Thor protector) ; *Dch.* Doorman ; p.n.

DORR. Dour ; a loc. n., Belg. Or *see* Dore

DORRELL. *See* Darrell

DORRINGTON. A loc. n., Lincs

DOTT. *D., Dch.* Dodt ; a p.n. *See* Dodd

DOTTRIDGE. *See* Dodderidge

DOUBIKIN. *See* Dowbiggin

DOUBLE. *Dch.* Dubbel, Dubbeld ; *Fl.* Duballe, Dubal ; *G.* Dubiel ; p.n. ; *N. dubba* (to smite)

DOUBLEDAY. *Fr.* Doublet. A Hugt. n., Lond. 1685

DOUDS, DOWDS. *See* Dod

DOUGHTY. *N.-Fr.* De Oughtia (?) ; a p.n. ; *G.* Daute ; *Dch.* Dothée, Daudeij ; *Fr.* Daudé ; *Fl.* Dotheij ; p.n. Hugt. n., Lond. 1687. *See* Dodd
De Dote in Rot. Hund.

DOUGLAS. A loc. n., Lanark

DOULTON. From Dolton ; a loc. n., Devon

DOUSE. From Ussey ; a loc. n., Norm.

DOUTHWAITE. A loc. n., Cumb., Yorks

DOVE. *N.* Dufan ; *S.* Dufva ; *D.* Duvier ; *Fl.* Dufey ; *Dch.* Douwe ; *G.* Dove ; p.n. *See* Duff

DOW, DOWE. *See* Duff.
Dow is the Scottish form of Dove.

DOWDESWELL. A loc. n., Glost.

DOWDING. *A.S.* Dud, Thinda, Dudding ; p.n. *See* Deed

DOWDNEY. *See* Dudeney

DOWLEY. From Dowlais ; a loc. n., S. Wales

DOWNES. From Downies ; a loc. n., Kincardinesh.

DOWNING. A loc. n., Worc.

DOWNTON. A loc. n., Hants, Wilts

DOWNWARD. From Downhead (?) ; a loc. n. in Somerset

DOWSING. *D.* Duusen ; a p.n. *See* Dowse

DOWTELL. *Fl.* Dautel ; a p.n.

DOXEY. A loc. n., Staffs

DOY. *Fl., Fr.* Doy. From Douy and Douai ; loc. n. Hugt. Lond. 1618

DOYLE. From Doel ; a loc. n., Belg.

DRABBLE. *N.-Fr.* D'Arables ; a p.n.
Norm. 12th cent. In Rot. Hund. 1272.

DRAKE. *N.-Fr.* Fitz Draco, Fitz Drogo ; *A.S.* Draca, Drag, Thrag ; *D.* Dræger, Dracke ; *S.* Draghi, Drake ; *Dch.* Drager ; *Fl.* Draecke ; p.n. (force, strength). Prot. ref. n., Lond. 1618

DRAKEFORD. From Drayford (?) ; a loc. n., E. Worlington, Devon

DRANE. *N.* Þráin; *D.* Trane; *S.* Trana; *G.* Trenner; p.n.; *A.S. thrægian* (to run)

DRAPER. *A.S.* Drabba; *Fr.* Drapier; *Dch.* Draper; p.n. (a slayer). Hugt. n., Dover, 1622

DRAY. *N.-Fr.* Droie, Drey; p.n.

In Rot. Hund.

DRAYTON. A loc. n., Heref.

DREDGE. *See* Drake

DREW. From Dreux; a loc. n., Normandy. *See* Druse. Hugt. n., Norwich, 1622

DREWITT, DRUITT. *See* Drought

DREWRY. From Roueray; a loc. n., Norm. Or *A.S.* Thrudheri; a p.n. (a true warrior); *N.-Fr.* De Rouvray
Sire Niel Drury, Ald. of Lond., 1312.

DRIFFIELD. A loc. n., Yorks

DRING. From Tring; a loc. n., Herts. Or *A.S.* Dreng; a p.n. (a young soldier); *N. drengr* (a youth)

DRINKALL, DRINKHILL. *A.S.* Dringhel; a p.n. (a young soldier)

DRINKWATER. *Dch.* Drinkwaard (?); a p.n.
The warden of the scot-ale or lord's ale. It has been suggested that it is a corruption of Derwentwater, Cumb. At Eustone, Oxon, the earliest spelling is Derwenkwater.

DRIVER. *N.-Fr.* De Rivers; *Dch.* Druyve, Drijver; p.n.

DROOSTEN. *Dch.* Druivestein; a p.n.

DROUGHT. *N.* Þóriða (?); *A.S.* Drud, Druht, Thrud, Thryth; *G.* Drath; *N.-Fr.* Droart, Drouet, Drueth; p.n. (a true friend). A Hugt. n., Lond. 1618
R. D. in Rot. Hund.

DROZIER. *Fl.* Drogeir. Ref., Lond. 1618

DRUCE. *See* Druse

DRUMMOND. A loc. n., Ross, Scotl. Or *A.S.* Thrythmund, Truhmund; p.n. (true protector)

DRURY. *See* Drewry

DRUSE. *D.* Drews; *G.* Drusche; *Dch.* Dros; *D.B.* De Dreuues; p.n. *See* Drew
Herman de Drewes held many manors under the Conqueror in Glost., Heref., Worc., Wilts.

DRY. *See* Dray

DRYDEN. A loc. n., Lasswade

DRYSDALE. A loc. n., Dumfries

DUBBLE. *See* Double

DUBBLEDICK. From Doubledykes, Stonehouse, Lanark

DUBERLEY. *Fr.* Duboulay; a p.n.

DUCAT. *See* Duckett

DUCE, DUCIE. *See* Douse

DUCK. *N.-Fr.* Le Duc; *Dch.*, *Fl.* Duc; *G.* Duch; *S.* Ducke; p.n. *See* Duke

DUCKER. *S.* Ducke, Dücker; *Dch.* Duker; p.n. *See* Tucker

DUCKETT. *N.-Fr.* Duchet; a p.n.

DUCKHAM. A loc. n., Devon

DUCKWORTH. A loc. n., Camb.

Held by D'Abernon. The name was anciently written Dykewarde

DUDD. *N.* Þjóðar; *A.S.* Thiuda, Dudda; *theod* (people); *G.* Duda; p.n.

DUDDERIDGE. A loc. n., near Alwinton, Devon

DUDDING. From Dudden; a loc. n., Ches. Or *A.S.* Duding; a p.n. (descendants of Dod, Dud, Theod)

DUDENEY. *Fr.* Dieudonné; a p.n. (God-given)

DUDGEON. *See* Dodgson

In the north of England Dodgson is frequently so pronounced.

DUERDON. *Fr.* Dourdoigne; a p.n.

DUFF. *N.* Dufan; a p.n. adapted from the Gaelic in the 10th century; Irish *dubh* (black), *dubhoda* (dark)

DUFFETT. *Fr.* Duffaut; a p.n.

DUFFIELD. A loc. n., Derbysh.

DUFFILL. Duffel ; a loc. n., Belg. Or *see* Duffield

DUFFUS. A loc. n., Elgin

DUFFY. Irish O'Duffy. *See* Duff

DUGDALE. A loc. n., Staffs

DUGGAN. Irish Duibhcenn ; a p.n. (black head)

DUIGNAN. From the Irish O'Duibh-gennain (of the family of Black Gennan)

> The O'Duigenans descend from Mainé, fourth son of Niall of the nine host-ages, King of Ireland, who died A.D. 405. They were historians (Ollamhs) from remote times. Maelpeter O'D., Archdn. of Briefny, 1296. (Ann. Four Masters).

DUKE. *A.S.* Dug, Tuc, Tucca ; p.n. From *A.S. dugan* (to be doughty). *See* Duck. Fl. Prot. ref., Lond. 1618

DUKINFIELD. From Dunkinfield ; a loc. n., Ches.

DULLEY. *Fr.* D'Ully or Doullé ; p.n.

DUMBLETON. A loc. n., Glost.

DUNBAR. A loc. n., Haddington-shire

DUNCAN. Gaelic Donnachu (brown chief)

DUNCE. From Dunse ; a loc. n., Berwick

DUNCOMBE, DUNCUM. From Dun-comb ; a loc. n., Dur.

DUNDAS. A loc. n., Dalmeny, Scotl.

DUNDONALD. A loc. n., Ayr

DUNFORD. A loc. n., Yorks

DUNGER. *Dch.* Duncker ; a p.n. From Dunckhart

DUNGEY. From Dengie ; a loc. n. in Essex. Or Dangu, a loc. n. in Normandy

DUNHAM. A loc. n., Norf., Notts

DUNHILL. A loc. n., Waterford

DUNKIN. From Dunnichen (?) ; a loc. n., Forfar. Or *N.-Fr.* Doni-can ; a p.n.

DUNKLEY. From Dinkley ; a loc. n., Lancs

DUNLOP. A loc. n., Ayr

DUNN. From Dun ; a loc. n., Forfar. Or Irish Duine ; *A.S., S., Dch.* Dun ; p.n. (brown) De Dun in Rot. Obl. et Fin.

DUNNETT. A loc. n., Scotl.

DUNNICLIFF. *See* Tunnicliffe

DUNNING. A loc n., Perth. *See* Dunn

DUNSTALL. A loc. n., Staffs

DUNSTAN. A loc. n., Devon, Northbd.

DUNTHORN. *See* Donithorne

DUNTHORPE. A loc. n., Oxf.

DURBRIDGE. From Dwrbach (?) ; a loc. n., Pembroke

DURDEN, DURDON. From Dourdan ; a loc. n., France

DURIE. *See* Dury

DURNFORD. A loc. n., Wilts

DURRANT. *D.* Durandin ; *Fr.* Durand, Durant ; p.n. (enduring) Durand in Roll of Battell Abbey. *D.B.* Durand.

DURRELL. *Fr.* Durell. A Hugt. n., Lond. 1687. *See* Darrell

DURST. A Germ. p.n. Or *see* Durston

DURSTON. A loc. n., Somers

DURY. From Durie ; a loc. n., Fife. Or *Fr.* Duray, Duré ; p.n. (durable)

DUTHY. *Fr.* Du Thais ; p.n. Or *see* Doughty

DUTT. *A.S.* Dud, Thiuda ; p.n. *See* Dade

DUTTON. A loc. n., Ches., Lancs

DWIGHT. *N.-Fr.* Doit ; a p.n. Or *see* Thwaite

DYAS. *See* Dyce

DYBALL, DYBBELL. *See* Tipple

DYCE. A loc. n., Aberdeen

DYE. *G.* Thei ; p.n. *See* Tye

DYER. *N.* Dýri (a deer) ; Diore ; *D.* Dyhr ; *A.S.* Deór, Dyre ; *S.* Dyr ; *G.* Dier ; *N.-Fr.* ; p.n.

DYKES. A loc. n., Scotl.

DYMOCK, DYMOKE. A loc. n., Glost.

DYMOTT. *Fr.* Demotte; a p.n.;
N.-Fr. de la Motte (fosse, moat)
DYOTT. *A.S.* Dœgheard; *Fl.* Dey-
aert (glorious strength); p.n.

DYSART. *See* Disart
DYSON. From Dison; a p.n., Belg.
Dch. Diessen; a p.n.

E

EACHER. *A.S.* Ecga, Egeor (point,
edge); *D.* Egger; *Dch.* Eger;
p.n.
EACOTT. *A.S.* Ecgheard; *D.*
Eckert, Eigaard; *G.* Eckardt; *Fl.*
Eekhout; p.n. (strong edge)
EADE. From Ede; a loc. n.,
Holland. Or *A.S.* Eadd; *F.*
Edde; *S.* Ed; *G.* Eder; *Dch.*
Ede, Edie, Ide; *Fl.* Ide; *Fr.*
Ede; p.n. *See* Addy
EADIE, EADEY. From Eday; a loc.
n., Orkney. Or *see* Addy, and
Eade

Edie is used in Ireland for Adams.

EAGLE. A loc. n., Lincs; *D.B.*
Aycle. Or *see* Diggles
EAGLESHAM. A loc. n., Renfrew
EAGLETON. A loc. n., Rutland
EAGLING. *N.* Egill; *A.S.* Egel
(Ethel), Eagling; a fam. n.; *S.*
Egelin; *Dch.* Eggeling; p.n.
(noble)
EAKEN. *See* Eykin
EALES. *See* Eels
EALY. From Ely; a loc. n., Camb.
Or *see* Healy
EAMES. *See* Ames
EARDLEY. From Eardisley; a loc. n.,
Heref. Or Eardlew, Staffs
EARL. *N.* Erli, dimin. of Erlingr.
From *jarl* (an earl); *N.-Fr.* Le
Erl; *S.* Erling; *G.* Erle, Erler;
A.S. Erlechin, Erlenc; p.n.
In Rot. Hund.
EARNSHAW. A loc. n., Lancs. Or
Ernsheugh, Berwick
EARP. From Erpe; a loc. n.,
Belgium. Or *N.* Erpr; *A.S.*
Eorp (a wolf); *Dch.* Erp, Herpe;
G. Erpff; *Fr.* Herpin; p.n.

EARWAKER, EARWICKER. *A.S.* Eur-
wacer, *efor wacer* (boar watcher),
Eureuuacre, Euroac, Euuacre;
G. Ehrich; *D.* Eyrich; p.n.
EASDALE. *See* Esdaile
EASLEE. From Eastlee; a loc. n.,
Hants
EAST. *N.-Fr.* D'Est; a p.n.

Rich. de E. Essex, W. Est, 31 Edw. I.

EASTALL. From Eastwell; a loc. n.,
Kent
EASTER. From L'Estre; a loc. n.,
Norm. Also a loc. n., Ess.
EASTERBROOK. A loc. n., Devon
EASTGATE. A loc. n., Dur.
EASTHAUGH, EASTO, EASTOE. *See*
Easter
EASTLAKE. A loc. n., Devon
EASTON A loc. n., Devon, Ess.,
Herts, Northants, Yorks
EASTWOOD. A loc. n., Devon, Ess.,
Notts, Renfrew, Yorks
EASTY. *See* Easter
EASY, EASEY. *Old G.* Eso; *A.S.*
Es, Esa, Esi; *F.* Eisse; p.n.
See Ess
EATWELL. From Etwall; a loc. n.,
Derbysh.
EAVES, EAVIS. A loc. n., Lancs,
Staffs, and other counties. Or
N.-Fr. Ivas; *D.* Ivers; *Dch.*, *Fl.*
Eves, Ivers; p.n.. *See* Eve.
Prot. ref., Lond. 1622
EBBAGE. From Abridge (?); a loc.
n., Ess.
EBBERN. *See* Hepburn
EBBLETHWAITE. *See* Ablewhite
EBBRELL. *See* Abrahall
EBBS. *A.S.* Eb, Ebba; *F.* Ebbe;
D. Eber; *Dch.* Ebers; *S.* Ebbes;
p.n. *See* Epps (strong wild boar)

EBBUTT. *See* Hebbert

EBDEN. From Hebden; a loc. n., Yorks

EBRILGE. *See* Ebbage

EBSWORTH. From Ibsworth; a loc. n., Hants

ECCLES. A loc. n., Berwick, Lancs

ECKERSHALL. From Eccleshall; a loc. n., Staff.

ECKERSLEY. *See* Exley

EDDINGTON. A loc. n., Berks, Somers

EDDLESTONE. A loc. n., Peebles

EDDY, EDEY. From Aidie; a loc. n., Normandy. Or *see* Eade

EDEN. A loc. n., Durham

EDGAR. *A.S.* Eadgar; a p.n. (prosperous spear)

EDGCUMBE. A loc. n., Devon

EDGE. A loc. n., Glost., Salop, Yorks

EDGELL. From Edgehill; a loc. n., Somers

EDGELOW. A loc. n. *See* Edgerley

EDGERLEY. A loc. n., Ches., Salop

EDGINTON. *See* Egginton

EDGLEY. A loc n., Salop

EDGWORTH. A loc. n., Glost., Lancs

EDINTON. A loc. n., Somers, Wilts

EDLESTON. From Egliston (?); a loc. n., Dorset

EDMASTON. From Edmonstone; a loc. n., Edinbg.

EDMUNDS. *A.S.* Eadmund; *S.* Edman; *N.-Fr.* de St Edmond; p.n. (happy protector)
In Rot. Hund.

EDRIDGE. *See* Etrige

EDWARDS. *A.S.* Eadweard; *D.* Edvard, Edwards; *Fr.* Edouard; p.n. (happy guardia)

EELS. *A.S.* Il, Ille; *G.* Ilse; p.n. (a hedgehog)

EGARR. *N.* Heggr (a kind of tree, *prunus padus*); *F.* Egge; *S.* Eger, Eggers; *Dch.* Eggers; *G.* Eger; p.n. Or *L.S.* Egger, Æthelgar (noble spea)

EGERTON. A loc. n., Kent, Lancs

EGGETT. *A.S.* Ecgheard; *G.* Eggert; p.n. (hard edge or point)

EGGINTON. A loc. n., Derbysh.

EGGLETON. A loc. n., Heref.

EGGS. *See* Egarr

EGLETON. A loc. n., Rutland; Egletons, France

EGLIN. *See* Eagling, Egelen; a loc. n., Pruss.

EGLINGTON. From Eggleton (?); a loc. n., Heref.

EGREMONT. A loc. n., Cumb.

EKE. *D.* Ek; *N.* Eik; *Dch.* Eik; *A.S.* Eaca; p.n. (an oak)

EKINS. *See* Eykins

ELAM. *See* Ellam

ELAND. A loc. n., Northbd. Or *Dch.* Elandt; a p.n.

ELBOROUGH, ELBROW, ELBURY. A loc. n., Somers

ELCOAT. From Elcot; a loc. n., Berks, Wilts

ELDERDICE. *See* Allardyce

ELDERSHAW. *See* Oldershaw

ELDERTON. A loc. n., Ross. Or Alderton, Northants

ELDRID. *See* Aldred

ELDRIDGE. From Eldrig; a loc. n., Wigton. Or *see* Aldridge

ELENGER. *N.* Erlinger; a p.n. *See* Earl

ELGAR. *N.* Álfgeirr (elf-spear); *S.* Elg; *D.* Helge; *G.* Elga, Elger; *Dch.* Elgers; p.n.; *D.B.* Elgar, Elfgar, Algar. *See* Algar

ELGEE. *See* Elgar

ELGOOD. *A.S.* Æthelgeard; *D.* Ellegaard; *B.D.* Elgert; p.n. (noble guardian)

ELKINGTON. A loc. n., Lincs, Northants

ELLABY. From Ellerby; a loc. n., Yorks. Or *D.* Elleby; a loc. and p.n.

ELLACOMBE. A loc. n., Devon

ELLAM. From Elham; a loc. n., Berwick, Kent

ELLAND. A loc. n., Yorks
ELLER. *A.S.* Ealhhere; *D.* Eller; p.n. (hall warrior)
ELLERAY. A loc. n., Westmd.
ELLERBECK. A loc. n., Yorks
ELLERD. *A.S.* Ealhweard; a p.n. (palace guard)
ELLERSHAW. From Elishaw; a loc. n., Northbd., Yorks
ELLERTON. A loc. n., Salop, Yorks
ELLICOMBE. From Ellicum; a loc. n., Belg. Or *see* Ellacombe
ELLICOT. From the Irish Mac Elligott; a p.n.; *Scot.* Mac Leod. Or *see* Elcoat
ELLINGHAM. A loc. n., Norf.
ELLINGTON. A loc. n., Hunts
ELLINGWORTH. *See* Illingworth
ELLIOT. *F.* Elle, Eilert; *A.S.* Ailward, Ailuert, Ailiet, Eli, Eliard, Eliert, Eliet; *N.-Fr.* Eliot; p.n. *See* Aylward
ELLIS. From Alis; a loc. n., Norm. Or Welsh Elias, Eliseus; a p.n. Or *A.S.* Elsa, Elsi, Ælfsige; p.n. (elf victory)
ELLISON. *See* Allison or Elliston
ELLISTON. From Elston; a loc. n., Wilts. Or *A.S.* Elstan, Ælfstan; p.n. (elf stone, *i.e.* firm elf)
ELLWICK. From Eldwick; a loc. n., Yorks
ELLWOOD. *Dch.* Elewoud; *Fl.* Elewaut; p.n. *See* Aylward
ELLYARD. *See* Aylward
ELMAR. *N.* Hjálmr (a helmet); *F.* Helmer; *S.* Hjelm; *Dch.* Helmer; *G.* Elmers. Or *A.S.* Elmar, Æthelmær (famous noble)
ELMHIRST. A loc. n., Staffs
ELMY. From Elmley; a loc. n., Kent
ELNAUGH, ELNEY. From Ellenhall; a loc. n., Staffs
ELPHEE. *A.S.* Ælfa; a p.n. (elf)
ELPHIC. *A.S.* Alfeage, Alfec, Ælfheah; p.n. (high elf)

ELPHINSTONE. A loc. n., Haddington
ELSDEN. From Elsdon; a loc. n., Northbd.
ELSE. *See* Ellis. Elys in 1327
ELSLEY. From Allesley; a loc. n., Warw.
ELSMERE. From Ellesmere; a loc. n., Salop
ELSTON. A loc. n., Devon, Yorks
ELSWORTH. A loc. n., Camb.
ELTON. A loc. n., Lancs
ELVEY. From the Irish M'Elvie
ELVIN. *A.S.* Elwi, Eluenc, Alfwin, Elfin; *S.* Elfwin; *Dch.* Elven; p.n. (elf-friend). Or Irish M'Elveen
ELVIS, ELWES. *A.S.* Ælf (elf); *N.-Fr.* Helouis; *S.* Elvers; *D.* Elvius; p.n.
ELWELL. A loc. n., Dorset
ELWYN. *See* Elvin
ELY. *N.-Fr.* Fitz Elie; a p.n. Also a loc. n., Camb.
EMBLETON. A loc. n., Cumb., Dur., Northbd.
  Anciently Elmdene Elmedon, Emeldon, Emleton.
EMBURY. From Emborough; a loc. n., Somers
EMERIDGE. A loc. n., Devon
EMERSON. *See* Anes
EMERTON. A loc. n., Devon
EMERY. *Dch.* Emmerie; *Fl.* Emery. From Emmerin; a loc. n. Hugt. n., Lond. 1685
EMES. *See* Ames
EMLY. From Elmley; a loc. n., Kent
EMMETT. From Amiot; a loc. n., Norm
  William A. in Rot. Hund.
EMMS. *See* Anes
EMSDEN. From Elmstone; a loc. n., Kent
ENDACOTT. A loc. n., Devon
ENDERBY. A loc. n., Leics
ENDERWICK. *See* Inderwick
ENDICOTT. A loc. n., Devon
ENEFER, ENEFER. From Henfynyw; a loc. n.

ENGLAND. *D.* Engelund; *S.* Englund; *N.-Fr.* Anglicus; p.n. *See* Inglis

ENGLEDOW. *See* Ingledew

ENGLEFIELD. A loc. n., Berks

ENGLEHEART. *See* Ingleheart

ENGLISHBY. *See* Ingoldby

ENNIONS. *See* Onions

ENNIS. From Enys; a loc. n., Cornw.

ENRAGHT. *A.S.* Eanred; a p.n.; *a'nræd* (one-minded)

ENSBY. From Ensbury; a loc. n., Dorset

ENSELL, ENSOLL. From Hensall; a loc. n., Yorks

ENSOR. From Edensor; a loc. n., Derbysh.

ENTECOTT. *See* Endicott

ENTICKNAP. From Endikeknap; a loc. n., Yorks, E.R.

ENTWISTLE. A loc. n., Lancs

EPPS. *A.S.* Eppa, Eappa; *F.* Ebbo, Eppo; p.n. *See* Ebbs.

EPTON. From Heppington; a loc. n., Kent

ERDINGTON. A loc. n., Worcest.

ERLAM. From Earlham; a loc. n., Suss.

ERRINGTON. From Erringden; a loc. n., Yorks. Or *see* Harrington

ERSKINE. A loc. n., Renfrew

ERT. *See* Hart

ESAM. From East Ham; a loc. n., Ess.

ESBALD. *See* Archibald

ESCOTT. A loc. n., Devon

ESDAILE. From Eskdale; a loc. n., Cumb.

ESHELBY. From Exilby; a loc. n., Yorks

ESLER. *See* Easlee

ESLING. *S.* Esselin; a p.n. Or Eastling; a loc. n., Kent

ESMOND. *See* Osmund

ESPIE. *D.*, *G.* Espe; a p.n. *See* Hesp

ESPIN. From Hespen; a loc. n., Belg.

ESPLEY. A loc. n., Northbd.

ESS. *F.* Eisse, Aisse; *G.*, *D.*, *Fl.* Esser; *Dch.* Es; *A.S.* Æs, Æsc (ash); p.n.

ESSINGTON. A loc. n., Staffs

ESTCOURT. *See* Escott

ESTWICK. A loc. n., Herts

ETCHELL. From Nechells; a loc. n., Staffs; anciently Echeles. Or *see* Edgell

ETCHES. *D.*, *Dch.* Eggers; *G.* Egers; p.n. *See* Egar

ETHERIDGE. From Etterick (?); a loc n., Selkirk

ETHERINGTON. From Atherington; a loc. n., Devon

ETRIDGE. *See* Etheridge

ETTLES. From Etal; a loc. n., Northbd. Etalle, Belg.; or Etaieles, France

EVANS. Welsh; *Fl.* Evens; p.n.

EVE. *A.S.* Æffa, Eafa, Ef, Efe (elf); *N.-Fr.* Ive; *F.* Eve; p.n. *See* Eaves. Prot. ref., Lond. 1618

EVELEIGH. From Everley; a loc. n., Wilts

EVELY. From the Irish M'Evely. Or *see* Eveleigh

EVELYN. *Dch.* Evelein; *N.-Fr.* Ivelyn; p.n. *See* Aveling

EVENS. *See* Ivens

EVERARD, EVERED, EVERETT, EVERITT. *A.S.* Eoforheard, Eoferard, Efrard, Ebrard (a strong wild boar); *Fl.*, *Dch.* Everard; *Fr.* Evrard; *S.*, *D.* Evert; *G.* Eberhardt; p.n.

In Rot. Hund.

EVERINGHAM. A loc. n., Yorks

EVERS. *See* Ivers

EVERSFIELD. A loc. n.

EVERSHED. From Evershot (?); a loc. n., Dorset

EVERSON. *N.* Evarr; *A.S.* Efer, Eofer (a boar); *S.*, *Fl.* Evers; *D.*, *Dch.* Eversen; p.n. Prot. ref., Lond. 1618

EVERTON. A loc. n., Beds

EVERY. From Ivry; a loc. n., Norm.

    D.B. de Iveri.

EVILL. From Yville; a loc. n., Normandy

EVINGTON. A loc. n., Glos., Leics

EVISON. *See* Everson

EWAN, EWEN. *A.S.* Euing; *Dch.* Ewing, Euwen; *G.* Euen; *D.B.* Ewen; p.n. Prot. ref., Lond. 1618. Scotch M'Ewen. From *A.S.* Eo, Eowa, Ewa; p.n. (ancient)

EWART. *N.-Fr.* De Huart; a p.n.

EWBANK. From Yewbank. A loc. n., Cumb.

EXELBY. A loc. n., Yorks

EXELL. A loc. n., Belgium. Or from Exwell; a loc. n., Rutland

EXLEY. A loc. n., Yorks

EXON. The ancient name of Exeter

EXTON. A loc. n., Devon, Rutland, Somers

EYES. From Huysse; a loc. n., Belg. *Fl.* Eyers; a p.n. Hies, a Prot. ref., Norwich, 1622

EYKIN. From Iken; a loc. n., Suff. Or *F.* Eke, Eike; *D.* Eiche, Eicken, Eken; *A.S.*, Ecca; *Dch.* Eck, Eik, Eijken; p.n. Also an Irish form of Aitken. Or fam. n. of Eke

EYKINS. *Fl.* Eykens; a p.n. *See* Eykin

EYLES. *See* Eels

EYRE. *See* Ayre

EYTON. A loc. n., Heref., Salop

    Held by Warin, relative of Pantulf, Baron of Wem, *D.B.*

F

FABB. *D.*, *Dch.*, *Fl.*, *G.* Faber; *Fr.* Fabri, Fabry; *D.B.* Faber, Fabri; p.n. (a smith). Fabre, a Hugt. n., Lond. 1678

FACER. *N.-Fr.* Fessart; a p.n.

FACHNEY. *Fr.* Fauconnier; a p.n. (a falconer)

FACON. *Fr.* Facon; a p.n. (falcon)

FADDY. *See* M'Fadden

FAGAN. From St Fagan; a loc. n., Glamorgan. Irish p.n. Or *A.S.* Fagin; a p.n.; *fægen* (joyful)

FAGE, FAGG. *A.S.* Fagg, Fac, Feg; p.n.; *N.-Fr.* De Fago; p.n.

FAIERS. *See* Fayers

FAIL. *D.* Feill; *Fl.*, *Dch.* Weel, Vael; p.n.; *A.S. væl* (good, true). Or *see* Fell

FAILES. *See* Felce

FAINT. *Dch.* Vendt; *Fl.* Vent; *G.* Fende; p.n. *See* Went

FAIRALL, FAIRHALL. *See* O'Ferrall

FAIRBAIRN. From Fairburn; a loc. n., Yorks

FAIRBROTHER. *A.S.* Færbeorht; a p.n. (illustrious traveller). Verbore, Prot. ref., Sandwich, 1622

FAIRCHILD. *Fl.* Verschilde; a p.n.

FAIRCLOTH. *See* Fairclough

FAIRCLOUGH. A loc. n.

FAIRFAX. From Ffairfach; a loc. n., Carmarthen. Or Irish Fearfassa, a form of Francis. *N. fögr-fax*; *A.S. fæger-feax*; means fair mane, but it is in no list of p.n.

FAIRFOOT. From Fairford; a loc. n., Glos.

FAIRHEAD. *Fl.* Verheide; a p.n. Or *A.S. fægr-heófod* (fair head)

FAIRHURST. From Fairest; a loc. n., Yorks

FAIRLEY. *Dch.* Verlee; *Fl.* Verlegh, Verley; p.n. Or *see* Fairlie

FAIRLIE. From Fairlee; a loc. n., Hants. Or Fairlie, Ayrshire

FAIRMAN. *See* Fearman

FAIRS, FAIREE. *See* Fayers

FAIRWAY. From Farway; a loc. n., Devon

FAIRWEATHER. From Fairwater; a loc. n., Glamorgan

FAIRY. From Verrey; a loc. n., France. Or *Fr.* Ferry, Féré; p.n. (shod with iron). Hugt. n., Lond. 1618. Also a loc. n., Scotl.

FAITH. *N.-Fr.* de St Faith. Or *S.* Feith; *D.* Faith; *G.* Veith; p.n.; *A.S. fétha* (a foot soldier). Hugt. n., Lond. 1618

FAKES. *D.* Fack; *D.B.* Fech; *F.* Feyke; *Fl.* Feykens; p.n. *See* Fagg

FALCONER. *See* Faulkner

FALKLAND. A loc. n., Scotl.

FALLE. *N. - Fr.* Falet; a p.n.; Fellie in Rot. Hund; Irish M'Fall

FALLENTIRE. *Dch.* Valender; a p.n. A Prot. ref., Colchester, 1622

FALLICK. *Fl.* Falck; *G.* Falk; p.n. (falcon)

FALLON, FALLOON. From Fologne; a loc. n., Flanders. Or Valognes, France; *Fl.* Falon; a p.n.

FALLOWS. From Falaise; a loc. n., Normandy. Also Fallais, in Flanders; *Fl.* Falise, Falloise; p.n.; *D.B.* de Faleise; p.n.
> William de Faleis in Rot. Obl. et Fin., K. John.

FALLS. *See* Fallows

FALLSHAW. From Fullshaw; a loc. n., Ches.

FALVEY. *A.S.* Fealwe (yellow)

FAMIN. *Fl.* Vermin; a p.n. *See* Fearman

FANCOURT. From Falencourt; a loc. n., Normandy

FANE. From Fains or Veynes; loc. n., France; *D.B.* Fenise (?); *F.* Feyen; *Dch.* Feen; *Fr.* Fainc; *Fl.* Fayen, Feyens; p.n.
> Thomas de Vein held lands in Glost. *temp.* K. John, A.D. 1207. Rot. Obl. et Fin. Sir Francis Fane of Fulbeck, Lincs, and Aston, Yorks, third son of Francis, first Earl of Westmd., made K.B. at coronation of Charles I., Feb. 1, 1625.

FANN, FANNER. *Dch.* Fane; *Fl.* Vane; a p.n. *See* Fagan

FANNING. From Faineant; a loc. n., Norm.

FANSHAWE. A loc. n., Derbysh.

FARADAY. An Irish form of Ferguson. Or from La Ferte; a loc. n., Norm.

FARDELL. A loc. n., Devon
> For some time the residence of Sir Walter Raleigh.

FARE. *See* Phair and Fayers

FAREY. *See* Fairy

FARGER, FARGHER. Gael. Fearachur (manly). *See* Fergus. Manx, contracted from Mac Fearghoir; *Ferg.* (brave). *See* Farquhar

FARIS, FARISH. *See* Ferrers

FARJON. *Dch.*, *Fr.* Fargeon; p.n. Hugt., Lond. 1685

FARLER. *See* Farley

FARLEY. A loc. n., Hants, Salop, Staffs, Surr., Wilts

FARLOW. A loc. n., Salop

FARMAN. *See* Fearman. Prot. ref., Colchester, 1605

FARMER. A loc. n., Somers (*D.B.* Ferramere). Or *Fr.* Fermier; *Dch.* Vahrmeijer; p.n.; *A.S. feormere* (a farmer)

FARNBOROUGH. A loc. n., Berks, Hants

FARNFIELD. From Farnsfield; a loc. n., Notts

FARNHAM. A loc. n., Ess., Hants, Surr., Yorks

FARNINGTON. From Farmington; a loc. n., Glost.

FARNLEY. A loc. n., Yorks

FARQUHAR. Gael. Fearachur (manly)

FARR. A loc. n., Sutherland. Or *see* Fayer

FARRAGUT. *Old G.* Faregaud; *Fr.* Farcot; p.n. (travelled Goth)

FARRALL, FARRELL. Irish Farrall, O'Farrell; Fearghal (?) man of strength)

FARRANCE, FARRANT, FARREN.
N.-Fr. Farrand ; *Fl.* Farin ; p.n.
FARRAR, FARRER. *D.* Farrer ; a
p.n. (a teacher). Or *see* Ferrers

FARRINGTON. A loc. n., Dorset,
Somers, Yorks

FARROW. *A.S.* Fara, Faro ; *Dch.*
Faro ; p.n. *See* Fayers

FARTHING. *A.S.* Færthegn, Far-
thein ; *Dch.* Fardon, Vaarting ;
Fl. Verdeyen ; *D.B.* Fardan,
Fardein (Saxon tenants) ; p.n.
See Varden (a traveller Thane)

FARWIG. A loc. n. in Kent

FASHAM. From Faversham ; a loc.
n., Kent (?)

FASSETT. *Fl.* Fassaert, Vassart ;
p.n. Or *see* Fawcett

FASTNEDGE. A loc. n.

FATHERS. *N.* Fjöder (a feather) ;
Dch. Vader ; *D., G.* Vater ; *A.S.*
Fader, Fæder ; *N.-Fr.* Le Feut-
rier ; p.n.

FATLING. *A.S.* Fad ; *Fr.* Vaudelin ;
p.n. *See* Fathers

FAUCIT. *See* Fawcett

FAUCUS. *See* Vaux

FAUGHT. *S.* Vought, Fought ; *Dch.*
Vogt ; *G.* Fauth ; p.n.

FAULCONBRIDGE. From Fauquembergues ; a loc. n., Normandy

FAULDING. *A.S.* Folthwine, Ful-
doin ; p.n. ; *feald, fold* (?) (field.
friend). Or the fam. n. of Fold,
Folth

FAULKE. *N.* Fálki (a falcon) ; *F.*
Fôlerk, Fôke, Fauke ; *S.* Falck,
Falk ; *D.* Falck ; *Dch.* Folkers,
Valk, Fok, Vokke ; *Fl.* Volck ;
G. Falk, Forcke ; *A.S.* Fale, Folc ;
N.-Fr. Fulcher, Fulk, Fulco, etc.;
p.n.

Fouke and Fitz Fouk are in the Roll
of Battell Abbey. Fulche, Fulc,
Fulco, tenants in chief in *D.B.*

FAULKNER. *Fr.* Fauconnier ; a p.n.
(a falconer) ; Hugt. n., Lond.
1681

FAUX. *See* Vaux

FAWCETT. From Fossard, France,
Forcett ; a loc. n., Yorks. Or
Farcet, Hunts
Gilbert de Forset, in Lib. Vit. Dur.

FAWELL. *See* Fowell and Vowell

FAWN. *See* Vaughan

FAY. From Fay ; a loc. n., Norm.
Or *D.* Faye, Feigh ; *G.* Fay,
Fei ; p.n. (a fairy)

FAYERMAN. *See* Fairman

FAYERS. From Vayres (?) ; a loc.
n., France. Or *S., D.* Fehr ; *G.*
Farr ; *Fl.* Feer ; *Dch.* Fehrs ; *A.S.*
Fara, Fær (traveller) ; p.n.

FAZACKERLEY. A loc. n., Lancs

FEA. See Fay

FEAKS. *See* Feek

FEAR. *Fr.* Feauer. *See* Fayers.
Hugt. n., Lond. 1618

FEAREY. *See* Fairy

FEARMAN. *S.* Fehrman ; *G.* Fuhr-
mann ; *A.S.* Faraman ; p.n.
(carter, traveller)

FEARNCOMBE. From Farncombe ;
a loc. n., Surr.

FEARNE. A loc. n., Ross. Or
A.S. Forn ; a p.n. ; *fearn* (fern)

FEARNHEAD. A loc. n., Lancs

FEARNLEY. From Fernilee ; a loc.
n., Derbysh.

FEARNSIDE. A loc. n.

FEARON. *N.-Fr.* Feron ; a p.n.
Ferun in Rot. Hund.

FEASEY. *See* Veasey

FEAST. *Fr.* Fisette ; a p.n.

FEATES. *See* Fetch

FEATHERSTONE. A loc. n. in Yorks

FEATHERSTONEHAUGH. A loc. n.,
Northumbd.

FEAVERYEAR, FEAVIOUR, FEAVYER.
From Favières ; a loc. n., France.
Fr. Favière ; a p.n.
Richard Feverer in Rot. Obl. et Fin.,
K. John. Also Hugt. n.

FEEK. From Vicques ; a loc. n.,
Norm. Or *A.S.* Fec, Feg, Fig ;
S., D. Fick ; *Dch.* Ficke ; *F.*
Feyke, Fekke ; p.n.

FEEN. *See* Fane

FEENEY.　*See* Finney

FEETHAM, FEETUM.　A loc. n., Yorks

FELCE.　*A.S.* Wælisc (?); *Dch.* Fels, Velse; *G.* Felsch; p.n. Felles, Hugt. n., Lond. 1687.　*See* Wallis

FELDWICK.　*Dch.* Veldwijk; a loc. and p.n.

FELGATE.　From Fellgate; a loc. n., Westmd.

FELL.　*N.-Fr.* Faiel; *D.* Fjel; *Dch.* Vel, Velde, Veldt, Wel; *G.* Feldt, Feleer; *Fl.*, *Fr.* Velle; p.n.; *A.S. feld* (field)

　Richard de-la-Felda occurs in Rot. Obl. et Fin., K. John, A.D. 1201 (Yorks). W. de Fall, Rot. Hund. 1272.

FELLOWES.　*See* Felce

FELTHAM.　A loc. n., Middlx., Dorset

FELTON.　A loc. n., Northbd., Somers

FELTWELL.　A loc. n., Norf.

FENDER.　*A.S.* Wenda; *G.*; p.n. (a Vandal)

FENN.　*See* Fane. Fene, a Hugt. n., Norwich, 1622
　In Rot. Hund.

FENNELL.　*Fr.* Venelle; a p.n.

FENNELLY.　*See* Finlay

FENNER.　From Feneur; a loc. n., Belg.　*See* Venner

FENNIMORE.　From Fennemore; a loc. n., Salop. Or Fenemere or Finmere, Oxon

　Gilbert de Finemere held lands there in Oxon, A.D. 1208.

FENSHAM, FENSOM.　From Vinchem; a loc. n., Fland.

FENTHAM, FENTUM.　*See* Phantom

FENTON.　A loc. n., Cornw., Lincs, Notts, Yorks

FENWICK.　A loc. n., Ayrshire, Yorks

FENWRICK.　*D.* Wendrick; *G.* Fenrich; *Dch.* Vendrik; *A.S.* Wenric; p.n. (wend-ruler)

FEREDAY.　*See* Faraday

FERGUS.　Scot., Celt. Fearghus (man of strength)

FERGUSON.　*See* Fergus

FERNIE.　*N.-Fr.* Vernie; a p.n. From Vernai; a loc. n., Norm.

FERNIHOUGH.　From Fernihalgh; a loc. n., Lancs

FERNLEY.　*See* Farnley

FERRABY, FERREBO.　From Ferriby; a loc. n., Lincs, Yorks

FERRETT.　*A.S.* Færheard; *Fl.* Feraert; *Fr.* Ferrett; *G.* Fereth; p.n. (strong traveller). Hugt. n., Dover, 1622

FERRIE.　*See* Fairy

FERRIER.　From Ferrières; a loc. n., Norm. and Fland.; *Fl.* Ferier; a p.n.

FERRIES, FERRIS.　*Fl.* Verraes; a p.n. *See* Faris

FERRIMAN.　*See* Fearman

FERRY.　*See* Fairy

FERTEL.　*G.* Virtel; a p.n. Dim. of Wird; a p.n. (fate)

FESSENDEN.　A loc. n.

FESSEY.　*See* Veasey

FETCH.　From Vietz; a p.n., Germ. Or Fesches, France; *G.* Vietsch, Fietz, Fitza; *D.* Fitzer; p.n.; *N.-Fr.* Fitz; *Fl.* Vits; *D.B.* Fitheus (?); p.n. *See* p. 8, footnote

FEW.　*See* Pugh

FEWKES.　*G.* Fuchs; a p.n. (a fox). Or *see* Foggo

FEWSTER.　*Fl.* Deveuster and Devuyster; p.n.

　William Fuster in Rot. Obl. et Fin., K. John.

FEWTRELL.　*N.-Fr.* Vautrel; a p.n. (a hunter)

　Ralph Futerel, Herts, 1198. Rot. Cur. Reg.

FFOLKES.　*See* Faulke

FFOOKS.　*See* Fewkes

FFYTCHE.　*See* Fetch

FICKLING.　*N.-Fr.* de Wyclyne; a p.n.

FIDDAMAN, FIDDEMAN.　*See* Fiddyman

FIDDES, FIDDY. *N.-Fr.* St Fides
FIDDYMAN. *D.*, *G.* Wiedemann;
S., *Dch.* Wideman; *Fl.* Widmer,
Wydeman; p.n. *See* Fiddy
FIDDYMONT. From Wideumont;
a loc. n., Fland.
FIDGEON. An Irish form of
Pidgeon. Or *Dch.* Viegen; *Fl.*
Vigen; p.n.
FIDGETT. From *Fr.* Fichet; a p.n.
Dim. of Fig. *See* Feek
In Roll of Battell Abbey. Perhaps
from the loc. n. Vichte, Belg.
FIDLER. Le Fidelaire; a loc. n.,
Norm. Or *A.S.* Fitela; *G.* Fiedler;
p.n. (a fiddler). *See* Vidler
FIDOE. *See* Fiddy
FIELD. *D.* Fjelde; a p.n. *See*
Fell
FIELDING. *S.* Felldin; *Dch.* Vel-
den; p.n.; fam. n. *See* Faulding
FIEN, FIENNES. *See* Fane
FIFETT, FIFOOT. *Fr.* Fivet; a p.n.
FIFIELD. A loc. n., Ess., Hants,
Wilts
FIGGINS. *Dch.* Viegen; *Fl.* Vigen;
p.n.
FIGGIS. *Fl.* Figeys; a p.n. *See*
Feek
FIGURES. *See* Vigors
FILBERT. From St Philbert; a
loc. n., France. Or *A.S.* Fil-
brith; *D.* Filbert; p.n. (fully
bright, illustrious). Also *Fr.*
Philibert; *A.S.* Wilbeorht; *Old*
G. Willibert (resolute brightness)
FILGATE. From Villegats; a loc.
n., Normandy
FILL. *A.S.* Fili; *G.* Filla; *Fr.*
Ville; p.n. Or dimin. of Philip (?)
FILLINGER. *N.* Veljungr (?); a n.n.
(a wailing child); *D.* Felling;
Dch. Fellinger; *D.B.* Felaga;
p.n.
FILLINGHAM. A loc. n., Lincs
FILLISTON. A loc. n. Or *Dch.*
Vilsteren (?); a p.n. (?)
FILLMORE, FILMER, FILMORE. *See*
Phillemore

FINBOW. From Finborough (?); a
loc. n., Suff. Or Irish Finbo;
N. Finnbogi; p.n. (white bow)
FINCH. From Vynkt; a loc. n., Belg.
De Vinck, Prot. ref., 1622. *Fl.*
Finch, Vinck; *G.*, *Dch.* Finke;
p.n.; *A.S. finc* (a linnet)
FINCHAM. A loc. n., Norf.; Finchém,
Belg.
FINCHETT. *Fr.* Vinçotte (?); a
p.n. Or dim. of Finch
FINDLATER. A loc. n., Banff
FINELLY. *See* Finlay
FINIGAN. From the Irish O'Finne-
gan; a p.n. (fair)
FINKELL. *Dch.* Finkel, Vinkel.
See Winkel
FINLAY. Celtic Fionnlaoch (white
soldier)
FINNEMORE. *See* Fenimore
FINNEY. *N.* Finni; *A.S.* Fin;
D. Finne; *Fl.* Finné; *S.* Finn;
p.n. (a Finn); Celtic (fair)
FINNIS. *See* Fiennes. Ulf Finisc;
a p.n. in *D.B.*
FIRBANK. A loc. n., Westmd.
FIRK, FIRKINS. *A.S.* Furic; a
p.n. Dim. of *fýr* (fire). Or
fircynu (race of men)
FIRMAN. *Dch.* Ferman; a p.n.
See Fearman
FIRMIN. *Fl.* Vermin; a p.n. *See*
Fearman
FIRMINGER. *Fl.* Verminger; a p.n.
FIRMSTONE. A loc. n.
FIRTH. A loc. n., Scotl.
FISH. *D.*, *S.*, *G.* Fisch; a p.n.
See Fiske
FISHBOURNE. A loc. n., Dur.,
Suss.
FISHENDEN. A loc. n.
FISHER. *G.* Fischer; *D.* Fisker;
Dch., *Fl.* Visscher; p.n.; *A.S.*
fiscere (a fisher)
FISHWICK. A loc. n., Lancs. A
hamlet in the creek of the Ribble.
D.B. Fiscuic
Johannes de Fyschwyke in Lib. Vit.
Dur.

FISHLOCK. From Fishlake; a loc. n., Yorks

FISHPOOL. A loc. n., Lancs, Notts

FISKE. *S.* Fiske; *D.* Fisker; *G.* Fisch; *Fl.* Fisco; *D.B.* Fisc; p.n. (fish)

FITCH. *See* Fetch

FITCHEW. Fitz Hugh (?)

FITHIAN. *See* Vythian

FITT. *Dch.* Vieth; a p.n. *See* Fiddy

FITZPATRICK. *See* Patrickson

FIVASH. A loc. n. Or *see* Vivish

FIX. *D.*, *Fr.*; p.n.; *A.S.* Fex, Feax; p.n. (hairy)

FLACK. *See* Flagg

FLADGATE. A loc. n.

FLAGG. *G.* Flach, Flack; *Dch.* Vlak; p.n. *See* Flegg

FLAMANK. *Fl.* Flamand, Flament, Vleminck; p.n. (a Fleming)

FLAMSTEAD. A loc. n., Herts

FLANDERS. The country of the Flemings

FLANNAGAN. Irish. Young Flann (ruddy)

FLATHER. *A.S.* Flæda; *G.* Flauder, Flatau; p.n. *See* Flatt

FLATLEY. From the Irish Flattley and Flattholy

FLATMAN. *A.S.* Floteman; *Dch.* Flotman; *G.* Flottmann; p.n. (a shipman (?)). Or *see* Flatt

FLATT. *A.S.* Flad, Flæd, Flod; *G.* Flatt; p.n.; *N.* fliôd; *Old G.* flat (beauty). Or *N.-Fr.* Floet; a p.n. From La Flotte, near Rochelle

FLAVELL. *N.-Fr.*, *Lat.* Flavilla (yellow)

FLAXMAN. *Dch.* Vlasman; a p.n.

FLECK. Or Affleck. *See* Flegg

FLEECE. *Dch.* Vlies; *G.* Fleege; p.n. (a fly)

FLEET. A loc. n., Lincs. Or *Dch.* Vliet; a p.n.

FLEETWOOD. A loc. n., Lancs

FLEWELLEN. *See* Llewellyn

FLEGG. *N.* Flóki (hairy, woolly); *D.* Vlak, Fleck; *Dch.* Vleck; *G.* Fleck, Fleger; p.n. Or *N.* fláki (?) (flat moorland)
  G. and *W.* Flegg are hundreds in Norf.

FLEMING. *S.* Flemming; *Dch.* Vlaming; *Fl.* Vleminck; *G.* Flemming; *D.B.* Flamand, Flandren; p.n.
  William le Fleming received the Manor of Aldingham, Lancs, from the Conqueror. Also a Prot. ref. n., Sandwich, 1622.

FLETCHER. *N.-Fr.* Le Flechier; a p.n. (arrow-maker)

FLEURY. *Fr.* Fleury; p.n. (florid). Hugt. n., 1687

FLEWITT. *See* Floyd.

FLEY. From Fly, Norm. *Dch.* Vlie; *D.* Flye; p.n.

FLICK. *Dch.* Flick; *D.* Flig; p.n. (a patch). Or *see* Flegg

FLIGHT. *D.* Flycht; *Dch.* Vliet; p.n.; *A.S.* flit (?) (strife)

FLIN. *See* Flynn

FLINDERS. *See* Flanders

FLINT. A loc. n., Wales. Or *D.* Flindt, Flint; p.n. (a fire-lock)

FLITT. From Fleet; a loc. n., Hants, Lincs. Or *see* Flight

FLITTEN. *See* Flitton

FLITTON. A loc. n., Beds

FLOGDELL. A loc. n.

FLOOD. Atte Flode, Court of Hustings 1258. Or *see* Flatt. *A.S.*, *S.* Flod; *D.* Flott; *G.* Flöte, Fluder; p.n.

FLOOK. *N.* Flóki; *D.* Floecke; p.n. *See* Flegg

FLOOKS. *See* Flux

FLORY, FLOREE. A loc. n., Flanders. *Fl.* Flory; *Fr.* Floris; p.n. A Hugt. n., Cant. 1622

FLOWERS. From Fleurus; a loc. n., Flanders; *Fl.* Floris, Vloors; *Dch.* Florus; p.n. Hugt. n., Lond. 1618
  Elyas Flur in Rot. Obl. et Fin., K. John.

FLOWERDAY, FLOWERDEW. *Fr.* Fleureau (?) ; a p.n. (flowery)
FLOYD. *See* Lloyd
FLUCK. *See* Flook
FLUDE. *See* Flood
FLURRY. *See* Flory
FLUTTER. *A.S.* Flodhere, Floter ; *G.* Fluder ; *Fr.* Floutier ; p.n. (sea warrior)
FLUX. *G.* ; p.n. Floques ; a loc. n., Normandy
FLY. *See* Fley
FLYNN. Irish O'Flynn ; *N.* Fleinn ; a p.n.
FOALE. *See* Fowell
FODDY. From the Irish *Fodha*, the equivalent of Long
FOGARTY. The Irish equivalent of Swift ; a p.n.
FOGG. *N. fok* (flight). *See* Foggo
FOGGIN. *Dch.* Focken, Vogin ; p.n.; fam. n.
FOGGO. A loc. n., Scotl. Or *A.S.* Focco, Focga ; *N.* Foka ; *fok* (flight) ; *F.* Fokke, Fokko ; p.n. ; *G.* Fökke, Vocke ; *S.* Fock ; *D.* Fog ; p.n. ; *Fr.* Foucaut. Hugt. n., Lond. 1685
FOGWELL. From Vogwell ; a loc. n., Devon
FOISTER. *See* Fewster
FOL, FOLEY. From La Folie, Norm.; *Fr.* Folie ; *D.B.* Folet ; p.n.
Folet in Rot. Obl. et Fin., K. John.
FOLJAMBE. From Fulgent ; a loc. n., Norm.
In Hund. Roll.
FOLKARD. *A.S.* Folcheard (Falc the strong) ; *Fl.* Volckaert ; *G.* Folkert ; p.n.
FOLLETT. *Fr.* ; p.n. *See* Foley
FOLLIOTT. *N.-Fr.* Foliot ; a p.n.
In Roll of Battell Abbey and Rot. Obl. et Fin., K. John.
FOLLOWES. *F.* Fôlers ; a p.n. Or *see* Fallows
FOLLY. *See* Foley
FOLTROP. From Felthorpe ; a loc. n., Norf.

FOOKS. *See* Fewkes
FOOT. *Dch.* Wout ; *G.* Wuthe ; *S.* Futy ; *D.B.* Fot ; p.n. ; *A.S. fôte* (nimble(?))
FOOTER. *Dch.* Wouter ; a p.n. *See* Foot
FOOTMAN. *A.S.* Wudeman ; *Dch.* Woutman ; p.n. (woodman). *See* Foot
FOOTTIT. *N.-Fr.* Fotet ; a p.n.
FORBES. A loc. n., Aberdeensh.
FORD. A loc. n., Devon, Dur., Salops, Staffs, Voorde, Fland.
De Ford in Rot. Obl. et Fin.
FORDER. A. loc. n., Devon. Or *A.S.* Forthere ; a p.n. (warrior)
FORDHAM. A loc. n., Ess.
FORDOM. *See* Fordham
FORDYCE. A loc. n., Banff
FORFEITT. *Fl.* Forfert ; a p.n. (fault)
FORGAN. A loc. n., Fife
FORGE. *N.-Fr.* ; p.n. (smithy) ; Forges ; a loc. n., France and Flanders
FORKER. *See* Farquhar
FORKES. *See* Faulke
FORMAN, FORMON. *D.* Formann ; *Dch.* Foreman ; *Fr.* Formont ; p.n. Hugt. n., Lond. 1618. *See* Farman
FORMBY. A loc. n., Lancs
FORMES. *G.* ; p.n. Contr. of *A.S.* Formannus. *See* Fearman
FORREST. A loc. n., Cornw., Norm., Salop
FORRESTER. From Forestarius ; an officer of feudal times
FORSAITH. A loc. n., Scotl.
FORSBREY. *See* Fosbery
FORSBROOK. A loc. n., Staffs ; *D.B.* Fotesbroc
Osbert de Focebroc was living 3 John, A.D. 1201. Pipe Roll, under Staffordshire. Effigy of John de Fossebroke, Cranford Ch., Northants, A.D. 1418.
FORSCUTT. A loc. n., Somers. Or *see* Foscote

FORSDICK. *See* Fosdyke

FORSGATE. A loc. n.

FORSHAM. From Fosham; a loc. n., Yorks

FORSHAW. From Faugeres; a loc. n., France. Or *D.* Fourchou; a p.n. From *N. Fagriskbgr* (Fairwood); a loc. n. Or *Fr.* Faucheur, Fauchois; p.n. (a mower, reaper)

FORSYTH. *See* Forsaith

FORT, FORTY. *N.-Fr.* le Forte. Or *A.S.* Forth, or Ford; *Dch.* Voort; p.n. *See* Fought

FORWARD. *See* Forwood

FORWOOD. A loc. n., Glost.

FOSBERRY, FOSBERY. From Fosbury; a loc. n., Berks, Wilts

FOSBROOKE. *See* Forsbrook

FOSCOTE. A loc. n., Bucks

FOSDYKE. A loc. n., Lincs

FOSSETT. *See* Fawcett

FOSTER. *Dch.*, *G.* Forster; *Fl.* Fostier; *D.B.* Forst; p.n. (a forester)

FOTHERBY. A loc. n., Lincs

FOTHERGILL. A loc. n.

FOTHERINGHAM. A loc. n., Inverarity, Scotl.

FOULE. *N.* Fugl; *A.S.* Fugel, Ful.; p.n. (a fowl)

FOULIS. A loc. n., Perthsh.

FOULGER. *See* Fulcher

FOULSHAM. A loc. n., Norf.

FOUNTAIN. *Fr.* Fontaine. A Hugt. n., Lond. 1688. A loc. n., Norm.

FOURACRE. A loc. n., Devon

FOWELL, FOWLE. *See* Foule

FOWERAKER. *See* Fouracre

FOWKES. *See* Folkes, or Vaux
Faucus in 1327.

FOWLER. *A.S.* Fula; *G.* Vogler; *Dch.* Vogelaar; p.n. Or Foula; a loc. n., Scotl. *Fr.* Fouiller; a p.n. (a bird-catcher). *See* Fuller
Le Fowelere in Rot. Hund., Ess., Oxon; le Feulere in 1327.

K

FOX. *Fl.* Fockx; a p.n.; fam. n. of Fokko
H. Fox in Rot. Obl. et Fin., K. John. A Prot. ref. n., Lond. 1618; Norwich, 1622. The old English broadsword was called a fox. *See* Vaux and Foggo.

FOXALL, FOXHALL. A loc. n., Suff.

FOXCROFT. A loc. n.

FOXLEY. A loc. n., Devon, Hants, Norf., Staff.

FOXTON. A loc. n., Camb.

FOXWELL. A loc. n., Devon

FOY. From Foye; a loc. n., Heref. Also a Hugt. n. *See* Faith

FOYSON. *See* Fyson

FOYSTER. *See* Fewster

FRADGLEY. From Fradley; a loc. n., Staff.

FRAKES. *See* Freeke

FRAME. *A.S.* Fram; *Dch.* Vreem; *D.* Frahm; *N.-Fr.* Fitz Fram; p.n; *N. fram* (?) (forward)

FRAMPTON. A loc. n., Dorset, Lincs

FRANCIS. *Fr.*; p.n.
R. le Franceis in Rot. Obl. et Fin., K. John.

FRANE. From Fresnes; a loc. n., France

FRANKLAND. A loc. n., Devon

FRANKLANDS. A loc. n., Cumb.

FRANKS. *Fl.* Francus, Francx, Vranckx; p.n. (free)
Francus in 1327.

FRAREY. *See* Freer

FRASER. Fraize; a loc. n., France. *Fr.* Fraiseur; a p.n. From *fraiser*, to plait or to fortify with stakes. Or fraisier (a strawberry)

FRAY. *See* Fry

FRAYLLE. From Fresles; a loc. n., Normandy. Hugt. n.

FREARSON. *N.* Freyer (the god Freyr); *S.* Fria; *G.* Freier; *Fl.* Frey; p.n.

FRECKLETON. A loc. n., Yorks

FREEBODY. *Old G.* Frithubodo; a p.n. (peaceful messenger)

FREEBORN. *A.S.* Freobeorn, Frebern (free bear) ; *G.* Frieben ; p.n.

FREEKE. *A.S.* Fric ; *Fr.* Friche, Fricot ; *Fl.* Frick ; *G., D.* Frich, Fricke ; p.n. (fresh, lusty, bold)

FREELOVE. *N.* Freyleif or Friðleifr ; *A.S.* Frealaf, Frithulaf ; p.n. (peaceful love)

FREEMAN. *A.S.* Freoman ; *D.* Frieman ; *S.* Friman ; *G.* Friedemann ; *Fl.* Freyman ; p.n. Prot. ref., Norwich, 1622

FREEMANTLE. From Fromanteau ; a loc. n., France. Nigel de Fremantel; Northants, 1216; a loc. n., Hants

FREEN. From Vrigne ; a loc. n., France

FREER. *See* Frere

FREMONT. *N.* Friðmund ; *A.S.* Frithumund ; *Fr.* Frémont ; p.n. (peaceful director)

FRENCH. *Fl.* Frentz; *Dch.* Fransche; p.n.

FRERE. Fraire ; a loc. n., Flanders. Or *N., S., D., Dch.* Freyr ; *G.* Freier ; *Fr.* Frère ; *Old G.* Friher (free lord) ; *N.-Fr.* Le Frere; p.n.

FRESHFIELD. A loc. n., Lancs. Or *N.-Fr.* De Freshville ; a p.n.

FRESHWATER. A loc. n., I. of Wight

FRESTON. A loc. n., Lincs, Suff.

FRETWELL. From Freteval ; a loc. n., France

FREUER, FREWER, FREW. From Freux ; a loc. n., Belg. *See* Freer

FREWIN. *A.S.* Freawine, Frithuwine ; p.n. (peaceful friend)

FRICKER. *See* Freeke

FRIGGENS. *A.S.* Frig ; *G.* Frigge ; p.n. (free) ; a fam. n. ; *N.-Fr.* Frigant ; a p.n.

FRIGHT. *S.* Freit ; *G.* Freiheit ; p.n. (freedom)

FRISBY. A loc. n., Leics

FRISWELL. From Freshwell ; a loc. n., Ess. Or *see* Freshfield

FRITCHLEY. A loc. n., Derbysh.

FRITH. *A.S.* Frith ; *D.* Fryd ; p.n. (peace)

FRODSHAM. A loc. n., Ches.

FROGGATT. A loc. n., Derbysh.

FROGLEY. A loc. n.

FROHAWK, FROHOCK. From Frowick (?) ; a loc. n., Ess.

FROMANT, FROMOW. From Froidmont ; a loc. n., Belg. Or *A.S.* Freomund, Fromund (free protector) ; *Fr.* Fromment ; *D.B.* Frumond ; p.n. Fromeau, Hugt., Lond. 1618

FROOM. From Frome ; a loc. n., Somers

FROSDICK. *See* Fosdyke

FROST. A loc. n., Devon. Or *D., G., Dch.* p.n.

FROSTICK. *See* Fosdyke

FROUDE, FROWDE. *N.* Fróði, *fródr* (clever); p.n. ; *D.* Froede ; *S.* Frode ; *A.S.* Froda, Frodo ; p.n.

FRUSHER. *A.S.* Frithugeard (peaceguard) ; *Fl.* Fruchart ; *Dch.* Froschart ; *D.B.* Froissart ; p.n. Fruschart, Prot. ref., Lond. 1687

FRY. From Fry ; a loc. n., Normandy. Or Icel. Frey ; a fam. n. ; *Dch.* Vree ; *Fl.* Frey ; *D.* Frey, Freij, Frie ; *D.B.* Vruoi (?) ; *G.* Frei, Frey ; *A.S.* Freâ (a lord) ; p.n.

FRYER. *N., S., D., G.* Freyer (the name of the god Freyr) ; a p.n. *See* Frere

FUDGE, FUGE. From Foug, France; Fuidge ; a loc. n., Devon. Or Fouches, Belg.

FUDGER. From Fougères ; a loc. n., France

FUGGLE, FUGILL. *A.S.* Fugel ; *N., D.* Fugl ; *S.* Fogel ; *Fl., Dch., G.* Vogel; p.n. (a fowl, bird)

FULCHER. *A.S.* Fulcherus, Folchere ; p.n. (falcon warrior) ; *G.* Fulge. Or from Fougeres or Fulgiers ; a loc. n., Bretagne.

FULFORD. A loc. n., Devon, Yorks

FULKE. *See* Faulke

FULLAGAR. *See* Fulcher

FULLALOVE. *A.S.* Ful-leof; *Old G.* Filuliub; p.n. (very dear)

FULLARTON. A loc. n., Ayr, Hants

FULLBROOK. From Fullerbrook; a loc. n., Devon

FULLER. *See* Fowler. Or *A.S. fullere* (a bleacher); *Fr. fouleur* (a cleanser of cloth).
Le Fulere, Rot. Hund.

FULLERTON. *See* Fullarton

FULLMER. A loc. n., Bucks, Devon

FULLWOOD. A loc. n., Lancs, Notts, Yorks

FULSHAW. *See* Fulcher

FULTON. *See* Fullerton

FUNGE. *D., G., S., Fl., Dch.* Funck, Funke; a p.n. (a spark)

FUNNELL. From Fundenhall; a loc. n., Norf.

FURBER. *A.S.* Fulbeorht; a p.n. (very illustrious); *Fr.* Foubert; A Hugt. n., Lond. 1618

FURBY. From Firby; a loc. n., Kent, Yorks

FURLEY. A loc. n., Devon

FURLONG. A loc. n., Devon

FURNER. *Fr.* Fournier; a p.n. (oven-keeper, baker)

FURNESS. A loc. n., Flanders, Ess. N. Lancs

FURNISH, FURNISS. *See* Furness

FURSDON. A loc. n., Cornw., Devon

FURSE. A loc. n., Devon. Or *N.-Fr.* Foursey (?); a p.n.; *D.B.* Fursa
Forz in Roll of Battell Abbey.

FUSEDALE. A loc. n., Westmd.

FUSSEY. *N.* Fusi. *See* Fyson

FUSSLE. *N.-Fr.* Fuise; *D., G.* Füssel; a p.n. Dim.

FUSTLING. *D.* Füsterling; a p.n.

FUTCHER. *G.* Füger; a p.n. *See* Fudger

FUTLER. *See* Footer

FYFFE. From Fife, a county in Scotland

FYLER. *A.S.* Fula; *G.* Feiler; p.n. *See* Fuller

FYNES. *See* Fiennes

FYSON. *N.* Fusi (dimin. of Vigfús); *G.* Fuhs, Fuss; *Fl.* Fussen; p.n.

G

GABB, GABE. *N.* Gapi; a n.n. (heedless); *A.S.* Gab; *N.-Fr.* Gaipi; *D.* Gabe; p.n. *See* Gape

GABBESEY. A loc. n., Ess.

GABBETT. *Fr.* Gabet; a p.n. Hugt. n., Lond. 1688

GABLE. *G.* Gebel; a p.n. *See* Gabb

GABY. *Fr.* De Gabay. Hugt. n.

GACE. *See* Gaze

GACHES. From Gages; a loc. n., Flanders. Or *Fr.* Gauchez; a p.n. Hugt. n., Lond. 1688

GADD. *A.S.* Gad, Gadelo; *D.* Gad, Gade; *G.* Gade; p.n.; *N. gaddr*; *A.S. gád* (a goad, spear)

GADNEY. From Gedney; a loc. n., Lincs

GADSBY. From Gaddesby; a loc. n., Leics

GADSDEN, GADSDUN. From Gaddesden; a loc. n., Herts

GADSWORTHY. From Godsworthy; a loc. n., Devon

GAFF, GAFFER. From Cavre; a loc. n., Fland. *Fr.* Gaffé; a p.n.

GAGE. *See* Gaches. *S.* Gagge; *Fl.* Gegers; p.n.

GAGEN. *A.S.* Gagan; a p.n. Or *N. gagn* (gain)

GAIGER. *See* Gage

GAINSFORD, GAISFORD. From Gainford; a loc. n., Dur., Yorks

GAITSKELL. From Gaitsgill; a loc. n., Cumb.

GALBRAITH. A loc. n., Scotl.

GALE. A loc. n., Devon, Lancs, Yorks. Or Gheel, Belg.

GALILEE. *Dch.* Gallé, Gallee, Galjee; *Fr.* Gailly, Gailliet, Gailliez, Gaillait; *G.* Galley; p.n. (cheerful)

GALL. *N.-Fr.* Gal; *D.* Gall; *Fr.* Galle; *Fl.* Gal; p.n. (valour). Or Irish M'Gall; Scot. M'Call

GALLAGHER. From Gellygaer; a loc. n., S. Wales; Irish p.n.

GALLAND, GALLANT. *Fr.* Gaillande; *Fl.* Galland; *G.* Gallant; *D.* Galen; p.n. (lively, spirited). A Hugt. n., Lond. 1687

GALLEY. From Gallaix, Belg. *Fr.* Gallais, Gallait, Gallay, Gallet, Gally; p.n. Hugt. n., Lond. 1687

GALLICK. *See* Garlick

GALLIMORE. From Gallemar
A Walloon Hugt. n., *temp.* James I., Canterbury. *Old G.* Gelemir (pledge of fame).

GALLING. *Dch.* Galen; p.n. *See* Gall; fam. n.

GALLOP. *See* Gollop

GALLOWAY. A loc. n., Kirkcudbright

GALLYON. *N.-Fr.* Gaillon; a p.n. A loc. n., Normandy. Hugt. n., Lond. 1618

GALPIN. *Fr.* Galopin; a p.n. Chalopin, a Hugt. n., Lond. 1684. *A.S.* Galba = Abba. *See* Abbs

GALSWORTHY. A loc. n., Devon

GALT. *See* Gault

GALTON. A loc. n., Somers

GAMBLE. *N.* Gamli; *D.* Gamel; *N.-Fr.* le Gemel; *G.* Kammell; *A.S.* Gamel; p.n. (old)

GAMBLING. *Fr.* Gamblin; a p.n.; *N.-Fr.* dim. *See* Gamble

GAME, GAMES. From Cambes; a loc. n., Norm. Or *A.S.* Gamas; *D.* Gemz, Gjems; *G.* Gems; *Fl.* Geemers, Gemers; p.n.

GAMGEE. *See* Gammage

GAMMAGE. From Gamaches; a loc. n., Normandy
Gamages in Roll of Battell Abbey.

GAMMON, GAMON. *N.* Geir-mundr (spear-protector); *F.* Gërman; *G.* Gehrmann; *D.* Garman, Germund; *N.-Fr.* Gamain, Germain; *Fl.* Germon; *A.S.* Garmund; p.n.

GANDY. *N.-Fr.* De Candy; *G.* Gande; p.n.; *Old G.* Ganthar (wolf warrior)

GANE. *Dch.* Geen; a p.n. *See* Gagen

GANLY. From Ganilly; a loc. n., Scilly Isles

GANNAWAY. *See* Knevitt

GANT. *N.-Fr.* De Gand; *Dch.* Gant; p.n. A loc. n., Fland.
De Gand, tenant in chief in *D.B.*

GANTREY. *Old G.* Gendirih; a p.n. (wolf-ruler)

GAPE, GEPP. *A.S.* Gab, Geb, Geppa, Geppo; p.n. *See* Gabb

GAPP. A loc. n., France. Or *see* Gabb

GAPPER. *G.* Gaber; *D.* Gabe; p.n. *See* Gabb

GARD. *See* Garth

GARDEN. A loc. n., Kirkcudbright; Gardonne, France

GARFIT. *See* Garforth

GARFORD. A loc. n., Berks

GARFORTH. A loc. n., Yorks

GARIOCH. A loc. n., Aberdeen

GARLAND. A loc. n., Devon. Or *N.-Fr.* de Garlande; a p.n.

GARLICK. From the Irish M'Gorlick. Or *G.* Gawlick; *Old G.* Gerlac; p.n. (spear-play); *N.-Fr.* Garlayk; a Breton n.

GARMAN. *See* Gamon

GARNER. *A.S.* Garn, Gern, Georn; *D.* Gerner; *N.-Fr.* Garnier; *D.B.* Garner; p.n. (careful warrior)

GARNHAM. A loc. n., Merioneth

GARRARD. Fr. Hugt. n., Lond. 1618. *See* Garrod

GARRETT. *N.-Fr.* Garet

GARRICK. From Gerrick; a loc. n., Yorks. Or *Fr.* Garrigues; a p.n.

GARROD. *N.* Geirröðr (spearwarrior); *A.S.* Gærheard (firm spear); *Dch.* Gerhard, Gerardts, Geraets; *Fl.* Gheeraerts, Geeraerts, Geerts; *G.* Gerhard, Gerhardt; *Fr.* Garet, Garot, Gérard; p.n.

GARSIDE. A loc. n., Yorks

GARTH. *N.* Garðr; *A.S.* Gard, Geard; *S.* Gardt; *Fl.* Gard; *G.* Görth; p.n. A loc. n., S. Wales (a guard, protection)

GARTHWAITE. From Gawthwaite; a loc. n., Lancs

GARTLEY. A loc. n., Aberdeensh.

GARTON. A loc. n., Yorks

GARWOOD. From Garswood; a loc. n., Lancs

GASCOIN, GASCOYNE. *See* Gaskin

GASELEE. *See* Gazeley

GASKARTH. From Geitaskarth; a loc. n. in Iceland. Also Cumbd.(?)

GASKELL. From Gaisgill; a loc. n., Westmd. Or Gascuil, Norm.

GASKIN. *N.-Fr.* De Gascoigne; p.n. (a native of Gascony)

GASS. From Gacé (?); a loc. n., France. *Fr.* Gassé; a p.n. Or *G.* Gasse; *Dch.* Gase; p.n.

GASTON. *A.S.* Gest, Gesting; *Fl.* Gasten; *Fr.* Gaston; p.n. (stranger)

GATAKER. From Goatacre; a loc. n., Wilts

GATEHOUSE. A loc. n., Kirkcudbright

GATES. From Geet; a loc. n., Belg. Or *A.S.* Getius; *N.-Fr.* de Geyt; *Fl.* Gets; p.n. (a Goth)

GATFIELD. A loc. n.

GATH. *D.*; a p.n. *See* Gadd

GATHERCOLE. *A.S.* Gaddo; a p.n.; *gád-col* (a pointed helmet)

GATLAND. From Garthland; a loc. n., Renfrew

GATTENBY. From Gatenby; a loc. n., Yorks

GATTY. *Old G.* Gatto; a p.n. *See* Gadd

GAULT. *N.* Galti (a boar). Or *A.S.* Gald; *Fr.* Gâlt; contr. of Garrelt (Gerhold); p.n.

GAUNT. *See* Gant

GAVIN. Celtic (hawk of battle); *Fr.* Gauvin (?); a p.n.

GAWKROGER. A Scot. term for a foolish wanderer

There is also *rodge*, an old word for a small water-fowl. *See* Gowk.

GAWMAN. *See* Gamon

GAWTHORPE. A loc. n., Yorks

GAY. *N.-Fr.* De Gai; *Fr.*, *Dch.* Gay, Gee; *G.* Gey; p.n.

GAYFER. *See* Gayford

GAYFORD. From Gateford; a loc. n., Notts

GAYLEARD. *Fl.* Gellaert; a p.n.

GAYTHORPE. From Garthorpe; a loc. n., Lincs

GAYTON. A loc. n., Lincs, Norf., Staffs

GAZE. From Gays; a loc. n., Devon. Or *see* Gass

GAZELEY. A loc. n., Suff. Gossellies; a loc. n., Belg. Or *Fr.* Gasly; a p.n.

GEAR. *A.S.* Gær; *Dch.* Gier; p.n. (a spear)

GEARING. *See* Guerin

GEARY. From St Géry; a loc. n., Belg. Or *N.* Geiri (fire); *Fr.* Géry; *D.* Gjeraae; *Fl.* Giers; *G.* Gierig (eager); *D.B.* Gheri; p.n.

GEATER. From Guitres; a loc. n., France

GEDDES. A loc. n., Nairn

GEDGE. *See* Gage

GEE. From Gits; a loc. n., Belg. *Fr.* Ghys; Gy, France; p.n. Or Irish M'Gee

GEEN. From Guines; a loc. n., France. Or *see* Ginn

GEERS. *N.-Fr.* De Guerres; a p.n.

GELASPY. *See* Gillespie

GELDART, GILDART. Irish. Servant of Arthur

GELL. *Fr.*, *Fl.* Geill; *Dch.* Geel; p.n. *See* Jelly

GELLATLY. From Gelly-dy (?); a loc. n., Carmarthen

GELSTHORPE. A loc. n., Notts. *D.* Gjelstrup; *Dch.* Geldorp; loc. and p.n.

GELSTON. From Geldeston; a loc. n., Norf.

GEMLEY. From Gembling; a loc. n., Yorks

GEMMILL. *G.* Gemmell; a p.n. *See* Gamble

GENGE. From Genck; a loc. n., Belg. *Fr.* Gence; a p.n. Or *see* Ginger

GENN. *See* Geen

GENNEY. From the Irish Gennach, M'Kenney

GENT. *Dch.* Gendt; a p.n. *See* Gant

GENTLE. From Gentilly; a loc. n., France. *Fr.* Gentil; a p.n.
In Rot. Obl. et Fin. J. Gentyl, Longdon, Staffs, 1341.

GENTRY. *See* Gantrey

GEOGHEGAN or MACGEOGHAGAN. From the Irish MacEachagain or MacEoghagain (young warrior)
The MacGeoghagans were hereditary marshalls of Meath.

GERDAN. *See* Jordan

GERLING. *A.S.*, *Dch.* Gerling; a p.n.; fam. n. from *N. geirr*; *A.S. går* (a spear)

GERMAN. St Germain; a loc. n. in Normandy and Belgium. *Fr.* Germon. Hugt. n., Lond. 1618. *See* Gamon

GERRISH. *Dch.* Gerrets, Gerrits; p.n. *See* Garrod

GERVASE. *N.* Geirfuss (?); *N.-Fr.* Gervais; p.n. (spear eagerness)

GERY. *See* Gearey

GETGOOD. *A.S.* Geatgod (a Jute Goth)

GETHING. From Geddiug; a loc. n., Suff.; Gedinne; Belg.; or Geithain, Germ. *Fl.* Goetinck; p.n.

GETTEN, GETTING. *See* Gething

GIBBENS, GIBBINGS. Irish M'Gibben. Or *F.* Jibbo, Jibben; *Fl.* Giebens, Gibbs; *Dch.* Gebbing; p.n.

GIBBS. *D.* Gieb; *F.* Gibbs; *Dch.* Gips; p.n.; a contr. of Gilbert. Or *A.S.* Geb, Geppa, Gibbius; p.n.; *geben* (to give)

GIBERNE, GIBBON. *See* Gibbings. *N.-Fr.* Gibon

GIBLET. *N.-Fr.* Gibelot. *See* Gibbs

GIDDENS, GIDDINGS. From Gidding; a loc. n., Hunts. Or *D.* Giede; *Fr.* Guidon; *A.S.* Ghida, Gidding; p.n.
Guidon in Rot. Obl. et Fin., K. John. Stephen Guitan, a Hugt. n., London, in 1687. *N.* Gydinga (?) (Jew).

GIDLEY. From Gidleigh; a loc. n., Devon

GIDNEY. From Gedney; a loc. n., Lincs

GIEN. *See* Geen

GIFFEN. A loc. n., Ayrsh.

GIFFORD. *A.S.* Gifheard; a p.n. (give hard). Or *N.-Fr.* Giffard; a p.n. (full-cheeked). Or Gifford, a loc. n., Haddington
Giffard in Roll of Battell Abbey. Gifard, a tenant in chief in *D.B.*

GIGGLE. *See* Jiggle

GILAIN. From St Ghislain; a loc. n., Belg. Or *see* Gilleny

GILBERT. *N.* Gisli-bjártr; *Fl.* Gillebaert; *Fr.* Gibert, Gilbert; *D.B.* Chilbert, Ghilebrid, Giselbert; p.n.; *N. gísl* (hostage), *bjártr* (bright)

GILBEY. From Gilby; a loc. n., Lincs

GILBODY. *N.* Gisl-bodi (?) (hostage envoy)

GILCHRIST. From the Irish Giolla Chriosd (the servant of Christ). *A.S.* Gilcrist; *S.* Gillqvist; p.n.

GILDEA. From the Irish *Giolla Dé* (the servant of God)

GILDEN. *Dch.*; p.n.

GILDERSLEEVES. From Gelder-sleeuw; a loc. n., Holland

GILES. St Gilles; a loc. n., Flanders. *Fl.* Gilis; *Fr.* Gilles; *D.* Giles; p.n. *N. gisl, gils* (a hostage)

GILFILLAN. A loc. n., Wigtownshire. Or servant of St Fillan

GILHAM. From Gillingham; a loc. n., Dorset, Kent. Or *S.* Gilljam; *Fr.* Gillaume; p.n.

GILL. From the Gaelic *giolla* (a servant or disciple). *G.* Gilla; *Fr.* Gille; *S.* Gihl; *D.* Gille; *A.S.* Gilo, Gile, Ghil; p.n.; Irish M'Gill

GILLAM. *See* Gilham

GILLAN, GILLEN, GILLENY. From the Irish M'Gullian, Gillen, Killen; *gill Oin* (the servant of John)

GILLESPIE. From Gillesbie; a loc. n., Dumfries. Or from the Gaelic Gillescop and Gillespie (the bishop's servant)

GILLETT. *Fr.*; p.n. *See* Gillott

GILLFOYLE. From the Irish *Giolla Phoil* (the servant of Paul)

GILLIBRAND. *A.S.* Gislbrand (hostage sword)

GILLINGHAM. A loc. n., Somers;

GILLINGS. *A.S.* Gilling; a fam. n.; *S.* Gillen; *Dch.* Gilling; *Fl.* Gillain; p.n. *See* Gill

GILLINGTON. A loc. n.

GILLITLIE. *See* Gellatly

GILMARTIN. *See* Kilmartin

GILLOT. *Fr.* Huguenot n., Lond. 1618. Dimin. of Gill

GILMORE. A loc. n., Yorks. Or from the Irish Mac Giolla Muire; a p.n. (son of the great servant)

GILMOUR. *See* Gilmore

GILPATRICK or KILPATRICK. *D.B.* Ghilepatric. From the Irish Giolla Padraig; a p.n. (devoted to St Patrick)

GILPIN. *See* Kilpin

GILSON. *Fl.*; p.n. *See* Gill

GILSTRAP. *See* Gelsthorpe

GILYARD. *A.S.* Gislheard (strong hostage); *Fr.* Gilliard; p.n. Goilard, Hugt. n., Lond. 1687

GIMLETT. *Fr.* Gimlette. A Huguenot n., Lond. 1618. Dim. of *Gimm* (gem)

GINDER. *A.S.* Geanthryth (a true giver); *Fl.* Gindra (?); p.n.

GINGEL. *G.* Ginschel; p.n.

GINGER. *A.S.* Geng (traveller); *Dch.* Genger; p.n.

GINN. From the Irish M'Ginn. Or *Fr.* Gynn; *D.* Gihn; *Dch.* Gijn; *G.* Gins; p.n.; *N. ginn* (a jester); *N.-Fr.* Guines
W. de Gene, Rot. Hund.

GIPPS. *See* Gibbs

GIRDLER. *See* Curtler

GIRDLESTONE. A loc. n.

GIRLING. *See* Gerling

GISBOURNE. From Gisburne; a loc. n., Yorks

GISBY. From Girsby (?), Lincs; a loc. n.

GISCARD. *A.S.* Gislheard (firm hostage); *Fl.* Gischard; p.n.

GISSING. A loc. n., Norf.

GISSON. *See* Gissing

GITTENS, GITTINGS. *See* Giddings

GITTUS. From Gits; a loc. n., Flanders. *Dch.* Gidts; a p.n.

GIVEEN, GIVEN. *See* Giffen or Gavin

GLADDING. *See* Gladwin

GLADSTONE. *See* Gledstanes

GLADWELL. A loc. n.

GLADWYN. *N.* Glað-vinnr (a gladsome friend); *A.S.* Gladewin, Gladuin, Gledwin; p.n.

GLAISHER. *N.* Glæsir (shining); *D.* Glæser; *G.* Gläser; *Fl.* Glaser; p.n.

GLANVILLE. A loc. n., Norm.

GLASFUIRD. A loc. n., Lanark

GLASS. *Dch., S.* Glas; *D.* Glase, Glass; *G.* Glass, Glees; *Fr.* Glace; p.n.; Celtic (blue). A Hugt. n., Lond. 1618; a loc. n., Scot.

GLASHBY. *See* Gillespie

GLASPY. *See* Gillespie

GLASSCOCK. Dimin. of Glass. Or Glascote; a loc. n., Staffs

GLASSINGTON. From Glasserton; a loc. n., Wigtonshire

GLASSON. A loc. n., Lancs. Or Celtic Glasan (blue). *See* Glass

GLASSPOLE, GLASSPOOL. A loc. n. *B.* glâs (grey), pwll (a pool)

GLASSUP. *See* Glossop

GLATWORTHY. *See* Clapworthy

GLAZEBROOK. A loc. n., Lancs

GLAZIN. From the Irish M'Glashin; a p.n. *See* Glass

GLAZZARD. From Glasoed; a loc. n., Monmouth

GLEAD. *See* Gleed

GLEADAH, GLEADOWE. From Gleadhow; a loc. n., Yorks

GLEASON. From Gleaston; a loc. n., Lancs

GLEDSTANES. A loc. n., Scotland

GLEED. *N.* Glædir (a red-hot coal, fiery); *D.* Glad; *G.* Glied; p.n.; *A.S.* Glæd (cheerful)

GLENDINNING. A loc. n., Dumfries

GLENHAM. From Glentham; a loc. n., Lincs

GLENNIE. From the Celtic Gleannau (a little upland glen). Or *see* Glynne

GLEW. Gheluwe, a loc. n., Belg. *D.* Gleu; *G.* Glauer; *A.S.* Gleu; gleaw (skilful, wise); p.n. Or *see* M'Glew

GLISTER. *D.* Glistrup; a loc. and p.n.

GLITHROW. *See* Clitheroe

GLOAG. *See* Cloake

GLOSSOP. A loc. n., Derbysh.

GLOVER. *N.-Fr.* Gantier; a p.n.

GLYDE. *See* Gleed

GLYNNE. A loc. n., Cornw. Ghlin; a loc. n., Belg. Or *N.* Glenna, n.n.; *S.* Glenne; *D.* Glyhn; *Fr.* Glin; *Dch.* Glindt; p.n.; Irish M'Glynn

GOACHER. *Fr.* Gaucher; *N.* Valgeir; *A.S.* Walcher; p.n. (foreign spear). Hugt. n.

GOAD. *N.* Goddi (dimin. of comp. names, as Guð-run, etc.). Or *S.* Godha Gohde; *G.* Göde; *D.* Goth; *Fl.* Gody, Gœdde; *Fr.* Godde, Goudé, Got; *Dch.* Goede, Götte; *A.S.* Gode, Godde, Gote, Goda (a Goth), Goti, Gouti; p.n.

Walter Gode in Rot. Obl. et Fin. W. Godio in Rot. Hund.

GOADBY. A loc. n., Leics

GOATE. *See* Goad

GOATLEY. From Godeley; a loc. n., Ches.

GOBBETT. From Gobit; a loc. n., Worcest. Or *A.S.* Godbeort; *G.* Gutbier, Göbert; *Fl.* Gobert, Gobbet; *Dch.* Gobits; p.n. *See* Gotobed

GOBBY. *See* Gobbett

GOBLE. *G.* Göbel; p.n. Or *Fr.* Goupil (a young fox). *See* Godbold

GODBEER, GODBER. *See* Gobbett

GODBOLD, GODBOLT. *N.* Guðbaldr; *D.B.* Godebold; p.n. (good-bold)

GODBY. *See* Goadby

GODDARD. *N.* Guð-rödr (good strength); *Fl.*, *N.-Fr.* Godart; *Dch.* Goddard; *D.*, *G.* Gotthard; *A.S.* Godard, Godheard; p.n. Hugt. n., Lond. 1618

GODFREY. *N.* Guðfriðr; *D.* Godfred; *A.S.* Godfrith; *Fr.* Godefroy; p.n. (good peace). A Hugt. n., Lond. 1681

GODING. *A.S.*, *Dch.*, *Fl.* Godding; a p.n. *See* Goad. A Prot. ref. n., Lond. 1685

GODLEE, GODLEY. A loc. n., Ches.

GODSON. From Godstone; a loc. n., Staffs. Or *see* Goad, Goodson

GOE. From Goé; a loc. n., Belgium. Gouy, a Prot. ref., Lond. 1688. Or *see* Goy

GOFF. *Fl.* Goffe; *G.* Göffi; p.n.;
A.S. geof (a gift). *See* Gough

GOFFEN, GOFFIN. *Fl.*, *Dch.*
Goffin; p.n.

GOFT. *See* Goff

GOGGS. *A.S.* Gogo; *Dch.* Gog,
Gokkes; p.n. *See* Coggan

GOLD. *A.S.* Golde; *D.* Gold; *G.*
Golde; p.n. (value)

GOLDBY. From Coleby; a loc. n.,
Kent, Lincs

GOLDING. *G.* Golding; a p.n.

GOLDINGHAM. From Coldingham;
a loc. n., Berwick

GOLDRIDGE. From Coleridge (?); a
loc. n., Devon

GOLDRING. A *G.* p.n.; *A.S.* Golde-
win (valued friend)

GOLDSBURY. From Goldsborough;
a loc. n., Yorks

GOLDSWORTHY. A loc. n., Devon

GOLDTHORPE. A loc. n., Yorks

GOLDUP. *See* Goldthorpe

GOLDY. *See* Gold

GOLIGHTLY. *See* Gellatly

GOLL, GOLLE. *A.S.* Gol; *G.*
Golla, Golli; p.n.; *N. gull* (gold)

GOLLEDGE. *See* College

GOLLOP. From Gollup; a loc. n.,
Germ. *G.* Gollob; a p.n.

GOMERY. From the *N.-Fr.* De
Cambray

This family came from Cambray in
Normandy, and were tenants in
chief (*D.B.*) of eighty-one manors.
Comp. Lee Gomery or Legh Com-
brey, Salop.

GOMM. *G.*; p.n. *See* Game

GONNER. *A.S.* Gonhard, Gonnar,
Gonuerd; p.n. (strong soldier).
Or *see* Gunn

GOOBY. *See* Guby

GOOCH. *See* Gowk

GOODACRE. *A.S.* Godwacer (?);
D. Goedecke; *Dch.* Goudecke;
p.n. (watchful Goth); *G.* Godeck;
p.n. (Goth watcher). Or from
Goatacre; a loc. n., Wilts. Or
see Gataker

GOODA. From Gouda; a loc. n.,
Holland. *Fr.* Goudeau; a p.n.
See Goad

GOODALL. *N.-Fr.* Godel; a p.n.

Godhale, 1199; Godehil in Rot
Hund.

GOODAY. *D.* Goday; *N.-Fr.* Godet,
Goudé; *A.S.* Goda, Godœg;
p.n. (illustrious Goth)

GOODBAN. *N.* Guðbrandr (good
sword); a p.n.

GOODBARNE. *See* Goodban

GOODBODY. *A.S.* Godbodi (Goth
envoy)

GOODCHAP. From Goodcheap; a
loc. n., Kent

GOODCHILD. From Goodchill; a
loc. n., Westmd. Or *A.S.* Godc-
cild; a p.n. (Goth soldier (?))

GOODDY, GOODE, GOODEY. *See*
Gooday

GOODENOUGH. *Fr.* Godineau; a
p.n. (deformed)

Mr Ferguson thinks it comes from an
old Frankish Godenulf (Goth wolf).

GOODFELLOW. *N.-Fr.* Bonenfant;
A.S. godfelaw (?)

GOODGE. *See* Goudge

GOODGER. *See* Goodyer

GOODHART. *See* Goddard

GOODHEW. *A.S.* Godo; *N.-Fr.*
Gaudiou; *Fr.* Godeheu, Gode-
aux; p.n. *See* Goad

GOODING. *See* Goding

GOODLAD. A *Dch.* p.n.

GOODLIFFE. *N.* Guð-leif; *A.S.*
Guthlaf; p.n. (good inheritance)

GOODMAN. *N.* Guðmundr; *A.S.*
Gudmund; *D.* Gudmann; *F.*
Goddeman, Goodman; *G.* Gutt-
mann; *N.-Fr.* Godeman; *D.B.*
Godman, Godmund, Gudmund;
p.n. (good protector)

GOODRICH. A loc. n., Heref.

GOODRICK. *N.* Guðrikr (good
mighty one); *D.B.* Godric;
p.n.

GOODRUM. *N.* Guð-ormr (war-serpent); *A.S.* Guthrum; *G.* Gudrum; *Dch.* Gottmer; p.n.

GOODSON. A loc. n., Norf.

GOODWILL. From Goderville; a loc. n., Normandy

GOODWIN. *N.* Guð-vinr; *A.S.* Godwin, Godwine, Guthwine (good friend or battle friend); *Fl.* Goddyn, Goetvinck, Guttin; *N.-Fr.* Godvinne; *Fr.* Goudinne, Godefin; *G.* Guttwein; p.n.

> *N.-Fr.* Goduin, a tenant in chief; *D.B.* Goduin, Gotwin, under-tenants at time of Survey. Goduin, Saxon tenant, Edw. Conf. Godwine, Rot. Hund. For varieties of spelling *see* Introduction, page 2. Otto Abel thinks it is equivalent to Theophilus.

GOODYER. *A.S.* Godhere (good warrior); *Fr.* Goudier; p.n.

GOOSE. From Goes; a loc. n., Holland. A Hugt. n., Norwich, 1622. *See* Goss

GOOSEY, GOOZEE. From Gozée; a loc. n., Belg.

GOPP. A loc. n., Flint. *See* Guppy

GOPSILL. From Gopsall; a loc. n., Leics

GORDON. A loc. n., Berwick

GORE. From Goor; a loc. n., Holland. *N.* Gorr (gore); *Dch.* Goor; p.n. Or *see* Gower

GORHAM. A loc. n.

GORING. A loc. n., Oxf., Suss.

GORMAN. *Dch.* Gortman; *Fl.* Gouman; *Fr.* Gourmont; p.n. *See* Gamon

GORNALL. A loc. n., Staffs

GORRILL. *D.* Gorell; *G.* Gorille; p.n. Dim. of Gorr. Or Welsh Gwril (lordly)

GORST. From Jort; a loc. n., Norm. Sire de Jort at Hastings

GORTON. A loc. n., Lancs

GOSFORD. A loc. n., Haddingtonshire

GOSLING. *A.S.* Gozlin, Goscelin, Godzelin; *Dch.* Goseling; *N.-Fr.* Gosselin; p.n. Prot. ref., Lond. 1622. *See* Goss

GOSS. *S.* Gooes; *G.* Gosse; *Dch.* Goos, Goes; *Fl.* Gosse, Gossy; *A.S.* Gos; p.n. From *Old G.* Gauzlind; *goz*, a form of *gaud* (Goth), *lind* (gentle)

GOSSETT. *See* Gozzard

GOSTELLOW. *See* Costello

GOSWELL. From Goosewell, Plymstock, Devon

GOTHORP. *See* Gawthorpe

GOTLEY. From Godley; a loc. n., Ches.

GOTLING. *See* Goad

GOTOBED. *N.* Guðbjártr (good-bright); *A.S.* Cuthbert, Godebert, Guthbeorht, Gutbert; p.n.

GOTSON. *See* Goodson

GOTTO, GOTTS. *See* Goad

GOUDGE. *Fr.* Gouge; a p.n.

GOUGH. From the Irish M'Gough; a p.n. (the red)

GOUK. *See* Gowk

GOULBURN. From Goulborn; a loc. n., Ches., Lancs

GOULD. *See* Gold

GOULDER. *See* Gold

GOUNDRY. *N.-Fr.* de Gundres. Or *A.S.* Gundræd (war counsellor); *Fr.*, *Fl.* Gondry; p.n.

GOURLAY, GOURLEY. *See* Curly

GOVANE. A loc. n., Lanark

GOW. Irish Gobha (a smith). Or *Dch.* Gouw; a p.n.

GOWEN. Irish M'Gowan. *See* Gow

GOWER. From Goher; a loc. n., Norm.

> Thomas de Gaweia in Rot. Obl. et Fin., K. John. Gower in Roll of Battell Abbey.

GOWERS. *Dch.* Govers; *Fl.* Govaerts; p.n. Gouers, a Prot. ref., Lond. 1618

GOWING. A loc. n., Devon. Or *see* Gowen

GOWK. *N.* Gaukr; *G.* Gauck; *Fr.* Gouche; p.n. (a cuckoo)

> Couk in Rot. Obl. et Fin.

GOWLAND. *See* Garland

GOWTHORPE. A loc. n., Yorks

GOWTHWAITE. A loc. n., Yorks
GOWTRIDGE. *See* Gutteridge
GOY, GHOY. A loc. n., Belg. *Fl.*
Goye; *Dch.* Goey; *Fr.* Gouy;
p.n. Gouy; a loc. n., Normandy.
Hugt. n., 1687. *See* Goe
GOYDER. *G.* Geuther; *Dch.* Goede;
p.n. *See* Goad or Gwyther
GOYMER. *See* Guymer
GOZZARD. *Old G.* Gozhart (strong
Goth); *N.-Fr.* Gocet, Gozet, Gos-
set; p.n.
GRABHAM. From Graban (?); a
loc. n., Brecon
GRACE. *See* Gracie
GRACEY, GRACIE. *Fr.* Gresy; p.n.
From Graçay; a loc. n., France
GRADDON. *See* Gratton
GRADWELL. A loc. n., Yorks. *D.B.*
Cradeuuelle
GRAFHAM. A loc. n., Hunts
GRAFTON. A loc. n., Warw., Wilts,
Yorks
GRAHAM. From Grantham or
Graham; a loc. n. in Kesteven,
Lincs
William de Graham settled in Scotland
in the twelfth century.
GRAIN. *N.-Fr.* De Grana; *Fr.*
Graine; a p.n.
GRAMMER. From Gramat; a loc.
n., France
Latinised into Grammaticus, Pipe
Roll., Middleton, Yorks, 1189
GRAND. *Fr.* Grand; a p.n.
Graunt in Roll of Battell Abbey; Le
Grant in Rot. Obl. et Fin.
GRANDIGE. *Fr.* Graindorge; a p.n.
GRANDISON, GRANDCHAIN. A loc.
n., France. *Fr.* Grandjean; a
p.n.
In Roll of Battell Abbey.
GRANGER. *Fr.* Grangé; a p.n.;
N.-Fr. granger (farmer of a
grange)
GRANT. *See* Grand
GRANTHAM. A loc. n., Lincs
GRANTLEY. A loc. n., Yorks
GRANVILLE. *See* Grenville

GRAPES. *N.* Greipr (?); *S.* Grape;
G. Gräber; *Dch.* Graap; *Fl.*
Greps; p.n.; *A.S. grœp* (a ditch).
A Prot. ref. n., Lond. 1618
GRASBY. A loc. n., Lincs
GRATTAN. *See* Gratton
GRATTON. A loc. n., Devon
GRATTRIDGE. *See* Greatrex
GRAVATT. *Fl.* Grauwet; *Fr.* Gravet,
Gravot; p.n. Dim. of Grave
GRAVE. *N.-Fr.* De la Gréve; *D.B.*
Greve; p.n.
GRAVENER. From Greven; a loc.
n., Germ. *Fl.* Greven; p.n.
GRAVER. *Dch.* Greve; *Fr.* Gravé;
p.n. *See* Grave
GRAVES. *Fl.* Gravis; a p.n. *See*
Grave
GRAVESTON. A loc. n. *See* Grave
GRAY. A loc. n., Normandy. *Fr.*
Grey; *G.* Graye; *D.B.* De Grai;
p.n.
De Gray or Grai in Rot. Obl. et Fin.,
K. John. A Hugt. n., Lond.
1618.
GRAZEBROOK. From Gresbroke or
Greasbrough; a loc. n., Yorks
GREABY. From Grebby; a loc. n.,
Lincs
GREAGSBY. A loc. n.
GREAM. *D.*, *Dch.* Grim; a p.n.
See Grimmer. A Hugt. n., Nor-
wich, 1622
GREATHEAD. *N.-Fr.* Grosteste; a
p.n.
In Rot. Hund. 1272. Robt. G., Bp.
of Linc. Gretheved, Grethed in
1327.
GREATREX. From Great Rakes;
a loc. n., Cumb., Derbysh., Staffs.
Or Gayteric (Catterick), Yorks
GREBBY. *Dch.* Grebe; a p.n. *See*
Grubb
GREEDAY. *A.S.* Grid; *Dch.* Greede;
p.n. *See* Crate
GREEF. *D.* Greiff; *Dch.* Griev;
G. Grief; p.n.; *A.S. gerefa*
(sheriff)

GREELY, GRELLY. From Gresillé; a loc. n., Anjou.
  Sir T. de Grelly, 1307.
GREEN. A freq. loc. n. Or *A.S.* Gron, Grun; *D.* Grün; *Dch.* Grin, Groen; *D.B.* Grene, Greno, Grino; p.n.; Green, in the sense of young, fresh
  H. del Grene in Lib. Vit. Dur.; Atte Grene, Court of Hustings, 1258.
GREENAWAY. A loc. n., Devon. Or *N.* Gronveg; *Dch.* Groeneweg; loc. and p.n.
GREENHALGH. A loc. n., Lancs
GREENHOW. A loc. n., Yorks
GREENLAW. A loc. n., Berwick, Kirkcudbright, Edinb.
GREENLEAF. *A.S.* Granulf (?). Perhaps a corruption of the *N.* Grímólf (stern wolf)
GREENLEES. A loc. n., Scotl.
GREENSLADE. A loc. n., Devon
GREENSTREET. From Greenstead; a loc. n., Ess.
GREENWAY. A loc. n., Devon
GREENWELL. A loc. n., Dur., Yorks. Or Grenville
GREENWOOD. A loc. n.
GREER, GREIR. *Dch.* Greijr, Greier, a p.n. Prot. ref., 1687
GREET. A loc. n., Glost., Salop
GREETHAM. A loc. n., Rutland
GREEVES. *See* Grave
GREGG, GREIG. From Gréges; a loc. n.; France, Graig, Monmouth. Or *G.* Kreck, Krex; *Fl.* Greck; p.n.; Celtic *greg* (fierce)
GRENHAM. From Greenham; a loc. n., Berks
GRENTO. *N.-Fr.* De Grento
GRENVILLE. From Greinville; a loc. n., Norm.
GRESHAM. A loc. n., Norf.
GRESLEY. A loc. n., Leics, Notts
  Nigel, second son of Nigel de Toigni (afterwards de Stafford), took the name of de Gresley from his lordship of Gresley, Leics. De Grisele in Rot. Obl. et Fin., K. John.
GRESSWELL. *See* Cresswell

GRETTON. A loc. n., Glost., Northants, Salop
GREW. *Fr.* Grieu, Grout; p.n. (a little dog). Or Le Grue (a crane)
GREX. *See* Gregg
GREY. *See* Gray
GRIBBEN. Fam. n. of *A.S.* Grippo; a p.n. (a gripper). Or from M'Robin
GRIBBLE. A loc. n., Devon
GRICE. *N.-Fr.* De Grisy, Grise. Or *D., G., Fl.* Gries, Greis (grizzled, grey); p.n.
GRICKS. *See* Grix
GRIDLEY. A loc. n.
GRIEF. *See* Greef
GRIFFIN. Welsh Gruffin; a p.n. (ruddy)
GRIFFITH. Welsh Gruffydd; a p.n. (ruddy)
GRIGG. *See* Grix
GRIGGS. A loc. n., Cornw. Or *see* Grix
GRIGSBY. *See* Greagsby
GRIGSON. *See* Grigg
GRIMBLE. *N.* Grimbald (stern, fierce, and bold); *A.S.* Grimbeald; *Fr.* Grimoult; p.n.
GRIMDITCH. A loc. n.
GRIME, GRIMER, GRIMES. *See* Grimmer
GRIMLEY. A loc. n., Worcest.
GRIMMER. *N.* Grímr (stern); *D., S., Dch., G.* Grimm, Grimmer; *D.B.* Grim; p.n.
GRIMMETT. *Fr.* dimin. of Grim
GRIMMOND. *N.* Grimmundr; *Fr.* Grimont; *Dch.* Grimmon; p.n. (stern director)
GRIMOLDBY. A loc. n., Lincs
GRIMSDALE. From Grinsdale; a loc. n., Cumb.
GRIMSEY. From Grimsby; a loc. n., Lincs
GRIMSHAW. A loc. n., Yorks
GRIMSON. *N.* Grimssynr; a p.n. Or *see* Grimston
GRIMSTON. A loc. n., Leics, Norf., Yorks

GRIMTHORPE. A loc. n., Yorks

GRIMWADE. *See* Grimwood

GRIMWOOD. A loc. n., Suff.

GRINDLEY. A loc. n., Staffs

GRINDROD. A loc. n., Lancs. Anciently Grenerawde (Fishwick)

GRINHAM. From Grittenham (?); a loc. n. Wilts

GRINLAW. *See* Greenlaw

GRINLING. Dim. of Green

GRINSLADE. From Greenslade; a loc. n., Devon

GRINSTED. From Grinstead; a loc. n., Kent, Suss.

GRINT. *A.S.* Grind; *Fl.* Grinaert; *G.* Grünert; p.n.

GRISENTHWAITE. From Gristwaite; a loc. n., Yorks

GRISKS. *G.* Grischke; a p.n. Dim. of Grice

GRISS. *See* Grice

GRISSAM. *See* Gresham

GRISSELL. *Fr.* Grisel; a p.n.

GRISTOCK. From Greystock; a loc. n., Cumb.

GRISTON. A loc. n., Norf.

GRITTON, GRITTEN. *See* Gretton

GRIX. *Fl.* Krickx; *Dch.* Griek, Kriek; a p.n.; *A.S. grig* (grey)

GRIZEDALE. A loc. n., Lancs, Yorks

GROCOTT, GROWCUTT. *See* Groocock

GROGAN. A loc. n., Queen's Co., Ireland

GROMIT. *See* Groom

GROOCOCK. *G.* Groche; a p.n. *See* Grew

GROOM. *A.S., D.* Grum; *Dch.* Grummer; *Fr.* Grummeau; *G.* Crumm, Grummich; p.n. (fierce, severe)

GROSS. *D.* Gross; *Fl.* Groos, Gros; *Fr.* Grosse; *Dch.* Grosz; *D.B.* Grossus; p.n. (big, tall)

GROSVENOR. *Fr.* Grovenour; a p.n. *Lat.* Grandis Venator (chief huntsman)

GROTE. *See* Croote

GROUND. *S., G.* Grund; a p.n. Or *see* Grand

GROUT. *N.* Graut (groats); *G.* Grutz, Kraut; *Dch.* Groot; *Fl.* Groeters; *D.* Grude; p.n.; *D.B.* Grutt, Grud. *See* Croote

GROVES. *D.* Grove; a p.n.; *grov* (big). Or Atte-groves; a loc. n.

GROWSE. From Graux; a loc. n., Belg. *Dch.* Graus; a p.n.

GRUBB. *D.* Grubb; *G.* Grube; *Dch.* Grob; p.n. Grube; a loc. n., Holstein (a ditch). Or Irish M'Crub. Prot. ref., Lond. 1618.

GRUEL. *D.* Groule; *S., Dch.* Grewell; *Fr.* Gruelle; *G.* Greul, Grüel (fright); *D.B.* Gruel; p.n. Hugt. n., Lond. 1628

Griuel in Roll of Battell Abbey.

GRUGGEN. *See* Grogan

GRUNDY. *D.* Gruntvig; *S.* Grundin; *G.* Grundey, Grundig; p.n. (solid, well-grounded). Or *see* Goundry

GRYLLS. *S.* Grill; *G.* Griehl; *Fr.* Grille; p.n.; *N. grylla* (?) (dim sight)

GUBBINS. *N.-Fr.* De Gobion; a p.n. Hugt., Lond. 1618

GUBBY. *A.S.* Guba; *G.* Gubig; a p.n. (scarred). *See* Guppy

GUDGE. *See* Gooch

GUDGEON, GUDGIN. *Fl.*; p.n.; *D.* Gude; a p.n. Dimin. Gudchen. *See* Gooda

GUERIN. From Gueron; a loc. n. in Normandy. A Hugt. n., Lond. 1621

Gurry in Roll of Battell Abbey. Gerin, a tenant in chief in *D.B.*

GUEST. A loc. n., Norm. *Fr.* Guest; *Dch.* Gest. Or *A.S.* Gest; p.n. (a stranger)

GUIHEN. The Irish form of Wynne

GUINNESS or MACGUINNESS. From the Irish Aongusa (excellent virtue)

Ancient lords of Iveagh, co. Down.

GUIVER. *A.S.* Wigbeorht (?) (illustrious victor) ; *Fr.* Guibert, Quivy (?) ; *D.B.* Guibert ; p.n.

GULL. *N.-Fr.* Goles, Gouel, Gule ; p.n.

In Rot. Hund.

GULLIFORD. A loc. n., Devon

GULLY. From Golley or Golet ; a loc. n., Norm. Or *N.* Guðleifr ; *A.S.* Guthlaf (divine relic) ; *D.* Gulleiv ; *Fr.* Gually, Gulley ; p.n.

W. Gollay in Rot. Hund., 1272.

GUMBLETON. From Gomeldon ; a loc. n., Wilts

GUMLEY. A loc. n., Leics

GUMMER. *D.* Gummer ; *A.S.* Gummœr ; p.n. (excellent, famous)

GUNBY. A loc. n., Yorks

GUNDRY. *See* Goundry

GUNN, GUNNS. *N.-Fr.* Gons, Goun, Gun ; *A.S.*, *Fl.* Guns, Gun ; p.n. *See* Gunner

GUNNELL. *N.* Gunnólfr (warrior wolf) ; *A.S.* Gunnulf ; p.n.

GUNNER, GUNNERY. *N.* Cunnarr ; *A.S.* Gunhere, Gunner (warrior)

GUNNING. *A.S.* fam. n. *See* Gunn

GUNSON. *S.* Gunnarson ; *D.* Gunarson ; p.n. *See* Gunn

GUNTON. A loc. n., Norf., Suff.

GUPPY. *N.-Fr.* Coupil ; *Fl.* Goupy ; p.n. *See* Gubby

GURLING. *See* Gerling

GURNER. *A.S.* Georngœr ; *D.* Gerner ; *Fl.* Gernet ; *Fr.* Gurnort ; p.n. (eager spear). Hugt. n., Lond. 1618

GURNEY. From Gournai ; a loc. n., Normandy
Hugo de Gurnai, tenant in chief in *D.B.* (Essex). Also a Hugt. n.

GURR. From the Irish M'Girr (short). Or *see* Gower

GURRIN. *See* Guerin

GUSCOTTE. From Goscote ; a loc. n., Staffs

GUSH. *See* Gooch

GUTHRIE. A loc. n., Forfar

GUTTERIDGE. *See* Goodrich

GUTTERY. *See* Guthrie

GUYMER. *A.S.* Widmœr ; Frankish Guidomer ; *Fl.* Ghémer ; p.n. (famous sense)

GWATKIN. The Welsh form of Watkin

GWILLYAM. *Fr.* Guillaume ; p.n. Or the Welsh form of William

GWYTHER. From Gwydyr ; a loc. n., South Wales. *B. gwydden* (a tree), *gwyther* (a dweller in the woods)

GYE. *Dch.* Guye ; *G.* Goy ; *Fr.* Gay ; p.n. Hugt., Lond. 1684. *See* Goy

GYFORD. *See* Gifford

GYTON. *See* Gayton

H

HABERNATHY. *See* Abernethy

HABGOOD. *See* Hopgood

HACKBUT. *N.* Hagbarðr ; *A.S.* Agabeorht, Ecgbert, Hagbert ; p.n. (bright edge)

HACKER. *N.* Hákr ; *A.S.* Hacca ; *S.* Hake ; *D.* Hackhe ; *D.*, *G.* Hacke ; *Fl.* Hacker ; *Dch.* Hakker ; p.n. (a battle-axe wielder). Prot. ref., Norwich, 1622

HACKETT. *N.-Fr.* Haket ; *N.* Haki a myth. p.n. (a hook); *D.* Haak ; *G.* Hake ; *Dch.* Hackert ; *Fl.* Acket, Hack ; p.n. Dim. of Haki. *See* Hatchett

Haket in Roll of Battell Abbey and Rot. Obl. et Fin., K. John. W. Achet, 1086, under-tenant of Giffard, Bucks. Bertram Haget founded Helaugh Abbey, York, 1200.

HACKNEY. A loc. n., Devon, Middlx.
HACKSHAW. *See* Hawkshaw
HACKWELL, HACKWILL. A loc. n., Devon
HACKWOOD. A loc. n., Devon
HACKWORTH. *See* Ackworth
HACON. *N.* Hákon (name of a king); *F.* Hagen, Heiko, Heiken; *Fl.* Haaken; *Fr.* Hacquin; *A.S.* Hacon, Haco, Hago; p.n.
HADDAH. *A.S.* Hadda, Heathu; *D.* Hader; *Dch.* Ader; *S.* Hadders; *G.* Hader; p.n. (warrior)
HADDAWAY. *See* Hathaway
HADDEN. *See* Haddon
HADDER. *See* Haddah
HADDESLEY. A loc. n., Yorks
HADDOCK. *See* Adcock
HADDON. A loc. n., Beds, Derbysh., Middlx., Northants.
  De H. in Rot. Hund.
HADFIELD. A loc. n., Derbysh.
HADLEY. A loc. n., Herts, Middlx., Staffs
HADLINGTON. *See* Adlington
HADOW, HADDOW. *See* Haddah
HADWIN. *A.S.* Haduuine; a p.n. (war friend)
HAGG. *See* Aggs
HAGGARD. *A.S.* Ægheard, Ecgheard; *Old G.* Agihard; *D.* Aaggaard; *S.* Hagert; *Dch.* Hageraats, Hakkert, Hagers, Hagoort, Hagt; *G.* Hoeger; *Fl.* Hager; p.n. (firm edge, *i.e.* of sword or axe)
HAGGER. *See* Haggard
HAGGIE. *F.* Agge; *D.* Agier; p.n. *See* Aggs
HAGGIS. *See* Aggs
HAGGIT. *See* Haggard
HAGON. *See* Hacon
HAGRAM. From Hargham (?); a loc. n., Norf.
HAGREEN. *See* Haygreen
HAGUE. *A.S.* Hac, Hag; *Fl.* Haege, Huyghe; *Dch.* Hage; *Fr.* Hague; p.n. Le Heegue, Prot. ref., Lond. 1621. *See* Haggard

HAILL. *See* Hale. Or *Fl.* Heyl; a p.n.
HAILSTONE. From Aylestone; a loc. n., Leics
HAIME. *F.* Eime, Eme; *Dch.* Hemme; *A.S.* Eamer; *G.* Heim; p.n. *See* Ames
HAINES. *See* Haynes. Or *N.*, *F.*, *G.* Hein, Hain, Heine; *Dch.* Hens; *Fl.* Hennes; p.n. Dim. of Heinrich
HAIRS. From Heers (?); a loc. n., Belg. *See* Ayers
HAKE. *See* Haycock
  De Hake in Rot. Obl. et Fin.
HAKEN. *See* Hacon
HALBROOK. *See* Holbrook
HALCRO. A loc. n., Scotl.
HALDANE. *N.* Hálfdan (name of a king); *A.S.* Haldan (half Dane); *N.-Fr.* Alden; p.n. *See* Alldin.
HALE. A loc. n., Ches., Cornw., Hants, Lincs, Somers, Staffs, Yorks. Haisle, Norm.
HALES. A loc. n., Norf. Or *Dch.* Hales; *D.* Hallas, Halse, Hels; p.n.; *A.S.* Hel, *i.e.* Ælf (elf)
HALESTRAP. *D.* Alstrup; a loc. and p.n.
HALFACRE. A loc. n., Devon. Or *N.* Hálfrekkr; a p.n. (the champion of King Half)
HALFHEAD. *A.S.* Ælfheard; *Old G.* Alfaid; p.n. (strong elf)
HALFNIGHT. *A.S.* Ælfnoth; *G.* Elvenich (?); p.n. (elf-bold)
HALFORD. A loc. n., Devon, Warw.
HALFPENNY. Irish Alpin, Halpin, M'Alpin; p.n. Or *Dch.* Alphenaar; a p.n.
HALFYARD. *A.S.* Ælfgeard (elf-protected)
HALKET. A loc. n., Scotl. Or from Halcote, Northants.
HALL. From Hal; a loc. n., Belg. Or *N.* Hallr (a hill); *D.*, *Dch.*, *S.* Hall; *Fl.* Hal; p.n. A Prot. ref., Lond. 1899
  De Aule and de la Haule in Rot. Obl. et Fin., K. John; Atte Hall, 1327.

HALLACK. *See* Hollick
HALLETT. A loc. n., Belg. *N.-Fr.*
p.n. *See* Allott
HALLIDAY. From Halyday, Norm.
S. Helleday; a p.n.
In Rot. Obl. et Fin., K. John. De
H., Rot. Cur. Reg. 1194.
HALLIFAX. From Halifax; a loc.
n., Yorks
HALLIWELL. A loc. n., Lancs
HALLOCK. *See* Hall. Dimin.
HALLSTEAD. From Halstead; a
loc. n., Ess., Kent, Leics. *D.*
Alsteed; *S.* Hallstedt; loc. and
p.n.
HALLUM. From Hallam; a loc. n.,
Derbysh., Notts, Yorks
HALLWARD. *N.* Hallvarðr (hill-
ward); *S.* Hallbahr; *G.* Halfar;
D. Halvor; *Fl.* Hallart; *Dch.*
Haller; *A.S.* Halweard; *D.B.*
Alward, Aluert; p.n.
HALLWORTH. From Halworthy; a
loc. n., Cornw.
HALLYBONE. *See* Allbone
HALPIN. *See* Halfpenny
HALTON. A loc. n., Bucks
HAM. A loc. n., Belg., Norm.,
Dorset, Glost., Hants, Somers,
Wilts
De H. in Rot. Hund.
HAMAWAY. From Hamoir; a loc.
n., Belg.
HAMBLETON. Leics, Lincs, Surr.,
Yorks
HAMBLETT. *N.* Ambloði (Hamlet),
the mythical prince of Denmark;
Fl. Hamlett; p.n. A Hugt. n.,
Lond. 1618
HAMBLIN. *A.S.* Hama, Hamelin;
F. Amel, Amelung (descendants
of the mighty one); *Dch.*
Hamerling; p.n.
HAMBY. From Hanby; a loc. n.,
Yorks. *N.-Fr.* De Hambeia
HAMER. A loc. n., Lancs. Or
N. Heimir (name of a Jarl); *F.*
Heimo; *Fl.* Haemer; *D.B.*
Haemer, Haimer; p.n. (houselord)

HAMERTON. *See* Hammerton
HAMEY. *Fr.* Ameye, Hamiet; p.n.
Dim. of Hama
HAMILTON. A loc. n., Scotl. Or
Hambleton, Lincs; Hamelton,
Yorks
HAMMACK. *Fl.* Hamecher; *Dch.*
Hamacker; p.n. Dim. of Hama
HAMMANT. *See* Hammond
HAMMERSLEY. *D.* Hammerlev; *S.*
Hammarlöw; *Dch.* Hamerslag;
loc. and p.n.
HAMMERTON. A loc. n., Yorks
HAMMON, HAMMOND, HAMONT. A
loc. n., Belg. *N.* Hámundr (high
protector); *D.* Hamann; *G.*
Hammann; *D.B.* Hame, Hamon,
Hamine, Amund; *Dch.* Ormondt;
Fr. Aumont; p.n.
In Roll of Battell Abbey; under-tenant
in *D.B.*
HAMPSON. *D.* Hampe; a p.n.
HAMPTON. A loc. n., Middlx.,
Warw., Worcest. *N.-Fr.* De
Hantona
HAMSHAW, HAMSHIRE. From
Hampshire, the county
HANBURY. A loc. n., Staffs,
Worcest.
HANCER, HANCHETT. *A.S.* Haneca;
Fl. Hannecart, Hansett; p.n. *See*
Hankey. Hanser, Prot. ref. n.,
Lond. 1618
HANCOCK. From Hencot or Hen-
goed; a loc. n., Salop
W. de Sprenchaux, from S. in Bur-
gundy, lord of H., *temp.* K. Steph.
(Eyton's, Salop).
HAND. *A.S.* Han, Hand; *G.*
Hander; p.n.
HANDFIELD. From Hanningfield;
a loc. n., Ess.
HANDFORD. A loc. n., Staffs
HANDLEY. A loc. n., Derbysh.,
Staffs. Or from Andelys, Norm.
HANDOVER. From Andover; a
loc. n., Hants
HANDS. *A.S.* And; a p.n. (against).
Or *G.*, *Dch.*, *Fl.* Hans, Hannes;
p.n. (Jack)

HANDYSIDE. A loc. n.

HANEY. *See* Heney

HANFORD. A loc. n., Dorset, Staffs

HANHAM. A loc. n., Glost.

HANINGTON. A loc. n., Hants, Wilts

HANKEY. From Anché, in Poitou. Or *see* Hanks
    T. de Hanchet, Camb. 1316

HANKINSON. *See* Hanks

HANKS. *F.* Anke; *Dch.* Hanke; *Fl.* Hancke, Hancq; *G.* Hanke, Hanko; p.n. *See* Hanchett

HANLON. From the Irish O'Hanlon (champion)

HANMER. A loc. n., Flint

HANNAFORD. *See* Hanford

HANNAH. *N.* Hani (a cock); n.n.; *D.* Henne; *S.* Hanc, Hanner; *A.S.* Hana; *Fr.* Hany, Hannay; *G.* Hanner; p.n. Or *see* Henn

HANNAM. *See* Hanham

HANNANT. *See* Hennant

HANNATH. From Hanworth; a loc. n., Suff.

HANNATT. *Fl.* Hanart, Hannot; p.n. Dim. of Hanno. *Old G. ano* (ancestor). Or *see* Hannah

HANNAV, HANNER. *See* Hannah

HANSELL. *S.* Hansell; a p.n.

HANSOM. *A.S.* Anselm (?) (god's helm); *Fr.* Anceaume; p.n.

HANSON. *D.* Hansen; *S.* Hanson; p.n. (Johnson)

HANWELL. A loc. n., Middlx. Or Andeville, Norm.

HARBARD, HARBORD. *N.* Há-bjártr; *A.S.* Heahbeorht (illustrious chief); *Dch.* Harbord; p.n.

HARBOTTLE. A loc. n., Northbd.

HARBOUR, HARBUTT. *See* Harbard

HARCOURT. A loc. n., Normandy
    Harecourt in Roll of Battell Abbey.

HARCUM. From Harcomb; a loc. n., Devon

HARDACRE. *A.S.* Hardgear; *G.* Hardtke; p.n. (strong spear)

HARDAWAY. From Hardway; a loc. n., Hants, Somers

HARDBOARD. *See* Harbard

HARDCASTLE. From Hardencastle (?), Roxburghshire

HARDEN. *See* Horden or Arden

HARDIMENT. *N.* Hjörtmundr (stag protector); a p.n. Hartieman, a Fl. Prot. ref., Lond. 1618

HARDING. *N.* Haddingr (a mythical hero); *A.S., D.* Harding; *S.* Hardin; p.n.
    Harding, a tenant in chief in *D.B.*, held lands which he had occupied *temp.* Edw. Conf. in Glost., Somers, Wilts.

HARDMAN. *A.S.* Heardman; *D.*, *Fl.* Hardman; *Dch.* Hardeman; *G.* Hartman; p.n. (strong man). Prot. ref., Lond. 1618

HARDMEAT. From Hardmead; a loc. n., Oxf.

HARDWICKE. A loc. n., Camb., Derbysh., Dur., Norf., Northants, Staffs, Warw., Worcest., Yorks

HARDY. *N.-Fr.* Hardi; p.n. (bold, strong). Hugt. n., Lond. 1684
    In Rot. Hund.

HARE. Heer; a loc. n., Belg. Or *N.-Fr.* Le Hare; *N.* Hár; *F.* Hére; *D.*, *G.* Herr; *Dch.* Haar; *Fl.* Hery; *D.B.* Her, Har; p.n. (soldier, hero)

HARFORD. A loc. n., Devon, Somers

HARGRAVE. A loc. n., Suff., Northants

HARGREAVES. A loc. n., Lancs

HARIOTT. *See* Herriott

HARKAN. *See* Hacon

HARKER. A loc. n., Cumb. Or *A.S.* Hardgær, Heregær; p.n. (strong spear)

HARKNESS. From Hackness; a loc. n., Yorks

HARKORT. *See* Harcourt

HARLAND. A loc. n., Caithness

HARLE. *N.* Erli; *F.* Harl; *A.S.* Erle, Hærle, Herle; *G, Dch.* Harlaar; *N.-Fr.* Harel; p.n. *See* Earl

L

HARLEY.   A loc. n., Salop.   Or *Fr.*
Harlé; a p.n.   *See* Hurly

HARLOCK.   A loc. n., Lancs

HARLOW.   A loc. n., Ess.

HARMAN.   *A.S.* Hereman; a p.n.
(soldier man)
N.-Fr. Herman in Rot. Hund.

HARMER.   *A.S.* Heremær; a p.n.
(famous soldier)

HARMSWORTH.   *See* Armsworth

HARNAGE.   A loc. n., Salop

HARNESS.   *G.* Harnisch; a p.n.
(armour)

HARNEY.   *A.S.* Arnwi, Earne, Earn-
wíg; *Fr.* Hahné, Hanet; p.n.
(war eagle)

HARPER. *N.* Erpr, *harpari* (a harper);
S. Arpi, Hjerpe; *D.*, *Dch.* Arp;
A.S. Herp, Herpo, *herpere* (a
harper); p.n.

HARPHAM.   A loc. n., Yorks

HARPLEY.   A loc. n., Norf. and
Worcest.

HARR.   *A.S.* Har; *F.* Hâre; *Dch.*
Haar; p.n. (a soldier)

HARRADEN,   HARRADINE.   From
Harrowden; a loc. n., Northants

HARRALL.   *See* Harrald

HARRALD.   *N.* Haraldr; *Dch.*
Herold; p.n.   Harrald; a loc,
n., Beds; name of a king (host-
wielder, a leader)

HARRINGTON.   A loc. n., Cumb.,
Northants. Anciently Haverington

HARRIS, HARRISON.   *N.-Fr.* Heriz,
Fitz Herice, Hairez, Harys; *Dch.*
Harries; *Fl.* Hariche; p.n.; *A.S.*
harra (a lord)

HARROD.   *See* Harwood.   Or *A.S.*
Heahred; a p.n. (high counsel)

HARROP.   From Harehope; a loc.
n., Northbd.

HARRY.   *Fr.* Harrye.   A Hugt. n.,
Lond. 1621.   *See* Harris

HARSAM.   *See* Hearsum

HARSANT.   *A.S.* Hærsand; *Old G.*
Hersand; *D.* Herschend; *Fl.*
Herssen; p.n. (battle envoy)
N.-Fr. Harsent in Rot. Hund.

HARSTON.   A loc. n., Cumb., Leics,
Northants

HART.   *N.* Hjörtr (a hart, stag); *S.*
Hjerta; *D.* Harth; *Dch.*, *G.*
Hart, Herte; p.n.   Or *A.S.* Hart,
Heard; p.n. (strong)

HARTCUP.   *G.* Hastkopf; p.n.
(strong head)

HARTLEY.   A loc. n., Kent, Northbd.
Or Hardley, Norf.

HARTOPP.   From Hartoft; a loc. n.,
Yorks

HARTSHORNE.   A loc. n., Derbysh.

HARTWELL.   A loc. n., Bucks,
Devon, Northants

HARTWRIGHT.   *A.S.* Heardric, Har-
teric; p.n. (strong ruler)

HARVARD.   *See* Harward

HARVEY.   From Hervé; a loc. n.,
Belg.   *Fr.* Hervé; p.n.   Hugt. n.
Lond. 1618

Herveus, a tenant in chief in *D.B.*
William Hervei in Rot. Obl. et Fin.,
K. John.

HARWARD.   *A.S.* Hereweard; *S.*
Herouard; *Dch.* Herwaarde; p.n.
(army warden)

HARWOOD.   A loc. n., Lancs and
Yorks

HASE.   *G.* Hase; *Dch.* Haas; p.n.
(a hare).   Or *A.S.* Has, Haso
(livid)

HASELL.   From Hasle; a loc. n.,
Yorks.   Or *see* Hazle

HASKETT.   *See* Hesketh

HASLAM.   From Asheldam (?); a loc.
n., Ess.

HASLEDEN,   HASELDINE.   From
Hazledine; a loc. n., Worcest.

HASLEHAM.   *See* Haslam

HASLEWOOD.   A loc. n., Yorks

HASLOCK, HASLUCK.   From Hass-
loch; a loc. n., Germ.   Or *N.*
Asleikr; *A.S.* Oslac; p.n. (god's
play)

HASLOP, HASLUP.   *See* Heslop

HASSALL.   A loc. n., Ches.   Hessell,
Prot. ref., Sandwich, 1622

HASSARD. *D.* Hassert; *Fl.* Hasaert; *N.-Fr.* Hasart; p.n. (the gods' strong one)

HASSETT. *N.-Fr.* Hassot; a p.n.
> Rot. Hund. 1272. Haste and Hest, Norm., 1180.

HASTED. From Ashstead ; a loc. n., Surr. Or Hawstead, Suff.

HASTELOW. A loc. n.

HASTIE. *See* Hassett

HASTING. From an island off the coast of Normandy
> In Roll of Battell Abbey. De Hasting in Rot. Obl. et Fin., K. John.

HASTINGS. A loc. n., Suss.
> Held by De Venoix in 1086.

HASTWELL. *See* Eastall

HASWELL. A loc. n., Dur.

HATCH. A loc. n., Beds, Kent, Somers
> Atte Hach in 1327.

HATCHAM. A loc. n., Middlx.

HATCHER. *G.* Hatscher ; a p.n. (a halberdier). Or *see* Hatchett

HATCHETT. *Fr.* Hachette ; a p.n. *See* Hacket
> Achet, under-tenant at survey in *D.B.*

HATE. *A.S.* Hat, Hæth ; *Fl.* Het ; p.n. *See* Hatt

HATFIELD. A loc. n., Ess., Herts, Worcest., Yorks

HATHAWAY. *A.S.* Heathuwig, Heathewi (victory in war)

HATHERLEY. From Hatherleigh ; a loc. n., Devon

HATHORNTHWAITE. A loc. n., Westmd.

HATT. *N.* Höttr (a hood) ; *D.* Hatte ; *F.* Hatto ; *A.S.* Hat, Heathu ; p.n. (war)

HATTEN. *See* Hatting or Hatton

HATTERLEY. A loc. n., Ches.

HATTERSLEY. *See* Haddesley

HATTING. *D.* ; p.n. *See* Atto, Hatt

HATTON. A loc. n., Middlx., Staffs

HAUGHTON. A loc. n., Dur., Staffs

HAVELL, HAVILL. *See* Hovel

HAVELOCK. *N.* Hafleikr ; a p.n. ; *haf* (sea), *leik* (sport)

HAVERS. *N.-Fr.* De Auvere. Or *N.* Hávarr, *há-vörr* (?) (high lip) ; *Dch.* Havers ; *A.S.* Hæfa ; p.n.

HAVILAND. *G.* Haveland ; a p.n. Or Haverland ; a loc. n., Norf.

HAWARD. *N.* Hávarðr ; *A.S.* Haward, Hahweard, Heahweard ; *Fl.* Havaert, Havard, Hauwaert ; *Dch.* Houwaard ; *G.* Hofert, Hoffarth ; p.n. (high warden). Or *see* Hayward
> A Saxon tenant in *D.B.*

HAWEIS. *A.S.* Hathewis ; a p.n. Hathwise (war leader)

HAWKE. *A.S.* Hafoc, Heafeca ; *Fl.* Hauke ; p.n. A Prot. ref. n., Norwich, 1622. *See* Auker

HAWKES. From Hawkers ; a loc. n., Northbd. Or *see* Auker

HAWKINS. From Hawking ; a loc. n., Kent
> Osbert de Hawking, *temp.* Henry II.

HAWKRIGG. A loc. n., Westmd.

HAWKSHAW. A loc. n., Lancs
> Rob' de Hauconesheu in Rot. Obl. et Fin., K. John, A.D. 1199.

HAWKSLEY. A loc. n., Somers. Or Hauxley, Northbd.

HAWKSWORTH. A loc. n., Yorks

HAWLEY. From La Haulle ; a loc. n., Norm.

HAWORTH. A loc. n., Yorks

HAWS. From Hawes ; a loc. n., Yorks

HAWTAYNE. *Fr.* Hautein ; a p.n. From Autigny (?) ; a loc. n., Normandy. Or *N.-Fr.* Le Hautain ; a p.n. (the proud)
> In Roll of Battell Abbey.

HAWTHORN. A loc. n., Lincs

HAWTREY. From Hauterive ; a loc. n., Norm.

HAXALL, HAXELL. From Exwell (?) ; a loc. n., Rutl. Hackensall, Lancs

HAY. A loc. n., Cornw., Staffs. *N.-Fr.* De la Haye. A Hugt. n., Dover, 1622.
  Atte Hay, Court of Husting, 1258.

HAYCOCK. A hill in Cumb. Or *F.* Heike; *Fl.* Haeck; *A.S.* Hecca; *Dch.* Heek, Haeij-Koch; p.n. Dim. of *F.* Hayo. *See* Heyhoe

HAYCROFT. A loc. n., Dorset

HAYES. A loc. n., Norm., Salop; Hees, Belg. *Dch.* Hees; a p.n. Hugt. n., Lond. 1618

HAYGREEN. A loc. n., Yorks

HAYLES. A freq. loc. n. *See* Hales

HAYLEY. From Haylie; a loc. n., Largs, Scotl.

HAYLOCK. From Haylake (?) Cheriton Bishop, Devon

HAYMAN. From Heman; a loc. n., Germany. *Dch.* Heiman; *Fl.* Heman, Heyman; p.n. Or *A.S.* Æceman (edge-man)

HAYNES. From Haiene, Norm.; a loc. n., Beds, Devon. *See* Haines.
  Hugh de H., 12th century.

HAYTER, HAYTOR. A loc. n., Derbysh.

HAYWARD. From Hauwert; a loc. n., Belg. *Fl.* Hauwaert, Heywaert; p.n. *See* Haward
  Hayward in Roll of Battell Abbey. This being a loc. n. is more likely to be the origin of the noble name of Howard than that of a Saxon tenant. The Conqueror had many Flemings in his army.

HAZARD. *See* Hassard

HAZELRIGG. A loc. n., Northbd.

HAZLE. *S.* Hasle; *D.* Hassel; *Dch.* Hazel; *G.* Hessell; *D.B.* Hezelin; p.n. *See* Hassall

HAZLETT. *See* Haseldine

HAZZARD. From Hazard; a loc. n., Devon. *See* Hassard

HEACOCK. *See* Haycock

HEAD. *A.S.* Headda, Hedde; *G.* Hede; *D.* Heede; p.n. (warrior). Prot. ref., Norwich, 1622
  Hedde in Rot. Hund.

HEADEACH, HEADECH. *See* Hedach

HEADIN. *S.* Hedin; *Dch.* Hedden; *G.* Hedin; p.n.; fam. n. of Head

HEADLAM. A loc. n., Dur.

HEADLEY. A loc. n., Hants, Surr., Worcest.

HEAGREEN. *See* Haygreen

HEAL. A loc. n., Surr.

HEALEY. A loc. n., Northbd., Yorks

HEANEY. *See* Henny

HEAP. *A.S.* Ibba, Ippa; *F.* Ippe; *G.* Hippe; *Dch.* Hiep; p.n. *See* Abbs

HEARD. *See* Ard

HEARNE. From Heron; a loc. n., Norm.; a loc. n., Kent, Surr.

HEARSUM. From Hersham; a loc. n., Surr.

HEASELL. *See* Hasell and Hazle

HEASLIP. *See* Heslop

HEATH. A loc. n., Derbysh., Devon, Yorks, etc.

HEATHCOTE. A loc. n., Derbysh.

HEATHER. A loc. n., Leics

HEATLEY. A loc. n., Staffs

HEATON. A loc. n., Ches., Lancs, Staffs

HEAVEN, HEAVENS. From Heffen(?); a loc. n., Belg. Or *see* Evans

HEAVER. *See* Heffer

HEBB. *A.S.* Ebba; *Fl.* Hebbe; *F.* Ebbe; p.n. *See* Abbs

HEBBERT. *N.-Fr.* Hebart; *A.S.* Hygebeorht; a p.n. (bright mind). Higbert, bp. of Worcester. Prot. ref., Lond. 1685

HEBBLETHWAITE. *See* Ablewhite

HEBGIN. *F.* Ebo, Ebbo, Ebbe, Ebken; *S.* Hebbe; *G.* Ebbeke; p.n. Dimin. of Hebbe

HECKFORD. From Hackforth; a loc. n., Yorks. *D.B.* Acheford. Also Hackford; a loc. n., Norf.
  John de Hackford, A.D. 1340; Sir W. de Hakeford, *temp.* Hen. I. (Norf.).

HEDACH. *G.* Heyduck, Hedicke; p.n. Dim. of Head. *See* Hettich

HEDDERLEY. *See* Adderley

HEDDERWICK. From Hedrick (?); a loc. n., Dur.

HEDDLE. *Dch*. Hedel; a p.n. Dim. of Head

HEDERTON. *See* Hetherington

HEDGE. *Dch.*, *G.* Heege; a p.n. Or *see* Edge

HEDGECOCK. *A.S.* Hecca; *G.* Hedtke (?); a p.n.; *ecg* (edge, sword). Dim.

HEDGELAND. *D.* Hegeland, Hegge-lund; *S.* Hägglund; loc. and p.n.

HEDGES. *See* Etches

HEDLEY. A loc. n., Dur.

HEEPS. *See* Heap

HEFFER. From Hever; a loc. n., Belg. Or *N.* Evarr; *A.S.* Hefa; *F.* Eve; *G.* Heffe; p.n. *See* Havers

HEFFILL. Dim. of Hefa

HEFFORD. *D.* Heerfordt; a p.n.

HEGGS. *D.*, *Dch.* Eggers; a p.n. *See* Eggs

HELLELEY. From Hellingly; a loc. n., Suss.

HELLERAY. *See* Elleray

HELLIER. From St Hellier, near Rouen, Norm.

HELLING. *F.* Elle (strong, brave), Ellen; a fam. n.; *S.* Helin, Hell-ing; *Fl.* Hellin, Hellings; p.n.

HELLINGS. From Helions; a loc. n., Normandy.

Upton Helions, Devon; in old deeds U. Hyllyngs.

HELM. From Helme; a loc. n., Dur. Or Halme, Norm.; *N.* Hjálmr (a helmet), Hjelm; *Fl.*, *G.* Helm; *A.S.* Helm; p.n.

HELMER. *See* Helm

HELMORE. From Elmore; a loc. n., Glost. Or *A.S.* Helmœr; *Fl.*, *S.* Helmer; p.n. (famous helmet)

HELMSLEY. A loc. n., Yorks

HELPS. *N.-Fr.* De Helpe; a p.n.

Helbe in Rot. Hund.

HELSHAM. From Hailsham; a loc. n., Suss.

HELY. *See* Healey

HEMAN. *See* Hayman

HEMANS. *See* Hemmans

HEMERY. *See* Emery

HEMINGWAY. From Hemingby; a loc. n., Lincs

HEMMANS. *N.* Hemingr (an adopted son); a p.n.; *Dch.* Hem-minga; *F.* Emmen, Emminga; *Fl.* Heman; *G.* Hemens; *S.* Hemming; p.n.

HEMMANT, HEMMENT. *See* Ham-mond

HEMMINGTON. From Hemington; a loc. n., Leics, Northants

HEMPSHALL. From Hempshill; a loc. n., Notts

HEMS. *See* Ames

HEMSLEY. *See* Helmsley

HEMSTEAD, HEMSTED. From Hemp-stead; a loc. n., Ess., Glost.

HEMSWORTH. A loc. n., Yorks

HEMUS. *See* Ames

HENCHMAN. *G.* Heinzmann; a p.n. (a page, footman). Heinz, dimin. of Heinrich

HENDERSON. *See* Hendry

HENDRA, HENDREY, HENDRY. A loc. n., Cornw. Or *N.* Endriði; *A.S.* Henthryth; p.n. (chief rider (?))

HENEY. From Henis; a loc. n., Belg. Or *see* Henny

HENGULF. *N.* Ingolf; *A.S.* Ingulf; p.n. (Ingswolf)

HENN. *F.* Enno; *A.S.* Hen (old, ancestral); *D.* Henne; *Fl.* Hen; p.n.

HENNANT *Dch.* Hent; a p.n.

HENNELL. From Henlle; a loc. n., Salop

HENNESY. From the Irish O'h Aengusa; a p.n. *See* Guinness

HENNIKER. *A.S.* Haneca; a p.n. (ancient spear); *Old G.* Anager, Enegar; p.n.

HENNY. A loc. n., Ess. *See* Henn

HENSHAW. A loc. n., Northbd.
HEPBURN. A loc. n., Northbd.
HEPHER. *See* Heffer
HEPPLESTON. From Eppleton (?);
a loc. n., Dur.
HEPPLEWHITE. *See* Ablewhite
HEPTONSTALL. A loc. n., Lancs
HEPWORTH. A loc. n., Suff., Yorks
Stephen de Hepworth, Chancellor of
Cambridge University A.D. 1257-99.
Adam de Heppeworth, Yorks (formerly de Belmont) assumed the
name with the manor A.D. 1303.

HERBAGE. From Herbisse ; a loc.
n., France. Or *G.* Herbich, Herbig ; p.n.
HERBERT. *N.-Fr.* Herbart, Herbet ; p.n. ; *A.S.* Hearra - beorht
(bright lord)
D.B. tenant in chief and under-tenant.
Freq. in Rot. Obl. et Fin., K. John.
Hugt. n., Cant. 1622.

HERCY, HERSEE, HERSEY. From
Hericy ; a loc. n., Norm.
In Roll of Battell Abbey. Hugo de
Hersi vel Hersy in Rot. Obl. et
Fin., K. John. Hugh de Hercy,
1135, Wingram, Bucks.

HEREPATH. A loc. n., Devon
HERIOT. A loc. n., Edinburgh.
Or *N.-Fr.* De Ariete ; a p.n.
HERN. *See* Hearne. Or *A.S.*
Arne, Earn ; p.n. (eagle)
HERON. *Fr.* Héron ; a p.n. ; *D.B.*
de Herion. Le Héron ; a loc. n.,
Normandy
In Roll of Battell Abbey.

HERRICK. *N.* Eireker (peaceful
franklin) ; *A. S.* Herric ; *Fr.* Héricher ; p.n.
D.B. Eric, tenant in chief. Heryce
in Roll of Battell Abbey.

HERRING. *D.* Herring ; *Fl.* Herinckx ; *Fr.* Herinne ; *G.* Häring ;
p.n. From *N.* Hæringr (hoary
men), Hérinnes ; a loc. n., Belg. ;
Herin, France
HERRIOTT. *See* Heriot
HERSUM. *See* Hearsum
HESELTINE. *See* Haseldine

HESFORD. From Hessenford ; a
a loc. n., Cornw.
HESKETH. A loc. n., Lancs
HESLAM. *See* Haslam
HESLOP. A loc. n., Derbysh.
HESP. *A.S.* Esber, Esbeorn ; *Dch.*
Hesper ; *G.* Espe ; p.n. *See*
Osborne
HETHERINGTON. A loc. n., Cumb.
HETTICH. *See* Headach
HEUGH. *See* Hughes
HEUSTICE. *See* Eustace
HEWARD. *A.S.* Hugihard ; *Old G.*
Hugihart, Hugard ; *Fr.* Houard,
Huard, Huart ; p.n. (firm mind)
Houard and Huard, tenants at Survey
in *D.B.* Prot. ref., Lond. 1618.
HEWES. *See* Hughes
HEWETT. *N.-Fr.* Huet, Huett ;
p.n. (little Hugh). Hugt. n.,
Lond. 1621. Or from Huest or
Huet, near Evreux, Norm.
HEWISH. From Huish ; a loc. n.,
Devon, Somers. Or *Dch.* Huis,
Huysse ; *Fr.* Hugues, Huez ; p.n.
See Hughes
HEWITT. *See* Hewett
HEWKE. *See* Hook
HEWLETT. *See* Hullett
HEWSON. *Dch.* Huessen ; a p.n.
See Hughes
HEXTALL, HEXTELL. A loc. n.,
Staffs
HEY. *See* Hay
HEYCOCK. *See* Haycock
HEYGATE. *A.S.* Heahgyth ; *G.*
Heygütte ; *Dch.* Hegt ; p.n. (noble
Goth)
HEYHOE. *A.S.* Heio ; *F.* Hayo,
Heie, Hei ; *S.* Ey ; *Dch.* Heij ;
G. Hey, Heyer ; p.n. (high)
HIBBERT. *See* Hebbert
HIBBINS. *F.* Ibo, Ibe ; fam. n.,
Ibben ; p.n. *See* Abbs
HIBBIT. *See* Hebbert
HIBBLE. *A.S.* Higelbald (bold
mind), Higbald, bp. of Lindisfarne ; *Dch.* Hibbel ; *G.* Hiebel ; p.n.
HIBGANE. *See* Hebgin

HIBLING. *Dch.* Hibelen

HICHENS. *S.*; p.n. *See* Higgins

HICK. *F.* Iko, Ike, Iken; *Dch.* Hikke; *Fl.* Ickx; *A.S.* Hicca, Hig; p.n.

HICKEN. *See* Higgin

HICKEY. *N.-Fr.* Hequet; a p.n.

HICKLING. A loc. n., Notts

HICKMAN. *See* Higman

HICKORY. *A.S.* Hygehere; a p.n. (Hugh the warrior)

HICKS, HICKSON. *See* Hick

HIDDELSTON. *See* Huddleston

HIDE, HIDES. From Hyde; a loc. n., Middlx.; Heyd, Belg. Or *N.* Heidr; *D.*, *G.*, *Dch.* Heide, Heyde; p.n.

HIGGETT. From Highgate (?); a loc. n., Lond. Or *see* Huggett

HIGGIN. *A.S.* Hyge; *F.* Iggs, Iggen; *N.-Fr.* Hicun; p.n.

HIGH. From Huy; a loc. n., Belg.; or Haigh, Lancs

HIGHAM. A loc. n., Kent, Lancs, Northants, Leics

HIGMAN. *See* Hugman

HIGNETT. *A.S.* Hugon; *Fr.* Hugnot, Hognet; p.n. *See* Hughes

HILARD. *See* Hildyard

HILDERSLEY. From Yeldersley; a loc. n., Derbysh.

HILDYARD. *A.S.* Hildegeard (warguard); *D.* Hilleraad; *G.* Hilger; *Fr.* Guillard; p.n.; *D.B.* Hildeuert, Guluert, Wielard, Willard

HILES. *F.* Eilerts, Eilts, Eils; a fam. n.; *A.S.* Æthelheard; *D.* Heil; *Dch.* Heillers; *Fl.* Heilaerts; p.n. (strong noble)

HILEY. From Highley; a loc. n., Salop

HILL. A loc. n., Devon, Germ., Hants, etc. Or *F.*, *D.*, *G.* Hille; *Fl.* Hil; p.n. *Dch.* ref. n., Lond. 1618

HILLARY. From St Hilaire; a loc. n., France

Stephen de St Hillary in Rot. Obl. et Fin., K. John.

HILLEN. A *Dch.* p.n. *See* Hill

HILLIARD, HILLYARD. *See* Hildyard

HILLYER. *See* Hellier

HILTON. A loc. n., Derbysh., Dorset, Dur., Lancs, Staffs

HIMUS. *See* Ames

HINCHLIFFE. A loc. n., Yorks

HINCKLEY. A loc. n., Leics

HINDE. *Fl.* p.n. Prot. ref., Lond. 1618

HINDLE. *Dch.* Hindael; a p.n.

HINDLEY. A loc. n., Lancs

HINDRIE. *See* Hendry

HINDSON. *S.* Hinderson; a p.n.

HINE, HINER. *D.* Hein; *G.* Heine; p.n. (Harry). Prot. ref., Lond. 1618

HINGE. From Irish M'Hinch. Or dim. of Hinc; *G.*, *Dch.* Hinse; p.n.

HINKS. *A.S.* Hengst; a p.n. (horse)

HINNEL. *See* Hennell

HIPKIN, HIPPER, HIPPERSON. *F.* Hibbo, Hibbe; *G.* Hippe, Hipper, Ibich; *Dch.* Hipken; *Fl.* Hippert; *A.S.* Ibbo, Ibi; p.n. *See* Abbs

HIPSLEY. From Ipsley, a loc. n., Warw., Worcest.

HIRD. *A.S.* Hirde; *D.* Herth; *S.* Hierta; *Fl.* Herdies; *Dch.* Heerde; *G.* Hirt; p.n. *See* Hart

HISBENT. *D.* Isbrand; a p.n. (iron sword)

HISCOX. *A.S.* Eisc; a p.n. (icy)

HISLOP. A loc. n., Scotl.

HITCH, HITCHCOCK. *F.* Hiddo; *A.S.* Hidda, Hiddi; akin to *had* (war); *Fl.* Hittecher; a p.n. Dimin.

HIVES. St Ives; a loc. n., Cornw., Hunts. Or Hives, Belg.

HOADLEY. From Hoathley; a loc. n., Suss.

HOARE. From Oare; a loc. n., Kent; Ore, Suss. Or Aure, Auray, Bretagne

HOBART. *See* Hubbard. Hugt. n., Lond. 1618

HOBBES, HOBBS. *See* Hobson

HOBBINS. *Dch.* Obbens; a p.n. *See* Hoben

HOBBIS. From Hobbies; a loc. n., Norf. Or *Dch.* Obbes; a p.n.

HOBBLE. *D.* Hobolth; *Dch.* Hobbel; *Fl.* Houbel; p.n. *See* Hubble. Prot. ref., Sandwich, 1621

HOBEN. *G.* Hoben; *Dch.* Hobben; *Fl.* Hobin, Hœben; p.n.

HOBHOUSE. *See* Hobbis

HOBKIRK. A loc. n., Roxburghsh.

HOBLYN. From Aublain; a loc. n., Belg. *Fr.* Houblinne, Oblin; *G.* Uebelin; p.n.

HOBOURN. From Holborn; a loc. n., Middlx.

HOBSON. *A.S.* Oba; *N.* Ubbi (?) (wild); *D.* Obbe; p.n.
   Leuric Hobbesune, a Saxon tenant in *D.B.* (Suff.).

HOCKIN. *A.S.* Hoc; a p.n.; Hocing; a fam. n.; akin to *N.* Hugi; *A.S.* Hoga; p.n.; *F.* Okko; a p.n. *See* Hughes.
   Okken, Okking, fam. n., seems to be derived from Odoko. *See* Oddy.

HOCKLEY. A loc. n., Derbysh., Ess.

HODDS. *Dch.* Hoddes; a p.n. Prot. ref., Lond. 1618

HODDY, HODY. A loc. n., Belg. Or *N.* Oddi (a leader); *F.* Ode, Oddo; *D.* Odde, Odder; *N.-Fr.* Audé; *Fl.* Hody; *A.S.* Oda, Odda; p.n.
   In Rot. Hund.

HODGE, HODGSON. *N.* Hugi; *A.S.* Hoc, Hoce, Hoga; *Dch.* Hocke; p.n. (mind). *See* Hogg and Hughes

HODGERS. *See* Odgers

HODGKIN. *A.S.* Hogcin; a p.n. Dim. of Hodge. *See* Hughes and Odger

HODGKINSON. *See* Hodgkin

HODGSON. *D.B.* Odesune; a p.n. Or *see* Odgers and Hodge

HOFF. *A.S.* Hof, *hófer* (?) (a humpback); *S., D., Fl., Dch., G.* Hoff; p.n.

HOGAN. From the Irish O'h-Ogain; a p.n. Or *Dch., Fl.* Hoogen; a p.n. *See* Huggins

HOGARTH. *See* Hoggarth

HOGBEN. *A.S.* Hagbeorn; a p.n. (clever bear). Or *see* Ogben

HOGG. *N.-Fr.* De Hoga. From La Hogue, Norm. Or *Dch.* Hog; *Fl.* Hogge; *A.S.* Hog, Hoc, *hog* (prudent); *G.* Hoch, Hocher; p.n. *See* Hughes

HOGGARTH. *N.* Hofgarðr; *N.-Fr.* Hogart; *Fl.* Hogger, Hoogaerts; *D.* Hofgaard; *A.S.* Hoga; *Fr.* Hocquart; p.n. (castle warden)

HOGGER. *Fl.*; p.n. *See* Hoggarth

HOGGETT. *N.-Fr.* De la Hoguette, *i.e.* Howe. Or *see* Hoggarth

HOGGINS. *See* Huggins

HOLBECHE. From Holbeach; a loc. n., Lincs. Or *D.* Holbech; a loc. and p.n.

HOLBECK. A loc. n., Notts

HOLBROOK. A loc. n., Derbysh., Yorks

HOLCOMBE. A loc. n., Devon, Dorset, Somers

HOLCROFT. A loc. n., Lancs

HOLDAM. From Oldham; a loc. n., Lancs

HOLDAWAY. From Holdawit (?); a loc. n., Cornw.

HOLDEN. A loc. n., Yorks. Or *S.* Hollden; *D.* Holten; p.n.

HOLDERNESS. A loc. n., Yorks

HOLDITCH. A loc. n., Devon, Dorset

HOLDOM. *See* Holdam

HOLDON. *See* Holden

HOLDRON. *See* Oldring

HOLDSWORTH. A loc. n., Yorks

HOLE. A loc. n., Cornw., Devon
   Rich. de la Hole in Rot. Hund.

HOLEYMAN. *A.S.* Hallmund; *Dch., Fl.* Hollemann; p.n. (hill protector)

HOLEHOUSE. A loc. n., Dumfries

HOLGATE. A loc. n., Lancs, Yorks

HOLKER. A loc. n., Lancs

HOLKHAM. A loc. n., Norf.

HOLL. A loc. n., Germ. Or *A.S.* Holl ; *Dch.* Holl ; p.n. *See* Hall

HOLLAND. From Hulland (*D.B.* Holund) ; a loc. n., Derbysh. Or *Dch., Fl.* Holland ; a p.n.

HOLLEY. *Fl.* Holle ; a p.n. *See* Holl

HOLLICK. *D.* Holck ; *Dch.* Hollak ; *G.* Holleck ; p.n. Dim. of Holl

HOLLIDAY. *See* Halliday

HOLLINGHAM. From Holdingham ; a loc. n., Lincs

HOLLINGSHEAD. From Hollingsend ; a loc. n., Yorks. Or Hollingside ; a loc. n., Dur.

HOLLINGSWORTH. *See* Hollingworth

HOLLINGWORTH. A loc. n., Lancs

HOLLOMON, HOLLYMAN. *See* Holeyman

HOLLOWAY. A loc. n., Devon, Warw.

HOLMES. A loc. n., Lancs, Lincs. ; Atte Holmes. Or *D., S., Dch., G.* Holm ; *Fl.* Holms ; p.n. From *N. hólmr* (an islet in a lake or river)
D.B. de Holmo, a tenant in chief.

HOLROYD. Anciently de Howrode ; a loc. n., Yorks

HOLT. A loc. n., Norf. ; Atte Holt. Or *Dch.* Holt ; *S.* Holter ; *D.* Holte, Holde ; *G.* Holdt ; p.n. (a wood)
De Holt in Rot. Obl. et Fin.

HOLTBY. A loc. n., Yorks

HOLTHOUSE. *Dch.* Holterhuis ; *G.* Holthaus ; p.n.

HOLTHUM, HOLTOM. From Haltham ; a loc. n., Lincs. Or *D.* Holtum ; a loc. and p.n.

HOLYOAKE. A loc. n., Staffs

HOMBERSLEY. From Ombersley ; A loc. n., Worcest.

HOME. A loc. n., Holland. *See* Hume

HOMFRAY. *N.* Hólmfríðr, *hólm* (islet), *friðr* (peace) ; *G.* Humpfer, Humphrey ; p.n.

HONE. An Irish form of Owen. Or from Hogne ; a loc. n., Belg. Also *N.* Aun ; *A.S.* Hon, On ; p.n. (old, ancestral)

HONEYBUN. *See* Hunneybun

HONEYCHURCH. A loc. n., Devon

HONSLOWE. From Hounslow ; a loc. n., Middlx. Or *see* Onslow

HONYWILL. From Honeywell ; a loc. n., Devon

HOOD. A loc. n., Devon ; Hude, Germ. Or *N.* Udi ; *F.* Udo, Ude ; *D.* Hude; *G.* Hudy; *Dch.* Ouda ; *A.S.* Hud, Hudda, Udi ; p.n. Udo, a Hugt. n., Lond. 1618. *See* Hudson

HOOK. A loc. n., Devon, Hants. Or *A.S.* Huc, Huch, Hyge ; *F.* Uko, Uke (?) ; *G.* Huck ; *S.* Huch ; *Dch.* Hoek ; *Fr.* Huc, Hucq ; p.n.
This is one of the French forms of Hugo. *See* Hughes. A Prot. ref. n., Lond. 1618.

HOOKER. *A.S.* Hucco; *G.* Hucke ; *N.-Fr.* Hucherer ; p.n. *See* Hook
There is a *N.* n.n. Húkr (one who sits on his hams), but it hardly applies. J. Hochard in Rot. Hund.

HOOKWAY. A loc. n., Devon

HOOLE. A loc. n., Lancs

HOOLEY. *Fr* Houllet ; a p.n. *See* Hullett or Howley

HOOPER. A loc. n., Cornw.

HOOPPELL. A Hugt. n., Dover, 1622

HOPE. A loc. n., Derbysh., Salop, Heref., Yorks, N. Wales

HOPGOOD. *N.* Ubbi (wild) ; *A.S.* Ubba ; *Old G.* Hopi ; p.n. ; *gaut* (a Goth)

HOPKING, HOPKINS. *Dch.* Hoppe, Hop, Höpken ; p.n. Dimin. of Hob. *See* Hobson

HOPKIRK. *See* Hobkirk

HOPPER. *D.*, *Dch.* Hoppe, Hopper; *G.* Hoppe; p.n. *See* Hobson

HOPPS. *See* Hobbs

HOPSON. *See* Hobson

HOPTON. A loc. n., Yorks

HOPWOOD. A loc. n., Lancs

HORBURY. A loc. n., Yorks

HORDEN. A loc. n. (a manor), Dur.

HORN. *D.*, *S.*, *A.S.*, *Dch.*, *G.* Horn; p.n. (a horn or trumpet)

HORNBLOW, HORNBLOWER. From Hornblotton (?); a loc. n., Somers. Or Horninglow, Derbysh.

HORNBY. A loc. n., Lancs, Yorks

HORNER. *S.* Horner; a p.n. *See* Horn

HORNEY. *S.* Horney; a p.n. *See* Horn

HORNINGHOLD. A loc. n., Rutl.

HORNSBY. *See* Ormsby

HORNSEY. A loc. n., Middlx.

HOROBIN. *N.* Örrabeinn; a n.n. (scar-leg)

HORREX. *N.* Oraekja; *A.S.* Orric; *Dch.*, *Fl.* Horrickx; p.n. Or *N.* Örrek; n.n. (swift driver (?))

HORSEBURGH. A loc. n., Tweeddale

HORSELL. A loc. n., Surr.

HORSENAIL. From Orsmael (?); a loc. n., Belg.

HORSEPOLE. From Herspool; a loc. n., Cornw.

HORSEY. A loc. n., Ess., Norf.

HORSFALL. A loc. n., Yorks, near Hebden Bridge

HORSFIELD. From Hersfeld; a loc. n., Prussia

HORSFORD. A loc. n., Norf.

HORSHAM. A loc. n., Norf., Suss.

HORSINGTON. A loc. n., Lincs, Somers

HORSLEY. A loc. n., Camb., Surr., Yorks

HORSWELL. *See* Horsell

HORTH. From Horwath or Hoath; A loc. n., Kent. Or *See* Hart

HORTON. A loc. n., Devon, Kent, Northants, Surr., Yorks

HORYAN. *Fr.* Horion; a p.n. (a thumb). Also a loc. n., Belg.

HOSGOOD. *N.* Ásgautr (a name of Odin, or divine Goth); *A.S.* Asgot, Osgot, Osgod; p.n. Tenant in chief in *D.B.* Richard Ausgod in Rot. Obl. et Fin., K. John.

HOSKINS, HOSKYNS. *Dch.* Huskens; a p.n. *See* Hodgkinson

HOSTE. *G.* Ost; *Dch.* Haust, Hoost, Oost; *Fl.* Hoste; p.n. Hoost, a Prot. ref., Lond. 1618 The Osti (Estonians) were a people of Germany.

HOTCHKIN. *See* Hodgkinson

HOTCHKISS. *See* Hodgkinson

HOTHAM. A loc. n., Yorks

HOTINE. *Fr.* Autin; a p.n. From Austin, Augustin. Or *see* Hawtayne

HOTSON. From Hoddesdon; a loc. n., Herts. Or *see* Hoddy

HOTTEN. *See* Hotine or Outon

HOUCHEN. *See* Huggin

HOUGH. A loc. n., Ches., Lincs

HOUGHTON. A loc. n., Beds, Dur., Lancs, Norf., Northants

HOULDERSHAW. *See* Oldershaw

HOULGRAVE. From Youlgreave; a loc. n., Derbysh.

HOULSTONE. From Holstone; a loc. n., Devon

HOULTON. *See* Hulton

HOUSTON. A loc. n., Scotl. *See* Owston

HOVELL. From Houville; a loc. n., France. *Dch.* Hoevel; a p.n. In Roll of Battell Abbey. Huwell in Rot. Obl. et Fin.

HOW. *See* Howe

HOWARTH. A loc. n., Lancs

HOWE. A loc. n., Norf., Yorks. From *N.* haugr (a cairn over one dead). Or *D.* Hau, Hou; p.n. Thomas de Hou in Rot. Obl. et Fin., K. John.

HOWARD. *See* Haward and Hayward

> This name does not occur in *D.B.* as a tenant in chief. Haward is a Saxon tenant. Houard and Huard are tenants at the Survey, but they may be the *N.-Fr.* forms of Hugihard. *See* Heward. Hayward is in the Roll of Battell Abbey, but neither name appears in Rot. Obl. et Fin., K. John. Burke does not trace Howard farther back than Edw. I. Dugdale suggests that the name took its origin from a high office in Saxon times or from the name of a place.

HOWELL. Name of a Welsh prince in *D.B.* Hoel (lordly). Also a Hugt. n., Lond. 1618

HOWES. From Housse; a loc. n., Belg. *Dch.* House; a p.n. Prot. ref. n., Cant. 1622

HOWCHIN. *See* Huggin

HOWITT. From Houyet; a loc. n., Belg. *D.* Howitz; *Dch.* Hoet; p.n. Hugt. n., Cant. 1622. *See* Hewett

> A younger branch of Hewet of Killamarsh, Derbysh., acquired Wansley, Notts, and changed the name to Howitt. De Hoet in Rot. Obl. et Fin.

HOWLETT. *See* Hullett

HOWLEY. *N.-Fr.* De Houlei; a p.n. John Houle in Rot. Hund.

HOWSE. A Cornish form of Haweis. Or *see* Howes

HOWSTON. *See* Owston

HOY. *See* Heyho

HOYLAND. From the Irish Hyland; a p.n.

HOYNE. An Irish form of Owen

HUARTSON. *See* Heward

HUBBALL, HUBBLE. *A.S.* Hygebeald, Hubald; p.n. (bold mind, or mind prince)

HUBBARD, HUBERT. *A.S.* Hygebeorht, Hubert; *G.* Huber, Hubert; *Fl.* Houba, Houbard; *N.-Fr.* Houbart; *Dch.* Huber; p.n. (bright mind). Hugt. n., Lond. 1618

HUBBLE. *N.* Hugi-baldr (foremost in thought); *A.S.* Hygebald; *Fl.* Houbel; *G.* Hübel; *D.B.* Hubald, Hubold; p.n.

HUBY. *N.* Ubbi; *F.* Ubbe, Ubbo; *A.S.* Hubi; p.n. *See* Hobson

HUCKER. *See* Hooker

HUCKERBY. From Huckaby; a loc. n., Devon

HUCKLE. From Ughill; a loc. n., Yorks. Or Uccle, Belg.; *A.S.* Hicel, a dim. of Hugo; *N.-Fr.* Hogel, Hockell; p.n.
> In Rot. Hund.

HUCKLEBRIDGE. *Fl.* Hucklenbroich; a loc. and p.n.

HUDBUD. *See* Hubbard

HUDD. *See* Hood

HUDDEN. From Houdain; a loc. n., France. Or *Dch.* Uden; *Fl.* Utten; *S.* Udden; p.n. *See* Hood

HUDDLESTONE. From Huddleston; a loc. n., Yorks

> Nigel de Hudelston was Provost of the Archbishop of York, A.D. 1110. Sir Richard de Hodelston was living at his manor-house of Huddleston in 1262.

HUDGELL. *See* Hugill

HUDSON. *N.* Udr (a son of the night); *D.* Hude; *N.-Fr.* Hudesent; *F.* Udo, Ude; *Dch.* Uden, Udsen; *Fl.* Hudson, Hudsyn; *A.S.* Hud, Udda, Udi; p.n.

HUFF. From Hough; a loc. n., Yorks. Or *A.S.* Hufo (Offa(?)); a p.n.

HUFFEN. From the Irish Houghegan, Hogan; a p.n.

HUGGARD. *See* Hoggarth

HUGGETT. From Huggate; a loc. n., Yorks. Or *N.-Fr.* Hugot, dim. of Hugo

HUGGINS. *F.* Uken; *Dch.* Hoogen, Huygens; *Fl.* Hugens; p.n.; fam. n. of Hugh

HUGH. *N.* Hugi; *F.* Uko, Uke; *G.* Huge, Hugo; *Fr.* Hue, Hugé; *A.S.* Huc, Hug, Hugi, Hyge; p.n. (mind, thought)

HUGHES. *D.* Huhs ; *Dch.* Hugues ;
p.n. *See* Hugh

HUGHSTON, HUSTON. *See* Houston

HUGILL. A loc. n., Westmd.

HUGMAN. *A.S.* Humman, Hyge-
mund ; *G.* Hieckmann ; *Fr.*, *Dch.*
Human ; p.n. (thoughtful protector)

HUKE. *See* Hook

HULKE. *N.* Hugleikr (Hugh the
player) ; *A.S.* Hygelac ; *Fr.*
Hulek ; *G.* Ulke ; p.n.

HULLAH. From the Irish O'h-
Oiliolla ; a p.n. Or *A.S.* Ulla ;
a p.n. (wolf)

HULLETT. *Fr.* Houllet, Hulet
(owl) ; *D.* Uhlott ; *Dch.* Uloth ;
p.n.

HULLEY. *A.S.* Ula ; *G.* Uhle ; *Fr.*
Hulet ; p.n.

HULLOCK. *See* Hulke

HULTON. A loc. n., Lancs
Bleythen de Hulton was lord of the
manor *temp.* Hen. II. Jorvet de
Hulton in Rot. Obl. et Fin., K.
John, A.D. 1199.

HULME. A loc. n., Lancs

HULYER. *See* Hildyard

HUMAN. From Humain ; a loc. n.,
Belg. Or *see* Hugman

HUMBLE. *A.S.* Hunbeald ; *G.*
Humbolt (Hun the bold) ; *D.*
Humble, Hummel ; *Fr.* Hum-
blet ; p.n.

HUMBY. A loc. n., Lincs

HUME. A loc. n., Berwick

HUMM. *G.*, *Dch.* Humme, p.n.
From Humme ; a loc. n. in Hesse
Cassel

HUMMERSTON. From Hum-
berstone ; a loc. n., Leics, Lincs

HUMPAGE. From Humphage ; a
loc. n., Hants

HUMPHREY. *See* Homfray

HUNN. *A.S.* Hun (a giant), the
nation ; *G.* Huhn ; p.n.

HUNNIBELL. From Anneboult ; a
loc. n., Norm. Or *D.*, *Fr.*
Hannibal ; *Fl.* Hennebel ; p.n. Or
A.S. Andbeald (bold opponent)

HUNNYBUN. From Honeybourne ;
a loc. n., Worcest.

HUNT. *N.* Hundi (a dog) ; *N.-Fr.*
le Huant ; *G.* Hund, Hundt ;
Dch. Hunt ; p.n.

HUNTER. *A.S.* Hunta ; *G.* Hunder ;
Dch. Hunter ; p.n. (a hunter)

HUNTINGDON. County town, Hunts

HUNTLY. A loc. n., Aberdeensh.,
Staffs

HUPTON. From Upton ; a loc. n.,
Devon, Norf., etc.

HURD. *See* Heward

HURLESTONE. A loc. n., Ches.

HURLOCK. From Harlock ; a loc.
n., Lancs

HURLOW. *See* Harlow

HURLY. From Hurley ; a loc. n.,
Berks. Or Irish O'Herlihy

HURN. *See* Hearn and Horn

HURNARD. *Fl.* Arnoeyd ; *Fr.*
Arnaud (Arnold) ; p.n.

HURNDALL. *See* Arundel

HURRAN. *See* Uren

HURRELL. *Fr.* Hurel ; a p.n.
Dim. of Urr

HURRING. Fam. n. of Urr.

HURSAM. *See* Hearsum

HURST. A freq. loc. n.
De la Hurst in Rot. Obl. et Fin.

HURY. A loc. n., Yorks. Or from
Urray ; a loc. n., Ross. Or *Fr.*
Huré, Huret, Hurey ; p.n.
(boar's head)

HUSBAND. From Husborne (?) ; a
loc. n., Beds. Or *N.* hús-bóndi
(a house-master)
Simon Huseband in Rot. Obl. et Fin.,
K. John.

HUSE. *See* Hughes

HUSKISSON. *See* Hodgkinson

HUSON. *See* Hughes

HUSSEY. *Fr.* Houssaye. From
N.-Fr. de Hossé or de Heuzé ; a
p.n. Houssaye ; a loc. n., Norm.
Husee in Roll of Battell Abbey.

HUSTHWAITE, HUSTWAIT, HUST-
WITT. A loc. n., Yorks

HUTCHINGS, HUTCHINSON. *See*
Huggins

HUTH. *A.S.*, *D.*, *Dch.* Huth ; *Fl.*
Hutt ; a p.n. (guard, keeper)
HUTHWAITE. A loc. n., Cumb.,
Notts
HUTT. *See* Huth
HUTTON. A loc. n., Berwick, Dumfries, Somers, Westmd., Yorks
Alan Bussel held it in Yorks in 1153.

HUXFORD. A loc. n., Devon
HUXHAM. A loc. n., Devon

HUXLEY. A loc. n., Ches.
HYAM. From Eyam ; a loc. n.,
Derbysh. Or *see* Higham
HYATT. From Ayott ; a loc. n.,
Herts. Or *Fl.* Hyart ; a p.n.
HYE. *See* High
HYLTON. From Hilton ; a loc. n.,
Dur., Staffs, Suff.
HYMERS, HYMUS. *See* Ames
HYNE. From the Irish O'h-Eidhin ;
a p.n. Also Heyne

I

I'ANSON. *See* Johnson
IBBERSON. *A.S.* Ib, Ibba ; *F.* Ibo,
Hibbo ; *D.* Ibson ; p.n. *See* Abbs
IBBETSON, IBBOTSON. *See* Hibbert
ICELY. From Isley ; a loc. n., Leics
ICKE. *A.S.* Icca, Ycca ; *Dch.* Icke ;
F. Ikke ; p.n. (sharp-edged)
IDDON. *N.* Iðunn (name of a
goddess) ; *S.* Idun ; *F.* Hiddo,
Ide, Hidden, Iden ; p.n. Or
Iden ; a loc. n., Suss. Hiden, a
Prot. ref., Lond. 1618
IDE. A loc. n., Devon. Or *F.*,
D., *Dch.* ; p.n.
IDLE. A loc. n., Yorks
IFE. *See* Ivy
IGGLESDEN, IGGULDEN. From Ickleton (?) ; a loc. n., Camb. Or
Hickleton, Yorks
ILBERRY. From Hilbury ; a loc.
n., Ches. Or Hilborough, Norf.
ILDERTON. A loc. n., Northbd.
ILES. *See* Eels
ILETT. *See* Aylett
ILIFF. *See* Ayliffe
ILLING. *A.S.* Illing ; a fam. n. ;
G. Illing ; *Fl.* Hillen ; p.n. Or
see Hillen
ILLINGWORTH. A loc. n., Yorks
ILOTT. *See* Alyett
ILSLEY. A loc. n., Berks. Or
Hillsley, Glost.
IMAGE. *G.* Immich, Immig ; p.n. ;
A.S. Imma ; *F.* Immo, Emma ;
p.n. *See* Ames

IMLAY. From Himley. A loc. n.,
Staffs
IMRAY, IMRIE. *See* Emery
INCE. A loc. n., Lancs. Or *see*
Innes
INCHBALD. *A.S.* Ingelbald ; a p.n.
(Ingel the bold)
INCHBOARD. *A.S.* Ingibeorht ; a
p.n. (the bright or illustrious son)
INCKLE. *See* Ingle
INCLEDON. From Ingleton ; a loc.
n., Dur., Yorks
IND. *See* Hinde
INDERWICK. From Innerwick ; a
loc. n., Haddington
INESON. *A.S.* Hinn, Ina, Inno
(domestic (?)) ; *F.* Ino, Ine ; *S.*
Hinnerson ; *Fl.* Hinnsen ; p.n.
ING. *N.* Ingi, a contraction of
compounds in Ing, as Ingimundr,
etc. *A.S.* Ing, Inga ; p.n.

Ing was identical with the god Freyr

INGALL. *See* Ingle
INGAMELLS. From Ingoldmels ; a
loc. n., Lincs
INGATE. A loc. n.
INGELOW. From Inchigeelagh ; a
loc. n., Cork. Or *S.* Engellau ;
a p.n.
INGERSOL. From Inkersall ; a loc.
n., Derbysh.
INGLE. *See* Inglis
INGLEDEW. *A.S.* Angêltheow ; a
p.n. (Engel-servant)

INGLEHEART. *N.-Fr.* Engeart ; a p.n. (strong angle)
Ingelard in Rot. Hund.

INGLESANT. *Old G.* Ingilsind ; a p.n. (Angle companion)

INGLESBY. *See* Ingoldby

INGLET. Dim. of Ingle

INGLETON. A loc. n., Dur., Yorks

INGLIS. *A.S.* Angel, Engel, Ingel ; *Fl.* Inghels ; *Dch.* Ingelse, Inckel ; *S.* Ingelson ; p.n.
One from the country of the Angles, between Flensburg and the Schley, in Denmark.

INGOLDBY. From Ingoldsby ; a loc. n., Lincs

INGPEN. *See* Inkpen

INGRAM. A loc. n., Northbd. Or *A.S.* Ingiram ; a p.n. (Ingsraven) ; *N.-Fr.* Ingelram

INGREY. From Ingrave ; a loc. n., Herts

INKER. *F.* Ino, Ine, Inke ; p.n, *See* Hinks

INKERSOLE. *See* Ingersoll

INKERSON, INKSON. *A.S.* Ingwar (Ing guarded) ; *D.* Ingverson ; *Dch.* Ingwarsen ; p.n.

INKLEY. *See* Hinckley

INKPEN. A loc. n., Bucks

INKSTER. From Ingestre ; a loc. n., Staffs

INMAN. *N.* Ingi-mundr (Freyer's protection) ; *S.* Ingman ; *D.* Ingemann ; *Dch.* Ingerman ; *Fl.* Indeman ; *A.S.* Ingimund ; p.n.

INN. *F.* Ine, Ino ; *A.S.* In, Ina ; p.n.
A.S. king, A.D. 727.

INNES, INNIS, INNS. A barony in Elgin

INNOCENT. *Fr.* Innocent ; *A.S.* Enisan, Enisant ; p.n.; *ean sind* (?) (companion defender)
Enisant in Rot. Obl. et Fin., K. John.

INSKIP. A loc. n., Lancs

INSLEY. *See* Hingeley

INSOLE. From Inzell (?) ; a loc. n., Germ. Or *see* Ensell

ION. *N.-Fr.* De Aion ; a p.n.
Ion in Rot. Hund.

IRBY. A loc. n., Lincs. Or Ireby, Cumb.
Held by De Amondeville.

IREDALE. From Airedale ; a loc. n., Yorks

IRELAND. *N.* Erland ; *Old G.* Heriland ; *Fl.* Irlen ; a p.n. (*er, out* ; the banished man)

IREMONGER, IRONMONGER. *D.* Irminger ; *A.S.* Eormengær ; p.n. (great spear)

IRONS. From Airan ; a loc. n., Norm. *Fr.* Ayrenx ; a p.n.

IRTON or IRETON. From Ireton ; a loc. n., Derbysh. *D.B.* Hiretune, Iretune

IRVIN, IRVING, IRWIN. From Irvine ; a loc. n., Ayr

ISDELL. From Easdale ; a loc. n.

ISHERWOOD. From Ishlawrcoed or Ushlawrcoed ; a loc. n., Monmouth

ISLE. From Isell ; a loc. n., Cumb.

ISLIP. A loc. n., Northants, Oxf.

ISMAY. *See* Ames

ISOM. From Isham ; a loc. n., Northants

ISON. *See* Izon

ISSITT. *See* Izzard

IVATT, IVETT. *Fl.* Heyvaert ; p.n. Dim of Iva

IVENS. Celtic, *Fr.* Yueins ; Breton, Yvain ; Irish, Yyon ; Welsh, Ywain ; p.n. (young warrior, archer). *See* M'Ivor and Owen

IVERS. From Iver (?) ; a loc. n., Bucks. Or *see* Ivor

IVES. *See* Hives

IVOR. *N.* Ivarr ; a p.n. (yew warrior, archer)

IVORY. From Ivry ; a loc. n., Normandy

IVY. *A.S.* Ifa, Iffi, Yffi ; *N. yfa* (?) (to rage) ; p.n.

IXER. *See* Ixworth

IXWORTH. A loc. n., Suff.

IZOD. *See* Izzard

IZON. From Isen ; a loc. n., Germ, Esson, Norm. Or *F.* Eisse. ; Eissen ; *D., S.* Eisen ; *A.S.* Isen (iron) ; p.n. *N.-Fr.* De Aison J. De Eisenne in Rot. Hund.

IZZARD. From Essarts ; a loc. n., Norm. Or *A.S.* Isheard, Ishard (iron firm) ; *Fl.* Izouard ; *D.B.* Iseard ; p.n.

J.

JACK. *F.* Jak ; *G.* Jache, Jach ; *Fr.* Jacques ; p.n. ; *Old G.* Jacco, perhaps from *jagon* (to hunt). Or from Jacob
   W. Jak in Rot. Hund.
JACKMAN. *G.* Jachmann ; *Fl.* Jacqmain; *Fr.* Jacquemont; p.n. Hugt. n., Canterbury, 1622 (huntsman)
JACKSON. *F.* Jak, Jäckchen ; p.n.
JACOB. *N.* Jakob ; *F.* Jakub, Jakup ; *D.* Jacob ; *Fr.* Jacob ; *D.B.* Jacob ; p.n.
JACOBS, JACOBSON. *D., Dch., S., Fl.*; p.n. *Fl.* Prot. ref., Lond. 1618
JACQUES. *See* Jack
JAFFRAY. *See* Geoffry
JAGGARD. *Fr.* Jacquard; *G.* Jagode; *Dch.* Jagt, Jacot ; p.n. (hunt ward)
JAGGERS, JAGGS. *See* Jaggard
JAKES. *See* Jacques
JAKYLL. *See* Jekyll
JALMAN. *S.* Hjelman ; a p.n. *See* Helmer
JAMES. From St James, Norm. *Fl.* James ; *D.B.* James ; p.n. Prot. ref., Lond. 1621
JAMIE, JAMY. From Chimay (?) ; a loc. n., Belg. *F.* Jimme ; *N.-Fr.* Jamet ; *Fr.* Gimai ; p.n. Or dim. of James
JANE. *A.S.* Gen ; *Fl.* Jegn ; *Fr.* Janet, Jean, Jeanne ; p.n. ; *Old Fr. gens* (gentle)
JANES. *N.-Fr.* De Genez or Gennys ; a p.n. ; *Dch.* Janse ; *G.* Jensch ; *Fl.* Jennes, Jeyens ; p.n.
JANNEY. *G.* Jani ; a p.n. *See* Janc
JANNINGS. *S.* Jahn ; *F.* Jan ; *D.* Janniche ; *Dch.* Janning ; *D.B.* Junain (?) ; a p.n. (John's descendants)

JARDINE. *Fr.* Jardin ; a p.n. (garden)
   Jarden in Roll of Battell Abbey.
JARMAIN, JARMAN. *Fr.* Germain ; a p.n. *See* Gamon
JARRED. *A.S.* Garheard (firm spear) ; *F.* Gerd, Gerhard ; *G.* Jerathe ; *Dch.* Gerhardt, Gererts ; *D.B.* Girard, Gerard ; p.n. St Gérard ; a loc. n., Belg.
JARROLD. *A.S.* Garweald (spear ruler) ; *F.* Garrelt, Gerrelt ; p.n.
JARVIS. *N.-Fr.* Gerveis ; a p.n. ; *N. geir-ves* ; *A.S. gar-was* (spear-keen). Hugt. n., Lond. 1688.
JARY. *F.* Djure ; *G.* Jury, Jurei ; *Fr.* Jarry. *See* Jarrett
JASPER. From Chassepierre (?) ; a loc. n., Belg. *Dch.* Jasper, Jaspers ; *Fl.* Jaspar ; p.n. Or *Fr.* Gaspard (?) (treasure - master). Prot. ref., Lond. 1621
JAWINS. *A.S.* Jouin, in *D.B.* ; *Fr.* Jouen, Jouvin ; p.n.
   Jouve is a *Fr.* form of Job, Jopp.
JAY. A loc. n. Heref. Or *F.* Gayo ; *Dch.* Jay, Jehee ; *Fl.* Jeyens ; p.n. *See* Gay and Gee
   Jay is in the Roll of Battell Abbey.
JEAFFRESON. *See* Geoffrey
JEAKES. *See* Jacques
JEALOUS. *Dch.* Jaulus ; *G.* Gelse, Jelsch ; p.n.
JEARY. *See* Jary
JECKELL. *See* Jekyll
JECKS. *See* Jacques
JEE. *See* Gee
JEEVES. *See* Jeffs.
   Peter de Cheef, Norm. 1180.
JEFFCOCK, *See* Jeffery
JEFFERSON. *See* Jeaffreson

JEFFERY, JEFFREY. *Fr.* Geoffrey, Jaffré; *N.* Guðfriðr; *D.B.* Godefrid; p.n. *See* Godfrey
JEFFS. *See* above
JEKYLL. Jacle (a fief), Normandy. Or *N.* Jökull (an icicle); *D.* Jœkel; *A.S.* Gicel, Jcel; *G.* Jäckel, Jäkel, Jagel; *Dch.* Jeekel; p.n.

Iuichel or Iuikel, a Presbyter (Norf.), a tenant in chief in *D.B.* W. Jackel, 1180; J. Jacel, 1198. Mag. Rot. Scaccarii, Normanniœ. W. and R. de Jakele, Rot. Hund., 1272.

JELF. *See* Jelly
JELLETT. *See* Gillett
JELLICOE. *A.S.* Geleca; *Old G.* Jeliko. Dimin. of *F.* Jelle; *Dch.* Gellecum; p.n.
JELLY. From Jelliffe, a form of *N.* Eilífr (enduring). *F.* Jelle; *Fl.* Jelley; p.n.
JEMPSON. *See* James
JENEWAY. *Fr.* Genvier; a p.n., From St Geneviève; a loc. n., Normandy
JENKIN, JENKINS. *Dch.* Jenck, Jenk, Jenkens; *G.* Jenke; p.n. (little John)
JENNER. St Genois (?); a loc. n., Flanders. Or *A.S.* Gener; *Old G.* Genear; p.n. (a refuge, protection); *G.* Jenner; *Fl.* Jenar, Jenart; *Dch.* Jener; p.n.
JENNERY. *A.S.* Genere; *Old G.* Ginhari (?); p.n. (protector lord)
JENNEY. *Fl.* Genis; a p.n. *See* Jane
JENNINGS, JENNYNS. *See* Jannings
JENNIS. *See* Janes
JENNISON. *See* Jennis
JEPHSON. *D.* Jeppesen, Jepsen; *S.* Jepsen, Jippson; a p.n. *See* Ibberson
JERAM. *Fr.* Jerome; a p.n. (holy name)
JERDAN. *See* Jordan
JERMY, JERMEY, JERMYN. *See* Jarmain

JERNINGHAM. *N.-Fr.* Jernegan or Fitz-Jarnegan; p.n.
Forestarius in Bretagne, 1083.
JERRETT. *See* Jarred
JERROLD. *See* Jarrold
JERVIS. *See* Gervase
JESSON. From Jessains; a loc. n., France. OrJessen,Germ.; *D., N., Dch., Fl.* Jessen; p.n. *See* Chase
JESSOP. *D.* Jess; a p.n. Jesshope; a loc. n.
JESTY. *Fr.* Jestin; a p.n. *See* Jewson
JEUNE. *N.-Fr.* Le Jovene; a p.n. In Rot. Hund.
JEVON. Welsh Jevan (young warrior)
JEWELL. *See* Jouel
Juhel, a sub-tenant in *D.B.*
JEWKES. *See* Jukes
JEWSBURY. *See* Dewsbury
JEWSON. *F.* Juist; *Dch.* Joosten; *Fl.* Jossen; *D.* Justesen; *A.S.* Justeign, Justen, Justan, Justin (guest soldier); p.n. *See* Just
JEX. *See* Jacques
JICKLING. *See* Hickling
JIGGENS. *See* Juggins
JIGGLE. *A.S.* Cich; *Old G.* Gigio; *Fl.* Gigault; a p.n.; *N.gygr* (agiant)
JILBERT. *See* Gilbert
JILLINGS. A loc. n., Yorks. *See* Gillings
JOBLIN. From Jublains; a loc. n., France
JOCKEL. *See* Jekyll
JODDRELL. *S.* Jordell (?); a p.n.
JOEL. *See* Jouel
JOHN, JOHNS. *N.* Jón; *F.* Jan; *G., Fl., Dch., D.* Jan, Jans, Jahn, Jahns, Jen, Johan, Johans, John, Johne, Johns, Jons, Jones; *N.-Fr.* Joannes; *Fr.* Jean, Jouan, Jouen; p.n. Contr. of *Lat.* Johannes. *See* St John.
In Rot. Hund.
JOHNSON. *D.* Johannsen, Johanson, Johnssen, Johnson; *S.* Jansen, Johnsson; *Dch.* Jannissen, Jansen, Johannissen, Johanson; p.n.

JOLLIFFE. *N.-Fr.* Giolif, Jolyf ; p.n.

JOLLY. Hugt., Lond. 1681. *See* Jouel

JOHNSTONE. A loc. n., Dumfries, Renfrew

JONAS, JONES. *D.*, *Dch.*, *G.*, *S.* ; p.n. *See* Johns

JOPE. From St Job ; a loc. n., Belg. *D.* Job, Jopp ; *Dch.* Job, Joppe ; *Fl.* Job, Jobin ; p.n.

> Adam de Jope in 1334 ; Walter Joop, reeve of Marlborough, 1388.

JOPLING. *See* Joblin

JORDAN. *D.*, *G.*, *Dch.* Jordan ; *Fl.* Jordaen ; p.n.

JOSH. From St Josse ; a loc. n., Belg. *G.* Josch ; a p.n.

JOSSELYN. *See* Goss

JOUEL. *N.* Jólfr (?) (from Jólfuðr, a name of Odin) ; *A.S.* Ialf, Iaul, Iol, Yol ; *D.* Hjul, Juell, Juhl, Juul ; *S.* Juel ; *Fr.* Juhel ; *Dch.* Jolle, Jolly, Joly ; *N.-Fr.* Fitz-Juel ; *G.* Jouly, Joul ; p.n.

> Johol de Lincoln, 1068.

JOYCE, JOYES. From Joyeuse ; a loc. n., Normandy

> Johais in *D.B.* (St Judocus), undertenant. Ric. de Jorz, 1200 ; Gaufrid de Jorz, 1207, in Rot. Obl. et Fin. (Notts.) ; Simon de Jorce, John Jorse (Hoton, Leics), Lay Sub. R., 1329 ; Ranulph de Jorz, Rob. de Jors, Testa de Neville. Also Sim. de Joyce (Wymeswold) held lands. François de Joyeuse was Abbot of Mont-Saint-Michael in 1594.

JOY. From Goi or Gouy ; a loc. n. Norm. *Fr.* Joet ; a p.n. Hugt., Lond. 1685

JUDD, JUBY, JUBEY. *G.* Jube, Juppe, Jupe ; *Fl.* Jubin ; *D.* Juby ; p.n. *See* Jupp

JUDD. *F.* Udo, Ude ; *Dch.* Joode ; *Fl.* Jude ; *D.* Jud ; *A.S.* Jud, Udi ; p.n.

JUDGE. *Fr.* Juge (a judge) ; *G.* Chutsch ; p.n.

> According to Ferguson, Judge, Jugg, and perhaps Jukes may be possibly derived from *Old G.* Jugo, referred by Stark to Gothic *jiukan* (to combat).

JUDKINS, JUDSON. *See* Judd

JUGG. *D.* Joeg ; a p.n. *See* Judge

JUGGINS. *D.* Jürgens (?) ; a p.n. ; fam. n. of Jugg

JUKES. From Choques ; a loc. n., Fland. Or *see* Judge

JULER. *N.* Jólfr ; *G.* Julich, Jouly ; *D.* Juhler ; *Fr.* Julez ; p.n. *See* Jouel

JULIAN. *Fr.* Julien ; a p.n.

JULIER. *Fr.* Juliard ; a p.n.

JULIET. *Fr.* Hugt. n., Lond. 1618

JUMP. A loc. n., Devon, Yorks

JUNIPER. *Dch.* Jongeboer (?) ; a p.n. (young rustic)

JUPP. *G.* Jupp ; *Fr.* Chupé ; p.n. *See* Jubb, Jope, Chope

JURDAN. *See* Jordan

JURY. *See* Jary

JUST. *A.S.* Iust ; *D.* Just ; *G.* Just ; *Dch.* Juist ; *Fl.* Juste ; p.n. *A.S.* gyst (?) (a guest, or just, right, straight)

K

KAIL. *A.S.* Ceol, Cil ; *Fl.* Kuyl ; *D.* Keil ; *Dch.* Kehl ; *G.* Keyl ; p.n. (ship)

KAINE. Irish M'Kain. *See* Caine

KARSLAKE. *See* Carslake

KAVANAGH. From the Irish O'Caomhanach ; a p.n. (comely (?))

KAY. *D.B.* Kee ; *A.S.* cœg (a key) ; *D.* Kai ; *S.* Key ; *Fl.* Kai, Key ; *Dch.* Kea ; p.n. Or Scot. M'Kay

KAYNES. *See* Keynes

KEABLE. *See* Keble

KEAL. *See* Keel

KEALEY. Manx. Originally Mac Gilla Ceallaigh. *See* Kelly

M

KEAN. *See* Keen
KEAREY. *See* Carew
KEARNEY. *See* Cairns
KEARNS. *See* Cairns
KEAT. *See* Keith
KEATS. From Kitts; a loc. n., Devon. Or *G.* Keitz; a p.n.
KEBLE. *A.S.* Cædbeald; *Fr.* Quibel; *N.-Fr.* Cabal; *G.* Kiebel; p.n. (war bold)
KECK. *A.S.* Cæc; *D.* Keck; *Dch.* Koek; *Fl.* Koecke; p.n.; *cæg* (key). Prot. ref., Norwich, 1622
KEDGE. *See* Gedge
KEDGLEY. *See* Keighley
KEED. *See* Kidd
KEEFE. Irish O'Keefe. Or *D.* Kieffer; p.n.; *D.B.* Chevre; *A.S. ceafor* (a beetle)
KEEL. From Keele; a loc. n., Staffs
KEELER. *A.S.* Ceola; *Dch.* Kiella; *G.* Kieler, Kille; p.n. (a sailor)
KEELEY. *See* Kieley
KEELING. From Killing or Keeling (*D.B.* Chellinge); a loc. n., Yorks
KEEN. *A.S.* Cen, Cyne (noble); *D.* Kiehn; *Fl.* Kien; p.n.
KEEP. *D.B.* Cepe, Ceppa; *Dch.* Kiepe, Kip; p.n.; *A.S. ceap* (a merchant). Prot. ref., Lond. 1618
KEEPING. Fam. n. of Keep. Or *see* Kippen. *D.B.* Cheping; a p.n. *See* Chipp
KEER. *See* Keir
KEETLEY. *See* Keightley
KEEVIL. A loc. n., Wilts
KEFFORD. *Fr.* Quifut (?); a p.n. *See* Gifford
KEGGIN. From the Irish Keghan, M'Keogh; p.n.
KEGLEY. *See* Quigley
KEHOE. *Fr.* Cahot, Cahut, Cayeux; p.n. Or *see* Keogh
   W. de Keheu in Rot. Obl. et Fin., K. John.
KEIGHLEY. A loc. n., Lancs, Yorks
KEIGHTLEY. A loc. n., Yorks

KEINCH. *S., D.* Kinch; *Fl.* Kints; *G.* Kensche; p.n. Or Irish M'Kinch. Dim. of Keen
KEIR. A loc. n., Dumfries
KEITH. A loc. n., Elgin
KEKEWICH. From Kekwick; a loc. n., Ches.
KELF. *A.S.* Ceolf, Ceolwalf (ship wolf); *Dch.* Kalff, Kalf, Kelfkins; p.n.
KELK. A loc. n., Yorks
KELL. *A.S.* Cel, Ceol; a p.n. (a keel, ship). *See* Kill
KELLAWAY, KELLEWAY. A loc. n., Wilts
KELLETT. A loc. n., Lancs
KELLIE. A loc. n., Fife
KELLS. A loc. n., Kirkcudbright
KELLY. A loc. n., Renfrew. Or Irish O'Killy-Kelly, Giolla Cheallaigh (the disciple of Ceallach)
KELSEY. A loc. n., Lincs
KEMBLE. A loc. n., Wilts. Or *A.S.* Cynbald; a p.n. (bold noble)
KEMP. *See* Camp
KEMPSON, KEMPSTER. From Kempston; a loc. n., Beds, Norf.
KEMPTHORNE. A loc. n., Devon
KEMPTON. From Kemberton; a loc. n., Salop. Or *see* Kimpton
KEMSHEAD. From Kempshott; a loc. n., Hants
KEMSLEY. A loc. n., Kent
KEMSTEAD. *See* Kemshead
KEN, KENN. A loc. n., Somers
   John and Richard de Ken in Rot. Obl. et Fin., K. John.
KENDRICK. *See* Kenrick
KENISTON. From Kenstone; a loc. n., Salop
KENNARD. From Kennarth; a loc. n., S. Wales. Or *A.S.* Cyneheard; a p.n. (noble strong)
KENNEDY. From the Irish O'Ceannfhada or O'Cinnidh; p.n. Cineadh (a nation). *See* Kenneth
KENNERLEY. From Kennerleigh; a loc. n., Devon

KENNETH. Irish Caoinnach (peaceable man)

KENNEWAY. From Kennoway; a loc. n., Fife. Or *see* Knyvett

KENNEY. Irish M'Kenny. Or *Fr.* Kenis, Kennis; p.n.; *A.S.* Cyne (noble)

KENNION. *See* Kenyon

KENRICK. From Kenwrick; a loc. n., Salop. Or *A.S.* Cynric; *D.B.* Chenric; p.n. *A.S. cyn* (race, tribe), *ríc* (dominion, power)

KENT, KENTISH. The county

KENYON. A loc. n., Lancs

KEOGH. From the Irish MacEochaidh; a p.n. (horseman). *See* Kehoe

KEPPEL. *N.-Fr.* Capel; *Dch.* Keppel; p.n. *See* Capel

KERBY. *See* Kirkby

KERLIN. *See* Carlin

KERMODE. The Manx form of the Celtic MacDiarmaid; Irish M'Dermott; p.n.

KERNS. *See* Cairns

KERR. *See* Carr and Keir

KERSHAW. A loc. n., Lancs. Anciently Kyrkeshagh

KERSWELL. A loc. n., Devon

KESSANLY. From Kessingland (?); a loc. n., Norf.

KESTERTON. From Casterton; a loc. n., Westmd.

KESTEVEN. A loc. n. (tithing), Lincs

KETCHER. *Dch.* Kegge (?); a p.n.

KETLEY. A loc. n., Salop

KETT. *See* Catt

KETTERIDGE. From Catterick; a loc. n., Yorks. Or Irish M'Kitterick

KETTERING. A loc. n., Northants

KETTLE. A loc. n., Fife. Or *N.* Ketill; *Dch.* Ketel; p.n. (the kettle of the gods)

KETTLEBOROUGH. A loc. n., Suff.

KETTLEBY. A loc. n., Yorks

KETTLEWELL. A loc. n., Yorks

KEWLEY. Manx. A contraction of MacAulay, the shortened form of MacAmhlaibh (Aulaf's or Olaf's son)

KEY. From the Irish M'Kee. *See* Kay

KEYLOCK. From Killough; a loc. n., co. Down, Ireland

KEYMER. A loc. n., Ess.
Symon de Kyma in Rot. Obl. et Fin., K. John.

KEYNES. *D.* Kiens; a p.n. Or *see* Caine

KEYWORTH. A loc. n., Notts

KIBBLE. *See* Keable

KIDALL, KIDDELL, KIDDLE. From Kiddall; a loc. n., Yorks

KIDD, KIDDY. *A.S.* Cydd, Cydda, Cyddi; *D.* Kidde; *Dch.* Kidd; p.n. (a striver)
R. Kide in Rot. Obl. et Fin., K. John. Kede in Rot. Hund.

KIDGELL. *G.* Kitschelt; a p.n.

KIDGER. *N.* Kygeir (people's spear); *Dch.* Kigge; *G.* Kitscher; p.n.

KIDNER. From Kitnor (now Culbone); a loc. n., Somers

KIDNEY. From the Irish Kedney; a p.n. Or *see* Gidney

KIELEY. From the Irish O'Caolidh; a p.n.

KIERNAN. From the Irish Kernaghan; a p.n.

KIGHTLY. *See* Keightley

KILBOURN. From Kilburn; a loc. n., Middlx.

KILBRIDE. *D.B.* Ghilbrid. From the Irish Giolla Bridghid (the servant of Bridget)

KILBY. A loc. n., Leics, Lincs

KILL. *A.S.* Ceol (a ship); *G.* Kille; p.n.

KILLEN. From Killin; a loc. n., Perth

KILLICE. From Killisk; a loc. n., Wexford

KILLICK. *See* Kilwick

KILLMAN. *A.S.* Ceolmund; a p.n. (a ship director)

KILMARTIN. A loc. n., Argyll

KILMINSTER. A loc. n., Caithness

KILMISTER. From Kilminster; a loc. n., Caithness

KILNER. A loc. n., Somers

KILPACK. From Kilpeck; a loc. n., Heref.

KILPATRICK. *See* Gilpatrick

KILPIN. A loc. n., Yorks

KILVERT. From the Irish M'Ilrath; a p.n.

KILVINGTON. A loc. n., Yorks

KILWICK. From Kildwick; a loc. n., Yorks

KIMBELL. *See* Kimble

KIMBERLEY. A loc. n., Notts

KIMBLE. A loc. n., Bucks. Or *A.S.* Cinebeald; *G.* Kimbel; *Dch.* Kimpel; *Fl.* Quimbel; p.n. (noble bold)

KIMM. From Kyme; a loc. n., Lincs

KIMPTON. A loc. n., Hants

KINABLE. *A.S.* Cynebil; a p.n. (noble sword). Or Cynebeald (noble bold)

KINCH. Irish M'Kinch; a p.n. (islander)

KINCHIN. *Fl.* Kinkin; *G.* Kinsing; p.n. Dimin. of Cyn

KINCHLEY. *See* Kingerley

KINDRED. *A.S.* Cynered; a p.n. (noble counsel)

KING. *D.* Kinck, Kink; p.n. Dim. of Cyn. Or *A.S.* cyng, cyning (a king). Perhaps from the character in a mediæval play. *See* official names. A Flem. ref. n., Lond. 1618

KINGDOM. From Kingham; a loc. n., Oxf. Or *see* Kingdon

KINGDON. A loc. n., Devon

KINGERLEY. From Kingley; a loc. n., Warw. Or Kinsley, Yorks

KINGSBURY. A loc. n., Warw.

KINGSFORD. A loc. n., Devon, Worcest.

KINGSLEY. A loc. n., Hants, Staffs

KINGSMILL. A loc. n., Hants

KINIPPLE. *Fr.* Kinable; a p.n. *See* Kimble

KINLOCH. A loc. n., Fife

KINNAIRD. A loc. n., Perth, Stirling

KINNAVY. From the Irish *cnamh* (a bone)

KINNISH. *See* Kinch

KINSEY. *A.S.* Chinesi, Cynesige (noble victor); *D.* Kinzi; p.n. Kynsy, Bishop of Lichfield, A.D. 960.

KIPLING. From Kiplin; a loc. n., Yorks. *D.B.* Chipeling

KIPPEN. A loc. n., Stirling

KIRBY. *See* Kirkby

KIRK. From Atte-kirk (at or near the church), 1327, Lay, Sub. R.

KIRKBY. A freq. loc. n.

One family of this name lived for eighteen generations at the Old Hall, Kirkby in Furness, Lancs.

KIRKCALDY. A loc. n., Scotl.

KIRKLAND. A loc. n., Cumb., Fife, Lancs, Westmd.

KIRKLEY. A loc. n., Suff.

KIRKPATRICK. A loc. n., Dumfries

KIRKUP. From Kirkthorpe; a loc. n., Yorks

KIRKWOOD. A loc. n., Dumfries, Lanark

KIRSHAW. *See* Kershaw

KIRTLAND. *See* Kirkland

KIRTLEY. From Kirtling; a loc. n., Camb.

KIRTON. A loc. n., Lincs, Suff., Devon. Also a loc. corr. of Crediton

KIRWAN. Irish p.n. (dark visaged)

KISBEE. From Kisby; a loc. n., Hunts

KISSACK, KISSICK. Manx; contracted from MacIsaac. Or *Fr.* Queyssac; a p.n.

De Cussack in Rot. Obl. et Fin., K. John.

KITCAT. From Kitcott; a loc. n., Devon

KITCHEN, KITCHIN. *D.* Ketjen ; *S.* Kitzing ; *Dch.* Ketjen ; *Fl.* Kitson, Kitzen ; p.n. A double dimin. of Christopher. *See* Kitt. Or Irish M'Cutcheon, McEachen, Ketchen. Hutcheon, the Gaelic form of Hugon. *See* Hutchings

KITCHINGMAN. *G.* Kitschmann ; a p.n.

KITLEY. A loc. n., Devon

KITT. Dimin. of Christopher. *D.B.* Chit ; *G.* Kitt ; *Dch.* Kits, Chits ; p.n. Or *see* Kidd

KITTEBY. *See* Kettleby

KITTERIDGE. *See* Ketteridge

KITTERMASTER. A corruption of Kidderminster ; a loc. II.

KITTLE. *See* Kiddle

KNAGGS. *A.S.* Cynech (?) ; *Fl.* Knage ; p.n. Dim. of Cyn (noble)

KNAPP. A loc. II., Devon. Or *N.* Knappi (a knob) ; *A.S.* Cnapa (a bag) ; *G.* Knappe ; *D.* Knaap ; *Fl.* Knapp ; p.n. Knaby ; a loc. n., Sweden

De la Cnapp in Rot. Obl. et Fin.

KNAPPIT. *See* Knapp. Dim.

KNAPTON. A loc. II., Leics, Norf.

KNEE. *A.S.* Cyne (?) (noble) ; *G.* Knie ; p.n.

KNEEBONE, KNEEBORN. *A.S.* Cynebeorn ; a p.n. (noble bear)

KNEVITT, KNYVETT. From St Pierre de Canivet ; a loc. n. Norm.,

KNEWSTUBB. From Knostrop ; a loc. n., Yorks

KNIBB. *A.S.* Cnebba, Cnibba (neb, beak) ; it was used of the prow of a vessel, so might mean a sailor ; *Dch.* Knibbe ; p.n.

KNIFE. *N.* Kneif ; a n.n. (nip). Cniva, the n. of a Gothic king, 3Id cent. Perhaps from *A.S.* Cynefar ; a p.n. (noble traveller) Knif in Hund. Rolls.

KNIFTON. *See* Kniveton

KNIGHT. *A.S.* Cniht ; *Dch.* Knegt ; *G.* Knecht (a servant) ; Irish M'Knight ; p.n.

KNIGHTLEY. A loc. n., Staff.

KNIGHTON. A loc. n., Devon, Leics

KNILL. From Knylle or Knill ; a loc. n., Heref.

Sir John de Braose received the Manor of Knille, *temp.* K. John.

KNIPE. *See* Knibb. *Dch.* Knip ; *D., G.* Kniep ; p.n.

KNIVETON. A loc. n., Derbysh.

KNOCK. Knocke, a loc. n., Belg. Or *N.* Knjúkr (a fighter, striker) ; *G.* Knoch ; *Dch.* Knoek ; *D.* Knock ; p.n. (a knock, stroke)

KNOTT. *N.* Knöttr (a ball, knob) ; *D.* Knodt ; *G.* Knoth ; a p.n. *See* Nute

KNOWLE. A freq. loc. n. De la Cnoll in Rot. Obl. et Fin.

KNOX. A loc. n., Renfrew

KNYVETT. *See* Knevitt

KVBIRD. *A.S.* Cybeorht, Cynebeort ; *Dch.* Kiberd ; p.n. (illustrious, noble)

KYD. *See* Kidd

KYFFIN. Welsh Cyffin ; a p.n.

KYLE. *See* Kail

KYNASTON. A loc. n., Salop, Staffs

KVRLE. From Criol or Crieul, near Eu, Norm.

KYTE. *A.S.* Cyta ; *Dch.* Kuyt ; *Fl.* Kayaert ; p.n. (a kite)

L

LACHLAN. From the Gaelic *laochail* (warlike)

LACK. From Lacq; a loc. n., France

LACY. From Lessay; a loc. n., Normandy. *D.B.* de Laci, a tenant in chief
De Lacy and De Lascy in Rot. Obl. et. Fin., K. John.

LADBROKE, LADBROOKE. From Ladbrook; a loc. n., Warw.

LADBURY. From Ledbury; a loc. n., Heref.

LADD. *A.S.* Lad, Leod; *Dch.* Laddé; p.n. (people)

LADLER, LADLY. *See* Laidlaw

LAFFEATY, LAFFERTY. *See* Laverty

LAIDLAW. A loc. n., Selkirk

LAIDLAY. *See* Laidlaw

LAILEY. *See* Lely

LAING. *See* Leng

LAITY. A loc. n., Cornw. *See* Leuty

LAKE. From St Martin du Lac, Burgundy; a loc. n., Devon, Hunts, Salop, Wilts. Leke; a loc. n., Belg.

LAKIN. From Lacon, Norm.; Laeken, Belg. Or *A.S.* Læcing; a fam. n.; *Dch.* Leyking; p.n.

LALOR. *Fr.* Lalot, Lalou; p.n.

LAMB. *N.* Lambi (a lamb); *S.* Lamby, Lamm; *Dch.* Lam; *Fl.* Lamme; *D.B.* Lambe; p.n.

LAMBERT. From St Lambert; a loc. n., Belg. and France. *A.S.* Lambeorht, Landbeorht; *Fr.* Lambard, Lambert, Lambret; *D.* Lamberth; *Dch.* Lambert, Lambrecht, Lammerts; *G.* Lambart; *D.B.* Lambert, tenant in chief; p.n. (the country's illustrious one). Also a Flem. ref. n., Lond. 1618
Gen. Lambert, Governor of York, A.D. 1531.

LAMBERTH. *See* Lambert

LAMBETH. A loc. n., Surr.

LAMBOURNE, LAMBURN. From Lamborne; a loc. n., Berks, Cornw.

LAMBSON. From Lambston; a loc. n., S. Wales

LAMBTON. A loc. n., Dur.

LAMERTON. A loc. n., Devon

LAMPARD. *Fl.* Lampaert; *G.*, *Dch.* Lampert; p.n. *See* Lambert

LAMPLUGH. A loc. n., Cumb.

LAMPSON. *See* Lambson

LANCASTER. The county town

LANCE. From Lanz; a loc. n., Prussia. *Dch.*, *G.* Lanz; a p.n. Also a dimin. of Lancelot or Laurence

LANCUM. *See* Langham

LAND, LANT. From Landes; a loc. n., Normandy; Land, Devon. Or *A.S.* Land; a p.n. *See* Lound

LANDER. From Landres; a loc. n., Burgundy. Or *D.*, *Dch.*, *G.* p.n.; *A.S.* Landweard; a p.n. (Landwarden)

LANDFEAR. *See* Lanfear

LANE. A loc. n., Devon. Or *D.* Lehn; *Fl.* Leyn; *Dch.* Leijn; p.n. From Laignes; a loc. n., France
In Roll of Battell Abbey.

LANEY. *See* Delaney

LANFEAR. From Llanfair; a loc. n., N. Wales. Or *A.S.* Landfrith; a p.n. (land peace)

LANG. *A.S.*, *D.*, *Dch.*; p.n.

LANGDALE. A loc. n., Cumb.

LANGFORD. A loc. n., Devon, Notts, Somers, Wilts

LANGHAM. A loc. n., Devon, Ess., Norf., Rutld., Suff.

LANGHORNE. *D.* Langhorn; *Dch.* Lankhoorn; a loc. and p.n.

LANGLEY. A loc. n., Derbysh. and other counties

LANGMAID. *See* Langmead

LANGMEAD. A loc. n., Devon

LANGMORE. From Langmere; a loc. n., Norf.

LANGRIDGE. A loc. n., Devon, Somers

LANGSHAW. A loc. n., Dumfries

LANGSTER. *See* Lancaster

LANGSTON. A loc. n., Devon

LANGTON. A loc. n., Devon, Leics, Somers

LANGTREE, LANGTRY. A loc. n., Devon

LANGWORTHY. A loc. n., Devon

LANKESTER. *See* Lancaster

LANSDELL. *See* Lonsdale

LANSDOWNE. A loc. n., Somers

LANYON. A loc. n., Brittany and Cornw.

LAPPER. *See* Lepper

LAPSLEY. From Lapley; a loc. n., Staffs

LAPTHORNE. A loc. n., Devon

LAPWORTH. A loc. n., Warw.

LARCHER. *N.-Fr.* Le Archier; a p.n. (the archer)

LARCHIN. *See* Larkin

LARCOMBE. A loc. n., Devon

LARDER. *See* Lawder

LARGE. *N.-Fr.* De Largo; a p.n. In Rot. Hund.

LARK, LARKE. *A.S.* Leofric, Leoric; *S.* Larka; *G.* Lerch, Lorke; *D.* Larcher; *Fl.* Larock; *D.B.* Lorch; p.n. *See* Laveric

LARKIN. Dim. of Laurence. Or *N.-Fr.* Largan; a p.n.

LARLHAM. From Laleham; a loc. n., Middlx.

LARMETT. *Fr.* Lermytte; a p.n.

LARTER. From Latour; a loc. n., France. *Fr.* Latour; *Fl.* Latteur; p.n. Le Tour, Hugt. n., Lond. 1618

LASCELLES. From Lacelle; a loc. n., Norm. *N.-Fr.* De Lascelles, under-tenant in *D.B.* In Roll of Battell Abbey and Rot. Obl. et Fin., K. John.

LASHAM. A loc. n., Hants

LASHMAR. *See* Latchmore

LAST. *Dch.*; p.n.

LATCH. *A.S.* Lac, Lec; *G.* Lach, Lache; p.n. (a leech, surgeon)

LATCHFORD. A loc. n., Ches.

LATCHMORE. From Letchmore; a loc. n., Herts

LATER. *See* Larter

LATHAM. From Letham; a loc. n., Fife; Lathom, Lancs; or Laytham, Yorks

LATHBRIDGE, LETHBRIDGE. *See* Lathbury

LATHBURY. A loc. n., Bucks

LATTA, LATTER. *See* Larter

LAUDER. *See* Lawder. Or from the Irish *laidir* (strong)

LAUGHLAND. From Lawkland; a loc. n., Yorks

LAUGHTON. A loc. n., Lincs, Yorks

LAURENCE. *Fr.*; p.n. From *Lat.* Laurentius (crowned with laurel). Hugt., Lond. 1618

LAURIE. *See* Lowry In Rot. Hund.

LAVENDER. From Lavendon; a loc. n., Bucks. Or *Fr.* Lavandier; a p.n.

LAVER. *See* Leaver

LAVERICK. *Fr.* Levreux (?); a p.n. Or *A.S.* Leofric, Leuuric (?); p.n. (beloved ruler); *laferc* (lark) does not occur as a p.n.

LAVERTON. A loc. n., Somers, Yorks

LAVERTY. From the Irish O'Labhradha; a p.n.

LAVIES. *Fr.* Lavie, La Vie; *Fl.* Lavies; Prot. ref. n., 1683

LAVIN. *Fr.* Lavigne; a p.n. (a vineyard)

LAVINGTON. A loc. n., Wilts

LAW. A loc. n., Dur., Lanark; Lauwe, Belg.

LAWDER. A loc. n., Berwick

LAWFORD. A loc. n., Warw.

LAWLER. *See* Lalor

LAWLESS. From Loulas (?); a loc. n., S. Wales

LAWLEY. A loc. n., Salop
LAWMAN. From the Irish Laman, Lamon, a form of Lamont; p.n. Or *A.S.* Lagman; a p.n. (lawman)
LAWN. *See* Lound
LAWS. From St Lowe (?), Norm.; p.n. Prot. ref., Norwich, 1622
LAWSON. *N.-Fr.* Loison; a p.n.
LAWTON. A loc. n., Salop
LAXTON. A loc. n., Northants, Notts, Yorks
LAY. From Lea, Lee, Leigh; freq. loc. n. Or *D.* Leigh; *Dch.* Lee; *S.* Leja; p.n.
LAYBORN, LAYBOURN. From Labourn; a loc. n., Surr. Or Leybourne, Kent
LAYCOCK. From Laycock; a loc. n., Wilts, Yorks (*D.B.* Lacoc). Or *Fr.* Lecocq; a p.n. La Cock, Hugt. n., Dover, 1622. *See* Cock
LAYLAND. A loc. n., Cornw., Lancs, Somers
LAYMAN. *Fl.* Leman; a p.n. Prot. ref., Lond. 1618. *See* Leman
LAYT. *A.S.* Let, Leod, Leth; p.n. (people)
LAYTON. A loc. n., Ess.
LAZEL. *Fr.* Lasalle; a p.n. *See* Lascelles
LAZENBY. A loc. n., Yorks. Comp. Lazonby, Cumb.
LEA. *See* Lee and Lay
LEACH, LEECH. *A.S.* Laic, Lec; *G.* Liche; a p.n. *A.S. læce* (a healer)
LEACROFT. A loc. n., Staffs
LEADBEATER, LEADBITTER. *See* Lebetter
LEADER. *A.S.* Lida, Leodhere (people's warrior); *G.* Lieder; p.n. *See* Leather
LEAF. *See* Leefe
LEAGE. From Liege; a loc. n., Belg. Hutg. n., Lond. 1687
LEAK. From Leak; a loc. n., Lincs (*D.B.* Leche). Comp. Leek, Staffs

LEAKEY. From Lickey; a loc. n., Worcest. Or Irish p.n.; *G.* Lichey; a p.n.
LEAN. From Ligne; a loc. n., Belg. *Dch.* Lien; a p.n.
LEAPMAN. *D.*, *Dch.* Lipman; *G.* Lipman, Liebermann; p.n. (a goodly man)
LEAR. From Liers; a loc. n., Belg.; or Lyre, Norm. *G.* Liehr; *Dch.*, *D.* Lier; p.n.
LEARNER. *Fr.* Lernoud (?); a p.n.
LEAROYD. A loc. n.
LEARY. Irish O'Leary
LEASE. A loc. n., Devon
LEASK. *G.* Lieske; a p.n. Dim. of *A.S.* Lis, Lissa; p.n.; *liss* (happy)
LEAT. *See* Leete
LEATHER. *A.S.* Leodhere, Leother; Old *G.* Lethar; *G.*, *Dch.* Leder, Lieder; p.n. (people's warrior)
LEATHERDALE. From Leverdale (?); a loc. n., Staffs
LEATHLEY. A loc. n., Yorks
LEATHWAITE. *See* Lewthwaite
LEAVER, LEVER. *A.S.* Leofhere, Lifher; *Dch.* Lever, Liever; p.n. (a deliverer, beloved warrior)
LEAWOOD. A loc. n., Devon
LEBETTER. *Fr.* Lebouteux (?); a p.n.
LECK. A loc. n., Yorks
LECKY. *See* Leakey
LEDGER. From St Legère; a loc. n., Norm. and Belg. Or *A.S.* Leodgœr; a p.n. (people-spear); *Fl.* Leger; p.n.
LEDSON. From Ledstone; a loc. n., Yorks. Or *A.S.* Led, Leod; p.n. (people)
LEDYARD. *N.* Lidvard; *A.S.* Lidgeard; p.n. (gate ward)
LEE. A loc. n., Ess., Kent, etc.
LEEDHAM. *See* Latham
LEEFE. From Liff (?); a loc. n., Forfar. Or Lives, Belg.
LEEMING. A loc. n., Yorks
LEES. A loc. n., Lancs

LEESON. *See* Licence

LEETE. *A.S.* Let; *Dch.* Liet; p.n. *A.S. læt* (a freeman)

LEETHAM. From Leatham; a loc. n., Yorks

LEEVERS. A loc. n., Lincs. Or *Dch.* Lievers; a p.n. *See* Leaver

LEEVERSUCH. *See* Liversage

LEFGOOD. *A.S.* Leofgod; *Dch.* Lievegoed; p.n. (beloved Goth)

LEFTWICH. A loc. n., Ches.

LEGGATT. *N.-Fr.* Legat; a p.n.; *Lat.* Legatus

LEGH. A loc. n., Ches.

LE GRICE. *Fr.* Legris; a p.n. (grey)

LEIGH. A loc. n., Lancs. Or *D.* Leigh; a p.n. *See* Lay

LEIGHTON. A loc. n., Devon

LEITCH. *See* Leech

LELY. *A.S.* Lil, Lilla; *N.-Fr.* Lele, De Lelay; *Dch.* Lely; p.n. (lily)

LEMAN, LEMMON. *A.S.* Leofman, Leman; *G.* Lehman; *D.* Lejman; *Fl.* Leman, Lemmen; *S.* Lemon, Leman; p.n. (beloved man)

LEMPSTER. From Leominster; a loc. n., Heref.

LENDRUM. A loc. n., Aberdeen

LENG. *Dch.* p.n. *See* Lang

LENNEY. From Lennai; a loc. n., Norm.

LENTHALL. From Leinthall; a loc. n., Heref. Or *G.* Leinethall; a loc. and p.n.

LENTRON. From Lentrathen (?); a loc. n., Forfar

LEONARD. From St Leonard; a loc. n., Norm.

LEPPARD. *A.S.* Leofheard, Lipperd; *G.* Liepert; a p.n. (beloved strong)

LEPPER. *N. Fr.* Lepère; a p.n. Hugt. n., Lond. 1618. *See* Leppard

LESLIE. A loc. n., Aberdeen, Fife, Stirling

LESSELS. *See* Lascelles

LESSEY. Lesee, a Hugt. n., Lond. 1621. *See* Lacy

LESTER. From Leicester; a loc. n.

LESTRANGE. *N.-Fr.* Bretagne

LETCHWORTH. A loc. n., Herts

LETHAM. A loc. n., Fife, Forfar

LETT, LETTY. *Dch.* Leth; *Fl.* Lette; p.n. *See* Layt

LETTIS, LETTS. *G.* Letsch, Lettig; p.n. Dim. of Lett

LEUTY. *A.S.* Leod, Leot; *Dch.* Loeté; a p.n. (people)

LEVENSTON. *See* Livingstone

LEVER. *N.-Fr.* Lievre; a p.n. A loc. n., Lancs

LEVERETT. *A.S.* Liboret, Leofred; *Dch.* Levert; p.n. (beloved counsellor)

LEVERMORE. *See* Livermore

LEVERS. *See* Leevers

LEVERSON. From Levasson; a loc. n., Norm. Or *see* Leaver

LEVERTON. *See* Laverton

LEVETT. From Livet; a loc. n., Norm.

LEWIN. *A.S.* Leofwine, Leowine, Lewin; *Dch.* Leeuwen; p.n. (dear friend)

LEWIS. *N.-Fr.* De Lues, Luiz, Lews, Lewes; p.n. Or *A.S.* Leodwig; *Fr.* Louis; *Lat.* Ludovicus; *G.* Ludwig; p.n. (defender of the people). A Hugt. n., Norwich, 1622

LEWTHWAITE. From Lowthwaite or Lothwaite; a loc. n., Cumb.

LEY. *See* Lee and Lay

LIBBIS, LIBBY. *A.S.* Leof; *Old G.* Liub; *Fl.* Libois; *G.* Libas, Liebes; p.n. (dear)

LIBERTY. A loc. n., Fife. Or *D.* Libbert, Lippert; *N.-Fr.* Livardé; p.n.

LICENCE. *A.S.* Lis; *Fl.* Liessens, Lissens, Lyssens; *G.* Lieson; *Dch.* Leyssens; p.n.; *liss* (happy)

LICKFOLD. A loc. n., Suss.

LICKORISH. From Lickerigg; a loc. n., Galway

LIDDARD, LIDDIARD, LIDIARD, LID-
YARD. From Lydiard; a loc. n.,
Wilts. Or *A.S.* Lidgeard; a p.n.
(people's guard)

LIDDELL. From Lydale; a loc. n.,
Scotl.

LIDDICOTT. From Lidcott; a loc.
n., Cornw.

LIDDON. From Lidden; a loc. n.,
Kent. Or Lidon, Aquitaine

LIDGEY. From Lidsey; a loc. n.,
Suss.

LIDSTONE. A loc. n., Oxf.

LIELL. From Lisle; a loc. n.,
France. *Fr.* Lille; *Dch.* Lil; p.n.

LIGERTWOOD. *See* Lightwood

LIGHTBAND, LIGHTBOWN. From
Lightbounds; a loc. n., Lancs

LIGHTBODY. *A.S.* Liht; a p.n.;
liht-bodi (nimble messenger)

LIGHTFOOT. *Old G.* Lytfuss; *Dch.*
Ligtvoet; p.n.; *A.S. lyt fot*; *F.
ligt fôt* (nimble footed)

LIGHTOLLER, LIGHTOWLER. A loc.
n., Lancs (Fishwick)

LIGHTWOOD. A loc. n., Staffs

LILL. *A.S., Dch.* Lil; p.n. Or *see*
Liell

LILLINGTON. A loc. n., Dorset

LILWALL. A loc. n., Heref.

LILY. From Lilley; a loc. n.,
Berks, Yorks; Lilly, Norm. Or
D. Lillie; *G.* Lilie; *S.* Lilje;
Dch. Lelie, Lelij; p.n. *See* Lely

LILYWHITE. From Liliethwaite or
Littlethwaite; a loc. n.

LIMBY. *See* Limbeer. Or Linby, Notts

LIMEBEER. From Limber; a loc.
n., Lincs

LIMMER. From Limours; a loc. n.,
France. *N.-Fr.* Limers; *G.*
Limer; *Fl.* Lemaire. Or *A.S.*
Lemmer, Leofmær; p.n. (famous
beloved)

Limers in Roll of Battell Abbey;
and Leimar, a tenant in *D.B.* at
the Survey.

LIND. From Lynde; a loc. n.,
Fland.

LINDLEY. A loc. n., Yorks

LINDOW. A loc. n., Ches. Or *G.*
Lindau, Lindow; *S.* Linder, Lindau; *Fl.* Linters; *Fr.* Lintot;
loc. and p.n.

LINDSAY. *See* Linsey

LINE, LINES, LYNES. From Luynes;
a loc. n., Normandy, or Ligne,
Belg.

LINFOOT, LINFORD, LINFORTH.
From Lynford; a loc. n., Norf.

LING. A loc. n. in Norf. Prot.
ref., Lond. 1618

LINGARD. *D.* Lyngaard; a p.n.

LINGFER, LINGFORD. From Linford; a loc. n., Bucks, Leics

LINGHAM. A loc. n., Ches.

LINKLATER. A loc. n., Scotl.

LINNELL. *Fr.*; p.n. From *N.-Fr.*
lignel or *l'isnel* (prompt)

LINNIKER. From Lenacre; a loc.
n., Yorks

LINNINGTON. A loc. n.

LINSCOTT. A loc. n.

LINSDELL. From Linsdale; a loc.
n., Westmd.

LINSELL. From Lindsell; a loc.
n., Ess. Or *Fl.* Linseele. A
Hugt. n., 1618

LINSEY. From Lindsey; a loc. n.,
Ess., Lincs, Norf.

LINSTEAD. A loc. n., Kent

LINTHWAITE. A loc. n., Yorks

LINTON. A loc. n., Camb., Derbysh.,
Devon, Haddington, Heref., Kent,
Peebles, Roxburgh, Yorks

LINTOTT. From Lintot; a loc. n.,
Normandy

LIPPINCOTT. From Luffingcot; a
loc. n., Devon

In ancient documents Loghyncote,
Loffyngcote, Loginggetot, Lough-
wyncote, Loyhingcote, Luffingcott,
Luffyngcote, Lughencot, Leffyng-
cote, Lippingcote. Robert de
Lywenscot, *temp.* Ed. I., A.D.
1296. Lef, Lefa, Liaf, Lib, Lip,
Liob, Lub, Luf are all variations
of the *A.S.*; Leof, a p.n. (beloved);
Leofing is the tribal n.

LIPSCOMBE. A loc. n.
LIPTON. *See* Lupton
LIQUORISH. *See* Lickorish
LISHMAN. *A.S.* Liseman; a p.n.; *liss* (happy)
L'ISLE. A loc. n., Vaucluse, France
LISTER. Old Scot. Litster (a dyer)
LISTON. A loc. n., Ess.
LITHERLAND. A loc. n., Lancs
LITTLE. Lutel; a p.n. in 1327
LITTLEBOY. *Fr.* Lillebois (little wood); a loc. n.
LITTLEDALE. A loc. n., Lancs. Or from Liddeldale; a loc. n., Roxburgh
LITTLEJOHN. From Littlejoy (?); a loc. n., Devon. Or *Fr.* Petitjean
LITTLEMORE. A loc. n., Oxf.
LITTLEPROUD. From Littleport (?); a loc. n., Camb.
LITTLER. *See* Laidlaw
LITTLETON. A loc. n., Derbysh., Glost., Hampsh., Middlx., Surr., Somers, Suss., Wilts, Worcest.
LITTLEWOOD. A loc. n., Lancs
LIVERMORE. From Livermere; a loc. n., Suff.
LIVERSAGE, LIVERSIDGE. From Liversedge; a loc. n., Yorks
LIVESEY. A loc. n., Lancs. Or *A.S.* Leofsi, Lefsi; *N.-Fr.* Lenveyse; p.n. (dear victory)
LIVING. *Fl.* Livain; *A.S.* Leofing, Lifing, Lyfing; fam. n. of Leof (dear). Or Leaven; a loc. n., Yorks. A Hugt. n., Norwich, 1622
LIVINGSTONE. A loc. n. near Linlithgow
LIVOCK. *Fl.* Levacq; *Fr.* Levaque; *N.-Fr. le vaquier* (cowman). Or Levêque; a p.n. Hugt., Norwich, 1622
LLEWELLYN. Welsh; p.n. (like a lion, or perhaps lightning sword)
LLOYD. From Welsh *llwyd* (grey)
LOADER, LODER. *N.* Lióði (a singer); *G.* Lode; *D.B.* Lodi, Loda; *Dch.* Lodder; p.n.
  La Lodere in Rot. Hund.

LOADES. *A.S.* Loding; a fam. n.; *Fl.* Lodens; a p.n. *See* Loader
LOAKE. *See* Lock
LOANE. From Lohne; a loc. n., Germ. *Dch.* Loon; a p.n.
LOASBY. From Lowesby; a loc. n., Leics
LOBB. A loc. n., Devon, Oxf. Lobbes; a loc. n., Flanders. Or *N.-Fr.* De la Lobe; *A.S.* Lob; *Dch.* Lobbe; *G.* Lobe; p.n. *A.S. lobb* (spider)
LOBBETT. Dimin. of Lobb
LOBLEY. A loc. n.
LOCH, LOCK. A loc. n., Cornw. Loches, Norm. Or *N.* Loki (a giant god); *D.B.* Lochi; p.n.
LOCKER. *A.S.* Locær; *G.* Locker; *Dch.* Lokker; a p.n. Or from Locre; a loc. n., Belg. *See* above
LOCKETT. *Fr.* Locquet; a p.n. *See* Lockhart
LOCKHART. *N.* Loki; a p.n. (a giant god), *hard* (strong); *N.-Fr.* Locard; a p.n.
LOCKWOOD. A loc. n., Yorks
LOCKYER. *See* Locker
LOCOCK. From Lovetot (?), Norm. Or *see* Luccock
LODBROOK. *See* Ludbrook
LODGE. From les Loges; a loc. n., Normandy. *Fr.* Logé; a p.n.
  De Loges, a tenant in chief, *D.B.*
LOE. *Dch.* Louw; *Fr.* de Lo; *G.* Lohe; p.n. Hugt., Lond. 1618
LOFTE. *See* Lovett
LOFTHOUSE. A loc. n., Yorks. *D.B.* Lofthus
LOFTING. *A.S.* Leofthegn; a p.n. (dear soldier). A Prot. ref. n., Lond. 1688
LOFTS, LOFTUS. *See* Lofthouse
LOGAN. A loc. n., Scotl. Or from the Irish O'Leochain; a p.n.
LOGIE. A loc. n., Fife
LOGUE. *See* Logie

LOMAS, LOMAX. *Fr.* Lammas, Lamusse; *Fl.* Lammers; *Dch.* Lommerse; p.n. (time of birth (?)), (famous)
   Lammasse in Rot. Hund. Lamisso, a Lomb. king, 5th century.

LONDY. *See* Lundy

LONG. *N.-Fr.* De Longa, De Longues; p.n. Also Prot. ref., Lond. 1621
   In Rot. Hund.

LONGBOTTOM. From Longbeddom; a loc. n., Dumfries

LONGBOURNE. A loc. n.

LONGCAKE. From Longacre; a loc. n., Somers. Or Lankaker; a loc. n., Westmd.

LONGDEN. A loc. n. Staffs, Worcest.

LONGFELLOW. From Longueville; a loc. n., Normandy. Also Hugt. n., Lond. 1685
   In Roll of Battell Abbey.

LONGFORD. A loc. n., Derbysh., Glost., Salop, Wilts

LONGHURST. A loc. n., Northbd.

LONGLEY. A loc. n., Yorks

LONGMAID. *See* Langmead

LONGMAN. A loc. n., Banff

LONGMIRE. A loc. n., Westmd.

LONGMORE. *See* Longmire

LONGRIDGE. A loc. n., Lancs

LONGSHANKS. From Longchamps; a loc. n., Normandy
   It was a n.n. of Edward I.

LONGSTAFF. From Longstow (?); a loc. n., Camb. Or Longstock, Hants

LONGSTON. A loc. n., Staffs

LONGTON. A loc. n., Lancs, Staffs

LONGWORTH. A loc. n., Berks, Lancs

LONSDALE. A loc. n., Lancs and Westmd.

LOOKER. *See* Locker

LOOMES. *N.-Fr.* Lomme, Lomb; p.n. *See* Lumb

LOOSE. Los, Norm.; Looz, Flanders; or a loc. n., Kent. Or *Fr.* Luce; *Dch.* Loose, Loos; *Fl.* Loze, Lus; p.n. Lúce, a Prot. ref., Lond. 1618
   Luse in Roll of Battell Abbey. De Lorz in *D.B.* (?).

LORAINE. From Lauraine; a loc. n., Norm.

LORD. *A.S.* Lord, Lorta; *N.-Fr.* le Lavord; p.n.; *hláf-ord* (a lord)
   In Rot. Hund.

LORKIN. *See* Larkin

LOSH. From Loches; a loc. n., France
   Losse in Rot. Hund.

LOTHERINGTON. From Lotherton; a loc. n., Yorks

LOTHIAN. A loc. n., Edinbgh., Haddington, Linlithgow

LOTT. *Fr.* Loth; *G.* Lott; *Fl.* Lotte; p.n. From Loth; a loc. n., Flanders. Or *A.S.* Loth, Hloth; p.n. (spoil, plunder)

LOUCH. *See* Losh

LOUDON. A loc. n., Ayrsh.

LOUGHTON. A loc. n., Salop

LOUND. *N.* Lundr (a grove); *D.* Lundt, Landt; *S.* Lund; *Dch.* Lund, Lonte, Lantz; *A.S.* Lant; *N.-Fr.* de la Lounde; p.n.

LOVAT. A loc. n., Inverness

LOVE. *A.S.* Leof, Lof; *D.*, *Dch.* Luf; *Fl.* Loef; p.n. (dear)

LOVEBOND. John Lovingsbone, Hugt., Lond. 1621

LOVEDAY. From Loudet; a loc. n., Toulouse, France. Or *A.S.* Leofdæg, Leuedai; p.n. (glorious beloved); *Fl.* Lovatty; p.n.; *Fr.* Lovedain. Hugt., Canterbury, 1622

LOVEGROVE. A loc. n.

LOVEJOY. *A.S.* Leofgifu, Lifgiue; *Fr.* Laugeois, Lobjois; p.n. (beloved giver)

LOVELACE, LOVELESS. *See* Lawless

LOVELL. *N.-Fr.* Louvel; *Fr.* Lovel; p.n. Dimin. of Love. A Hugt. n., Lond. 1618
   In Roll of Battell Abbey. Luvel in Rot. Obl. et Fin., K. John.

LOVER. From Louviers; a loc. n., Norm. Or *A.S.* Leofhere; a p.n. (dear warrior)

LOVERIDGE. From Loughrigg; a loc. n., Westmd.

LOVEROCK. *See* Laverick

LOVESEY. *A.S.* Leofsige, Lylsye; p.n. (dear victory)

LOVETT. *N.-Fr.* Louvet (a young wolf); a p.n.
  D.B. tenant in chief. Luvet in Rot. Obl. et Fin., K. John.

LOVEWELL. *See* Lovell

LOVIBOND. *See* Lovebond

LOVICK. From Lowick; a loc. n., Lancs; anciently Lofwic. Or *A.S.* Leofic, Leofwig; p.n. (dear warrior)

LOW. A Prot. ref. n., Lond. 1621. *See* Lowe

LOWDEN. *See* Loudon

LOWE. A loc. n., Salop. Or St Lo, Norm.

LOWELL. *See* Lovell

LOWER. From Lauwe (?); a loc. n., Belg. *Fl.* Lauwers, Louwers; *Dch.* Lauwer, Louwer; *N.-Fr.* De Luera; p.n. Prot. ref., Lond. 1618
  In Rot. Hund.

LOWESBY. A loc. n., Leics.

LOWLESS. *See* Lawless

LOWMAN. *A.S.* Lagman (a lawyer); *G.* Lohmann; *Fl.* Loomans; p.n. Or *see* Leman.

LOWNDES, LOWNES. From Lounds; a loc. n., Lincs

LOWRY. From Lurre, Luri, Lury, or Loury; a loc. n., Norm.

LOWTHER. *A.S.* Hlodhere; *G.* Lothar, Luther; *Fr.* Lothaire; p.n. *See* Clothier. A loc. n., Cumb.

LOWTHIAN. *See* Lothian

LOXDALE. A loc. n., Yorks

LOXLEY. A loc. n., Staffs, Warw., Yorks

LOYDELL. *See* Lydal

LUBBOCK. *A.S.* Leof, Lub; *Old G.* Liub; *F.* Lübbo; *G.* Löbe, Löbbecke; *Dch.* Lub, Lubke; *Fl.* Lubcké; p.n. Dimin. (little dear)

LUCAS. *A.S.* Ludgoz; *Old. G.* Luitgoz, Luikoz; *Fr.* Lucas; p.n. (beloved Goth)

LUCCOCK. *Fr.* Lucq; *G.* Lücke; p.n. Dimin. of Lucas

LUCK. *Fl.* Luc; *Fr.* Lucq; p.n.

LUCKETT. A loc. n., Cornw.

LUCKEY, LUCKIE. *A.S.* Yuca; *Fr.* Lucké; *G.* Lücke; p.n. Dim. of Lucas

LUCKHURST. *Fl.* Luckhaus (?); a p.n.

LUCKING. *Dch.*; p.n. (Luck's descendants)

LUCRAFT. *See* Leacroft

LUCY. A loc. n., Normandy. *Fr.* Louiset; *Fl.* Lucie; p.n. Prot. ref., Lond. 1634
  Lucy in Roll of Battell Abbey. De Lucy in Rot. Obl. et Fin., K. John.

LUDBROOK. A loc. n., Devon

LUDFORD. A loc. n., Salop

LUDLOW. A loc. n., Salop

LUFF. *See* Love

LUGG. *Old G.* Lugius; *G.* Luge; *Dch.* Lugt; *Fl.* Luig; p.n. *See* Lucas

LULHAM. *See* Larlham

LUMB. A loc. n., Lancs, Yorks. Or *G.* Lumbe; *Old G.* Lumpe; p.n. *See* below and Loomes

LUMBARD. *A.S.* Lunbeorht, Lumpert (poor, bright); *Dch.* Lombart; *Fl.* Lombaert; p.n. Hugt., Lond. 1687

LUMBY. A loc. n., Yorks

LUMLEY. A loc. n., Dur.
  Johannes de Lomley in Lib. Vit. Dur.

LUMMIS. *See* Lomas

LUMSDEN. A loc. n., Aberdeen, Berwick

LUNAN. *A.S.* Luning; a fam. n.; *Fl.*, *Dch.* Loonen; a p.n. *See* Lunn

LUND. A loc. n., Yorks. *See* Lound

LUNDY. From Lundie; a loc. n., Fife, Perth

LUNN. *A.S.* Lun; a p.n. (poor)

LUNNON. *See* Lunan

LUNNY. *See* Lunn
LUNT. A loc. n., Lancs (*D.B.* Lont). *See* Lund
LUPSON. *See* Lubb
LUPTON. A loc. n., Westmd.
LUSBY. *See* Lowesby
LUSCOMBE. A loc. n., Devon
LUSH. *See* Losh
LUSHER. *N.-Fr.* De Lusoris. From Lisores, Norm.
LUSHINGTON. Formerly Lussyntone, Kent; a loc. n.
LUSK. From Lussac (?); a loc. n., France
LUSON. *See* Lusson
LUSTY. *A.S.*, *Fl.* Lust; *G.* Lustig; p.n. (powerful)
LUTLEY. A loc. n., Staffs
LUTRIDGE. From Lutheridge; a loc. n., Glost.
LUTT. *A.S.* Leod, Lud, Lude; p.n.; *Dch.* Lut, Luth; p.n.; *A.S.* *leod* (people)
LUTTRELL. From Loudervielle; a loc. n., Normandy. *Fr.* Latreille; *N.-Fr.* Lottrel; p.n.
Lutterell in Rot. Obl. et Fin.

LUXON. A loc. n., Devon
LUXTON. *See* Luxon
LYALL. A loc. n., Scotl.
LYCETT. A loc. n., Staffs
LYDAL, LYDLE. *See* Liddell
LYE. A loc. n., Devon, Worcest.
LYNCH. A loc. n., Devon, Somers, Suss.
LYNDALL. A freq. loc. n., Sweden, Lancs, etc.
LYNE. A loc. n., Peebles
LYNES, LINES. From Luynes; a loc. n., Normandy
LYNN. A loc. n., Norf., Staffs
LYON. From Lions, Norm. *Fr.* Lion, Lyon; a p.n. Prot. ref., Norwich, 1622
LYSACHT. From the Irish Mac-Giolla Josacht; a p.n.
LYSONS. From Lison, Norm. Or *see* Licence
LYTHABY. A loc. n.
LYTTON. From Litton; a loc. n., Yorks
LYWOOD. *See* Leawood or Lythwood, Salop

M

MABB. From Mabe; a loc. n., Cornw. Or *Fl.* Mabbe; p.n.; Welsh *mabb* (?) (a male child)
MABBOTT, MABBUTT. *N.* Módbjartr; *D.B.* Modbert, Motbert; *Fl.* Mabeyt; *Fr.* Maubert; p.n. (bright courage)
MABER. *See* Mabb
MABSON. *Fl.* Mabesoone; *A.S.* Mapeson; p.n.
MACAULAY. From the Irish Mac-Amhailgaidh; a fam. n. Also MacAuley, MacAwley, MacAuliffe, Macgawley (work, labour)
MACBETH. Gael. son of Beth (life)
MACBRIDE. From the Irish McGill Bride; a p.n. *See* Kilbride
MACCHEYNE. Irish MacShane; a p.n. (Jackson, Johnson)
MACCLELLAN. *See* Gilfillan

MACCLOSKEY. From the Irish Mac-Blosgaidh; a p.n.
MACCORMACK. Irish; son of *Corb*, *i.e.* (charioteer)
MACCULLAGH. From the Irish MacCeallach; a p.n. *See* Kelly
MACDERMOTT. From the Irish MacDiarmada; a p.n. (freeman)
MACDONALD, MACDONNELL. From the Irish MacDomhnaill; a p.n. (great chief)
MACDUFF. *See* Duff
MACE. *F.* Mês or Mewes (contraction of Bartolomæus); *G.* Mais, Mese; *Dch.* Mes, Mees; *Fl.* Maes, Mees; *D.* Maes, Mess; p.n. Or from Meysse; a loc. n., Belg.; Mes, Norm. Hugt. n., Lond. 1618
In Rot. Hund.

MACER. *A.S.* Mæssa; *G.* Meser; p.n. *See* Mace

MACGILLIAN. Gael. (son of the servant of John)

MACHELL. *A.S.* Mægenweald; *Old G.* Magoald; *F.* Machelt; *S.* Mæchel; *Fl.* Machiels; *Dch.* Mäschel, Machielse; *G.* Machol; *D.B.* Machel; p.n. (power wielder) Machel held lands at Crackenthorpe, Westmd., *temp.* Edw. Conf. William Mauchel was living *temp.* K. John, A.D. 1201.

MACHREE. Irish; p.n. (king's son)

MACK. *N.* Mögr (boy, brother, kinsman); *A.S.* Mac, Mæg; Gaelic Mac; *G.* Mache, Mack; *D.* Maak; *Dch.* Mack; p.n. Or *see* Madge

MACKAREL. *N.-Fr.* Makerel; *Dch.* Makkreel; p.n. Makerell in Rot. Obl. et Fin., K. John. Mackrell, Hugt., Norwich, 1622.

MACKARETH. From the Irish Mac-Craith, Macgrath, Magrath; Scot. Macreath; p.n.; *craith* (to weave, the son of a weaver). Or *A.S.* Mægred; a p.n. (strong counsel)

MACKARNESS. *See* Magness and Guinness

MACKENZIE. *See* Kinsey or Kenneth

MACKLEY. Scotch MacLae or Mac-Leay; p.n. Flem. Prot. ref., Lond. 1618

MACKREATH. *See* Mackareth

MACKROFF. *See* Rolf

MACKWORTH. A loc. n., Derbysh.

MACLEAN. From the Gaelic Mac-Gillian; a p.n. (son of the servant of John)

MACNAUGHTON. From the Gaelic McNachtan (strong as a bull)

MACOUN. From the Irish Mac-Gowan; a p.n. Or *see* McKeown

MACRAE. *See* Machree

MACY. *See* Maisey

MCALPIN. *See* Alpin

MCANALLY. From the Irish McInally; a p.n. (teacher's son)

MCANDREW. From the Irish Mac-Aindris; a p.n. (the son of Andrew)

MCBEAN. Gael. McVean; a p.n. (a hillman)

MCCALL. Irish McGall; Scot. McCall; p.n. From *cathal* (battle, valour)

MCCALLUM. *See* Callum

MCCLAVE. From the Irish *lamh* (a hand)

MCCLEVERTY. *See* Laverty

MCCLYMONT. *See* Clement

MCCOMBIE. *See* Cumby

MCCOSH. From the Irish *cos* (a foot)

MCCRAITH. *See* Mackareth

MCCREEDY. *See* Read

MCCROBIE. Robert's son

MCCUE. *See* McHugh

MCELGUNN. *See* Gunn

MCENERY. *See* Hendry

MCFADDEN. From the Irish Mac-Paidin; a p.n. (the son of little Patrick)

MCFARLANE. Bartholomew's son

MCGIRR. From the Irish *gor* (short)

MCGLEW. Irish *clow* (?) (wise)

MCGOWAN. From the Irish *Gobha* (a smith)

MCGREGOR. Gaelic *grig* or *garig* (the fierce)

MCHUGH. From the Irish Mac-Aedha; a p.n. (the son of Hugh)

MCILVAIN. Irish McGillbain (son of Bain's servant)

MCINNES. Gael. Johnson

MCINTOSH. Sons of the chief

MCINTYRE. From the Irish *Mac-an-t-saoir* (the son of a workman)

MCIVOR. *See* Ivor

MCKANE. *See* Caine

MCKECHNIE. Gael. Euchrain (son of a horseman)

MCKEOWN. The son of Eoin, an Irish form of John

MCKERROW. *See* Hare

MCKILLOP. Philip's son

MCKINLAY. *See* Finlay (fair hair)

McKINNON. Gael. Finnan; a p.n. (fair, blonde)

McLARTY. *See* Laverty

McLEAREY. Irish McGill Cabhair (the clerk's servant's son)

McLEOD. From the Gaelic *llwyd* (grey or brown). *See* Lloyd

McLURE. *See* McLearey

McMANUS. Irish *manus* (great)

McNAB. *See* Abbs

McNAIR. Gael. Macaire; p.n. (son of the heir)

McNAMARA. Irish (son of the sea)

McNAUGHT. Gael. McKnight

McNEILL. *See* Neale

McPHERSON. Sons of the parson

McPHIN. Gael. (fair)

McQUILLAN. *See* Wilson

McRANNAL. *See* Reynolds

McRORY. From the Irish Mac-Ruadhri; a p.n. (red)

McSHANE. From the Irish Mac-Shawn; a p.n. (the son of John)

McTAVISH. Gael. Thomson

McTEAGUE. *See* Teager

McTEAR. *See* McIntyre

McVICAR. *See* Viccars

McWHANNON. *See* Buchanan

MADDEN. From the Irish O'Mada-dhain (a wolf (?)). Madden; a loc. n., Armagh

MADDER. *G.* Mader; p.n. *See* Mather

MADDICK. *See* Maddox

MADDIN. *See* Madden

MADDISON. *D.* Madsen; p.n. *See* Maddy

MADDLE. *A.S.* Madal; *Fl.* Mad-yol; *Fr.* Madoulé; p.n.; *mæthel* (speech)

MADDOCK. *See* Madocks

MADDY, MADDEY. *A.S.* Mada; *D.* Madie; *Dch.* Maade, Made; *Fr.* Madou; p.n.; *A.S. mæth* (dignity, authority)

MADELL. *See* Maddle

MADEWELL. From Maidenwell; a loc. n., Dorset, Lincs

MADGE. *N.-Fr.* Magis; *A.S.* Mæg, Mecga; *Fr.* Maggi; p.n. (strength)

MADGETT. *See* Matchett

MADGIN. *A.S.* Mægen; *D.* Magens; *Fl.* Magnin; *Fr.* Magin; p.n.; fam. n. of Mag, Mac

MADOCKS, MADOX, MADDOX. From Maddocks; a loc. n., Devon. Or *Fr.* Madoux; *D.B.* Madoc; Welsh Madoch (good); p.n.

MAGEE. From the Irish O'Maol-gaoithe; a p.n.
　　Chief of Muintir Maolgaoithe (*gaoth,* wind; pronounced 'ghee').

MAGER, MAUGER. *N.* Magr; n.n.; *A.S.* Mæghere; *D., S.* Mager; p.n. (able warrior)

MAGGS. *See* Madge

MAGINN. *N. meginn* (strong). Or *see* Guinness

MAGINNES. *See* Guinness

MAGNAC. A loc. n., Upper Vienne, France

MAGNAY. *Fr.* Magny, Magnée; p.n. Magnée; a loc. n., Belgium

MAGNESS. *N.* Magnús; *A.S., G.* Magnus; *Fr.* Magniers, Magniez; p.n. (great). Or *see* Guinness

MAGNIAC. *See* Magnac

MAGRATH. *See* Mackareth

MAGUIRE or MACGUIRE. From the Irish of MacUibhir or Maguibhir, chief of Fermanagh (goat (?)). Also MacIvir, MacIvor

MAHAFFY. Irish McGuffee; a p.n. *See* Duffy

MAHON, MAHONY, MACMAHON. From the Irish MacMathgham-hain; a p.n. (a bear)

MAIDWELL. *See* Madewell

MAINWARING. From Mesnilwarin or Menil Garin; a loc. n., Norm.
　　In Roll of Battell Abbey.

MAISEY. A loc. n., Wilts, or Mezy, France

MAITLAND. From Maltalent, near Nantes, or Mautland, Scotl.
　　Thomas de Matulant settled in Scotland in 1220.

MAJOR. *N.-Fr.* Major; a p.n. Hugt., Lond. 1688
Le Magere, Rot. Hund.

MAJORIBANKS. A loc. n., Scotl.
The barony of Ratho formed the marriage portion of Marjorie, only daughter of Robert Bruce. It was called Terra - de - Marjorie - Banks (Lower).

MALAN. From Malain; a loc. n., France

MALCOLM. From the Gaelic MacGillecalum (the son of the servant of Columba)

MALE. From Melle; a loc. n., Belg. *Dch.* Mell; *Fl.* Mail; *N.-Fr.* De Maisle; a p.n. Hugt. n., Dover, 1622
Mayle in Rot. Hund.

MALET, MALLET. *N.-Fr.*; a p.n. From Melet (?); a loc. n., Flanders
The Conquerer, after the battle of Hastings, committed the body of Harold to W. Malet to see it buried. His son Robert was a tenant in chief in *B.D.* (Surr.). He founded the Monastery of Eye. Malet held lands *temp.* K. John.

MALINS. *Fl.* Maelens, Melens; p.n. Mallines and Mellin, Prot. ref. Lond. 1618. From Melin; a loc. n., Fland.

MALLORY. A loc. n., Flanders. *Fr.* Mellery; a p.n.

MALLOWS. *See* Marlow

MALPAS. A loc. n., Ches., Cornw., Flint

MALT. *Dch.* Molt; a p.n. *A.S.* Malte; *Old G.* Magoald (powerful ruler)

MALTBY. A loc. n., Lincs, Yorks

MALTON. A loc. n., Yorks

MAMMATT. *N.-Fr.* Mamignot; a p.n. A fief of Norm.
Robt. Maminot, Sire de Corbespine, near Bernai, was father of Gilb. M., bp. of Lisieux, and Ralph, de C., of Kent, Willm. I. M., tenant in chief in *D.B.*

MANBY. A loc. n., Lincs

MANCLARKE. *Fr.* Mauclerc (?); a p.n.
Rot. Obl. et Fin., *temp.* K. John, 1208.

MANDER. *Dch.* Mandere; *Fr.* Mandre; p.n. Manders; a loc. n. in Normandy

MANGAN. From Mannacan; a loc. n., Cornw. Or *N.-Fr.* Mangcant, Mangon; p.n.

MANGER. *A.S.* Mægengær (strong spear); *Fr.* Mangez; p.n. Or *A.S. mangere* (a merchant)

MANHILL. *N.-Fr.* Manneville; a p.n. From Mandeville; a loc. n. in Normandy
Maundeville or Meneville in Roll of Battell Abbey. Manneville, a tenant in chief in *D.B.*

MANIFOLD. From Mannofield; a loc. n., Aberdeen

MANISTY. *D.* Mannstead; a loc. and p.n.

MANLEY. A loc. n., Devon

MANLOVE. *A.S.* Manleof; a p.n. (man beloved)

MANN. *N.* Manni (a man, manly); *F.* Manne, Manno; *G.* Mann; *D.B.* Man, Manna, Manne, Manus; *D.* Mann; *Dch.* Mahn, Man; p.n.

MANNERING. *See* Mainwaring

MANNERS. From Mesnieres; a loc. n., Norm. Or *Fl.* Mannaers, Mannaerts; p.n. (strong man)

MANNING. *A.S.*; fam. n.; *Dch.* Manen, Mening; p.n. *See* Mann
In Rot. Hund.

MANSELL. A loc. n., Heref. Or *N.-Fr.* Mancel; a p.n.
Robert Le Mansel held lands in Leics. *temp.* K. John. *N.-Fr. mancel* (a rural proprietor)

MANSER. *N.-Fr.* Manesier; a p.n. Or *see* Mansergh

MANSERGH. A loc. n. (manor), Westmd.
Nicholas de M., 12 Ed. I. 1283 (de Banco Rolls). Thomas de M., 12 Edw. II. 1319. John de M. represented Westmd. in Parliament 7 Ric. II. 1384.

N

MANSFIELD. A loc. n., Notts

MANSON. From Manston; a loc. n., Devon, Yorks. Or *A.S.* Mansuna; *Dch.* Manson; p.n. *See* Mann

MANT. *D.* Manthey; *A.S.* Mantat; *G.* Manth; *Dch.* Mandt, Mante; p.n. (tender man (?)). Or from Mantes; a town of Seine and Oise, France. Fr. Prot., Lond. 1618.

MANTELL, MANTLE. From Mantel; a loc. n., Norm. *Fr.* Mantel ; a p.n.

Tenant in chief, *D.B.*

MANTHORPE. A loc. n., Lincs

MANTON. A loc. n., Lincs, Notts, Wilts

MANWARING. *See* Mainwaring

MANWELL. *See* Manhill

MAPLE. From Mepal; a loc. n., Camb; or Meppel, Holland. *See* Maypole

MAPLESTON. From Mapleton; a loc. n., Derbysh.

MAPLEY. From Mapperley; a loc. n., Derbysh.

MAPP. *See* Mabb

MAPPIN. *N.-Fr.* Magnepeine; a p.n.

MARCH. A loc. n., Camb. Or Marché, Norm.

MARCON. *Fr.* Marquant. A Hugt. n., Cant. 1622

MARDEL, MARDLE. *See* Maddle

MARDEN, MARDON. A loc. n., Heref., Suss., Wilts

MARE. From La Mare; a loc. n., Norm.

MAREHAM. A loc. n., Lincs

MARGETTS. *Sec* Madgett

MARGRIE. *N.-Fr.* De St Marguerie; *Dch.* Magerey ; p.n.

In Rot. Hund.

MARIS, MARRIS. *N.-Fr.* Mariess, Maris; p.n. From le Marais; a loc. n., Normandy. Mares, a Hugt. n., Lond. 1682

MARJORAM. From Margam; a loc. n., Glamorgansh.

MARKETT. *A.S.* Mearcweard (a boundary warden); *Fl.* Merkaert; *Fr.* Marquet ; p.n.

MARKEY. From the Irish *marcach* (a horseman); hence a synonym for Knight

MARKHAM. A loc. n., Notts

MARKIN. From Marquain; a loc. n., Belg.

MARKWELL. A loc. n., Cornw.

MARLER. *N.-Fr.* le Marler ; a p.n. Or *see* Marlow

In Rot. Hund.

MARLEY. From Merlai; a loc. n., Norm.

MARLOW. A loc. n., Herts ; or Marlieux, France

MARMION. *N.-Fr.* ; a p.n.

MARNEY. From Marigny ; a loc. n., Norm. Or *see* Murnane

MARPLE. A loc. n., Ches.

MARQUIS. *Fr.* ; p.n.

MARR. A loc. n., Yorks ; La Mare, Norm. Or *A.S.* Mar, Mær; *S.* Mars; *Dch.* Mar; *Fl.* Maere ; *Fr.* Marre ; p.n. (famous). Hugt. n., Lond. 1618

MARRABLE. From Mirabel; a loc. n., Norm.

MARRACK. *Fr.* Marique ; a p.n. Hugt., Lond. 1688. Or *see* Merrick

MARRIAGE. A loc. n., Devon ; Merridge, Somers ; Maurage ; a loc. n., Belg. Or *Fr.* Mariage ; *D.* Mariager ; p.n. (famous spear)

MARRIFIELD. From Merrifield ; a freq. loc. n.

MARRIOTT, MARRITT. From Merriott; a loc. n., Somers ; or *Fr.* Marriette ; a p.n. Hugt. n., Lond. 1685. Or *see* Marryat

MARRYAT. A loc. n., Yorks

MARSDEN. A loc. n., Lancs, Yorks

MARSH. A loc. n., Devon, Lancs ; Marche ; a loc. n., Belg. *See* March

MARSHALL. Celtic Marchell; *Fl.* Marchal; *Fr.* Maréchal; p.n. (horse servant). Hugt. n. Lond. 1618

MARSHALLSAY. From Marshallsea (near Crewkerne); a loc. n., Wilts

MARSHAM. A loc. n., Norf.

MARSLAND. A loc. n., Cornw.

MARSTON. A loc. n., Ches., Heref., Lincs, Northants, Staffs, Warw., Yorks

MARTER, MARTYR. *N.-Fr.* Le Martre; a p.n.

MARTIN. From St Martin; a loc. n., Norm. Hugt. n., Lond. 1688

MARTINDALE. A loc. n., Lincs

MARTINEAU. *Fr.* Martiny, Martinais, Martinant, Martinet; p.n. From Martigne; a loc. n. of Ille and Vilaine, France

MARVIN. *A.S.* Maruuen, Merefin, Meruin; p.n. (famous friend)

MARWOOD. A loc. n., Devon, Dorset, Dur.

MARYON. From Marines or Marinis; a loc. n., Normandy

Werricus de Marines in Rot. Obl. et Fin., K. John, A.D. 1205. Hertford, Marwyn in Rot. Hund.

MASE. *See* Mace

MASH. A loc. n., Dur.

MASHAM. A loc. n., Yorks

MASHEDER, MASHITER. From Meschede; a loc. n., Germany. *G.* Meschter; *Fl.* Mestdagh; p.n.

MASKALL, MASKELL. *See* Marshall

MASKELYNE. *Fr.* Masquelin; a p.n. (masking or disguising)

MASKEW. *G.* Maschke; *Fr.* Mascot; p.n. (a masker)

MASKREY. *Fr.* Mascre, Mascrier; p.n.

MASLEN, MASLIN. From Meslin (?); a loc. n., Flanders. *N.-Fr.* Masselin; a p.n.

In Rot. Hund.

MASSEY. From Macey; a loc. n., Normd. Hugt. Lond. 1684

MASON. *N.-Fr.* Mavesyn, from Malveysin or Malvoisin; a p.n. Or *Fl.* Meessen; *Fr.* Maçon, Le Mazon, Masson; p.n. Hugt., Lond. 1618

MASSINGBERD. From Massingham; a loc. n., Norf.

In the will of Ælgyfu, A.D. 1012, it is Mæssanwyrð. The ending often occurs as *wurde*, *vrde*. *A.S.* Mæssing, a fam. n., is freg. in local n. Massenberg is a loc. and p.n. in Germany.

Alan Massyngberd in Lay Subsidy Roll, Lincoln, 1 Edw. III. Sir Thomas M., Gunby, Lincs, 1405.

MASSINGER. *See* Messenger

MASSINGHAM. A loc. n., Norf. *D.B.* Massingeham, but earlier Mæssanwyrð

MASTERS. *N.-Fr.* le Maystre; p.n.

MASTERTON. From Mastertown; a loc. n., Fife

MATCHAM. From Masham; a loc. n., Yorks.

MATCHETT. *Fr.* Machotte; a p.n. Dimin. of Mag. *See* Madge

MATE. *A.S.* Mæth; *Dch., Fl.* Met; *Fr.* Mette; p.n. (dignity). Hugt., Lond. 1618

MATHER. *A.S.* Mæthhere (revered lord); *D.* Mathe, Mather; p.n. Hugt., Lond. 1618. *See* Madder

MATHEWS. *Dch.* Matthes, Matthies; *Fl.* Mathys; p.n. Hugt., Lond. 1618

MATSELL. From Mattishall; a loc. n., Norf.

MATTISON. *D.* Matteson, Mathiessen; *Dch.* Mathiesen; a p.n.

MATTIX, MATTOCKS. *See* Maddox

MAUDE. *N.-Fr.* De Mouhaut; a p.n.; a loc. n., Aberdeensh; St Mard, Belg.

John Maud was living *temp.* K. John.

MAUDSLEY. A loc. n., Lancs

MAUGHAM. A loc. n., Monmouth

MAUGHAN. From Mawgan, Cornw. Or Irish Mahon

MAULE. A loc. n., France. Hugt., Lond. 1618. *See* Moll

MAULKIN. An old dimin. of Mary

MAUN. *See* Maughan

MAUNDER. *See* Mander

MAW. From Mawr; a loc. n., Glamorgan. Or St Maur; a loc. n., Belg.

MAWBERY. *See* Mowbray

MAWBY. From Moorby; a loc. n., Lincs. Or Mautby, Norf.

MAWDESLEY. A loc. n., Lancs

MAWLEY. From Mauley, Poitou.

MAXELL. *See* Maxwell

MAXLOW. From Muxloe; a loc. n., Leics; or Moxley, Staffs; formerly Moceslow

MAXSE. From Maxey; a loc. n., Northants

MAXTON. A loc. n., Roxburgh

MAXWELL. A loc. n., Roxburgh; anciently Maccusville

MAY, MAYS. A loc. n., France. Or *A.S.* Mæg, Mei (power); *Dch.* Maij, Mee, Mei; *Fl.* Mahy, May; *D., G., S.* May; p.n.

MAYALL. Irish Mael; *Dch.* Meijll; *D.* Meil; *Fr.* Meyelle; p.n. Celtic *mael* (bald, tonsured disciple)

St Mael, Bishop of Ardagh and founder of the monastery there, died *circa* 488.

MAYBERRY. From Mayborough; a loc. n. Or Mabire, Norm.

MAYCOCK. *F.* Maike; *G.* Mäcke; p.n. A dimin. of Mary

MAYDEW. From Meadow; a loc. n., Surr. Or *A.S.* Mægtheow (strong servant)

MAYER. *See* Myers

MAYGER. *A.S.* Mægenheard; *Fr.* Mégard; p.n. (strong power)

MAYHEW. *Fr.* Mahieu, Mayeux; p.n. Hugt., Norwich, 1622

MAYNE. A loc. n., Scotl. Or from Mayenne, France. Hugt. n., Lond. 1687

MAYNARD. Mainharŏt; a loc. n,. Germ. *D.* Meinert; *Dch.* Meijnhardt; *Fl.* Meynaert; *D.B* Mainard; *Fr.* Ménard; p.n. *See* Mayger. Hugt. n., Dover, 1622

Maniard in Roll of Battell Abbey.

MAYO. *N.-Fr.* Maio; a p.n.

MAYPOLE. From Maybole; a loc. n., Ayrsh. *See* Maple

MAYS. *See* Mace

MAYSENT. *See* Mason

MEACHAM. From Mitcham; a loc. n., Surr.

MEACHEN, MEAKIN, MEEKIN. *N.-Fr.* Le Meschin. Or *Dch.* Meegen, Meeken; *G.* Michan; p.n. Dimin. of May

MEAD. A loc. n., Somers

MEADOWS. A loc. n., Surr.

MEADWAY, MEDWAY. A river, Kent

MEADWELL. From Meadenwell; a loc. n., Cornw.

MEALL. *N.* Mjöll (meal); *A.S.* Mil, Mul; *D.* Moyell; *Fl.* Mylle; *Fr.* Mille; p.n. *See* Mayall

MEAN. *See* Meen

MEANS. *Fl.* Minnens; a p.n. *See* Meen. Prot. ref., Lond. 1687

MEAR. A loc. n., Devon. Or *see* Meer. Hugt. n., Lond. 1618

MEARA. Irish Meaghar; a p.n.; *mear* (merry)

MEARS. *See* Meers

MEASE. *See* Mace

MEASURES. From Mèzières; a loc. n., Normandy. Maziers; a Hugt. n., Lond. 1687

MEATYARD. *N.-Fr.* Le Meiteier; a p.n.

MEAUX. A loc. n., Belg. Yorks. *See* Mew

MECK. *See* Meek

MECRATE. *See* Mackereth

MEDCALF. *See* Metcalf

MEDE. *See* Mead

MEDEX. *See* Madox

MEDHURST. From Midhurst; a loc. n., Suss.

MEDLEY. A loc. n., Oxon

MEDLICOTT. A loc. n., Salop

MEDLOCK. A loc. n., Lancs

MEDWELL. *See* Meadwell

MEDWIN. *A.S.* Medwine; a p.n. (revered friend). *See* Methven

MEDWORTH. *Dch.* Medevoort; a loc. and p.n.

MEE. From My; a loc. n., Fland. Or *see* May

MEECH, MEEK. *N.* Mikill (much, great); *D.* Micha; *Fr.*, *Dch.* Miche; *G.* Micke; a p.n.

MEEKING. *See* Meachen

MEEN. From Migne; a loc. n., France. Or *A.S.* Min, Minna (love); *Fr.* Minnes; *G.* Miny, Minner; *Dch.* Minne, Mijn; *Fl.* Mine, Minne, Min; p.n. Prot. ref., Lond. 1618

MEER. A loc. n., Wilts

MEERS. A loc. n., Worcest.

MEESON. *See* Mason

MEFFEN. *Fl.* Meeuwens; a p.n.

MEGGATT. A loc. n., Peebles

MEGGINS. *See* Maginns

MEGGS. *See* Maggs

MEINS. *F.* contr. of Meinert

MELBOURNE. A loc. n., Derbysh., Herts

MELDRUM. A loc. n., Aberdeensh.

MELLER. Mellier; a loc. n., Belg. Hugt., Cant. 1622

MELLERSH. *See* Melluish

MELLIN. *See* Malins

MELLIS. A loc. n., Suff.; Melles, Belgium. *Fr.* Mellisse; a p.n.

MELLISH. *See* Melluish

MELLON. From Melon; a loc. n., Norm.

MELLOR. A loc. n., Derbysh., Lancs

MELLOWS. *See* Mellis

MELLUISH. A loc. n., Devon

MELSOM. A loc. n.

MELVILLE. From Malleville; a loc. n., Normandy

MENDS. Mendez, Hugt. n., London, 1682

MENHINNICK. From Menhynnet; a loc. n., Cornw.

MENLOVE. *See* Manlove

MENTEITH. *See* Monteith

MENZIES. A loc. n., Scotl. Anciently de Mengues, *de maneriis*

MERCER. *See* Merser

MERCY. *See* Merser

MEREDITH. From Mirridith; a loc. n., Heref. Or Welsh p.n. (the roaring of the sea)

MEREST. *A.S.* Meresuuet; *Fr.* Merresse (?); p.n. (a sea-guard)

MERRELLS. *N.-Fr.* De Merel; a p.n.

MERRICK. From Marrick; a loc. n., Yorks. Or *see* Meyrick

MERRIDEW. *See* Meredith

MERRINGTON. A loc. n., Dur., Salop

MERRISHAW. *Fr.* Maréchal or Marescot; p.n. *See* Marshall

MERRISON. *Dch.* Merisson; a p.n.

MERRITT. *A.S.* Merehwit; *Fl.* Marit; a p.n. (sea white)

MERRY. *Fr.* Méret, Mery; p.n. Merrey; a loc. n., Normandy

MERRYDEW. *See* Meredith

MERRYFIELD. A loc. n., Devon

MERRYWEATHER. From Mereworth; a loc. n., Kent. *A.S.* Mereweorðig, merewurðe
Dōms Johannes de Merwrthe in Lib. Vit. Dur.

MERSER. *Fr.* Mercier. Hugt. n., Lond. 1618; Mercere, 1327

MERWYN. *D.B.* Maruen, Maruuen, Merefin, Meruen. Meruin; Saxon tenant. Mereuuin; tenant in chief. Mereuin; under-tenant. *A.S. mæra-wyne* (illustrious friend)

MERYMAN. From Miremont; a loc. n., France
It is also an Irish form of Marmion.

MESS. From Meese; a loc. n., Staffs. Or *D. F.* Mess; a p.n. *See* Mace

MESSENGER. From Messingham; a loc. n., Lincs. Or *see* Leggatt

MESSETER. *See* Mashiter

METCHIM. *See* Meacham

METFORD. *See* Mitford

METHVEN. A loc. n., Perthsh.

METTAM. From Metham; a loc. n., Yorks

MEW. *Dch.* Mewe; *Fr.* Mieux; p.n. From Meux; a loc. n., Belg.

MEYER. *See* Myers

MEYNELL. From Mesnil; a freq. loc. n. in Normandy

MEYRICK. *Fl.* Meryck; *N.-Fr.* De Meric; a p.n. Prot. ref. Lond. 1621.

MIALL. *See* Mayall

MICHELL. *Fr.*; p.n. Hugt., Lond. 1618

MICKLESON. *S.* Michaelson; *Dch.* Michelson; *D.* Mikelsen; p.n.

MICKLETHWAITE. A loc. n., Yorks

MIDDLEBROOK. A loc. n.

MIDDLEDITCH. A loc. n.

MIDDLEMASS, MIDDLEMISS. From Middlemarsh; a loc. n., Lincs

MIDDLEMORE. A loc. n., Worcest.

MIDDLETON. A loc. n., Derbysh., Edinbgh., Dur., Lancs, Norf., Northants, Yorks

MIDDLEWEEK. From Middlewich; a loc. n., Ches.

MIDGLEY. A loc. n., Yorks

MIDWINTER. Possibly the first to bear the name was born at that time

MIELL. *See* Miall.

MIGEON. *A.S.* Mic; a p.n. (midge); *Fr.* Migeon; p.n.

MIGGS. *N.* Myg; *A.S.* Mæg, Mec, Meg, Mic; p.n.; *N. mý*; *D. myg*; *A.S. mcg* (a gnat, a midge). Or *mæg* (strength, power)

MIGHT. *N.-Fr.* Miette, Myte; p.n. W. Mite in Rot. Hund.

MILBORROW. From Millbrook; a loc. n., Cornw., Hants

MILBOURN, MILBURN. From Milborne; a loc. n., Dorset, Wilts

MILDMAY. *Fr.* Mildmé; a p.n.

MILEHAM. A loc. n., Norf.

MILES. *N.-Fr.* Miles; *Fl.* Milis; p.n.

MILESON. From Milson; a loc. n., Salop. Or *Fr.* Milsan; a p.n.

MILESTONE. *G.* Milostan; a p.n.

MILFORD. A loc. n., Devon, Hants, Salop, Staffs, Surr., S. Wales

MILICAN. A loc. n., Scotl. Or *Dch.* Milligen, Milikan; *Fl.* Milecan; p.n. Dimin. of Miles

MILK. *G.* Milich, Milke; *D.B.* Melc; p.n. Dimin. of Miles

MILL. *See* Miall. Or Atte Mill

MILLER, MILNER. *N.-Fr.* Le Mouner; a p.n.; *Lat.* Molendinarius

MILLERCHIP, MILLERSHIP. From Millichope; a loc. n., Salop

MILLETT. *Fr.*; p.n. Dim. *See* Miall

MILLIGAN, MILLIKIN. *See* Milican

MILLINGER. *See* Mullinger

MILLINGTON. A loc. n., Ches., Yorks

MILLS. A loc. n., Devon. Or *Dch.* Mills; *Fl.* Miles, Millis; *G.* Milisch; *D.B.* Milo, Miles; p.n. Prot. ref., Norwich, 1622. *See* Miles

MILNE. From Millen; a loc. n., Belg.

MILNTHORPE. A loc. n., Westmd.

MILSOM. From Melksham (?); a loc. n., Wilts

MILSON. *See* Mileson

MILTON. A loc. n., Devon, Dorset, Fife, Hants, Kent, Northants, Oxf., Westmd., Yorks, etc.

MILWARD. *D.* Moellgaard; *Fl.* Moulaert; *Fr.* Milliard; p.n. (mill-keeper)

MIMMACK. From the Irish Mimnagh; a p.n.

MIMMS. A loc. n., Herts and Middlx.

MINCHER. *A.S.* Min, Mina; p.n.; *myn* (love, affection); *G.* Minschke; a p.n. Dimin.

MINCHIN. *See* Minnikin

MINES. *See* Meen. Hugt. n., 1688

MINETT. *Fl.* Minnaert; *G.* Minuth; *Fr.* Minet; p.n. Hugt. n., Lond. 1688

MINGAY. *Fr.* Minquet; a p.n.

MINNIKIN. *F.* Menken; *G.* Mennicke; *Fl.* Minique; *Dch.* Mennecken; p.n. *See* Meen. Dim. (little love)

MINNISH. From M'Nish

MINNITT. *See* Minett

MINNS. *See* Mines

MINSHULL. A loc. n., Ches.

MINTER. *G.* Minte; *Fr.* Minder (a minor); p.n. Mint., Prot. ref., Lond. 1618

MINTERN. A loc. n., Dorset

MINTEY. *See* Minter

MINTING. A loc. n., Lincs

MINTON. A loc. n., Salop. Or *Fl.* Minten; a p.n.

MISSEN. *Fl.* Misson; a p.n. Hugt. n., Lond. 1687. Or Misson; a loc. n., Staffs. *See* Mace

MIST. *Dch.* Misset; a p.n. Dim.

MITCHAM. A loc. n., Surr.

MITCHELL. *See* Michel

MITCHINSON. *See* Meachen

MITFORD. A loc. n., Northbd.

MITTON. A loc. n., Staffs, Yorks. *D.B.* Mutone

MOATE. *See* Mott

Mote in Hund. Rolls.

MOBBS. *Fl.* Mobers; a p.n. *See* Mabb

MOBERLEY. From Mobberley; a loc. n., Ches., Staffs

MOCHRIE. From the Irish M'Rae, M'Cree; p.n.

MOCKLER. *A.S.* Mogla (?); *Fr.* Mauclere. A Hugt. n., Lond. 1689

MODGERIDGE, MODGRIDGE, MODRIDGE. From Modrydd; a loc. n., Brecon

MOELLEDON. From Moel-y-don, Menai Straits, N. Wales

MOFFAT. A loc. n., Dumfries

MOGER. *Fr.* Mauger; a p.n. *See* Mogg

MOGG, MOGGS. *N.* Mögr; *D.* Maag; *Dch.* Mock, Mok; *Fl.* Moke; *G.* Moch; p.n. *See* Madge

MOIR. *N.-Fr.* De Moire; a p.n.

MOLD. A loc. n., Flint

MOLDEN. From Malden; a loc. n., Surr. Or Maldon, Ess.

MOLE. *G.* Mohl; *Fr.* Molé; p.n. *See* Moll

MOLESWORTH. A loc. n., Hunts

MOLINEUX. From Moulineaux; a loc. n., Normandy. Moliner, a Hugt., Lond. 1618

MOLL. *A.S.*, *Dch.*, *Fl.*, *G.* Moll; p.n. A loc. n., Norm., Belg.

MOLLET. *Fr.* Mollet; a p.n.

Mulet in Rot. Hund.

MONCKTON. A loc. n., Devon, Dorset, Kent, S. Wales, Wilts, Yorks

MONCRIEFF. A hill in Perthsh.

MONCUR. A loc. n., Perth

MONDAY. *See* Mundy

MONEY. *N.-Fr.* Monnaye, Muny; p.n. Mauny, Monnaie; loc. n., Norm. Hugt. n., Lond. 1618

MONEYPENNY. *N.-Fr.* Magnepeine; a p.n.

Roger M., Norm., 1180-95; Hubt. Manipeni, 1272. Rot. Hund.

MONGER. *A.S. mongere* (a merchant, dealer). Or Mongour; a loc. n., Kincardine. *See* Manger

MONK. *N.* Munki; n.n. (monk); *D.* Munck; *Dch.* Monch, Monk; Munk; *Fr.* Moncq; p.n. *See* official names, p. 12

MONKHOUSE. A loc. n., Northbd.

MONKSFIELD. A loc. n.

MONKTON. A loc. n., Dur.

MONNINGTON. A loc. n., Heref.

MONSER. Monceau; a loc. n., Belg. Or *see* Mountseer

MOUNSEY. *See* Mountseer or Mounsey. A Hugt. n., Lond. 1618

MONSON. From Montzen (?); a loc. n., Belg. Or *A.S.* Mon; a p.n. (man)

MONTAGUE. From Montaigu; a loc. n., France, Belg.
In Roll of Battell Abbey. Tenant in chief, *D.B.*

MONTEITH. A loc. n., Perth

MONTFORD. A loc. n., Salop

MONTGOMERY. A loc. n., Norm.
In Roll of Battell Abbey. Tenant in chief in *D.B.*

MONUMENT. From Mornimont (?); a loc. n., Belg.

MOODY. *G.* Mude; *D.* Muthe; *Dch.* Mudde; *A.S.* Mōd; p.n.; *mōdig* (proud, courageous)

MOON. From Moyon or Mohun; a loc. n., Normandy. Or *Dch.* Moen; *Fl.* Moine; p.n. Hugt. n., Sandwich, 1622

MOONEY. Irish, from Mahoney (?)

MOOR. A freq. loc. n. *N.* Mór (a Moor); *Dch.* Moor; *Fl.* Morre; *G.* Mohr; p.n. Or Celtic Morre. Or Atte-moor. Moer, a loc. n., Fland. More, a Hugt. n., Lond. 1618

MOORBY. A loc. n., Lincs

MOORHOUSE. A loc. n., Dur. Or from Muirhouse; a loc. n., Forfarsh.

MOPPET. *Fr.* Moppert; a p.n. *See* Mabbut

MORAN. From Morannes; a loc. n., France
Tenant in chief and under-tenant in *D.B.*

MORBEY. *See* Mawby

MORCOM. *Fr.* Marcomb; a p.n. Or Morecambe; a loc. n., Lancs

MORDAUNT. *N.-Fr.* Mordant; a p.n.

MORDEY. From Morda (?); a loc. n., Salop

MORELAND. A loc. n., Westmd.

MORELL, MORRELL. *N.-Fr.* Morel; a loc. n., Normandy
In Roll of Battell Abbey. Philip de Morel in Rot. Obl. et Fin., K. John. Also a Hugt. n., Lond. 1618.

MOREWOOD. From Moorwood; a loc. n., Yorks

MORFATT. *See* Moffat

MORGAN. From the Irish O'Muiregain; Welsh Morgwn; p.n. (a mariner, sea-dweller)

MORKHAM. *See* Morcom

MORLEY. A loc. n., Derbysh., Devon, Yorks, etc.; Morlaix, France

MORRALL. *See* Morell

MORRISS. From St Maurice d'Etelan; a loc. n., Normandy. *Fr.* Maurice, Morisse; p.n.; *D.B.* Mauric, tenant in chief. Meurisse, a Hugt. n., Cant. 1622
Morreis in Roll of Battell Abbey; Morice in Rot. Hund.; de Moris in Rot. Obl. et Fin., K. John. Harvey de Monte Morisco of Beaumaris, nephew to Richard, Earl of Chepstow, commonly called "Strongbow," went with his uncle to Ireland *temp.* Hen. II.

MORSE. A loc. n., Glost. Or *Dch.* Mors; a p.n.

MORTER. Mortier; a loc. n., Belg. Or *Fr.* Mortiaux, Mortier, Mortoire; p.n. Morteaux; a loc. n., Normandy. A Flem. ref. n., Lond. 1622

MORTIMER. From Mortemer; a loc. n., Normandy. *D.B.* De Mortemer, a tenant in chief
In Roll of Battell Abbey, and Rot. Obl. et Fin., K. John.

MORTLOCK. From Mortlach; a loc. n., Banff. Or Mortlake, Surr.

MORTON. A loc. n., Derbysh., Dumfries, Lincs, Northants, Yorks. Mortagne, France

MOSEDALE. A loc. n., Cumb. Also *D.* Mosdal; a loc. and p.n.

MOSELEY. A loc. n., Lancs

MOSER. From Museres; a loc. n., Norm. *See* Mouser

MOSS. *N.-Fr.* De la Mosce; a p.n.

MOSSOP. *Dch.* Masdorp, Massop loc. and p.n.

MOSTYN. A loc. n., N. Wales

MOTHERSIL, MOTHERSOLE. From Mottishall (?); a loc. n., Suff. Or Moddershall, Staffs

MOTION. *N.-Fr.* Moisson; *Fr.* Maussion; a p.n. (little bird)

MOTT. *Fr.* Motte and De la Motte. From Motte, a town of Cotes du Nord, France. A Hugt. n., Lond. 1621

MOTTERWAY. Welsh Mawddwy; a loc. n. Or Mauduit, Norm. Or *A.S.* Modher, Motheri; p.n. (courageous warrior)

Gilbert de M. in Rot. Obl. et Fin.

MOTTON. *See* Mutton

Sir William Moton, knight, was living at Peckleton, Leics, A.D. 1174. Sir Robert Moton was killed at the battle of Evesham, A.D. 1265. Motten, a Prot. ref., Norwich, 1622.

MOTUM. From Mottingham (?); a loc. n., Ess.

MOUAT, MOWAT. From Mouet; a loc. n., Norm.

MOUEL, MOWLE. *See* Mole

MOULD. Moult; a loc. n., Norm. *See* Mold

MOULES. *See* Mole

MOULTON. A loc. n., Norf., Suff.

MOUNSEY. From Monchy; a loc. n., Norm. *Dch.* Monsee; *Fr.* Montoisy (?); p.n. Mountsey, a Hugt., Lond. 1618

MOUNSHER. *See* Mountseer

MOUNT. *N.-Fr.* De Monte; a p.n.

MOUNTAIN. *Fr.* Montaigne. Hugt. n., Lond. 1618

MOUNTSEER. *Fr.* Monseur. Hugt. n., Lond. 1685

MOUSE. *D.* Muus; *G., Dch., Fl.* Maus, Mus; *Fr.* Mousse; p.n.; *Old G.* form Muoza, from *môd* (courage). Moze, a Hugt. n., Lond. 1687

MOUSER, MOUSIR. *Fr.* Moussier; a p.n. *See* Moser

Mow. A loc. n., Roxburgh

MOWBRAY. From Moutbray; a loc. n., Normandy; or Maubray in Flanders

Moribray and Mowbray in Roll of Battell Abbey. William de M. held lands in Notts. Rot. Obl. et Fin.

MOWCHER. From Mouchard; a loc. n., France

MOXEY. *See* Maxse

MOXON. *D.* Mogensen; *Dch.* Mock, Mok; p.n. *See* Mogg

MOY. *N.-Fr.* De Moeia; p.n.

MOYSE, MOYSEY. From Moissac (?); a loc. n., France. *N.-Fr.* Moisy; a p.n.

MOZLEY. From Moseley; a loc. n., Staffs

MUCKALL. *N.* Mikill; *A.S.* Mucel (big); *D.* Muxoll; *S.* Michal; *Fl.* Michils; p.n. Or from Mucholls; a loc. n., Kincardine

MUCKLEBREED. *See* Kilbride

MUCKLESTON. A loc. n., Salop, Staffs

MUCKLOW. From Mucklagh (?); a loc. n., Kerry, Ireland

MUDD. *See* Moody

MUDDLE. From Muthill (?); a loc. n., Perthsh.

MUDGE. *See* Mogg

MUDIE. *See* Moody

MUELUISH. *See* Mellish

MUFFET. *Fl.* Muffat; a p.n. Or see Moffat

MUGFORD. From Mogford; a loc. n., Devon

MUGGE, MUGGS. *See* Moggs

MUGGERIDGE, MUGRIDGE. *See* Modridge

MUGGLESTON, MUGLISTON. *See* Mucklestone

MUGGLETON. From Muckleton; a loc. n., Salop

MUIR. A loc. n., Scotl. *See* Moor

MULHOLLAND. From the Irish O'Maolchallain; a p.n. (descendant of the disciple of Caellin)

MULINGER. *See* Molineux. *Fr.* Moulinier (a silk-mill man). A Hugt. n., Lond. 1618

MULLALLY. From the Irish *eala* (a swan)

MULLEN. *Fr.* Moulin ; *Dch.* Mullen ; *G.* Mühlan ; p.n. (a mill). *See* Mullins

MULLEY. *A.S.* Mula ; *Fr.* Mullie ; p.n. (miller)

MULLIGAN. Irish (servant of the bald-headed man, *i.e.* priest)

MULLINER. *See* Molineux

MULLINS. From Moulins ; a loc. n., Normandy

MULLIS. *G.* Mulitz ; a p.n.

MUMBY. A loc. n., Lincs

MUMFORD. From Mundford ; a loc. n., Suff.

MUMMERY. *Fr.* Momerie ; p.n. (masquerade)

MUNCASTER. A loc. n., Cumb.

MUNCH. *G.* Münch, Münich ; *D.* Munnich ; p.n. *See* Monk

MUNCY. *See* Mounsey

MUNDAY, MUNDY. From Mondée or Mondaye (Mons Dei) ; a place and abbey in the diocese of Lisieux, parish of Bayeux, Normandy. French Gazeteer, 1791. Or *N.* Mundi ; *A.S.* Munda ; *Fl.* Mondis, Munday ; *G.* Mund, Munder ; p.n. (protection). Also Monedy ; a loc. n., Perthsh.

> Thomas de Mondaye, abbé de Ardenne, 1282 ; Geoff. de M., abbot of M., 1290 ; Gilles de M., 23rd abbot, 1477. Robert de Mundeye, 1258, in deed, Balliol Coll. report, Roy. Hist. Com.

MUNGY. From Montjoye ; a loc. n., France

MUNN. *A.S.* Mun ; *Dch.* Munne ; p.n. Or *see* Moon. A Prot. ref., Lond. 1618

MUNNING. Descendants of Munn

MUNT. *Dch.*, *S.* Munthe ; *A.S.*, *G.* Mund ; p.n. Or from Munte ; a loc. n., Flanders

MUNTING. *See* Mountain

MURCH, MURCHIE. From the Gaelic Murdoch (sea power)

MURCHISON. From Merchiston ; a loc. n., Edinburghsh.

MURCOTT. A loc. n., Northants, Wilts

MURE. *See* Moor

MURGATROYD. A corruption of Moorgate Road, Yorks

MURLEY. From Moorly ; a loc. n., Wilts

MURNANE. From the Irish Marnane, Mournane (Warren) ; a p.n.

MURPHY. From the Irish MacMurchada ; a p.n. MacMorrow, MacMurrogh (sea warrior)

MURR. *See* Moore or Muir

MURRAY. From Moray ; a loc. n., Scotl. Or Irish O'Muiredhaigh ; a p.n. (sea protector)

MURRELL. *See* Morell

MURROW. A loc. n., Camb. Or *see* Murphy

MURSELL. From Moorsel ; a loc. n., Fland. Prot. ref., Dover, 1622

MURTHWAITE. A loc. n., Westmd.

MUSCHAMP. From Moschaus ; a loc. n., Norm.

MUSCHET. *N.-Fr.* de Montfichet ; a p.n. *See* Mussett

> In Roll of Battell Abbey.

MUSCOTT. A loc. n., Northants

MUSGRAVE. A loc. n., Cumb., Westmd.

MUSGROVE. From Mucegros ; a loc. n., Norm.

MUSK. From Moussac ; a loc. n., France. *Dch.*, *Fl.* Musch ; *G.* Muske ; p.n.

MUSKETT. From Mousquette ; a loc. n., France. *Fl.* Musschaert, Musschot ; *G.* Muskat ; p.n.

> In Rot. Hund.

MUSSETT. From Mozet (?) ; a loc. n., Flanders. *Fr.* Moussett, Musset ; *Dch.* Mussert ; p.n.

> Musett in Roll of Battell Abbey.

MUSSON. From Mouçon; a loc. n., Norm.; Musson, Flanders. Or Muston, Leics, Yorks

MUST. *See* Mussett

MUSTERS. From Moustier; a loc. n., Flanders. *Fr.* Mustière; a p.n.

Robert de Mosters, a tenant in chief in *D.B.* Gaufrid de Musters, *temp.* K. John, Rot. Obl. et Fin.

MUTIMER. *See* Mortimer

MUTTON. From Motons; a loc. n., Norm. *N.-Fr.* Mouton; a p.n. Or *see* Mitton and Motton

Hugo de Mutton, Rot. Obl. et Fin.

MUTTITT. *Fr.* Mottet; a p.n. (a hillock)

MVCOCK. *See* Maycock

MYERS. *Old G.* Magher; *A.S.* Mæghere (valiant warrior); *D., S.* Meyer; *Dch.* Meier; *G.* Mayer, Meyer; *Fl.* Meyers, Miers; p.n.

MYERSCOUGH. A loc. n., Lancs

MYHILL. *See* Miall. Hugt. n., Lond. 1618

MYLCHREEST. The Manx form of the Celtic Mac Giolla Chriosd. *See* Gilchrist

MYLNES. *See* Mullins

MYNOTT. *See* Maynard

N

NADIN. *Fr.* Nadine; a p.n.; Slavonic (hope). Hugt. n.

NAGGS. *N.-Fr.* De Nages; a p.n.

NAGLER. *N.* Nagli (a nail); *A.S.* Nægel; *D.* Nagel; *G.* Niegel; *Fr.* Naglée; p.n. Nagle; a loc. n., Normandy

NAILER. From Nesle (?); a loc. n., France

NAISH. *See* Nash or Neach

NALDRETT, NOLDARITT, NOLDWRITT. From *N.-Fr.* de Maldrett; a p.n.

NALL. *See* Neale

NANCE. *A.S.* Nan, Nansige (doughty victor); *Fr.* Nens; p.n. *See* Nanney

NANGLE. *See* Angle

NANKIVEL. From Nanckivel; a loc. n., Cornw.

NANNEY. *F.* Nanno, Nanne; *A.S.* Nan, Nennius; p.n.; *N. nenna* (energy)

NAPIER. *N.-Fr.* le Naper, le Napier; p.n.

The officer of the king's household who had charge of the napery or table linen.

NAPKIN. *G.* Knabechen; a p.n. Dim. of Napp

NAPLETON. A loc. n., Worcest.

NAPP. *N.* Knappi (a servant, boy); n.n.; *A.S.* Cnapa; *Old G.* Hnabi; *D., Fl., Dch.* Knapp; *G.* Knapp, Knabe, Knappe, Knaps, Knop; p.n.

NAPPER. *See* Napier

NAPTHEN. From Napton (?); a loc. n., Warwicksh.

NARES. *N.-Fr.* De Neirs; a p.n.

NASH. A loc. n., Heref., Kent

NASLEN. *See* Nesling

NASSAN. *A.S.* Nas, Neri (a protector); *Dch.* Nussen; *D.* Nissen; *Fl.* Niesen; p.n.

NATERS. *See* Nattrass

NATT. *A.S.* Nata; *Dch.* Nat; *G.* Nath; p.n. Contr. of Nadal (needle)

NATTRASS. *Fl.* Nateris, Natris; p.n.

NAUGHTON. A loc. n., Suff.; Nawton, Yorks

NEACH. *A.S.* Nytta; *G.* Nietch, Nische; p.n. Dim. (useful)

NEAGLE. *See* Neale

NEALE. *N.-Fr.* de Neel. Or *N.* Njáll (from the Gaelic); *S.* Nihl; *D., A.S., Dch.* Niel; *Fl.* Niels, Nille; *Fr.* Nesle; p.n. The original meaning is a noble, or *niadh* (champion), but the *N.-Fr.* Latinised it to Nigellus, supposing it to mean black. Niel; a loc. n., Flanders

Neile in Roll of Battell Abbey; and Nigel, a tenant in chief in *D.B.* Also a Hugt. n., Lond. 1688.

NEAME. *A.S., D.* Nim; a p.n. (holder, keeper)

NEARY. *A.S.* Neri; a p.n. (deliverer)

NEATE. *N.-Fr.* De Nits; *A.S.* Nith, Nid, Nytta, Nyding; p.n.; *nyd* (necessity)

NECK. *Dch.*; p.n. *See* Noakes

NEEBE. From Newby; a freq. loc. n. Or *see* Neighbour

NEECH. *See* Neach

NEED, NEEDES. *See* Neate

NEEDELL. *A.S.* Nadal; *D.* Nedahl; *G.* Niedel; *Fr.* Nidoul; p.n.; *nædel* (needle)

NEEDHAM. A loc. n., Norf.

NEEP. *A.S.* Cnebba, Cnibba; *G.* Kneip; *Dch., Fl.* Knip; p.n. (nipper)

NEEPER, NEIPER, NEPER. Irish forms of Napier

NEESON. *See* Nassan

NEGUS. *G.* Niegisch, Nikish; *Fr.* Nigaise, Nicaise; p.n. Or *see* Naggs

NEIGHBOUR. *D.* Nyeboe; *G.* Neubauer, Neuber, Niebour, Niebuhr; *S.* Neijber, Nieber; *Dch.* Nieubuur, Nueboer; p.n.

NELL. *Dch.*; p.n.; *N. hnalla* (to beat). Or *see* Neale

NELSON. *D.* Neilson, Nielson; *S.* Nelson, Nelzon; *Dch.* Nelson, Nielsen; p.n. *See* Neale

NEOBARD. *A.S.* Nithbeorht (bright need); *Fr.* Néaubert; *G.* Neubert; p.n.

NERTIGAN. *Fl.* Neutgens; *Dch.* Neutegem; p.n. Dimin. of Neute. *See* Nute

NESBET. A loc. n., Dur., Northbd.

NESLEN, NESLIN, NESLING. *A.S.* Nesta; a p.n. (a neighbour); *nestling* (?)

NESS. *D., S.*; p.n. Also a loc. n., Ches., Salop, Yorks. Or from Nas; a loc. n., Norm. Hugt. n., Rye, 1622.

De Nes in Rot. Hund.

NETHERCLIFT. From Nethercleugh; a loc. n., Dumfries

NETHERCOTT. A loc. n., Devon, Somers

NETHERSOLE. From Netherseal; a loc. n., Leics

NETTLE. *Fr.* Niatel; a p.n. *See* Needell

NETTLEFOLD, NETTLEFIELD. From Netherfold (?); a loc. n., Yorks. Or from Netreville; a loc. n., Norm.

NETTLETON. A loc. n., Lincs, Wilts

NEVARD. *Fr.* Nivard; a p.n.

NEVAY. A loc. n., Forfar

NEVE. From Nives; a loc. n., Belg. Or *see* Nevison

NEVELL. *See* Neville

NEVILLE. From Néville; a loc. n., Normandy

Nevill in Roll of Battell Abbey and in Rot. Obl. et Fin., K. John.

NEVISON. *N.-Fr.* Le Neve; *D.* Neve; *Dch.* Neef, Neeve, Neff; *Fl.* Neefs, Neave; p.n.

NEWALL. From Newhall; a loc. n., Ches.

NEWARK. A loc. n., Notts

NEWBEGIN. *See* Newbiggin

NEWBERRY. From Newbury; a loc. n., Berks

NEWBIGGIN. A loc. n., Dur., Fife, Forfar, Lanark

NEWBOLT. *See* Newbould

NEWBOULD. From Newbold; a loc. n., Leics, Yorks. Or *A.S.* Nubold, Nybald; p.n. (new, fresh, bold)

NEWBY. A loc. n., Yorks, etc.

NEWCOME. *A.S. niwe-cuma* (a new comer, a stranger); a n.n.

NEWDICK. A loc. n. (?)

NEWDIGATE. A loc. n., Surr.

NEWELL. From Nieul; a loc. n., France. Or *see* Newall

NEWHAM. A freq. loc. n.

NEWITT. *See* Newt

NEWLING. *G.* Neuling; a p.n. Dim. of *nyr* (young)

NEWLOVE. From Newlaw (?); a loc. n., Kirkcudbright

NEWMAN. *G.* Neumann; *Dch.* Nieman, Numan; *S., D.* Nyman; p.n. le Neuman in 1327.

NEWNES. A loc. n., Salop

NEWNHAM. A loc. n., Glost., Hants, Northants., Salop, Warw., Worcest.

NEWNUM. *See* Newnham

NEWPORT. A loc. n., Bucks, Glost., Hants, Montgy, Salop, Somers, S. Wales. Nieuport; a loc. n., Flanders

NEWSAM. *See* Newsome

NEWSOME. A loc. n., Lincs, Yorks

NEWSON. *Dch.* Nussen, Nijssen; p.n. *See* Nassan

NEWSTEAD. A loc. n., Lincs, Notts, Staffs

NEWT, NEWTH. *See* Nute

NEWTON. A freq. loc. n.

NIBBS. *A.S.* Cnibba; *G.* Nibisch; p.n. (a beak)

NIBLET. *See* above

NICE. From Neisse; a loc. n., Germ. *D.* Niss; *Fl.* Neys, Nys; *Dch.* Nies; *G.* Kneis; p.n. Prot. ref., Lond. 1618

NICHOLAS, NICHOLLS, NICHOLS. *See* Nicker

NICHOLSON. *S.* Nicolausson; *D.* Nikelsen; p.n. Prot. ref., Lond. 1618

NICKER, NICKERSON, NICKLESS, NICKOLS, NICOL. *N.* Nikolás; *D.B.* Nicolaus, Nicol; *G.* Nick, Nicke, Nickel; *Fl.* Nicole; *D.* Nickels; *N.-Fr.* Nicholas; p.n.

NICKLIN. Dim. of Nicholas

NIEL. *See* Neale

NIGHTINGALE. *N.-Fr.* Nightyngale; *G.* Nachtigall; *Dch.* Nagtegaal; *Fl.* Nachtergael; p.n. Nytingall, Flem. refugee, Lond. 1618

NIKER. *See* Nicker

NIMMO. *Dch.* Nimmo, Niemer (Nieman); p.n. *See* Newman

NINCE. From Ninnes, Ninnis; loc. n., Cornw. Or *G.* Nintz; a p.n.

NIPPER. *Fl.* Nepper; a p.n. *See* Neeper

NISBET. A loc. n., Berwick, Haddingtonsh., Roxburgh

NIX, NIXON. *See* Nicker

NOAKES, NOAKS. Noke; a loc. n., Oxf. Or from Atten oak; *D.* Knoak; *Dch.* Noack; p.n.

NOAR. *N.-Fr.* De Noa; or *D.* Nohr; p.n.; *Norra* (a Norseman)

NOBBS, NOBES. *N.* Knappi; n.n. (a knob); *G.* Nabe; *Fl., D.* Knop; *Dch.* Knobbe, Noppe; p.n. *See* Napp

NOBLE. *N.-Fr.* le Noble; *D., Dch.* Nobel; *Fl.* Nobels; p.n.

NOCK. *See* Nonkes

NOCKALL, NOCKLES, NOCKOLDS. *Fl.* Nockels; p.n. *See* Noakes

NODDER. *A.S.* Nod, Noth (bold); *Fr.* Nodé; p.n.

NODE, NODES. *N.-Fr.* Node; *A.S.* Nod, Noth; p.n. (daring, bold)

Note in Rot. Hund. Not in Rot. Obl. et Fin.

NOEL. From Noailles; a loc. n., Normandy

NOKES. *See* Noakes

NOLAN. Irish O'Nuallain; a p.n.; *nuala* (fair shoulders)

NOLLOTH. *D.* Nolleroth; *Fr.* Nolleau, Nollett; *G.* Nolte; p.n. Hugt. n., London, 1687

NOON. From Noyon; a loc. n., Norm.

NOOTT *See* Nute
NOPS. *See* Nobbs
NORBURY. A loc. n., Ches., Derbysh., Salop, Staffs
NORDEN. *D.* Norden; *Dch.* Noorden; p.n. (North)
NORFOR. *N.* Narfi (the n. of a giant); *G.* Nafe, Nave, Naveau; *D.B.* Novi; *Fl.* Noeve; p.n.
NORKETT. From Norracott; a loc. n., Devon. Or *see* Northcote
NORMAN. *S.* Nordman; *G.* Nordmann; *D.*, *N.-Fr.* Norman; *Dch.* Normant; p.n. (Northman)
NORMINGTON. From Normanton, Derbysh., Leics, Lincs, Wilts, Yorks
NORRINGTON. A loc. n., Wilts
NORRIS. *Fr.* Noris; a p.n.

Norice in Roll of Battell Abbey. Le Norreis, Rot. Obl. et Fin.

NORSWORTHY. *See* Nosworthy
NORTHCOTE. A loc. n., Devon. Or Northcott, Somers.

Held by De Colville.

NORTON. A freq. loc. n.
NOSWORTHY. From Knaworthy; a loc. n., Devon
NOTCUTT. *See* Northcote
NOTLEY. A loc. n., Ess.
NOTSON. *Fl.* Knudsen; a p.n. *See* Nott and Nute
NOTT. *Fr.* Notte; a p.n. *See* Node
NOTTAGE. A loc. n., S. Wales. Or *Fl.* Notez; *G.* Nöthig (needful); p.n.
NOTTIDGE. *See* Nottage
NOURSE. *See* Nowers
NOWELL. *See* Noel

NOWERS. From Noyers; a loc. n., Norm.

De Noiers, de Noies, de Nouuers, tenants at the time of the Survey, *D.B.* Noers is on the Roll of Battell Abbey. Simon de Noers in Rot. Obl. et Fin., K. John. Sir Robert de Nowers was Lord of the Manor of Knossington, Leics, in 1278.

NOY. *A.S.* Neue; *Dch.* Noy; p.n. (fresh, young)
NOYCE, NOYES. *G.* Neuss; a loc. and p.n. Or *see* Nowers
NUDD, NUDDS. *See* Nute
NUELL. *See* Noel
NUGENT. From Nogent; a loc. n., Normandy

De Nugent, Rot. Obl. et Fin.

NUNN. *A.S.* Nun; *Old.G.* Nunno; *G.* Nunn; p.n. (an orphan)
NUNNELEY. From Noneley; a loc. n., Salop
NURSE, NURSERY, NURSEY. *See* Nourse
NUTBEAM, NUTBEAN. *G.*, *Dch.* Nussbaum; a p.n. (nut tree)
NUTCHER. *G.* Knutsche; p.n. Dim. of Knut
NUTE, NUTH, NUTT. *N.* Knútr (a knot, hill); *A.S.* Canud, Cnud, Cnut; *D.* Knudt; *Dch.* Noot, Nut, Knuijt; *G.* Knuth; *Fl.* Cnudde; p.n.
NUTMAN. *A.S.* Nothmund; *Dch.* Nootman; a p.n. (daring director)
NUTTAL. From Nuttall; a loc. n., Notts (*D.B.* Notele)
NUTTER. *See* Nute
NUTTING, NUTTY. Tribal n. of Cnut
NYE. *Dch.* Nije, Nuy; p.n. *See* Noy

O

OAFS. *A.S.* Of, Offa, Wufa; p.n. (n. of a king)
OAK. A loc. n., Devon, Somers. Or *A.S.* Oc, Oca, Ocg; p.n. *See* Ogg
OAKDEN. *See* Ogden

OAKES. A loc. n., Derbysh., Lancs. Atte Oaks (?)
OAKEY. From Hockai; a loc. n., Belg. *Fr.* Ocket; *Fl.* Ogy; *G.* Ocke; p.n.

Oky; Seal, Leics. 1327.

OAKHAM. A loc. n., Notts, Rutland, Warw.

OAKLEY. A loc. n., Beds, Berks, Bucks, Ess., Hants, Northants, Staffs, Suff., Worcest., etc.

OAKSHETTE, OAKSHOTT. From Oxshott; a loc. n., Surr.

OATES. *N., Fl.* Ots; a p.n. *See* Oddy

OATLEY. *See* Ottley

OBBARD. *See* Hobart

OBEE. From Obaix; a loc. n., Belg.

OBORNE. A loc. n., Dorset

O'BRIEN. From the Irish *brian* (strong)

OCLEE. From Ockley; a loc. n. in Surr. Or Oakley, Ess.

ODAM. A manor in Devon

ODAMS. *Dch.* Odcms; a p.n.

ODDIN. From Odeigne; a loc. n., Belg. Or *Dch.* Oddinck; a p.n. *See* Oddy

ODDY. *N.* Oddi (a leader); *F.* Ode, Odo; *D.* Odde; *Dch., Fl.* Otte, Hody; *N.-Fr.* Aude; *G.* Otho, Other, Ott, Otte, Otto; *A.S.* Oda, Odda, Odo, Otha; p.n.

ODEL, ODELL. A loc. n., Bucks, Devon. Or *N.* Oddkell or Ottkel (Ketel the leader); *D.B.* Odel, Oudchell, Ouetel; *G.* Hodel; p.n.

ODGER. *N.* Oddgeir (leader spear); *Fl.* Oger; *A.S.* Eadgar; *Fr.* Audiger; p.n. Prot. ref., Lond. 1622

ODLING. *D.B.* Odelin; a p.n. (Saxon tenant); *N. öðlingr* (?) (a landowner); *N.-Fr.* Fitz-Odeline

O'DONOGHUE. From the Irish O'Donchada or O'Donchu; p.n. (brown chief)

O'FERRALL. Irish *O'Feargail. See* Farrell

OFFIN. From Offagne or Ophain; loc. n., Belg.

OFFLEY. A loc. n., Herts

OFFORD. A loc. n., Hunts

OGBEN. *See* Ogbourne

OGBOURNE. A loc. n., Wilts

OGDEN. A loc. n., Lancs

OGG. *N.* Ögurr (?) (terrible); *A.S.* Og, Ogga; p.n. Or *see* Oak

O'HART. Irish p.n.; *arta* (great). *See* Carter

O'KANE. *See* Caine

OKES. *See* Oakes

OLCOTT. From Holcott; a loc. n., Northants

OLD. A loc. n., Northants. Or *A.S.* Ald, Eald, Old, Weald (rule, power); *Dch., S.* Olde; p.n.

OLDACRE. From Aldecar; a loc. n., Derbysh. Or *A.S.* Ealdgar; a p.n. (ruler spear)

OLDERNESS. From Holderness; a loc. n., Yorks

OLDERSHAW. From Aldersholes; a loc. n., Yorks

OLDFIELD. A loc. n., Worcest.

OLDHAM. A loc. n., Lancs

OLDING. *D.* Olden; a p.n. Fam. n. of Old

OLDMAN. *A.S.* Ealdman; *G.* Ohlmann; *S.* Ollman. *See* Old

OLDRIDGE. A loc. n., Devon

OLDRING. *A.S.* Aldran (old strength); *Dch.* Olderen; p.n.

OLDROYDE. *See* Holroyd. Or *A.S.* Ealdred (ruler counsellor); *Fl.* Oldrade; p.n.

OLET, OLLETT. *Fr.* Oliette; a p.n. *See* Olyott

OLIFFE. *See* Oliver

OLIPHANT. *Dch.* Ollcfen; a p.n.

The Scot. and Old Engl. form of elephant. Chaucer has "Sire Oliphaunt." Old Norse *olifant* was used for the unicorn, but was a foreign word. Olifant in Roll of Battell Abbey.

OLIVER. *N.* Óláfr or Óleifr; *A.S.* Olaf; *S.* Olof; *Dch.* Olfers; *Fl.* Oleff; *Fr.* Olivier; p.n. Hugt., Lond. 1682

The original form was Anleifr (inheritance of the gods).

OLLAY, OLLE, OLLEY. From Oleye; a loc. n., Flanders. *D.B.* de Ole, de Olgi, Oiley, de Oilli; p.n.; tenants in chief

OLLIFFE. *See* Oliver

OLNEY. A loc. n., Bucks

OLPHERT. *Fr.* Olivert; a p.n.

Olivard in Roll of Battell Abbey. David de Oliphard, Scotl. 1142.

OLYOTT. *A.S.* Olfgeat, Oluiet; *Fl.* Holliette; p.n. *See* Olett (wolf-gate (?)

OMANT. *Fr.* Omont; a p.n. *See* Osmund

OMASH. *Fr.* D'Ormasse; a p.n.

OMER. A loc. n., Devon

OMMANEY. A loc. n., Hants

ONES. *A.S.* Ona; *F.* Onno; *Dch.* Onasse; p.n.; fam. n. Or One-house; a loc. n., Suff.

ONG. *N.* Ungi (?) (the younger); *F.* Onke, dimin. of Onno; *G.* Unger; *Fl.* Ongers; p.n. Or Ongar; a loc. n., Ess.

ONGLEY. *See* Onley

O'NIELL. *See* Neale

ONIONS. From Angiens (?); a loc. n., Normandy. Or Welsh Eignion (just)

ONLEY. A loc. n., Northants, Staffs

ONSLOW. A loc. n., Salop. *D.B.* Ondeslow

OPENSHAW. A loc. n., Lincs

OPIE. *Fr.* Aupée; a p.n. Or *see* Obee

ORAM. From Owram; a loc. n., Yorks. Or Horham, Suff.

ORBY. From Orbais; a loc. n., Belg.

ORCHARD. A loc. n., Devon, Somers. Or *see* Archard

ORD. A loc. n., Northbd. Or *A.S.* Ord, Weard; *D.* Orth; *Dch.* Oort, Ort; p.n. (guard)

ORDERS. *A.S.* Orde, Ordarus; *F.* Ordgies; p.n. Akin to *A.S. weard* (a guard)

ORFEUR. *N.-Fr.* Orfrere (Auri-faber); a p.n. (a goldsmith)

ORFORD. A loc. n., Lancs, Lincs, Norf., Suff.

ORGILL. A loc. n., Cumb. Or Orguil, Norm.

ORGLES. *See* Argles

ORLEBAR. From Orlingbury (?); a loc. n., Northants. Or *A.S.* Herlebeorht; *Dch.* Haleber; p.n. (illustrious earl)

ORMAN, ORMANDY. *See* Ham-mond

ORME. *N.* Ormr; a p.n. (snake)

ORMEROD. A loc. n., Lancs

ORMISTON. A loc. n., Edinbgh.

ORMOND. *See* Ormandy

ORMS. From Ormes; a loc. n., Normandy

ORMSBY. A loc. n., Lincs, Norf., Yorks

ORR. *N.* Orri (heathcock), *tetras tetrix*; n.n.; *D.* Orr; *Dch.* Orri; *Fl.* Ories, Orys; *G.* Oehr; *D.B.* Ori; p.n.

ORRELL. A loc. n., Lancs

ORRIDGE. From Horridge; a loc. n., Devon

ORRIS. *See* Orr

ORROCK. A loc. n., Scotl. Or *see* Horrex

ORTH. *See* Ord

ORTHORPE. From Authorpe; a loc. n., Lincs

ORTNER. *A.S.* Ordnoth; a p.n.

ORTON. A loc. n., Cumb., Hunts, Leics, Staffs, Westmd.

ORVIS. From Avize (?); a loc. n., France. *Dch.* Avis; *Fr.* Avice, Avisse; p.n.

OSBALDESTONE. A loc. n., Lancs

OSBASTON. A loc. n., Salop

OSBORNE. *N.* Ás-Björn (the gods' bear); *D.* Osborn; *N.-Fr.* Os-bern; p.n.

OSLAR, OSLER. *N.-Fr.* le Oiselor. Or *A.S.* Osla; a p.n. (Oslaf (?), the gods' relict)

OSMAN, OSMENT. *See* Osmund

OSMONT. *See* Osmund

OSMOTHERLEY. A loc. n., Lancs, Yorks

OSMUND. *N.* Ásmundr (under the guardianship of the gods); *A.S.*, *D.*, *Fl.* Osmund; *Dch.* Osseman; *Fr.* Osmont; *G.* Ossmann; p.n.

OSSINGTON. A loc. n., Notts

OSTICK. *Dch.*, *Fl.* Oosterwijk; p.n. Also a loc. n. in Flanders

OSWALD. *N.* Ásvaldr; *Fl.*, *D.*, *G.*, *A.S.* Oswald; p.n. (power of the gods)

OTTAWAY. *A.S.* Othwig, Eadwig (prosperous victory); *G.* Ottawa; *Fl.* Ottevaere; p.n.

OTTLEY. A loc. n., Salop, Suff., Yorks

OTTY. From Othée; a loc. n., Belg. Or *see* Oddy

OTTYWILL. From Outwell (?); a loc. n., Norf.

OTWAY. *See* Ottaway

OULTON. A loc. n., Cumb., Norf., Yorks

OUNSTEAD. From Houndstreet (?); a loc. n., Somers

OURY. *Fr.* Oury; *G.* Ury; p.n. *See* Orr

OUSELEY. A loc. n., Northants

OUSEY. *See* Hussey

OUTHWAITE. *See* Huthwaite

OUTLAW. From Oathlaw; a loc. n., Forfar

OUTON, OUTTAN. *A.S.* Othin; *F.* Otten; *Dch.* Ouden; *Fr.* Othon; p.n. Fam. n. of Oth, Oddy. Or *see* Houghton

OUTRAM. *Old G.* Audram; a p.n. From *aud*, *A.S. eád* (prosperity), *ram* (strong)

OVENS. *A.S.* Offa, Ofing; *S.* Ovens; *Fl.* Ovyn; *Dch.* Oven; p.n. (wolf's descendants)

OVENSTONE. A loc. n., Fife

OVER. A loc. n., Camb.

OVERALL, OVERELL, OVERILL. From Overhill; a loc n., Worc. Or *N.-Fr.* Avril, de Avrilla; p.n.

OVERBURY. A loc. n., Suff., Worcest.

OVEREND. A loc. n., Worcest.

OVERMAN. *N.* Oframemni (a champion); *Dch.* Overman; *D.B.* Offram; p.n.

OVERTON. A loc. n., Ches., Derbysh., Hants, Lancs, Staffs, Wilts, Yorks

OVERY. A loc. n., Oxf. Or *Fr.* Ouvry; a p.n. Hugt. n., Lond. 1618

OVINGTON. A loc. n., Ess., Norf.

OWEN. British p.n. (a prince). Also *D.* Owen; *Fr.* Ouin; *D.B.* Ouen; p.n.

OWERS. A loc. n., Hants

OWGAN. *See* Hogan

OWLES. A loc. n., Suff.

OWSTON. A loc. n., Dur., Leics, Lincs

OWTHWAITE. *See* Huthwaite

OXBORROW. A loc. n., Norf.

OXENHAM. From Oxnam; a loc. n., Roxburghsh.

OXER, OXIER. From Auxerre; a loc. n., France

OXLADE. From Oxlode; a loc. n., Camb.

OXLEY. A loc. n., Lancs, Staffs

OXX. *N.* Oxi; *Dch.* Ox; p.n.

OYLER. *N.-Fr.* Huelier. Or *G.* Eule; a p.n. (an owl). Hugt. n., Lond. 1618

P

PACE, PACEY. A loc. n., Norm.

PACKER. *A.S.* Baghere (a contentious soldier), Bægeras (the Bavarians)

PACKE. *A.S.* Bag, Pæcg, Pag; *Dch.* Pak; *Fl.* Paké; *G.* Pache; p.n. *See* Bagge
In Rot. Obl. et Fin.

o

PACKHAM. A loc. n., Devon

PACKMAN. *Fl.* Packman; *G.* Pachmann; a p.n. (a farmer)

PADBURY. A loc. n., Oxf.

PADDAY. *N.* Pade; *A.S.* Pada, Peada; *D.*, *G.* Pade; p.n. *See* Badcock

PADDON. From Patton; a loc. n., Yorks (*D.B.* Patun). Or *Dch.* Paddinge; a p.n.

PADEY. *See* Padday

PADFIELD. A loc. n., Derbysh.

PADGET. *See* Paget

PADLEY. A loc. n., Derbysh.

PADMORE. From Pedmore; a loc. n., Worcest.

PAFFEY. *See* Pavett

PAGAN. *A.S.* fam. n.; *D.B.* Paganus, Pagen; p.n.
In Rot. Obl. et Fin. *A.S. bagan* (to contend).

PAGE. *Fr.* Page; a Hugt. n., Lond. 1688; *N.-Fr.* Le Page. Or *see* Packe

PAGET. *N.-Fr.* Pachet; a p.n.
In Rot. Hund.

PAGNAM. *See* Pakenham

PAICE. *See* Pace

PAINE, PAYEN. A loc. n., Normandy. Or *A.S.* Pag, Pagan, Pagen; *G.* Pein; *Fr.* Pain; *Fl.* Payen, Pien; *Dch.* Pen, Penn; p.n. Also a Hugt. n., Lond. 1618
Wm. Paen, *temp.* K. John.

PAINELL. *N.-Fr.* Paganel, Paynel; p.n.

PAINTER. *A.S.* Pender, Pendhere; *D.* Penter; *Fl.* Pinter; p.n. (crowned warrior)

PAKE. From Pecq; a loc. n., Flanders. *Dch.* Peek, Pek; p.n.
Pecche in Rot. Obl. et Fin.

PAKENHAM. A loc. n., Suff.

PALETHORPE. From Pallathorp; a loc. n., Yorks. Or Perlethorpe, Notts

PALEY. *Fr.* Pelay, Pelet, Pelez; p.n.; *pelé* (a bald-headed man)

PALGRAVE. A loc. n., Norf., Suff.

PALIN. *A.S.* Palling, Palig; *N.-Fr.* Palain; p.n. *See* Pelling
In Rot. Hund.

PALK. A loc. n., Devon

PALLETT. From Paillette; a loc. n., France. A Hugt. n., Lond. 1688

PALMER. *N.-Fr.* le Paumier; *Fl.* Palmaert; *Dch.* Pallme; *G.* Palmer; p.n. Flem. ref. n., Lond. 1618
Richard Palmer held lands in Worcest. *temp.* K. John.

PALMES. A loc. n., Languedoc

PANCHEN. From Paunchin; a loc. n., Devon. Or *A.S.* Bana (a slayer); *S.* Panchéen; *Fr.* Panquin; p.n. Dim. *See* Banner

PANGBOURNE. A loc. n., Berks

PANK, PANKS. *A.S.* Panga; *D.*, *S.* Pang; *G.* Pancke; p.n. Dim. of Bana

PANKHURST. A loc. n., Suss.

PANNELL. *See* Painell

PANTER, PANTHER. *A.S.* Band, Panti; *Fr.* Pante, Panthou; *Dch.* Pante; *G.* Panter; p.n. *See* Bond

PANTIN. *See* Panton

PANTON. *N.-Fr.* De Panton; a p.n.
In Rot. Hund.

PANTRY. From Penterry; a loc. n., Monmth.

PAPE. *A.S.* Papo; *Fr.* Pepe; a p.n. *See* Poppy. *N. papi* (a priest). Papper, a Prot. ref., Lond. 1618

PAPWORTH. A loc. n., Camb.

PARADISE. *A.S.* Berrardus (?), Bernardus; *Fl.*, *Fr.* Paradis; p.n. *See* Pardoe

PARAMAN. *See* Pearmain

PARAMORE. From Paramé (?); a loc. n., Norm. *N.-Fr.* Paramor

PARCELL. *Fr.* Parisel; a p.n.

PARCHMENT. *G.* Pergament; a p.n.

PARDOE. *A.S.* Beradus; *Old G.* Peradeo; *Fr.* Pardieu; *Dch.* Pardo; *D.* Pardi; p.n. (bear firm)

PARDON. *Fr.* Pardant, Pardon; *Fl.* Pardaen; *G.* Pardon; p.n.

PARFITT. *N.-Fr.* Parfait; a p.n. (perfect)

PARISH. *See* Parritch or Parris

PARK, PARKE, PERCK. A loc. n., Flanders; Parc, near Valognes; *Dch.* Park; *Fr.* Parc; p.n.
Richard de Parco held lands in Lincs, *temp.* K. John.

PARKER. *N.-Fr.* le Parker; *G.* Parke; *Dch.* Parker; p.n.; *Fr. parquer* (a park-keeper)
Parcher, tenant in chief, *D.B.*

PARKES. From Les Perques; a loc. n. near Valognes. *N.-Fr.* Bertram De P.; a p.n.

PARKHOUSE. A loc. n., Northbd.

PARKHURST. A loc. n., I. of Wight

PARKINS, PARKINSON. *Fl.* Parcyns; a p.n. *See* Perkins

PARLET. *See* Pallett

PARLOUR. *G.* Parlow; a p.n.

PARMETER, PARMINTER. *N.-Fr.* Parmentier; a p.n. (a tailor)

PARNELL. From Pernelle; a loc. n., Norm. *Fr.* Purnelle; p.n.

PARR. A loc. n. in Lancs. Or *Dch.* Parre, Paare; p.n. *See* Barr

PARRINGTON. A loc. n., Ess.

PARRIS. *N.-Fr.* Parez, Paresse, de Paris, Parys; p.n. Or Welsh ap Harris

PARRITCH. From Parwich; a loc. n., Derbysh.

PARROT. *See* Perrott

PARRY. *Fr.* Parré; a p.n. Or Welsh Ap Harry. *See* Parris. A Hugt n., Lond. 1687

PARSLEE, PARSLEY, PARSLOW. *See* Purslow

PARSON, PARSONS. *Dch.* Parson, ~~ Passon, Passens; *D.* Pass, ~~ Parr or Pass ~~

PART. *See* Pert

PARTINGTON. A loc. n., Ches.

PARTON. A loc. n., Camb.

PARTRIDGE. From Pettridge (?), a loc. n., Kent. Or *A.S.* Beorhtric; *Old G.* Perhtric; p.n. (illustrious ruler); Partrick de la Lande, Norm.
Partryk in Dur. Liber Vitæ. Partriche in Hund. Rolls. Patrickes in 1327.

PASCOE. *Fr.* Pasque; a p.n. (Easter)

PASH, PAISH. *Dch.* Pashe; *G.* Pasch; p.n. *See* above

PASHLEY. From Pasley, the Irish form of Paisley

PASK, PASKE. *See* Pascoe (time of birth (?))

PASKELL. *Fr.* Pascal; a p.n.; Hugt. n., Lond. 1687
De Peschall in Rot. Obl. et Fin.

PASS. *A.S.* Passa; *D.* Pass; *Fl.* Pas; *S.* Passy; *Dch., G.* Pas, Pass, Passe; p.n. *See* Bass

PASSMORE. From Peasemore; a loc. n., Berks

PATCH. *A.S.* Pecga; *G.* Patsch; p.n.

PATCHING. A loc. n., Suss.

PATCHITT. *See* Paget

PATE. *A.S.* Pade, Pata; *Fl.* Patte, Peet, Piette; *Dch.* Pet, Peet; p.n. Hugt. n., Canterbury, 1622. *See* Badcock

PATERNOSTER. *Dch., Fl.*; p.n.

PATEMAN, PATMAN. *G.* Patermann; a p.n. *See* Badman

PATON. *See* Peyton. Hugt. n., Canterbury, 1622

PATRICK. *Lat.* Patricius; *N.* Patrekr; Irish Padrig; p.n. (a nobleman) Or *see* Partridge

PATTEN, PATTON. A loc. n., Salop, Yorks. *N.-Fr.* Patin, Patun; p.n.
In Rot. Hund.

PATTERSON. *See* Pate

PATTISON. *Fl.* Patte, Petterson, Patesson; p.n. *See* Pate. Flem. ref., Lond. 1618

PATTLE. From Pathull or Pattishall; a loc. n., Staffs

PAUL. *N.-Fr.* de St Paul. Or *N.* Páll; *D.* Poul, Pauli, Paulin; *Fl.* Pauwels, Pauly, Poel, Pol, Polet, Poly, Polyn, Spoel; *Dch.* Pool, Pouwels, Spall, Spoel; *G.* Pohl, Pohler, Pollack, Poli, Pohlit, Pollok, Paul; *D.B.* Pauli; p.n. A Hugt. n., Lond. 1618

PAULETT. From Poolet; a loc. n., Somers. Or *Fr.* Poulet; a p.n. Dim. of Paul. A Hugt. n., Lond. 1687

PAULGER. *A.S.* Polga; *Dch.* Poelje; a p.n. Dim. of Paul

PAUNCEFOTE. *N.-Fr.* Pancevolt; a p.n. *See* Penfold

PAUSE, PAUSEY. *G.* Pause; a p.n. *See* Poysey

PAVETT. *Fr.* Pavot; *Fl.* Pevaert; p.n. (a poppy)

PAVEY. *N.-Fr.* Pavie, Peyveye; p.n.

PAVIS. *Dch.* Pavias, Paviers; p.n.

PAWLETT. *See* Paulett

PAWLEY. *N.-Fr.* Pauly; *D.* Pauli; p.n. *See* Paul

PAWSEY. *See* Pause

PAWSON. *D.*, *Dch.* Paulsen; a p.n.

PAXTON. A loc. n., Berwick

PAYNE. *See* Paine

PAYTON, PEYTON. From Paythorne; a loc. n., Yorks. *See* Paton

PEABODY. *See* Peberdy

PEACE. *Dch.* Piesche, Pees; p.n. *See* Pace

PEACHE, PEACHEY. *G.* Pietsch; a p.n.

　N.-Fr. Peche in Roll of Battell Abbey; Pecehaie, a tenant in chief, in *D.B.*; Peeche in Rot. Obl. et Fin.

PEACOCK. From Peakirk (?); a loc. n., Northants. Or *G.* Piechocki; a p.n. *See* Peak. Flem. ref. n., Lond. 1618

PEAD. *D.* Pied; *Fl.* Piette; p.n. *See* Pedder

PEAK. *N.* Pík (a peak (?), pike, pick, point of a sword, etc.); *Dch.* Pieck, Piek; *G.* Pick; *D.* Picker; *A.S.* Pic; p.n. *See* Pigg

PEALL. *See* Peel

PEAR. From Peer(?); a loc. n., Belg. *Dch.* Peer. Or *Fr.* Pièrre; p.n. Hugt., Lond. 1687

PEARD. *Fr.* Pirard; a p.n.

PEARETH. A loc. corruption of Penrith; a loc. n., Cumb.

PEARL. From Perl (?); a loc. n., Germ. Or *D.* Perle; *G.* Perl, Pirle; *N.-Fr.* Perol; *A.S.* Perlo; *Dch.* Perlee; *Fl.* Perlau; p.n. (pearl)

　Perles in Rot. Hund.

PEARMAIN, PEARMAN. *Old G.* Berman; *D.* Permin; *S.* Perman; *Fl.* Pierman; p.n. (bear man)

PEARS, PEARSE. *Fl.* Piers; *Dch.* Peere, Pierse; *D.* Pers; *N.-Fr.* De Piris; p.n. Peres, a Hugt. n., Lond. 1688

　Pers in Rot. Hund.

PEARSON. *Dch.*, *Fl.* Pierson, Pirson; *D.* Persson; *G.* Person; *Fr.* Pierresenné; p.n. Prot. ref., Lond.

PEASCOD. Welsh Pyscoed. From Dinbych-y-Pys-god, the ancient name of Tenby

PEASE. *See* Peace

PEASGOOD. *See* Peascod

PEASLEY. A loc. n., Lancs

PEBERDY. *N.-Fr.* Pabode or Pappedæ; p.n.

　Dur.. *temp.* Will. I.

PECHEY. *See* Peachey

PECK. *See* Pake

PECKETT. *See* Pickett

PECKHAM. A loc. n., Surr.

PECKOVER. A loc. n.

PEDDER, PEDDIE. *A.S.* Peada; a p.n. (K. of Mercia) *D.* Peder; p.n. *Se*

PEDDLE. From Pedwell; a loc. n., Somers

PEDLAR, PEDLEY. *See* Padley

PEEBLES. A loc. n., Scotl.

PEED. *See* Pead

PEEK. *See* Peak

PEEL. A loc. n., Lancs; Pyle, Normandy. Or *A.S.* Pil (pile, dart); *S.* Piehl, Pihl; *G.* Piel; *Dch.* Piël; *D.* Pihl, Piell, Pille; p.n.

PEEN, PEENY. *N.-Fr.* Peigne; a p.n.; *Fr.* Pin; a p.n.

PEEPS. *See* Pape

PEERLESS. *G.* Pieles (?); a p.n.

PEET. *See* Pead and Pitt

PEGG. *A.S.* Pega, Pæga; *Dch.* Peck, Pek; p.n. *See* Pigg

PEGLAR. *S.* Pegelow; a p.n.

PEILL. *See* Peel

PEIRSON. *See* Pearson

PELGRAM. *A.S.* Pilgrim, Piligrim; p.n. (fierce dart); *Fl.* Pelgrim; p.n.

PELHAM. A loc. n., Herts

PELL. Pael; a loc. n., Belg. *G.* Pell; *Fl.* Pelle; *Dch.* Pel; p.n.

PELLEW. From Pelwe; a loc. n., Norm.

PELLING. From Pelyn; a loc. n., Cornw. Or Pellaines, Belg. *See* Palin

PELLY. *See* Paley

PEMBER. *See* Pembury

PEMBERTON. A loc. n., Lancs

PEMBURY. A loc. n., Kent. Or from Pehembury, Devon

PENDER. *A.S.* Pendhere; a p.n. (a crowned or decorated warrior)

PENDERED. *A.S.* Pendræt; *Old G.* Bandrad; *Dch.* Pendraat; a p.n.; *bend* (chaplet), *rad* (counsellor)

PENDERGAST. *See* Prendergast

PENDERLEIGH. From Plenderleith (?); a loc. n., Scotl.

PENDLEBURY. A loc. n., Lancs

PENDLETON. A loc. n., Lancs

PENDREIGH. From Pendrea; a loc. n., Cornw.

PENFOLD. *A.S.* Pendweald, Penweald, Pineweald; p.n. (crown ruler)

Penvald, moneyer, K. Offa; *D.B.* Pancevold, a tenant in chief; Pancefolt, under-tenant at Survey.

PENGELLY. A loc. n., Cornw.

PENGLAZE. A loc. n., Cornw.

PENKETT. From Penketh; a loc. n., Lancs

PENLEY. From Pendley; a loc. n., Herts. Or Penly, Normandy

PENMAN, PENMAIN. From Penmain; a loc. n., Monm. Or Penmaen, S. Wales

PENN. A loc. n., Bucks, Staffs; Penne, France. Or *see* Paine

PENNEFEATHER. From Pontfathew; A loc. n., Merioneth

PENNINGTON. A loc. n., Lancs

PENNISTON. From Penistone; a loc. n., Yorks

PENNY. *N.* Peini; n.n.; *N.-Fr.* Penné; *D.* Peine; *Fl.* Penet; *Dch.* Pen, Penha; *Fr.* Peigné, Penna; p.n. Peno, Prot. ref., Norw. 1622

Peny in Rot. Hund.

PENNYCOOK, PENNYCUICK. From Penicuik; a loc. n., Edinburgh

PENRHYN. A loc. n., Cornw., N. Wales

PENRICE. A loc. n., S. Wales

PENROSE. A loc. n., Cornw.

PENSTONE. *See* Penniston

PENTECOST. From Pentecostes-Castel in Normandy

Roger Pentecost in Rot. Obl. et Fin., *temp.* K. John. Or from time of birth.

PENTELOW. From Pentlow; a loc. n., Ess.

PENTLAND. A loc. n., Edinburgh

PENTON. A loc. n., Hants

PENTREATH. From Pentraeth; a loc. n., N. Wales

PENWALL. From Penwell; a loc. n., Devon

PENWARNE. A loc. n., Cornw.

PEPLAR, PEPLER, PEPLOE. *See* Peplow

PEPLOW. A loc. n., Lincs, Salop

PEPPER. *A.S.* Pippa; *N.-Fr.* Pipart; *Dch.* Peper; *Fl.* Pepet, Piepers; *S.* Piper; *G., D.* Pieper, Piper; p.n. (a piper)

PEPPERCORN. *Dch.* Peperkoorn; a p.n.

PEPPERDAY. *See* Peberdy

PEPPERELL. From Pepperhill; a loc. n., Salop. Or *Fr.* Piperelle; *D.B.* Piperel; a p.n. Comp. Peverel

PERCY. From Percy; a loc. n., Normandy
In Roll of Battell Abbey; tenant in chief, *D.B.*

PERFECT, PERFETT, PERFITT. *See* Parfitt

PERKINS. *Fl.* Peterkin (little Peter); p.n.

PERKIS, PERKS. *See* Parkes

PERNIE. A loc. n., France

PEROWNE. *Fr.* Peronny; a p.n. From Perronne; a loc. n., France. Or Péronne, Belg. Hugt., Lond. 1618

PERREN, PERRIN, PERRING. *N.-Fr.* Perrin; *G.* Piering; *Dch.* Perrin; p.n.
In Rot. Hund.

PERRIAM. A loc. n., Somers
De Puryham in 1327.

PERROTT. A loc. n., Wilts. Or *A.S.* Pirot; *Fr.* Perot; p.n.

PERRY. *Fr.* Perrée; *Dch., D.* Perry; p.n.
Pery on the Roll of Battell Abbey; and Peret, a tenant in chief in *D.B.*

PERT. *A.S.* Pert, *beorht* (bright); a p.n.

PERTWEE. From Pertuis; a loc. n., France (a defile, narrow pass)

PESCOD. *See* Peascod

PESKETT. *See* Peascod

PESTALL, PESTELL. *Fr., S., Dch.* Pestel; *G.* Pessel; p.n. (a staff of office (?))

PETCH. *G.* Petsch; a p.n. *See* Patch

PETCHELL. *Fr.* Pechell; p.n. (a fishery). Or dim. of Peche

PETEL. *Fr.* Petel, Pettell; p.n.

PETERS. *D., G.* Peters; *Dch.* Peters, Peeters; *Fl.* Peeters; p.n. Prot. ref., Lond. 1618

PETERSON. *S.* Pedersen; p.n. *See* Pattison

PETHERBRIDGE. From Pethybridge; a loc. n., Devon

PETHERHAM. From Petham; a loc. n., Kent

PETHERICK. A loc. n., Cornw.

PETHERIDGE. *See* Partridge

PETHICK. *See* Petherick

PETLEY. From Peterly; a loc. n., Bucks

PETO. From Poitou, Normandy. Or *Fr.* Piteaux (merciful), Pitot; p.n.
Peito in Roll of Battell Abbey.

PETRE. *See* Pate

PETT. A loc. n., Suss. Or *Dch.* Pet; a p.n. *See* Pate

PETTAR, PETTER. From Pettaugh; a loc. n., Suff. *Fr.* Petteau; a p.n. Or *see* Pate

PETTENGILL. From Portingal; an old name for a Portuguese (Lower)

PETTIFER, PETTIFORD. A loc. n., Worc.

PETTIGREW. From Pettigoe (?); a loc. n., Fermanagh

PETTIT. *Fr.* Petit; a p.n. Hugt. n., 1618

PETTY. A loc. n., Inverness. Or *see* Pettit

PEW. *See* Pugh

PEXTON. *See* Paxton

PEYTON. A loc. n., Ess. Or Pieton, Belg.

PHAIR. Gaelic; p.n. (valour)

PHANTAM, VENDOME. A loc. n., France. Or *Fl.* Vandam; a p.n. Prot. ref., Lond. 1618

PHARE. *See* Phair and Fayers

PHARO, PHAROAH. *See* Farrow

PHAYRE, PHEAR. *See* Phair

PHEASANT. From Peissant; a loc. n., Belg. Or *N.-Fr.* le Paisant; *Fr.* Paysan; p.n. (a peasant)

> Peysan in Rot. Hund.

PHELPS, PHIBBS. *See* Phillips

PHILBRICK. *A.S.* Fulbric (very bright); a p.n.

PHILCOX. Dimin. of Philip

PHILLIMORE. From Fullamore; a loc. n., Devon. Or *A.S.* Filmær, Filimar; *Old G.* Filomor; p.n.; *N. fylmærr* (full of fame)

> Wm. Fylymore, of Dursley, 1460, will proved 1491. The will of Henry Fylymore, of Wickwar, dated 1546, and proved at Glost., 1562, is endorsed Henry Fynymore. In the registers of Cam, Glost., from 1640 to 1680, Phillimore and Phinimore are used interchangeably.

PHILLIPS. *N.* Philippus; *N.-Fr.* Fitz Philip; *Dch.* Philipps, Philipsen; *Fl.* Phlups; *S.* Philp; p.n. Prot. ref., Lond. 1618

PHILPOTT. Dimin. of Phillip

PHIPPS, PHIPSON. *See* Phillips

PHIZACKERLEY. *See* Fasacklea

PHYSICK. From Figeac; a loc. n., France. Or *G.* Fiescheck, Fietzek; p.n. Or *see* Fisk

PICARD. *N.-Fr.* Picard; *Fl.* Pickert; *Dch.* Piekart (strong fighter); p.n. Hugt. n., Lond. 1621. *See* Peake

PICKEL. *A.S.* Püchel; *N.-Fr.* Pigole; *G.* Pickel; p.n. Or from Pickhill; a loc. n., Yorks. *See* Peake

> Pikel in Rot. Hund.

PICKEN. The fam. n. of Pic. Or *N.-Fr.* Picon; a p.n.

PICKERING. A loc. n., Yorks

PICKESS. *See* Peake

PICKETT. *A.S.* Picced; *Fr.* Piquet; *Dch.* Piket; *N.-Fr.* Picot; p.n. *See* Pigott

PICKFORD, PICKFORTH. *See* Pitchford

PICKLES. *See* Pickel

PICKUP. A loc. n., Lancs

PICKWICK. A loc. n., Wilts

PICTHALL. A loc. n. Or *A.S.* Pcthœth, Pictel, Picthad; p.n. (war Pict)

PICTHORN. A loc. n., Salop

PICTON. A loc. n., Flint, Yorks

PIDCOCK. From Pittcott (?); a loc. n., Somers

PIDDING. *A.S.* fam. n. From Peada; *D.* Pied; p.n. *See* Pedder

PIDDINGTON. A loc. n., Northants

PIDGEON. *N.-Fr.* Pichon; *Fr.* Pigeon; p.n.

> Pigun in Rot. Hund.

PIDWELL. From Piddle; a loc. n., Worc.

PIERSON. *See* Pearson

PIGG. *A.S.* Pic (a slasher), *bichen* (to slash). *See* Peak and Pegg

PIGGIN. *See* Pidgeon

PICONY. From Picquigny; a loc. n. near Amiens, France. *Fr.* Pichonnier, Pigné, Pigny; p.n.

PIGOTT. *Fr.* Pegeaud, Pegot, Pichot, Picot; *G.* Pigotta; *D.B.* Picot, Pecoe; p.n. *See* Peake or Bygot

> Reginald Pigot held lands in Norf. *temp.* K. John. Hugt. n., Lond. 1685.

PIKE. *See* Peake

PIKESLEY. From Pickersleigh; a loc. n., Worcest. Or Pigsley, Devon

PILBOROUGH. From Pulborough; a loc. n., Surr.

PILCH. *S.* Piltz; *G.* Pils, Pilz; p.n.; *A.S. pylce* (a fur garment). Or dim. of Pil

PILE. *See* Peel

PILGRIM. *See* Pelgram

PILKINGTON. A loc. n., Lancs

PILL. A loc. n., Cornw., Glost., Somers. Or *see* Peel

PILLANS. *Fl.* Pilaen; *Fr.* Pillon; p.n. *See* Peel

PILLINGER. From Pillinge; a loc. n., Beds

PILLOW. From Pilhough; a loc. n., Derbysh. Or *N.-Fr.* Pilot; a p.n. Pilloe, a Hugt. n., Colchester, 1622

PILSON. *S.* Pylsson; a p.n. *See* Peel. Pilison, Fl. ref., Lond. 1618

PILTON. A loc. n., Devon, Northants, Rutland, Somers

PIM. *A.S.* Pymma; *G.* Pimmer; p.n. (speckled (?))

PINCH. From Binche (?); a loc. n., Belg. Or dim. of Pinn. *Dch.* Pink, Pinks, Pinkse; *G.* Pintsch

PINCHARD. *Fr.* Pinchart; *Fl.* Pinchaert; p.n. From Pinchardon or Punchardon; loc. n., Normandy

In Roll of Battell Abbey.

PINCHBACK, PINCHBECK. A loc. n., Lincs

PINCHEN. *Fl.* Pingeon, Pinson; *N.-Fr.* Pinçon (finch); *D.B.* Pinc'u'n, Pinchengi; p.n. Pinchon, a Hugt. n., 1622

PINCHES. *G.* Pincus, Pinkas; p.n. *See* Pinch

PINCHING. *See* Pinchen

PINCOMBE. From Pinnacombe; a loc. n., Devon. Or Bincom, Belg.

PINCOTT. *See* Penkett

PINDAR, PINDER. *G.* Pinder; *N.-Fr.* le Pinder; *Fl.* Pinter; p.n. *See* Pender

PINE. *G.* Pein; a p.n. *See* Payne

PINHEY. A loc. n. (?). *See* Paine

PINK. *See* Pinnock or Pinch

PINKERTON. From Pontcardon (?); a loc. n., Norm.

PINKHAM. *See* Pincombe

PINKNEY. A loc. n., Northants, Wilts

PINN. A loc. n., Devon. Or *Fr.* Pin; *G.* Pinn; *D.B.* Pin; p.n. *See* Peen

PINNEGAR. *A.S.* Pinegear = Winegear; *G.* Pinger; p.n. (friendly spear)

PINNER. A loc. n., Middlx. Or *Fr.* Pineur; a p.n. (a painter). Prot. ref., Norwich, 1622

PINNION. From Pignan; a loc. n. in France. *Fl.* Pingeon, Pinon; p.n. Or *see* Binyon

PINNOCK. A loc. n., Glost.

PINSENT, PINSUN. Pinston; a loc. n., Devon. Or *see* Pinchen

PIPE. A loc. n., Heref., Staffs. Or *Fr.* Pipe; a p.n.

PIPER. *See* Pepper

PIPPET. *Fl.* Pipart; a p.n. (strong piper)

PITCAIRN. A loc. n., Perth

PITCHER. *N.-Fr.* Pichere; a p.n.

PITCHES. *See* Peache

PITCHFORD. A loc. n., Salop

PITE. *See* Pitt and Pyatt

PITFIELD. From Petiville; a loc. n., Norm.

PITKIN. Dimin. of Peterkin

PITMAN. *Dch.* Piderman; *G.* Pitschmann; p.n.

Piteman in Rot. Hund.

PITT. A loc. n., Cornw., Devon. Or *Dch.* Piet, Pitt; *Fr.* Pitte; p.n. *See* Pead

PITTOCK. *See* Pidcock

PITTY. *See* Pettit

PIXEL. From Pickshill; a loc. n., Somers. Or Picts-hill, Yorks

PIXLEY. A loc. n., Dur., Heref.

PIZEY, PIZZEY. *G.* Peysey; a p.n. Or *see* Poysey

PLACE, PLAICE. Le Places; loc. n., Norm. *D.* Plees; *G.* Pless; *Fl.* Pleis; *Dch.* Ples; *Fr.* Place; p.n.

PLAMPIN. *Fl.* Blampain; a p.n.

PLANE. From Pleine; a loc. n., Norm. Or *G.* Plener; *D.B.* Pleines; p.n.

PLANK. From le Planquay; a loc. n., Norm. Or *D.* Planck; *Dch.*, *Fl.* Plank; *Fr.* Planche, Planque; p.n. Prot. ref., Dover, 1622

PLANT. *N.-Fr.* De la Plante; a p.n.

PLANTIN. *Dch.* Planten; a p.n.

PLASTOW. From Plaistow; a loc. n., Derbysh., Ess., Kent, Suss.

PLATT. From Plathe; a loc. n., Germ. (a plain). Or *A.S.* Blæd (glory); *G.* Platt; *D., S.* Plaate; *Dch.* Platte; p.n.

PLATTEN. *D., S.* Platen; *Fl.* Plétain, Plettinck; p.n.; fam. n.

PLAW. *See* Plow

PLAYER. *A.S.* Pleghere; *Dch.* Plieger; *Fr.* Plehiers; p.n. (war player)

PLAYFAIR. *G.* Plewa; a p.n.

PLAYFORD. A loc. n., Suff.

PLAYLE. *G.* Pleul; p.n.

PLEASANCE, PLEASANTS. *N.-Fr.* Plaisance; a p.n.

PLEDGER. *See* Player

PLENTY. *G.* Plantier; a p.n.

PLEWS. *Fl.* Pluys; p.n. *See* Plow

PLIMPTON. From Plympton; a loc. n., Devon

PLIMSAUL, PLIMSOLL. From Plemstall or Plemonstall; a loc. n., Ches.

PLOW. From Plau; a loc. n., Germ. Or *D.* Plógr, Ploug; *G.* Plew, Pluge, Plohs; *Dch.* Ploos; *Fl.* Pluys; p.n.

PLOWDEN. A loc. n., Salop

PLOWMAN. *S.* Ploman; p.n.

PLOWRIGHT. From Plougouvert (?); a loc. n., Norm.

PLUCKROSE. *D.* Plockross; a p.n.

PLUM, PLUMB. *D., Fl.* Plum; *N.-Fr.* Plumme; p.n.

PLUMBRIDGE. A loc. n., Kent

PLUME. *See* Plum

PLUMMER. *N.-Fr.* le Plumer, Plumier; p.n. (plume maker). Hugt. n., Lond. 1682

PLUMPTRE. A loc. n., Notts

Originally De Clerfai, from Clarfait, near Avesnes, Fland. Afterwards Fitz William of Plumtre.

PLUMSTEAD. A loc. n., Norf.

PLUNKETT. From Plouquenat, near Rennes, Bretagne. *N.-Fr.* De Plugenet; a p.n.

PLYMSELL. *See* Plimsaul

POATE. *Dch., Fl.* Poot; a p.n.

POBJOY. *See* Popjoy

POCHIN. *N.-Fr.* Pocin; a p.n.

POCKETT. *Fr.* Pauchet, Pochet; p.n. Dim. of Pook

POCKLINGTON. A loc. n., Yorks

POCOCK. *D.* Pock; *G.* Pocha; p.n. *See* Pook. Dim.

PODD. *See* Paddy

PODGER. Welsh Ap Odger; a p.n.

PODMORE. A loc. n., Staffs

POGSON. *See* Pook

POINTER. *Fr.* Pointier; a p.n. (a maker of points). Or *see* Pont

POINTIN. *See* Poynton

POINTS. From Pontoise (?); a loc. n., Norm.

Ponz, under.tenant in *D.B.* Nicholas Puintz held land in Glost. *temp.* K. John.

POLDEN. A loc. n., Somers

POLE. A loc. n., Devon. Also from St Pol de Leon; a loc. n., Norm.; de la Pole. Or *see* Paull

POLES. *See* Paul

POLEY. *D.* Pol, Poli; *Fr.* Pollet; p.n. *See* Paul

POLGLAZE. A loc. n., Cornw.

POLHILL. A loc. n.

POLKINGHORNE. A loc. n., Cornw.

POLL. *See* Pole

POLLARD. *A.S.* Boldheard (?) (bold, strong); *Fl.* Pollaert; *Fr.* Pollard; p.n. *See* Bollard

Gaufrid Pollard on Rot. Obl. et Fin., *temp.* K. John. Also a Hugt. n., Lond. 1618.

POLLITT. *Fr.* Polet, Pollet; *Dch.* Politz; p.n. *See* Paul. A Hugt. n.

POLLOCK. A loc. n., Renfrew. Or *Dch.* Polak; a p.n. *See* Paul

POLLY. *Fr.* Pollet; *Fl.* Polly; *D.* Poli; p.n. *See* Paul

POLLYN. *See* Paul

POLSUE. Cornish p.n.

POLWARTH. A loc. n., Berwick

POLWHELE. A loc. n., Cornw. (*D.B.* Polhel)

POMFREY. A loc. corruption of Pontefract; a loc. n., Yorks. Or *see* Pumphrey

POND. From Pont; a loc. n., Belg., Cornw. *Dch.* Pont; a p.n. Prot. ref., Lond. 1618

PONDER. *N.-Fr.* le Pondere; *D.B.* Ponther; *G.* Punde; p.n.

PONSFORD. A loc. n., Devon. Or Pontesford, Salop

PONSONBY. A loc. n., Cumb.

PONT. *See* Pond

PONTIFEX. *D.* Pontavice; a p.n.

PONTING. *N.-Fr.* De Pontin; a p.n.

PONTON. A loc. n., Lincs

POOK. From Poucques; a loc. n., Fland. Or *N.* Púki (Puck); *D.* Pogge; *A.S.* Pucca, Puch; *G.* Puche; *S.* Puke; p.n. Also a contraction of Pollock

POOLE. A freq. loc. n., Dorset, Yorks, etc. From *N.* Pollr; *B.* pwl (a pool). Or *see* Paul. Poule, a Prot. ref., Lond. 1621

POORE. From Puers (?); a loc. n., Belg. *G.* Pur; *D.B.* Pur; p.n.
John le Poer held lands in Yorks, *temp.* K. John, 1201.

POOS. *A.S.* Bos; *Dch.* Poesse; *Fl.* Pues; p.n. (a stall)

POPE. *N.* Papar; *A.S.* Papo; *F.* Poppe; *D.* Pop; *S.* Pape; *Fl.* Papy, Poppin; *Dch.* Paap, Pop; *G.* Pape, Papke, Poppe, Poper; p.n. (father)
Poppe was the name of a Duke of Friesland, slain in battle by Charles Martel, A.D. 734.

POPHAM. A loc. n., Devon, Hants

POPJOY. *Fl.* Papegaey; a p.n.; *G.* papagei (a parrot)

POPKIN. *See* Pope. Dimin.

POPLE, POPPLE. A loc. n., Belg. *Dch.* Poppel; a p.n.

POPPLETON. A loc. n., Yorks

POPPY. *See* Pope

PORCHER. *N.-Fr.*; p.n. (swine-herd)

PORLEY. *See* Pawley

PORT. Portes; a loc. n., Norm. *Fr.*, *G.* Port; *Dch.* Porth, Porte; p.n.

PORTAL. *Fr.*; p.n. Hugt. n., Lond. 1687

PORTEOUS. From Portways (?); a loc. n., Oxf.

PORTER. *Dch.* Poorter; *Fr.* Portier; p.n. (a door-keeper). Hugt. n., Norwich, 1622
Ad Porta', 1327.

PORTLOCK. From Porlock; a loc. n., Somers

PORTWAY. A loc. n., Worcest.

PORTWINE. *Fr.* Potvin (good-will). Or *A.S.* Peohtwine (Pict-friend); *Dch.* Portheine; p.n.

POSEY. *Fr.* Pousset; a p.n.

POSSELT. *See* Postlethwaite

POSTEL, POSTLE. *N.-Fr.*; p.n.; petit poteau (post, stake)
In Rot. Hund.

POSTLETHWAITE. A loc. n. A clearing enclosed with stakes. *D.* Poselt; a p.n.

POSTON. A loc. n., Heref., Salop

POTCHETT. *See* Pockett

POTHECARY. From Apothecary; the occupation
Laurencius Ypotecarius occurs among the tenants of Ipswich Priory in the thirteenth century.

POTT. *Fl.*, *Dch.* Pot; *S.* Pott; p.n. Prot. ref., Lond. 1618. *See* Body

POTTAGE. From Potheridge; a loc. n., Devon

POTTER. *Dch.* Potter, Potters; *Fr.* Potier, Pottier; p.n. (a potter)
Le Potere in Rot. Hund.

POTTINGER. Fam. n. of Pott. *Dch.* Pottinga; a p.n.

POTTON. From Potterne; a loc. n., Wilts

POTTOW. *Fr.* Poteau, Pottaux; p.n. (a post)

POTTS, POTTES. A loc. n., Belg. *Dch.*, *Fl.*; p.n. *See* Pott

POULTER. *G.* Polte; *Fr.* Poultier; p.n. (a poulterer). Hugt. n., Canterbury, Jas. I.
Le Poleter in Rot. Hund.

POULTNEY. A loc. n., Leics. A hamlet of Misterton
   Sir John de Poultney, knight, Lord Mayor of London, bur. St Paul's, 1349.

POULTON. A loc. n., Glost., Kent, Lancs

POUNCEBY. *See* Ponsonby

POUND. A loc. n., Devon

POUNTNEY. A loc. n., Suff.

POWELL. Welsh ab Howell; *Fr.* Puel; a p.n. Hugt. n., Lond. 1618

POWER. *Fr.* Pouyer; a p.n. (grand). *See* Poore

POWLEY. *See* Paul

POWNALL. A loc. n., Ches.

POYNINGS. A loc. n., Surr.

POYNTER. *See* Pointer

POYNTON. A loc. n., Lincs

POYSER. *A.S.* Boзo, Buзa, Pusa (stall keeper); *G.* Peiser, Peuser; *Fl.* Pizar; *Dch.* Peyser; p.n.

POYSEY. From Poissy; a loc. n., Norm. Hugt. n., Lond. 1681

PRAHL, PRALL. *D.*, *G.*, *Dch.*; p.n. (bounce, brag). Or Prawle; a loc. n., Devon

PRAILL. From Presles; a loc. n., Belg. *Dch.* Prell; a p.n.

PRATT. A loc. n., France. *N.-Fr.* Du Prat; *Fr.* Du Pré (meadow), Prat; *Fl.* Praet. A Hugt. n., Lond. 1687

PRECIOUS. *Dch.* Preussiche (?); a p.n. (Prussian)

PREDAM. *Fr.* Predhom; a p.n. *See* Prodham

PREDDY, PREEDY. *See* Priddy

PREESE. A loc. n., Lancs. Or *see* Price

PRENDERGAST. A loc. n., Pembroke

PRENTICE, PRENTIS. *A.S.* Prentsa or Prentisa (?); a p.n. *See* Prince

PRESCOTT. A loc. n., Devon, Lancs, Salop

PRESENT. *Fr.* Présent; a p.n.

PRESLAND. *Dch.*; loc. and p.n.

PRESLEY. *See* Priestley

PRESOW. *Fr.* Preseau; a p.n. Or Presall; a loc. n., Lancs. Bressoux, Belg.

PRESS. *G.*; p.n. Or *see* Preece

PRESSEY. From Precy; a loc. n., France

PREST. *See* Priest

PRESTIGE. From Prestwich; a loc. n., Lancs

PRESTON. A loc. n., Kent, Lancs, Mid-Lothian, etc.

PRETTEJOHN. *Fr.* Petitjean; a p.n.

PRETTY. *See* Priddy

PRETYMAN. *A.S.* Beorhtman, Brihtman; *G.* Brettman; p.n. (illustrious man)

PREVOST. *Dch.* Prevost; *Fr.* Prévost; p.n. (a provost). A Hugt. n., Rye, 1621

PREWETT. *Fr.* Prevet; a p.n.

PRICE. Welsh Ap Rhys; a p.n. Prise; a loc. n., Yorks. Preece, Denbigh
   Roger Preise in Rot. Obl. et Fin., *temp.* K. John.

PRICKETT. *See* Prichard

PRIDDEN. From Priding; a loc. n., Glost. Welsh Pryddyn (?)

PRIDDY. A loc. n., Somers

PRIDHAM. *See* Predham

PRIDMORE. *A.S.* Beorhtmær (illustrious famous); *D.* Bredmore; p.n.

PRIEST. *A.S.* Preost; *N.* Prestr; *Fl.* Prist; p.n. From the office

PRIESTLEY. From Priestcliffe (?); a loc. n., Derbysh.

PRIGG. *A.S.* Bric, Bright; *Fl.* Prick; a p.n. (illustrious)

PRIGGENS. *Dch.* Pricken; a p.n.; fam. n.

PRIKE. *See* Prigg

PRIM, PRIME. *A.S.* Brým; *Dch.* Priem; *D.* Prime; p.n. (the sea). Hugt. n., Lond. 1618

PRIMROSE. A loc. n., Fife

PRINCE. *Fr.*, *Fl.* Prins; *Dch.* Prince, Prins; *G.* Prinz; p.n. Hugt. n., Lond. 1618. *See* official names

PRING. *N.* Brynki, from Brynjólfr (mailed Jólfr); *G.* Bring; *Dch.* Brink; p.n.

PRINGLE. From Hop-Pringle (?); a loc. n., Scotl. Pringel, a Prot. ref., Lond. 1687

PRINSEP. From Brinsop; a loc. n., Heref. Or Princethorpe; a loc. n., Devon

PRIOR, PRYER. *Fl.* Preier; *Fr.* Prier; *D.* Prior; p.n. (prior, priest)

PRITCHARD. Welsh Ap-Richard

PRITTY. *See* Priddy

PROBART, PROBERT. Welsh Ap-Robert; a p.n.

PROBY, PROBYN. Welsh Ap-Robin

PROCTER. *Lat.* Procurator (an apparitor); *Fr.* Procureur; a p.n.

PRODGERS. Welsh, Ap-Rodgers

PRODHAM. *Fr.* Prodhomme; a p.n. (gallant, brave)

PROFFITT. *G.* Proft, Prophet; *Fr.* Profit; p.n. Or *see* Proudfoot (?)

PROPERT. *See* Probert

PROSSER. *G* Preusser; a p.n.

PROTHEROE. *See* Prydderch

PROUD. *N.* Pruði; *Fr.* Praud; *A.S.* Pruð; p.n.

PROUDFOOT. *N.* Pruði-fótr; *G.* Prowit (stately foot); a n.n.

PROUDHAM. *Fr.* Prudhomme; a p.n. *See* Prodham

PROUDLOVE. *Fr.* Prioleau (?). A Hugt. n.

PROUT. *See* Proud

PROWSE. A loc. n., Devon. Or *G.* Praus; *Dch.* Prousse; p.n.

PRUDAMES. *See* Proudham

PRUDENCE. *Fr.* Prudans; a p.n. (honest)

PRUDHOE. A loc. n., Dur., Northbd.

PRUDHOM. *Fr.* Prudhomme; a p.n. (a skilful man)

PRUE. *Fr.* Preux; a p.n. (brave). Hugt. n., Lond. 1687

PRUEN. *A.S.* Brun, Bryne, Prun (brown); *Dch.* Preün, Prooijen; p.n.

PRUST. *Fl.* Proust; a p.n. *See* Prevost

PRY. A loc. n., Belg. Prey, Norm.

PRYDDERCH, PRYTHERCH. Welsh Ap-Rhydderch, the son of Roderick (the red). *See* Brodrick

PRYKE. *See* Prigg

PUCKETT. *G.* Puchat; a p.n. *See* Pook. Dim.

PUCKEY. From Puchay; a loc. n., Norm. Or *see* Pook

PUCKLE. *G.* Puchelt; *Fl.* Puckle; p.n. (humped (?)). Or dim. of Puck

PUCKRIDGE. A loc. n., Herts

PUDDEFOOT, PUDDEPHATT. From Puddephats; a loc. n., Herts

PUDDICOMBE. From Pudcombe; a loc. n., Devon

PUDNEY. *See* Putney

PUGH. From the Welsh Ap-Hugh (son of Hugh). Or *A.S.* Puh, Puch; p.n. *See* Pook

PUGSLEY. From Puxley; a loc. n., Northants

PULESTON. A loc. n., Heref.

PULFORD. From Pulsford; a loc. n., Devon

PULHAM. A loc. n., Devon, Norf.

PULL. A loc. n., Belg.

De la Pulle in Rot. Obl. et Fin.

PULLBROOK. From Polebrook; a loc. n., Northants. Or Pullabrook, Devon

PULLEIN, PULLYN. *Fr.* Poullain; a p.n. *See* Paul. A Hugt. n., Lond. 1622

PULLEY. From Pullay; a loc. n., Norm. Or *Fr.* Poullet; a p.n.

PULLUM. *See* Pulham

PULVER. *See* Bulwer

PUMFRIT. *See* Pomfrey

PUMPHREY. From the Welsh Ap-Humphrey (?). Or *see* Pomfrey

PUNCH. *N.-Fr.* Pointz, Ponce, Punce; p.n. Or Irish corruption of Ponsonby

PUNCHARD. *Fr.* Ponchaut; a p.n. *See* Pinchard

PUNG. *Dch.* Puncke; a p.n. *A.S.* *pung* (a purse)

PUNNETT. *G.* Pundt; a p.n.

PUNSHON. *Fr.* Ponchon; a p.n. Puncin in Rot. Obl. et Fin.

PUNT. *A.S.* Punt; *G.* Pundt; p.n.; *pund* (a mole). *See* Pond

PUNTER. *G.* Punte; a p.n.

PURBROOK. A loc. n., Hants

PURCELL. *N.-Fr.* Pourcel; a p.n. (little pig) Radulph Purcel held land in Bucks, *temp.* K. John.

PURCHAS. *N.-Fr.* Perahgoz (?) (bear-Goth); *Fr.* Pourchez; a p.n. (a poor knight) Andreas Purchaz held land in Kent, *temp.* K. John.

PURDAY, PURDEY, PURDIE, PURDUE, PURDY. *See* Pardoe

PURDON. From Purton; a loc. n., Glost., Wilts. Or Pirton, Herts, Staffs., Worcest.

PURFITT. *See* Perfitt

PURGOLD. *A.S.* Burgweald, Burwold; p.n. (the castle ruler)

PURITAN. From Puriton; a loc. n., Somers

PURKHAM. From Purcombe; a loc. n., Devon

PURKIS. *See* Purchas or Perkis

PURR. *A.S.* Bur; *G.* Pur; p.n. *See* Poore

PURRIER. *A.S.* Burhicher (secure warrior). Or *Fr.* Perrier; a p.n. (a quarryman (?))

PURSER. *Fr.* Perseau; a p.n. *See* Purss

PURSLEY. *See* Purslow

PURSLOW. A loc. n., Salop

PURSS. *G.* Pursche; a p.n. (sound). Dim. of Pur

PURTON. A loc. n., Glost.

PURVES, PURVIS. A loc. n., Berwick. Pervyse; a loc. n., Flanders

PUSEY. A loc. n., Berks

PUTLEY. From Putloe; a loc. n., Glost.

PUTNAM. From Puttenham; a loc. n., Herts, Surr.

PUTNEY. A loc. n., Surr.

PUTT. A loc. n., Belg. Or *A.S.* Putta; *G.* Puth; *Dch.* Put; p.n. *See* Pott

PUTTERILL. *Fr.* Poutrel (?); a p.n. (a beam); or a loc. n.

PUTTOCK. *A.S.* Puttoc; *G.* Puttke; p.n. Dim. of Putt

PUXON. From Puxton; a loc. n., Somers, Worcest.

PYATT. *See* Pyett

PYBUS. *Dch.* Pijpers; a p.n.; fam. n. *See* Pepper

PYE. From Pois (?); a loc. n., Belg. Or *D.* Pii; *Fl.* Peys, Pye; *G.* Poyer; p.n.

PYEMONT. *Fr.* Pimont; a p.n.

PYETT. *A.S.* Pyht, Peoht (Pict); *Fl.* Piette; p.n.

PYGALL. *G.* Biegal; *Dch.* Biegel; p.n.

PYKE. *Fl.* Pycke; a p.n. *See* Peak

PYLE. A loc. n., Norm. *See* Peel

PYM. *See* Pim

PYMAN. *See* Pyemont

PYMAR, PYMER. From Pyemoor; a loc. n., Camb.

PYNE. *See* Paine

PYTCHES. *See* Peake

PYWELL. From Bywell; a loc. n., Northbd.

Q

QUADLING, QUODLING. Dimin. of *D.* Quaade; a p.n. *See* Wadd

QUAIE. *Fr.*; p.n. Or Irish M'Qua

QUAIL. A Manx contraction of the Irish MacPhail (Paul's son). Or *A.S.* Wealh; *N.-Fr.* Cuala (a stranger); *G.* Quiel; *D.* Quehl; p.n.

QUAIN. *A.S.* Cwen (an inhabitant of Quenland, a vandal); *Fr.* Quenne; *Dch.* Quien; p.n. Or Irish M'Queen

QUAINTANCE. *Fl.* Quintins; a p.n.

QUALTER. From M'Walter

QUANT. *A.S.* Wand, Want; *Dch.* Kwant; *G.* Quandt; p.n. (Wend). Prot. ref., Lond. 1618

QUANTOCK. A loc. n., Somers

QUANTRELL. *See* Cantrell

QUARMAN, QUARMANE. *A.S.* Wærman; *Fr.* Querment; p.n.; *war* (cautious)

QUARMBY. A loc. n., Yorks

QUARRELLE. *See* Carrell

QUARRINGTON. A loc. n., Dur., Lincs

QUARRY. *A.S.* Cwara; *Fr.* Quarré; a p.n. (wary). Or Scotch M'Quarrie

QUARTERMAIN. *A.S.* Weardman; *Fr.* Quatremains; p.n. (guardman)

In Oxon, Rot. Obl. et Fin.

QUARTLEY. A loc. n., Devon

QUASH. *A.S.* Waso, Wassa; *G.* Quass; p.n. (waterman (?))

QUAY. *See* Quaie

QUAYLE. *See* Quail

QUECKETT. A loc. n., Wilts. Or *A.S.* Wigheard (war firm); *G.* Quickert; a p.n.

QUELCH. *See* Welch

QUENBY. A loc. n., Leics

QUESTED. From Quenstadt; a *G.* loc. and p.n.

QUICK. A loc. n., Yorks. Or *A.S.* Cwic; *Fr.* Guiche; *Old Fr.* Guige; *Fl.* Kwick; *S.* Qvick; *Dch.* Kuijk; *G.* Quicker; p.n. (active)

QUIGLEY. From Quedgeley; a loc. n., Glost. Or *Old G.* Wigilo; *A.S.* Wigelin. Dim. of Wig

QUILLAN. From the Irish *cuileann* (holly)

QUILTY. From the Irish *coillte* (woods)

QUINBY. *See* Quenby

QUINCEY. From Quincé; a loc. n., Maine

Quinci in Roll of Battell Abbey. De Quency, Leics, *temp.* K. John.

QUINN. A loc. n., Killaloe, Ireland. Also M'Quin, from the Irish *Con* (the descendant of Con)

QUINNEY. From Queney; a loc. n., Camb. Or Irish M'Quiney; a p.n.

QUINTOCK. *See* Quantock

QUINTON. A loc. n., Glost., Northants, Warw., Worcest.

QUIRK. A Manx contraction of the Irish MacCuirc (Cork's son); a p.n.; *coirce* (oats)

QUIXLEY. *See* Quigley

R

RABAN. *N.-Fr.* De Rabayne. Or *A.S.* Hraban; = *ram* (strong); *Fr.* Raban, Raband; *Dch.* Rabanus; p.n.

RABBETH, RABETT. *A.S.* Radbod; *G.* Rabat; *Dch.* Rappart; p.n. (counsel messenger)

RABBIDGE. *A.S.* Raba; *G.* Rabisch; *N.-Fr.* De Rabes, Rabace; p.n.

RABBITS. D. Rabitz; a p.n. Also a corruption of Roberts. *See* above

RABEY, RABY. From Raby; a loc. n., Ches., Norm. Or Rebaix, Belg.

RABLEY. A loc. n., Herts

RACE. *See* Reece

RACKETT. *See* Reckett

RACKHAM. A loc. n., Suss.

RACKLEY. A loc. n.

RACKSTRAW, RACKSTRAY. *D.* Rockstroh; a p.n.

RADCLIFFE. A loc., n. Notts

RADFORD. A loc. n., Devon, Notts

RADLEY. A loc. n., Notts, Staffs

RADMALL. From Rathmell; a loc. n., Yorks

RADMORE. From Rathmore; a loc. n., Killarney. Redmire, Yorks. Or *A.S.* Rædmær, Rademar; p.n. (famous counsellor)

RADNALL. From Rednal; a loc. n., Worcest.

RADWILL. *A.S.* Rædwealh; a p.n. (a foreign counsellor)

RAE. *See* Ray

RAEBURN. A loc. n., Dumfries

RAFFE. *See* Rolf

RAFFETY. From the Irish O'Rafferty; a p.n.

RAFFLES. *Fl.* Raphaels; a p.n.

RAGG. *N.* Ragi (a king); *A.S.* Rag, Wraca; *D.* Rager; *Dch.* Rack; p.n. (an exile)

RAGGETT. *N.-Fr.* Ragot; *G.* Rackette; p.n. Dim. of Ragg

RAIKES. A loc. n., Lincs

RAILTON. *See* Relton

RAIN. *N.* Hreinn (reindeer); *A.S.* Wrenna; *Fr.* Raine, Reine; *G.* Renn; p.n. *See* Wren

RAINBIRD. *A.S.* Regenbeort, Regenbert (very bright); *G.* Reinbardt; *N.-Fr.* Reinbert; p.n.

RAINBOW. *A.S.* Regenbod; *G.* Reinboth; *N.-Fr.* Rainbaut; p.n. (chief messenger)

RAINEY. A loc. n., France

RAINHAM. A loc. n., Ess.

RAINS, RAINES. A loc. n., Ess.

RAINSFORD. From Rainford; a loc. n., Lancs

RAIT. A loc. n., Perth

RAITHBY. A loc. n., Lincs

RAKE. A loc. n., Devon

RALEIGH. From Rayleigh; a loc. n., Ess. Or *Fr.* Ralet; a p.n.

RALF. *See* Rolfe

RAMAGE. *D.* Rames; *Fl.* Ramuz; p.n. *A.S.* Hranig(?) (a reindeer). Dim. of Hran

RAMM. *N.* Ramr; n.n. (strong); *D.B.* Ram; *D.*, *G.* Ramm; p.n. Rame, Hugt. n., Lond. 1687

RAMPLEN. *Fr.* Rampillon; a p.n.

RAMSAY. A loc. n., Ess., I. of Man, S. Wales

RAMSBOTHAM, RAMSBOTTOM. A loc. n., Lancs. Comp. *Fl.* Ransbotyn; a p.n.

RAMSDEN. A loc. n., Ess., Herts, Oxf.

RAMSHAW. A loc. n., Dur., Northbd.

RAMSHAY. *See* Ramshaw

RAMSTEAD. *D.* Ramstad; a loc. and p.n.

RAMYELL, RANYELL. *N.* Rafnkell; *A.S.* Ramcytel, Ramechil; *Fr.* Ramioul (?); p.n. (Ketel the strong)

RAND. A loc. n., Lincs. Or *A.S.*, *D.* Rand; a p.n. (a shield)

RANDALL. *A.S.* Rendel; *D.*, *G.* Randel; a p.n.; *N.* Röndolfi (shield-wolf). *See* Rendell

RANDOLF. *See* Randulph

RANDS. From Raunds; a loc. n., Northants. Or fam. n. of Rand

RANDSFORD. *See* Rainsford

RANDULPH. *D.* Randulff; *G.*, *S.* Randel; *A.S.* Randolf, Randulf, Randwuff; p.n. (shield-wolf)

RANGER. *A.S.* Regengar; *N.-Fr.* Reignier; *D.* Rannje; p.n. (chief spear)

RANKIN. A loc. n. Scotl. Or *N.-Fr.* Roncin; *Fl.* Renkin; p.n. Dim. of Renn

RANNALS. *See* Reynolds

RANNEY. From Renaix; a loc. n., Fland. *N.* Hrani (a blusterer); *Fr.* René; p.n. Renie, Hugt. n., Lond. 1688

RANSDALE. From Ravensdale (Raunsdale); a loc. n., Derbysh.

RANSLEY. From Ramsley; a loc. n., Devon

RANSOME, RANSON. *N.-Fr.* Rançon; a p.n. (ransomed)

RANSTEAD. A loc. n.

RANT. *Dch.*; p.n. *See* Rand

RANTELL. *See* Randall

RANTON. A loc. n., Staffs

RAPER. *See* Rope

RAPKIN. *G.* Rappke; a p.n. Dimin. of Rapp

RAPP. *A.S.* Raba; *D.*, *Dch.*, *G.* Rapp; *Fl.* Rappe; p.n. (strong). Hugt. n., Lond. 1681

RAPLEY. *Fr.* Raparlier (?) ; a p.n.
RAPPARD. *See* Rabbeth
RAPSON. *See* Rapp
RARP. *See* Rapp
RASH. *D.* Rask ; *Fl.* Rasse ; *G.* Rasch ; p.n. Dim. of *A.S.* Ras ; a p.n. (rash)
RASHLEIGH. A loc. n., Devon
RASP. *A.S.* Rasbeort, Raspert (illustrious assailant) ; *G.* Rasper; p.n.
RASTALL. From Rusthall (?) ; a loc. n., Kent
W. Rastel in Rot. Obl. et Fin.
RATHWELL. *See* Rothwell or Radwill
RATTEE. *A.S.* Rad, Ratho (counsel); *D.* Rathje ; *G.* Ratay, Rathay ; *Dch.* Ratté ; p.n.
RATTRAY. A loc. n., Aberdeensh.
RATTY. An Irish corruption of Ratcliffe. Or *A.S.* Ræd, Rat, Ratho ; p.n. (counsel)
RAVEN. *N.* Hræfn ; *S.* Ravn ; *D.* Rafn, Raun ; *Dch.* Raven ; *A.S.* Ræfen, Rauen ; p.n. (a raven)
RAVENHILL. From Ravenel ; a loc. n., Norm.
RAVENSCLIFFE. A loc. n., Staffs
RAVENSCOURT. A loc. n.
RAVENSCROFT. A loc. n., Ches.
RAVENSWORTH. A loc. n., Dur.
RAVEY. *Fr.* Revet ; a p.n. *See* Rivett
RAW. *A.S.* Raue, Ræf ; p.n. (raven); *D.*, *Fl.*, *G.* Rau ; p.n. *See* Roe, Rowe
RAWCLIFF. A loc. n., Yorks, Lancs
RAWDON. A loc. n., Yorks
RAWKINS. *G.*, *Dch.* Rauch, Raucke; p.n. Dim. of Raw
RAWLE, RAWLL. *Dch.* Rohol; a p.n. *See* Rolfe
RAWLENCE. *N.* Hródland (famous land) ; *A.S.* Rolland ; *Fl.* Roulandt; *S.* Roland; *Dch.* Roelants; p.n.
RAWLEY. *See* Raleigh or Rowley

RAWLINGS. *Dch.* Rohling ; a p.n. (descendants of Rolfe)
RAWLINSON. *See* Rolfe
RAWSON. *N.* Rauðssynir (children of the "red ") ; *Fl.* Raussens ; p.n.
RAY. *See* Reay
RAYBOULD. *N.* Rögnvaldr (the keeper of the gods) ; *A.S.* Rainbald ; *G.* Rebohl ; *N.-Fr.* Ribald ; p.n.
RAYCRAFT. *See* Ryecroft
RAYDEN, RAYDON. A loc. n., Suff. Or *Dch.* Reeden ; a p.n.
RAYMENT, RAYMOND. *N.* Hrómundr (famous protector) ; *D.* Reymann ; *Dch.* Reiman ; *G.* Rehmann ; *D.B.* Raimund ; p.n. Raimond in Roll of Battell Abbey.
RAYNARD. *A.S.* Ragenheard ; *D.* Reinhard ; *G.* Rennert ; *Dch.* Renard ; *Fr.* Renaud ; p.n. (wise firmness)
RAYNER. *N.* Hreinnarr (reindeer). Or *A.S.* Regenhere (wise warrior); *D.* Reiner ; *G.* Renner ; *N.-Fr.* Ranier ; *Fl.* Rener ; *D.B.* Rayner ; p.n.
RAYNHAM. A loc. n., Norf.
RAYNOR. *See* Rayner
RAYSON. From Rasen ; a loc. n., Lincs. Or *see* Ray
READ. A loc. n., Yorks. Or *see* Reid
READY, RETHY. A loc. n., Belg. *Dch.* Riede ; a p.n.
REAM. *N.* Hreimr ; n.n. (noisy) ; *S.* Reimers; *Dch.* Riem, Reimers; p.n.
REAP. *A.S.* Rip ; *Dch.* Reep ; a p.n. *See* Ribbans
REARDEN. From Ruardean ; a loc. n., Glost. Or *see* Riordan
REASLEY. *See* Risley
REASON. From Ressons ; a loc. n., France. *Dch.* Riessen ; a p.n. De Reasne, a Prot. ref. n., Lond. 1618
In Rot Hund.
REAVELEY. A loc. n., Northbd.
REAVELL. *See* Revill

REAY. A loc. n., Caithness, Kirkcudbright. Or *D.* Reeh; *S.*, *Dch.* Ree; *Fl.* Rey, Reh; *N.-Fr.* De Rea; *Fr.* Ray, Rayé; p.n. A Hugt. n., Lond. 1688

REBBECK. From Rebecq; a loc. n., Fland. Rebache, Hugt. n., Lond. 1688

RECKITT. *Fr.* Requette; *Dch.* Reket; p.n.; *N.-Fr. requette* (a stick). Or *A.S.* Ricard, Ricart; *Fl.* Reyekeart, Richet; *N.-Fr.* Racate; p.n. (firm rule)

REDAWAY. A loc. n., Devon

REDDAN, REDON. *Fr.* Redant; a p.n. (toothed)

REDDIE, REDDY. *See* Ready

REDDING. From Reading; a loc. n., Berks. Or *see* Reid

REDDISH. A loc. n., Ches. Or Redditch, Worcest.; or *G.* Rettisch; a p.n. *See* Reid

REDFORD. From Retford; a loc. n., Notts

REDGRAVE. A loc. n., Norf., Suff.

REDHEAD. *A.S.* Rædhæard, Rathart; p.n. (strong counsellor)

REDMAN, REDMAINE. *N.* Raðmaðr or Raðmann (counsellor); *D.* Raadman; *Fl.* Redeman; *A.S.* Rædman; *G.* Rathmann; p.n.

REDMOND. *A.S.* Rædmund (counsel protector)

REDPATH. A loc. n, Northbd.

REDWOOD. A loc. n., Devon

REECE, REESE. Welsh Rhys. Or *N.* Hrísi; a n.n. (illegitimate); *D.* Rüs; *Fl.* Reisse; *G.* Riess; *Dch.* Rees; p.n.

REED. A loc. n., Suff. Or *see* Reid

REEDER. *N.* Hreidarr (?) (a wreath); *D.* Redder; *A.S.* Rædhere, Reder; *G.* Reder; *Dch.* Reeder; p.n. (wise warrior)

REEKIE. *A.S.* Ric (rule); *Fr.* Ricquier; *D.* Rieck; *G.* Ricke, Rieck; *Dch.* Rieke; p.n. Rycke; loc. n., Belg.

REEKS. *Fl.* Rykers; a fam. n.

REEMAN. *Dch.* Rieman; a p.n.

REEVE. *G.* Riewe; *Dch.* Rieuwe; p.n. Rèves; a loc. n., Belg.; Rives, France. Or *A.S. réfa* (a tax gatherer). *See* Sheriff

REFFELL. *Fl.* Revael; a p.n. *See* Revill

REGAN. From Irish O'Regan; a p.n. Royeoghan (Roy's son)

REGESTER. A loc. corruption of Rochester (Lower)

REID. La Reid; a loc. n., Belg. *G.* Ried; *Dch.* Riede; *D.* Read; p.n. Or *A.S.* Ræd (red, also counsel)

REILLY. From the Irish Radheolagh or Raghalach; p.n. Comp. Reuilly; a loc. n., France. *D.B.* Ruhilie; a p.n.

REITH. From Reeth; a loc. n., Yorks

RELPH. *F.* Rôlf; *Dch.* Reelfs; *A.S.* Radulf, Ralf; p.n. *See* Rolfe

RELTON. From Wrelton; a loc. n., Yorks

REMINGTON. *See* Rimmington

REMNANT. *Fr.* Remont (?); a p.n. Remand, a Hugt. n., Lond. 1687

RENDALL, RENDEL. A loc. n., Orkney. Or *see* Randall

RENNALLS *See* Reynolds

RENNIE. *See* Rainey

RENNISON. *Fl.* Renson; a p.n. *See* Rain

RENSHAW. From Renishaw; a loc. n., Derbysh.

RENTON. A loc. n., Dumbarton. Or Rennington, Northbd.

RENWICK. A loc. n., Camb.

REPINGTON. From Repton; a loc. n., Derbysh. *D.B.* Rapendune

REPUKE. *Dch.*, *G.* Rehbock; *Fr.* Reboux (?), p.n. Or *see* Rebbeck

RESTALL. *See* Rastall

RESTHER. *N.-Fr.* Fitz-Reste; a p.n. Resteau, a Hugt. n., Lond. 1688

RETALLACK, RETALLICK. A loc. n., Cornw.

REVELEY. *See* Reaveley

P

REVEN. *See* Ruthven

REVILL. From Reville; a loc. n., Norm. *Fr.* Revel, Revelle; p.n. Hugt. n., Lond. 1618
Revel in Rot. Obl. et Fin., K. John.

REW. A loc. n., Devon. Rue, Dorset; Rue, France; Roux, Belg.

REYNOLDS. *N.* Rögnvaldr; *A.S.* Regnald; *D.*, *S.* Reinhold; *Dch.* Reinold, Rennel; p.n. (gods' wielder or ruler)

RHIMES. *See* Ream

RHIND. A loc. n., Perth

RHODES. From Rhodez; a loc. n., Aquitaine. A loc. n., Lancs. *N.-Fr.* De Rodes, 1202

RHYS. Welsh p.n. (a warrior)

RIBBANS, RIBBONS. *A.S.* Rip (reaper, also spoiler); *Dch.* Ribbink; *G.* Rippin; p.n. Or *see* Raban

RIBICK. *See* Rebbeck

RICE. *See* Rhys

RICH. From Riche; a loc. n., Lorraine

RICHARDS. *A.S.* Ricard; *Fr.* Richard; *F.* Rikkerd, Rikkert, Rikkerts; *Dch.* Ricard, Richards; p.n. (strong ruler). Contr. of Ricardus

RICHARDSON. *See* Rix

RICHBELL. *A.S.* Ricbeald (bold ruler)

RICHES. *A.S.* Richere, Ricerus; p.n. (ruler-warrior). *See* Rich

RICHFIELD. From Richeville; a loc. n., France

RICHFORD. From Rickford; a loc. n., Somers

RICHMOND. A loc. n., Surr., Yorks

RICKARBY. A loc. n., Cumb.

RICKET. *See* Reckitt. Ricquart, Hugt., Canterbury, 1622

RIDALL, RIDDEL, RIDDLE. A loc. n., Scotl. Or *D.* Riedel; *S.* Rydall; *Fr.* Ridel, Ridelle; a p.n. (wrinkle). Or dim. of Rid
Richard Ridel in Rot. Obl. et Fin., K. John. Also de Ridal.

RIDDETT, RIDET. *N.-Fr.*; p.n. Dim. of Rid (knight)

RIDDLESWORTH. From Roddlesworth; a loc. n., Lancs

RIDER. *See* Ryder

RIDGARD. *See* Rudyard. Or *A.S.* Ricweard; a p.n. (rule protector)

RIDGE. A loc. n., Devon, Glost., Salop, Wilts

RIDGELY. From Rugeley (?); a loc. n., Staffs

RIDGWAY. A loc. n., Devon, Somers

RIDGWELL. A loc. n., Ess.

RIDLEY. A loc. n., Ches., Kent, Northbd.

RIDOUT. *Fr.* Redouté; a p.n. (dreaded)

RIDPATH. *See* Redpath

RIDSDALE. A loc. n., Northbd.

RIGBY. A loc. n., Yorks (*D.B.* Rigbi)

RIGG. A loc. n., Dumfries

RIGGLESWORTH. *See* Riddlesworth

RIGGS. *See* Ridge

RILEY. *See* Reilly

RILLETT. *Fr.* Rouillet (rusty); *Fl.* Rielaert; Rillaert; p.n.

RIMMINGTON. A loc. n., Yorks (*D.B.* Renitone)
William de Rimington was Prior of Sawley Abbey and Chancellor of Oxford, A.D. 1372.

RING. *N.* Hringr (a ring); *Dch.* Ring; *G.* Ring; p.n.

RINGER. *A.S.* Hringware; *Old G.* Rincar; *Dch.* Rincker; *G.* Ringer p.n. (a warrior defended by rings or chain mail)

RINGROSE. *N.* Hringr; a p.n. ring); *hrós* (praise); *A.S.* Rin a p.n. (warrior)
Stephen Ryngros, Chaplain of Mary's, Scarborough, 1582. Y Wills.

RINTOUL. *Dch* Rintel; a p.n. Randall

RION. A loc. n., France. Ryan; *Fl.* Rion; p.n.

RIORDAN. Irish O'Riordan

RIPLEY. A loc. n., Derbysh., Ess., Surr., Yorks

RIPPER. *Dch.* Rippe; *Fl.* Ripet; p.n. *See* Reap

RIPPIN. *G.* Rippin; *Dch.* Ripping; a p.n.; fam. n. of Rip

RIPPINGILLE. From Rippingale; a loc. n., Lincs

RIPPON. From Ripon; a loc. n., Yorks

RIPSHER. *G.* Rippke; a p.n. Dim. of Rip

RISELEY. A loc. n., Derbysh.

RISING. A loc. n., Norf. Or *S.* Rising; a p.n.

RIST. *N.* Reistr (a twist); *G.* Rister; *D.*, *Fl.*, *Dch.* Rist; p.n.

RITCHIE. *A.S.* Righeah; *Fr.* Richet; p.n. (high ruler)

RITSON. A loc. n., Devon

RIVERS. *Fr.* Rivez; *D.* Rievers; p.n. From Rivière; a loc. n., Belg.

> Rivers in Roll of Battell Abbey. *D.B.* Riveire, a tenant in chief.

RIVETT. *N.-Fr.* Rivet; *Fl.* Riffaert; p.n.; *A.S.* Riu; a p.n. Contr. of Riculf (ruler-wolf)

RIVINGTON. A loc. n., Lancs

RIX. *G.* Rietsch; *Dch.* Rikke, Rikkers; *Fl.* Richez; p.n. *See* Riches

ROBB. *Fl.* Robbe; a p.n. *See* Roberts

ROBBINS. *Fl.* Robyns; a p.n; fam. n.

ROBERTS. *N.* Hró-bjartr; *A.S.* Rodbeort; *Fr.* Robert; *Dch.* Robart, Roberts; p.n. Robert's, for *N.-Fr.* Robertus (illustrious fame). *See* Christian names

ROBEY, ROBY. A loc. n., Derbysh., Lancs, Yorks

ROBIN. *Fr.*; p.n. Robain, Hugt., Lond. 1687

ROBINETT. *Fr.* Robinet. Dimin. of Robin

ROBINSON. *N.* Robbi, from Hró-bjartr (Robert); *Fl.* Robyns, Robson, Robisson; p.n. *See* Roberts. Prot. ref., Lond. 1618

ROBSON. *Fl.*; p.n.

ROCHE. *Fr.*; loc. and p.n. Hugt., Lond. 1687

ROCHEFORT. A loc. n., Belg. and Norm.

ROCKE. *A.S.* Roc; *N.-Fr.* De la Roca; *Dch.*, *G.* Rock; *Fr.* Rocque; p.n. (a rook)

> Roger Roc in Rot. Obl. et Fin., K. John; and Rot. Hund.

ROCKETT. From Rogate; a loc. n., Suss. Or *Fr.* Rochette, Roquet; p.n. From Roquette; a loc. n., Normandy

ROCKLEY. A loc. n., Herts, Notts, Wilts. *N.-Fr.* De Rokela; a p.n.

RODD. *A.S.* Rod, Rodda, Hrod, Rud, Rudda; p.n.; *N.* hróð (famous)

RODGERS. *N.* Hróð-geirr; *D.* Roedeger, Rodgers; *Fl.* Roger; *Fr.* Rogier; *G.* Roger; *A.S.* Rodgar, Roger; p.n. (famous spear)

RODNEY. From *N.-Fr.* Reyney or Radenay

RODWELL. *See* Rothwell

ROE. A loc. n., Herts. Or *see* Raw, Rowe

ROEBUCK. *See* Rebbeck

ROFFE. *N.-Fr.* De Rof; a p.n. *See* Rolfe. Hugt., Lond. 1687

ROGERS. *See* Rodgers

ROGERSON. *See* Rodgers. Or from Rogerstone; a loc. n., Monmouth (?)

ROKEBY. A loc. n., Yorks

ROLFE. *N.* Hródólfr, Hrólfr; *A.S.* Rodulf; *G.* Roll, Rolle, Rolof, Roff, Ruff; *D.B.* Ralf, Roulf, Rolf; *F.* Rôlf; *D.* Rohlf; *Fl.*, *Dch.* Roll, Rolff, Rol; p.n. (glorious wolf)

ROLL, ROLLE. Roly; a loc. n., Belg. *N.-Fr.* De Rouel; a p.n.

ROLLES. *See* Rowles

ROLLESTON. A loc. n., Staffs (*D.B.* Roolfeston)

ROLLING. *Fr.* Rollin; a p.n. *See* Rawling

ROLLINSON. *See* Rawlinson

ROLPH. *See* Rolfe

ROMER. From Roumare; a loc. n., Norm. Or *N.* Ramr (strong); *A.S.* Rom; *G.*, *Dch.* Römer; *Fl.* Romer; a p.n.

ROMILLY. A loc. n., Normandy. Romiley; a loc. n., Ches.
William de Romillé was the first Baron of Skipton, Yorks.

ROMNEY. A loc. n., Kent

RONALD. Scot. Ranald; a p.n. (power of judgment)

RONEG. From the Irish Mulrooney; a p.n.

RONEY. *N.-Fr.* De Roenai; a p.n.

ROOFE. *See* Roffe

ROOK. *N.* Hrúkr; p.n. *See* Rocke

ROOM. Rumes; a loc. n., Belg.; Ruoms, France. Or *A.S.* Rom, Rum; *G.* Ruhm; *Fl.* Rooms; p.n.

ROOPE, ROPE. *N.* Hrappr (a yeoman); *G.* Rupp; *A.S.* Hroppa, Rop, Roppa; *D.* Rupe; *Fl.* Roup; *N.-Fr.* de Rupe; p.n.

ROOT. *See* Rutt

ROPER. From Rupiere; a loc. n., Norm.

RORKE. From the Irish O'Rorke; a p.n.

ROSCOE. A loc. n., Yorks

ROSE. From Ros (now Rots); a loc. n., Norm. Or *N.* Hross, *hrósa* (praise); *A.S.* Ros; *D.*, *G.*, *Dch.*, *Fr.* Rose; a p.n. A Hugt. n., Lond. 1684

ROSHER. From Rochers; a loc. n., France. *Fr.* Rocher. Or *Dch.* Rosier; *Fl.* Rosaer; *D.* Roscher; *G.* Roescher; p.n. (praised warrior)

ROSKILL. From Rosskell or Hrosskell; a loc. n., Cumb. Also *N.* Hrosketel; *A.S.* Roschil; p.n. (horse-kettle)

ROSLYN. A loc. n., Edinburgh

ROSS. A loc. n., Heref., Perth, Yorks. *See* Rose

ROSSALL. A loc. n., Lancs, Yorks

ROSSER. *See* Rosher

ROSWELL. *Fr.* Rousselle; a p.n. *See* Russell. Hugt. n., Cant. 1622

ROTH. *See* Routh

ROTHERHAM. A loc. n., Yorks

ROTHWELL. A loc. n., Lincs, Northants, Yorks (*D.B.* Rodowelle)
Held by De Warneville.

ROTTER. *A.S.* Hroth; *Dch.* Rotte; *Fr.* Routier; p.n. (experienced)

ROTTON. *Dch.* Rooten; a p.n.; fam. n. of Rotte. Or *see* Roughton

ROUCH. *See* Rouse

ROUGH. *See* Ruff

ROUGHTON. A loc. n., Lincs, Norf., Salop

ROUNCE, ROUND. *N.-Fr.* Rotundus; a p.n. *See* Rands

ROUNTREE. From Rowantree; a loc. n., Cumb.

ROUPEL. *G.* Ruppel; a p.n.; *A.S.* Rup. Dim. (a tuft of hair)

ROUSBY. A loc. n., Yorks. *D.B* Rozebi

ROUSE. A loc. n., Cornw.; Roux Belg. *N.-Fr.* Le Roux; *Dch.* Rous; *G.* Rausch; *Fr.* Rousse Rouse; p.n. A Hugt. n., Lond 1618

ROUT. *N.* Rauðr (red); *G.* Ruth Roth, Rauter; *D.B.* Rot; Rauth; *Dch.* Root; *Fl.* Rowe p.n.

ROUTH. A loc. n., Yorks
Held by De Scruteville.

ROUTLEDGE. A loc. n., Cumb.

ROUTLEY. From Rothley; a n., Leics. Or *see* Routledge

Row, Rowe. From Roeux; a loc. n., France; or Roux, Belg. *Fr.* Raux, Réaux; p.n. An Irish p.n.; *ruadh* (red). A loc. n., Dumbarton, Somers, Yorks. *See* Raw, Roe

Rowan, Rowen, Rowing. *Dch.* Rouwen; *Fr.* Rouen; p.n. Hugt., Lond. 1618

Rowarth. A loc. n., Ches.

Rowbotham. From Robotham; a loc. n., Lancs (near Ashton-under-Lyne)

Robert Robotham of Raskyll, Yorks, received a grant of arms Dec. 1560. Compare Rowbarton, Somers.

Rowdon. From Rowden; a loc. n., Devon, Leics

Rowell. A loc. n., Glost. Or from Rouelles, France. A Hugt. n., Lond. 1687

Rowland. A loc. n., Derbysh. Or *see* Rawlence. Hugt., Dover, 1622

Rowlatt. From Rowlett; a loc. n., Kent. Or *Fr.* Roulet; a p.n.

Rowles. From Rolles; a loc. n., Ess. Or Rouelles, France

De Rolles in Rot. Obl. et Fin.

Rowley. From Reuilly; a loc. n., Norm. Also a loc. n., Dur., Staffs, Wilts

Rowling. *See* Rawlinson

Rowney. From Rosny; a loc. n., France. *Fr.* Rouneau; a p.n. Or *see* Roney

Roworth. A loc. n., Derbysh.

Rowsell. *Fl.* Roussel; a p.n. *See* Russell. A Hugt. n., Lond. 1618

Rowson. From Rowston; a loc. n., Lincs

Lowton. A loc. n., Salop, Yorks

Oxburgh. The county town

Oxby. A loc. n., Lincs, Yorks

oy. From Roye; a loc. n., France. Or *N.* Hroi; *Dch.* Rooij; *Fr.*, *G.* Roy; p.n. A Hugt. n., Lond. 1688. A loc. n., Belg.

Royal, Royle. *Fr.*; p.n. From Roisel; a loc. n., France

Galfrid Roille in Rot. Obl. et Fin., K. John.

Royce. *G.*, *Dch.*, *Fl.* Reuss; a p.n. *See* Rouse

Roycroft. *See* Rycroft

Royston. From Ryston; a loc. n., Herts, Norf., Yorks

Roythorne. From Rowthorne; a loc. n., Derbysh.

Rubery. A loc. n., Worcest.

Rubie. From Roubai; a loc. n., France. *Dch.* Rube; *G.* Rubie; *Fr.* Ruby; p.n. De Rewbay, a Hugt. n., Lond. 1618

Rudall. From Rudhall or Rudhale; a loc. n., Heref.

Rudd. *A.S.*, *D.* Rud; a p.n. Prot. ref., Lond. 1621. *See* Rutt

Ruddle. *See* Rudall

Ruddock. Dimin. of Rud

Rudgard. *See* Rudyard

Rudge. A loc. n., Devon, Somers, Staffs, Wilts

Rudland. From Rutland. Or *see* Rawlence

Rudrum. From Rotherham; a loc. n., Yorks (*D.B.* Rodreham)

Rudyard. A loc. n., Staffs

Ruff. *G.*; p.n.; Ruffus (red). Prot. ref., Lond. 1618

In Rot. Obl. et Fin.

Ruffell, Ruffles. *Fr.* Rouval; *G.* Rouvel; p.n.

Ruffitt. *Fr.* Rouffart; a p.n.

Ruggles. From Rugeley; a loc. n., Staffs. *D.B.* Rugehala, Rugelie. Or it may be from Rugles; a loc. n., Norm.

The final "s" is a recent addition. Members of the family who emigrated to New England, U.S.A., in 1637, spelled the name Ruggle, and their descendants have it both with and without the "s." It occurs also as Rogyll and Rugelay. The arms of Rugeley and Ruggles are identical.

RULE, RULLES. A loc. n., Belg.; Rull, Devon. *Fr.* Ruelle; *Dch.* Rühl; p.n.

RUMBALL. *G.* Rumpel; *Fl.* Rummel; p.n. *See* Rumbold

RUMBELOW, RUMBLOW. From Tromelow or Rumbelow (Atte-Trumelow); a loc. n., Wednesfield, Staffs

Stephen Rummelowe or Rumbilowe was governor of Nottingham Castle, A.D. 1369. The sailors' "Heave, oh, rumbylow" is a coincidence, and refers probably to the grog in prospect.

RUMBLE. *See* Rumbold

RUMBOLD. *A.S.* Rumbald, Rumbeald, Rumbold; p.n.; *D.B.* under-tenant; *Old G. hrom, hruam* (glory, praise), *bald* (bold) Stephanus Rambald in Rot. Obl. et Fin., K. John, 1207 (Hants).

RUMLEY. From Romilly; a loc. n., Norm.

RUMMINGS. *Dch.* Roumen; *S.* Rumin; *Fl.* Rumens, Rummens; p.n. Rummen; a loc. n., Belg.; fam. n. of Room

RUMNEY. *Dch.* Rummenie; a p.n. Or *see* Romney

RUMP. *D.* Rump; *G.* Rumpe, Rumpf; *Dch.* Rumpff; p.n. (body)

RUMSEY. From Romsey; a loc. n., Ess.

RUNACRES. *A.S.* Runwacer (?) (running guard); *Fl.* Runacher; p.n.

RUNDELL, RUNDLE. *S.* Rondahl; *Dch.* Rouendal; a loc. and p.n.

RUNHAM. A loc. n., Norf., Kent

RUNNACLES, RUNNECKLES. *G.* Runkel; *Dch.* Runckel; p.n. Dim. of *A.S. rynig* (runner)

RUNNALL. From Runhall; a loc. n., Norf.

RUNNICUS. *See* Runacres

RUNNIFF. *D.* Roennov; a p.n.

RUSBY. *See* Rousby

RUSCOE. *See* Roscoe

RUSE. From Roose; a loc. n., Lancs. Or *see* Rouse

RUSH. A loc. n., Dublin. Or *D., G., Dch.* Rusch; a p.n.

RUSHBROOK. A loc. n., Suff.

RUSHBURY. A loc. n., Heref.

RUSHTON. A loc. n., Ches., Dorset, Northants, Salop, Staffs

RUSHWORTH. From Rishworth; a loc. n., Yorks

RUSKIN. *A.S.* Ruscing; fam. n.; *Fl.* Raskin; *Fr.* Rasquin; p.n. Or *N. roskinn* (?), met. (vigorous, doughty, valiant), lit. (ripe, mature). *See* Rose

RUSS. A loc. n., Germ. *G., Dch., Fl.* Russ, Russe; p.n. *See* Rouse

RUSSELL. From Rosel; a loc. n., Norm.

Rushell or Rosel is in the Roll of Battell Abbey, and Huges de Rozel occurs as one of the benefactors of the abbey of St. Étienne at Caen, founded by William the Conqueror. Rozel, a tenant in chief in *D.B.*

RUST. *A.S.* Roswith (?) (greatly praised); *D., G., Dch.*; p.n.

RUSTON. A loc. n., Norf.

RUTH. *See* Routh

RUTHERFORD. A loc. n., Roxburgh. Also Ruddervoorde in Flanders

RUTHERGLEN. A loc. n., Lanark

RUTHVEN. A loc. n., Perth

RUTLAND. The county

RUTLEY. A loc. n., Worcest.

RUTT. *A.S.* Hrod, Rut; *Dch* Ruth (famous); p.n. *See* Rudd Rutes, Hugt. n., Lond. 1618

RUTTEN. *Dch.*; p.n.; fam. n. c Rutt

RUTTER. *N.* Hrútr (a ram); *Dc.* Rutter; p.n. Prot. ref., Lon⟨ 1618

RUTTLEGE. *See* Routledge

RUTTY. *Fr.* Routier; a p.n. ⟨ Rutter

RYALL. A loc. n., Devon. ⟨ Ryhall, Worcest. *See* Royle

RYAN. From Royan; a loc. n., Normandy; or Ruyen, Flanders. *D.* Ryan; *Fr.* Royon; p.n.

RYDER. From Ryther; a loc. n., Yorks. Or *N.* Hreidarr; *A.S.* Rid, Rida; *G.* Reuter, Reiter; *D.* Ryder; *Dch.* Ruijter; p.n. (horse soldier, knight)

RYE. A loc. n., Suss. Or Rie, Norm.

RYECROFT. A loc. n., Lancs, Yorks

RYGATE. From Reigate; a loc. n., Surr.

RYHOPE. A loc. n., Dur.

RYLAND. A loc. n., Lincs. Rylands; loc. n., Notts

RYLE. A loc. n., Northbd. *See* Royle

RYMAN. *See* Raymond

RYMER. A loc. n., Suff. Or *G.* Reimer; a p.n.

S

SABERTON. From Sapperton; a loc., Derbysh. Or Soberton, Hants

SABEY. *N.-Fr.* Saba, Sabe; *A.S.* Saba, Sæba, Sæbeorht; *Fr.* Sabbe; *D.* Saaby; p.n. (sea illustrious). *See* Sebright

SABIN. *Fl.* Saapin; a p.n.; fam. n.

SACH. *N.* Saxi (Saxon); *G.* Sacha, Sack; *Dch.* Saacke, Sak; *D.* Sack; *N.-Fr.*, *Dch.* Sac; *Fl.* Seck; p.n. Prot. ref., Lond. 1618

SACKVILLE. From Sacquenville; a loc. n., Normandy

De Sacheuilla in *D.B.*, Soohevill, Sekeville in Rot. Obl. et Fin., K. John.

SACRET. *Fr.* Secret; a p.n.; *sakeret* (a hawk)

SACRISTAN. From Sacriston; a loc. n., Dur.

SADD. A loc. n., Devon

SADDINGTON. A loc. n., Leics

SADDLE. A loc. n., Argyll

SADGROVE. *See* Sitgreaves

SADLER. *G.* Sattler; a p.n.

SAFFELL. *See* Saville

SAFFERY. *See* Savery

SAFFORD. From Salford; a loc. n., Lancs

SAGE. *N.-Fr.* le Sage (Sapiens), a p.n.

SAGGERS. *A.S.* Sægær, Sagar; *Fl.* Sagaer, Segers, Sager; p.n. (sea spear)

SAINSBURY. From Saintbury; a loc. n., Worcest.

ST AUBYN. From St Albino, near Evreux, Norm.

Granted tithes to St Taurin, Evr. 980. Witness found. chart. Barnstaple Abbey, *temp.* Will. I.

ST CLAIR. A loc. n., Normandy

Sent Clere in Roll of Battell Abbey. *D.B.* de Sent Cler.

ST GEORGE. From St Georges; a loc. n., Norm. and Belg.

In Roll of Battell Abbey.

ST JOHN. *Fr.* Seuntjens; *Fl.* Vansintjan; a p.n

Three local names in Flanders are Saint Jean (lez-Ypres), Saint-Jean-Geest, Saint-Jean-in-Frems. Sent John in Roll of Battell Abbey.

ST LEGER. From Saint-Léger; a loc. n., Norm.

Sent Legere in Roll of Battell Abbey.

ST QUINTIN. A loc. n., Norm.

Sent Quintin in Roll of Battell Abbey and *D.B.*

SAINTY, SAINTES. A loc. n., Brabant. *Dch.* Sante; *Fl.* Senty; *Fr.* Saintais; p.n.

SAIR, SAIRS. *See* Sayer

SAITE. *A.S.* Sæta; *N.-Fr.* Saiete; *Fr.* Sethe; p.n, (a settler)

Seyot in Rot. Hund.

SALE. *N.-Fr.* De Salle; a p.n. A loc. n., Ches.; Zele, Belg.

SALES. From Seilles; a loc. n., Belg.

SALINGER. *N.* Sælinger; a n.n. (a wealthy man); *G.*; p.n. Prot. ref., Lond. 1618

SALISBURY. The city of that name

SALKELD. A loc. n., Cumb.

SALL. *A.S.* Sal, Sele; *Fr.* Salles; p.n. *See* Sale

SALLIS. From Sallys; a loc. n., Heref. Or *Dch.* Salis; *Fr.* Salles; p.n. Salles; a loc. n., Belg.

SALLOWS. From Sallowes; a loc. n., Norf.

SALMON. *N.* Sölmundr (sallow protector); *Fl.* Salman, Salmain, Solmon; *G.* Sallmann; Scot. Salmond; *A.S.* Salomon; *N.-Fr.* Salmon; p.n.

SALT. A loc. n., Staffs. Or *Dch.* Solt; a p.n.

SALTER. *N.-Fr.* le Salter; *S.* Solter; *Dch.* Selter; p.n.

SALTHOUSE. A loc. n., Lancs, Norf.

SALTWELL. A loc. n., Lincs

SALVIDGE. *A.S.* Selewig; *D.* Selvig; *N.-Fr.* Salvage; p.n. (dark, swarthy)

SAMBRIDGE. *See* Sambrook

SAMBROOK. A loc. n., Salop

SAME. From Seaham; a loc. n., Dur.

SAMERS. *See* Sammars

SAMES, SAMS. From Seames; a loc. n., Yorks. Or *D.*; p.n.

SAMMARS. From Samarés; a loc. n., Jersey

SAMMON. *See* Salmon or Seaman

SAMPLE. *See* Sempill

SAMPSON. From St S.; a loc. n., Norm.

SANDAY. From St Die, France; or Sandy; a loc. n., Beds. Or *see* Sandys

SANDBACH. A loc. n., Ches. Or *D.* Sandbech; a loc. and p.n.

SANDBROOK. *See* Sandbach

SANDELL. From Sendall; a loc. n., Yorks. Or *D.*, *S.* Sandell; a p.n.

SANDEMAN. *Dch.* Sandman; a p.n. *See* Sandys

SANDERSON. *S.* Sanderson. *See* Sandys

SANDFORD. A loc n., Devon, Lanark, Salop, Somers, Westmd.

SANDHALL. *See* Sandell

SANDHAM. From Sandholme; a loc n., Lincs, Yorks

SANDIFER. From Sandiford; a loc. n., Staffs

SANDILANDS. A loc. n., Lanark

SANDLANT. *S.* Sandlund; a loc. and p.n.

SANDS. *See* Sandys

SANDWELL. A loc. n., Devon, etc.

SANDWITH. A loc. n., Cumb.

SANDYS. *N.* Sandi; n.n.; *G.*, *D.*, *S.* Sand, Sander; *Dch.* Sande, Sanders; *Fl.* Sannes, Sanders; *A.S.* Sand, Sanda, Sendi; p.n. (a messenger)

SANGER. *A.S.* Sangere (a singer); *Fr.* Sangier; *Dch.* Sanger; p.n.

SANGSTER. *Dch.* Sangstier; a p.n.; *A.S.* Sangstere (a female singer)

SANKEY. A loc. n., Lancs. Or *Fl.* Sancke; *Fr.* Sanchez; *Dch.* Sanches; p.n. Dim. of Sand.

SANN. *See* Sandys

SANQUHAR. A loc. n., Dumfries

SANSOM. *Fr.* Sanson; *D.B.* Sanson and de St Sansone; p.n.

SANXTER. *See* Sangster

SAPEY. From Cepie; a loc. n., France. Or *see* Seapey

SAPSED, SAPSEID. From Shepshed; a loc. n., Leics

SAPSWORTH. *See* Sopworth

SAPWELL. From Sopewell; a loc. n., Herts

SARE. From Sarre; a loc. n. Kent. *See* Sayer

SARLL. *See* Serle

SARSON. A loc. n., Hants. O *N.-Fr.* Sarazin; a p.n.

SARTAIN. *Fr.* Sarton; a p.n.

SARTORIS or SARTRES. *Fl.* Sa torius; a p.n. A Hugt. n., Lon 1684

SASSE. *A.S.* Sas, Sahs, Sæx ; *N.-Fr.* De Sace ; *D.* Sass ; p.n. (a Saxon)

SATCHELL, SATCHWELL. A loc. n., Hants. *See* Setchell

SATTERLEIGH. A loc. n., Devon

SATTERTHWAITE. A loc. n., Lancs

SATTLEY. *See* Satterleigh

SAUCHIE. A loc. n., Perth

SAUL. From Saughall ; a loc. n., Ches. Saul ; a loc. n., Glost. Or *N.* Sjölfr, contr. of Sæ-úlfr (sea-wolf) ; *G.* Saul, Sauler ; *D.B.* Saulf, Seulf, Saul ; *Dch.* Scholl, Saul ; *Fl.* Swolf, Soualle ; p.n.

SAUMAREZ. *See* Sammars

SAUNDERS. *See* Sandys

SAURY. *See* Sawrey

SAVAGE. *Fr.* Sauvage ; a p.n. *See* Salvidge

Le Sauvage in Rot. Obl. et Fin., K. John. A Hugt. n., Lond. 1687.

SAVERY. *Fr.* Savary, Sevrey. From Sivry ; a loc. n., Belg. De Savary, a Hugt. n., Lond. 1687

SAVILLE. *N.-Fr.* De Sevele, De Sayville ; *D.* Sevel ; p.n. From Serville (?) ; a loc. n., Belg.

SAVORY. *See* Savery

SAW. *Fr.* Saut ; a p.n. (a leap). Or *A.S.* Sawata ; a p.n. (sower)

SAWBRIDGE. A loc. n., Warw., Westmd.

SAWER. *See* Sawyer

SAWREY. A loc. n., Lancs. Sorée, Belg.

SAWYER, SOHIER. A loc. n., Belg. *Fr.* Soyer ; a p.n.

SAWYERS. A loc. n. in Essex. Or Sahurs, Norm.

SAXBY. A loc. n., Leics, Lincs

SAXELBY. A loc. n., Leics

SAXTON. A loc. n., Yorks

SAY. Séez ; a loc. n., Norm. Or *A.S.* Se, Sæ, Sig (victory) ; *Fr.* Saye ; *Fl.* Saey ; *Dch.* See ; p.n.

SAYCE. *Fr.* Sayes ; *Dch.* Seys ; p.n.

SAYER. *A.S.* Sihar (victorious warrior) ; *G.* Sehr ; *Old G.* Sigheri ; *Fl.* Sehier ; *D.*, *Fr.* Seyer ; p.n. Or St Saire ; a loc. n., Norm. Serre, Hugt. n.

SAYLE. *See* Sale

SAYMER. *A.S.* Sigemær (victory famous), or Sæmœr (sea-famous) ; *D.B.* Semar, Samar ; *Dch.* Seemer, or St Maur (?) ; p.n. Simore, Hugt. 1618

SCADDING. *D.* Schad, Skade ; p.n.

SCAGELL. *See* Scargill

SCAIFE. *N.* Skeifr ; a n.n. (askew) ; *Fl.* Scaff ; *G.* Skiefe ; *D.* Skife ; p.n. Skive ; a loc. n., Den.

SCALES. A loc. n., Lancs

Or from Hardwin de Scalers or D'Echellers, a follower of the Conqueror, and tenant in chief in *D.B.* William de Escales in Rot. Obl. et Fin., K. John.

SCAMBLER. *G.* Schammler ; a p.n. *See* Scammell

SCAMMELL. *N.* Skam-háls ; a n.n. (short neck). Or dim. of *N.* Skammi ; *A.S.* Scamma (the short) ; *G.* Schammel ; a p.n.

SCANES. *A.S.* Scan ; a p.n. (shiny) ; *Dch.* Schans ; a fam. n.

SCARBOROUGH. A loc. n., Yorks

SCARCE. From Skears ; a loc. n., Dur. Or *see* Shears

SCARD. *See* Scarth

SCARE. *G.* Schar ; *Dch.* Schier ; p.n. ; *N. sker* ; *A.S. scear* (share)

SCARFE. *A.S.* Sceorf ; *G.*, *D.*, *Dch.* Scharf ; a p.n. (sharp). *See* Sharpen

SCARLES. *See* Scarll

SCARLETT. From Escarlat ; a loc. n., Norm. *G.* Scharlot ; a p.n.

SCARLL. From Scarle ; a loc. n., Notts

SCARSBROOK. From Scarisbrick ; a loc. n., Lancs

SCARTH. A loc. n. (a mountain pass). Or *N.* Scarði ; n.n. (harelip) ; *D.* Scard ; *G.* Scharte ; p.n.

SCARVELL. From Escardeville; a loc. n., Norm.

SCATTERGOOD. *See* Shadgot

Schatregod, Rot. Hund. 1273; Scatergude, Test. Ebor. 1481.

SCHICKLE. *N.* Skekill (shank); *G.* Schichel; p.n.

SCHOFIELD. From Scholefield; a loc. n., Lancs. Or Escoville, Norm.

SCHOLES. A loc. n., Yorks. Or *Fl.* Schoels; a p.n. *See* Scully

SCHOLEY. *See* Scully

SCHOOBERT. *G.* Schubart; a p.n.

SCHUSTER. *D.* Schuster; a p.n. (a shoe-mender)

SCOBEL. A loc. n., Devon

SCOGGINS. *N.* Skaggi; a p.n. (skew); *A.S.* Scacca; *D.* Schackinger; *Dch.* Schokking; *Fl.* Schaekens, Shoukens; fam. n.

SCOONES. *Dch.* Schoen; a p.n.

SCOPES. *A.S.* Scop (a poet, minstrel); *G.* Schoppe; p.n.

SCORER. From Scorrer; a loc. n., Cornw. Or *A.S.* Scorra; a p.n. (scarred)

SCOTCHER. *A.S.* Scot (an arrow); *Dch.* Schotse; p.n. Dim of Scot

SCOTCHMER. *A.S.* Scotmær (famous archer); *Dch.* Schottemeijer; p.n.

SCOTT. *N.* Skati (a lordly man), or Skotti (archer); n.n.; *G.* Schotte; *Dch.* Schot; *Fr.* Scotti; *S.*, *D.* Skotte; p.n.

Jordan Scot in Rot. Obl. et. Fin., K. John.

SCOTTER. A loc. n., Lincs

SCOTTOW. A loc. n., Norf.

SCOURFIELD. *See* Schofield

SCOVELL. From Escoville (now Ecoville); a loc. n., Normandy

Radulph de Scovill held land in Wilts, *temp.* K. John.

SCRACE. *See* Scrase

SCRAFIELD. From Scrayfield; a loc. n., Lincs

SCRAGGS. *See* Scroggs

SCRAGIE. *See* Scroggie

SCRASE. *A.S.* Scræwa; a p.n (a shrewmouse). Or *N.* Skreyja; a n.n. (a boaster); *Fl.* Schreyers (?); a fam. n.

SCREETON. From Screveton; a loc. n., Notts; locally pron. Screeton

SCRIME. *N.* Skrymir (n. of a giant); *G.* Schrimmer; p.n.

SCRIMGEOUR. A loc. n., Scotl.

SCRIMSHAW, SCRIMSHIRE. *See* Skrymsher

SCRIVEN. A loc. n., Yorks

SCRIVENER. Belonging to Scriven. Or a law-writer

SCROGGIE. From Scrogie; a loc. n., Perth

SCROGGS. A loc. n., Cumb., Dumfries

SCROGHAM. A loc. n.

SCROTTOW. A loc. n.

SCRUBY. From Scrooby; a loc. n., Lincs, Yorks

SCRUTON, SCRUTTON. A loc. n., Yorks

SCRYMGEOUR. *See* Skrimgeour

SCUDAMORE. From Escudimore; a loc. n., Norm.

Sent Scudamore in Roll of Battell Abbey. It is not in *D.B.*, unless Scudet, a tenant in chief, be the same.

SCULLY. *N.-Fr.* De Scoleio. Or *N.* Skuli (a protector); *G.* Schylla; *A.S.* Scule, Scula; p.n.

SCUPHAM. From Scupholme; a loc. n., Lincs

SCURLL. *N.* Skirvill (?) (the name of a dwarf); *G.* Skeurell; p.n. Or *see* Scarll

SCURRAH, SCURRY. *See* Scorer

SCUTT. *D.* Skytt; *Dch.* Schutt; p.n. *See* Skeat. Hugt. n., Lond. 1687

SEABER. *Fr.* Sibert; a p.n. *See* Seabright

SEABOURNE. *N.* Sæbjörn; *A.S.* Sigbeorn; a p.n. (victorious bear)

SEABRIGHT. *A.S.* Sæbeorht ; *G.* Seibert, Siebert ; p.n. (sea-illustrious)

SEABROOK. A loc. n., Kent

SEABURY. *A.S.* Sæburh ; a p.n. (sea-protection)

SEADON. *Fr.* Sidon ; a p.n.

SEAFORD. A loc. n., Suss.

SEAGER, SEAGO. *N.* Siggi, dimin. of Sigurðr ; *A.S.* Secgga, Sigar ; *Dch.* Segar, Seger, Sieger ; *F.* Sikke ; *D.* Sekker, Seeger ; *S.* Seger ; *Fl.* Segher ; *G.* Sieg ; p.n. (victory spear)

SEAGRAVE. A loc. n., Leics, Northants

SEAKER. *See* Seager

SEAL. A loc. n., Kent, Leics, Surr. Or *see* Sill

SEALBY. From Selby ; a loc. n., Yorks

SEALEY. *See* Seeley

SEAMAN, SEAMON. *A.S.* Sæmann ; *Dch.* Seeman ; p.n. (a sailor)

SEAPEY. *N.* Sibbi, pet n. of Sigbaldr (foremost in victory) ; *F.* Sebo, Sibo ; *A.S.* Sibba, Sibbi, Sibold ; *G.* Siber, Seppe ; *Dch.* Siep, Sepp, Seepe ; p.n. *See* Sapey

SEAR, SEARS, SEEAR, SEER. From Cire ; a loc. n., France. *G.* Zier ; a p.n. Or *see* Sayer

SEARBY. A loc. n., Lincs

SEARCH, SERWECH. *N.-Fr.* De Cherches. Or *A.S.* Siric, Sigeric ; *Dch.* Sierich ; p.n. (victorious ruler)

SEARLE. *See* Serle

SEARY. From Cirey ; a loc. n., France

SEATLE. A loc. n., Lancs

SEATON. A loc. n., Cumb., Devon, Dur., Nairn, Northbd., Ross, Yorks. *D.B.* Seton

SEAVERS. *Dch.* Sieverts ; *D.*, *G.* Sievers ; *Fl.* Severs, Seyffers ; p.n. *See* Seward

SEAWARD. *A.S.* Sæweard ; a p.n. (sea warden). Or *see* Seward

SECCOMBE. A loc. n., Devon. Or Seacombe, Ches.

SECKER. *See* Seager. Prot. ref., Lond. 1618

SEDDING. *A.S.* Sidewine (?) ; *Fr.* Sedyn ; p.n. (a great friend)

SEDDON. *See* Sedding

SEDGER. *Fr.* Segers ; a p.n. *See* Seager

SEE. *See* Say

SEELEY. From Sillé ; a loc. n., Normandy ; Silly ; a loc. n., Belg. Or *G.* Siele, Sille ; *Fr.* Sillyé ; p.n. *See* Sill. Hugt., Lond. 1621

SEEVILL. *See* Civill

SEFTON. From Sephton ; a loc. n., Lancs

SEGON. *A.S.* Segen, Segwine, Sigen, Sigewine ; *Fl.* Seghin ; p.n. (victorious friend). Seguin, Hugt. n., Lond. 1688

SEGRAVE. *See* Seagrave

SEGRE. *A.S.* Sigar ; a p.n. *See* Segon

SEILY. From Zele ; a loc. n., Belg. Or *see* Seeley

SELBY. A loc. n., Yorks

SELDEN. From Seldon ; a loc. n., Devon

SELF. *N.* Sjölfr, a contr. of Sæ-ulfr (sea-wolf) ; *Fl.* Swolf ; *A.S.* Seolf, Seulf ; p.n.

SELKIRK. A loc. n., Scotl.

SELL. From Celles ; a loc. n., Belg. *Dch.*, *G.* Selle ; *Fl.* Sell ; p.n.

SELLERS. *Dch.* Zeller ; *Fl.* Selders ; *N.-Fr.* Selchar ; *Old G.* Salahar. Or *A.S.* Sellier (dark warrior) ; *Fr.* Sellau ; p.n.

SELLEY. *Fr.* Sailly ; a p.n. Or from Selly ; a loc. n., Salop

SELLICK. From Sellack ; a loc. n., Heref. Or Zellick, Belg.

SELLINGER. *See* St Leger

SELWY, SELWYN. *A.S.* Selui, Selwine ; *Fl.* Sallewyn ; p.n. (dark friend)

Saxon tenant in *D.B.* William Selveyn held land in Oxon, *temp.* K. John.

SEMAIN, SEMMENCE, SEMMENS, SEMON. *Fr.* Sement; a p.n. *See* Symonds. Hugt., Lond. 1618

SEMPER. *G.*; p.n. Or *Fr.* Saint-Pierre

SEMPILL, SEMPLE. A loc. n., Scotl. Or *Fl.* Sempels ; a p.n.
Robert de Sempill, of Renfrew, *temp.* Alex. III., Scotl.

SENDALL. *D.* Sandell; *Fl.* Sendall ; p.n.

SENIOR. From Signau (?); a loc. n., Switz.

SENNETT, SENNITT. From St Neot ; a loc. n., Cornw.

SENTANCE. From St Anne's ; a loc. n., Cornw. Or *Fr.* Seuntjens ; a p.n. *See* St John

SEPPINGS. *See* Seapey

SERJEANT. *Fr.* Sergeant ; a p.n. ; *Lat.* Servientem

SERLE. *A.S.* Særle ; *Fr.* Serlé, Serlui ; *D.B.* Serlo ; *Dch.* Sarlie ; *S.* Serling ; p.n. (a suit of armour)
Magister Serlo in Rot. Obl. et Fin., K. John (Devon), A.D. 1205.

SERMON. *Fr.* Serment ; Hugt. p.n. Also Sermain ; *A.S.* Saraman ; *N.-Fr.* Sireman ; p.n. (armour man)

SERRES. From Serez ; a loc. n., Norm. *N.-Fr.* De Siry ; *Fr.* Serès ; *Fl.* Serruys ; p.n. A Hugt. n., Lond. 1622

SERVANT. *Fr.* Serviant ; a p.n. *See* Serjeant

SERVICE, St Servais ; a loc. n., Belg. *Fr.* Servais ; a p.n.

SESSENS. *See* Sisson

SETCHELL. From Setchell ; a loc. n., Camb. Or Sachville, Norm.

SETON. *See* Seaton

SETTERINGTON. A loc. n., Yorks

SETTLE. A loc. n., Yorks

SEWARD. *N.* Sigvatr (bold in victory), a name of Odin ; *D.* Sivert ; *S.* Sivard ; *G.* Sievert, Siewert ; *Fl.* Siffert ; *Dch.* Sieuwerts ; *D.B.* Siward, Seward, Suert ; p.n.

SEWILL, SEWELL. *A.S.* Sæweald (sea ruler). *See* Saville

SEXTON. *See* Saxton

SEYMOUR. From St Maur; a loc. n., Norm. Or *see* Saymer
In Roll of Battell Abbey.

SHACKLE. *Dch.* Schakel ; a p.n. ; *A.S.* sceacul (a shackle)

SHACKLETON. From Shakerton (?) ; a loc. n., Dur.

SHACKSBEE. From Skegby (?) (*D.B.* Schegebi) ; a loc. n., Notts. *D.* Schacke ; *A.S.* Scæcca ; p.n. ; *bær* or *byr* a (dwelling). Comp. Shakerly, Shackerston, Exbear, Ailsbeare, Shebbeare, etc.
In Rot. Obl. et Fin. it is Scheggeby. Shacksbee is a p.n. in Mass., U.S.A.

SHACKSON. *D.* Schacke ; *Dch.* Schaik, Schake ; *G.* Schach ; *Fl.* Schack, Schaeck, Schaek; p.n. *A.S.* Sceacca (brandisher)

SHADBOLT. *A.S.* Cædbeald ; a p.n. (war prince, or bold in war)

SHADDICK, SHADDOCK. *G.* Schadeck ; p.n. Dim. of Chad

SHADE. *See* Sheedy

SHADFORD. From Shadforth ; a loc. n., Dur.

SHADGOT. *Old G.* Hadugot ; *Fr.* Chagot ; p.n. ; *A.S.* Ceaddagod, Chadgod (war Goth)

SHADRAKE. *A.S.* Ceadric ; *Old G.* Chadric ; *G.* Schadrich ; p.n. (war ruler)

SHADWELL. A loc. n., Middlx., Salop, Yorks

SHAFT. *N.* Skapti (a shaft-maker) ; *A.S.* Sceaft ; *D.* Skafte ; *G.* Schaffert ; p.n.

SHAFTO. From Shaftoe ; a loc. n., Northbd. Or *see* above

SHAKERLEY. A loc. n., Lancs, Salop

SHAKESPEARE. *See* Shacksbee
Or *N.-Fr.* Saquespée ; a p.n., from *saquer* (to shake), *spée* (a lance.) *Lat. spatha* (a long sword.) Hence the personal name Saquespée or Sache-Espée.

SHAKESPEARE—*continued*

A.S. scæccaspeare means one who shakes or brandishes a spear, but there is no such personal name in any known list.

The *N.-Fr.* form, however, appears in the Norman records.

In 1195 Roger Sakespee paid a fine of 10s. in the bailifry of the Caux near Lillebonne. In 1198 William Sakespee occurs in the same bailifry. In 1195 William Sakespee owed two marks as security for Reginald le Blaier in the bailifry of Hiesmes. In 1203 Roger Sacespee paid a fine in the bailifry of Coutances, and Godfrey Saccspee another fine at the same time and place. (Great Rolls of the Exchequer, Normandy.)

The Archives du Calvados relate a donation made in 1241, by Roger de Rupiere, to the Abbey of Villers-Canivet of all the land which Thomas Sach - Espée held of him in Grenteville. Another gift is recorded, made in 1250, to the Abbey of Troarn, by Robert, called Saquespée, of certain rights in corn in the parish of Touffréville. Again, Robert Saquespée, in 1257, sells to Troarn divers rents, and a sale is made in 1294 by Raoul de Noerville to Master Philippe Saquespée of a rent.

M. Jal, in his *Glossaire nautique*, mentions one Robin Saque-Espée, a pilot of a galliot (Anthoine-Nègre), and in the *Memorial de la Chambre des Comptes* of Paris, 1424, Ducange refers to a canon bearing the name of Jacob Saque-espée. Lastly, it occurs as a local name. There is a gorge or defile in la Manche, near Mortain called " Pertuis de Saque-spée," which, according to an ancient tradition, was the scene of a battle ; and there is also another place of the name in the commune of Cérences, in the same department. (Moisy, *Glossaire Anglo-Normand.*)

The question arises—did a branch of the Norman family return to Normandy after acquiring the English local name ?

SHALDERS. *N.* Skjöldr ; *A.S.* Scald, Sceald (a shield) ; *Fl.* Scholders ; p.n. *See* Skelt

SHALE. *See* Skeels

SHALLESS. *Dch.* Schallies ; *G.* Schallisch ; p.n. *See* Callis

SHAMBROOK. *See* Sambrook

SHAND, SHANDY. From Chanday ; a loc. n., Normandy

SHANKS. *D., Dch.* Schank ; *Fl.* Schangh ; p.n. ; *sceanca* (leg)

SHANNON. Irish Shanahan ; a p.n. (a fox)

SHAPCOTT. A loc. n., Devon

SHAPLAND. From Shopland ; a loc. n., Ess.

SHARDALOW, SHARDLOW. A loc. n., Derbysh.

SHARLAND. From Shirland ; a loc. n., Derbysh. (?)

SHARMAN. From Charmont (?) ; a loc. n., France. Or *G.* Scharmann ; *Dch.* Schürman ; *D.* Schauman ; *D.B.* Sceman (?) ; p.n. (Shearman). *See* trade names, p. 13

SHARP. *A.S.* Scearp, Scerp ; *N.-Fr.* Poinant ; *Dch.* Scharp ; p.n. (sharp, quick, skilful)

Scarp in Rot. Hund.

SHARPEN, SHARPINS. *N.* Skarp-heðinn, Skarpin (dried goat-skin coat) ; *G.* Scharf, Scharfen ; p.n. ; *A.S.* Scerphuin

SHARPUS. *Dch.* Schaapes ; a p.n.

SHARR. *See* Shaw

SHARWOOD. *See* Sherwood

SHATTICK, SHATTOCK. *G.* Schattke ; a p.n. *See* Shaddick

SHATTON. A loc. n., Derbysh.

SHAUL. From Shawell ; a loc. n., Leics

SHAVE. From Chièvres (?) ; a loc. n., Belg. Or *D.* Schevers ; *Fl.* Schaeff ; *G.* Schäfer ; p.n. *See* Chafy

Chievre, tenant in chief, *D.B.*

SHAW. A loc. n., Lancs, Oxf., Wilts. From *N.* Skógr (a wood). Or *S.* Skog ; *D.* Schau, Shaw ; *Dch.* Schouw, Schowe ; *Fl.* Schaugh ; p.n. Sceaux ; a loc. n., France

SHAWFIELD. A loc. n., Lancs

SHAWNEY. *See* Shorney

SHEAR. From Shere; a loc. n., Surr. Or *see* Shears

SHEARER. *A.S.* Scira; a p.n. *See* Shires

SHEARHOD. *A.S.* Scirhód; a p.n. (bright hood)

SHEARS. *A.S.* Scir; *Dch.* Schier; *G.* Schierse; p.n. (glorious)

SHEAVYN. *A.S.* Sceafwine (sheaf friend); *S.* Schevin; *Fl.* Scheyvin; a p.n.

SHEEDY. From the Irish *sioda* (silk). *N.* Skíði (a kind of bird); *G.* Schiedeck; *Dch.* Scheijde; *D.* Scythe; p.n.

SHEEKEL. *See* Shickle

SHELDON. A loc. n., Derbysh., Devon

SHELDRACK, SHELDRAKE, SHELD-RICK. *A.S.* Scealdric; a p.n. (shield ruler)

SHELFORD. A loc. n., Warw.

SHELL. An Irish corruption of Shields, Shiel

SHELLEY. A loc. n., Yorks

SHELTON. From Skelton; a loc. n., Yorks (*D.B.* Scheltun). Or Shelton, Beds, Norf.

SHEMMILL. From Chemille; a loc. n., France

SHENSTONE. A loc. n., Staffs

SHEPHERD, SHEPPARD. From Cheb-bard; a loc. n., Dorset. Or *Dch.* Schappert; a p.n. *A.S. scephyrde* (a shepherd)

SHEPPEY. A loc. n., Kent

SHERATON. A loc. n., Dur.

SHERBORNE. A loc. n., Devon, Dorset, Glost., Hants, Somers

SHERBROOKE. From Shirebrook; a loc. n., Derbysh.

SHERIDAN. From Shrawardine; a loc. n. , Salop. Or *A.S.* Scerda; *S.* Scherdin; p.n.

SHERIFF. *N.* Greifi; n.n. *A.S.* Geréfa; *Engl.* Reeve, Shire-reeve; *G.* Schriefer; *D.* Schreve; p.n.; the office

SHERINGHAM. A loc. n., Norf.

SHERINGTON. A loc. n., Wilts

SHERLOCK. From Shurlach; a loc. n., Ches.

SHERRARD, SHERRATT. From Che-ratte; a loc. n., Belg. Or *A.S.* Scirheard; *N.-Fr.* Sirart, Scirat (clever, firmness), Gerhard; *Fr.* Gerard; p.n. (firm spear). Sher-aret, Flemish Prot. ref., Lond. 1618

SHERREN, SHERRIN. *See* Sherwin

SHERRINGTON. A loc. n., Bucks, Wilts

SHERRY. *See* Serres

SHERSBY. From Shearsby; a loc. n., Leics

SHERT. *See* Sherrard
  In old documents Short is sometimes spelled Shert.

SHERVIL. From Sherwill; a loc. n., Devon

SHERWIN. *A.S.* Sceorfwine, Scorphuin; *D.* Scherwin; *Fl.* Scheyvin; *Dch.* Scherren; *G.* Scherwing; p.n. (clever friend)

SHERWOOD. A loc. n., Notts

SHEW. *See* Shaw

SHEWILL. *Dch.* Schewel; a p.n.

SHEWRING. From Shering; a loc. n., Ess. Or *Dch.* Schuring; a p.n.

SHICKLE. *G.* Schickel; a p.n.

SHICLE. *See* Shickle

SHIELDS, SHIELLS. From Shields; a loc. n., Dur.

SHILDRICK. *See* Sheldrick

SHILLAKER. From Shellacres; a loc. n., Northbd.

SHILLCOCK. *G.* Schilke; a p.n. Dim of *A.S.* Scel, Sceld; p.n.

SHILLING. A loc. n., Dorset. Or *A.S.* Scilling, Scylding; *D., G., Dch.* Schilling; p.n. Descendants of Scyld (shield)

SHILLINGFORD. A loc. n., Devon

SHILLITOE. *A.S.* Scealda; *Dch.* Schilte; *G.* Schilter; p.n. (shield bearer). Or *Ital.* Sillito (?)

SHILTON. A loc. n., Northants, Oxf., Worcest.

SHIMMIN. *D.* Schieman; a p.n. *See* Skey

SHINGLE. *Dch.* Schenkel; a p.n.

SHINGLETON. *See* Singleton

SHINN, SHINNER. From the Irish Shinan, originally O'Shanahan; a p.n. (Lower). Or *A.S.* Sin; a p.n. = *sig* (victory)

SHIPP. *A.S.* Scepi; *D.* Schipke; *Dch.* Schipper; a p.n. (a sailor)

SHIPPARD. *See* Sheppard

SHIPPEY. From Shiphay; a loc. n., Devon

SHIPPING. From Shippon; a loc. n., Oxf. Or fam. n. of Shipp

SHIPLEY. A loc. n., Derbysh., Salop, Yorks

SHIPSIDES. From Shepshed (?); a loc. n., Leics

SHIPTON. A loc. n., Glost., Oxf., Salop, Yorks

SHIPWASH. From Sheepwash; a loc. n., Devon, Northbd.

SHIPWAY. *See* Shippey

SHIRES. *A.S.* Scir; a p.n.; *Fl.* Scheyers; a fam. n. (sheer, bright)

SHIRLEY. A loc. n., Derbysh., Hants, Kent, Surr., Worcest.

SHIRT. *See* Sherrard

SHIRTCLIFFE. *See* Sutcliffe

SHIVES. A loc. n., Scotl.

SHOEBRIDGE, SHOOBRIDGE. From Shewbridge; a loc. n., Lancs

SHOESMITH, SHOOSMITH. A shovel or spade-maker

SHOLL. *N.* Skjöldr; *A.S.* Scald (shield); *G.*, *Dch.* Scholl; a p.n.

SHONE. *Dch.* Schoen; a p.n.; *A.S.* *scóne* (beautiful)

SHOOLBRED. From Shulbred; a loc. n., Suss.

SHOPPEE. *A.S.* Scop; *D.* Schoppe; p.n. (a minstrel); *Fr.* Shoppée. Hugt. n.

SHORE. From Shoore; a loc. n., Fland. *Dch.* Schoor; a p.n.

SHOREY. *Fr.* Chourrier (?); a p.n.

SHORING. *See* Shewring

SHORLAND. A loc. n., Devon

SHORMAN. *See* Sharman

SHORNEY. *Fl.* Schournoy; a p.n.

SHORROCK. *A.S.* Særic, Saric, Seric; p.n.; *serc*; Scot. *sark* (a shirt of mail)

SHORT, SHORTER. *A.S.* Scorta; *D.* Schorti; *G.* Scharte, Schorter; p.n. (short)

SHORTEN, SHORTING, SHORTINS. *Fl.* Scharten; fam. n. of Short

SHORTRIDGE. From Shortbridge; a loc. n., Suss.

SHOTBOLT. *See* Shadbolt

SHOTLIFF. *See* Shirtcliffe

SHOTTER. From Shothaugh; a loc. n., Northbd. Or *G.*, *Dch.* Schotte; a p.n. *See* Scott

SHOTTIN. From Shotten; a loc. n., Dur. Or Shooten; a loc. n., Belg.

SHOUT. *Dch.* Schout; a p.n.; *Fl.*; p.n. *See* Skcat

SHOVE. From Echauffour; a loc. n., France. Or *A.S.* Scuff, Scuffa (a shover); *Fr.* Chauveau (?) (bald); *Dch.* Schouw, Schuver; *D.* Schow; p.n.

SHOVELLER, SHOWLER. *See* Shuffle

SHOWEL. *See* Shuffle

SHOWERING. *See* Shewring

SHOYE. Irish form of Joyce

SHREEVE. *See* Sheriff

SHRIGLEY. A loc. n., Ches.

SHRIMPLING. *G.* Schrempel; a p.n.; *schrumpel* (a wrinkle)

SHRIMPTON. A loc. n.

SHROSBREE. From Shrewsbury; a loc. n., Salop

SHRUBSOLE. A loc. n., Staffs

SHUBROOK. From Shobrook; a loc. n., Devon

SHUCKBURGH. A loc. n., Warw.

SHUDD. *See* Scutt

SHUELL. *See* Sewill

SHUFFLE. *Dch.* Schewel; *Fr.* Chauvel, Chouville, Chaville; p.n.

SHUFFREY. *Fr.* Chaufouraux (?) ; a p.n.

SHUGAR. *See* Seager

SHUM. *A.S.* Sceomma; *G.* Schumm; p.n. (bashful, modest)

SHURMAR. *G.* Schirmer; *Dch.* Schermer ; p.n. (protector, screener)

SHURY. *See* Shorey

SHUTE. A loc. n., Devon. Or *A.S.* Sceot ; *Dch.* Schoot, Schut ; *G.* Schütt ; *D.* Skytte ; p.n. *See* Skeat

SHUTER. *A.S.* Scytta ; *Dch* Schuter ; p.n. *See* Skeat

SHUTLER. *G.* Schüttler ; a p.n. (shaker)

SHUTTLEWORTH. A loc. n., Yorks. *D.B.* Scitelesuuorde

SIBBERIN. *Fr.* Sibron, Sibrin. A Hugt. n., 1681

SIBBETT, SIBBIT. *Dch.*, *G.* Siebert; p.n. *See* Sigbert

SIBEL. *N.* Sig-baldr (foremost in victory) ; *A.S.* Sibba, Sibi, Sibbold, Sigbeald ; *F.* Sibo ; *G.* Sibe, Siebe, Sieber, Siebler, Seppelt, Sebald ; *Dch.* Sibbelee ; *Fl.* Siebels, Sibille ; p.n.

SIBERT. *See* Sibbett

SIBLEY. From Sible ; a loc. n., Ess. Or *Dch.* Sibbelee ; a p.n.

SIBTHORPE. A loc. n., Notts

SIBUN. *A.S.* Sibban; *Fl.* Sibon; p.n.

SICH. *See* Sitch

SICKLEMORE. From Sicklemere ; a loc. n., Suff.

SICKLIN. *See* Suckling

SIDDALL. A loc. n., Lancs. Or *see* Sydal

SIDDERS. *Dch.* Sieders ; a fam. n. (Side)

SIDDON. *See* Seadon and Seaton

SIDE. A loc. n., Glost. Or *A.S.* Sida ; *G.* Seite ; p.n. (broad, great)

SIDEBOTTOM. A loc. n.

SIDEWAY. From Sidway ; a loc. n., Staffs

SIDLE. *See* Sydal

SIDNEY. From St Denis (?) ; a loc. n., France. A loc. n., Suss. Originally Sithney

SIDWELL. A loc. n., St Sativola

SIELEY. *See* Seeley

SIEVEWRIGHT. *A.S.* Sefrith, Sœfrid, Sefred ; p.n. (sea peace)

SIGBERT. *N.* Sigbjartr ; *A.S.* Sigbeorht, Sigibert ; p.n. (victory bright)

SIGGE, SIGGERS. *N.* Sig-urðr (fated to victory) ; *D.* Seyghers ; *Dch.* Seegers ; p.n. *See* Segon

SIGGINS. *See* Segon

SILCOCK. *Dch.* Sielcken ; a p.n. Dim. of Sill. *See* Silk

SILENCE, SILLENCE. *D.* Seiling, Sillin ; *A.S.* Sœling ; p.n.

SILITOE. *See* Shillitoe

SILK. *A.S.* Sigelac, Silac, Sylc ; p.n. (victory sport). *See* Silcock

SILL. *A.S.* Sil ; *D.* Sillo ; *S.* Sillow ; *Fl.* Siegel ; *G.* Siele, Sille ; *Dch.* Siehl ; p.n. *Sigel* (the sun)

SILLETT. *See* Sillitoe

SILLIS. From Seilles ; a loc. n., Belg. *Dch.* Silles ; p.n.

SILVER. *N.* Silfra (silver, greyhaired) ; n.n. ; *D.* Silfver ; *Dch.* Silva ; *Fl.* Silver ; p.n.

SILVERLOCK. *D.* Silberloh ; a p.n.

SILVERSIDE. A loc. n.

SILVERSTONE. A loc. n., Northants

SILVERTON. A loc. n., Devon

SILVERTOWN. A loc. n., Ess.

SILVESTER. From St Sylvestre ; a loc. n., Norm. *Fl.*, *G.* Silvester ; *Fr.* Silvestre ; p.n.

SILVEY. *See* Silver

SIMCOCK, SIMCOE, SIMKIN. Dimin. of Simmund, Simmon, Simon. From *N.* Sigmundr ; a p.n. (victorious protector)

SIMMENS. SIMMONS, SIMMS. *See* Symonds

SIMPER. *G.* Semper, Simba ; a p.n. Or from St Pierre

SIMPLE. *G.* Zimpel ; a p.n. Or *see* Semple

SIMPSON, SIMSON. *N.* Simba, dim. of Sigmundr; *G.* Simba, Simm; *D.* Simeon; *S.* Simson; p.n. *See* Symonds

SIMVIL. *See* Somerville

SINCLAIR. *See* St Clair

SINEMON. *See* Symonds

SINGER. *Dch.*, *Fl.*; p.n.; *A.S.* Isenger (?) (iron spear); *singere* (singer)

N.-Fr. Le Chaunter in Rot. Hund.

SINGLEHURST. *See* Swindlehurst

SINGLETON. A loc. n., Yorks

SIRER. *Fr.* Sirier; a p.n. (lordship)

SIRGOOD. *See* Sirkett

SIRKETT. From Cercottes; a loc. n., France. A Hugt. n., Lond. 1688

SIRR. From Seurre; a loc. n., France. *Dch.* Suur; a p.n.

SISLEY. From Sysseele; a loc. n., Fland. *Dch.* Sisselar; a p.n. *See* Cecil

SISON. From Syston; a loc. n., Leics

SISSENS, SISSON. From Siston; a loc. n., Glost.; Seesen (?); a loc. n., Germ. *Fl.* Sisen; *Dch.* Sisseren; p.n.

SITCH. From Sytch; a loc. n., Salop

SITDOWN. From Seatown; a loc. n., Dorset. Or *see* Seadon

SITGREAVES. From Seagrave; a loc. n., Leics. *D.B.* Satgrave

SITWELL. *See* Sidwell

SIVIL. *See* Civill

SKAE. *Dch.* Schee; a p.n.

SKAIFE. *See* Scaife

SKAKEL. *See* Shackle

SKAYMAN. *D.*, *Dch.*, *G.* Schiemann; a p.n.

SKEAT, SKEET. *N.* Skyti; *A.S.* Scytta, Sceit; *D.* Skytte (archer); p.n. (a shooter, marksman). Scate, a Dch. Prot. ref., Lond., 1621

SKEDGE. *See* Skegg

SKEELS, SKELLS. From Schelle; a loc. n., Belg. *D.* Skeel; *Dch.* Schell; *Fl.* Schoels (shell); p.n. Or *A.S. scel*

SKEEN. *See* Skene

SKEFFINGTON. A loc. n., Leics

SKEGG. *N.* Skaggi; *A.S.* Scæcca, Scacca; *D.* Schek; *Dch.* Scheick; *G.* Schech; *Fl.* Schaek; p.n. (a shaker, brandisher)

SKELT. *Dch.* Scheltes; a p.n. *See* Child

SKELTON. A loc. n., Cumb., Yorks

SKENE. A loc. n., Aberdeen

SKERRITT. From Skirrid; a loc. n., Monmouth; Skerwith, Cumb.

SKERRY. A loc. n., Antrim. Or *see* Skerritt

SKETCHLEY. A loc. n., Leics

SKETT. *See* Skeat

SKEVINGTON. *See* Skeffington

SKEWES. A loc. n. (manor), Cornw. Or *Dch.* Schüss; a p.n.

SKEY. From Scy; a loc. n., Belg. *Dch.* Schey, Schie; p.n.

SKIDMORE. *See* Scudamore

SKIFFENS. *A.S.* Scefing; a fam. n.; *Dch.* Schiewink; *G.* Skiefe; p.n. (sheaf)

SKILBECK. From Skellbeck; a loc. n., Yorks

SKILES. *See* Skoyles

SKILLINGTON. A loc. n., Lincs

SKILLITO. *See* Shillitoe

SKILTON. *See* Skelton

SKINNER. *A.S.* Scinna, Scyn (bright, splendid)

SKIPPER. *Dch.* Schipper; a p.n.

SKIPPINS. *A.S.* Scepi (a sailor); *G.* Skiba, Skiebe; *D.* Schipke; p.n.

SKIPTON. A loc. n., Yorks

SKIPWITH. A loc. n., Yorks

SKIPWORTH. *See* Skipwith

SKIRLING. A loc. n., Peebles

SKIRROW. *See* Scorer

SKITT. *See* Skeat

SKITTERY. *A.S.* Sceotheri, Scyttaheri; *Dch.* Schutterij; p.n. (shooter, archer-warrior)

Q

SKONE. *See* Scone

SKOULDING. *Dch.* Scholten. *See* Skelt

SKOYLES. *Fl.* Schoels; *Dch.* Schuil; a p.n. *See* Skeels

SKRINE. From Skreen; a loc. n., Sligo

SKRYMSHER. *G.* Schremser; a p.n. Or *see* Scrime

SKUCE. *See* Skewes

SKUDDER. *See* Shutter

SKULL. *N.* Skuli (from *skjol*, a shelter, protector); *Dch.* Schule; *Fl.* Schul; *D.B.* Scule; p.n.

SKULTHORPE. A loc. n., Norf.

SKUSE. *See* Skewes

SKY. *See* Skey

SLACK. A loc. n., Derbysh., Yorks

SLADDEN, SLADEN. *A.S.* Sledda; a p.n. (a dweller in the plain (?)). Or from Slaidburn; a loc. n., Yorks

SLADE. A loc. n., Devon, Suff. Or from Slad; a loc. n., Glost.

SLAPP. *N.* Slappi (a lump-fish); *G.* Schlappe; p.n.

SLARK. *G.* Slach; a p.n. *See* Slack

SLATCHER. *See* Slaughter

SLATER. *D.* Schlytter; *Dch.* Schlette, Sluyter, Sluiter; p.n. (striker)

SLATFORD. From Slaughterford; a loc. n., Wilts

SLATTER. *See* Slaughter

SLAUGHTER. A loc. n., near Sherborne, Glost. Or *G.* Slotta; *Dch.* Slooter; *Fl.* Slotte; p.n. (a privileged hunter)

SLEDDALE. A loc. n., Yorks

SLEEP. From Sleepe; a loc. n., Heref.; Sleap, Salop; or Slepe, Dorset. Or *Dch.* Schlipp, Sloep; *Fl.* Sleyp; *D.* Schlippe; a p.n. Slype; a loc. n., Flanders. *See* Slipper

SLEIGH. *D.* Schlie; *Dch.* Sluy; p.n.; *A.S. slýh* (a slayer)

SLEIGHT. A loc. n., Wilts

SLINGSBY. A loc. n., Yorks

SLIPPER. *N.* Sleppi; n.n. (one who lets slip); *D.* Schlippe; *G.* Schleppe; *Dch.* Schleper; p.n. Or an inhabitant of Slype. *See* Sleep
Ric. Sliper in Rot. Obl. et Fin., K. John.

SLOCOMBE. A loc. n., Devon

SLOGG, SLOGGER. *See* Slugg

SLOPER. *Dch.* Sloeper; a p.n. (a sleeper)

SLOUGH. A loc. n., Berks

SLOW. From Sloo; a loc. n., Devon. Or *see* Slough
Atte-Slo, Court of Husting.

SLOWMAN. *D.* Slomann; a p.n.; *N. slá-mann* (?) (a slayer, fighting man)
Lower thinks this is a disguise of the Jewish name Solomon.

SLUCE. *Fl.* Sloos, Sluys; p.n. Prot. ref., Lond. 1618

SLUGG. *Dch.* Sloog; a p.n. (slayer)

SLY. *See* Sleigh

SLYPER. *See* Slipper

SMAIL, SMALE. From Esmael (?); a loc. n., Belg. Or *A.S.* Smala; *Fl.* Smal; *Dch.* Smale; *G.* Schmehl; p.n. *A.S. smæl* (small, slender). Hugt. n., Lond. 1618

SMAILHOLM. A loc. n., Roxburgh

SMALLBONE. *N. smá-beinn*; *A.S. smæl-bán* (dwarfish)

SMALLEY. A loc. n., Derbysh.

SMALLFIELD. A loc. n., Yorks

SMALLMAN. *A.S.* Smaleman; a p.n.; *N. smá-menn* (mannikin)

SMALLPAGE. *See* Smallpiece

SMALLPIECE. *See* Malpas
Francis Smalpece, Mayor of Norwich, 1622.

SMALLWOOD. A loc. n., Ches., Staffs

SMART. *D.* Smart; *A.S.* Smert; p.n. (pain). Hugt. n.

SMEATON. A loc. n., Inverness, Cornw., Yorks

SMEDDLES. *See* Smethills

SMEE. *G.* Smy; a p.n.

SMELLIE. From Smeley; a loc. n., Ess. Or Semilly, Norm. *See* Smail

SMELT. *A.S., Dch.*; p.n. (mild). Prot. ref., Lond. 1618

SMETHILLS. A loc. n., Lancs

SMETHURST. A loc. n.

SMILES. *See* Smail

SMILEY. *See* Smellie

SMIRKE. *Fl.* Smerche; a p.n.; *A.S. smærc* (a smile)

SMITH. *N.* Smiðr; *D.* Schmidt, Schmith, Smidt, Smidth, Smit, Smith; *Dch.* Smid, Smiet, Smith, Smitt; *Fl.* Smet, Smit; *G.* Schmidt, Schmitt; p.n.

John ye Smyth on a brass at Brightwell Baldwin, Oxon, A.D. 1400.

SMITHERS. *See* Smithies

SMITHIES. A loc. n., Yorks. Or *Dch.* Smithuis; a p.n.

SMITHSON. A loc. n., Devon

SMOUT. *Fl.*; p.n. (smooth)

SMURTHWAITE. From Smirthwaite; a loc. n., Cumb.

SNADHORST. From Snadhurst; a loc. n., Kent

SNAGGE. *A.S.* Snoc; *D.* Schnack; p.n. (a snake)

SNAITH. A loc. n., Yorks

SNAPE. A loc. n., Devon, Norf., Suff., Yorks. Or *Dch.* Sneep; *Fl.* Schnepp; p.n. (a peak)

SNAPPER. *Dch.*; p.n.; *N.* Sneypir (?) (a snipper)

SNARE. *N.* Snori; *D.* Snaaijer; *D.B.* Snerri; *G.* Schnier; *Dch.* Snoer, Schnaar; *Fl.* Sneyers; p.n. (active, quick)

SNART. A local corruption of Snargate, Kent. Or *A.S.* Snahard; *N.-Fr.* Senart; p.n. (snow firm); *N. snart* (swift, keen)

SNASDALL. A loc. n.

SNAZLE. From Snedshill; a loc. n., Salop

SNEAD. A loc. n., Worcest.

SNEATH. *See* Snaith

SNEE. *A.S.* Snæ; *G.* Snay; p.n. (snow)

SNEEZUM. From Snettisham; a loc. n., Norf.

SNELGROVE. A loc. n.

SNELL. *N.* Snjallr; n.n.; *A.S., Dch.* Snel; *G.* Schnell, Schnelle; p.n. (swift, courageous)

SNEPP. *See* Snape

SNEYD. A loc. n., Staffs, Worcest. Or Snaith, Yorks

SNOAD. *A.S.* Snod; a p.n. (a cap, hood)

SNODDON. *See* Snowdon. Or *A.S.* Snoding; a p.n. (descendants of Snod)

SNODGRASS. A loc. n., Scotl.

SNOOK. *N.* Snákr; n.n.; *A.S.* Snoc; *D.* Snog; *Dch.* Schnücke; *Fl.* Snoek; *D.B.* Snoch; p.n. (a snake)

SNOOKS. A loc. n., Devon. Or *Fl.* Snoeckx; a fam. n. of Snook

Lower thinks it is a corruption of Sevenoaks, Kent.

SNORE. *See* Snare

SNORING. A loc. n., Norf.

SNOWDEN. A loc n., Yorks

SNOWDON. A loc. n., Staffs, Wales

SNOXALL, SNOXELL. A loc. n.

SNUGGS. *See* Snooks

SNUSHALL. From Snowshill; a loc. n., Somers

SOAM. From Soham; a loc. n., Camb.

SOAMES. *See* Somers

SOANE. *A.S.* Son; *G.* Sohn; *Dch.* Son; p.n.

SOANES. *G.* Sohns; *Fl.* Soons; p.n.

SOAR. From Sore; a loc. n., France. Or *N.* Sárr (a wound); *Dch.* Soer; *G.* Sohr; p.n.

Sor in Rot. Obl. et Fin.

SOBEY. From Soubie; a loc. n., France. Or *N.* Sópi; a n.n. (a sweep); *A.S.* Sop; *Dch.* Sobbe; p.n.

SODDY. *See* Soder

SODEN. *Dch.* Soeding; a fam. n.

SODER. *A.S.* Sodda; *Fr.* Sodeau; *Dch.* Soede; p.n. (truthful)

SOFFE. *Fr.* Soffie; a p.n.

SOFLEY, SOFTEY, SOFTLEY. A loc. n., Dur.

SOLE. *N.-Fr.* De Sola; a p.n. In Rot. Hund.

SOMERFIELD. *D., S., G.* Sommerfeld; a p.n. *See* Summerville

SOMERFORD. A loc. n., Hants, Wilts

SOMERS, SOMES. From Sommeri; a loc. n., Norm. Or *A.S.* Som, Somar; *Fl.* Somme, Somers; *N.* *Sómi* (honour); p.n.

SOMERSET. The county

SOOBY. *See* Sobey

SOOLE. *See* Sole

SOONS. *See* Soanes

SOPER, SOPPER. From Sober; a loc. n., Yorks. Or *A.S.* Soppa; *G.* Sober; *Fl.* Sopers; p.n. *See* Sobey

SOPPET, SOPWITH. From Sopworth; a loc. n., Wilts

SORBEY, SORBY. A loc. n., Yorks

SORE. *See* Soar

SOREL. *N.-Fr.*; p.n. (yellow) In Rot. Hund.

SOTHAM. From Southam; a loc. n., Warw.

SOTHEBY. From Sotby; a loc. n., Lincs

SOTHERN. From Sotherton; a loc. n., Suff.

SOTHERS. From Southease; a loc. n., Suss.

SOUL. *See* Sole

SOULBY. A loc. n., Westmd.

SOULSBY. *See* Soulby

SOUNDY. *See* Sanday. Or *N.* Sjaundi; a p.n. (the seventh child)

SOUPER. *See* Soper

SOUTH. Hugt. n., Lond. 1618

SOUTHALL. A loc. n., Middlx.

SOUTHAM. A loc. n., Glost., Warw.

SOUTHARD. *See* Southward

SOUTHBY. *See* Sotheby

SOUTHCOMBE. A loc. n., Devon

SOUTHCOTT. A loc. n., Cornw., Devon. Or from Southcote; a loc. n., Devon, Yorks
Michael S., of S., Devon, 27 Hen. III. (1242); Will. S., of S., 19 Ed. III. (1345), Harl. MSS.

SOUTHERN. From Southton; a loc. n., Wilts

SOUTHERWOOD. *See* Southwood

SOUTHEY. A loc. n., Devon. Or *Fr.* Souday; a p.n.

SOUTHGATE. A loc. n., Middlx.

SOUTHWARD. From Southworth; a loc. n., Lancs. Or *see* Southwood

SOUTHWELL. A loc. n., Dorset, Notts

SOUTHWOOD. A loc. n., Somers

SOUTTARR. *See* Sowter

SOWARD. *See* Southward

SOWELS. *See* Saul

SOWERBUTTS. A loc. n., Lancs. Or *A.S.* Sarabeorht, Sarbert; p.n. (bright armour)

SOWERBY. A loc. n., Lancs, Yorks. *D.B.* Sorebi

SOWLER. From Soliers; a loc. n., Norm.

SOWTER. From Sautour (?); a loc. n., Belg. *A.S.* Sota; *G.* Sotta, Sauter; *Dch.* Soeter, Souter; *Fl.* Suttor; *Fr.* Sutter; p.n. Or *A.S.* sutere (a shoemaker). Sotteau, Hugt., Cant. 1622

SOWTON. A loc. n., Devon

SPAIN. *N.-Fr.* De l'Espagne; *Dch.* Spaan; p.n.

SPALDING. A loc. n., Lincs

SPALL. From Sporle; a loc. n., Norf. Or *Dch.* Spall, Spoel; p.n. *See* Paul

SPANKIE. *Fl.* Spanoghe; or *G.* Spanger; p.n. (a buckle-maker); *A.S.* spange (a clasp)

SPANSWICK. A loc. n.

SPANTON. From Spaunton; a loc. n., Yorks

SPARHAM. A loc. n., Norf.

SPARKE. *A.S.* Spearhafoc, Sperauoc; *Dch.* Sporck; p.n. (spar-hawk)

SPARROW. *A.S.* Spar; *S.* Sparre; p.n. *See* Spurr

SPARSHOTT. From Sparsholt; a loc. n., Hants

SPAULL. *See* Spall

SPEAIGHT. *See* Speight

SPEAK, SPECK, SPEKE. From Speke; a loc. n., Lancs. Or *N.-Fr.* Espec; a p.n.
> Le Spec in Rot. Obl. et Fin.

SPEAKMAN. *Dch.* Spiekerman; a p.n. (a spikeman)

SPEAR, SPEER, SPEIR. *A.S.* Spar, Sper; *Fl.* Spiers (small); *G.* Speer; *Dch.* Spier; p.n. Prot. ref. n., Lond. 1622

SPEARING. *Dch.* Spiering; a fam. n.

SPEARMAN. It is said to be a corruption of Aspromont
> Surtees, Hist. Dur., vol. i. p. 94. Aspermound in Roll of Battell Abbey.

SPEECHLY. From Spetchley; a loc. n., Worcest.

SPEED, SPEEDY. *N.-Fr.* De Spada; a p.n.
> Sped in Rot. Hund.

SPEIGHT. *A.S.* Spieta; *Old G.* Spiz; *G.* Spiess (spear); *S.* Spethz, Spitz; *D.* Speich; *Dch.* Spigt; *Fl.* Specht; p.n.

SPELLER, SPELLS. *Fl.*, *Dch.* Spellers; a p.n. (speaker)

SPELLMAN. *Dch.* Speelman; *G.* Spielmann; *Fl.* Spelmans; p.n. (a musician)

SPENCE, SPENCER. From Despenser (*Lat.* Dispensator); a steward
> Dispensator, a tenant in chief in *D.B.*

SPENCELEY. A loc. n.

SPENDLOVE. *A.S.* span-leof (?) (alluring dear)

SPERLING. *G.*; p.n. Dimin. a young sparrow. *See* Spurr

SPICE, SPICER. *Old Fr.* Espicier (?); *G.* Spiess; p.n.
> Benedict le Spicer in Rot. Obl. et Fin., K. John.

SPIKINGS. *Old G. spiz* (a spear). *See* Speight. Dimin. *A.S. spicyng* (a nail)

SPILL. *Dch.*; p.n. (a spoiler (?))

SPILLANE. *See* Spilling

SPILLER. *G.*; p.n. *See* above

SPILLING. *D.* Spelling; a p.n.

SPILSBURY. A loc. n., Worcest.

SPINK. *S.*, *D.* Spincke; *Dch.* Spaink; *Fl.* Spinnock; p.n. (a fieldfare)

SPITE. *See* Speight

SPITTA. *See* Speight

SPITTAL. A loc. n., Derbysh., Ess., Lincs, Northbd., S. Wales, Yorks

SPITTLE. A loc. n., Yorks

SPITTY. A British loc. n., Spyddid or Spytty. From the Latin *hospitium,* a hospital, as in Yspytty Ystwith (Card.) and Llan-spyddid (Brecons). Or *see* Speedy

SPLAINE. *See* Spillane

SPOER. *See* Spurr

SPOFFORD. *See* Spofforth

SPOFFORTH. A loc. n., Yorks

SPOKES. *Dch.* Spook; a p.n.; *N. spakr* (?) (wise)

SPON. A loc. n., Staffs.

SPONG. *D.* Sponneck (?); a p.n.; *N. spöng* (spangle)

SPOONER. *G.* Sponer; a p.n.; *N. Spánn* (?) (a Spaniard)

SPORE, SPOURS, SPOUS. *See* Spurr

SPORLE. A loc. n., Norf.

SPORTON. From Sproughton (?); a loc. n., Suff.

SPOTTISWOODE. A loc. n., Berwick

SPRAGG, SPRAGUE. *See* Sprake

SPRAGGETT. *See* Sprake

SPRAKE. *A.S.* Sperauc; a p.n. (sparrow-hawk). Or *N. sprakr* (active, sprightly); or *A.S. spræca* (a speaker, counsellor)

SPRANGE. *Dch.* Sprang; a p.n.; *N. spranga* (sprightly)

SPRATLEY. From Sproatley; a loc. n., Yorks

SPRATLING. *A.S.* Spræcaling; a p.n.; *N. sprakr* (active)

SPRATT. *Dch.* Spruit; *G.* Sprotte; p.n. *See* Sprott

SPRAY. *See* Spry

SPRECKLEY. *N.* Spræklegr; *A.S.* Spræcaling (sprightly); *D.* Spechler; p.n.

SPRIGGINS, SPRIGGS. *A.S.* Spræca (a speaker); *Dch.* Sprik; p.n.

SPRING. *G.*, *Dch.*, *D.* Springer; a p.n. (a leaper). Prot. ref., Dover, 1622

SPRINGALL, SPRINGHALL. From Springhill; a loc. n., Lancs. Or *Fl.* Springael; a p.n.; *A.S.* *springlic* (lively)

SPRINGBELT, SPRINGETT. *Dch.* Springveldt; a p.n.

SPRINGTHORPE. A loc. n., Lincs

SPRINKS. *G.* Springst; a p.n. *See* Spring

SPROAT, SPROD. *See* Sprott

SPROSTON. A loc. n., Ches.

SPROTT. *A.S.* Sprat, Sprot (a stick, spear), Spretman (a spearman); *G.* Sprotte; p.n.

SPRUCE. *Dch.* Spross; *G.* Sprosse; p.n. (a sprout)

Hence the old term Prussian or spruce beer, made from pine sprouts.

SPRULES. From Spreull; a loc. n., Scotl.

SPRY. *Dch.* Spree; *G.* Spreu; p.n. (chaff (?))

SPUNNER. *See* Spooner

SPURGE, SPURGEON, SPURGIN. Dim. of Sporre (Spörrechen). *See* Spurr

SPURR. *N.* Spörr; n.n. (a sparrow); *D.* Sporré; *Dch.* Spoor; *D.B.* Spur, Sperri, Sporri; p.n.

SPURRELL. From Spurwell; a loc. n., Devon. Or *G.* Spörel; a p.n. *See* Spurr

SPYER. Spy; a loc. n., Belg. *G.* Speier; *Dch.* Spijer; p.n. Belonging to Spy

SQUANCE. *G.* Schwanitz; a p.n. (tail)

SQUARE, SQUAREY, SQUIRE. *Fr.* Esquier; a p.n.

John le Squier in Rot. Obl. et Fin., K. John. Also a Huguenot n.

SQUIRELL. *A.S.* Scirweald, Scirold, Scirrell; p.n. (bright ruler) glittering, as applied to armour

SQUIRL. *See* Squirell

STABLE. From Staple; a loc. n., Devon, Kent. Or *see* Steble

Alex. de Stapele, Worcs., in Rot. Obl. et Fin., K. John.

STABLEFORD. A loc. n., Salop, Staffs

STACEY. *Fr.* St Eustace; a loc. n.

STACPOOLE. A loc. n., Pembrokesh.

STADDON, STADEN. A loc. n., Devon; also a loc. n., Flanders. *Dch.* Staden; a p.n.

STAFF. Stave; a loc. n., Belg. Or *D.* Staw; *S.* Staaf; *G.*, *Fl.*, *Dch.* Staff; p.n.

STAFFORD. The county town

STAGG. *D.* Stage; *Fl.* Stache; *G.* Stach; p.n.; *A.S.* *stác-a* (a stake)

STAGOLL. *See* Steggall

STAIGHT. *See* Stead

STAINER. Steener; a loc. n., Flanders. Or *N.* Steinnar; *A.S.* Stenhere; *Fl.* Stanier; *G.* Steiner; p.n. (firm warrior). Prot. ref., Lond. 1618

STAINES. A loc. n., Middlx.

STAINNS. *See* Staines

STAINTON. A loc. n., Cumb., Dur., Lancs, Yorks

STAIR. A loc. n., Ayrsh. Or *A.S.* Ster; *D.* Stæhr, Sthyr; *G.* Stähr, Stehr; p.n.; *A.S.* *stær* (a starling)

STALEY. A loc. n., Ches.

STALKER. *Dch.* Stolker, Stolkert; p.n.; *N.* *stál-görr* (?) (made of steel)

STALLABRASS, STALLEBRASS. From Stallingbusk (?); a loc. n., Yorks. Or *N.* *stál-brass* (hardened steel)

STALLARD, STALLER. *Fl.* Stallaert; *Dch.* Staller; p.n.; *A.S. steallere* (a steward); *Fr.* de Stailleurs. Hugt. n., Lond. 1618

STALLION. *S.* Stahlin; *Fl.* Staelens; *G., Dch.,* Stalling; *Fr.* Stalin; p.n.

STALLWOOD, STALLWORTHY. Loc. n. (?)

STAMER, STAMMERS. *D.B.* Stam; *G.* Stammer; *Dch.* Staamer; p.n. (family, race). Or *A.S. stamor* (stammering)

STAMFORD. A loc. n., Lincs

STAMP. From *N.-Fr.* D'Estampes; a p.n.; Stampes, a ville, Norm. Or *D., G.* Stampe; p.n. (a stamper). Prot. ref., Lond. 1622

STAMPER. Stembert; a loc. n., Belg. Or *Dch.* Stamperius; *Fl.* Stampaert; p.n.

STANBOROUGH. From Stainborough; a loc. n., Yorks

STANBRIDGE. A loc. n., Beds, Dorset, Ess., Yorks; Steenbrugge, Fland.

STANBURY. A loc. n., Devon, Yorks

STANCLIFFE. From Staincliffe; a loc. n., Yorks

STANCOMBE. A loc. n., Devon, Dorset

STANDEN. A loc. n., Wilts

STANDIDGE. A loc. n., Yorks

STANDISH. A loc. n., Glost., Lancs

STANDFAST. *G.* Standfuss; a p.n.

STANESBY, STANSBY. From Stonesby; a loc. n., Leics

STANFORD. A loc. n., Norf.

STANGER. *D., G.* Stanger; *S.* Stange; p.n. Or a loc. n., Cumb. (a pole, stake)

STANHAM. *See* Stoneham

STANHOPE. A loc. n., Dur.

STANIFORD. A loc. n., Devon, Salop

STANIFORTH. From Stainforth (*D.B.* Stenforde); a loc. n., Yorks

STANILAND. From Stainland; a loc. n., Yorks

STANLEY. A loc. n., Staffs, Dur., Glost., Lancs, Lincs, Yorks

The name of this manor was assumed by the Norman knight Valescherville. *D.B.* de Valuille.

STANNARD. *N.* Steinröðr (stone, *i.e.* firm glory); *G.* Steinert, Steinhardt, Stanner; *Fl.* Standaert; *D.B.* Stanard, Stanart, Stanhert; p.n.

STANNERS, STANNETT. *See* Stannard

STANPFLY. From Stanfree (?); a loc. n., Derbysh.

STANSFIELD, STANFIELD. A loc. n., Camb., Lancs, Suff., Yorks. *D.B.* Stanesfelt

STANSHAW. A loc. n. Or *see* Stanger

STANTON. A loc. n., Derbysh., Heref., Salop, Somers, Wilts

STANWAY. A loc. n., Ess., Glost., Salop

STANWELL. A loc. n., Middlx.

STANYON. A loc. n., Northants

STAP. *A.S.* Steapa; *Fl.* Staps; *Dch.* Stappes; p.n. *See* Staff

R. Stape in Rot. Obl. et Fin.

STAPLES. From Staplers; a loc. n., Hants. Or Staple, Devon. *See* Stable

STAPLETON. A loc. n., Glost., Salop, Somers, Wilts

STAPLEY. A loc. n., Ches., Devon

STARBUCK. From Starbeck; a loc. n., Yorks. Or Stabroeck, Sterrebeek; loc. n., Flanders

STAREY. *See* Sterry

STARK. *N.* Starkaðr; a p.n. *Sterk-Höör* (strong warrior), a mythical Danish hero; *A.S.* Starc; *D.* Starck; *G.* Stark; *Fl.* Starck, Sterck, Storck; *Dch.* Stark, Sterk, Stork, Sturk; *D.B.* Stercher, Stergar; p.n.

STARKEY. *See* Stark

STARLEY. From Stawley (?); a loc. n., Somers

STARLING. Dimin. *D.B.* Saxon tenant. Or Easterling. *See* Starr

STARNE. *N.* Stjárn (a star); *G.*, *D.*, *Fl.*, *Dch.* Stern; p.n.

STARR. *N.* Starri (starling); *D.B.* Stari, Stori, Stare; *Dch.* Storre, Starre; *G.* Stöhr, Stör, Stahr; *S.* Stahre, Star, Stare; *D.* Stahr; p.n.

START. A loc. n., Devon

STARTIN. From Starton; a loc. n., Warw.

STARTUP. *D.*; loc. and p.n.

STATHAM. A loc. n., Ches.

STATHER. *See* Stathern

STATHERN. A loc. n.

STATTER. *See* Stather

ST AUBYN. From St Aubin; a loc. n., Normandy

STAUNTON. A loc. n., Glost., Heref., Leics, Worcest.

STAVELEY. A loc. n., Derbysh., Yorks, Westmd.; also Flanders

STEABBEN. From Stebbing; a loc. n., Ess.

STEAD, STEED. From Stidd; a loc. n., Lancs. Or Stydd, Derbysh. *See* Studd

STEAMSON. *See* Stephenson

STEANE. A loc. n., Belg., Northants

STEARN. *See* Starne

STEBBENS, STEBBINGS. *See* Steabben

STEBLE. *N.* Styr-baldr; *S.* Stiebel; *D.* Stabel, Stibolt; *Dch.* Stapel; *D.B.* Stable; *G.* Stebel, Stiebahl; a p.n. (war bold, or battle prince)

STED. *See* Stead

STEDALL. *G.* Steidel; a p.n.

STEED. *See* Stead

STEELE. A loc. n., Northbd., Salop. *Dch.*, *G.* Stiel; a p.n.

STEER. *N.* Styrr (battle); *D.* Stühr, Stæhr; *S.* Stühr; *G.* Steer, Stehr, Stier; *Fl.* Stiers; *Dch.* Steer; *A.S.* Ster, Sterr, Stir, Stur, Styr; p.n.

Styr, a thane at the court of Ethelred II., mentioned in Royal Letters Patent. Also in Hardicanute's reign.

STEGGALL, STEGGLES, STEGGOLD. *N.* Stag-näl (?); n.n. (a darning-needle); *S.* Stagnell; *G.* Steckel; *Dch.* Stechel, Stiggel; p.n.

STEMBRIDGE. A loc. n., Somers, S. Wales

STENHOUSE. A loc. n., Stirling. Also Steenhuyze; a loc. n., Flanders

STENSON. A loc. n., Derbysh. Or *D.* Stensen; *S.* Stennsson. From Stephenson; p.n.

STENT. *See* Stunt

STEPHENS. Hugt. n., Lond. 1618

STEPTOE. *A.S.* Stepiot; *G.*, *Fl.* Steppe, Stiphoudt; a p.n. *See* Stibbard

STERLING, STIRLING. A loc. n., Scotl.

STERRY. *See* Steer

STEVENSON. *See* Stiffin

STEWARD, STEWART. *D.* Stigaard (war guard); *S.*, *Dch.* Stuart; *Fl.* Steyaert, Stuywaert; p.n. Or *A.S. stiweard* (steward)

The descendant of Alanus Dapifer, son of the Norman Fitzalan, styled himself *Senescellus Scotiæ* from the hereditary office. Q. Mary first spelled the name Stuart, *temp.* David I.

STIBBARD. *A.S.* Stithbeorht; *Dch.* Stibbe, Stiphout; *G.* Stibor; p.n. (firm illustrious)

STIBBON. *N.* Styr-björn; *D.* Stybe; *G.* Stibane; p.n. (war-bear)

STICHBURY. *See* Stutchbury

STICHLEY. From Stirchley; a loc. n., Salop

STICHLING. From Stickillin; a loc. n., co. Louth. Or *D.* Stick; *G.* Stich; a p.n. Prot. ref., Norwich, 1622

STICKLAND. A loc. n., Dorset

STIFF. *S.* Styffe; *G.* Steffe, Stief; *Dch.* Stiev, Stiffij; *Fl.* Steuve; *D.B.* Stefan; p.n. *See* Stiffin

In the Midland counties Stiff is used as a contraction for Stephen.

STIFFIN. *D.* Steffens, Steffin ; *Dch.* Stieven ; a p.n. *See* Stephens

STIGGANT. *N.* Stigandi ; n.n. (a stepper) ; *A.S.* Stigand ; a p.n.

STIGGINS. Stekene ; a loc. n., Fland. Or *N.* Stigandi ; n.n ; *D.* Stikken ; *Fl.* Stickens ; p.n.

STIGGLE, STIGGLES, STIGLE. *See* Steggall

STILES, STYLE, STOYLE. From Styal ; a loc. n., Ches. Or *G.* Steil ; a p.n.

STILL. *G.*, *Dch.* Stille ; a p.n. (quiet)

STILLINGFLEET. A loc. n., Yorks

STILWELL. A loc. n. (manor), Surrey. Stilewell, Styelwell

STIMSON. *See* Stephens

STINSON. *See* Stenson

STIRK. *Dch.* Sterk ; *Fl.* Sterck ; *G.* Stercke ; p.n. ; *N.* sterkr ; *A.S.* stearc (strong)

STIRRUP. From Styrrup ; a loc. n., Notts. Or *D.* Stürup ; a p.n. *See* Steer

Stürup is the Danish form of Styrthorp, a loc. n.

STIVELEY. *See* Staveley

STOBBS. A barony in Roxburgh. *See* Stubbs

STOCK, STOCKS. A loc. n., Salop. *D.*, *Fl.*, *G.* Stock ; *Dch.* Stok ; *D.B.* Stochi, Stoches ; p.n.

De Stok and De Stokes occur several times in Rot. Obl. et Fin., K. John.

STOCKBRIDGE. A loc. n., Dorset, Hants

STOCKDALE. A loc. n., Cumb.

STOCKEN. *See* Stocking

STOCKER. *Fl.* Stocquart ; *G.* Stöcker ; *D.* Stoker, Stokker ; p.n. ; *A.S.* stocc (a trumpet), stoccheard (?) (strong trumpeter)

STOCKFORD. From Stokeford ; a loc. n., Dorset

STOCKHAM. A loc. n., Ches., Devon ; Stockhem, Belg.

STOCKING, STOCKINGS. A loc. n., Herts. Or *Dch.* Stokkink ; p.n. ; fam. n. of Stock. Prot. ref., Norwich, 1622

STOCKTON. A loc. n., Dur., Salop, Warw., Worcest.

STOCKWELL. A loc. n., Devon, Surr.

STOFER. *A.S.* Stuf ; *Fl.* Stoove, Stouffe ; *Dch.* Stoffers, Stöver ; *G.* Stöffer ; p.n. ; *A.S.* stof (a club, stake)

STOKE. A loc. n., Ches., Devon, Heref., Kent, Northants, Salop, Somers, Staffs, Surr.

STOKELY. A loc. n., Cornw.

STOKER, STOKEY, STOKOE. *See* Stocker. Hugt. n.

STOKES. A loc. n., Devon

STOLLERY. *G.* Stolareyck (?) ; a p.n.

STONARD. *See* Stannard

STONE. A loc. n., Kent, Staffs, etc. Or *N.* Steinn ; *D.* Steen ; p.n.

STONEHAM. A loc. n., Hants. Or Stonham, Suff.

STONEHOUSE. A loc. n., Devon, Hants, Glost.

STONELAKE. From Stoneleigh ; a loc. n., Warw.

STONELEY. A loc. n., Hunts, Warw.

STONES. *D.* Steen ; *S.* Stein ; *N.* Steinn (stone) ; *A.S.* Stan, Sten ; *Fl.* Steens ; p.n. A freq. loc. n.

Atte Stunnes, 1327.

STONEX. From Stanwix ; a loc. n., Chesh.

STONEY. A loc. n., Warw.

STOOP, STOPP. *See* Stubbs

STOPFORD. A loc. n.

STOPHER. *See* Stofer

STOPS. From Stopes ; a loc. n., Lancs

STOREY. *Fl.* Storie, Story ; *Fr.* Stora ; *A.S.* Stori ; p.n. (sturdy)

STORK. A loc. n., Yorks. *D.B.* Estorch

STORMONT. From Stoumont ; a loc. n., Belg. *Fl.* Stoumon ; a p.n.

STORR. *D.* Stahr; *Dch.* Stor; p.n. *See* Starr

STORRS. A loc. n.,Westmd.

STORRY. *See* Storey

STOTE. *Fl.* Stoht; *Dch.* Stout; p.n. *See* Stott

STOTESBURY. From Stottersbury; a loc. n., Northants

STOTHERS. From *G.* Stoddart; a p.n.

STOTT. *N.* Stóti (a bull); *A.S.* Stotte; *Dch.* Stoete; p.n.

STOURTON. A loc. n., Wilts

STOUT. A loc. n., Devon, Somers. Or *Dch.* Stout; *G.* Staudte; p.n. *See* Stott

STOVELL. *See* Stowell

STOVING. From Stoven; a loc. n., Suff.

STOW. A loc. n., Ess., Northants, Salop, Staffs

STOWELL. A loc. n., Glost., Somers, Wilts

STOWER. A loc. n., Dorset. Or *Dch.* Stower; a p.n.

STOWERS. *See* Stower

STRACHAN, STRAHAN. A loc. n., Kincardine

STRAKER. *A.S.* Starc, Strac; *Dch.* Stracke; p.n. (straight, erect). *See* Stark

STRANG. *A.S., N.* Strangr (strong); *Dch.* Strange; p.n. Streing, Hugt. n., Lond. 1688
John le Strange held land in Staffs, *temp.* K. John.

STRANGE. *N.-Fr.* L'Estrange; a p.n.

STRANGER. *A.S.* Strangher (strong hero)

STRANGWAYS. A loc. n., Lancs

STRANGWICH. *See* Strangways

STRAPP. *D.* Starup; or *Dch.* Straub; p.n.

STRATFOLD. From Stratfield; a loc. n., Hants

STRATFORD. A loc. n., Oxf., Suff., Warw., Wilts

STRAWBRIDGE. A loc. n., Somers

STRAWSON. *D.B.* Struostun; a p.n.

STREATFIELD. *N.-Fr.* De Strata-villa or Estreville; a p.n. Or Stratfield, Hants

STRECKLE. *G.* Streckel; a p.n. *See* Straker. Dim.

STREDWICK. *See* Strudwick

STREET. A loc. n., Devon, Hants, Somers, Suss.

STREETER. *A.S.* Struth; *Old G.* Striter; *D.* Stræter; *G.* Streda; p.n. (a fighter, warrior)

STREETON, STRETTON. A loc. n., Derbysh., Staffs, Warw., etc.

STRELLEY. A loc. n., Notts. *D.B.* Strahlei
Walter de Straley in Rot. Obl. et Fin., K. John.

STRETCH. *G.* Streich; a p.n.; Stric in *D.B.*; *N.* strjúka; *D.* stryge; *A.S.* strica (a stroke)

STRIBLING, STRIPLING. Dimin. of Stripp

STRICKLAND. A loc. n., Cumb.

STRICKSON. From Strixton; a loc. n., Northants. Or *see* Stretch

STRICKSTOCK. A loc. n.

STRIDE. *G.* Streit; a p.n.; *A.S.* striδ (strife)

STRINGER. *Dch.* Strenger; *G.* Stringer; p.n. (strict, vigorous, firm, brave). *See* Stranger

STRIP, STRIPP. *D.* Stripp; *Dch.* Streep; p.n.; *N.* stripr (a stripling, youth)

STRODE. *See* Stroud

STRONG. *See* Strange

STRONGITHARM. *See* Armstrong

STROTHERS. A loc. n., Dur.

STROUD. A loc. n., Dorset, Glost., Hants, Middlx.

STROVER. *G.* Struwe; *Dch.* Stroeve, Struwer; p.n.; *Fl.* struve; *Goth.* struban (proud)

STROWGER, STROWYER. *D.* Stroe-yer; *Fl.* Strohouwer; p.n. (strewer (?))

STRUDWICK. *Dch.* Strodijk; a p.n.

STRUMPSHAW. A loc. n., Norf.
STRUTHERS. A loc. n., Scotl.
STRUTT. *A.S.* Struth; *Fl.* Stroot;
p.n. (strife, battle); hence *G.*
Struttmann; a p.n. (a fighting
man, a spoiler)

> In the pedigree of Baron Rayleigh
> Burke derives this name from God-
> frid Strutz de Hinkelred of Unter-
> walden in Switzerland.

STUART. *See* Stewart
STUBBINGS. A loc. n., Berks
STUBBS. A loc. n., Yorks (*D.B.*
Stubuzan, Stubbsham). Or *N.*
Stubbi; n.n.; *D.B.* Stubart; *G.*
Stöbe; *D.* Stüb; *Dch.* Stoop,
Stübbe; p.n. (branch) of lineage (?)

> Adam de Stubber in Rot. Obl. et Fin.,
> K. John.

STUCK, STUCKEY. *A.S.* Stuca; *Dch.*
Stucki; p.n. (a pikeman (?))
STUCKBERY. *See* Stutchbury
STUDD. *A.S.* Stedda, Stid, Stith,
Stut; *D.* Stuhde; *G.* Studer,
Studt; p.n. *stíð* (firm)
STUDHOLME. From Studham; a
loc. n., Herts
STUKELEY. From Stewkley; a loc.
n., Bucks, Hunts
STUMORE. *See* Sturmer
STUNT. *G.* Zunz; a p.n.
STURCH, STURGE, STURGES. From
Sturridge; a loc. n., Devon. Or
A.S. Styrgar; a p.n. (battle spear)
STURGEON. *Fr.* Lestourgeon; a
p.n. Hugt. n., Lond. 1683
STURMER. *N.* Styrmir; *A.S.* Styr-
mær (famous fighter); *G.* Stür-
mer; p.n.
STURROCK. *Dch.* Sturk; a p.n.
See Stark
STURT. *See* Stuart
STUTCHBURY. A loc. n., Northants
STUTFIELD. From Estouteville (?);
a loc. n. near Yvetot, Norm.
STUTTER. *A.S.* Stuthere; *G.* Stut-
zer; p.n. (firm warrior). *See*
Studd
STUTTLE. *See* Stutfield

STYAN. *N.* Steinn (stone, firm); a
p.n.
STYGLE. *See* Steggall
STYTH. *See* Studd
SUART. *See* Seward
SUCKER. *G.*; p.n. *See* Sugg
SUCKLING. *F.* Sikke, Sikko; *A.S.*
Sycling; *S.* Syk; *Dch.* Suchtelen,
Sukkel; *G.* Suche, Suckel; p.n.
See Sugg
SUDBURY. A loc. n., Middlx., Suff.
SUDLOW. From Sudeley, Glost.
SUEL. *See* Sewill
SUFFELL, SUFFIELD. A loc. n., Norf.,
Yorks
SUFFLING. *A.S.* Swefling; a p.n.
Swæf (Suabian)
SUGARS. *See* Sugg. Fl. ref., Lond.
1618
SUGDEN. A loc. n., Salop
SUGG. *A.S.* Sucga, Suga, Sig, Syg;
G. Suge; p.n. (victory)
SUGGATE, SUGGETT, SUGGITT. From
Southgate; a loc. n., Derbysh.,
Middlx.
SULLIVAN. Irish O'Suillobhean (the
one-eyed man)
SULLOCK. *See* Sellick
SULLY. A loc. n., S. Wales. Or
Fr. Soulé; a p.n.
SUMERIL. *See* Somerville
SUMMERBEE. From Somerby; a
loc. n., Lincs
SUMMERFIELD. *See* Somerfield
SUMMERS. A loc. n., Ess. Or *N.*
Sumarliði; *A.S.* Somar (summer
sailor); *Fl.* Somers; p.n. Prot.
ref., Lond. 1618
SUMMERSBY. *See* Summerbee
SUMMERSUN. From Somersham; a
loc. n., Hants. *D.B.* Summer-
sham
SUMMERVILLE. From Sommerville;
now Sommervieux, Norm.
SUMNER. An apparitor, a sum-
moner

> Halliwell, quoting Nominale MS.
> Nomina dignitatum clericorum,
> gives "*Aparator* (a summunder)."

SUMPTER. From Sometour, a sumpterman

SUMPTON. From Summerton; a loc. n., Camb., Norf., Oxf., Somers. Sommethone; a loc. n., Belg.

SUNMAN. *A.S.* Suneman (sunman); *Dch.*; p.n.

SURFLIN. *See* Suffling

SURREY. The county. Or *Fr.* Surée, Sury; p.n. Sury; a loc. n.

SURRIDGE. A loc. n., Devon

SURTEES. A loc. n., derived from the river Tees, Durham

> The name of an ancient family which long resided there. Dominus Thomas Suyrtayse *miles*, in Lib. Vit. Dur.

SUSSENS. *See* Sisson

SUTCH. *G.* Suche; a p.n. *See* Zouch

SUTER, SUTRE. *See* Sowter

SUTHERLAND. The county

SUTLIFF. From Southcliffe; a loc. n., Lincs, Yorks

SUTTABY. *See* Sutterby

SUTTERBY. A loc. n., Lincs

SUTTLE. From Southill; a loc. n., Beds. Or *see* Southwell

SUTTON. A loc. n., Ches., Devon, Lancs, Notts, Yorks, etc.

SWABY. A loc. n., Lincs

SWAIN. *N.* Sveinn (a boy); *Dch.* Swen; *D.* Svenne; *Fr.* Suin; *Fl.* Svenne; *A.S.* Swegen, Swen, Swain; p.n.

SWAINSON. *S.* Svenson; *D.* Svenssen; p.n. *See* Swain

SWALLOW. A loc. n., Lincs

SWALLWELL. A loc. n., Dur.

SWAN. *N.* Svanr (a swan); *D.* Swane, Svane; *D.B.* Suuan, Suan; *Dch.* Swaan; *S.* Svan; p.n.

SWANSTON. A loc. n., Edinburgh

SWASH. *N.* Svasi (n. of a giant); *A.S.* Suauis; *G.* Swazina; p.n.

SWAYNE. *See* Swain

SWEARS. *A.S.* Swar; a p.n.; *Old G. suari* (important); *Gothic swers* (honourable). Or *see* Swyre

SWEENEY. A loc. n., Salop

SWEET. *A.S.* Suid, Suith, Swet, Swid, Swith, *swið' (strong, power-ful, great); *Dch.* Swidde; p.n.

SWEETAPPLE. *Dch.* Zoetappel is the corresponding word, but there is not the certainty of its being a p.n.

SWEETING. *Dch.* Swieten; *A.S.* Sweting; p.n. *See* Sweet

SWEETLAND. A loc. n., Devon. Comp. Swithland

SWEETMAN. *A.S.* Suetman, Swet-man; *Dch.* Soetman; p.n. *See* Sweet

SWEETSER. *G.* Schweitzer; *Fl.* Switser; p.n. (a Swiss). Swiss ref., Lond. 1618

SWEPSTONE. A loc. n., Leics

SWETENHAM. From Swettenham; a loc. n., Ches.

SWIFT. *A.S.*; p.n. (swift, nimble)

SWINBORNE. *See* Swinburn

SWINBURN. A loc. n., Northbd. Or *N.* Sveinbjörn; a p.n. (boy-bear)

SWINDELL. From Swindale; a loc. n., Cumb.

SWINDLEHURST. From Windlehurst; a loc. n., Ches.

SWINDLEY. *See* Swindell

SWINEY. *See* Sweeney

SWINFEN. A loc. n., Staffs

SWINGER. *G.* Schwinger; a p.n. (a brandisher)

SWINGLEHURST. *See* Swindle-hurst

SWINGLER. *G.* Schwingel; a p.n.

SWINHOE. From Swinhope; a loc. n., Lincs

SWINNARD. From Swynearde; a loc. n., Fland.

SWINNERTON. From Swynnerton; a loc. n., Staffs

SWINSON. *See* Swainson

SWINSTEAD. A loc. n., Cumb., Lincs

SWINTON. A loc n., Berwick

SWIRE. *See* Swyre

SWITHINBANK. A loc. n.

SWORD. *A.S.* Sward, Sweart, Swert, (black); or *sweord* (sword); *N.* Svertingr; *F.* Sweerd; *Dch.* Sweertz; *Fr.* Sourdes; p.n. Fl. ref., Lond. 1618

SWORN. *See* Swan

SWYRE. A loc. n., Dorset

SYDAL. *A.S.* Sidel; *D.* Seidel; *G.* Siedel; p.n. Dim. of Side

SYDENHAM. A loc. n., Devon, Kent

SYDER. *See* Side

SYER. *See* Sayer

SYFERT. *N.* Sighvatr; *A.S.* Sigweard; *D.* Sievert; *G.* Seiffert, Seyffert; *Fl.* Seyffers; *Dch.* Seyffardt; p.n. *See* Seward

SYKES. A loc. n., Yorks. Also Fl. ref., Lond. 1618

SYME, SYMES, SYMS. *Dch.* Seijm; a p.n. *See* Simms

SYMINGTON. A loc. n., Ayrsh.

SYMONDS. *N.* Sigmundr; *A.S.* Sigemund, Simond (victorious protector), ; *G.* Siegmund, Siegmann, Siemens, Siemon, Siems, Simmon; *N.-Fr.* Fitz-Simon; *Dch.* Semeins; *Fl.* Symon; p.n. Hugt., Lond. 1618

SYPHER. *See* Syfert

SYRES. *See* Sayer. Or St Cyres; a loc. n., Devon

SVRETT. From Sarratt; a loc. n., Herts

T

TABB. *A.S.* Tæbba; *F.* Tebbe; *Dch.* Tappe; *G.* Taube (?); p.n.; *N. táp* (?) (brave)

TABBERER. *N.* Tabarŏr (a tabard, a herald's coat); *N.-Fr.* Taborer; p.n.; Tabourier (a tambouriner). Ref. n., Lond. 1678

TABER, TABOR. *Fr.* Tabur; a p.n. *See* Tabberer

TABERNACLE. *Dch.* Tabbernal; a p.n.

In old records *tabernaculum* (a public inn).

TABNER, TABINER. *Lat. tabernarius* (a tavern-keeper); *N.-Fr.* Tabernar; a p.n.

TABRAM. A loc. n.

TABRAR. *See* Tabberer

Scholars in Queen's Coll., Oxon, were called Tabardiers, from Tabard, a short gown which they wore.

TACK. *S., D., Fl.* Tack; *Dch.* Tak; *N.-Fr.* Tac, Tagg; p.n.; *A.S. tácn* (?) (a standard)

TACKLEY. A loc. n., Lancs. Or Takeley, Ess.

TACON. *Dch.* Takken; a p.n. *See* Tack

TADD, TADDY. *A.S.* Tad, Tadda; *F.* Tade; *Fr.* Thadée; p.n. from Thaddeus. Or Goth. *thiuda* (father)

TADHUNTER. Scot. a foxhunter

TAFF. A loc. n., S. Wales. Also Welsh dim. of David, and used as a dim. of Theophilus

TAGART. From Scot. McTaggart; p.n. Or *A.S.* Dægweard; *Old G.* Taganwart (day guard)

TAGG. *See* Tack

TAHOURDIN. Fr. Hugt. n., Lond. 1685

TAILBY. *N.-Fr.* Taille-bois; *Fl.* Talgebosch; *D.B.* Tailgebosc, Talliebosc; p.n. (wood-cutter)

TALBOT. *Fr.* Talbot; *Fl.* Talabot; *D.B.* Talebot; p.n. (a dog with a turned-up tail)

In Roll of Battell Abbey. The *A.S.* form would be Talbot (speech or tale envoy), but there is no such name recorded. It is more likely to be from *A.S.* Dallbeorht or Tallbeorht, *Old G.* Dalbert (illustrious), the badge or cognisance being assumed later.

TALER, TALL. *A.S.* Tella; *F.* Tale; *Dch.* Tal, Tall; p.n. (a reckoner)

TALLACK. From Tallach; a loc. n., Scotl.

TALLBOYS. *See* Tailby

TALLEMACH. *See* Tollemache

TALLENT. From Talland; a loc. n., Cornw.

TALLON. *A.S.* Tæling; *S.* Talén; *Fr.* Talon; p.n.; fam. n. of Tall

TALMADGE, TALMAGE, TALMIDGE. *See* Tollemache

TAMBLYN, TAMLYN. *Fr.* Tamberlain; a p.n. *See* Tombling

TAME. From Thame; a loc. n., Oxf.

TAMMADGE, TAMMAGE. *See* Tollemache

TAMPEN, TAMPIN, TAMPLIN. *See* Tamblyn

TANCRED. *N.* Þakk-raðr (grateful counsel); *D.* Tanggaard; *D.B.* Torncrd; *G.* Tancred; *Dch.* Tanker (?); p.n.
  Latinised in Norman times into Tancredus.

TANDY. *Fr.* Tantais; a p.n. (dyed)

TANEY. From Tany; a loc. n., Norm.

TANGYE, TANK. *N.* Þenja (?); n.n. (an axe); *D.* Tang, Tange, Teng; *Dch.* Tang, Tenger, Tinga, Tinke; *Fl.* Tanghe; *Fr.* Tanguy; p.n.

TANKARD. *See* Tancred

TANKLIN. Dimin. of *D.* Tang; a p.n.

TANN. From Thann; a loc. n., France. Or *N.* Tanni (toothed); *F.* Tanno; *G.* Tanne; *Fr.* Tanne; p.n.

TANNER. *G.* Tanner; p.n.
  Le Tanur in Rot. Obl. et Fin.

TANSLEY. A loc. n., Derbysh.

TAPHOUSE. A loc. n., Devon

TAPLEY. A loc. n., Devon

TAPLIN. *N.-Fr.* Topelin; a p.n.

TAPLOW. A loc. n., Bucks

TAPP. *See* Tabb

TAPPER. *A.S.* Teappa, Tapa (a vintner); *Dch.* Tappé; *D.* Tappert; *G.* Tapper; p.n.

TAPPIN. Fam. n. of Tapp

TAPSCOTT. A loc. n.

TAPSFIELD. From Toppesfield; a loc. n., Ess.

TAPSON. *N.-Fr.* D'Abison (?); a p.n.

TAPSTER. The Scot. and N. Engl. form of Tapper. *A.S. tæppestre* (a female tapper)

TARBART, TARBET, TARBUTT. From Tarbat; a loc. n., Ross

TARDY. *Fr.*; p.n. (slow). Hugt., Lond. 1688

TARGETT. *N.* Þorgautr; *A.S.* Turgot; p.n. (Thor's Goth). Hugt. n., Lond. 1681

TARLTON. A loc. n., Glost.

TARN. From Thearne; a loc. n., Yorks. *N.-Fr.* Taurne; a p.n.

TARPEY. From the Irish Torpey; a p.n.

TARR. A loc. n., Somers

TARRANT. A loc. n., Dorset

TARRAS, TARRIS. *G.* Tarras; a p.n.

TARRY. *See* Terry

TARTAR, TARTE. *Fr.* Thard; a p.n.

TARVER. *N.* Þorvarðr (Thor's guard); *D.B.* Toruerd, Toruert, Torht; p.n. Or from Torver; a loc. n., Lancs

TASH. *A.S.* Tæsa; *Fr.* Tassy; *G.* Tasche; *Fl.* Tesch; p.n. (kind)

TASKER. *N.-Fr.* Taskier; *Dch.* Teske; a p.n.

TASSELL. From St German de Tassell, Norm. *Fr.* Tassel; *D.B.* de Taissel; p.n.
  Tassilo, n. of a Bavarian k., 6th century.

TASWELL. A loc. n.

TATE. *N.-Fr.* Teste (Tête); a p.n.

TATHAM. A loc. n., Yorks

TATTENHALL. A loc. n., Staffs

TATTERSHALL. A loc. n., Lincs

TATTON. A loc. n., Ches.

TAUNTON. A loc. n., Somers

TAVERNER, TAVINER, TAVNER. *N.-Fr.* Tavernier; *Dch.* Taverne; p.n. Hugt., Lond. 1622

TAY. *N.-Fr.* De Toie; *Fl.* Tay; *Fr.* Téhy; p.n.

TAYLOR. *N.-Fr.* le Telier; *Fr.* Tailleau, le Tailleur, Taillir; p.n. Or *A.S.* Telia; a p.n. (a dealer, divider). Or *see* Tyler
Silvester Taillor in Rot. Obl. et Fin., K. John.

TAYNTON. A loc. n., Glost.

TEAGER. Irish McTeague. Or *G.* Tiecke; *Dch.* Tieger, Tickc, Tiggers; *S.* Tiger; *A.S.* Tic, Tig, Tiger, Tigga; *Fr.* Tigé; p.n. (secure, fast)

TEAGLE. *G.* Tiegel; a p.n. *See* Tickle

TEAGUE. Irish McTeague. Tadhg (a poet)

TEAKLE. *See* Tickle

TEALE. From Theale; a loc. n., Somers. Or *see* Teele

TEAPE. *A.S.* Tib; *Dch.* Teepe, Tip; p.n. (timid)

TEAR, TEER. From Thiers; a loc. n., France. *Fr.* Thier, Thiers; *Dch.* Thier; p.n. Or *A.S.* Tir; a p.n. (a leader)

TEARLE. *Dch.* Terlet; a p.n.

TEASDALE. A loc. n., Dur.

TEASDELL, TEASDILL. *See* Teasdale

TEASEL. *G.* Ticsler; *D.* Thysel; *S.* Tisell; *Dch.* Tessel; p.n. *See* Tash

TEATHER. *See* Tedder

TEAZE. *See* Tice

TEBAY. A loc. n., Westmd.

TEBB, TEBBS. *F.* Tebbe; a p.n. *See* Tibbetts

TEBBATTS, TEBBITT, TEBBUT. *A.S.* Tatbeorht, Tedbert; *Fl.* Tybaert; *Fr.* Thibaut; p.n. (illustrious Tad)

TEDDER. *A.S.* Tathere; a p.n. (Tad the warrior). *See* Tate

TEDDY. *See* Tedder

TEE. *See* Tye. Or *Fr.* Thys; *D.* Thyc; p.n.

TEECE. *See* Tice

TEED. *See* Tidd and Tate

TEELE. From Thiel (?); a loc. n., France. Or *A.S.* Thyle, Tilla, Dil, Til; *G.* Tille, Tylle; *D.B.* Tihel, Tehel; *Dch.* Tiele, Til; *Fr.* Thil; p.n. (good)

TEEVAN. *See* Tiffen

TEGART. *See* Taggart

TEGG. *Dch.*; p.n. *See* Day

TELFER. *N.-Fr.* Taillefer, Tailfer; a p.n. (iron-worker)

TELFORD. A loc. n., Kent

TELLET. *See* Tillett

TELLING. Tellin; a loc. n., Belg. *Fl.* Telen, Tellin; *D.*, *Dch.* Telling; p.n.

TEMME. *G.* Themme; a p.n. Or *see* Tame

TEMPANY. *D.* Tempenau (?); a p.n.

TEMPERLEY. From Timperley; a loc. n., Ches.

TEMPEST. *Fl.* Tempst; a p.n.

TEMPLE. A loc. n. near Caen, Norm. *Dch.*, *G.* Tempel; *Fl.* Tempels; p.n.

TEMPLETON. A loc. n., Devon

TENCH. *Dch.* Tenge; a p.n. *See* Tangye

TENNENT. Dinant; a loc. n., Belg. *G.* Thenen; a p.n.

TENNET. *See* Dennett

TEPPER. *A.S.* Teppa; *Dch.* Tepe; *G.* Tepfer; p.n. (brave). *See* Tabb

TERRELL. *See* Tyrrell

TERRINGTON. A loc. n., Norf.

TERRY. *A.S.* Theoderic; *F.* Tiaderik (people's ruler); *Fr.* Terris, Therry, Thery, Thierry; p.n. Hugt., Lond. 1618

TESTER. *Fl.* Testaert, Testar, Teste; p.n. (a test, witness, will; also a head-piece). Testard, Hugt. n.

TETLEY, TETLOW. *See* Titley

TETSALL. *See* Tattersall

TETT. *See* Tate

TEULON. From Toulon ; a loc. n., France

TEVERSON. From Teversham ; a loc. n., Camb.

TEWELS. *Fl.* Tevels ; a p.n.

TEWKESBURY. A loc. n., Glost.

TEWSON. *See* Tyson

TEXTOR. *Dch.* ; p.n. *See* Thatcher

THACKER. *A.S.* Dæcca, Dæghere ; *Fl.* Dacker ; *Dch.* Dekker ; p.n. (glorious warrior)

THACKERAY, THACKWRAY. *See* Tancred

THAIN. *N.* Þegn (a thane); *D.* Thiene ; *Fl.* Thein ; *Dch.* Theyn ; *G.* Thien, Thenen ; *D.B.* Tain, Taini, Teini, Teigni ; p.n.

THAIRLWALL. *See* Thirlwall

THAKE. *See* Thacker

THANE, THAYNE. *See* Thain

THARP. *See* Thorpe

THATCHER, THAXTER. *See* Thacker

THEAKSTON. A loc. n., Yorks

THEED. *See* Tidd

THELWALL. A loc. n., Ches.

THEOBALDS. *See* Tipple

THEW. From Thieu ; a loc. n., Belg. Or *A.S.* Þeow (a serf)

THEXTON. *See* Theakston

THICK. *G.* Dicke ; a p.n. (stout)

THICKBROOM. A loc. n., Staffs

THICKNESSE. *Fr.* Xhignesse ; a p.n.

Robert Thicknesse was lord of Balterley, Staffs, Ed. I. 1274. Also said to be derived from Thickens, *Gent's. Mag.*, Nov. 1809.

THIN. Thynes ; a loc. n., Belg. *A.S.* Dynne, Thynne ; a p.n. (thin, lean), Dux, Kent ; *Dch.* Thijn ; *D.*, *G.* Thien ; *Fr.* Thin ; p.n.

Burke states that "John Boteville, *temp.* K. John, resided in one of the Inns of Court, and was styled John o' th' inne." De Thain in Rot. Obl. et Fin.

THING. *A.S.* Thing ; a p.n. ; perhaps Thingman (a Danish soldier)

THIRGOOD. *See* Toogood

THIRKETEL, THIRKETTLE, THIRTLE. *N.* Þórketell (Thor's kettle) ; *D.B.* Torchetel, Torchil, Turchil ; *S.* Torkels ; *D.* Therchil, Terkel, Thorkel ; *N.-Fr.* Fitz Turquetil ; p.n.

THIRLWALL. A loc. n., Northbd.

THIRST. *G.* Durst ; a p.n. (thirst); probably a contr. of *N.* Þorsteinn ; *A.S.* Thurstan (Thor's stone)

THISTLE. *D.* Thysel ; *S.* Thiesel ; *Dch.* Dissel ; p.n.

THISTLETHWAITE. A loc. n.

THISTLETON. A loc. n., Cumb ; Lincs, Rutland

THODAY. *D.* Thode ; a p.n. *See* Todd

THOM, THOMPSON. *N.* Tumi (pet name for Thomas); *S.* Tomasson ; *D.* Thomassen ; *Dch.* Thomson ; *D.B.* Tumi, Tumme, Tombi., p.n. Prot. ref., Lond. 1618

THORBURN. *N.* Þór-björn (Thor's bear) ; *S.* Torbiörn ; *D.* Thorbjoern ; *A.S.* Thurbeorn, Torbern ; p.n.

THORLEY. A loc. n., Dorset, Hants, Herts

THORNBER. *See* Thornborough

THORNBOROUGH. A loc. n., Cumb., Northbd., Oxf., Yorks

THORNE. A loc. n., Devon, Yorks, Suff. *D.B.* Torn. Or *N.* Thórny (a thorn); *D.* Thorning ; *Dch.* Thorn ; p.n.

THORNHILL. A loc. n., Derbysh., Dorset, Wilts, Yorks

THORNICROFT. A loc. n., Ches.

THORNLEY. A loc. n., Dur., Lancs

THORNS. *See* Thorne

THORNTON. A loc. n., Devon, Lancs, Leics, Yorks

THORNTOUN. A loc. n., Edinburgh

THOROLD. *N.* Þóraldr (Thor's ruler) ; *D.B.* Tored, Torold, Tori, Torol, Toi, Thori ; *Fr.* Thorel, p.n.

THOROUGHGOOD. *See* Toogood

THORPE. A freq. loc. n., Lincs, Yorks, etc.

THORRINGTON. A loc. n., Ess.

THOULESS. *See* Thurlows

THOYTS. *See* Thwaites or Toats

THRASHER, THRESHER. *D.* Drescher; a p.n.

THREADGALE, THREADKELL, THREADKILL. *See* Trudgil

THRELFAL. From Threlfield; a loc. n., Yorks. *D.B.* Threlfeld, Trelefelt

THRESH. *G.* Drescher; a p.n.

THRIDGOLD, THRIDGOULD. *See* Trudgil

THRIFT. *Dch.* Drift; a p.n.

THRING. *D.*, *S.* Thorin; *Fl.*Thurin; *G.* Thöring; p.n.; fam. n. of Thor. Or. *A.S.* Dreng; a p.n. (soldier, guard)

THRIPP. *See* Thrupp

THROCKMORTON. A loc. n., Warw.

THROOP. A loc. n., Dorset, Hants, Somers, Wilts

THROSSEL. *G.* Drossel; a p.n; *A.S.* þrostle (a thrush)

THROWER. *See* Trower

THRUPP. A loc. n., Glost., Northants

THUNDER. *A.S.* Thunar; *Fl.* Tunder; p.n.

THURBURN. *See* Thorburn

THURGAR, THURGUR. *N.* Þorgeirr (Thor's spear); *A.S.* Thurgar; p.n.

THURKETTLE, THURKLE. *See* Thirkettle

THURLAND. From Thurgoland; a loc. n., Yorks

THURLES. *See* Thurlows

THURLEY. From Thurleigh; a loc. n., Beds

THURLOW, THURLOWS. A loc. n., Suff.

THURRELL. *Fr.* Thorel; a p.n. *See* Thirkettle

THURSBY. A loc. n., Cumb.

THURSFIELD. A loc. n., Staffs

THURSTON. A loc. n., Lancs, Norf., Suff. Or. *N.* Þorsteinn; a p.n.

THURTELL. *See* Thirketel

THURWOOD. *N.* Þorvarðr; *A.S.* Thurweard; *G.* Thorwardt; p.n. (Thor-protector)

THWAITES. A loc. n., Cumb., Yorks

THWING. A loc. n., Yorks

THYER. *N.* þyr; *A.S.* þeowa (a bond-woman); *D.* Thyre; p.n. Or *A.S.* Thyrra; a p.n. (withered (?))

THYNNE. *See* Thin

TIARKO, TIARKS. *F.*; p.n. Perhaps from *N.* jarki, jaðrki, metaph. (the highest, best)

TIBB, TIBBS, TIBBY. *A.S.* Tib, Tibba; p.n. *See* Tipple

TIBBALD. *See* Tipple. Hugt. n., Lond. 1688

TIBBETTS, TIBBITTS, TIBBITT. *Dch.* Dibbetts; p.n. *See* Tebbut

TIBBLES. *See* Tipple. Tiboles, Hugt., Lond. 1618

TIBNAM. From Tibbenham; a loc. n., Norf.

TICE. *Fl.* Thyes; *Dch.* Theijs; *Fr.* Thiess; *G.* Thys; p.n. A contr. of Mathias. Prot ref., Lond. 1618
Teice in Rot. Obl. et Fin.

TICHBON. *See* Tichborne

TICHBORNE. A loc. n., Hants (formerly Itchenborne)

TICK. *See* Tigg

TICKELL. *See* Tickle

TICKETT. From Tecket; a loc. n., Northbd.

TICKLE. From Dickele; a loc. n., Fland.; Tickhill; a loc. n., Yorks. *Dch.* Tikkel; p.n.

TICKLEPENNY. From Dickelvenne (?); a loc. n., Fland. Or Gaelic (overhanging hill)

TICKNER, TICKNOR. From Ticknall; a loc. n., Derbysh.

TIDBALL. *See* Tibbald

TIDBURY. A loc. n., Hants

R

TIDD. A loc. n., Camb., Lincs. Or *see* Tidder

TIDDER, TIDDY, TIDEY, TIDY. From Tydee; a loc. n., Monmouth. Or *F.* Tide; *A.S.* Tida; *theod* (people); p.n.

TIDMAN. *A.S.* Theodman, Tidman (people's man); *D.* Thideman; *G.* Thiedemann; *Dch.* Tiedeman; p.n.

TIDSWELL. From Tideswell; a loc. n., Derbysh.

TIERNAY. Irish Tighearnach; a p.n.; *tighearn* (a king)

TIFFEN. *Fr.* Thifane, Tiphaigne, Typhaigne; *N.-Fr.* Epiphany. Hugt., Lond. 1618

TIGG. *A.S.* Tic, Ticca; *N.-Fr.* Tike; p.n.

Tig in Rot. Hund.

TIGHE. *See* Teager or Tye

TIGHT. Irish Tuite; *G.* Ticht; *Dch.* Tuit; *D.* Teitge; p.n. *See* Tite

TIGWELL. *See* Tugwell

TILBROOK. *See* Tilbury

TILBURY. A loc. n., Ess.

TILDESLEY. From Tyldesley; a loc. n., Lancs

TILKE. *D.* Tillge; *A.S.* Tilluc; *G.* Tilke; p.n. Dimin. of Till

TILL. *See* Teele

TILLARD, TILLEARD. *D.* Theilgaard, Theilade; *G.* Tillert; *Dch.* Tillaard; *Fr.* Thillard; p.n. (good protection)

TILLCOCK. *See* Teale. Dimin.

TILLETT. A loc. n., Belg. *Fr.* Tillot; a p.n. Or dim. of Till

TILLEY. A loc. n., Somers. Or *see* Tilly

TILLING. *A.S.* p.n.; fam. n. of Till; *Fl.* Thielen; a loc. and p.n.

TILLS. *See* Teele

TILLY. From Tilly; a loc. n., Belg. *Fr.* Thillais, Tilley; p.n. Or *see* Teele

Geoffroy de Tilly occurs as one of the benefactors of the abbey of St Étienne, Caen, Normandy, founded by William I. Henry de Tilly held Marshwood, Somers, *temp.* K. John.

TILLYER, TILYARD. *See* Tilleard

TILNEY. A loc. n., Norf.

TILSON. From Dilsen; a loc. n., Belg. Or *see* Teele

TIMBERLAKE. From Timperley (?); a loc. n., Ches.

TIMBERS. *A.S.* Tima; a p.n.; *Dch.* Timmers; a fam. n.; *A.S. tyma* (a leader)

TIMBRELL. From Timble; a loc. n., Yorks

TIMBS, TIMES, TIMMS. *See* Tims

TIMEWELL. A loc. n., Devon

TIMGATE. A loc. n.

TIMS. *D.*, *S.* Thim, Timm; *Dch.* Tim, Tims; *G.* Thimm; p.n. *See* Timbers

TINCKHAM. *See* Tingcombe

TINDALL, TINDALE, TINDELL. *Dch.* Tindal; *S.* Tengdahl (?); a loc. and p.n.

TINGCOMBE. From Teigncombe; a loc. n., Devon

TINGEY. *See* Tangye

TINGLE. A loc. n., Yorks

TINHAM. A loc. n.

TINK, TINKER. From Dinker; a loc. n., Germ. *Dch.* Tinke, Tuinker; p.n. Or *see* Tangye

TINKLER. From Dinklar; a loc. n., Germ. *Dch.* Dinkelaar; a p.n.

TINKLEY. From Dingley; a loc. n., Northants

TINN. *Fl.* Tinne; *Dch.* Tijn; *Fr.* Thin; p.n. *See* Thin

TINNEY. *Fl.* Tinne; a p.n. *See* Thin

TINSLEY. A loc. n., Yorks

TINWORTH. From Timworth; a loc. n., Suff.

TIPP, TIPPELL, TIPPER. A loc. n., Kildare. Or *A.S.* Tibba; a p.n. *See* Tibb, Tipple

TIPPETT, TIPPETTS. *See* Tibbitt

TIPPING. *Dch.* Tieben, Tippen; a p.n. Fam. n. of Tib

TIPPLE, TIPLER. *A.S.* Theodbald; *D.* Theobald; *Fl.* Thicbauld; *Fr.* Thibault; *G.* Thepold, Tiepolt, Thiebau; *D.B.* Tidbold, Tebald; p.n. (people's prince). *See* Tibbles

TIPTAFT, TIPTOFT. *See* Tiptod

TIPTOD. From Thibtot; a loc. n., Norm.

Tibtote in Roll of Battell Abbey.

TIREBUCK. *G.* Tirbach; a loc. and p.n.

TISSINGTON. A loc. n., Derbysh.

TITCHEN. *G.* Titsche; *Dch.* Titsingh; p.n. Dim. of Tide, Tidy

TITCHMARSH. A loc. n., Northants

TITCOMB. A loc. n., Wilts

TITE. From Thuit; a loc. n., Norm. *N.-Fr.* Tiet, Titte; *Fl.*, *Dch.* Tuyt; p.n. *See* Tight

De Tuit in Rot. Obl. et Fin.

TITFORD. From Thetford; a loc. n., Camb., Norf.

TITLEY. A loc. n., Heref.

TITLOW. *See* above

TITMAS. From Tidmarsh; a loc. n., Oxf. Or *see* Titchmarsh

TITT. *A.S.* Tid, Tit; *D.* Thiede; *G.* Tita; *Dch.* Tiedt, Tito; *Fl.* Tits; p.n. *See* Tiddy and Tite

TITTERTON. From Titterstone; a loc. n., Salop

TITTLE. *A.S.* Titel; *G.* Tietel, Tittel; p.n. Dim. of Tid

TIVEY. Irish Tavey, McEtavey; p.n.

TOALE. *See* Toghill or Toll

TOAS. *See* Tosar

TOATS. *D.* Thott; *Fl.* Toto; *D.B.* Toti; p.n. *See* Dodd

TOBIN. *See* St Aubyn

TOBY. *Fr.* Tobie, Toby; *Dch.* Tobi, Tobé; p.n. From Tobias

TOCK. *See* Tooke

TODD. *N.* Tjod; *F.* Todo; *G.*, *Dch.* Tode; *D.* Thode; *D.B.* Dodd, Toda, Todi, Tot; p.n. Or *A.S.* Theod; Goth. *thiuda* (people's ruler). *See* Dodd

Todd is the Scottish for a fox; but *A.S.* Dod seems to be the original form of the name.

TODHUNTER. *See* Tadhunter

TOFTS. A. freq. loc. n. *See* Tuffs

TOGHILL. From Taghill; a loc. n., Derbysh. Or *see* below

TOGWELL. From Touqueville; a loc. n., Norm.

TOINTON. From Torrington; a loc. n., Devon, Lincs

TOLD. *D.*; p.n. (toll)

TOLER, TOLLER. *G.*; p.n. Or from Toller; a loc. n., Dorset. *A.S. tólere* (a tax gatherer)

TOLFREE, TOLFREY. From Tollervey (?); a Cornish p.n. Or *A.S. tól-fréo* (toll free)

TOLL. *A.S.* Thola, Tol, Tola, Thol; *Dch.*, *D.*, *S.*, *G.* Toll; p.n. *A.S. tól*; *N. tollr*; *D. told* (tax); or *þól* (patient)

TOLLADY. From Tolladine (?); a loc. n., Worcest. *N.-Fr.* De Toleta; *Dch.* Toledo; p.n.

TOLLEMACHE, TOLMASH. *Fr.* Toulmouche; a p.n. Or from Tollmarsh; a loc. n., Buckfastleigh, Devon; Toulemer, Norm.

Tollemach in Roll of Battell Abbey. Richard Talamag, Talamasch, or Talemasch, held lands in Ess. and Oxon, *temp.* K. John, Rot. Obl. et Fin. Talmach, a benefactor to Ipswich Priory, 13th century.

TOLLINGTON. From Tallington; a loc. n., Lincs

TOLVER. *Fr.* Tolleve. Hugt. n., Norwich, 1622

TOMBE. *See* Toombs

TOMBLESON, TOMBLIN, TOMLINE, TOMLINSON. *See* Tombling

TOMBLING. From Tomblain; a loc. n., Norm.

TOMPKINS. *See* Toombs

TONGUE. A loc. n., Sutherland. Or Tonge, Leics; Tong, Yorks

TONKIN, TONKS. Dim. of Antonius. *F.* Tönjes; p.n. *See* Town

TONSON. *See* Townson

TOOBY. *See* Tubby

TOOGOOD. *N.* Þorgautr (Thor's Goth); *D.* Thuge; *Fl.* Tycknert; *G.* Tückert; *Dch.* Tuke; *D.B.* Thurgod, Turgot; p.n.

TOOHEY. Irish Tuohig, Tuohy, Tooey; *Dch.* Tahey, Tooy; p.n. *See* Toy

TOOKE. *N.* Tóki (foolish, simple); *D.* Tyge or Thuge; *Lat.* Tycho; *G.* Tuch; *Dch.* Tuck, Tuk, Tuke, Tukker; *A.S.* Tochi, Toc, Tuc; *Fr.* Touq; p.n. Or from Touques; a loc. n., Norm.
<small>Touke in Roll of Battell Abbey. De Toke in Rot. Obl. et Fin.</small>

TOOLE, TOOLEY. From the Irish O'Tuathail; a p.n. (lordly). *A.S.* Tula (a bard). Or *D.* Thule; *Dch.* Tulle; *S.* Tul; *Fl.* Toullet; p.n.

TOOMBS. *A.S.* Tomus; *Dch.* Toom, Thoms; *D.* Thom; *G.* Thomas, Tomisch; p.n.

TOOMEY. *N.* Tumi (pet n. for Thomas); *D.B.* Tumie, Tumme, Tombi; p.n.

TOONE. From Thuin; a loc. n., Belg. Or *Dch.* Tuin; *D.* Thun; p.n. *See* Town

TOOP. *See* Topp

TOOSEY. From Thuisy; a loc. n., France. *Fr.* Touzé, Touzet; p.n. Tuse, Prot. ref., Lond. 1622

TOOT, TOOTH. From Tot, a fief in Norm. Or *N.* Toti; n.n.; *Fr.* Touté; *A.S.* Tota, Toti; p.n.
<small>Tut in Rot. Hund.</small>

TOOTAL, TOOTEL, TOOTLE. *See* Tuthill

TOOVEY. *N.* Dufva; *S.* Thufva; *Fl.* Dufey; *Fr.* Tuvée, Tuffay; *A.S.* Tof, Tuffa; p.n.; *D. tove* (a dove)

TOP. *See* Topp

TOPHAM. From Topsham; a loc. n., Devon

TOPLER, TOPLEY. From Topcliffe (?); a loc. n., Salop, Yorks

TOPLIS. From *G.* Toplitz; a loc. and p.n.

TOPP. *Dch.*, *Fl.* Top; *S.*, *D.* Topp; *A.S.* Tope, Topp; p.n.; *top* (a tuft)
<small>Top in Rot. Obl. et Fin.</small>

TOPPING. A descendant of Topp. Or *Fr.* Taupin; a p.n. (tawny)
<small>In Rot. Hund.</small>

TOPPLE. *See* Topley

TOPPS. *Dch.* Tops; a p.n. *See* Topp

TOPSOM. From Topsham; a loc. n., Devon

TORBET, TORBITT. *A.S.* Thurbeorht, Torbert; *G.* Taubert; p.n. (Thor bright, illustrious)

TORR. A loc. n., Cornw., Devon. Or *A.S.* Thor, Tor; p.n. (the god)

TORRANCE. A loc. n., Stirling

TORRENS. *Dch.*; p.n. Or *see* Torrance

TORRINGTON. A loc. n., Devon

TORROP. *D.* Thorup, Torup; loc. and p.n.

TORRY, TORRIE, TORREY, TORY. *N.* Þóri; a n.n. (a young bull); *A.S.* Thorri; *Fl.* Thorez; *Fr.* Thouret; p.n. Prot. ref., Lond. 1618. Turry, a castle and barony, Norm.

TOSAR. *Dch.* Tuser; *D.B.* Tosard; p.n. *See* Toosey

TOSH. *N.-Fr.* De Tosca; a p.n. Or McIntosh

TOSSELL. *See* Tassell

TOSSELYN. *D.B.* Tascelin, Tezelin; *Dch.* Teeseling; p.n. *See* Teasel

TOSWILL. *See* Tassell

TOTHERICK. From Todridge; a loc. n., Northbd.

TOTHILL. A loc. n., Lincs

TOTTENHAM. A loc. n., Middlx.

TOTMAN. *A.S.* Dodman; a p.n. (the people's man)

TOTTERDELL. A loc. n.

TOTTLE. *See* Tothill

TOUCH. *G.* Tusch; *Fr.* la Touche; p.n. *See* Took

TOUGH. A loc. n., Aberdeen. Or *Dch.*, *A.S.* Tof, Tofig, Tou, Tuff, Touw; p.n.

TOULD. *D.B.* Torold, Touilt; p.n. *See* Thorold

TOULMIN. *Fl.* Tolleman; a p.n. (tax, toll, or customs officer)

TOVELL. *N.-Fr.* Tavel; a p.n.

TOVEY. *See* Toovey

TOW. From Thou; a loc. n., Normandy. Or *N.* Tofi, Toui; *Dch.* Touw; *G.* Thau, Toui, Tou; p.n. Or *see* Thew

TOWELL. A loc. n., Devon. Or *see* Tovell

TOWERS. From Tours; a loc. n., Normandy

    W. de Tours had the manor of Lowick or Lofwick, Lancs, from W. de Taillebois, baron of Kendal, after the Conquest, and assumed the name of de Lofwick.

TOWLER. *See* Toler

TOWN. *N.* Tónn; n.n. (a tune); *D.* Tonn; *S.* Tuné; *Dch.* Tuin; *A.S.* Ton, Tone, Toni; p.n. Or *Dch.* Toon, dimin. of Anthony; a p.n.

TOWNDROW. From Town Row (?); a loc. n., Sussex

TOWNS. *Fl.* Teuns; a p.n. *See* Toone

TOWNSEND. A loc. n., Devon
    Atte Tounesende, 1327.

TOWNSON. *N.-Fr.* Tunçon; *D.* Tonnesen; p.n. *See* Town

TOWSE, TOWSEY. *See* Toosey

TOY, TOYE. *See* Tye

TOZE, TOZER. *See* Tosar

TRACEY. From Tracy, a barony near Vire, Norm.
    Tracy in Roll of Battell Abbey. De Traci and de Trascy in Rot. Obl. et Fin.

TRAFFORD. A loc. n., Lancs

TRAILL. *See* Tyrrell

TRAIN. From Treignes (?); a loc. n., Belg. *N.-Fr.* Traine; a p.n. *See* Drane
    Simon T. in Rot. Hund.

TRAINER, TRAYNER. Irish Tremfear (strong man). Or *see* Treanor

TRAISE. *See* Tracey

TRAPP. From Trappes; a loc. n., France. Or *Fl.*, *D.*, *Dch.*, *S.*, *G.*; p.n. (a bustard)

TRAQUAIR. A loc. n., Peebles

TRASK. *G.* Treske; a p.n. Dim. of Trass

TRASS. *N.* Þrasi; *Dch.* Traus; p.n. (pugnacious)

TRATT. *See* Troutt

TRAVELL, TRAVIL. From Traffell; a loc. n., Cornw.

TRAVERS. From Trevieres; a loc. n., Norm.

TRAVIS. *See* Travers

TREACHER. *See* Treasure

TREADGOLD. From Tregolds; a loc. n., Cornw. Or *see* Thridgold

TREADWELL. From Tredgarville; a loc. n., S. Wales

TREANOR. From Trenear or Trenower; loc. names, Cornw.

TREASURE. *G.* Tresser; p.n.; *tressor* (treasure). Or *see* Thrasher

TREBECK. *Dch.* Traarbach; a p.n.

TREBLE. A loc. n., Devon. Or *N.-Fr.* Trepel; a p.n.

TREBY. From Trebigh; a loc. n., Cornw.

TREDGETT. From Treguth (?); a loc. n., Cornw.

TREE. *Dch.* Tree; *Fr.* Tré; p.n. Prot. ref. n., Lond. 1618. *See* Drake

TREEBY. *See* Treby

TREEN. A loc. n., Cornw.

TREETON. A loc. n., Yorks

TREFFRY. A loc. n., Cornw.

TREFUSIS. *Fr.* Tréfousse (?); a p.n.

TREGARTHEN. A loc. n., Cornw.

TREGEAR. A loc. n., Cornw.

TREGELLAS. A loc. n., Cornw.

TREGENZA. From Tregenna ; a loc. n., Cornw.

TREGIDGO. From Tregidhoe ; a loc. n., Cornw.

TREGO. From Tregue ; a loc. n., Cornw.

TREGONING. A loc. n., Cornw.

TREGURTHA. From Tregotha ; a loc. n., Cornw.

TREHARNE, TREHEARNE, TRE-HERNE. From Trehane ; a loc. n., Cornw.

TREINEN, TRINEN. From Trinent ; a loc. n., Monm.

TRELAWNY. A loc. n., Cornw.

TRELEASE. A loc. n., Cornw.

TRELEAVEN. From Trelaven ; a loc. n., Cornw.

TRELIVING. *See* Treleaven

TRELOAR. From Trelow ; a loc. n., Cornw.

TREMAIN, TREMAYNE. A loc. n., Cornw.

TREMBETH. From Trembath ; a loc. n., Cornw.

TREMBLE. *Fr.* Tremblay ; a p.n. From le Tremblay ; a loc. n., Norm. ; or Trembleur ; a loc. n., Belg. Or *see* Turnbull

TREMELLEN. From Tremellin ; a loc. n., Cornw. (the mill-town)

TREMENHEERE. A loc. n., Cornw.

TREMLETT. From Trembleth ; a loc. n., Cornw.

TRENAM. *See* Trenaman

TRENAMAN. From Trenmaen ; a loc. n., Cornw.

TRENBATH. From Trembath ; a loc. n., Cornw.

TRENCH. From La Trenche ; a seigneurie in Poitou, France. A loc. n., Salop
Trenchevile in Roll of Battell Abbey.

TRENDELL. From Trendeal ; a loc. n., Cornw.

TRENGROUSE. A loc. n., Cornw.

TRENGROVE. A loc. n., Cornw.

TRENNER. *See* Treanor

TRENOW. From Trenower ; a loc. n., Cornw.

TRENT. A loc. n., Somers. *D.B.* Trend, Trent ; p.n.

TRENTHAM. A loc. n., Staffs

TRENWITH. A loc. n., Cornw.

TREPESS. A loc. n., Cornw.

TRESHAM. A loc. n., Glost.

TRESIDDER. From Tresaddern ; a loc. n., Cornw.

TRESIZE. From Tresayes ; a loc. n., Cornw.

TRETHEWY. A loc. n., Cornw.

TRETT. *Fr.* Tréhet ; a p.n.

TREVALDWYN. A loc. n., Wales. Baldwin's dwelling

TREVALLION. *See* Trevelyan

TREVASKIS. A loc. n., Cornw.

TREVATT. From Trevarth ; a loc. n., Cornw. Or *see* Trevitt

TREVELYAN, TREVILLION. From Trevelgen or Trevellan ; loc. n., Cornw.

TREVENEN. From Trevennen ; a loc. n., Cornw.

TREVERTON. *See* Trevethan

TREVETHAN. A loc. n., Cornw.

TREVETT, TREVITT. *Fr.* Trevette ; a p.n. *See* Truwhitt
Trivet in Roll of Battell Abbey.

TREVOR. A loc. n., N. Wales ; or Trevoux, France

TREW. From Trou ; a loc. n., Norm. Or *see* Trow

TREWBY. *See* Treby

TREWINNARD. From Trewinard ; a loc. n., Cornw.

TREWREN. From Trewern, N. Wales. Or Truren ; a loc. n., Cornw.

TRIA. *Dch.* Trier ; a p.n. Trier, the *G.* n. for Trèves

TRIAIRE. From Trehire ; a loc. n., Cornw.

TRIBE. *Dch.* Treub ; *G.* Treiber ; p.n. (a driver)

TRICK, TRICKER, TRICKETT, TRICKEY. *N.-Fr.* Trichet ; *Fr.* Triquet ; p.n. (a small club, bat)

TRIFFITT. *See* Trevitt

TRIGG. *D.* Thrige, Trygg; *Dch.* Tright; *D.B.* Trec; p.n. *See* Trigger

TRIGGER. *N.* Tryggvi (faithful, true); *D.* Trygg, Træger; *A.S.* Tricga; *Dch.* Drieger; *Fl.* Trigot; *G.* Troeger; *S.* Trygger; p.n. Or Trigueres; a loc. n., France

TRIM. *Dch.*; p.n.; *A.S.* Trum. *See* Trumm

TRIMER, TRIMMER. From Tremeer; a loc. n., Cornw. Or *A.S.* Trumhere; a p.n. (firm warrior)

TRIMMING. *See* Trim

TRINDER. A Cornish p.n.

TRINGALL. *See* Drinkall

TRINGHAM. From Trimingham; a loc. n., Norf.

TRIPLOW. A loc. n., Camb.

TRIPP. *Dch.* Trip, Triep; p.n.

TRISTRAM. *N.-Fr.* Tristan, from the Celtic Trystan; a p.n. (herald)

In Rot. Hund.

TRITTON. *Dch.* Tritten; a p.n. Or *see* Treeton. Prot. ref., Lond. 1687

TRIXON. *See* Trigg

TROLLOP. A loc. n.

TROMP. *Dch.*; p.n. *See* Trumm

TROOD. *A.S.* Drud, Druht, Trud, Thryth; *Dch.* Traude; *Fl.* Truyt; *Fr.* Troude; p.n. (true)

TROST. *G.* Trost; *Dch.*, *Fl.* Troost; a p.n. (comfort)

TROTMAN. *G.* Trautmann; a p.n. *See* Trood

TROTT. *A.S.* Trot; *Dch.* Trots; *S.* Trotz; p.n. *See* Trood

TROTTER. *A.S.* Trothere (true warrior); *Dch.* Trottier; p.n.

TROUBRIDGE. *See* Trowbridge

TROUGHTON. From Trohoughton; a loc. n., Dumfries. Compare Trawden, Lancs; Treodythin, Llandaff; Trotton, Suss.

TROUNCE. *Fl.* Truyens; a p.n. *See* Trew

TROUP. A loc. n., Banffsh. Or *see* Throop

TROUSDALE. A loc. n., Yorks

TROUTBECK. A loc. n., Westmd.

TROUTT. *See* Trood

TROW. *See* Trew

TROWBRIDGE. A loc. n., Wilts

TROWELL. A loc. n., Notts

TROWER. From Troars or Troarn; a loc. n., Norm. Or *N.-Fr.* Trouvère; a p.n. (a troubadour)

TROWSE. *G.* Trautsch (?); *Fr.* Troussé; a p.n. (well-shaped)

TROY. *G.* Treu; a p.n. (truc)

TRUDGETT. *Fr.* Trugard (?); a p.n. Or *see* Tredgett

TRUDGILL. *A.S.* Thrythgild or Thrythhild; a p.n. (true value)

TRUE. *A.S.* Thruth, Thryth; *G.* Treu, Trew; *Dch.* Trouw; *D.* Thrue, Thrye; p.n. *A.S.* treów (trust, faith), trýw (true). Or *see* Trew, Trow

TRUEFITT. *N.* Þorvið; *D.* Turvid; p.n. (Thor's wood). Or *see* Truwhitt

TRUELL. From Trull; a loc. n., Somers. Or *see* Trowell

TRUELOVE. A loc. n., Devon

TRUETT. *See* Trood and Truwhitt

TRUMAN. *A.S.* Thrythman, Trutman; *Dch.* Trijman; *G.* Trauman; *D.B.* Trumin; p.n. (true man)

TRUMBALL, TRUMBLE. *A.S.* Trumbald; a p.n. (strong, bold); *Fl.* Trumpel; p.n.

TRUMM. From Drum; a loc. n., Aberdeen. Or *A.S.* Trum; *Dch.* Tromm; p.n. (firm, strong)

TRUMMER. *A.S.* Trumhere; a p.n. (strong warrior)

TRUMPER, TRUMPLER. *Fl.* Trumper; *Dch.* Trompee; *G.* Trümper; p.n. (a trumpeter). Or *A.S.* Trumbeort; a p.n. (firm bright)

TRUMPET. A loc. n., Heref.

TRUMPP. A loc. n., Glost. Or *see* Trumm

TRUNDEL. *N.* Trandill (a trundle); p.n.; *S.* Tranell; *Fl.* Trentels; a p.n.

TRUNDLEY. A loc. n.

TRUSCOTT. From Trescott; a loc. n., Staffs. Or Tresscoit, a manor in St Mabin, Cornw.

TRUSLER, TRUSLOW. From Trusley; a loc. n., Derbysh.

TRUSSON. *S.* Trysen; a p.n. *See* Try

TRUST. *Dch.* Troost; a p.n.

TRUSWELL. From Tresawell; a loc. n., Cornw.

TRUWHITT. From Trewhitt; a loc. n., Northbd. Or *see* Tyrwhitt and Trood

TRY. From Trie; a loc. n., Norm.

TRYON. *Fr.* Trion. Hugt. n., Broad Street, London, 1618

TUBB, TUBBS, TUBBY. Tubize (?); a loc. n., Belg. Or *A.S.* Dub, Tubba, Tube; *G.* Dube; *Dch.* Tubbing, Tupkin; *Fr.* Toubeau; p.n.; *N. dubba* (to smite)

TUBMAN. *G.* Taubmann; a p.n.

TUCK, TUCKEY. *See* Tooke

TUCKER. *A.S.* Dug, Tuc, Tucca; *Dch.* Tukker; p.n.; *A.S. dugan* (to be doughty). *See* Tooke

TUCKETT. *A.S.* Tuc, Tuca; *Fr.* Toquet; *G.* Tuckert; *Fl.* Tyckaert; p.n. *See* Tooke and Tuttiett

TUCKNESS. *See* Thicknesse

TUCKWELL. *See* Tugwell

TUDBALL. *See* Theobald

TUDDENHAM. A loc. n., Suff.

TUDGE. *See* Touch

TUDHOPE. From Tudhoe; a loc. n., Dur.

TUDOR. The Welsh form of Theodore. *A.S.* Theodhere; a p.n. (the people's warrior)

TUFF. *Dch.* Duif, Toff; p.n. *See* Toovey

TUFFEN, TUFFIN. *N.* Dufan (from the Gaelic); *S.* Dufven; p.n. Or *see* Tiffen

TUFFIL. *See* Duffill.

TUFFLEY. A loc. n., Glost.

TUFFNELL. *N.* Dufnial (from the Gaelic); *N.-Fr.* Tafernel; p.n.

TUFFS. *See* Tuff or Tufts

TUFNAIL. *See* Tuffnell

TUFTON. A loc. n., Hants

TUFTS. From Tofts; a loc. n., Norf.

TUGWELL. *See* Togwell

TUKE. *See* Tooke

TULEY, TULLEY, TULLY. *N.-Fr.* Tuelou, Tulye; p.n. Hugt. n., Lond. 1618

TULL. *See* Toole

TULLETT. From Tult; a loc. n., Devon. Or *Fr.* Toullet; a p.n.

TULLIDGE, TULLIS. From Tullich; a loc. n., Aberdeen

TULLOCH. A loc. n., Perth

TULLOCK. *See* Tulloch

TUMPENNY. *See* Tempany

TUNALEY. *See* Tunley

TUNBRIDGE. A loc. n., Kent

TUNGATE. From Tundergarth (?); a loc. n., Dumfries

TUNKIN, TUNKS. *See* Tonkin

TUNLEY. A loc. n., Somers

TUNMER. *See* Tunmore

TUNMORE. A loc. n. Eight places in Ireland and Scotland

TUNNEY. From Toesni; a loc. n., Norm.

TUNNICLIFFE. From Tonnacliff; a loc. n., Lancs

TUNSTALL. A loc. n., Dur., Kent, Staffs, Suff.

TUPHOLME. A loc. n., Lincs

TUPMAN. *See* Tubman

TUPP, TUPPER. *A.S.* Tub, Dub, Tubba (a striker (?)); *G.* Töpper (a potter); p.n. Or *see* Tubb

TUPPING. *Dch.* Tubbing; a p.n.; fam. n. of Tubb

TUR. *See* Torr

TURBAND. *N.* Þorbrandr; *D.B.* Torbrand, Turbrand (Thor's sword); *G.* Turbin; p.n.

TURBEFIELD. From Turberville or Troubleville; a loc. n., Norm.

TURBETT. *See* Torbet

TURBEY. *G.* Turbe; a p.n. *See* Thorburn

TURK. *A.S.* Turca; *N.-Fr.* Turkeis; *Fl.* Turck; *Dch.* Turk; *D.* Türck; *G.* Tourke, Türk; p.n. Dim. of Thor (?)

TURNADGE. *See* Turnidge

TURNBULL. From Tournebu; a barony in Norm.

TURNER. *Fr.* Tournaire, Tourneur, Turnier; *Fl.* Turner; p.n.

> *N.-Fr.* From the *tourn*, or feudal court, from attending which the tenant's deputy was styled an attorney. Turnerus, capellanus, in a grant to Croyland, A.D. 1051. Reginald le Turnur held land in Oxon *temp.* K. John.

TURNEY. From Tournay; a loc. n., France. *D.B.* de Torny; a p.n.

TURNHAM. A loc. n., Devon, Middlx.

> De Garlande held it.

TURNIDGE. From Turnditch; a loc. n., Derbysh.

TURPIN. From Turpin au Bois; a loc. n., Norm. *G.* Turbin; *Dch.* Torbein; *Fr.* Turpin; p.n.

> Walter Turpin held lands in Dorset *temp.* K. John, 1202.

TURRELL *N.-Fr.* Turel; a p.n.

TURTLE, TURTILL. *See* Thirketel

TURTON. A loc. n., Lancs

TURVEY. A loc. n., Beds

TURVILLE. A loc. n., Bucks. Or Tourville, Normandy

TUSHAW. *G.* Tusche; a p.n.

TUSON. *See* Tyson. Prot. ref., Lond. 1688

TUSTIN. *N.-Fr.* Fitz Tustin; *N.* Þorsteinn; *A.S.* Thorstan, Thurstan, Tustain, Tusten; p.n. (Thor's stone); or *A.S.* Thurstegn (Thor's soldier)

TUTCHER. *Fr.* Tousjours (?); a p.n.

TUTE, TUTT. *See* Tooth

TUTHILL, TUTILL, TUTTELL, TUTTLE. From Toothill; a loc. n., Hants, Lincs

TUTING. From Tooting; a loc. n., Surr.

TUTTIETT. From Touchet, near Mortaine, Norm.; a baronial n. Cephas Tutet, Hugt., Lond. 1681

> Ursin de T., 1082, Norm. Jocelin T., Ches., *temp.* W. I., Lords Audley, Earls of Castlehaven. Toget, Tuchet in Roll of Battell Abbey.

TWADELL. *See* Tweddel

TWAITS. *See* Thwaites

TWAMLEY. From Twemlow; a loc. n., Ches.

TWEDDEL. From Tweed-dale; a loc. n.

TWEED, TWEEDIE. *N.* Þveit; *D.* Tvede; p.n. *See* Thwaites

> At first a local n. (a piece of land cut off or reclaimed, *A.S. thwitan* (to cut)), it became a p.n.

TWEEN. Thuin; a loc. n., Belg. *N.-Fr.* Tuinc; *Dch.* Tuijn, Tuyn; p.n.

> Twin in Rot. Hund.

TWELLS. Originally Atte-Wells

TWIDDY. *See* Tweedie

TWIGG. *A.S.* Twicga; a p.n.; *tweg* (two, twin (?))

TWIGHT. *See* Twite

TWINBERROW. A loc. n., Worcest.

TWINER, TWINN. *See* Tween

TWINING. *See* Twyning

TWISDEN. From Twisten; a loc. n., Lancs

> Twisten was called Twysilton *temp.* K. John, at which period the family of that name were owners there.

TWISLETON. A loc. n., Yorks

TWISS. *Dch.*; p.n.; *Old G.* Zuiso; p.n.; *A.S. twis* (twin)

TWITCHELL. *See* Twitchwell

TWITCHIN, TWITCHING. From Twitchen; a loc. n., Devon, Norf.

TWITCHWELL. From Titchwell; a loc. n., Norf.

TWITE. From Thwaite; a loc. n., Norf., Yorks. Or *Dch.* Tuit; a p.n.

TWOGOOD. *See* Toogood

TWOO. *See* Tow or Thew

TWYCROSS. A loc. n., Leics

TWYDELL. *See* Tweddle

TWYFORD. A loc. n., Derbysh., Hants, Lincs, Norf., Salop

TWYNAM. From Twineham; a loc. n., Salop

TWYNING. A loc. n., Glost.

TWYSDEN. A loc. n., Kent. Formerly Twysenden

TYACK. *Fr.* Taiche; p.n. *See* Teager

TYARS, TYAS, TYCE. *See* Tice

TYDEMAN. *Dch.* Tydeman; a p.n. *See* Tidman

TYE. From Teigh; a loc. n., Rutld.; or Thy, Thys, Belg. *D.* Thye; a p.n. *See* Dye

TYERMAN. *Dch.* Tieman; a p.n.

TYLECOTE. From Tulket; a loc. n. on the Ribble, near Preston, Lancs (Brit. Tylcoed (?)). Or Holecote, Ullcote, Northants

Philip de Ulecot and Hugh de Bailiol, in 1216, sided with King John against his brother Richard. Persons

TYLECOTE—*continued*
of the name of Talkatt, Tallcot, Taylcote, Taylcott were living at Braintree, Essex, in 1623. John Tallcott occurs in a list of emigrants to America in 1632.

TYLER. From Tilers, a fief and castle in Norm. *N.-Fr.* De Telieres; a p.n.

De Tilere in Rot. Hund.

TYNDALE, TYNDALL. *See* Tindal

TYRER. *N.-Fr.* Terrer; a p.n.

TYRIE. A loc. n., Aberdeen

TYRRELL. A loc. n., Norm. *D.* Turrell; *Fr.* Thirel, Tirel; p.n.; *N.-Fr.* a little castle or tower

Tirell in Roll of Battell Abbey; and de Tirel, under-tenant, in *D.B.*

TYRWHITT. From Tywardreth; a loc. n., Cornw. Or *see* Truwhitt

TYSON, TYSSEN. *D.* Thuessen, Thyssen; *Dch.* Thijssen, Tijssen; *Fl.* Tison, Tyssen; *N.-Fr.* Tison, Tisun; p.n.

Gislebert Tison, a tenant in chief, *D.B.* (Notts, Yorks, Lincs), had twenty-nine manors forfeited upon the ravaging of Yorks by William I. Teison or Thisun in Rot. Obl. et Fin.

U

UBANK. *See* Ewbank

UDALL. *Fr.* Oudalle; a p.n. From Ouvedale; a loc. n., Norm.

UDEN. *N.* Uðr; *A.S.* Ud, Uda; *F.* Uda, Udden; *Dch.* Uden; *S.* Uddén; p.n. Trib. n. of Udo (the prosperous)

UDNEY. A loc. n., Aberdeen

UFF. *A.S.* Uffa, Wuffa; *D.* Uffe; p.n. *See* E. Angl. king (an owl, vulture)

UFFINDEL. A loc. n. Wo Uffendale

UGLOW. *S.* Uggla (?); a p.n.

ULLATHORNE. A loc. n.

ULLETT. *See* Hullett

ULLMER. *A.S.* Ulfmær, Ulmer; *D.*, *Dch.* Ulmer; p.n. (famous wolf)

ULP, ULPH. *N.* Ulfarr or Ulfr (wolf); *F.* Ulferd; *D.B.* Ulf, Ulfere, Ulfii; *G.* Uhl, Uhlfig, Ulfert; p.n.

ULYATT. *See* Ullett

UNCLE. A loc. n., Holland and Germ. *Dch.* Unkel; a p.n.

UNDERDOWN. A loc. n., Cornw.

UNDERHAY. From Underheugh; a loc. n., Cumb.

UNDERHILL. A loc. n., Devon

UNDERWOOD. A loc. n., Derbysh., Devon, Notts

UNGOOD. From Hengoed; a loc. n., Salop

UNITE. From Unity; a loc. n., Cumb.

UNSWORTH. A loc. n., Lancs

UNTHANK. A loc. n., Cumb. and Northbd.

UNWIN. *N.* Aun; *A.S.* Onwine, Unwen, Unwinus (friend of the gods); *Fl.* Unwin; p.n.

UPCHER. *See* Upsher

UPCOTT. A loc. n., Devon, Somers

UPFILL. From Uphill (?); a loc. n., Devon

UPHAM. A loc. n., Hants

UPJOHN. Welsh Apjohn (?); a p.n. (Johnson)

UPPERTON. A loc. n., Devon

UPSALL. A loc. n., Yorks

UPSDALL. From Upsall (?); a loc. n., Yorks

UPSHER. From Upshire; a loc. n., Ess.

UPSOM. A loc. n.

UPTON. A loc. n., Berks, Cornw., Devon, Dorset, Hants, Kent, Lancs, Northants, Somers, Wilts, Yorks

UPWARD. *See* Upwood

UPWOOD. A loc. n., Hunts

URE. From Urr; a loc. n., Kirkcudbright. Or *A.S.* Ur; *N.* Urr; p.n. (wild ox)

UREN. A contr. of Trewren; a loc. n., Cornw.; or Welsh Urien (heavenly). St Urien; a loc. n., Norm.

URIE. A loc. n., Inverness

URMSTON. A loc. n., Lancs

URQUHART. A loc. n., Elgin

URRY. *See* Hurry

URWICK. From Urswick; a loc. n., Lancs

Adam de Urswick, 6 Edw. III. (1332), was chief forester of Bowland. Sir Robert, knight of the shire, 5 to 20 Rich. II., and 1 and 2 Henry IV. Sir John de Urswick, 14 Rich. II., sheriff. Christopher, chaplain to Henry VII., the "Sir Christopher" of Rich. III., Act V. § 5, buried in Hackney Church.

USBORNE. From Husborne; a loc. n., Beds. Or *see* Osborne

USHER. From Ushaw; a loc. n., Dur. Or *A.S.* Hoshere, Oshere; p.n. (the gods' warrior)

The family of De Neville assumed the name of Le Uschere or Le Huissier, from the office granted to them by K. John.

USHERWOOD. *See* Isherwood

USILL. From Ussel or Uzel; loc. n., France. *Dch.* Husel; a p.n.

UTTERMARE. From Udimore; a loc. n., Kent

UTTERTON. From Otterton; a loc. n., Devon

UTTING. *N.* Udr; *F.* Udo, Ude, Uden; *G.* Otte, Oettinger; *Dch.* Ouden; *Fl.* Utten; *S.* Udden; *D.B.* Eudo, Udi, Othingar; p.n. Prot. ref., Sandwich, 1622. *See* Udden

UWINS. *See* Ewens

UZZELL. *See* Usill

V

VACHELL. From Vaucelles; a loc. n., Fland.

VAGG. *See* Wagg

VAIL. *See* Vale

VAISEY, VAIZEY. *See* Veasey

VALE. *N.-Fr.* De Vetula or De Veel; a p.n.

VALENTINE. *Fr.* Valentin; *Dch.* Valentien; p.n. Hugt. n., 1618

VALIANT. *Fr.* Vaillant; a p.n. Hugt. n., Lond. 1681

VALLER. From Valeres; a loc. n., Norm.

VALLANCE. From Valence; a loc. n., Norm.

VALLINGS. *A.S.* Wealing; a fam. n.; *D.B.* Wellen (strangers, foreigners); *D.* Wahlin, Wallin; *Dch.* Walen; *Fl.* Wallens; p.n.

VALPY. From *D.* Valby; a loc. n.

VANCE. A loc. n., Belg.

VANDELEUR. *Fl.* Vande Laer, Vanderloo; p.n. Theodorus Vanderlaugh, gent., Prot. ref., Lond. 1618

VANE. *See* Fane

VANNE. From Van; a loc. n., Glamorgan. Or *Dch.* Vane; a p.n.

VANNECK. *Fl.* Van Eck, Vanneck; p.n. Dch. ref., Lond. 1618

VARDEN. *A.S.* Weording; a fam. n.; *D.* Warding; *G.* Wardein; *Dch.* Vaarting; *Fl.* Verdeyen; *D.B.* Werden; p.n. Or *see* Verdon

VARDIGANS. *See* Vertigan

VARDY. *N.-Fr.* La Ferté; a loc. n. (barony), Norm., near Evreux

VARGUS. *See* Fergus

VARLEY. A loc. n., Ess. Also *Fr.* Varlez; a p.n.
R. de Verli, Norf. 1086.

VARLO. *See* Varley

VARNAM. *See* Farnham

VARNELL. From Verneuil (?); a loc. n., Norm. Or *Fl.* Fannell; a p.n.

VARNEY. *Fl.* Warny; a p.n.

VARNHAM. *See* Farnham

VARVILL. From Varaville; a loc. n., Norm. *Fr.* Vauville; a p.n.
Varuurile in Roll of Battell Abbey. De Warwell in *D.B.*

VASEY. *See* Veasey

VASS. *A.S.* Was; *Dch.* Vas, Vasse, Vassy; *Fl.* Fas; p.n. (water)

VASSAR. *Fr.* Vasseur; *Fl.* Vassert; *G.* Wasser; *A.S.* Waso; p.n.; *N.-Fr.* Levasseur (a vassal)

VATCHER. *N.-Fr.* Vachier; a p.n. (cow-keeper)

VAUGHT. *See* Faught

VAUS, VAUSE, VAWSE. *See* Vaux

VAUX. A loc. n., Belg. and Norm.

VAVASSOUR. *Fr.* Vavasseur, Le Vavasseur; p.n. *See* official names

VAWDREY. From Valdaré or Vaudaré; a loc. n., Norm.; or Waudrez, Belg. *N.-Fr.* De Valdairie: a p.n. Hugt. n., Norwich, 1622

VAWSER. *See* Vassar

VEAL. From Ville; a loc. n., Belg. *See* Viall

VEAR. *See* Vere

VEARS. *A.S.* Wær (wary); *Dch.* Weers; p.n.

VEASEY. *N.-Fr.* De Vaacy; a p.n.; *D.B.* de Veci
Vessay or de Vesci in Roll of Battell Abbey and in Rot. Obl. et Fin., K. John.

VEITCH. *See* Fetch

VELLUM. *See* Welham

VENABLES. A loc. n., Norm.
D.B. Gislebert de V., an under-tenant (Ches.), 1086. Richard de V. in Rot. Obl. et Fin. The barony of Kinderton continued in this family till 1676.

VENESS. *Fl.* Van Esse, Vanesse; a p.n. Or *N.-Fr.* De Venis; a p.n.

VENIMORE. *See* Fennimore

VENN. A loc. n., Cornw., Devon

VENNING. *See* Fane

VENTRIS. *N.-Fr.* Ventras or Vintras; a p.n.
Ralph de Vintyr in Rot. Hund.

VERDON. From Verdun; a loc. n. in France
Verdoune in Roll of Battell Abbey. Bertram de Verdun, a tenant in chief in *D.B.* (Staffs). In 1273 John de Verdun held lands in Belton, Leics. Bertram de Verdun founded Croxden Abbey, 23 Henry II., 1176.

VERE. From Ver; a loc. n., Norm. *D.B.* de Ver; a p.n.
In Roll of Battell Abbey and Rot. Obl. et Fin.

VERLANDER. *Fl.*, *Dch.* Verlant, Verlinde; p.n.

VERLEY. *See* Varley

VERNEY. *See* Fernie

VERNON. From Vernon; a loc. n., Norm. Hugt. n., Lond. 1618

Vernoun in Roll of Battell Abbey; *D.B.* de Vernon, tenant in chief.

VERRY. From Viry or Verrey; a loc. n., Norm. *Fr.* Wéry; *Fl.* Werry; *Dch.* Verre; p.n.

VERSCHOYLE. From Vascœuil; a loc. n., Norm. *Fl.* Veerschuijl; a p.n.

VERTIGAN. *B.* Vortigern (?) (great king)

VERTUE. *See* Virtue

VERVILL. *See* Varvill

VESEY. *See* Veasey

VESPER. *Dch.* Weesper; a p.n.

VESTEY. *A.S.* West; *D.* Westi; a p.n. *See* West

VIALL. From Vile or Vielles; a loc. n., Norm. *See* Veal. Viel, a Hugt. n., Lond. 1864

Vile and De Vile are in the Roll of Battell Abbey.

VIAN. A loc. n., Fland. and Norm. *Fr.* Viane; a p.n.

VIBERT. *A.S.* Wigbeorht; *Old G.* Wigbert, Wibert; p.n. (war famous)

VICARAGE. *A.S.* Wigric; *Old G.* Wigirich (war rule); *Fl.* Wichterich; p.n.

VICARY. From La Vacherie; a loc. n., Norm.

R. de Vickery in Rot. Hund.

VICKERMAN. *D.* Wickman; a p.n.

VICKERS. *N.* Víkarr (a viking (?)); *D.* Wick, Vickers; *Fl.* Wyckaerts; *Dch.* Wichers, Wiggers; *G.* Wickert; p.n.

VIDLER, VIDLOW. From Vis-de-lou, Norm. Or *see* Fidler

Vis-de-Lew, tenant in chief, *D.B.*, Berks.

VIGORS. From St Vigor; a loc. n., Norm. *Fr.* Vigor. *See* Wigger

Viger in Rot. Obl. et Fin.

VILLIERS. From Villiers; a loc. n., Belg. and Norm. *Fl.* Villers; *D.* Willer; *Dch.* Willaars; p.n.

VIMER. *D.B.* Wimer; *G.* Wimmer; p.n. *See* Wyman

VINCE. *A.S.* Winsi (Winsige); *Fl.* Vinche, Wyns; *Dch.* Wins; *G.* Vins; p.n. (victorious friend). Or from *N.-Fr.* De Vinas; a p.n.

VINCENT. *N.-Fr.* St Vincent; a loc. n., Norm. Hugt., Lond. 1618

VINE, VINN. From Veynes; a loc. n., France. *Fr.* Vin; *Fl.* Wion, Wyn; *Dch.* Vinne; p.n.

VINEY. From Vinhay; a loc. n., Devon; Vinney, Somers; or Vignie, Norm.

VINNECOMBE. From Venycombe; a loc. n., Hants

VINRACE. *See* Wainwright

VINT. *Fl.* Windt; *D.* Wind; p.n.

VIPOND, VIPONT, VIPAND. *N.-Fr.* De Vieuxpont; a p.n. (barons of Westmd.)

Thomas Vipont, Bishop of Carlisle, 1255.

VIRGIN. From Verchin; a loc. n., France. Or *S.* Virgin; *Fl.* Wirtgen (dimin. of *F.* Wêert); p.n.

VIRGO, VIRGOE. *Fl.* Vergote; *D.* Vergo; *Dch.* Vergouw; p.n.; *A.S. wær-gota* (?) (war Goth)

VIRTUE. From Vertou; a loc. n., France

R. de la Vertu, 1180.

VISE. *See* Wise

VISGERS. *Fl.* Visschers; a p.n. *See* Whisker

VISICK. *See* Physic

VITTERY. From Vitry; a loc. n., Belg. and France. *Fr.* Vitré and de Vitré; p.n.

VIVEASH, VIVISH. *Fr.* Fievez; a p.n.

VIZARD, VIZER. *Fr.* Visart, Viseur; *Dch.* Visser; p.n. (a vizard or vizor; a mask for the face, attached to a helmet)

VOISEY. *Fr.* Voisin; a p.n. (neighbour)

VOKES. *See* Vaux

VORES. *G.* Voras; a p.n. *See* Vears

VOS, VOSE. *D.*, *Dch.*, *Fl.*, *G.* Voss; a p.n. *See* Vass

VOWEL. *See* Fowell

VOWLES. *See* Foule

VOYCE. *Dch.* Voijs; a p.n. De Voyce, Hugt. n., Cant. 1618

VYE. *Fr.* Vuy, Vuye; p.n. De la Fuyé, Hugt. n., Lond. 1683

VYNER. *A.S.* Winehere (friend-soldier); a p.n.

VYSE. *See* Wise

W

WABE. *A.S.* Wæba; a p.n. (a weaver)

WACE, WACEY. *A.S.* Was, Wass, Wassa (water (?)); *G.* Weese, Wehse; *Dch.* Wees; *N.-Fr.* De Wasa; p.n.
In Rot. Obl. et Fin. and Rot. Hund.

WACKETT. *See* Waggett

WADD. *N.* Vaði (a wader); *D.* Wad; *A.S.* Wada, Wade, Wado; p.n.

WADDELL. A loc. n., Scotl. Or *A.S.*, *D.* Wadel; *S.* Wadell; p.n. Dim. of Wad

WADDELOW. *See* Vidler. Wadelo; a p.n. in *D.B.*

WADDESLEY. From Wadsley; a loc. n., Yorks

WADDILOVE. *See* Waddelow

WADDING. *See* Woodin

WADDINGTON. A loc. n., Devon, Lincs, Yorks

WADDUP. From Whadub; a loc. n., Cumb.

WADDY. *See* Wadd

WADE. A loc. n., Hants
De W. in Rot. Hund. In Rot. Obl. et Fin.

WADHAM. From Waddingham; a loc. n., Lincs. Or *Dch.* Wadum; a p.n.

WADLEY. A loc. n., Berks, Devon

WADMAN. *S.*; p.n.

WADSWORTH. A loc. n., Lancs, Yorks

WAGER. *A.S.* Wæghere (sea warrior); *G.* Wager; p.n.

WAGG. A loc. n., Somers. Or *N.* Vágr; *A.S.* Wag; *D.* Waage; *Dch.* Waag; *D.B.* Waga; p.n. (wave, sea; or in the sense of waving, *i.e.* brandishing a sword)

WAGGETT. *G.* Weckert; *S.* Vagt; p.n. Dim. of Wagg

WAGGON. *N.* Vagn; *A.S.* Wagan; *Fl.* Wagon; p.n.; fam. n. of Wagg (?)

WAIGHT. *See* Waite

WAILING. *See* Vallings

WAIN. *D.* Wain; *G.* Wehn; p.n. *See* Waggon

WAINER. *G.* Wehner; a p.n.

WAINWRIGHT. *D.* Weinrich; *G.* Weinerich; *A.S.* Wineric; p.n. (friendly ruler)

WAITE. *A.S.* Wet, Wetta, Hwæt; *D.* Vet, Wiet; *Fl.* Vets; *F.* Wêt, Wiet; *G.* Weth; p.n. (sharp, keen)

WAKE. *A.S.* Wac, Wacar; *D.* Weeke; *G.* Weck; *Fl.* Weeck; p.n. (watchful)
In Rot. Obl. et Fin.

WAKEFIELD. A loc. n., Northants, Yorks

WAKEFORD. A loc. n.

WAKEHAM. A loc. n., Dorset

WAKELIN, WAKELING. *N.-Fr.* Walchelin; *S.* Wacklin; p.n.

WAKELY, WAKLEY. A loc. n., Herts

WALCOTT. A loc. n., Lincs, Norf., Salop, Worcest.

WALDEGRAVE. From Walgrave; a loc. n., Northants; anciently Waldegrave

Held by De Maloure of Bretagne.

WALDEN. A loc. n., Yorks

WALDON. *See* Walden

WALDRON. A loc. n., Suss. Or *A.S.* Waleran; *Dch.* Woelderen; p.n. (powerful raven)

WALDUCK. *Dch.*, *G.* Waldeck; a loc. and p.n. (forest oak)

WALE. *A.S.* Wale, Wealh, Wel; *D.* Wehl; *Fl.* Weyll; p.n. (stranger, foreigner)

WALES, WAILES, WAYLES. From Wales; a loc. n., Yorks (*D.B.* Walise). Or *G.* Wels; a p.n.

WALESBY. A loc. n., Lincs, Notts

WALEY. *See* Whalley

WALFORD. A loc. n., Staffs

WALKDEN. A loc. n., Lancs

WALKER. *N.* Valka (a foreigner); *Dch.* Walkart, Walker; *Fl.* Walckiers; *G.* Walke, Walker; *A.S.* Walcher, Wealhere; p.n. (a stranger soldier)

It is a very old n. The tribe of Wealceringas was among the early settlers. *A.S.* *wealcere* (a fuller) is not so likely a derivation.

WALKERLEY. From Walkley; a loc. n., Yorks

WALKINGSHAW. A loc. n., Renfrew

WALL. A loc. n., Staffs. Or *A.S.* Wal, Weal; p.n. (a stranger)

WALLACE or WALLIS. *N.* Valir; *A.S.* Valas or Wealas (the Welsh, *i.e.* foreigners or strangers); *A.S.* Wealhisc; *Dch.* Walsch; *Fl.* Wallays; p.n.

There was an influx of Anglo-Normans into Scotland in the reign of David I. Among these was Richard Waleys, the ancestor of the great Wallace. He has left his name at Richardtun in Ayrshire. Valers is in the Roll of Battell Abbey; and de

WALLACE or WALLIS—*continued*

Vals, de Wals, Walo, Walise, Walscin are in *D.B.* The northwestern part of France was called by the Norsemen Walland.

WALLACH, WALLEDGE. *Dch.*, *D.* Wallich; a p.n. *See* above

WALLBRIDGE. A loc. n., Glost.

WALLER. *A.S.* Wealhere; *S.*, *Dch.*, *Fl.* Waller; p.n. (a stranger warrior)

WALLETT. From Waillet; a loc. n., Belg. *Dch.* Walet; a p.n.

WALLING. *D.* Wallin; *S.* Wallen; p.n.; descendant of Wall

WALLINGTON. A loc. n., Hants, Norf., Surr.

WALLIS. *See* Wallace

WALLMAN. *See* Whall

WALLOP. A loc. n., Hants

WALMSLEY. A loc. n., Lancs, Staffs

WALPOLE. A loc. n., Norf., Somers, Suff.

WALRON. *N.-Fr.* Waleran; a p.n. *See* Waldron

WALSH. From Wallash; a loc. n., Staffs. Or *see* Wallach

WALSHAM. A loc. n., Norf., Suff.

WALSINGHAM. A loc. n., Norf.

WALSOM. *Dch.* Walsem; a p.n. Or *see* Walsham

WALTERS. *A.S.* Walder, Walter, Wealdhere; *Dch.* Wolters; *Fl.* Wauters, Wouters; p.n. (ruler-warrior); a contr. of Walterus. Prot. ref., Lond. 1621

WALTHEW. *N.* Valþjóf (a foreign servant); *G.*, *Dch.* Walther; *A.S.* Wealtheow; *D.B.* Wallef, Waltef; p.n.

WALTON. A loc. n., Berks, Derbysh., Herts, Lancs, Norf., Somers, Staffs, Suff.

WAND. From Wandre; a loc. n., Belg. *D.B.* Wand; *G.* Wander; p.n. *See* Want

WANKLYN. *A.S.* Wan, Wana; *S.* Wancke; *D.* Wang; p.n. A dim. (pale)

WANNOP. From Wandhope; a loc. n., Cumb.

WANSBOROUGH. From Wanborough; a loc. n., Surr., Wilts

WANT. From Wanz; a loc. n., Belg. Or *N.* Vandráðr; *D.B.* Wand, Wanz, Wants; *G.* Wander; *Dch.* Wandt; *Fl.* Wanet; p.n. (zealous counsellor)

WARBEY, WARBY. From Warboys; a loc. n., Hunts. Or Verbois, Norm.

WARBRICK. From Warbreck; a loc. n., Lancs

WARBURTON. A loc. n., Ches.

WARD. A loc. n., Devon. Or *A.S.* Ward, Weard (guard); *Dch.* Waard. Warde; p.n. Garde; a loc. n., I. of France

WARDALE, WARDELL. *See* Wardle

WARDEN. A loc. n., Kent, Northants, Northbd. Wardin, Belg.

WARDLAW. A loc. n., Inverness

WARDLE. A loc. n., Lancs

WARDLEY. A loc. n., Rutland. Or Weardley, Yorks

WARE. A loc. n., Devon, Herts

WAREHAM. A loc. n., Dorset

WARFORD. *See* Walford

WARHURST. *D.* Warhus; *Fl.* Verhust; p.n. (wood warden)

WARING. *See* Wearing

WARLAND. *Fl.*; p.n.

WARLEIGH. A loc. n., Somers

WARLOW. From Wardlow; a loc. n., Derbysh.

WARMAN. *A.S.* Wearman (warman; or cautious, wary); *D.* Warming; p.n.

WARMER. *A.S.* Wærmær; *G.* Warmer (war famous). Or Walmer; a loc. n., Kent

WARMINGTON. A loc. n., Northants, Warw.

WARN, WARNE. From Waghen or Wawne; a loc. n., Yorks. Or *see* Wearing

WARNEFORD. A loc. n., Hants

WARNER. *A.S.* Warner, Wernhere; *N.-Fr.* le Warner; p.n.

WARNES. *A.S.* Warinus; *D.* Warns; p.n.

WARR. *A.S.* War, Wær; *D.* Warrer; p.n. (cautious warrior) Le Warre in Rot. Obl. et Fin.

WARRAM. From Warham; a loc. n., Norf. Held by De Vere.

WARREN. *N.-Fr.* Warin, Verenne; p.n. *See* Wearing Gundred de Warren or Warrenna held lands in Wilts *temp.* K. John, 1201.

WARRENER. From Garenne; a loc. n., Norm. W. de W., 1066; Earl of Surrey, 1089.

WARRINGTON. A loc. n., Ches.

WARRY. *See* Warr

WARSAP. *See* Worsop

WARTER. A loc. n., Yorks

WARTH. *See* Ward or Worth

WARWICK. A loc. n., Cumb., Hants, and the county town

WASE, WASEY. *See* Wace, Wasce (Wascheham (?)) In Rot. Obl. et. Fin.

WASHBOURN. A loc. n., Devon

WASHINGTON. A loc. n., Dur., Suss.

WASPE. *See* Warsap

WASTELL. A loc. n., Worcest.

WATCHAM. From Watchcombe; a loc. n., Devon

WATERALL. From Waterfall; a loc. n., Staffs

WATERFIELD. From Waterville; a loc. n., Norm.

WATERHOUSE. A loc. n., Staffs

WATERLOW. *Fl.* Waterloos; a loc. and p.n. Or *see* Waddelow

WATERS, WATERSON. *See* Walters. Prot. ref. n., Lond. 1618

WATERSTONE. A loc. n., Pembroke

WATFORD. A loc. n., Derbysh., Herts, Northants

WATKINS. *See* Watts

WATLER. *Fr.* Watelet; a p.n.

WATLING. *A.S.*; fam. n.

WATLOW. *See* Waterlow

WATMORE. *See* Whitmore

WATTON. A loc. n., Norf.

WATTS. *N.* Hvati (active); *A.S.* Wat; *D.* Watt; p.n. *See* Wait

WAUCHOPE. From Warcop (?); a loc. n., Westmd.

WAUD. *See* Wadd

WAUGH. *See* Wagg. Or from the Irish McWhaugh

WAUGHN, WAWN. *G.* Wahn; *Dch.* Waan; *D.* Wohn; p.n. *See* Waggon

WAVELL. *See* Weevill

WAY. A loc. n., Devon, Kent. Or *see* Wagg

WAYBORN. From Waybourne; a loc. n., Norf.

WAYCOTT. *See* Waygood

WAYGOOD. *A.S.* Wigod, Wigot; *Old G.* Wihgoz; p.n. (war Goth)

WAYHAM. A loc. n.

WAYLAND. A loc. n., Dorset. Or *Fl.* Weyland; a p.n.

WAYLES. *See* Wales

WAYMAN. *See* Wyman

WAYMOUTH. *See* Weymouth

WEAGER. *See* Widger

WEAKLEY, WEAKLIN. *See* Wakelin

WEAL. *A.S.* Wil; *Old G.* Willo; *Dch., Fl.* Wiel; *G.* Wiehl; p.n. (resolution)

WEARE. A loc. n., Somers

WEARING. *N.* Væringi; the name of the Warings or northern warriors who served as body-guards to the Byzantine Emperors; *A.S.* Wæring; a fam. n.; *Fl.* Vering; *D.B.* Warenger, Werinc, Wareng, Warinc, Warin; p.n.
The Varangian Guard was originally composed of this Scandinavian tribe, but was afterwards recruited from Northern Europe and England. There is a Varengafjord in Norway.

WEATHERALL. A loc. n., Camb. *See* Wetherall

WEATHERBURNE. *See* Wedderburn

WEATHERLEY. A loc. n., Warw. From Wetherley; a loc. n., Camb.

WEATHERS. *See* Withers

WEATHERSTONE. From Withersden; a loc. n., Kent

WEAVER. A loc. n., Ches., Devon. *N.-Fr.* De Wevre; a p.n. Or *D.* Wæver; a p.n (a weaver)

WEAVING. *Dch.* Wieffering; a fam. n.

WEBB, WEBBER. *Fl.* Webb; *D., Dch., G.* Weber (a weaver)

WEBSDALE. A loc. n.

WEBSTER. The Scot. and N. Engl. form of *D., G., Dch.* Weber (a weaver)

WEDD. *See* Weed

WEDDERBURN. A loc. n., Berwick

WEDDERSPOON, WITHERSPOON. *See* Wotherspon

WEDDING. *D.* Weden; *S.* Wedin; p.n; fam. n. of Weed

WEDDUP. A loc. n.

WEDGEWOOD. A loc. n., Staffs

WEDLAKE, WEDLOCK. *See* Widlake

WEDMORE. A loc. n., Somers

WEEDE. *D.* Wied; *A.S.* Wid, Widda; *Fl.* Widy; *S.* Wid; p.n. (famous)

WEEDEN. From Weedon; a loc. n., Northants

WEEDING. From Weeting; a loc. n., Norf. Or *see* Weeden

WEEDS. *F.* Wiets; *D.B.* Widius; p.n. *See* Weed

WEEKS. A loc. n., Ess.

WEEVILL. From Wauville; a loc. n., Norm.; Wyvill, Lincs. Or *N.* Vífill (a beetle); *D.* Wivel; *D.B.* Wifle; *Dch.* Wiwel; p.n. *See p. 2*
Viville, Wyville, Wivel, in Roll of Battell Abbey. Richard de Wyvill held lands in Yorks *temp.* K. John, A.D. 1200.

WEGG. *Dch.* Wegge; *D.B.* Wege, Weghe; p.n. Prot. ref., Sandwich, 1622. *See* Wagg

WEIGHTMAN. *A.S.* Wetman; a p.n. *See* Waite

WEIR. Scot. form of *N.-Fr.* de Vere

WELBORE. From Wellebue; a loc. n., Norm. *See* Wildbore

S

WELBORN. A loc. n., Lincs, Norf. Or *A.S.* Wilbeorn (resolute bear); *G.* Wilborn; a p.n.

WELCHER. *See* Wilscher

WELDON. A loc. n., Northants

WELFORD. A loc. n., Berks, Glost., Northants, Warw.

WELHAM. A loc. n.

WELLAND. A loc. n., Devon, Worcest.

WELLBY. A loc. n., Leics, Lincs

WELLINGHAM. A loc. n., Norf.

WELLINGTON. A loc. n., Salop, Somers

WELLS. A loc. n., Norf., Somers

WELLSPRING. A loc. n., Devon

WELLSTEAD. A loc. n. (?). Or *A.S.* Wealhstod; a p.n. (an interpreter)

WELLUM. *See* Welham

WELTON. A loc. n., Lincs, Northants, Somers, Staffs, Yorks

WEMBORN. From Wimborne; a loc. n., Dorset

WEMYS. A loc. n., Fife

WENBORN. *See* Wemborn

WENDEN. A loc. n., Ess.

WENHAM. A loc. n., Suff.

WENLOCK. A loc. n., Salop

WENT. *D.*, *G.*, *S.* Wendt; *Fl.* Vent; *Dch.* Went; p.n. (a vandal; a native of Jutland)

WENTWORTH. A loc. n., Camb., Yorks

Held by De Oissy.

WESLEY. *N.* Vestliði (a western sailor); *S.* Westlau, Wessling; *Dch.* Wesler, Wesseling; *G.* Wesely; *Fl.* Wesly; p.n. Or from the Irish MacUaislaidh; a p.n. *See* Westley

WEST. *N.* Vestarr (a western man); *D.*, *Dch.*, *Fl.* West; *D.B.* Westre; p.n. Prot. ref., Lond. 1621

WESTACOTT. A loc. n., Devon

WESTBEAR, WESTBEER. A loc. n., Devon, Kent

WESTBROOK. A loc. n., Berks, Norf., Wilts

WESTCOTT. A loc. n., Devon, Warw.

WESTERBY. *D.*; loc. and p.n.

WESTGATE. A loc. n., Yorks, Dur. Kent

WESTHORPE. A loc. n., Lincs, Northants, Notts, Suff.

WESTLEY. A loc. n., Camb., Salop, Suff.

De Westle in Rot. Hund.

WESTON. A loc. n., Herts, Northants, Staffs, Suff., Yorks

WESTRAY. A loc. n., Orkney. Or *N.* Vestarr, Vestre; *D.S.* Wester; *Dch.* Westra; *D.B.* Westre (Saxon tenant); p.n. *See* West

WESTREPT. From Westhorpe; a loc. n., Norf. *See* Westrop

WESTROP. A loc. n., Wilts. *D.* Westrup; a loc. and p.n.

WESTWATER. From Wastwater, Cumb.

WESTWOOD. A loc. n., Dur., Devon, Kent, Notts, Wilts, Yorks

WETHERALL. A loc. n., Cumb.

WETHERLEY. From Wetherby (?); a loc. n., Yorks

WETHERSETT. *S.* Wetterstedt; a loc. and p.n.

WETMORE. *See* Whetmore

WETTERN. *Dch.* Wetten, Wetteren; p.n.

WETTERTON. From Wetherden; a loc. n., Suff.

WEY. From Ways; a loc. n., Belg. Or *N.* Véi or Vé-geirr (woe-spear); *D.* Weyhe; *D.B.* Weghe, Wege, Waih; *Fl.* Wey; *Dch.* Weih; p.n. Or *See* Wagg

WEYMOUTH. A loc. n., Dorset

WHADCOAT. *See* Whatcott

WHAITES. From Weeze (?); a loc. n., Fland. Or *see* Waite

WHALE. *See* Wale

WHALEY. A loc. n., Derbysh., Hants

WHALL. *G.* Walla, Walle; *Dch.*, *S.* Wall; p.n. *See* Wall

WHALLEY. A loc. n., Derbysh., Lancs

WHARMBY. From Warmanbie; a loc. n., Dumfries

WHARNSBY. A loc. n.

WHARTON. A loc. n., Heref., Lancs, Lincs, Westmd.

WHATCOTT. From Whatcote; a loc. n., Warw.

WHATELEY. A loc. n., Warw.

WHATLEY. A loc. n., Somers

WHATLING. *A.S.* Watling; a fam. n. *See* Watts

WHATTON. A loc. n., Leics. Or Whaddon, Camb., Wilts

WHAYMAN. *See* Wyman

WHEALS. From Houilles; a loc. n., France

WHEATBREAD. *See* Whitebread

WHEATCROFT. A loc. n., Derbysh.

WHEATER. *Dch.* Witte; a p.n. *See* White

WHEATLEY. A loc. n., Devon, Dur., Lancs, Notts, Oxf., Yorks

WHEATON. A loc. n., Staffs

WHEATSTONE. From Whetstone; a loc. n., Leics, Middlx.

WHEDDON. From Whaddon; a loc. n., Glost.

WHEELER. *N.* Víl-raðr (confused) (?). Or *Dch.* Wielaerts; *G.* Wiehle; *D.* Vieler; *A.S.* Wilred (resolute counsel); p.n.

WHEEN. *See* Wynn

WHELAN. Irish Phelan. Or *Dch.* Wielen; p.n.

WHELHAM. From Whelnetham; a loc. n., Suff.

WHELPDALE. From Wheldale; a loc. n., Yorks

WHENT. *See* Went

WHERRY. *A.S.* Wær, Wer; *Fl.* Wéry; p.n. (cautious)

WHERWELL. A loc. n., Hants

WHETMORE. From Wetmoor; a loc. n., Staffs

WHETTAM. *Dch.* Wettum; a p.n. Or *see* Whitham

WHEWELL. *See* Weevill

WHIRLEY. From Weobley; a loc. n., Heref.

WHICHCOTE. A loc. n., Salop

WHICHELOW. A loc. n.

WHICHER, WHICKER. *See* Widger

WHIDBORNE. From Whitburn; a loc. n., Heref., Linlithgow

WHIDDEN. From Whiddon; a loc. n., Devon. Or *S.* Widen; a p.n.

WHIDDINGTON. *See* Whittington

WHIFF. *A.S.* Wif; *D.* Wiuff; a p.n. *See* Whipp

WHIFFLE. *See* Whipple

WHIGHAM. From Whickham; a loc. n., Dur.

WHILEY. From Wyley; a loc. n., Ess.; or Wylye, Wilts. *See* Wayles

WHIMPER. From Whymple; a loc. n. in Devon. Or Wimpole, Camb.

WHIN. Irish Quinn. Or *D.* Wiene; *D.B.* Wine; *Dch.* Win; *Fl.* Wyns; p.n. (a friend)

WHINCOP. A loc. n., Cumb. Or *A.S.* Wincuf; *Dch.* Wincoop; p.n. (strenuous friend)

WHINERAY, WHINNERAH. *A.S.* Wineræd; a p.n. (friendly counsel)

WHINYATES. From Wingates; a loc. n., Northbd.

WHIPHAM. From Wipham; a loc. n., Suss.

WHIPP, WHIPPS, WHIPPY. *N.* Vippa; n.n.; *D.B.* Wiber; *G.* Wippert; *A.S.* Wippa (a whip); p.n.

WHIPPLE. *A.S.* Wifel; *N.* Vívill (a beetle); *S.* Wibell; a p.n.

WHISH. *See* Hewish

WHISKER. *A.S.* Wiscar, Wisgar (wise spear); *N.-Fr.* Guiscard; p.n.

WHISSELL. From Oissel; a loc. n., Norm. Or *G.* Wissell; a p.n. Oisel in Rot. Obl. et Fin., K. John.

WHISTLECRAFT. *G.* Wesselhöft; a loc. and p.n.

WHISTLER.   *N.-Fr.* Oiselur.   Or *Dch.* Wissel, Wisselaar ; p.n. ; *A.S.* hwistlere (a whistler, piper)

WHISTON.   A loc. n., Cornw., Northants, Staffs, Yorks

WHITBREAD.   *See* Whitebread

WHITBURN.   A loc. n., Dur., Heref.

WHITBY.   A loc. n., Yorks

WHITCHER.   *See* Widger

WHITCHURCH.   From Whitechurch; a loc. n., Yorks

WHITCOMBE.   A loc. n., Devon, Dorset, I. of Wight, Somers

WHITE.   *N.* Hvítr ; *S.* Witt ; *Dch.* Witte ; *A.S.* Hwitta, Wit, Wita ; p.n.

WHITEAR.   *See* Whiterod

WHITEBREAD.   *A.S.* Wihtbrord ; *Fl.* Wittebord ; *D.B.* Witbert, Wibert ; p.n. (courageous sword).   Prot. ref., Norwich, 1622

WHITEHAND.   *N. - Fr.* Blanchesmains ; a p.n.
     Steph. Blanmong, 1272, Rot. Hund.

WHITEHEAD.   *See* Whiterod

WHITEHEART.   *A.S.* Wihtheard (strong, courageous)

WHITEHORN.   A loc. n., Devon

WHITEHOUSE.   A loc. n., Aberdeen. Or *Dch.* Withuis ; a p.n.

WHITEHURST.   A loc. n., Staffs

WHITELAM.   *A.S.* Wihthelm ; a p.n. (strong, heavy helmet)

WHITELAW.   From Whitlow ; a loc. n., Northbd.

WHITELEGGE.   *A.S.* Wihtlæg ; a p.n. (wise law)

WHITELEY.   A loc. n., Devon, Yorks

WHITELOCK, WHITLOCK.   *A.S.* Wihtlac ; *S.*, *Dch.* Witlok ; a p.n. (courageous sword player)

WHITEMAN.   *Dch.* Witman ; *D.B.* Wihtmar ; p.n.

WHITEROD.   *A.S.* Wihtræd ; *F.* Witerd, Withert ; p.n. (courageous counsellor)

WHITESIDE.   A loc. n., Cumb.

WHITEWAY.   From Whitway ; a loc. n., Hants

WHITFIELD.   A loc. n., Dorset, Kent, Northants, Salop

WHITHAM, WITHAM, WHITWHAM.   From Witham ; a loc. n., Ess., Lincs

WHITHARD.   *A.S.* Wihtheard ; *F.* Witherd ; *Dch.* Wittert ; p.n. (firm courage)

WHITING, WHITTING.   *A.S.* Witting ; a fam. n. ; *D.* Witten ; *S.* Witting ; p.n.

WHITLEY.   A loc. n., Northbd., Wilts, Yorks

WHITMARSH.   From Whitnash ; a loc. n., Warw.

WHITMORE.   A loc. n., Staffs

WHITNEY.   A loc. n., Bucks, Heref.

WHITTAKER.   From Whitacre ; a loc. n., Worcest. ; Wheatacre, Norf. Or *A.S.* Wightgar ; a p.n. (strong spear)

WHITTALL.   *See* Whittle

WHITTENBURY.   From Whittlebury ; a loc. n., Heref.

WHITTERIDGE.   *See* Witheridge

WHITTET.   *See* Whithard

WHITTICK.   From Whitwick ; a loc. n., Leics

WHITTINGHAM.   A loc. n., Haddingtonsh.

WHITTINGTON.   A loc. n., Norf., Salop, Staffs, Warw., Worcest.

WHITTLE.   From Whittle ; a loc. n., Lancs. Or Whitle, Derbysh. *See* Whitwell

WHITTLESEY.   A loc. n., Camb.

WHITTOME.   From Whittenham ; a loc. n., Oxf.

WHITTON.   A loc. n., Lincs, Norf., Salop, Staffs, Yorks

WHITRICK.   *A.S.* Wihtric ; a p.n. (courageous rule).   Or *see* Witheridge

WHITWELL.   A loc. n., Derbysh., Hants, Herts, Leics, Norf., Yorks

WHITWORTH.   A loc. n., Dur., Lancs

WHUR.   *See* Wyer

WHYART, WHYATT. *A.S.* Wigheard, Wiard; *D.* Wiegardt; *Dch.* Wijaarda, Wyatt; *F.* Wiaarda; *Fl.* Wuyts; p.n. (war strong). Prot. ref., Lond. 1622

WHYBORN. *See* Wayborn

WHYBREW, WHYBROW. From Wyeborough or Wyebrow; a loc. n. on the Wye. Or *see* Wybrow

WHYLE. *See* Wylie

WHYTLAW. *See* Whitelaw

WIBBERLEY. *See* Whibley

WICK, WICKS. *See* Wigger. Prot. ref. n., Sandwich, 1622

WICKENDEN. From Wichingdine; a loc. n., Rutland

WICKETT. *A.S.* Wigod; *Fr.* Wicot; p.n. (war Goth)

WICKHAM. A loc. n., Berks, Dur., Ess., Hants, Kent, Suff.

WIDDICOMBE. A loc. n., Devon

WIDE. *See* Weed

WIDGER, WIDGERY. *A.S.* Wichere, Wighere; *Old G.* Wigheri; p.n. (war soldier)

WIDLAKE. From Widelake; a loc. n., Cornw.

WIDNALE. From Widdenhall; a loc. n.

WIDNELL. A loc. n.

WIFFIN. *A.S.* Wif, Wifare; a p.n.; *Dch.* Wijvering; a fam. n.; *wifre* (a weaver)

WIGER. *See* Widger

WIGFALL, WIGFUL. From Wigfield (?); a loc. n., Yorks, W.R.

WIGG. *A.S.* Wig; *G.* Wick; *D.* Wigh; *S.* Wik; p.n. *See* Wigger

WIGGAN. From Wigan; a loc. n., Lancs

WIGGER. *A.S.* Wigar, Wicgar, Wiga; *G.* Wicke; *Dch.* Wiggers; *D.* Wiecke; p.n. (war-spear)

WIGGETT. *See* Wichett

WIGGIN. *N.* Víkingr (a sea rover); *N.-Fr.* Wiguen, Wygeyn; *S.*, *Fl.* Wiking; *Dch.* Wijking; *D.B.* Wicing, Wichin, Wiking; p.n. Or *A.S.* Wighen, a contr. of Wighelm (war helmet)

WIGGINGTON. A loc. n., Herts, Yorks

WIGHT. *See* Wiggett or White

WIGHTMAN. *See* Whiteman

WIGLEY. A loc. n., Hants

WIGMORE. A loc. n., Heref., Salop

WIGNAL. From Wiggenhall; a loc. n., Norf.

WIGRAM. *A.S.* (strong in battle)

WILBERFORCE. From Wilberfoss; a loc. n., Yorks

WILBOURN. *See* Welborn

WILBRAHAM. A loc. n., Camb.; anciently Wilburgham

WILBY. A loc. n., Norf., Northants, Suff.

WILCH. *See* Wilscher

WILCOCKS. *Fl.* Wilcockx; *D.B.* Willac; p.n. Dimin. of Will

WILD. *See* Wildee

WILDBORE. *A.S.* Wilburh; *Dch.* Wildeboer; p.n. (resolute protection)

WILDEE. *F.* Wildert, Wilt; *A.S.* Wild; *G.*, *D.*, *Dch.* Wilde; p.n.; *A.S. wyldde* (powerful)

Adam le Wilde in Rot. Obl. et Fin. W. le W. in Rot. Hund.

WILDGOOSE. *A.S.* Wilgils, Wildgis; p.n. (resolute hostage). Or *Old G.* Wildigoz (powerful Goth). Joseph Wildigos, a Prot. ref. n., London, 1688

WILDMAN. *Dch.*, *Fl.* Wildeman; a p.n. (a verderer, or powerful man)

WILDONE. From Wilden; a loc. n., Beds

WILEMAR. *N.* Víl-Hjálmr (resolute helmet); *F.* Wilhelm, Wilm; *D.B.* Wilmar, Willelm, Wilelmus, Willa; *G.* Wilhelm; *Dch.* Willemar; p.n.

WILES. *Fl.* Weyllas; a p.n. *See* Wales

WILFORD. A loc. n., Notts. Or Williford, Staffs

WILGOSS. *See* Wildgoose

WILGRESS. *N.* Vilgeirr (resolute spear); *A.S.* Wilga; *Dch.* Willekes, Willigers; *G.* Williger, Williges; p.n.

WILKE. *F.* Wilko, Wilke; fam. n. of Wilken; *Dch.* Wilke, Wilkes; p.n. Dimin. of Will

WILKEN, WILKENS. *D.*, *Dch.* Wilken, Wilkens; *Fl.* Wilkain; p.n.
Wileken in Rot. Obl. et Fin.

WILKERSON, WILKIE. *See* Wilke

WILKINS, WILKINSON. *See* Wilkens

WILLEMENT. *N.* Vil-mundr (resolute protector); *A.S.* Wilmund; *G.* Willigmann, Willman; *Dch.* Willeman; p.n.

WILLES, WILLIS, WILLS. From Wellis, a fief in Norm.
John de W. and R. W. in Rot. Hund.

WILLESEE. From Wilsey; a loc. n., Suff.

WILLETT. Dimin. of Will

WILLEY. A loc. n., Devon, Lancs; Velly, Norm. Or *D.* Wille, Willig; *Fl.* Wyllie; *G.* Wiehle, Wille, Willich; *Dch.* Wiele, Wille, Wijle; p.n.
In Rot. Hund.

WILLIAMS, WILLIAMSON. *See* Wilemar. Flem. ref., Lond. 1618

WILLIMONT. *See* Willement

WILLIMOT. *See* Wilmot

WILLING. *Dch.* Willing; a fam. n.

WILLOUGHBY. A loc. n., Leics, Lincs, Notts, Warw.
De Wilgeby in Rot. Obl. et Fin. Muschamp held it.

WILMOT. *Old G.* Wilmod; *Fl.* Wilmart, Wilmet; *Fr.* Wilmotte; p.n. (resolute courage)

WILMSHURST. A loc. n., Suss.

WILSCHER. *See* Wilsher

WILSDON. From Willesden; a loc. n., Middlx.

WILSHAK. *G.* Wilschek; a p.n. Dim. Or Wilsick; a loc. n., Yorks

WILSHEE, WILSHER. From Wilshaw; a loc. n., Staffs, Yorks. Or Wiltshire

WILSON. *D.* Will, Wilson; p.n. Prot. ref., Lond. 1622

WILTON. A loc. n., Cornw., Norf., Northants, Somers, Wilts, Yorks

WILTSHEAR, WILTSHIRE. The county

WIMBLE. From Wimpole; a loc. n., Camb. Or *A.S.* Winebeald; a p.n. (a strong friend)

WIMBUSH. From Wimbish; a loc. n., Ess.

WIMHURST. *See* Wilmhurst

WINCE, WINCH. A loc. n., Norf. Or *A.S.* Winc, Wing; *S.*, *D.* Winge; *Dch.* Wins; p.n. Dim. of Winger (a friendly spear)

WINCHCOMBE. A loc. n., Glost.

WINCKELS. *See* Winkel

WINCKLEY. From Winkleigh; a loc. n., Devon

WINCKWORTH. From Wingerworth; a loc. n., Derbysh.

WINCOP, WINCUP. *See* Whincop

WINCOTT. A loc. n.

WINDALL. *S.* Windahl; a loc. and p.n. Or *see* Windle

WINDER. *A.S.* Windhere, Winidhere; *D.* Winder; p.n. (a wend warrior)

WINDISH. *A.S.* Windæg, Windig; *G.* Windisch; p.n. (glorious friend)

WINDLE. A loc. n., Lancs

WINDLEY. A loc. n., Derbysh.

WINDOVER. From Wendover; a p.n., Hants

WINDSOR. A loc. n., Berks, Dorset

WINDUS, WINDUST. From Windrush (?); a loc. n., Glost. Or *see* Windish

WINDYBANK. A loc. n., Lancs

WINEARL. *See* Winnall

WINFIELD. *See* Wingfield

WING. A loc. n., Rutl. Or *see* Winch

WINGATE. A loc. n., Dur.

WINGFIELD. A loc. n., Derbysh., Suff.
Held by De Braiose.

WINGROVE. From Wingrave; a loc. n., Bucks

WINKEL, WINKLE. From Wynkel; a loc. n., Fland. *Dch.* Winkel; a p.n.

WINKFIELD. *See* Wingfield

WINKUP. *See* Whincop

WINMILL. A loc. n., Devon

WINN. *See* Whin and Wynne

WINNALL. A loc. n., Warw.

WINNINGTON. A loc. n., Ches.

WINSER, WINZAR. *See* Winsor

WINSLOW. A loc. n., Bucks, Heref., Yorks

WINSON. *See* Winston

WINSOR. A loc. n., Cornw., Hants. Or *see* Windsor

WINSPEAR. From Winceby (?); a loc. n., Lincs. *D.B.* Winzebi. *See* Shakespeare

Winsbær or Winsbyr is the Danish form.

WINSTANLEY. A loc. n., Lancs

WINSTON. A loc. n., Dur., Suff.

WINTER. *A.S.*, *D.*, *S.*, *Dch.*, *Fl.*, *G.* Winter; a p.n. *See* Winder

WINTERBORN, WINTERBOURNE. A loc. n., Glost.

WINTERBOTHAM, WINTERBOTTAM. *See* Winterbourne (?)

WINTERTON. A loc. n., Lincs, Norf.

WINTHORP. A loc. n., Lincs

WINTLE. *See* Windle

WIRE. *See* Wyer

WISBY. From Wiseby; a loc. n., Lincs

WISDEN. From Wissendine (?); a loc. n., Rutl.

WISDOM. *D.* Wisbom (?); a p.n.

WISE. *A.S.* Wis; *G.* Weis, Weiss; p.n. (wise)

WISEDALE. A loc. n.

WISEMANN. *Dch.* Wiseman, Wiseman; *G.* Weissmann; p.n. (sage, philosopher)

WISKER. *See* Whisker

WISSON. *See* Whiston

WHITCOMB. A loc. n., Somers

WITFORD. A loc. n., N. Wales

WITH. From Withy; a loc. n., Somers. Or *see* Withers

WITHALL. *See* Whittall. Or from Withiel; a loc. n., Cornw.

WITHERBY. A loc. n., Worcest.

WITHERIDGE. A loc. n., Devon

WITHERINGTON, WITHRINGTON. From Widdrington; a loc. n., Northbd.

WITHERN. A loc. n., Lincs

WITHERS. *N.* Viðarr (name of a god); *F.* Withers; *N.-Fr.* Witer; *G.* Wieder; *A.S.* Wider, Wihthere; p.n. (courageous warrior)

WITHNELL. *See* Widnell

WITT. A *Dch.* p.n. *See* White

WITTON. *See* Whitton

WITTY. *Fl.* Wittigh; a p.n. (wise)

WIX. A loc. n., Ess.

WIXLEY. From Whixley; a loc. n., Yorks

WOAKES. *A.S.* Woc; *D.* Woges; p.n. (watchful)

WOBBE. *F.* Wobbo, Wobbe; *Dch.* Wubbe; p.n. (a weaver)

WOLLARD. *A.S.* Wolfhard; a p.n. (strong wolf)

WOLNO. *See* Woolnough

WOLSELEY. A loc. n., Staffs

WOLSEY. *See* Wolseley

WOLSTENCROFT. A loc. n.

WOLSTENHOLME. A loc. n., Lancs

WOLTON. *See* Walton

WOLVERIDGE. *See* Woolrych

WOLVERTON. A loc. n., Hants, Kent, Wilts

WOMACK. *A.S.* Wigmearc, Wihomarc, Wimarc; p.n. (a Mercian warrior)

WOMBWELL. A loc. n., Yorks

WONNACOTT. From Onecote; a loc. n., Staffs

WOOD. *A.S.* Wuda; a p.n. Or from Atte-wood; a loc. n. Fl. ref., Lond. 1618. *See* Uden

WOODALL. From Woodhall; a loc. n., Lincs, Worcest., Yorks

WOODARD. *A.S.* Wadweard; *D.* Wodder; *Fr.* Oudard, Oudart; *D.B.* Wadard; p.n.; *A.S. wuduweard* (a wood ward), or *wádweard* (ford guard)

Waudard in Rot. Obl. et Fin., K. John (Warwick), A.D. 1200.

WOODBERRY. *See* Woodbury

WOODBRIDGE. A loc. n., Camb., Suff.

WOODBURN. A loc. n., Northbd.

WOODBURY. A loc. n., Cornw., Devon, Hants

WOODCOCK. Dimin. of *F.* Ude (Udke). Or *A.S. wudu-coc* (the bird)

WOODEND. A loc. n., Staffs, and other counties

WOODERSON, WOODESON. *See* Woodard

WOODERSPOON. *See* Wotherspon

WOODFALL. A loc. n., Kent, Wilts

WOODFIELD. A loc. n., Dur.

WOODFORD. A loc. n., Ess., Glost., Northants, Somers

WOODGATE. A loc. n., Lancs, Staffs

WOODGER. *See* Woodard

WOODHAM. A loc. n., Ess.

WOODHEAD. A loc. n., Ches., Northbd.

WOODHOUSE. A loc. n., Derbysh., Hants, Lancs, Staffs, Somers

WOODIN, WOODING. *A.S.* Woden; *N.-Fr.* Waudin; *Dch.* Wouden; *Fl.* Wodon; p.n.

It is doubtful if this is the god Odin or Woden. It is more likely from *N.* Auðunn; a p.n. (charitable or prosperous friend).

WOODLAND. A loc. n., Devon, Lancs

WOODLEY. A loc. n., Devon, Hants

WOODMASON. From Woodmanstone; a loc. n., Surr.

WOODROFFE, WOODRUFF. *See* Woodrow

WOODROW. A loc. n., Dorset

WOODSTOCK. A loc. n., Oxf.

WOODTHORPE. A loc. n., Derbysh., Lincs, Oxf., Yorks

WOODWARD, WOODYARD. *See* Woodard

WOOF. *See* Uff

WOOKEY. A loc. n., Somers

WOOL. A loc. n., Dorset. Or *G.* Wolle; *D.* Uhl, Woll; p.n. (wolf)

WOOLAGE. From Woolwich; a loc. n.

WOOLARD, WOOLLARD. *A.S.* Wulfheard; *S.* Wollert; p.n. (strong wolf)

WOOLASTON. A loc. n., Heref., Northants, Salop, Staffs, Worcest.

WOOLCOCK. *G.* Wolke; a p.n. Dim. of Wulf

WOOLCOTT. From Woolscott; a loc. n., Staffs

WOOLDRIDGE. *See* Worledge

WOOLERSON. From Woolverstone; a loc. n., Norf. Or *see* Woolaston

WOOLFENDEN. A loc. n.

WOOLISCROFT. From Woolescroft; a loc. n., Staffs

WOOLLATT, WOOLLETT. *A.S.* Wulfhat; a p.n. (war wolf); *Fr.* Volett. Hugt. n., Dover, 1622

WOOLLEY. A loc. n., Derbysh.

WOOLMAN. *A.S.* Wulfman; *D.* Vollmann; *G.* Wollmann; p.n.

WOOLMER. A loc. n., Hants. Or *A.S.* Wulfmær; *D.* Vollmer; p.n. (famous wolf)

WOOLNOUGH. *N.* Ulf-njótr; *A.S.* Ulnod, Ulnoth, Wulfnoth; p.n. (bold wolf)

WOOLRYCH. *A.S.* Wulfric; a p.n. (wolf ruler)

WOOLSTON. A loc. n., Hants, Oxf.

WOON. A loc. n., Cornw.

WOOR. *See* Whur

WOOSNAM. *See* Wolstenholme

WOOSTER. From Worcester; the county town

WOOTON. *See* Wootton

WOOTTEN. A loc. n., Suff.

WOOTTON. A loc. n., Hants, Heref., Northants, Salop, Somers

WORBOYS. A loc. n., Camb., Hunts

WORBY. *See* Worboys

WORD. A loc. n., Kent, Suss.

WORDLEY. From Wordsley; a loc. n., Staffs

WORDSWORTH. From Wardysworth or Wadysworth, W.R., Yorks
Held by De Tilly.

WORLAND. A loc. n.

WORLEDGE, WORLLEDGE. From Warlage; a loc. n., Northbd.

WORLEY. *See* Whalley

WORM. *N.* Ormr; *A.S.* Orm, Ormar; *D.* Worm; *Dch.* Wormer; *G.* Wormt, Wurm; p.n. (a snake)

WORMALD. *A.S.* Wurmbeald; a p.n. (bold snake)

WORMER. *See* Warmer or Worm

WORMSLEY. A loc. n., Heref.

WORMULL. From Wormhill; a loc. n., Derbysh. Or *see* Wormald

WORN. *See* Warne

WORNER. *See* Warner

WORNUM. From Warnham; a loc. n., Suss.

WORPOLE. From Warpole; a loc. n., Devon

WORRALL. A loc. n., Yorks

WORROW. *A.S.* Worr; *D.* Worre; p.n. (defence)

WORSDELL. From Worsall; a loc. n., Yorks

WORSEY. *D.* Worsaae; a p.n. (victorious defender (?))

WORSFIELD. A loc. n.

WORSFOLD. A loc. n.

WORSHIP. From Warsop; a loc. n., Notts. Or *see* Wauchope

WORSLEY. A loc. n., Lancs

WORSSAM. A loc. n.

WORSTER. From Worstead; a loc. n., Norf. Or from Worcester

WORTH. A loc. n., Ches., Suss., Yorks. Also a Germ. loc. n.

WORTHAM. A loc. n., Suff.

WORTHING. A loc. n., Suss.

WORTHINGTON. A loc. n., Lancs, Leics

WORTLEY. A loc. n., Glost., Yorks

WORTON. A loc. n., Middlx.

WOSTENHOLME. *See* Wolstenholme

WOTHERSPON. A loc. n., Scotl.

WOTTON. A loc. n., Glost.

WRAGG. From Wragoe; a loc. n., Lincs. Or *see* Ragg

WRANGHAM. From Wrangham or Wrangholm; a loc. n., Lammermoor, Scotland
Radus de Wrengham in Rot. Hund., p. 198. Thos. Wrangh'm, 1565, York Wills.

WRATE. *D.* Wriedt; *S.* Wrede, Wret; p.n. *See* Wright

WRATTEN. From Wratting; a loc. n., Camb., Norf., Suff.

WREFORD. From Wreyford; a loc. n., Devon

WREN. From Rennes; a loc. n., France. Or *see* Rain

WRENCH. *G.* Wrensch; a p.n. Dim. of Wren. Or *see* Renishaw

WRENFORD. From Rainford; a loc. n., Lancs

WRENTMORE. A loc. n.

WRETHAM. A loc. n., Norf.

WRIGHT. *D.* Wright; a p.n.; *A.S.* wyrhta (a wright). Or Wryde; a loc. n., Camb.

WRIGLEY. A loc. n.

WRINCH. *See* Wrench

WRING. *See* Ring

WRISTBRIDGE. *D.* Wrisberg (?); a p.n.

WRITER. *G.* Reiter; a p.n. *See* Ryder

WRODT. A loc. n., Lincs

WROTTESLEY. A loc. n., Staffs

WURR. *See* Worrow

WYAND. *Dch.* Weijand; a p.n.

WYARD, WYATT. *See* Whyart

WYBROW. *A.S.* Wigburh; *D.* Wibroe; p.n. (war protection). *See* Whybrow

WYBURN, A.S. Wigbeorn, Wibern; p.n. (war bear). Or *see* Wayborn

WYCHE. A loc. n., Lincs

WYER. From Weyer; a loc. n., Belg. Or *A.S.* Wighere; *Old G.* Wiher (warrior); *Dch.* Weijer; *G.* Wier; p.n. Prot. ref., Lond. 1618

WYETH. *See* Wythe

WYGARD. *See* Wigger and Whyart

WYKE. A loc. n., Yorks

WYKEHAM. A loc. n., Hants, Lincs, Northants, Yorks

WYKES. A loc. n., Northants, Salop Surr.
De Wikes in Rot. Obl. et Fin.

WYLDE. *See* Wildee

WYLIE. *See* Whiley

WYMAN. *N.* Vémundr (temple protector); *D.B.* Wimund, Wimer; *Dch.* Weyman, Wijmen; *G.* Wim-

WYMAN—*continued*
mer, Weiman; *S.* Weman; *Fl.* Wyman; Weman; p.n. Or *A.S.* Wigman (war-man)

WYNDHAM. From Windham; a loc. n., Norf. Or Wymondham, Leics

WYNEKEN. *A.S.* Wineca; *Fl.* Vinken, Wynesken; p.n. Dim. of *wine* (friend)

WYNNE. *Welsh* Gwynn (white)

WYNYARD. *A.S.* Winegeard; *Fl.* Wyngaard; *Dch.* Wijngaart; p.n. (friendly protector)

WYON. *Fl.* Wion; a p.n. *See* Vian

WYRE. *See* Wyer

WYTHE. *D.* Wiethe; a p.n. *See* White

WYTTON. *D.* Witten; a p.n.

WYVILL. A loc. n., Lincs. *See* Weevill

Y

YALDEN. From Yalding; a loc. n., Kent. Or *A.S.* Ealdwine; a p.n. (old friend)

YALE. *F.* Jelle; *S.* Yell; *Fl.* Jell; p.n. *See* Jelly

YALLOP. *N.* Hjálp (help); *G.* Hallupp, Halop; p.n. *See* Gallop

YAPP. *A.S.* Gab, Geb; *F.* Jabbo, Jabbe; *G.* Jaap; *Fl.* Jabé; *D.* Jappe; p.n. *See* Gibbs

YARDE. A loc. n., Somers. *See* Youard

YARDLEY. A loc. n., Northants, Worcest.

YARHAM. From Yarm; a loc. n., Yorks

YARINGTON. A loc. n.

YARKER. *See* Tiarko
Jarkir is on a runic inscription quoted by Stevens.

YARLEY. *See* Yardley

YARMUTH. A loc. n., I. of Wight, Norf.

YARNALL, YARNEL. *A.S.* Iarna; *G.* Janel; p.n. Dim. *N. járn* (iron), *járna* (mailed)

YARR. From Yarrow; a loc. n., Somers

YARRAD. *See* Jarred

YARRANTON. From Yarnton; a loc. n., Oxf.

YARROD. *See* Jarred

YARROW. A loc. n., Scotl., Somers. Also Jarrow, Dur.

YATE. A loc. n., Glost.

YATES. *See* Gates

YAXLEY. A loc. n., Camb., Norf., Suff. From *F.* Jak

YEAMES. *See* James

YEAMON. *Fl.* Jemayne; a p.n. *See* Yeoman

YEARSLEY. A loc. n., Yorks

YEILDING. A loc. n., Worcest.

YELD. From Yelt; a loc. n., Cornw.

YELDHAM. A loc. n., Ess.

YELL. *See* Jelly, Yale

YELLAND. From Yealand; a loc. n., Lancs

YELLOLY, YELLOWLEE, YELLOWLEES. A loc. n., Scotl.

YELLON. From Yelling; a loc. n., Hunts. Or fam. n. of Yell

YELLOPP. *See* Yallop

YELVERTON. A loc. n., Norf.

YENDON. A loc. n., Staffs (Endon)

YEO. From Yea, *i.e. A.S. ea* (water). Or *see* Ewen.

Galfrida de la Ya held lands in Devon *temp.* Hen. III. It has been written Ya, Yaa, Yae, Yea, Yeo, and pronounced yaw.

YEOMAN. *G.* Jochmann; a p.n. (a bowman). Or *A.S.* Eomund; a p.n. (ancient protector)

YEOWELL. From Yeovil; a loc. n., Somers. Or *see* Jouel

YERBURY. From Yearby; a loc. n., Yorks

YERLING. *See* Yirling

YETTON. *See* Yatton

YEULETT. *See* Ullett

YEVES. *See* Jeeves

YEWDALL. From Yewdale; a loc. n., Lancs. Or *see* Udall

YEWENS. *Fl.* Juveyns; a p.n. *See* Ewen

YEXLEY. *See* Yaxley

YIRLING. *N.* Erlingr; *S.* Gjerling; *D.B.* Erlenc; a p.n. *See* Earl

YONGE. *D., Dch., Fl., G.* Jong, Jung, Junger; p.n. (young)

YORK. The city of that n.

YORSTON. From Yorton; a loc. n., Salop

YORWARTH. From Yoadwath; a loc. n., Yorks

YOUARD, YOUART. *See* Heward

YOUD. *See* Judd

YOUELL, YOUELS, YOUHILL, YOUILL. *See* Jouel

YOUENS. *See* Yewens

YOULDEN. *See* Youlton

YOULES. *See* Jouel

YOULTON. A. loc. n., Yorks

YOUNG. *See* Yonge

YOUNGER. *D.* Junker; a p.n.

YOUNGHUSBAND. *N.* Ungi-Ásbjorn (?); a p.n. Osborn the younger. *See* Osborne

YOUNGMAN. *D., Dch., G.* Jungman; a p.n.

YOUNGS. *Fl.* Junges; a p.n.

YOXALL. A loc. n., Staffs

YOXLEY. *See* Yaxley

YULE, YULL. *See* Jouel

Z

ZOUCH. From Sauchay (?); a loc. n., Normandy; or Jauche, Belg. Souch in Roll of Battell Abbey. De la Zuche in Rot. Obl. et Fin., K. Johh.

APPENDIX

THE following names are under consideration. Many of them are local names, but as they cannot be found in any existing gazetteer or county directory, they are very likely those of manors, which are not necessarily parishes, or small estates situated in different parts of the country.

Any information respecting them will be thankfully received by the author, as will any other suggestions for the improvement of this work in a future edition, should such be called for.

Alefounder, Allshorn, Artingstall, Ashmole, Ayerst.

Banthorpe, Bearcroft, Beardshaw, Bestman, Bidmead, Blackbeard, Brasnett, Broadbent, Budibent, Bulport.

Challingsworth, Corbishley, Cragild, Crickmer, Cruickshank, Cudby, Culpeper.

Dadfield, Dashwood. Densley, Dewsnap, Dibley, Dockerill, Drakeford, Drakeyoung, Dryland.

Everest, Eversfield.

Fairservice, Faithful, Fastnedge, Faulding, Faultless, Fessenden, Firmstone, Fishenden, Fladgate, Flear, Flindall, Flinders, Flintoff, Flogdell, Fothergill, Foxcroft, Fripp, Frogley, Furlo, Furmstone.

Gadum, Gallafent, Gatfield, Getcliffe, Gillington, Girdham, Girdlestone, Gisby, Gladwell, Gorham, Goswell, Greagsby, Greensmith, Gridley, Grigsby, Grimsdick, Grindrod, Grinham, Crinslade.

Hadgraft, Hainbon, Handyside, Harkaway, Havergal, Haylock, Heavyside, Hebditch, Helpman, Heritage, Ilignell, Hohday, Hogsflesh, Hoodless, Horlack, Horlick, Hostome, Hulcup, Huxtable.

Jeffcoat, Joyner.

Kenningham, Kethro, Kinglake, Kinstruck, Kirty, Kistrick, Knew.

Lamplin, Lasken, Lattey, Lealoyd, Leatherburrow, Lilliecrap, Linnington, Linscott, Lipscombe, Littlechild, Longbourne, Lovecraft, Love-grove, Lovelady, Lovelock, Lushington, Lythaby.

Maidment, Mainprice, Makemade, Manchip, Marrable, Melsom, Metcalf, Middlebrook, Middleditch, Monksfield, Mothersdill, Motters-head, Munnion.

Nall, Narraway, Nettleship, Nind, Norcross.

Orbell, Oxtoby.

Pagriff, Pedgrift, Penlington, Pieby, Pimlot, Popplewell, Prebble, Pummel, Pythian.

Rackley, Ranstead, Ravenscliffe, Ravenscourt, Reith, Remblance, Reside, Resther, Rexworthy, Ridler, Robjent, Rubrum.

Sculpher, Searson, Shalders, Shoard, Shrapnell, Shrimpton, Sidebottom, Silverside, Singlehurst, Sloggett, Slorach, Smethurst, Snelgrove, Snoxall, Snoxell, Spanswick, Spearpoint, Spenceley, Sperring, Sporton, Spyver, Squibb, Standeven, Stent, Stentiford, Stopford, Stradling, Strickstock, Strudger, Struggler, Stunt, Sturdy, Sunnuck, Supple, Swarbrick, Sweetapple, Swithinbank, Swivel.

Taffinder, Tapscott, Tarling, Tartelling, Taswell, Thickbroom, Timgate, Timlet, Tinham, Tinson, Tiplady, Todkill, Tofield, Tolhurst, Toplady, Totterdell, Trant, Tranter, Trapnell, Trimming, Trimy, Trinder, Triphook, Tripper, Trollope, Trubshaw, Truckle, Truelock, Trundley, Tumblety, Twelvetrees, Twentyman, Twisaday, Twyman.

Uffindel, Ullathorne, Umphleby, Uniacke, Ungless, Upsdall, Upsom.

Vamplew, Verity, Vousden.

Wagstaff, Wakeford, Wapshere, Warlock, Waterfield, Wayham, Waylet, Wellbeloved, Wharnsby, Whichelow, Widnell, Wimperis, Wildash, Wimpey, Wimpory, Wincott, Winship, Wisden, Wisedell, Wolstencroft, Wolveridge, Worland, Worsfield, Worssam, Wrentmore, Wrigley.

Yabsley, Yarnall, Yarnel, Yearren, Yeatman, Yendon, Yetman, Yeves, Yockney, Yount.

ELLIOT STOCK'S NEW PUBLICATIONS

Bound in cloth, gilt lettered, and profusely illustrated. **8s. 6d. net.**

Christt Lore:

The Legends and Traditions, Myths, Symbols, Customs, and Superstitions of the Christian Church.

By FREDK. WM. HACKWOOD, F.R.S.L.

In demy 8vo, handsomely printed and bound. **Price 7s. 6d. net.**

Proverb Lore:

A Manual Dealing with the History, Literature, Associations, and Significance of Proverbs in all Countries and Climes.

By F. EDWARD HULME, F.L.S., F.S.A.

Author of
"Mythland," "Wayside Sketches," "Natural History Lore and Legends."

In large 8vo, tastefully printed and bound in cloth, gilt lettered.
Price 10s. 6d. net.

Christmas: Its Origin and Associations

Together with its Historical Events and Festive Celebrations during Nineteen Centuries.

DEPICTED BY PEN AND PENCIL BY W. F. DAWSON

Memorable Celebrations, Stately Meetings of Early Kings, Remarkable Events, Picturesque Customs, Time-honoured Sports and Games, Royal Christmases, Coronations and Royal Marriages at Christmastide, Court Banquetings and Revellings, Christmas at the Colleges and the Inns of Court, Popular Festivities, and Christmas Keeping in different parts of the World, derived from the most authentic sources, and arranged chronologically.

CHEAP EDITION. In demy 8vo, illustrated, cloth gilt. **Price 5s.**

East Anglia and the Great Civil War.

The Rising of Cromwell's Ironsides in the Associated Counties of Cambridge, Huntingdon, Lincoln, Norfolk, Suffolk, Essex, and Hertford. With Appendices and Illustrations. By ALFRED KINGSTON, F.R.Hist.S., Author of "Herefordshire during the Great Civil War."

"The reader will find abundance of details, collected from many sources, that throw a great deal of light on particular incidents of the time ; and he will see that these minor details give the past a colour and liveliness which are not to be met with in some more pretentious histories."—*Pall Mall Gazette.*

"Every page of the work bears evidence of painstaking research and a desire to present an historically accurate picture. Some pages, indeed, may be regarded as parallel to the graphic pictures presented in the late Mr J. R. Green's notable volumes on ' The Making of England.' "—*East Anglian Daily Times.*

ELLIOT STOCK, 62 PATERNOSTER ROW, LONDON, E.C.

SECOND EDITION. Revised and Enlarged, with Index.

In crown 8vo, cloth, **price 6s.**

The Right to bear Arms

By "X," the Writer of the Series of Articles which appeared in the *Saturday Review* over that Signature.

" We cordially recommend this little book to those who are ignorant of such matters, and are not above learning something of the elementary rules of heraldry, even though they may be certain of their own right to use arms. The book is forcibly and clearly written, the arguments are unanswerable, and supported by extracts from ancient documents, and many common delusions about arms are exposed."—*Spectator.*

In crown 8vo, cloth, illustrated, **price 6s.**

Old English Social Life

AS TOLD BY THE PARISH REGISTER

By T. F. THISELTON DYER, M.A. (Oxon.), Author of " Church Lore Gleanings."

" Mr Thistleton Dyer's book is instructive and entertaining. He has a wide acquaintance with registers, and draws upon them for facts concerning parish life, the relations of parson and people, superstitions, parish scandals and punishments, marriage, death, and strange customs, and natural events. The result is an entertaining volume of small facts and curious diction."—*Academy.*

" One of the most fascinating books which has been issued for a long time."—*Genealogical Magazine.*

In large crown 8vo, cloth, fully illustrated, **price 10s. 6d. net.**

THE PEDIGREE OF SHAKESPEARE

Shakespeare's Family

BEING A RECORD OF THE ANCESTORS AND DESCENDANTS OF WILLIAM SHAKESPEARE

By CHARLOTTE C. STOPES.

" Mrs Stopes, by dint of industry and the detective instinct so valuable to the genealogist, succeeds in unearthing a vast number of hidden or unconsidered trifles having a direct or indirect bearing on the history of the greatest of dramatists."—*Scotsman.*

NEW EDITION. *In demy 8vo, cloth,* **price 8s. 6d.**

The House of Cromwell

A Genealogical History of the Family and Descendants of the Protector

By JAMES WAYLEN.

Revised by JOHN GABRIEL CROMWELL, M.A., Oxon., Hon. Canon of Durham.

" To those who are interested in such quaint lore Mr Waylen's book will yield a world of satisfaction."—*Morning Leader.*

" The work will be more than ever interesting to the student, especially to such as love the intricacies of genealogical research."—*Record.*

" A work of remarkable and painstaking research."—*Freeman.*

ELLIOT STOCK, 62 PATERNOSTER ROW, LONDON, E.C.